THE ANNOTATED CONSTITUTION OF PAPUA NEW GUINEA

The Constitution of the Independent State of Papua New Guinea (as altered to 1st January 1984) with Extracts from the Report of the Constitutional Planning Committee, Extracts from Leading Judgments, Case Annotations, Notes, Tables and Index

by

BRIAN BRUNTON, LLM

Barrister and Solicitor of the Supreme Court of Papua New Guinea
Lecturer in Law, University of Papua New Guinea
and

DUNCAN COLQUHOUN-KERR, LLB BA(Soc. W.)

Barrister and Solicitor of the High Court of Australia and of the Supreme Court of Papua New Guinea
Lecturer in Law, University of Papua New Guinea

University of Papua New Guinea Press 1984

Reprint edition published by:
The University of Papua New Guinea Press & Bookshop
Box 413
University Post Office
NCD 134
Papua New Guinea

ISBN-10: 9980-84-006-4
ISBN-13: 978-9980-84-006-6

CONSTITUTION AND AMENDMENTS

Legislation	*Gazette Published*	*In Operation*	*Manner of Commencement*
Constitution		16.9.75	see date in preamble
Amendment No.1 Provincial Government	G24 of 23.3.76	30.9.76	Certification
Amendment No.2 Provincial Government Elections	G24 of 23.3.76	31.12.76	Certification
Amendment No.3 Provincial Government (Consequential Amendments)	G29 of 1.4.76	31.12.76	Certification
Amendment No.4 Leadership Code	Nil — s14(6)	31.12.76	Certification
Amendment No.5 Citizenship	Nil — s14(6)	23.3.77	Certification
Amendment No.6 Benefits and Pensions	G65 of 4.10.79	2.9.80	Certification
Amendment No.7 Suspension and re-establishment of Provincial Government	15.11.83	15.11.83	Certification

CONTENTS

FOREWORD

The Constitution of Papua New Guinea is both a political statement and a legal document. As a legal document it has been subject to review and interpretation by the National and Supreme Courts and to amendment by the National Parliament. Yet it remains the supreme law of Papua New Guinea touching upon almost every area of public life. As a written Constitution it is rare, if not unique, in the detail of its expression. Because of its central place in the legal and political structure of the nation not only lawyers but also politicians and those involved in business or administration need to be aware of its provisions and how it has been interpreted.

For some years Goldring's *The Constitution of Papua New Guinea* (1978) has been the only available book to meet this need notwithstanding Goldring's disclaimer that his book was written not as a text on the law but as an analysis of the Constitution as an exercise in legal nationalism. However as Goldring noted:

> The Constitution of Papua New Guinea is complex, and full of words and phrases that will, no doubt, be the subject of very detailed consideration by the courts. What the courts and the legal profession of Papua New Guinea really need is a detailed annotated text, in the style — perhaps inimitable — of Quick and Garren's classic work on the Australian Constitution.

Responding to this need, Brian Brunton conceived in 1981 of producing, in a single volume, the up-to-date text of the Constitution annotated with the text of the Constitutional Planning Committee's *Final Report* 1974 — and a note of every relevant post-Independence decision of the National and Supreme Courts.

From the inception of this work the basic intention has remained constant: not to produce a text-book in the traditional sense, but to compile a book containing a comprehensive selection of primary materials coupled with such minimum editorial comment as is necessary to clarify obscure issues. In 1983 Duncan Colquhoun-Kerr joined Brian Brunton and the work subsequently developed collaboratively.

While the authors take joint responsibility for all that appears in these pages, Brian Brunton has had primary responsibility for preparing ss.32 to 63, and Duncan Colquhoun-Kerr for the remainder.

Methodology

The user of this volume will be assisted by the following description of the way in which it was compiled.

The Constitution has been divided into sub-parts, usually section by section, ocasionally into smaller sub-parts, sub-sections or sub-sub-sections. The text of the Constitution is highlighted by its being printed in ten point type.

Where a statute or an Organic Law has been passed pursuant to or affecting the Constitutional sub-part the reader is also referred to that statute.

Immediately following each sub-part of the Constitution we have included the complete text of any relevant parts of the C.P.C. Report. These extracts assist in clarifying the intention underlying particular provisions and, pursuant to s.24 of the Constitution, may be used 'as aids to interpretation where any question relating to the interpretation or application of any provisions of a Constitutional Law arises'. Where an extract from the C.P.C. Report is relevant to two or more sub-parts of the Constitution and cannot be severed, the text of the C.P.C. Report appears under the first major sub-part to which it is relevant. The C.P.C. Report is set in seven point type.

Under the extracts from the C.P.C. Report (if any) follow various subject headings. Subject headings are set in italic capitals. When we have found it impossible to group entries under a subject heading they have been included under the catch-all rubric *GENERALLY*.

Under each subject heading entries have been made in one of four styles:

Held

Entries under this heading are summaries of a relevant holding of one or more judges.

per Judge J.

Entries under this heading are direct quotations from a leading judgment. If the extract is from a dissenting judgment that fact is noted. Cross references to other relevant judgments in the case are also provided.

Comment

Entries under this heading contain the authors' contributions.

Referred to

Entries under this heading mention every instance not otherwise recorded in which a judge has referred to the relevant sub-part of the Constitution. If the judgment contains any observations of significance a brief note outlining the context of the observation appears in brackets after the reference.

The only variation in the format described above occurs between ss.32 to 56, the basic rights provisions. For those sections there is included, under the heading *CROSS REFERENCE* (after the C.P.C. Report but before the subject headings), references to analogous international human rights laws which, because of s.39, are relevant in determining whether a law of Papua New Guinea is 'reasonably justifiable in a democratic society . . .'.

In annotating the Constitution we have chosen to omit any reference to the records of debates and proceedings in either the Constituent Assembly or the pre-Independence House of Assembly. The omission is for pragmatic rather than principled reasons. No official published record of these debates exists, the unedited photo-copied transcripts that do exist are not generally accessible and the Courts almost never refer to them. For those reasons we decided that until the debates were published or otherwise made more accessible there was little point in over-burdening an already lengthy text with reference to material not available to most of our readers.

Acknowledgments

Financial assistance towards this project has been forthcoming from the University of Papua New Guinea Research Committee, the Melanesian Law Journal and the U.P.N.G. Press. For their assistance we are deeply grateful. For undertaking the thankless task of initial data collection we acknowledge the invaluable help of our principal research assistant, Phoebe Sangetari and of research assistants Judith Day and Regina Barton. For assistance in typing the manuscript we thank Joyce Kasokason, Ruth Lakani, Leobah Kuam, Didrie Nano, Gladys Wojeiba, Lavenga Kimbai, Janet Tau, Levana Dinda, Flavia Kimuli, Nancy Koriam, Celia Taylor and Haho Marjen. For assistance with proof-reading the text we thank Celia Taylor.

Dedication

This work is dedicated to Carol Brunton and Celia Taylor.

The Law

The law is stated as at the 1st January 1984.

Brian Brunton
Duncan Colquhoun-Kerr

Port Moresby

CONSTITUTION
OF
THE INDEPENDENT STATE OF PAPUA NEW GUINEA

PREAMBLE
Adoption of Constitution

WE, THE PEOPLE OF PAPUA NEW GUINEA —

- United in one nation
- pay homage to the memory of our ancestors — the source of our strength and origin of our combined heritage
- acknowledge the worthy customs and traditional wisdoms of our people — which have come down to us from generation to generation
- pledge ourselves to guard and pass on to those who come after us our noble traditions and the Christian principles that are ours now.

By authority of our inherent right as ancient, free and independent peoples

WE, THE PEOPLE, do now establish this sovereign nation and declare ourselves, under the guiding hand of God, to be the Independent State of Papua New Guinea.

AND WE ASSERT, by virtue of that authority

- that all power belongs to the people —
acting through their duly elected representatives
- that respect for the dignity of the individual and community interdependence are basic principles of our society
- that we guard with our lives our national identity, integrity and self respect
- that we reject violence and seek consensus as a means of solving our common problems
- that our national wealth, won by honest, hard work be equitably shared by all

WE DO NOW THEREFORE DECLARE

That we, having resolved to enact a Constitution for the Independent State of Papua New Guinea

AND ACTING through our Constituent Assembly on 15 August 1975

HEREBY ESTABLISH, ADOPT and GIVE TO OURSELVES this Constitution to come into effect on Independence Day, that is 16 September 1975.

C.P.C. Report Ch.15 p.2

Preamble

18. Our Constitution should contain an introduction or opening clause which sets out our basic beliefs. It is through the Almighty God that all our institutions and efforts are made. Our country should be based on basic principles of brotherhood which are found in our ancient customs and values and in Christianity. [p.3]

19. All power belongs to our people. National integrity and self-respect must not be limited. Our cultures should be promoted. Our material and spiritual benefits should be shared. We should respect every individual; encourage peaceful solutions to situations of conflict, instead of fighting to achieve our objectives; and always strive to be self-supporting at the community and national levels, and individually. By acting in these ways we will safeguard the rights and duties, powers and privileges of our people, and help to build a just society.

WE THE PEOPLE

per Frost C.J.

The Constitution itself is a truly autochthonous Constitution established, as the preamble recites, by the will of the people to whom 'all power belongs'. Its' authority is thus original and in no way derivative from any other source. Unlike the case of Australia where the first settlers brought with them the common law there is, to use the words of Sir Owen Dixon speaking of the *American Constitution*, 'no anterior law providing the source of juristic authority' for the institution of government now established.
The State v Mogo Wonom [1975] PNGLR 311 at pp. 315, 316.

per Pratt J.

The power wielded by any servant of the public, be he Minister, civil servant, judge or whatever stem from a delegation from the people.
S.C.R. No1 of 1982; Re Bouraga [1982] PNGLR 178 at p.203.

CHRISTIAN PRINCIPLES

per McDermott J.

I find it difficult to reconcile the Constitution's preamble that —
'We the people of Papua New Guinea pledge ourselves to guard and pass on to those who come after us our noble traditions and the Christian principles that are ours now', with the savagery, as exemplified in vindictive self-righteousness by which [the *Native Regulations* dealing with adultery] is availed of and enforced. If the aims of the legislation was to control native people and expediently deal with matrimonial squabbles, then it appears quite out of place in an independent and democratic country whose Constitution gives the same basic rights to men and women, without discrimination of colour.
Asi Burunge v John Kaupa (1983 Unreported) SC258 at pp.12, 13.

IN SO DOING WE, THE PEOPLE OF PAPUA NEW GUINEA, SET BEFORE OURSELVES THESE NATIONAL GOALS AND DIRECTIVE PRINCIPLES THAT UNDERLINE OUR CONSTITUTION:—

C.P.C. Report; Ch.2 p.1

The significance of Self Government and Independence

1. When a country achieves Self-Government and Independence, its constitution tends to be concerned largely with the tensions that exist at that time. While it is important that these tensions — reflected as they are in Papua New Guinea in the demands for secession, autonomy, restrictions on powers of the national government, etc. — be taken care of, partly through constitutional provisions if necessary, pre-occupation with this problem can have one unfortunate consequence. It is that the constitution does not face up to the problems of the future, and this tends to defeat the great opportunities presented by Self Government and Independence.

2. We believe that the significance of Papua New Guinea's attainment of Self-Government and Independence is that, by transferring power into the hands of the people of this country, it gives us a chance to define for ourselves the philosophy of life by which we want to live and the social and economic goals we want to achieve. If the Constitution is to be truly the fundamental charter of our society and the basis of legitimate authority, it should be an instrument which helps to achieve these goals and not one which obstructs. Our Constitution should

look towards the future and act as an accelerator in the process of development, not as a brake. It should be related to the national goals that we leaders of this country are enunciating. We have therefore framed our recommendations for the proposed Constitution with these goals in mind.

3. A clear definition of Papua New Guinea's most fundamental national goals, and a statement setting out the implications of their acceptance for the ways in which the Government seeks to achieve those goals, is of great importance to the welfare of our people and to the effectiveness of the Constitution in promoting it. Now that our country has become fully self-governing and its duly elected leaders have taken over virtually complete control of all internal governmental activity, the need for definite, widely known, long term objectives to guide them in their decision-making, is apparent. With the need for development so widespread, it is crucial that national priorities be in accordance with these objectives.

4. We leaders and people must know where we want to go before we can decide how we should get there. Before a driver starts a motor car, he should first decide on his destination. Otherwise his driving will be without purpose, and will achieve nothing. We Papua New Guineans are now in the driving seat. The road which we should follow ought now to be marked out so that all will know the way ahead. The Committee believes that at present our country's leaders have a unique opportunity to change the existing foreign-imposed system of government, which is widely recognised as being inappropriate to our needs. This opportunity must be firmly grasped.

5. Now is that historic moment in our search for identity and self-fulfilment to take the necessary measures to make substantial changes in all of our institutions, to create new ones and to redirect development when things are fluid and tractable. But for us to know clearly what measures should be taken, our objectives must be clearly established.

6. The Committee has decided that, as the Constitution is the basic charter of the country, it is essential that it incorporates the fundamental national goals towards which the people and we leaders are working. This should help to ensure that these objectives will become known throughout the country and provide a yardstick against which government performance can be judged.

What kind of society do we want?

The relevance of the Eight Improvement Aims

7. Over the last two years, there has been much discussion about the kind of society that our people want. There was a wide ranging debate on the socio-economic aspects of this topic in the House of Assembly last year resulting in the adoption by unanimous decision of certain fundamental guidelines for national improvement known as as the 'Eight aims'. These are:

- a rapid increase in the proportion of the economy under the control of Papua New Guinean individuals and groups, and in the proportion of personal and property income that goes to Papua New Guinea; [p.2]
- more equal distribution of economic benefits, including movement toward equalisation of incomes among people and toward equalisation of services among different areas of the country;
- decentralisation of economic activity, planning and government spending, with emphasis on agricultural development, village industry, better internal trade, and more spending channelled to local and area bodies;
- an emphasis on small-scale artisan, service and business activity, relying where possible on typically Papua New Guinean forms of economic activity;
- a more self-reliant economy, less dependent for its needs on imported goods and services and better able to meet the needs of its people through local production;
- an increasing capacity for meeting government spending needs from locally raised revenue;
- a rapid increase in the active and equal participation of women in all forms of economic and social activity;
- government control and involvement in those sectors of the economy where control is necessary to achieve the desired kind of development.

8. There are several basic principles which lie behind these aims. These have been summed up in the ideas of Equality, Self-Reliance and Rural Development. The Government has clearly stated its commitment to these aims in developing the country's human and natural resources to bring about improvement in the lives of our people, and there is general consensus on these principles all over the country.

9. In evolving the National Goals and Directive Principles of Policy which we propose should be incorporated

in the Constitution, we have taken full account of the Eight Aims. The Goals and Directive Principles we recommend are broader and more comprehensive than the Aims in that they provide for the full development of our people, whereas the Aims emphasize the economic aspects of our society. The Goals and Principles are generally consistent with the Aims but are more specifically aimed at achieving a free and just society in Papua New Guinea.

10. We did not determine these national goals in a matter of days or weeks. We have distilled them after a great deal of thought and discussion over the twenty-two months during which our Committee has been at work. During that time, as we have mentioned in our Introduction, we held well over one hundred public meetings in all parts of the country, and we received thousands of submissions, verbally and in writing, many of which were concerned either directly or indirectly, with the type of society we should seek to build for ourselves.

11. We believe that these goals, and the principles which should guide the government and our people in order to achieve them, express the needs and aspirations of our people in meaningful terms, and that they are stated in such a manner that people will readily understand and remember them. The particular form in which they have been cast — spelling out the goals first, and then stating the goals and the principles — is intended to assist our people to fully understand and appreciate them.

12. We consider that they should be given the widest possible publicity at all levels of government; in towns and villages, in schools and tertiary institutions; in churches and other organizations so that our people will become fully aware of them, discuss them and obtain a clear sense of the direction in which our country is heading. It should give each man and woman a clear appreciation of the need for him or her to participate fully in the building of our new nation — a nation which is firmly based on equality and social justice ... [p.25]

IMPLEMENTATION OF THE GOALS AND PRINCIPLES

All activities of the State and its institutions should be based on the directive principles and directed towards achieving the National Goals set out in this chapter.

The goals and principles as a guide in judicial interpretation

(1) All courts and other adjudicatory tribunals shall be guided in the exercise of their functions by the National Goals and Directive Principles.
(2) Except to the extent provided for in this recommendation, the National Goals and Directive Principles shall not be directly justiciable. However, these goals and principles should not be regarded by any court, other adjudicatory tribunal or institution of government as being of less weight than other directly justiciable provisions.
(3) Government (including institutions of Government) should make specific reference to the National Goals and Directive Principles indicating their relevance to national policies and programmes such as the Development Plan and the Budget.

Note: (i) To exemplify the manner in which Clause (1) of this recommendation is intended to be applied as an aid to interpretation, we envisage that where the meaning of a constitutional provision is in question, or any law or administrative action, or there is ambiguity in any law, or no particular law or principle of law appears to apply to the circumstances involved in any matter before a court, the court will give an interpretation which is consistent with the National Goals and Directive Principles rather than an alternative interpretation.

(ii) In Part 1 of Chapter 5, Human Rights and Obligations, the Committee has recommended that the proposed Law Reform Commission, or another body comprising Papua New Guinean public servants, and possibly politicians also, with appropriate skilled staff, and outside consultants (if needed), be established to review all existing legislation and policies with a view to achieving their conformity with the National Goals and Directive Principles in the chapter and the Human Rights and Obligations in Chapter 5.

SIGNIFICANCE AS AN AID TO INTERPRETATION

Comment

Section 25(3) provides:
Where any law, or any power conferred by any law (whether the power be of a legislative, judical, executive, administrative or other kind), can reasonably be understood, applied, exercised or enforced, without failing to give effect to the intention of Parliament or to this Constitution, in such a way as to give effect to the National Goals and Directive Principles; or at least not to derogate them, it is to be understood, applied or exercised, and shall be enforced, in that way.

The Supreme Court however has not as yet delivered a definitive judgment as to the correct approach of the courts to these materials prescribed as, inter alia, guides to judicial interpretation.

Instead this question remains unsettled. This lack of finality arises because of a schism between those judges who perceive it to be their duty to seek assistance from materials in every circumstance and those who believe they ought only turn to such aids if the law (or power conferred by law) cannot be construed or understood without ambiguity.

An example of each approach appears below. In the authors' opinion the approach illustrated in the judgment of Kearney J. is more consistent with the terms of the directions expressed in ss.24 and 25 of the Constitution.

Example 1: The judicial ingenuity approach.

per Kearney J

The process of statutory interpretation is essentially intuitive and subjective, in the absence of rules consistently applied. The Act is a Constitutional Law and thus subject to the general principles of interpretation set out in Constitution ss.10, 25(3), 63(3) and Basic Social Obligations ss.24, 109(4) when read with Sch. 1.2 and Sch. 1.5. In my opinion these provisions amount to a direction to the Court that in carrying out its functions under Constitution s.18(1) the words actually used in the Act do not have to be strictly adhered to but are to be construed with the assistance of the materials referred to in Constitution s.24, so as best to attain what Parliament intended. When Constitution ss.109(4) and 158(2) are themselves interpreted with the aid of s.24, this view is fortified: there are several references in Chapter 8 of the Report of the Constitutional Planning Committee which point against the Court taking a 'narrowly legalistic' or 'literal' approach, and thus sacrificing the 'spirit for the letter of the Constitution'. The 'dynamic character' of the Constitution is emphasized; in interpreting the laws, the judges are urged to use 'judicial ingenuity' in appropriate cases, to do justice. One consequence of this approach to interpretation is that the Court should not fail to give a provision the effect it considers the Parliament intended, by applying a literal or 'plain meaning' test nor should it attribute to the legislature an intention to produce a capricious or unjust result. The search throughout is for the intention of Parliament, a process which remains, formally at least, one of interpretation and not of legislation, and one in which the best guide remains the provisions of the Act itself.

The State v The Independent Tribunal: Ex parte Sasakila [1976] PNGLR 491, at pp.506-507.

Example 2: The 'Case of doubt' approach.

per Wilson J.

But, is a Committee of Review, appointed under s.7(1C)(sic) of the *Migration Act* 1963 charged with the responsibility of reviewing the Minister's notice of revocation and deciding whether or not to uphold the Minister's decision to revoke an entry permit, bound to follow the requirements of natural justice?

In order to find the answer to this question one needs to interpret the provisions of the Constitution itself. For the purpose of the interpretation of the Constitution the provisions of Sch.1 (Rules for Shortening and Interpretation of the Constitutional Laws) apply and, subject to that schedule, the underlying law applies (see s.8 of the Constitution). In interpreting the meaning of the language used in the Constitution it is necessary to read the Constitution, being a constitutional law in itself, as a whole (see Sch.1.5(1) of the Constitution) and to give to all provisions thereof and all words, expressions and propositions therein 'their fair and liberal meaning' (see Sch.1.5(2) of the Constitution). As there can be no doubt as to the interpretation of the provisions to which reference will be made, (i.e. this is not a 'case of doubt'), I find it unnecessary (indeed I think it inappropriate) to use the preamble to the Constitution, in particular, the national goals and directive principles 'as an aid to interpretation' and, in any event, the preamble, although forming part of the Constitution, 'must be read subject to any other provision' of the Constitution (see Sch.1.3(1) of the Constitution). As there appear to me to be rules of law that are 'applicable and appropriate to the circumstances' of this country, it is not part of this Court's duty to have particular regard to the national goals and directive principles and the basic social obligations (see Sch.2.3(1)(a)) .....

Premdas v Independent State of Papua New Guinea [1979] PNGLR 329 at p.375.

GENERALLY

Referred to

by Prentice Dep.C.J. in *Public Curator of Papua New Guinea v Public Trustee of New Zealand* [1976] PNGLR 427 at p.441 (See under Goal 2);

by Prentice C.J. in *Premdas v Independent State of Papua New Guinea* [1979] PNGLR 329 at pp.340, 341; see also Andrew J. at pp.395, 396 and Wilson J. (reproduced above) at p.375;

by Quinlivan A.J. in *Marben v Gesa* (1981 Unreported) N314(M) at p.7 (as enshrining 'democratic lesson of history').

National Goals and Directive Principles

WE HEREBY PROCLAIM the following aims as our National Goals, and direct all persons and bodies, corporate and unincorporate, to be guided by these our declared Directives in pursuing and achieving our aims:—

1. — INTEGRAL HUMAN DEVELOPMENT

We declare our first goal to be for every person to be dynamically involved in the process of freeing himself or herself from every form of domination or oppression so that each man or woman will have the opportunity to develop as a whole person in relationship with others.

WE ACCORDINGLY CALL FOR —

(1) everyone to be involved in our endeavours to achieve integral human development of the whole person for every person and to seek fulfilment through his or her contribution to the common good; and
(2) education to be based on mutual respect and dialogue, and to promote awareness of our human potential and motivation to achieve our National Goals through self-reliant effort; and
(3) all forms of beneficial creativity, including sciences and cultures, to be actively encouraged; and
(4) improvement in the level of nutrition and the standard of public health to enable our people to attain self fulfilment; and
(5) the family unit to be recognized as the fundamental basis of our society, and for every step to be taken to promote the moral, cultural, economic and social standing of the Melanesian family; and
(6) development to take place primarily through the use of Papua New Guinean forms of social and political organization.

C.P.C. Report Ch.2 p.3

The National Goals which we recommend should be incorporated in the Constitution are:—

INTEGRAL HUMAN DEVELOPMENT — LIBERATION AND FULFILMENT

1. ALL ACTIVITIES OF THE STATE SHOULD BE DIRECTED TOWARDS THE PERSONAL LIBERATION AND FULFILMENT OF EVERY CITIZEN, SO THAT EACH MAN AND WOMAN WILL HAVE THE OPPORTUNITY OF IMPROVING HIMSELF OR HERSELF AS A WHOLE PERSON AND ACHIEVING INTEGRAL HUMAN DEVELOPMENT.

1. *INTEGRAL HUMAN DEVELOPMENT — LIBERATION AND FULFILMENT*

14. We do not take development to be synonymous with material progress. For us the only authentic development is integral human development. This means that we use the term *development* to mean nothing less than the unending process of improvement of every man and woman as a whole person. We take our stand on the dignity and worth of each Papua New Guinean man, woman and child. In effect, this means that integral human development must reach out to and enrich Papua New Guineans in every part of the country.

15. All Papua New Guineans have an inalienable right to liberation and fulfilment through this process of development. This right does not depend on our Constitution. The Constitution is merely restating the right and explicitly confirming it.

16. No particular area or grouping of people should be developed at the expense of another, materially or in other ways. There should always be an equitable distribution and balanced sharing of all the benefits and opportunities the nation has to offer. For this type of development to come into being, it is necessary for such conditions to be created and to obtain throughout the nation at all times as to be conductive to that development. [p.4]

17. These conditions can only be brought about when the running of the country is in the hands of Papua New Guineans who cherish a genuine respect for the traditions of our country, and our people; who can distinguish those features of the peoples' traditions that should be retained from those that should be allowed to lapse; and who know how to discern what is good in what other nations and peoples have to offer to Papua New Guineans.

18. The best judges, therefore, of what contributes to the full human well-being of the people of Papua New Guinea are to be found among Papua New Guineans themselves. In probably no other matter is self-reliance more necessary. The Government will always have its proper and key role to play in helping to create the conditions in which Papua New Guineans can thrive and enthusiastically pursue their own full human development.

19. By tradition, Papua New Guineans are a spiritual people. This fundamental tradition must always be respected and given the conditions of freedom to develop and to be enriched. Closely tied with the spiritual and religious features of Papua New Guinea's traditions are the cultural elements of the nation. Here we are in touch with the spirit of the people, with their roots and with their authentic creative genius, the nurture of which will ensure our true national identity.

20. The social aspects of the life and progress of the people draw attention to how rich and deep is the meaning we give *development*.

21. Our National Goals and Directive Principles are intended to provide guidance for the full development of our people. People are the common denominators of progress, improvement and development. This is why all social, political, cultural, religious and economic activity should be directed towards the personal liberation and fulfilment of every citizen.

22. Although social progress is not synonymous with economic progress, economic development has meaning insofar as it promotes the well-being of the people in many of the important aspects of their lives as members of a community.

23. Without political development of the people of Papua New Guinea, the genuine progress of the nation will be seriously hindered. What is at stake is human freedom. One main key to political progress is the increasing participation of Papua New Guineans at all levels of political activity. This promotes human responsibility and enhances personal dignity as well as helping to safeguard personal freedom.

24. Acceptance of equality among Papua New Guineans with their active participation in the affairs of the nation will mean a substantial contribution to integral human development.

Education

25. We are concerned by the way in which in the past development and modern institutions have alienated our people from one another. Our schools have tended to make children strangers to their parents and their villages. Universities have furthered this process of alienation. At least until recently the whole education process was leading towards social stratification, increased difficulty in communication among members of a single social group, and a decline in the level of tolerance and interpersonal respect among our people.

26. To reverse this process of alienation is not an easy matter. We acknowledge this. The present government has begun the task, but it is one of great magnitude and will involve constant effort for real change to be achieved.

27. Education should be based on and should promote dialogue and co-operation. It should foster integral human development and tolerance among our people, awaken their social conscience, their awareness of the essential dignity of man, and their appreciation of the need to stand up for their rights, both as members of the

community and as individuals, in the face of pressures from foreign interests and arbitrary government. It should help develop a spirit of solidarity of one with another, and an appreciation of our inter-dependence.

28. We cannot build a democratic, just society unless our children's education and all educational institutions are geared to achieving these objectives.

International solidarity

29. In today's world it is essential for all countries industrialised and developing alike — to have effective links with other states. However, as our Government recognises, a new state such as Papua New Guinea needs to look very carefully at the kinds of relationships it forms with other countries. As a general rule we do not wish to become involved in formal alliances, or to become too closely linked with particular countries. [p.5]

However, we do believe that we should clearly recognize our position as a country of the Third World, and actively support initiatives aimed at improving the present underprivileged position of developing countries.

30. We recommend that our people should be encouraged and given greater opportunity, through education, the media and by other means, to increase their awareness of other emerging states. They should then obtain a greater realization of our government in joint international measures aimed at strengthening the solidarity of these states in the fight for 'the establishment of a new international economic order based on equity, sovereign equality, interdependence and co-operation to ensure economic and social development in peace and justice for present and future generations' in all countries, including our own.

31. A number of developments in the United Nations Organization and in different regions of the world in recent years give reason for optimism that the first positive steps are being taken towards changing the present grossly unjust international economic system which allows wealthy corporations and countries to exploit the people and resources of developing countries. We must play our part in strengthening the bargaining position of other developing countries and ourselves.

32. The principle of international co-operation which we recommend is similar to one which was adopted, by the General Assembly of the United Nations in May this year, at a Special Meeting called to find a way to reform the present world economic order which is so dominated by the wealthy industrialized countries, and heavily weighted in favour of their interests.

RECOMMENDATIONS

INTEGRAL HUMAN DEVELOPMENT — LIBERATION AND FULFILMENT

1. ALL ACTIVITIES OF THE STATE SHOULD BE DIRECTED TOWARDS THE PERSONAL LIBERATION AND FULFILMENT OF EVERY CITIZEN, SO THAT EACH MAN AND WOMAN WILL HAVE THE OPPORTUNITY OF IMPROVING HIMSELF OR HERSELF AS A WHOLE PERSON AND ACHIEVING INTEGRAL HUMAN DEVELOPMENT.
   (1) Everyone should be involved in our endeavours to achieve integral human development and each individual should seek fulfilment in his or her contribution to the good of all.
   (2) Education should be based on and should promote dialogue and co-operation. It should foster integral human development and tolerance among our people and encourage among them a spirit of solidarity and interdependence.
   (3) All forms of beneficial creativity and culture, both of individuals and groups; should be encouraged.
   (4) Improvement of the level of nutrition and of the standard of public health is essential to enable our people to attain self-fulfilment.
   (5) The people of Papua New Guinea should increase their awareness of, and solidarity with, the peoples of other emerging countries, with a view to the establishment of a new international economic order based on equity, sovereign equality, interdependence, common interest and co-operation to enable people everywhere to achieve full development.
   (6) The family is the fundamental unit of Papua New Guinea society and every step should be taken to protect and promote its moral, cultural, economic and social standing.

AS TO UNDERLYING CONSTITUTIONAL PRINCIPLES

Held

Paragraph 1 of Goal 1 is evidence that the Constitution is 'permeated by an underlying principle of free and equal participation by its citizens'.
S.C.R. No 2 of 1982; Re Organic Law [1982] PNGLR 214; see Kearney Dep.C.J. at p.230.

GENERALLY

Referred to

by Narakobi J. in *Tabo Sipo v Meli* (1980 Unreported) N240 at p.7 (Paragraph 5 of Goal 1 as relevant to the severity of sentence appropriate to impose for adultery).

2. — EQUALITY AND PARTICIPATION.

We declare our second goal to be for all citizens to have an equal opportunity to participate in, and benefit from the development of our country.

WE ACCORDINGLY CALL FOR —

(1) an equal opportunity for every citizen to take part in the political, economic, social, religious and cultural life of the country; and

(2) the creation of political structures that will enable effective, meaningful participation by our people in that life, and in view of the rich cultural and ethnic diversity of our people for those structures to provide for substantial decentralization of all forms of government activity; and

(3) every effort to be made to achieve an equitable distribution of incomes and other benefits of development among individuals and throughout the various parts of the country; and

(4) equalization of services in all parts of the country, and for every citizen to have equal access to legal processes and all services, governmental and otherwise, that are required for the fulfilment of his or her real needs and aspirations, and

(5) equal participation by woman citizens in all political, economic, social and religious activities, and

(6) the maximization of the number of citizens participating in every aspect of development; and

(7) active steps to be taken to facilitate the organization and legal recognition of all groups engaging in development activities; and

(8) means to be provided to ensure that any citizen can exercise his personal creativity and enterprise in pursuit of fulfilment that is consistent with the common good, and for no citizen to be deprived of this opportunity because of the predominant position of another, and

(9) every citizen to be able to participate, either directly or through a representative, in the consideration of any matter affecting his interests or the interests of his community; and

(10) all persons and governmental bodies of Papua New Guinea to ensure that, as far as possible, political and official bodies are so composed as to be broadly representative of citizens from the various areas of the country; and

(11) all persons and governmental bodies to endeavour to achieve universal literacy in *Pisin*, *Hiri Motu* or English, and in "*tok ples*" or "*ita eda tano gado*", and

(12) recognition of the principles that a complete relationship in marriage rests on equality of rights and duties of the partners, and that responsible parenthood is based on that equality.

C.P.C. Report Ch.2 p.3

EQUALITY AND PARTICIPATION

2. ALL CITIZENS SHOULD HAVE AN EQUAL OPPORTUNITY TO PARTICIPATE IN, AND BENEFIT FROM, THE DEVELOPMENT OF OUR COUNTRY. [p.5]

2. *EQUALITY AND PARTICIPATION*

33. As we have said in relation to the first goal — 'Integral Human Development — Liberation and Fulfilment', the kind of society which we believe our people want to build is one which is fundamentally based on the right of each one of our citizens, whether he or she lives in a village, a town, or a city; to fully develop himself or herself as a whole person.

34. We recognize that people are not born equal either in the talents they possess or in their determination to use them to the best of their ability. But everyone should have an equal chance to develop the talents he or she has whether they be in farming, teaching, the arts, technology or in any other field of human activity.

35. At present the place in which a child happens to be born is an extremely important factor in determining the opportunities he or she will have of obtaining any education at all, of winning a place in a high school, of obtaining health and other government services and of being able to participate in the cash economy.

36. This situation has resulted from the fact that some areas of the country have been very much neglected in the past — in their economic development and in the education, health and other services established there. Not surprisingly this situation has given rise to wide-spread resentment and has been a major underlying cause of disunity at this crucial stage of our country's development. The goal of achieving equality of opportunity and participation in our national life is not, then, something for which we may piously hope, but a vital necessity if we are to achieve genuine national integration.

37. Our present Government is seeking to reduce these inequalities of educational and economic opportunities and access to other government services in different parts of the country, and we fully endorse this policy.

38. But inequalities of opportunity as between different areas are not the only inqualities with which, as a nation, we should be concerned. There is also emerging a class structure which did not exist before — well-educated Papua New Guineans are tending to lose touch with their relatives in the villages, and gaining substantially greater opportunities to advance themselves than their village counterparts.

39. We must take firm steps to prevent this situation developing further. There is a clear need to reshape our society now before this emerging class structure becomes entrenched, so that all of our people have an equal opportunity to develop themselves; so that they can use their abilities to achieve personal fulfilment, and at the same time, make a full contribution to the welfare of the nation.

40. We do not underestimate the difficulties we face in seeking this goal of equality and participation, but we are convinced that now is the time to direct all major policies toward this end. Nothing less than a full scale effort will have any chance of success. [p.6]
Despite the recent steps taken by our Government to redirect development in this manner, the effects of the development policies which were vigorously pursued by the Australian Administration during the second half of the nineteen sixties and into the seventies, aimed at achieving the maximum economic return in the shortest possible time, are widespread and not easy to reverse.

41. But we must reverse these effects if we are to achieve this fundamental goal. Without equality of opportunity the level of participation in the political process and in other aspects of the life of our nation will be uneven. Those who have had the fewest opportunities will not be able to adequately press for their rights as against others who are more educated, have greater mobility, and more experienced in making their views known and taken into account by the national government. The more privileged groups will be in a position to dominate the less privileged and may well do so. Such a situation must not be allowed to develop. Action on a broad front must be taken now to begin about real equality of opportunity for all our citizens.

Political and administrative decentralization

42. Our political institutions must not only appear to be open to all citizens — they must in fact provide maximum opportunities for our citizens to be involved in decision-making that affects them. In our country,

which stretches over a substantial land area, includes many island groups, comprises a great number of different ethnic, cultural and language groups, and does not yet have well developed road links, we believe it is vital that political and administrative decision-making be decentralized to the maximum extent that is consistent with promoting and safeguarding the national interest. That is one of the main reasons why we have given so much thought to the need for the establishment of a new level of government — 'provincial government'.

43. In Chapter 10 'Provincial Government' we have spelt out this underlying philosophy and have set out our detailed proposals for putting it into practice. But we would emphasize here that without a fundamental change in our present system of government, it will be virtually impossible for the goal of 'equality and participation' to be fulfilled. As we point out in Chapter 10, the present governmental structure, inherited from the colonial administration, is one of the most centralized in the world, giving maximum opportunity to public servants, especially at headquarters, to influence policy, and minimum opportunity to our own people to be meaningfully involved in their own government. Most local government councils have not been able to provide a satisfactory avenue for the people's participation in their own development, as the councils have been dominated by the central administration for many years, and thus had much of their initiative and energy sapped.

44. We are convinced that only by establishing this system of provincial government at the district level will the undue dominance of centralized administration be broken, and the will of the people be adequately reflected in the policies and institutions of government in every part of the Papua New Guinean nation.

Equality of opportunity and equitable sharing of benefits

45. One of the most accurate measures of the degree to which a society is meeting the great challenge of attempting to achieve a just society is the evenness of the spread of the economic benefits of the country's development among those who live and work in that country. Few countries have gone very far in meeting this challenge. Even in the great majority of the most highly industrialised countries of the world the gulf between the richest and the poorest citizens is prodigious, and makes far less meaningful the fundamental rights and freedoms enshrined in the constitutions of some of these countries.

46. In many developing countries the contrast between the wealthy few and the mass of ordinary people, the great majority of whom are barely able to make out a subsistence living, is even more stark. Independent Papua New Guinea must be very different from this, and we have every confidence that it will be.

47. In seeking to build an egalitarian society, Papua New Guineans have two important advantages that many other countries lack. Firstly, we have no traditional ruling class whose members regard privilege and wealth as their rightful possessions. Secondly, the vast majority of our people have significant land rights which they have jealously guarded over centuries, and which enable a substantial number of them to obtain a basic living, quite apart from any involvement they may have in the cash economy.

48. The recent report of the Commission of Enquiry into Land Matters emphasized the need to ensure that our people are not deprived of their ancient land rights, stressing that Papua New Guinea does not want to see the emergence of a class of landless people as has occurred in so many other developing countries. [p.7]

49. We believe all Papua New Guineans want each of our people to have a decent standard of living, with no citizen living in luxury, enjoying a surplus of the benefits produced by the hard work of ordinary people. This aim is very much in keeping with the second of the Eight Aims, though it spells out more clearly the objective of substantial equality of incomes among all Papua New Guineans.

50. As we said earlier, we are well aware that no two people are exactly alike, in personality, ability or initiative. Some have more determination and drive than others. Certainly the reards which highly talented and hard working people receive should, in any system of government, be above the average level of incomes in the country, but consistently with the Eight Aims we consider that the disparities between those with the highest incomes and those with the lowest should be minimized as far as possible. The Government should actively seek to increase the proportion of the economic benefits of our country's development which goes to those who have the lowest incomes, whether they be living in villages or towns. We believe our people are firmly against 'elitism' which is both unjust and undemocratic, and leads to the kinds of social problems which we are experiencing now in our main towns, where disparities in wealth are most obvious.

51. We welcome and fully support the basis of the agreement recently reached between the Public Service Association and the Public Service Board for a flat pay increase for national public servants to take account of high inflation since their salaries were last increased. The amount involved, namely $350 per year, is to be paid irrespective of whether public servants are in a high position or at or near the base of the public service salary range.

52. The effect of such a salary increase is, of course, that the person on a lower salary benefits proportionately far more than does a person at a high level. Thus the gap between those public servants in responsible positions who earn high salaries and those who earn low salaries is being reduced. Already the ratio between the highest paid Second Division officers and the lowest paid Third Division officers has been reduced substantially since 1968. At that time the ratio between these two salary levels was 1:13. It is now 1:6.

53. We believe that practical examples of this type of forebearance on the part of our more privileged people can have a significant and very beneficial effect on the attitude of all of our people (including the Government) to greater equality of incomes. Such practical action carries far more weight than words can do. We believe action must be taken on a wide front to deal fully with this basic problem of income inequalities, and the initiative which the Public Service Association has taken to apply the principle of reducing wage and salary differentials between the highest and the lowest paid workers in the private sector as well as in the Public Service, deserves full support.

54. The incomes of expatriates should also be taken into account when looking at income levels in this country. It is not enough to hold down the incomes of our own senior people, if those of foreign citizens living and working here continue to rise with the same rapidity as they have been doing in recent years. There should be a firm policy on this matter developed immediately.

55. In seeking to achieve greater equality in the sharing of benefits, our Government should be particularly conscious of the present wide disparities between the standards of living of people in the various districts. To achieve this greater equality is an extremely urgent matter, but it will take a very substantial sustained effort to successfully change this situation.

56. We recommend that it should be a constitutional principle that the number of citizens participating in every aspect of development should be maximised. Thus co-operatives and general purpose corporations should be actively encouraged and promoted. The relatively few large scale enterprises which we allow to operate here should involve as many of our people as possible, in various capacities; not only as employees but as sub-contractors, suppliers, etc. Projects of any kind should meaningfully involve the people of the area in which they are being carried out.

57. The Government's recent legislation providing for the incorporation of land holding groups, and of groups that wish to involve themselves in development activities which are not necessarily linked with land, is a significant step in applying the directive principle which we purpose, namely, that "the organization and legal recognition of all groups engaging in development activities should be facilitated." It should help to stimulate more self-help business activity — something which is urgently needed if we are to become more self reliant. [p.8]

58. We believe it is a strongly held view of our people that no citizen should be deprived of the opportunity of performing any beneficial task which he or she does well, and particularly that, in the economic field, for example, a particular activity should not be monopolised by a single company or person. Our people are totally against allowing large enterprises, whether expatriate owned or Papua New Guinea owned to dominate a particular field for economic activity, such as the operation of fork-lift trucks, taxis or road transport, or marketing produce, thereby effectively depriving individual citizens or small groups of citizens, of the opportunity to complete.

Equal status and opportunity for women

59. We have also emphasized the importance of women being able to make their full contribution to the welfare of the country, on an equal footing with men. In recent years women have played a significantly greater part in the country's national life — in politics, in business, in social and cultural activities. But more effort should be made by government to hasten this development. Obstacles to educational and other opportunities which face women at present should be removed, and insofar as it is within the power of the Government to do so, the difficulties facing women who wish to involve themselves in the affairs of the nation should be reduced.

Broad representation in official bodies

60. Whilst we believe that it is of considerable importance that people chosen to fill positions of high responsibility in government such as in the National Executive Council, parliamentary committees and statutory authorities, etc., should be selected primarily on the basis of their personal qualities and experience, we recognize that another important factor should be taken into account. It is a strongly held view among many of our people that as far as possible official bodies should be composed of persons who are 'broadly representative of the various areas of the country'. If they are composed in this way the people of the different areas of Papua New Guinea will feel a greater sense of involvement than would otherwise be the case. Particularly at this stage of our development, this is a vital necessity.

National languages

61. We strongly recommend that the State clearly recognize Pidgin, Hiri Motu and English, as national languages. Literacy in these languages should be actively promoted to encourage better communication between many different groups of our people, and enable them to participate more fully in the affairs of the country.

62. Literacy in local languages should not, however, be discouraged as they should be safeguarded from falling into disuse. Thus we envisage that as many as possible of our people will be multi-lingual.

RECOMMENDATIONS [p.22]

EQUALITY AND PARTICIPATION

2. ALL CITIZENS SHOULD HAVE AN EQUAL OPPORTUNITY TO PARTICIPATE IN AND BENEFIT FROM THE DEVELOPMENT OF OUR COUNTRY.

(1) Every citizen should have an equal opportunity to take full part in the political, economic, social, religious and cultural life of the country.
(2) To provide for effective and meaningful participation by the people in their own development, a structure conducive to such participation must be evolved. In view of the diverse nature of Papua New Guinea and its peoples, that structure must provide for substantial political, economic and administrative decentralisation.
(3) Every effort should be made to achieve equalisation of incomes and equal distribution of the benefits of development among individuals and different areas of the country.
(4) Every citizen should have equal and effective access to all governmental services and legal processes. Therefore, strong emphasis should be placed on equalisation of services among different areas of the country.
(5) Women should be able to participate equally in all social, political, religious and economic activities.
(6) The number of citizens participating in every aspect of development should be maximised.
(7) The organisation and legal recognition of all groups engaging in development activities should be facilitated.
(8) No citizen should be deprived of the opportunity to perform any task that is beneficial and that he or she does well and, in particular, no citizen should be deprived of such an opportunity because of the predominance of another.
(9) Every citizen should be able to participate, either directly or through a representative, in the consideration of any matter affecting his interest or the interests of his community.
(10) The State should, as far as possible, ensure that official bodies are so composed as to be broadly representative of citizens from the various areas of the nation.
(11) The State should endeavour to achieve literacy in Pisin, Hiri Motu or English, and in 'tok ples' or 'ita eda tano gado'.
(12) Marriage rests on the equality of rights and duties of both spouses and responsible parenthood is based on that equality.

AS TO UNDERLYING CONSTITUTIONAL PRINCIPLES

Held

Paragraphs 1,2,5,8 and 9 of Goal 2 are evidence that the Constitution is 'permeated by an underlying principle of free and equal participation by its citizens'.
S.C.R. No 2 of 1982; Re Organic Law [1982] PNGLR 214; see Kearney Dep.C.J. at p.230.

AS GUIDANCE AS TO WHICH RULES OF COMMON LAW ARE INAPPLICABLE IN PAPUA NEW GUINEA

Held

Paragraph 11 of Goal 2 which distinguishes between written and unwritten languages is one indication that the common-law rule (that if a slander is alleged to have been published in a language foreign to the Court, when pleaded, it must be set out in writing in the foreign language and then followed by a literal translation in the language of the Court) is inapplicable to the circumstances of Papua New Guinea where many languages have yet to be reduced to writing.
Tei Abul v Anton Parau [1976] PNGLR 251, see Frost C.J. at p.254.

AS AN AID TO STATUTORY INTERPRETATION

per Prentice Dep. C.J.

Under National Goal No 2, that calling for Equality and Participation, the Constitution enacts as a directive, the 'equalization of services in all parts of the country, and for every citizen in all parts of the country, and for every citizen to have equal access to legal processes and all services, governmental and otherwise, that are required for the fulfilment of his or her real needs and aspirations ...'

Section 25 of the Constitution directs that:

25. (3) Where any law, or any power conferred by a law (whether the power be of a legislative, judicial, executive, administrative or other kind), can reasonably be understood, applied, exercised or enforced, without failing to give effect to the

> intention of the Parliament or to this Constitution, *in such a way as to give effect to the National Goals and Directive Principles, or at least not to derogate them*, it is to be understood, applied or exercised, and shall be enforced, in that way . . . .
>
> (emphasis mine)
>
> The desire to make proper testamentary disposition of his property comes within the legitimate needs and aspirations of citizens. Equalization of access to the legal processes and services necessary to achieve these needs and aspirations, including (1 conceive) the drafting making of effective wills of which probate can be granted by the Court is a declared aim. The legislators would have been fully seized of the difficulties put in the way of an intending willmaker by the geography, isolation, lack of easy (sic) and the cost of, travel facilities, the fewness of lawyers, prevailing in Papua New Guinea. They have intended I think, to provide that the ability to make a valid will without rigid compliance with formalities, should be more widely available.
>
> For each and all the above reasons I consider wide rather than a restricted interpretation of s.43, [of the *Wills Probate and Administration Act* 1967] to be called for.
> *Public Curator of Papua New Guinea v Public Trustee of New Zealand* [1976] PNGLR 427 at p.431.

AS CONSISTENT WITH TRANSFER OF PROPERTY OF WILL BY A CITIZEN

Held

Paragraph 3 of Goal 2 was not intended to prohibit or discourage a citizen from distributing his personal property and interests according to his wishes following death.
Timereke v Ferrie and Johns (1982 Unreported) N379; see Pratt J. at p.31.

Referred to

by Prentice Dep.C.J. in *Public Curator of Papua New Guinea v Public Trustee of New Zealand* [1976] PNGLR 427 at p.431;

by Kapi Dep.C.J. in *Re James Allan Sannga; Peter Yewie Umai Timereke v Duncan Martin Ferrie and anor* (1983 Unreported) SC255 at p.25; see also Kidu C.J. at pp.15, 16; Andrew J. at p.47.

GENERALLY

Referred to

by Prentice Dep.C.J. (dissenting) in *Peter v South Pacific Brewery Ltd* [1976] PNGLR 537 at pp.556, 557 (as support for the proposition that certain minor charges for which imprisonment is a potential penalty may be heard summarily in the absence of the defendent by consent);

by Pratt J. in *Minister of Lands v Frame* [1980] PNGLR 433 at pp.490, 491 (Paragraphs 1, 3, and 6 of Goal 2 to be considered by a court when determining 'just compensation' under s.53 of the Constitution);

by Narakobi J. in *Tabo Sipo v Meli* (1982 Unreported) N240 at p.7 (Paragraph 12 of Goal 2 considered in determining the penalty appropriate to be imposed for the offence of adultery);

by Narakobi J. in *Tongloe v Tongloe and ors* (1980 Unreported) N256 at p.3 (Paragraphs 5 and 12 of Goal 2 as evidence of the equality of duties and obligations of marriage partners owed towards each other);

by Kapi Dep.C.J. in *Re James Allan Sannga; Peter Yewie Umai Timereke v Duncan Martin Ferrie and anor* (1983 Unreported) SC255 at p.25 (preamble to the Constitution does not authorize a court to question the appropriateness of an allegedly inconsistent statute to the circumstances of Papua New Guinea).

3. — NATIONAL SOVEREIGNTY AND SELF-RELIANCE.

We declare our third goal to be for Papua New Guinea to be politically and economically independent, and our economy basically self-reliant.

WE ACCORDINGLY CALL FOR —

(1) our leaders to be committed to the National Goals and Directive Principles, to ensure that their freedom to make decisions is not restricted by obligations to or relationship with others, and to make all of their decisions in the national interest; and

(2) all governmental bodies to base their planning for political, economic and social development on these Goals and Principles, and

(3) internal interdependence and solidarity among citizens, and between provinces, to be actively promoted; and

(4) citizens and governmental bodies to have control of the bulk of economic enterprise and production; and

(5) strict control of foreign investment capital and wise assessment of foreign ideas and values so that these will be subordinate to the goal of national sovereignty and self-reliance, and *in particular* for the entry of foreign capital to be geared to internal social and economic policies and to the integrity of the Nation and the People; and

(6) the State to take effective measures to control and actively participate in the national economy, and *in particular* to control major enterprises engaged in the exploitation of natural resources; and

(7) economic development to take place primarily by the use of skills and resources available in the country either from citizens or the State and not in dependence on imported skills and resources; and

(8) the constant recognition of our sovereignty, which must not be undermined by dependence on foreign assistance of any sort, and *in particular* for no investment, military or foreign-aid agreement or understanding to be entered into that imperils our self-reliance and self-respect, or our commitment to these National Goals and Directive Principles, or that may lead to substantial dependence upon or influence by any country, investor, lender or donor.

C.P.C. REPORT Ch.2, p.3

NATIONAL SOVEREIGNTY AND SELF-RELIANCE

3. PAPUA NEW GUINEA SHOULD BE POLITICALLY AND ECONOMICALLY INDEPENDENT AND ITS ECONOMY SHOULD BE BASICALLY SELF-RELIANT. [p.8]

3. *NATIONAL SOVEREIGNTY AND SELF-RELIANCE*

63. It follows from what we have said that it is a fundamental goal of our people that Papua New Guinea should make its own decisions, and that its sovereignty should not be reduced by external political, economic or military dependence; that national leaders should always be free to make national decisions.

64. The economies of the developing countries of the world are in most cases strongly affected by foreign interests. Papua New Guinea is no exception. A study made last year by the Australian Government's Joint Intelligence Organization is reported to have found that almost two-thirds of the developed section of Papua New Guinea's economy is controlled by Australian companies and individuals. And with the rapidly increasing extent of Japanese involvement in large scale economic activity here, it is clear that we Papua New Guineans at present control only a very small part of our own economy, and will remain in this subservient position unless firm action is taken to change the existing situation in a meaningful way.

65. If Self-government and Independence are to have real meaning these milestones must be accompanied by a substantial measure of control by Papua New Guinea over economic enterprises throughout the country. In the present circumstances this can only be achieved by developing solidarity between all people within the country and giving second place to relationships with outsiders. It may well be that it will be necessary for us to forego some immediate material benefits which might be derived from dealings with outsiders, in order to enhance our own political sovereignty. [p.9]

66. Far too many countries of the Third World are forced, by economic relationships with industrialised countries, to build their societies more in accordance with the interests of the industrialised countries than with their own national wishes. We firmly believe that Papua New Guinea must avoid a situation where foreign capital controls the destiny of its people.

67. However, for many years Papua New Guinea's development has been steadily fitting into the type of development typical of many Third World countries. This is seen as basically a matter of obtaining money for development activities. To get this money, foreign investment (and foreign domination of the economy) is uncritically encouraged; inequality is often deliberately promoted so that there will be a band of rich people who (so it is argued) will reject their traditional obligations and retain money to invest. This kind of development has generally not been successful elsewhere and has led to very serious social inequalities, but it is still dominant in Papua New Guinea. It can be accurately called 'dominant development'.

68. Other trends in this country are opposed to dominant development. One such is the Eight Aims which we set out in full earlier in this Chapter. Another trend opposed to dominant development can be seen in the growth of development groups such as the New Guinea Development Corporation, Kabisawali Village Development Corporation, the Hiri Hanua Development Corporation, the Bena Association and the Komge Oro Association.

69. In comparison to these new trends, dominant development is much more effectively organised; it has a headstart, it is well entrenched and it has access to considerable resources and skills.

70. The fact that dominant development is better organised and well established means that it is in a superior position to take advantage of new situations. A most important emerging situation is 'provincial government' which, in Chapter 10, we recommend should be established throughout the country as soon as possible. We must be constantly aware of the danger of dominant development exercising an undue and improper influence on provincial governments, and take the necessary steps to ensure that such influence is firmly contained.

71. We should accept foreign investment only if it is in accordance with very strict controls, and to the extent that it does not overtax our capacity to cope with its direct and indirect effects. We have specifically provided in a directive principle under this goal of 'National Sovereignty and Self-Reliance' for full account to be taken of the skilled manpower resources which we have when we are deciding whether a particular foreign enterprise should be accepted. We believe it is seriously detrimental to the long-term interests of our people for large scale foreign enterprises to be established, employing substantial numbers of skilled expatriates, with our own people being involved only at the lower levels of management and operations for many years to come. We are also aware, however, that too many foreign enterprises can attract a substantial proportion of our highly skilled people, whose numbers are very small at present, thereby diverting these people away from governmental activities which are more directly relevant to the needs of the country.

72. Bringing foreign investment into our country at this stage of its development can be likened to using a bucket of water to fill a cup. The cup can only contain a small amount of the water in the bucket and the excess water simply overflows and runs away, as do the benefits of excessive foreign investment.

73. It is essential that we be highly selective as to the type of enterprise we allow into this country — not only should we very carefully consider whether the industry which a foreign company proposes to establish is in accordance with our national objectives, but we should thoroughly investigate the history of the company's activities in other countries. We must not allow any foreign enterprise to operate in our country unless we can be sure that it will fully abide by our laws, and will not make any attempt to interfere with our political and civic affairs.

74. Companies whose history shows that they have evaded substantial taxes by various unscrupulous means

should not be allowed to operate here. The recent allegations by the Leader of the Opposition, Mr. Abal, (which the Government has recently agreed are correct) that certain foreign companies operating here have, by 'juggling' their operations, evaded their obligations to Papua New Guinea, thereby costing this country millions of dollars in taxes, gives weight to this concern.

75. On a different plane, we know there have been too many instances of undue influence or even outright manipulation of the governments of developing countries (and some industrialized countries also) by multinational corporations sometimes backed by their home governments, to achieve their own ends. Foreign corporations which have interfered with any other government or taken steps to try to bring the government of any other country to its knees by economic pressure, should not be allowed to operate in this country. [p.10]

76. Foreign companies which fall into either of the above categories, but are already operating here should not be able to obtain any new agreement with our Government, and consideration should be given to whether any existing agreement between the Government and such company be cancelled.

77. We do not suggest that all foreign companies operate in this way, or that foreign investment in itself is necessarily bad. But we are concerned to ensure that foreign investment is firmly controlled in the interests of the majority of our people. When our economy is largely in the hands of foreign investors, as it is now, what real political power do we have, whether we are independent or not?

Impact of Multinational Corporations on development

78. The great problems which developing countries face in relation to the impact of the activities of multinational corporations, the largest and most powerful of the foreign investors, have been drawn together and analysed in a recent report (published on 9 June, 1974) prepared for the United Nations by a group of 'eminent persons', concerning the 'Impact of Multinational Corporations on Development and International Relations'. That Report (which we refer to below as 'the Report' makes reference to the benefits which such corporations can bring to a country, but emphasizes the dangers to developing countries if they do not —

(a) clearly spell out their national goals and priorities and their policies for the control and channelling of foreign investment; and
(b) ensure that all foreign investment accords with those policies.

79. The Report points out, on page 17, that multinational corporations generally continue to own and control the package of resources and capabilities which they introduce into a host country (the country in which they invest) —

> They also tap resources on a world-wide basis and syphon them off to markets where profitable possibilities exist. Their impact depends on the one hand on the nature of the package and the attitude and strategies of the multinational corporations, and on the other hand on the environment in which they operate. For example, foreign capital may augment the resources of the host country and relieve bottlenecks in foreign exchange; but it may also generate a series of large outflows in dividends and service payments. New technology may improve the utilization of resources, but may not always be appropriate for local needs such as for employment creation. Managerial and marketing skills may enhance productivity and the availability of goods, but they may also divert resources from where they are most needed to where they are most profitably sold.

80. The Report stresses the importance of looking at the total impact of multinational corporations on the host countries, and indicates that these corporations can increase the degree of dependence of host countries rather than strengthening their economic position.

81. As to the non-economic effect of these corporations on host countries, particularly developing countries, the Report says these are —

> frequently as important as or even more important than the economic impact. The effect of multinational corporations on the social institutions and cultural values of host countries may be especially striking if the tenor, tradition and stage of development of these countries differ considerably from those of the home countries. For example, the 'business culture', with its emphasis on efficiency, may be considered too impersonal in traditional societies. The very cultural identity and the entire social fabric may be at stake, especially if multinational corporations attempt to transplant their own models of social development to the host country.

82. The Report concludes that these problems are more pronounced in developing countries because most multinational corporations originate in countries with very different social and cultural backgrounds. The fact that multinational corporation feel that they can count on the support of a powerful home country or on the co-operation of a broad service network, strengthens their economic power.

83. Finally, the Report says, on page 18, that even in strictly economic terms, the benefits which the operations of multinationals confer on host countries is open to question.

> Spurs by multinational corporations to productive activities do not always [p.11] provide a basis for sustained and sound development. Isolated foreign enclaves have few linkages with the domestic economy. The extraction of natural resources may generate few processing industries or do little to raise the level of local skills. Branch plants which operate purely as off-shoots of their parent companies, such as component manufacturers, are unlikely to integrate fully into the local economy. Restrictions to competition may benefit the enterprise but not the individual countries in which its affiliates operate. Export market allocation and tied purchases affect the foreign exchange gained or saved by the host country. The attempts of host countries to raise taxes or to place limitations on foreign exchange remittances can be negated by vertically or horizontally integrated multinational corporations through transfer pricing and the use of tax havens.
>
> ..... even if a host country increases its share of benefits from the activities of multinational corporations and enjoys high rates of growth, its income distribution may not improve or may even deteriorate. Welfare standards for workers may be kept low, owing to weak or non-existent trade unions. Consumers may not benefit from low prices. High income obtained locally from the activities of multinational corporations may accrue largely to domestic elites associated with foreign interests. The vigorous sales efforts of the affiliate on behalf of products usually consumed in high-income countries may cater largely to upper income groups and promote consumption habits beyond the means of a poor country and unsuitable for the development of local industries. Basic needs of the population, such as food, health, education and housing, may be left unattended. The location of activities of multinational corporations in the developing countries may be influenced by more stringent requirements for protection of the environment in developed countries.

84. We have quoted extensively from this important Report because we believe the views expressed in it are very relevant to our situation. We have already experienced most of the detrimental effects both of foreign investment generally and of multinational corporations, in particular, to which the Report refers.

85. We believe strongly that the preservation of national sovereignty and integrity is crucial to our country's future well-being and that the Government must take a strong stand now to restrict the flow of foreign capital into our country if we are not to be overwhelmed by the influence of excessive foreign investment.

86. For this influence to be successfully contained, a thoroughgoing policy of self-reliance should be established to provide the basis of Papua New Guinea's attitude to foreign investment.

Self-reliance

87. The policy of self-reliance means various things: it means self-sufficiency in basic products, but also greater participation by Papua New Guineans in the economy, and an emphasis on small-scale business activity. We believe there is recognition throughout the country of the need for participation by the people in decision-making, and to open channels for the useful employment of the energies and enthusiasm of the people. This is reflected in the emphasis in the 'Eight Aims' on decentralisation and the typically Papua New Guinean forms of business activity.

88. It is clear that our people want economic development, but not just any kind of economic development. Our people are becoming increasingly aware that an obsession with economic development can lead to many harmful consequences; the disruption of traditional systems and values, the alienation of man, the exploitation of the poor by the rich, pollution of the environment and an unjustified depletion of our natural resources.

89. We believe that there is broad consensus among our people that economic development should not bring about disparities in incomes, either as between individuals or regions. Development above all, must be development of the people. It should be based on our people's own talents and hard work and emphasize Papua New Guinean ways in the manner we have explained earlier in this Chapter. True development is not to be measured by the Gross National Product. The degree to which people throughout the country have the opportunity to achieve personal fulfilment is a much more meaningful measure of a country's development. The total development of all our people, largely through their own efforts, should be our aim.

RECOMMENDATIONS [p.23]

NATIONAL SOVEREIGNTY AND SELF-RELIANCE

3. PAPUA NEW GUINEA SHOULD BE POLITICALLY AND ECONOMICALLY INDEPENDENT AND ITS ECONOMY SHOULD BE BASICALLY SELF-RELIANT.

(1) Leaders should be committed to the National Goals and should ensure that they are always able to freely make decisions in the national interest.
(2) The government should be responsible for the planning of social and economic development, based on principles of social justice, in the best interests of all Papua New Guineans.
(3) Internal interdependence and solidarity among citizens and between provinces should be vigorously promoted.

(4) The bulk of commercial enterprise and production should be controlled by citizens and the government.
(5) The entry and use of foreign investment capital must be subordinate to the goal of national sovereignty and self-reliance and, in particular, be geared to internal social and economic policies, and to the integrity of the nation and its people.
(6) The government should take strong and effective measures to control and actively participate in the national economy and especially to control major enterprises engaged in the exploitation of natural resources.
(7) Economic development should conform to the skills and resources that can be provided at any given time by citizens and by the government.
(8) Papua New Guinea's sovereignty must not be undermined by political, economic or military dependence on foreign countries or foreign capital. In particular, no investment, military or foreign aid agreement or understanding should be entered into that imperils the self-reliance and self-respect of the people and state of Papua New Guinea, or their commitment to these national goals and directive principles, or which may lead to substantial dependence upon or influence by any single country, investor, lender or donor (or any group of countries, investors, lenders or donors).

AS TO ALLEGED INCONSISTENCY WITH THE RULES OF NATURAL JUSTICE

per Miles J.

After very careful consideration of the National Goals and Directive Principles and of the Basic Social Obligations I am unable to see that they shed much light on the ... question as to whether the General Manager of Air Niugini has a right to be heard before he is removed from office under s.23(2) [of the *National Airline Commission Act*] .... I note that under the Constitution the third national goal of the people is expressed to be that of national sovereignty and self reliance and that the people accordingly call for the leaders of the nation 'to be committed to these National Goals and Directive Principles to ensure that their freedom to make decisions is not restricted by obligations to or relationships with others, and to make all of these decisions in the national interest'. I see this as a call for leaders to put aside personal obligations and relationships in favour of the national interest. It is not a charter for leaders to make decisions regardless of the rights accorded by law to other people. I agree with the view expressed by Greville Smith J. (*Fallsheer v Iambakey Okuk* [1980] PNGLR 101 at p.128) that it is not necessarily in the national interest that the chief executive of the national airline should be liable for dismissal without having an opportunity to be heard in his own defence.
Iambakey Okuk v Fallscheer [1980] PNGLR 274 at p.292.

GENERALLY

Referred to

by Narakobi J. in *Tabo Sipo v Meli* (1980 Unreported) N240 at p.7;

by Pratt J. in *Timereke v Ferrie and Johns* (1982 Unreported) N379 at p.30.

4. — NATURAL RESOURCES AND ENVIRONMENT.

We declare our fourth goal to be for Papua New Guinea's natural resources and environment to be conserved and used for the collective benefit of us all, and be replenished for the benefit of future generations.

WE ACCORDINGLY CALL FOR —

(1) wise use to be made of our natural resources and the environment in and on the land or seabed, in the sea, under the land, and in the air, in the interests of our development and in trust for future generations; and

(2) the conservation and replenishment, for the benefit of ourselves and posterity, of the environment and its sacred, scenic and historical qualities; and

(3) all necessary steps to be taken to give adequate protection to our valued birds, animals, fish, insects, plants and trees.

C.P.C. Report Ch.2 p.3

4. THE NATIONAL RESOURCES AND THE ENVIRONMENT OF PAPUA NEW GUINEA SHOULD BE CONSERVED AND USED FOR THE COLLECTIVE BENEFIT OF THE PEOPLE: AND SHOULD BE REPLENISHED IN THE INTEREST OF FUTURE GENERATIONS. [p.11]

4. *NATURAL RESOURCES AND THE ENVIRONMENT*

90. This goal is based on four fundamental principles. These are:-

1. In considering the natural resources of Papua New Guinea, our human [p.12] resources should be included. Our human talent should be directed to providing benefits to the majority of the people.
2. The basic concept in our society with regard to use of natural resources is that one generation holds and uses resources in the capacity of trustee for future generations. We, the generation of today, cannot squander our country's resources. We would clearly be failing in our responsibility if we sold our resources to foreigners for our own short term benefit, without regard to the needs of generations after us.
3. The resources of the world are limited. Our country and its resources are finite. For the sake of those who come after us, we must strictly limit the speed with which we exploit our natural resources. We must also replenish them as far as possible; (for example by replanting with new trees after mature trees have been cut down by a timber enterprise).
4. Our ancient animistic belief is that everything has a spirit. While this belief should not frighten us from 'subduing the earth' for our collective benefit, it should remind us that blind destruction of the environment will lead not only to pollution but to the 'death of the earth' which is vital to our nation.

91. Making the best use of the talents of our people, in the interests of the nation, is clearly of the highest importance. Particularly at our present stage of development when skills among Papua New Guineans which can usefully be aplied to the modern sector of productive activity, are scarce, we need to channel those skills into activities which will most effectively promote the welfare of our people. At the same time, the skills of the people in all kinds of traditional activities should be encouraged and further developed.

92. We believe that the people of Papua New Guinea, both of today and tomorrow, should be continually aware that in striving to improve their human lot they should not make the mistake of blindly destroying their rich natural environment — the land, the rivers, the sea, the fish, the animals, and the birds. Use of these resources should be weighed against the real cost to the country in terms of the damage which will be caused to the whole way of life of the people living in the vicinity of a particular project, the destruction of land, rivers and wildlife in the course of the operations of, for instance, a large mining or timber enterprise, the need for the integral development of man which also concerns spiritual, psychological, cultural and social development.

93. It is true that man can create a new landscape through reshaping the environment. But this should be done only with full regard to the natural scenic beauty of the environment. Man is inclined everywhere to use the modern tools of technology to demonstrate his mastery over matter. We believe that our mountains, our rivers and our valleys should not be destroyed for short term material benefits.

94. Historic sites, our objects of spiritual significance, for example, carved wood, spirit houses, etc. should be protected against deterioration and destruction. Everyone in our country should develop a true sense of pride and appreciation of our history and the objects which depict our yearnings, our struggles and our achievements.

95. We should develop a sense of respect for all our natural resources and the environment. We should not be afraid to use those resources to contribute to our development, but should be sure not to over-use them to the extent that they are rapidly exhausted, especially at this stage of our history when it is foreign interests who gain by far the most benefit from the exploitation of our natural resources. Our needs should be weighed against the needs of our children, their children and the generations which follow them.

96. The Government's recent establishment of the Ministry for the Environment is a welcome step towards the creation of effective institutions and policies for the adequate protection and improvement of the environment.

RECOMMENDATIONS. [p.24]

NATURAL RESOURCES AND ENVIRONMENT

4. THE NATURAL RESOURCES AND THE ENVIRONMENT OF PAPUA NEW GUINEA SHOULD BE CONSERVED AND USED FOR THE COLLECTIVE BENEFIT OF THE PEOPLE; AND SHOULD BE REPLENISHED IN THE INTEREST OF THE FUTURE GENERATIONS.

(1) The natural resources including land, forests, birds, animals, fish, water, sea, air and minerals should be used wisely in the interest of the integral development of all citizens throughout Papua New Guinea.

(2) The environment and its sacred, scenic and historical qualities should be conserved and replenished for the benefit of posterity.

5. PAPUA NEW GUINEAN WAYS.

We declare our fifth goal to be to achieve development primarily through the use of Papua New Guinean forms of social, political and economic organization

WE ACCORDINGLY CALL FOR —

(1) a fundamental re-orientation of our attitudes and the institutions of government, commerce, education and religion towards Papua New Guinean forms of participation, consultation, and consensus, and a continuous renewal of the responsiveness of these institutions to the needs and attitudes of the People; and

(2) particular emphasis in our economic development to be placed on small-scale artisan, service and business activity; and

(3) recognition that the cultural, commercial and ethnic diversity of our people is a positive strength, and for the fostering of a respect for, and appreciation of, traditional ways of life and culture, including language, in all their richness and variety, as well as for a willingness to apply these ways dynamically and creatively for the tasks of development; and

(4) traditional villages and communities to remain as viable units of Papua New Guinean society, and for active steps to be taken to improve their cultural, social, economic and ethical quality.

C.P.C. Report, Ch.2 p.3

PAPUA NEW GUINEAN WAYS

5. DEVELOPMENT SHOULD TAKE PLACE PRIMARILY THROUGH THE USE OF PAPUA NEW GUINEAN FORMS OF SOCIAL, POLITICAL AND ECONOMIC ORGANIZATION. [p.12]

5. *PAPUA NEW GUINEAN WAYS*

97. In Chapter 4 of our Second Interim Report dealing with Provincial Government, we said —
When Europeans settled in Papua New Guinea, they did not find a political vacuum on the shores and plains, and in the mountains of our islands. Our ancestors had well organised, self-sufficient communities or *wanples*, clans and tribes, to meet the needs of their times. The price of the impact of Western colonisation has been the sapping of the initiative of our people [p.13]

98. The process of colonisation has been like a huge tidal wave. It has covered our land, submerging the natural life of our people. It leaves much dirt and some useful soil, as it subsides. The time of independence is our time of freedom and liberation. We much rebuild our society, not on the scattered good soil the tidal wave of colonisation has deposited, but on the solid foundations of our ancestral land. We must take the opportunity of digging up that which has been buried. We must not be afraid to rediscover our art, our culture and our political and social organizations. Wherever possible, we must make full use of our ways to achieve our national goals. We

insist on this, despite the popular belief that the only viable means of dealing with the challenges of lack of economic development is through the efficiency of Western techniques and institutions.

99. We should use the good that there is in the debris and deposits of colonisation, to improve, uplift and enhance the solid foundations of our own social, political and economic systems. The undesirable aspects of Western ways and institutions should be left aside. We recognise that some of our own institutions impose constraints on our vision of freedom, liberation and fulfilment. These should be left buried if they cannot be reshaped for our betterment.

100. At the heart of our feelings is the Papua New Guinean human person. Full use should be made of the talent, skills and the abilities of our own people. We must place an unswerving trust in Papua New Guineans and their wisdom.

101. Our insistence that development should take place primarily through Papua New Guinean ways, should not be understood in its narrow, structural sense. What we mean is that since development is a process of growth in our people, it must take place through and in our human persons. Our social, political, economic and religious organisations are external manifestations of our human depth. Any development that is pursued outside our humanity is externally imposed and is inherently non-conducive to our true human development.

102. Development must take place through our people. It must be a process. It must not be a prefabricated, predetermined set of answers, formulae and solutions by foreigners to the problems and hopes we alone can feel and yearn for. Technology, scientific discoveries and institutions of the most recent times can, in many respects, be inappropriate for us. Proper development should take place through institutions and techniques that are not only meaningful to us, but also recognize our human dignity and enhance it.

103. Development through our ways should not be thought to involve stagnation. Papua New Guinean ways, contrary to a commonly held view, not only of foreign citizens but of our people also, are not stagnant and closed. Our ways have always been open to external influences. It is this inherent openness which has enabled us to achieve so much in such short time and adapt to the new structure which has existed since Europeans first arrived here. Our ability to cope with new demands, our ability to readjust our ancient ways to new needs, have enabled us to develop, though not in the manner which we are now striving for. It is this ability which is the centre of what we call 'Papua New Guinean ways'.

104. This ability to accept new ways is evident in the manner in which our people are quietly accepting the demands of a modern nation. There is the danger, however, that in so doing, we, as a people and as a nation, might become borrowers only. There is a danger that we might discard our ways or place them in subservience. No matter how hard we try to copy foreign ways, we will always end up being second-rate unless we make full use of our own traditions and institutions to achieve our national goals.

105. It is inevitable that we should make intelligent use of foreign ways. But we should do so only after we have set our national goals and priorities. The second step is to determine and make sound use of our own resources, both human and material. We should use foreign ways only to supplement our own resources. This is self-reliance. This is self-respect. It is our way, a Papua New Guinean way. It is a matter of our survival as a people to preserve our identity and still keep abreast of the changing times.

106. In this goal, we seek to promote our traditional ways such as participation, consultation and consensus and a willingness of privileged persons to voluntarily forgo benefits to enable those who are less privileged to have a little more. The example we have given earlier of the attitude of the Public Service Association to salary rises is a good example of this. We do not claim that these values are exclusive to Papua New Guineans. However, they are inherent in our people. Among friends, our way of life was to come to decisions by a long process of consultation and consensus. This process is the central element of true democracy and government by common will. This is a process which is most conducive to social harmony, co-operation and common good. [p.14]

107. This process may appear to be costly in time and in money. It is our firm belief, however, that if these processes of true mass involvement are not undertaken by our people, then in the long run, the new political institutions which we have either inherited or which the Committee has recommended in this Report will not take root. The result would be even more costly. Participation should grow out of commitment. Any commitment should grow out of an understanding of the real needs of the people and the measures being taken to meet these needs.

108. Consultation and consensus are inevitable where people recognise the need to depend on each other. They are based on respect for the individual and his dignity. Faced with real and pressing demands of one kind or another, we may despair and resort to drastic steps. And yet, the success of our labours will ultimately depend on the extent to which the masses understand our strategies and are able to identify with these.

109. Our colonisers have paid little regard to these values. They imposed their 'governments', their democracy, their institutions and their will with little or no regard to our own values and institutions. This way is a blatant denial of our humanity. By their practices, they have to some extent changed the natural growth of our human development and our organizations and forced them into positions of subservience.

110. We refer to the system of local government we have inherited. There can be little doubt that the effect of local governments has been, in some places, to reduce if not destroy the power of the traditional leadership and

government structure. A serious consequence has been the division of life into things political or governmental and things economic. Traditionally, life consisted of an integrated approach to our daily tasks. Law and morals, religion and spirituality, economics, politics and government were practised as a single system. In our societies there was not the word 'responsibilities'. We knew only of 'responsibility and authority'. Thus, whilst certain 'big men' or 'women' or chiefs assumed authority and responsibility, on the whole, men, women and children from a very early age assumed responsibility and authority.

111. Now, at this juncture of our development, we can do no less than to insist that the directive principles we have enunciated above should be renewed. We should seek to imbue all of our people with enthusiasm to work in the interests of the nation. They should be sufficiently motivated so that they are prepared to voluntarily accept the new authority required of them by new responsibilities.

112. Unless we revitalise those practices of participation, of consultation and consensus, and sacrifice for the common good, we are continuing the colonial process of holding our people subservient.

113. True democracy will not work until our people in every village and hamlet accept that they cannot be free and independent unless they actually think something, say something and take action about what should happen to their own lives and those of the people of our country. If we do not take development into our hands, we will become apathetic, disinterested, disillusioned and eventually destroyed. We will inevitably depend on others to supply us with answers to our problems — answers which only we, ourselves, are equipped to give.

114. We recognize our ethnic diversity and its varying forms of cultural expression as positive strengths. Despite our apparent differences, we are united in common spirit. All our people were deeply spiritual. Our technological achievements are similar. At this time, we can proudly claim that though in languages and in external forms of cultural practices we are diverse, we are, in essence, one people. We are a 'nation' within a nation, perhaps a model for a future world government.

115. Foreigners often say, 'but there are so many differences. What are the Papua New Guinean ways'? We recognize the legitimacy of this question. However, it betrays a lack of appreciation of what a Papua New Guinean person is. Our ways emphasize egalitarianism and commitment to the community. They recognize the individual as a member of his community. We place great stress on our obligations to our extended families. We share our wealth. We view life in an undivided total picture. These ways of thinking and acting should be encouraged, even in the face of the great emphasis of Western thinking on artificial differentiation between things spiritual or sacred and things physical or profane.

116. We see the darkness of neon lights. We see the despair and loneliness in urban cities. We see the alienation of man from man that is the result of the present machine orientated economy. We see true social security and man's happiness being diminished in the name of economic progress. We caution therefore that large-scale industries should be pursued only after very careful and thorough consideration of the likely consequences upon the social and spiritual fabric of our people. Great emphasis, we believe, should be given to small-scale, artisan services and business activity. That man should live decently in conditions fitting [p.15] to his dignity is an objective we cherish. We believe that humanity can be achieved in simplicity. There is overwhelming evidence to suggest that a significant number of people who live by the fruits of multi-million dollar multi-national corporations live in misery, loneliness and spiritual poverty. We believe that since we are a rural people, our strength should be essentially the land and the use of our innate artistic talents.

117. We should not be misunderstood. We are not here urging our people to become a nation of woodcarvers and banana-taro producers. What we say is that secondary and tertiary industries should be pursued only to supplement and to support our primary industries. Many of our people must, in time, become commercial entrepreneurs, capable of dealing with giant industries. But we should proceed in that direction with caution, and ensure that, in respect of each new large-scale enterprise it is conclusively established that the net benefit of the enterprise to Papua New Guineans as a whole will far exceed the net detriment in terms of our national goals and directive principles and to our human persons.

118. Our ways emphasize the needs of the community. We exercise our rights in the context of our obligations to our community. We consider our village and tribal units as our greatest elements for common care and support. Modern corporations, companies and business houses in our country should use the 'tribal spirit' to create a sense of solidarity and responsibility. In our village and tribal units, no-one is a master and no-one a servant, no-one is an employer and no-one an employee. Most of our societies are classless and egalitarian. This does not mean that, in earlier times, we were lawless or that we lived in anarchy.

119. Social obligations and customary laws governed our lives. We should redirect the government departments and the private sector to that 'tribal spirit' which is and can still be vital in efficiency, maximum output and eventual fulfilment.

120. Our rich variety in the cultural and artistic forms of expression should not be confused with our common unity. Making use of our ways, is a living process which places it beyond question that all material development is necessary only if it enhances the inherent good in ourselves and our social, religous, political, cultural and economic forms of organization. The fundamental premise is that we are a people. We are a race. We are a nation. It is through our ways that we should grow.

RECOMMENDATIONS [p.24]

PAPUA NEW GUINEAN WAYS

5. DEVELOPMENT SHOULD TAKE PLACE PRIMARILY THROUGH THE USE OF PAPUA NEW GUINEAN FORMS OF SOCIAL, POLITICAL AND ECONOMIC ORGANIZATION.

(1) To achieve our goals, there must be a fundamental re-orientation of the institutions of government, commerce, education and religion towards Papua New Guinean forms of participation, consultation and consensus. This re-orientation should be combined with a continuous renewal of the responsiveness of these institutions to the people, and a willingness on the part of those adversely affected by these changes to forgo disproportionate benefits for the good of all.
(2) In economic development particular emphasis should be placed on small-scale artisan, service and business activity.
(3) The cultural, communal and ethnic diversity of our peoples is recognized as a positive strength. There should be fostered a respect and appreciation for traditional ways of life and culture — including language — in all their richness and variety and a willingness to apply these ways dynamically and creatively for the tasks of development.
(4) Traditional villages and communities should exist as viable units of Papua New Guinea and every step should be taken improve their cultural, social, economic and moral quality.

HELD

Goal 5 (Papua New Guinean ways), does not justify a Minister interfering in the judical process.
Re Rooney (No 2) [1979] PNGLR 448; see Wilson J. at p.504.

Basic Rights

WE HEREBY ACKNOWLEDGE that, subject to any restrictions imposed by law on non-citizens, all persons in our country are entitled to the fundamental rights and freedoms of the individual, that is to say; the right, whatever their race, tribe, places of origin, political opinion, colour, creed or sex, but subject to respect for the rights and freedoms of others and for the legitimate public interest, to each of the following:—

(a) life, liberty, security of the person and the protection of the law; and
(b) the right to take part in political activities; and
(c) freedom from inhuman treatment and forced labour; and
(d) freedom of conscience, of expression, of information and of assembly and association; and
(e) freedom of employment and freedom of movement; and
(f) protection for the privacy of their homes and other property and from unjust deprivation of property,

and have accordingly included in this Constitution provisions designed to afford protection to those rights and freedoms, subject to such limitations on that protection as are contained in those provisions, being limitations primarily designed to ensure that the enjoyment of the acknowledged rights and freedoms by an individual does not prejudice the rights and freedoms of others or the legitimate public interest.

BASIC RIGHTS AS AN AID TO CONSTITUTIONAL/STATUTORY INTERPRETATION

per Frost J.

This reference by the Acting Public Solicitor relates to the Constitution, s. 42(2), which is contained in Pt. III, Div.3, Basic Rights. The section confers rights on a person who is arrested or detained. I shall refer later to its terms.
The question referred is:

Does failure to comply with the provisions of s.42(2) of the Constitution for that reason alone render subsequent admissions by an accused person inadmissible as evidence on his trial?

It is useful to refer first to the scheme of the constitution, in which that Division is placed. The Constitution commences with the Preamble which concludes with an Acknowledgment of Basic Rights and Declaration of Basic Social Obligations. The Preamble is significant in matters of construction of the Constitution because it is expressly provided that, in the manner stated, it may be used as an aid to interpretation in cases of doubt. Constitution, Sch. 1.3(1). Under the heading 'Basic Rights' it is acknowledged 'that, subject to any restrictions imposed by law on non-citizens, all persons in our country are entitled to the fundamental rights and freedoms of the individual, that is to say, the right, whatever their race, tribe, places of origin, political opinion, colour, creed or sex, *but subject to respect for the rights and freedoms of others and for the legitimate public interest*, to each of the following:

'(a) life, liberty, security of the person and the protection of the law; and . . .

and have accordingly included in this Constitution provisions designed to afford protection to those rights and freedoms, *subject to such limitations on that protection as are contained in those provisions, being limitations primarily designed to ensure that the enjoyment of the acknowledged rights and freedoms by an individual does not prejudice the rights and freedoms of others or the legitimate public interest.'* The portions I have [italicized] on the whole indicate that in the statement of the rights the legitimate public interest has been taken into account, and that the rights and freedoms have been included, subject only to the limitations on their protection as are expressly set out. It would be a wrong approach therefore further to cut down the operation of the Constitution, s.42(2), in the interest of ensuring, for example, that the guilty do not go unpunished. Of the Basic Social Obligations, it is necessary for the purposes of this case to refer only to (f), which, in respect of the rights and freedoms of others, puts the obligation no higher than to respect them, an obligation which is non-justiciable — Constitution, s. 63.

Reference No 1 of 1977 [1977] PNGLR 362 at pp.364, 365.

Referred to

by Andrew J. in *Premdas v Independent State of Papua New Guinea* [1979] PNGLR 329 at pp.395, 396; see also Prentice C.J. at pp.340, 341 but see Wilson J. at p.375 (circumstances in which recourse to the preamble as an aid to interpretation may be availed of referred to).

Basic Social Obligations

WE HEREBY DECLARE that all persons in our country have the following basic obligations to themselves and their descendants, to each other and to the Nation:—

(a) to respect, and to act in the spirit of, this Constitution; and
(b) to recognize that they can fully develop their capabilities and advance their true interests only by active participation in the development of the national community as a whole; and
(c) to exercise the rights guaranteed or conferred by this Constitution, and to use the opportunities made available to them under it to participate fully in the government of the Nation; and
(d) to protect Papua New Guinea and to safeguard the national wealth, resources and environment in the interests not only of the present generation but also of future generations; and
(e) to work according to their talents in socially useful employment, and if necessary to create for themselves legitimate opportunities for such employment; and
(f) to respect the rights and freedoms of others, and to co-operate fully

with others in the interests of inter-dependence and solidarity; and

(g) to contribute, as required by law, according to their means to the revenues required for the advancement of the Nation and the purposes of Papua New Guinea; and

(h) in the case of parents, to support, assist and educate their children (whether born in or out of wedlock) and in particular to give them a true understanding of their basic rights and obligations and of the National Goals and Directive Principles; and

(i) in the case of the children, to respect their parents.

IN ADDITION, WE HEREBY DECLARE that all citizens have an obligation to themselves and their descendants, to each other and to the Nation to use profits from economic activities in the advancement of our country and our people, and that the law may impose a similar obligation on non-citizens carrying on economic activities in or from our country.

C.P.C. Report Ch.5 Part 1 p.15

B. DECLARATION OF FUNDAMENTAL OBLIGATIONS

92. As well as entrenching in our Constitution the fundamental rights and freedoms which we recommend should be protected, we believe that certain basic obligations should also be incorporated in the Constitution as duties which all people in this country should accept if our goals are to be achieved.

93. Man's growth is based on his abilities and his personality, and how he uses and expresses them. We often assert that it is a person's right to do something and that no man or authority should interfere with that right unreasonably. We say that it is a motorist's right to drive his vehicle on a public highway. However, that right has to be exercised with the necessary restraints so that the motorist does not make difficult the exercise of the same right to use the road by other motorists or people on foot. In other words, the motorist has the obligation to drive safely, by obeying the laws of the road.

94. Before there were any written laws in Papua New Guinea the unwritten constitutions of our various communities were based on the acceptance of the concept of mutual responsibility. [p.16] Our responsibilities to each other and to our society stem from the recognition that in the long run the extent to which our rights and freedoms, whether they are of a social, spiritual, political or economic nature, are protected, will depend on the extent to which we recognise and respect the rights and freedoms of others.

95. These obligations or duties may be divided into different categories. Here we have divided them into constitutional, political, social and economic obligations. This categorization is artificial and is used for convenience only. We recommend that they should not themselves be legally enforceable, but that as in the case of the National Goals and Directive Principles, they should guide the courts in their interpretation of the Constitution or any law, and also the government in framing its policies.

1. *Constitutional Obligations*

96. Every person in Papua New Guinea whether he is a citizen or not, is obliged to uphold and obey the laws of our country. Our Constitution will become our fundamental law. All persons are expected to respect it and to act in accordance with its spirit. The Constitution should be a source of inspiration, freedom and justice for all of us. Respecting and acting in the spirit of the Constitution should not be a burden but a duty which all who live in our country should be glad to be able to carry out.

97. There may be times when an individual will be faced with alternatives of either fulfilling his constitutional or legal obligations against his better judgement, or pursuing a course which his conscience dictates. That is a matter for each individual to weigh up very carefully before deciding upon the action he will take. We feel that it would only be in circumstances in which there has been a distortion of the true spirit of the Constitution by amendment or suspension of crucial constitutional provisions, that it might be justified for a person to act in a way which is contrary to the provisions of the Constitution.

2. *Political Obligations*

98. The principles of freedom and democracy which our people wish to promote cannot become a reality unless we are prepared to protect and promote them. We believe our people have an obligation to exercise the political rights which are safeguarded by the Constitution, and in particular to participate in the government of our nation.

99. Participation in government means many things. In one very important aspect it means that every citizen who has reached the age at which he may do so, should take the opportunity of exercising the right to seek to become an elected representative or to share in the choice of representatives in the national, provincial, local and village governments.

100. Each person should contribute creatively and constructively to the political life of the country in one way or another. To fulfil this obligation may mean exercising our freedom of speech to criticise unjust or ineffective laws or policies. It may mean meeting our representative to put our point of view across. It may mean studying hard in school or college to enter government service to serve the public.

101. The governing of our country should be a collective and concerted effort. It is not a job for the ministers and members of parliament only. It is no simply a job for those in the Public Service. If we are to have good government in this country — government which is responsive to the needs and wishes of the people — all of our people should participate in accordance with rights they have under the Constitution and any law made in accordance with it. Not only political parties are involved — trade unions and other associations should make their contribution to political life also. So too should the media, churches and those in public employment and in private enterprise. But above all, our people as individuals, as members of village and urban commnities, and as citizens of our country should make their contribution however large or small if we are to have government of the people.

3. *Social Obligations*

102. That man is a social being is as true today as it was when this phrase was first articulated. Social ife consists of inter-actions between individuals. Traditional Papua New Guinean society gives prominance to *the individual in society*. A person is born into a family. He inherits many social obligations of his family and his community. Modern Papua New Guinea provides greatly increased opportunities for social inter-action. It also involves increased responsibilities and obligations. Man today is likely to despair if he pauses to count all the different demands placed on his life. The national and local governments, the church, the educational institutions, the family and the village — all of these institutions require each one of us to contribute in one way or another to meeting the [p.17] needs of others.

103. And yet, it is important to realise that real personal fulfilment, liberation and freedom lie in our commitment to the contribution towards fulfilling our community's needs. Since our country consists of different villages, tribes, language groups and districts, we must not forget that working conscientiously, in however small a village, to better the lives of one's people can completely fulfil the obligation to contribute usefully to the advancement of our nation.

104. Every person should be prepared to use his talents wisely to improve not only himself but others in his community, whether that community is small or large, local or national. Every person is born with talent he or she may use wisely or unwisely. Formal institutions such as schools exist to encourage individuals to refine their talents. They do not creat talent. In this country, which we are in the process of building into a nation, it is important that our people should be encouraged to take the initiative to use their talents and labour where no employment opportunities seem immediately available. At this stage of our development the government simply cannot provide all the employment opporutunities that our people would like, and this type of initiative is of great importance for our national wellbeing. At the same time, the government should give as much support as it can to those who use their initiative in this way.

105. Co-operation as opposed to confrontation should be our aim if we are to achieve all our objectives. Co-operation should stem from the appreciation of one's own rights and freedoms and respect for the rights and freedoms of others. There are, of course, times when co-operation is not possible because a matter of principle is at stake and a stand must be taken on that principle. We believe, however, that if emphasis is placed on co-operation the circumstances in which confrontation arises can be minimised.

106. As a nation we must have solidarity. That solidarity will be achieved only if we can develop a true sense of mutual trust and of personal and communal interdependence. That solidarity should be based on democratic principles. Every person who has something constructive to say or offer should be able to do so without unreasonable restriction. Government and community activity should be the result of our collective will.

107. The formation of a person's personality and character begins long before that person goes to a formal institution to receive instruction. It begins at home, among the family. In our country, the family is a much broader unit than the nuclear family. We believe it should stay that way. In our chapter on National Goals and Directive Principles, we stressed the need for strong, stable family life as the basis for our country's development. We believe that parents and all members of the family have a special obligation to support, assist, educate and teach their children.

108. We recognize that the changes in values which have taken place in our country and in the world generally in recent years have created what is popularly termed 'the generation gap'. Thus the members of one generation do not seem to share the same ideals as those held by the youth of a later generation. To some extent this is inevitable. However, we do believe that children should grow up and be responsible to their parents, respect them and care for them in their old age. Some children are born outside the marriage relationship, but they, too, should be cared for as far as possible as if they were born within marriage. The responsibilities of the parents towards these children are the same as those of other parents.

4. *Economic Obligations*

109. All of us should be aware that we are trustees for future generations of our people and have the fundamental duty of protecting the interests of our country by ensuring that its sovereignty and independence are not undermined by foreign interests. As we said in Chapter 2, we need to appreciate that the danger to our national integrity is less likely to come from military action than from foreign economic dominance which stems partly from our colonial heritage, and partly from our acceptance of too many large, highly capitalised foreign enterprises which appear to bring us attractive material benefits, but in reality exploit our resources for their own benefit, undermine our self confidence, and make us increasingly dependent on foreign capital, and foreign technical and managerial skills.

110. There is ample evidence that a substantial number of our people are already well aware of this danger and are taking steps to avoid it by opposing foreign controlled projects which they see as not being in their best interests. But there are many others who do not appreciate the long term implications of the activities of these enterprises. Only if the great majority of our people become fully aware of the implications for their children and grandchildren of the operation of these massive foreign enterprises — the rapid breakdown of [p.18] traditional societies, their values and customs; the encouragement of an attitude of dependence instead of one of self reliance; the irreparable damage which these enterprises can cause to the environment — will we be able to adequately protect ourselves from the old colonial and neo-colonial policy of 'divide and rule', which is often used by these enterprises to achieve their ends.

111. We believe that this obligation of protecting the State, safeguarding its wealth, its resources and the environment in the interests of future generations, is of crucial importance to the future of our nation.

112. A further basic obligation which we propose is that everyone should contribute to economic growth in our country to the extent that he is able to do so. All of us should work hard and help to advance the welfare of the local or national community by paying taxes lawfully required of us in accordance with our means. Active participation in economic as in other aspects of our society's development, is essential if we are to achieve our goals of equality and self reliance.

113. We so not mean to suggest that every person should strive to be self sufficient to the exclusion of others. That would be likely to lead to individualism and selfishness. We do believe that individuals should endeavour not to be unduly dependent on governments and the formal economic sector for their betterment. Instead, people should try to take the initiative in starting and expanding business activities to promote the collective well being of thier community. Where others can help in a project resulting from such initiative they should do so.

114. All our constitutional utterances will be empty unless our people are willing to do their part to make sure that the fundamental guarantees in the Constitution are meaningful and effective. We shall be going a long way towards making them so if all of us fully accept the obligations which we have proposed — obligations which everyone in our society owes to the other members of it.

Referred to

by Kearney J. in *The State v The Independent Tribunal, Ex parte Sasakila* [1976] PNGLR 507 at pp.506, 507 (Paragraph (a) of the Basic Social Obligations as supporting the general principle of statutory interpretation that words used in an Act do not have to be strictly adhered to but are to be construed with the assistance of the material referred to in Constitution s.24, so as to best attain what Parliament intended);

by Narakobi J. in *Tabo Sipo v Meli* (1980 Unreported) N240 at pp.7, 8 (as relevant to the seriousness and constitutionality of the offence of adultery).

PART I. — INTRODUCTORY.

Division 1. — The Nation.

1. — THE INDEPENDENT STATE OF PAPUA NEW GUINEA.

(1) Papua New Guinea is a sovereign, independent State by the name of the Independent State of Papua New Guinea.

(2) The name of the Independent State of Papua New Guinea and its variants shall be protected by an Act of the Parliament.

(*See*: *National Identity Act* Ch.9)

C.P.C. Report Ch.15. p.3

Name, Flag, Motto

20. We believe our country should be known as the Independent State of Papua New Guinea, with the present flag and emblem as the flag and emblem of our new nation. We should have a motto and anthem to be determined by the National Parliament.

2. — THE AREA OF PAPUA NEW GUINEA.

(1) The area of Papua New Guinea consists of the area that, immediately before Independence Day, constituted what was then known as Papua New Guinea, together with all internal waters and the territorial sea and underlying lands, and, subject to disclaimer by resolution of the Parliament at or before the end of its next meeting, includes such neighbouring waters and such lands underlying any such waters, and such additional lands and waters, as are declared by the Head of State, acting with, and in accordance with, the advice of the National Executive Council, to be part of that area.

(*See*: *National Seas Act* Ch.361)

(2) The sovereignty of Papua New Guinea over its territory, and over the natural resources of its territory, is and shall remain absolute, subject only to such obligations at international law as are freely accepted by Papua New Guinea in accordance with this Constitution.

C.P.C. Report Ch. 15 p.3

Sovereignty over natural resources

21. Because sovereignty over our natural resources is so basic to a nation, we recommend that this be asserted as a fundamental constitutional provision. This should serve to emphasize Papua New Guinea's right to exercise effective control over its resources and their exploitation, with means suitable to its own situation, including nationalization or transfer or ownership to our own citizens, this right being an expression of the full permanent sovereignty of our State.

Referred to

by Kapi J. in *S.C.R. No 4 of 1980 (No 2); Re Petition of M.T. Somare* [1982] PNGLR 65 at pp.75, 80 (as assisting in ascertaining the meaning of the words 'international obligations' in Section 202(b) of the Constitution).

3. — NATIONAL SYMBOLS.

(1) Acts of the Parliament may make provisions for and in respect of —
 (a) a National Flag; and
 (b) a National Emblem; and

(c) a National Motto; and
(d) a National Seal; and
(e) a National Anthem.

(*See: National Identity Act* Ch.9)

(2) Until such time as other provision is made in accordance with Subsection (1), the National Flag, National Emblem and National Seal are those that were in use immediately before Independence Day.

C.P.C. Report Ch.15 p.6

RECOMMENDATION

7. The flag for the Independent State of Papua New Guinea shall be the flag scheduled to the National Indentity Ordinance 1971.
8. The Papua New Guinea National Emblem shall be the emblem scheduled to the National Identity Ordinance 1971.
9. The Papua New Guinea National Motto shall be as determined by the National Parliament.

4. — NATIONAL CAPITAL DISTRICT.

(1) There shall be a National Capital District.

(2) The Seat of Government shall be in the National Capital District.

(3) The boundaries of the National Capital District shall be as defined by an Organic Law.

(*See*: *Organic Law on the boundaries of the National Capital District* Ch.1.)

(4) An Organic Law or an Act of the Parliament shall make provision in respect of the government of the National Capital District.

(5) in calculating the number of provincial electorates in accordance with Section 125 (*electorates*), the National Capital District shall be taken into account as if it were a province.

5. — PROVINCES.

(1) An Organic Law may declare, or make provision in respect of the declaration of, part of the country as provinces.

(*See*: *Organic Law on Provincial Boundaries* Ch.1.)

(2) An Organic Law may provide for, or make provision in respect of, the creation of new provinces by the amalgamation or division of existing provinces or for the variation of the boundaries of a province.

C.P.C. Report Ch.10 p.21

187. The Committee has explained in considerable detail — in both our *First* and *Second Interim Reports* and earlier in this Chapter — why provincial governments should be established on a district basis. We have also said that the constitutional framework for provincial governments should be flexible: that it should provide for change and variation in the circumstances and desires of the people of the various provinces. We therefore recommend that the Constitution should provide for the creation of new provinces, the amalgamation of existing provinces, and the alteration of provincial boundaries.

188. Existing district boundaries were drawn so as to meet the administrative requirements of a highly centralized colonial government. They acquired political significance later. This does not mean that we should ignore them, aş some of our critics have implied. The existing districts are of manifest importance to our people, as submissions made to the Committee have shown. We believe that district boundaries should be left intact when provincial governments are established, and that future changes to them should not be arbitrarily imposed. Provincial boundaries should henceforth be changed through a process in which elected leaders at both the provincial and national level of government have a say.

189. In Chapter 6, 'The legislature', the Committee made provision for the making of minor changes to provincial boundaries to bring national and provincial electoral boundaries into line. We are concerned here with the creation, amalgamation and other alterations, of provincial boundaries.

190. The Committee believes that the National Parliament should have the power to create, [p.22] amalgamate, and otherwise alter the boundaries of, provinces. The Constitution should ensure that local hopes, needs and affiliation should be taken into account. It should require that a bill to alter provincial boundaries be circulated to the provincial governments directly affected by it at least three months before it is presented in the National Parliament. In the case of a bill moved by a minister, the views of affected governments should be sought and incorporated in a submission to the National Executive Council before the bill is presented in parliament. The support of an absolute majority of the members of the National Parliament should be required for a bill to alter provincial boundaries to become law.

191. The Committee believes that it would be unwise for the National Parliament to agree to a bill to divide or amalgamate provinces or otherwise alter provincial boundaries without the agreement of the provincial assemblies of the provinces affected but, we recognize that it may not be possible to secure their agreement. We recommend that a bill to create a new province to amalgamate existing provinces, or otherwise alter provincial boundaries, should not become law unless it receives the support of a majority of the members of the Provincial Assemblies in all affected provinces. In the case of a bill wich affects more than one province and does not receive the support of all of the Provincial Assemblies concerned, the bill should be treated as the subject of a dispute between governments. If the dispute cannot be resolved through the procedures provided for the resolution of inter-governmental disputes, then the National Parliament should have the power to legislate on its own, provided that the bill is supported by an absolute majority of members.

192. The Committee believes that the procedures we have specified above provide vital safeguards for provincial governments, without preventing change. The many hundreds of submissions we have received indicate that our people want provincial governments to be set up on a district basis. Our proposals leave open the possibility that individual provinces might be divided into smaller units, each with its own provincial government, or combined to form larger units. The only ways in which we have qualified either possibility is by insisting that all of the governments directly affected by boundary changes — the National Government as well as provincial governments — should be consulted before such changes can be made, and if the change affects a single province, the provincial assembly of that province must support the change by a resolution passed by a simple majority.

193. The Committee recommends that the same general principles should be followed in respect of the naming and re-naming of the provinces, and legislation that provides for the making and alteration of the documents which establish provincial government. In both cases, the proposed measures should be circulated to the provincial assemblies affected at least three months before presentation in the National Parliament and the support of an absolute majority of the members of parliament should be required for such bill to become law. However, the National Parliament should not exercise its power to give a name to a province unless the provincial assembly of the province concerned has first passed a motion proposing a name. Legislation that provides for the making and alteration of the documents that establish provincial governments (which documents should specify, for example, the procedures for election and removal of each Provincial Council and Premier) make provision for both the National Government and provincial governments to take the initiative in proposing alterations to such documents.

6. — DECLARATION OF LOYALTY.

Where a law requires a Declaration of Loyalty to be made, it shall be made in the following form:—

'I, , realizing fully the responsibilities to which I am committing myself and the consequences of not living up to this Declaration and those responsibilities, freely and willingly declare my loyalty to the Independent State of Papua New Guinea and its People and to the Constitution of Papua New Guinea adopted by the Constituent Assembly on 15 August 1975, as altered from time to time in accordance with its provisions, and promise that I will uphold the Constitution and the laws of Papua New Guinea'.

C.P.C. Report Ch.14 p.2

13. It is important, we believe, that all constitutional office-holders should be publicly committed to uphold the Constitution, including the values embodied in the National Goals and Directive Principles in Chapter 2, and the Leadership Code in Chapter 3. They should, we recommend, take an oath or make an affirmation (according to individual conscience) in the form set out in Schedule 3 (sic) of this Report before they take up the duties of their offices. It should be impressed upon them that these pledges are no mere formalities: they have been carefully composed by and for those with a genuine personal commitment to the objectives they specify.

AS CONFERRING STANDING

per Kidu C.J.

[Members of Parliament] are required ... to ensure that laws they make are constitutional. They are also required, when taking office, to swear that they will uphold the Constitution of Papua New Guinea. This obligation must mean something. For people such as Members of the Parliament to make this declaration and ignore it afterwards makes a mockery of the Constitution ... I hold that the petitioner [a Member of Parliament] has the necessary standing to invoke the powers of this Court of determine the constitutionality (or otherwise) of the *Defence Force (Presence Abroad) Act* 1980.
S.C.R. No 4 of 1980; Re petition of M.T. Somare [1981] PNGLR 265 at pp.273, 274.

7. — OATH OF ALLEGIANCE.

Where a law requires an Oath of Allegiance or Affirmation of Allegiance to be made, it shall be made in the following form:—

'*Oath of Allegiance.*

I, , do swear that I will well and truly serve and bear true allegiance to Her Majesty Queen Elizabeth II, Her heirs and successors according to law.'

SO HELP ME GOD!

'*Affirmation of Allegiance.*

I, , do promise and affirm that I will well and truly serve Her Majesty Queen Elizabeth II, Her heirs and successors according to law.'

Division 2. — Interpretion.

8. — PRINCIPLES OF INTERPRETATION.

For the purpose of the interpretation of this Constitution and the Organic Laws, the provisions of Schedule 1 (*Rules for Shortening and Interpretation of the Constitutional Laws*) apply and, subject to that Schedule, the underlying law applies.

GENERALLY

Referred to

by Wilson J. in *Premdas v Independent State of Papua New Guinea* [1979] PNGLR 329 at p.375 (as [in conjunction with Sch. 1.5(2)] requiring all provisions in a Constitutional Law to be given their fair and liberal meaning);

by Miles J. in *S.C.R. No 4 of 1980; Re petition of M.T. Somare* [1981] PNGLR 265 at pp.302–305;

by Miles J. in *S.C.R. No1 of 1981; Re Inter-Group Fighting Act 1977* [1981] PNGLR 151 at p.169;

by Kaputin J. (dissenting) in *S.C.R. No 2 of 1982 In re Opai Kunangel Amin* (1982 Unreported) SC231 at p.16 (as relevant to the relationship between the Constitution and the Organic Laws).

PART II. — THE NATIONAL LEGAL SYSTEM.

Division 1. — The Laws of Papua New Guinea.

9. — THE LAWS:

The laws of Papua New Guinea consist of—

(*a*) this Constitution; and
(*b*) the Organic Laws; and
(*c*) the Acts of the Parliament; and
(*d*) Emergency Regulations; and
(*da*) the provincial laws; and (*Added by Constitutional Amendment No.1. — Provincial Government, s.2*)
(*e*) laws made under or adopted by or under this Constitution or any of those laws, including subordinate legislative enactments made under this Constitution or any of those laws; and
(*f*) the underlying law,

and none other.

UNDERLYING LAW

per Kapi J.

Strictly speaking, underlying law is different from the common law of England. Common law embodies the principles which apply in England. Underlying law embodies the principles established under Sch. 2 of the Constitution; so it includes adoption of custom under Sch. 2.1, adoption of common law principles under Sch. 2.2, creation of new principles under Sch. 2.3 and the development of these principles under Sch. 2.4.
S.C.R. No 1A of 1981; Re Motor Traffic Act [1982] PNGLR 122 at p.138.

DEVELOPMENT OF THE UNDERLYING LAW: JUDICIAL RESTRAINT

per Greville Smith J.

What 'the underlying law', within the meaning of s.9, presently is, and the manner in which such law may be 'developed' by the courts, is specified in s.20(2) of the Constitution, and by onward reference, in Sch. 2 ....

It follows from the foregoing that of what the Constitution in s.9 declares to be, and declares to be exclusively, 'the laws of Papua New Guinea', the courts are expressly, in the provisions I have mentioned, given power to provide only a part, and that by formulation and development of what may be described as the non-legislative law, namely the 'underlying law'. That the function of the courts should be confined even in this field is, I think, to be inferred from the following, namely, (1) the provision contained in Sch. 2.5 that the judges, in the reports they are required under the provisions of s.187 of the Constitution to make to the Head of State for presentation to Parliament, shall comment upon the state, suitability and development of the underlying law, (2) the provision contained in Sch. 2.14 that it is the special responsibility of the Law Reform Commission to investigate and report to the Parliament and to the National Executive, on the development, and on the adaption to the circumstances of the country, of the underlying law, and on the appropriateness of the rules and principles of the underlying law to the circumstances of the country from time to time, and (3) the fact that the duty placed upon the National Judicial System (by the provisions of Sch. 2.4) to ensure the development of the underlying law in the way specified, is circumscribed by the words 'except insofar as it would not be proper to do so by judicial act'.

As to the provision last mentioned, it is not proper by judicial act to invade the province of the legislature ..... In my view it was the intention of the legislature to impose ... restrictions upon the National Judicial System in the discharge of its duty to develop the underlying law.
S.C.R. No 2 of 1981: Re Section 19(1)(f) of the Criminal Code [1982] PNGLR 150 at pp.164,165. See also: annotations under Sch. 2.3.

AS INCONSISTENT WITH ANY JUDICIAL LAW MAKING FUNCTION UNDER SECTION 155(4) OF THE CONSTITUTION

per Greville Smith J.

Since the laws of Papua New Guinea are to consist, as stated in s.9 of the Constitution, of the categories set out in that section *and no other*, and since such law making powers as are given to the National Judicial System are, as we have seen, confined to the underlying law as set out in Sch. 2, it seems to me impossible to contend that the 'inherent power' referred to in s.155(4) is a power to make orders which have the effect of creating a 'law' in the sense that the plural of that term is used in s.9. The power in a court to create 'laws' or rules of law which shall become part of the laws of Papua New Guinea is clearly, by the terms of s.9, confined to the power conferred in Sch. 2.3(1).

It is inconceivable that the legislature intended to give any court the option, in any particular situation, of applying the 'laws of Papua New Guinea' as set out in s.9, or of resolving the situation before it according to the courts own individual and independent notion of justice. This being so the word 'justice' in s.155(4) means justice according to law, namely the law specified in s.9 .....

Seen in the light of the foregoing the provisions of s.155(4) declare that the National and Supreme Courts have power to make such orders as are necessary to jmplement the enforcement of the law, that is the law as established by s.9.
S.C.R. No 2 of 1981; Re Section 19(1)(f) of the Criminal Code [1982] PNGLR 50 at pp.166,167; see also annotations under s.155(4).

AS TO THE PRIORITY OF SOURCES OF LAW

per Kidu C.J. (Andrew J. concurring)

The development of our underlying law becomes relevant only where there is no statutory or accepted customary or common law .... The Court has no power to rule customary law overrides statutory law, where a statute has quite clearly and lucidly provided for a subject matter no custom or common law is applicable.
Re James Allan Sannga; Peter Timereke v Duncan Ferrie and anor (1983 Unreported) SC255 at p.17; see also Kapi Dep.C.J. at pp.25–26, 42.

per Kapi J.

The laws of Papua New Guinea are set out under s.9 of the Constitution, one of which is the underlying law. (s.9(f) of the Constitution.) The underlying law of Papua New Guinea is made up of three sources which are set out under Sch. 2 of the Constitution. Sch. 2.1, custom; Sch. 2.2, common law and Sch. 2.3, formulation of new law (development of the underlying law). The order in which these laws are listed under Sch. 2 is not without significance. In a case where the underlying law of Papua New Guinea is in question or is an issue, the enquiry should always begin with the examination of custom which is applicable under Sch. 2.1 of the Constitution. Custom which is adopted in accordance with Sch. 2.1 of the Constitution is superior to common law because common law is only applicable to the extent that it is not inconsistent with custom as adopted under Sch. 2.1 of the Constitution. (Sch. 2.2(1)(c) of the Constitution.) The extent to which common law is applicable cannot be determined without determining what the custom says.

Formulation of new law under Sch. 2.3 of the Constitution does not arise until it is established that custom under Sch. 2.1 and common law under Sch. 2.2 are inapplicable.
S.C.R. No 4 of 1980; Re petition of M.T. Somare [1981] PNGLR 265 at pp.285, 286. See also annotations under Sch. 2.1.

LAW DISTINCT FROM 'JUSTICE'

See *Comment* under Section 158(2)

GENERALLY

Referred to

by Kearney J. in *The State v Allan Woila* [1978] PNGLR 99 at p.100 (standard of proof on admissability of confessions);

by Bredmeyer A.J. in *Brown v Motor Vehicles Insurance (P.N.G.) Trust* [1980] PNGLR 409 at p.415;

by Miles J. in *S.C.R. No 1 of 1980;Re Section 22A(b) of Police Offences Act (Papua)* [1981] PNGLR 28 at p.47 (illuminating the meaning of the expression 'according to law' in s.37(4)(a) of the Constitution;

by Kapi J. in *Avia Aihi v The State* [1981] PNGLR 81 at pp.106, 107 (illuminating the meaning of the expression 'according to law' in s.37(15) of the Constitution;

by Kearney Dep.C.J. in *The State v Andrew Tovue* [1981] PNGLR 8 at p.11 (custom as part of the underlying law which may authorize, justify or excuse an assault);

by Kearney Dep.C.J. in *S.C.R. No 2 of 1981; Re Section 19(1)(f) of the Criminal Code* [1982] PNGLR 150 at p.157;

by Kapi Dep.C.J. in *Hetura Paz Development Co. Pty Ltd v Niugini Nius Pty Ltd and ors* [1982] PNGLR 250 at p.254 (circumstances in which freedom of expression may be regulated or restricted 'by law').

10. — CONSTRUCTION OF WRITTEN LAWS.

All written laws (other than this Constitution) shall be read and construed subject to —

(a) in any case — this Constitution; and
(b) in the case of Acts of the Parliament — any relevant Organic Laws; and
(c) in the case of adopted laws or subordinate legislative enactments — the Organic Laws and the laws by or under which they were enacted or made,

and so as not exceed the authority to make them properly given, to the intent that where any such law would, but for this section, have been in excess of the authority so given it shall nevertheless be a valid law to the extent to which it is not in excess of that authority.

RULE OF CONSTRUCTION ONLY

Comment

In *Peter v South Pacific Brewery Ltd* [1976] PNGLR 537 the Supreme Court held that s.10 provides for a rule of construction only. It was held that s.10 did not authorize the Court to propound any additional provision except as necessary to preserve that portion of the existing law which was not in excess of authority.

The Supreme Court drew considerable assistance in the interpretation of s.10 from decisions of the High Court of Australia interpreting s.15A of the *Acts Interpretation Act (Aust)* 1972.

per Frost C.J.

The effect of the Australian section, as it has been judicially interpreted, has been stated in Wynes, *Legislative, Executive and Judicial Powers in Australia*, 5th ed, at p.53, in a passage which commences with a citation from Sir Owen Dixon's judgment in *Bank of New South Wales v The Commonwealth* (1948) 76 CLR 1 at p.371 and which was cited in *The State v The Independent Tribunal; Ex parte Sasakila* [1976] PNGLR 491.

> .... His honour said: 'The effect of (severability) clauses is to reverse the presumption that a statute is to operate as a whole, so that the intention of the legislature is to be taken prima facie to be that the enactment should be divisible and that any parts found constitutionally unobjectionable should be carried into effect independently of those which fail. To displace the application of this new presumption to any given situation arising under the statute by reason of the invalidation of part, it must sufficiently appear that the invalid provision forms part of an inseparable context.' But once it appeared that rejection of the invalid part would mean a different operation of the valid part or produce a different result, the whole must fail. This consideration supplied a strong logical ground for holding provisions to be inseverable, since in such a case there was a strong inference that Parliament did not intend that anything less than the whole Act should be law. (76 C.L.R. at p.371). At a later stage his Honour refers to the rule 'that provisions are to be considered severable and general words distributable' (op cit).

There are, however, two additional considerations, which are that 'in no case can the Court be required to legislate nor should it do so', and, 'the reduced form or operation of the Act must result "in a consistent workable and effective body of provisions". *Strickland v Rocla Concrete Pipes Ltd.* (1971) 124 C.L.R. 468 per Barwick C.J. at p.493 ...

The only possible distinction between the Australian section and Constitution s.10, as it seems to me, is the enactment of the latter as part of the constitution rather than, as in the case of s.15A, as a direction by Parliament in relation to its own laws. But on the whole I do not consider that this distinction requires that s.10 be given effect otherwise than as a rule of construction. The significance of the enactment of s.10 as part of the Constitution is, in my opinion, to be seen in relation to a purported enactment by Parliament disclosing an intention inconsistent with the application of that provision to any particular law. If, as in Australia, the severability clause is to be found in an Act of Parliament, then the later Act would prevail and the clause would be excluded. Wynes, *Legislative, Executive and Judicial Powers*, (supra) at p.55. But in Papua New Guinea it is the severability clause found in s.10 which prevails because of its enactment as part of the Supreme Law.

Whether s.10 requires a different operation than is indicated by the Australian decisions, which I find of persuasive value, is a question which may be left for consideration in the future application of the section to the various types of enactments which may come up for decision. The citizen judges of this country may in the course of time prefer a different approach. In the meantime the considerations established by the High Court over many years in different types of cases, in my opinion, do provide valuable assistance in the interpretation of s.10 .... My view is that s.10 is a rule of construction in the sense that it provides a guide for the ascertainment of the intention of Parliament in the case of partial invalidity of a law; but for the particular legislative intention always to prevail in accordance with the spirit of the Constitution. This means that if from the terms of an Act it appears that Parliament intended that only the Act as a whole should come into operation, then the whole would fail if there was partial invalidity ....

The Deputy Chief Justice seems to have reached the same answer as I have excepting that in his opinion the section should be read and construed in such a manner as to permit an ex parte hearing in the case of offences punishable by imprisonment if the defendant consents to the charge being heard in his absence. To enable a proper answer to be given I should refer to his Honour's addition of an enabling jurisdiction in the case of consent. I regret that I am unable to agree with that construction for a number of reasons. First, on the plain meaning of s.10 its only operation is to preserve that portion of the law which remains valid; no power is given to the Court to propound any additional provision, except as is necessarily involved and therefore impliedly permissible under the section by way of words of qualification to preserve that portion of the existing law which is not in excess of authority. This extension of jurisdiction may be passed off as judicial legislation, but in Papua New Guinea, as I have said, the legislative power is vested in Parliament — Constitution s.100(1).

Peter v South Pacific Brewery Ltd. [1976] PNGLR 537 at pp.545–550; see also Kearney J. at p.560, Prentice Dep.C.J. (dissenting) at p.558 (below).

per Prentice Dep.C.J.

I appreciate that distinguished jurists of other countries shudder at the suggestion that recourse to a measure such as s.15A of the *Acts Interpretation Act* of Australia 1901–1973 would allow of 'judicial legislating' (see *Strickland v Rocla Concrete Pipes Ltd.* (1971) 124 CLR 468, Barwick C.J. at p.491, Menzies J. at p.497; *Pidoto and Others v The State of Victoria* (1943) 68 CLR 87). But with respect, I suggest that much of the interpretation by way of reading down *has* involved 'judicial legislating' in fact, even if the judges refuse or are unable constitutionally to recognize their offspring as such. And with respect, I consider that *any* solution which saved the operation of s.131 of the *District Courts Act* in regard to offences not carrying penalty of imprisonment, would involve in fact the deletion or insertion of words either in the definition of 'simple offence' or in s.131 itself and may frankly be recognized as 'judicial legislating' of a permissible kind.

Though it would not perhaps accord with the manner in which Acts of Parliament have been interpreted elsewhere, I think this court should be prepared and is empowered to, not only *eliminate* a phrase from an Act if by so doing constitutional validity could be secured in accordance with what it construed Parliament's intention; but also to add a phrase or change a phrase with the intent of construing (translating) an Act so that it is valid and still expressing the clear Parliamentary intent — 'legislating' though Constitutional experts of other lands might consider this process to be.

Peter v South Pacific Brewery Ltd [1976] PNGLR 537 at pp.558, 559; but see also Frost C.J. at pp.545–550 (above), Kearney J. at p.560.

Held

Section 30 of the *Corrective Institutions Act*, insofar as it purports to deny a right of appeal for corrective institutions offences, conflicts with s.37(15) of the Constitution and is invalid.
Constitutional Reference No.2 of 1978; Re Corrective Institutions Act 1957 [1978] PNGLR 404; per Curiam at p.409.

Held

A provision of the Constitution cannot be affected by the provisions of an Organic Law. Accordingly s.28 of the *Organic Law on the Duties and Responsibilities of Leadership* cannot take away the right of a Minister and a Member of Parliament to resign which is given by the Constitution.
S.C.R. No 2 of 1982; In the Matter of Opai Kunangel Amin (1982 Unreported) SC231; see Kapi Dep. C.J. at p.7, Bredmeyer J. at p.13, Kaputin J. (dissenting) at pp.17, 19.

Held

Section 220 of the *Organic Law on National Elections* which provides that a decision of the National Court upon an election petition shall be 'final and conclusive and without appeal and shall not be questioned in any way' is constitutionally valid to prohibit appeals but not as it purports to exclude the power of the Supreme Court to review the decision pursuant to s.155(2)(b) of the Constitution. Section 10 saves that much of the Organic Law as merely prohibits appeals.
In the matter of the Organic Law on National Elections: Malipu Balakau v Paul Paken Torato and anor (1983 Unreported) SC256; see Kidu C.J. at p.8, Andrew J. at p.26.

GENERALLY

Referred to

by Raine J. in *Cory v Blyth* [1976] PNGLR 274 at p.278;

by Kearney J. in *The State v The Independent Tribunal; Ex parte Sasakila* [1975] PNGLR 491 at p.506 (courts not to be narrowly legalistic in interpreting Constitutional Laws); see also Frost C.J. at p.497;

by Prentice Dep.C.J. in *In re Moresby N.E. Election Petition* [1977] PNGLR 429 at pp.432, 434; see also Pritchard J. at p.446;

by Prentice C.J. (dissenting) in *Constitutional Reference No 3 of 1978; Re Inter-Group Fighting Act 1977* [1978] PNGLR 421 at p.427;

by Greville Smith J. in *Re s.42 of the Constitution and Jacob Hendrich Prai* [1979] PNGLR 42 at p.44;

by Saldanha J. in *Premdas v Independent State of Papua New Guinea* [1979] PNGLR 329 at p.361; see also Andrew J. at p.401;

by Greville Smith J. in *The State v John Rumet Kaputin (No2)* [1979] PNGLR 544 at p.546;

by Kapi J. in *Minister for Lands v Frame* [1980] PNGLR 433 at pp.466, 470 (Constitution to override any Act which prescribes functions of Head of State inconsistent therewith);

by Kapi J. in *Avia Aihi v The State* [1981] PNGLR 81 at p.104 (Supreme Court Act has to be read subject to the provisions of the Constitution);

by Miles J. (dissenting) in *S.C.R. No1 of 1981; Re Inter-Group Fighting Act* [1981] PNGLR 151 at p.169 (s.10 does not displace the principle of the underlying law that any ambiguity or doubt is to be resolved in favour of the liberty of the person and, at p.174, it is not correct to refuse to sever laws if to do so would leave them ineffective or incomplete. A law is not unconstitutional if it is ineffective or incomplete);

by Miles J. in *S.C.R. No 4 of 1980; Re petition of M.T. Somare* [1981] PNGLR 265 at p.298 (the fundamental proposition that the National Parliament has no power to make laws which exceed or are inconsistent with the powers conferred by the Constitution); see also Kidu C.J. at p.273.

Division 2. — Constitutional Laws.

Subdivision A. — Supreme Law.

11. — CONSTITUTION, ETC., AS SUPREME LAW.

(1) This Constitution and the Organic Laws are the Supreme Law of Papua New Guinea, and, subject to Section 10 (*construction of written laws*) all acts (whether legislative, executive or judicial) that are inconsistent with them are, to the extent of the inconsistency, invalid and ineffective.

GENERALLY

Held

Section 10 governs the construction of written laws. Accordingly where any inconsistency arises between an Act of the Parliament and the Constitution, it is to be determined under s.10 rather than s.11.
Peter v South Pacific Brewery Ltd. [1976] PNGLR 537; see Frost C.J. at pp.541, 542.

Referred to

by Raine J. in *Cory v Blyth (No 1)* [1976] PNGLR 274 at p.278;

by Frost C.J. in *Peter v South Pacific Brewery Ltd.* [1976] PNGLR 537 at pp.541, 542;

by Frost C.J. in *The State v The Independent Tribunal; Ex parte Sasakila* [1976] PNGLR 491 at p.498;

by Kapi J. in *The Minister for Lands v Frame* [1980] PNGLR 433 at p.471;

by Andrew J. in *Avia Aihi v The State* [1981] PNGLR 81 at p.102;

by Andrew J. in *Milne Bay Provincial Government v Roy Evara and Anor* [1981] PNGLR 63 at p.66;

by Miles J. in *S.C.R. No 4 of 1980; Re petition of M.T. Somare* [1981] PNGLR 265 at p.298;

by Kapi J. in *S.C.R. No 1 of 1982; Re Bouraga* [1982] PNGLR 178 at p.195; see also Pratt J. at p.211;

by Kearney Dep.C.J. in *S.C.R. No 2 of 1982; Re Organic Law* [1982] PNGLR 214 at p.224;

by Bredmeyer J. in *S.C.R. No 2 of 1982; Re Opai Kunangel Amin* (1982 Unreported) SC231 at p.13;

by Bredmeyer J. in *Aundak Kapil v The Independent State of Papua New Guinea* (1983 Unreported) N435 at p.9.

(2) The provisions of this Constitution and of the Organic Laws are self-executing to the fullest extent that their respective natures and subject-matters permit.

SELF EXECUTING

Held

The direction in s.11(2) is subject to express or necessarily implied terms to the contrary. Accordingly Constitution s.28, which in terms directs provision to be made by an Organic Law, cannot be construed as self-executing.
The State v The Independent Tribunal; Ex parte Sasakila [1976] PNGLR 491; see Saldanha J. at p.503.

GENERALLY

Referred to

by Prentice Dep.C.J. in *In re Moresby North East Election Petition* [1977] PNGLR 429 at p.435;

by Kearney J. in *The State v Allen Woila* [1978] PNGLR 99 at p.117 (Constitution s.37 is self-executing);

by Pritchard J. in *Constitutional Reference No 1 of 1978 (s.19)* [1978] PNGLR 354 at p.377;

by Kaputin J. (dissenting) in *S.C.R. No 2 of 1982; Re Opai Kunangel Amin* (1982 Unreported) SC231 at pp.16, 17 (status of Organic Laws; requirement that they be read together with the Constitution).

12. — ORGANIC LAWS.

(1)For the purposes of this Constitution, an Organic Law is a law made by the Parliament that is —

(a) for or in respect of a matter provision for which by way of an Organic Law is expressly authorized by this Constitution; and
(b) not inconsistent with this Constitution; and
(c) expressed to be an Organic Law.

GENERALLY

Referred to

by Frost C.J. in *The State v The independent Tribunal; Ex Parte Sasakila* [1976] PNGLR 491 at p.495; see also Kearney J. at p.506;

by Prentice Dep.C.J. in *In re Moresby North East Election Petition* [1977] PNGLR 429 at pp.433–439 (as to alleged inconsistency between Constitution s.126(7) and the *Provisional Organic Law on National Elections* which provided, in respect of appeals to electoral matters, for the law to take effect as an ordinary Act); see also Williams J. at pp.439–441;

by Kaputin J. in *Constitutional Reference No 2 of 1982; Re Opai Kunangel Amin* (1982 Unreported) SC231 at pp.16, 17.

(2) An Organic Law may be altered only by another Organic Law, or by an alteration to this Constitution.

ONLY BY ANOTHER ORGANIC LAW

per Kidu C.J.

Section 12(2) ... says in no uncertain terms that an Organic Law may only be altered by another Organic Law or an alteration to the Constitution ... Once a provision is contained in an Organic Law ... the only way to alter [it] is categorically laid down by ... s.12(2). The only concession allowed by Constitution s.12(3) is that a provision contained in an Organic Law that might be made by an Act of the Parliament requires only the same *majority* required for any Act of Parliament. It does *not* say that the procedure laid down by s.14 [Making of Alterations to the Constitution and Organic Laws] does not apply. *S.C.R. No 2 of 1982; Re Organic Law* [1982] PNGLR 214 at pp.219,220; see also Kearney Dep.C.J. at pp.222–224.

(3) Nothing in this section prevents an Organic Law from —
 (a) making any provision that might be made by an Act of the Parliament; or
 (b) requiring any provision to be made by an Act of the Parliament that might otherwise be so made,

but any such provision may be altered by the same majority that is required for any other Act of the Parliament.

GENERALLY

Referred to

by Kidu C.J. in *S.C.R. No 2 of 1982; In re Organic Law on National Elections (Amendment) Act 1981* (1982 unreported) SC226 at pp.3, 4; see also Kearney Dep.C.J. at pp.6, 7.

Subdivision B. — Constitutional Alteration and Organic Laws.

13. — ALTERATIONS OF THE CONSTITUTION.

This Constitution may be altered only by law made by the Parliament that —
 (a) is expressed to be a law to alter this constitution; and
 (b) is made and certified in accordance with Section 14 (*making of alterations to the Constitution and Organic Laws*).

14. — MAKING OF ALTERATIONS TO THE CONSTITUTION AND ORGANIC LAWS.

(1) Subject to Sections 12(3) (*Organic Laws*) and 15 (*urgent alterations*), a proposed law to alter this constitution, or a proposed Organic Law, must be supported on a division in accordance with the Standing Orders of the Parliament by the prescribed majority of votes determined in accordance with Section 17 ("*prescribed majority of votes*") expressed on at least two occasions after opportunity for debate on the merits.

(2) Subject to Section 15 (*urgent alterations*), the opportunities for debate referred to in Subsection (1) must have been —
(a) during different meetings of the Parliament; and
(b) separated in time by at least two months,
and the proposed law must be published by the Speaker in full in the National Gazette, and circulated, in accordance with the Standing Orders of the Parliament, to all members of the Parliament not less than one month before it is formally introduced into the Parliament.

(3) Amendments to a proposed law to amend this Constitution or a proposed Organic Law shall not be moved unless they have been circulated to members of the Parliament before the end of the meeting of the Parliament at which the first opportunity for debate referred to in Subsection (1) occurs.

(4) Subject to Subsection (6), in his certificate given under Section 110 (*certification as to making of laws*), the Speaker must certify that the requirements of Subsections (1), (2) and (3) or Section 15 (*urgent alterations*), as the case may be, have been complied with.

(5) The certificate referred to in Subsection (4) shall state —
(a) the date on which each vote was taken; and
(b) in relation to each vote —
(i) the number of seats in the Parliament at the time; and
(ii) the respective numbers of members of the Parliament voting for and against the proposal, and where the requirements of Subsection (2) were waived under Section 15 (*urgent alterations*) for and against the motion for the waiver,
and is, in the absence of proof to the contrary, conclusive evidence of the matter so stated.

(6) Unless the Parliament decides otherwise in any particular case, Subsection (1) does not apply where the Speaker, after consultation with the Chief Justice or a Judge nominated by the Chief Justice for the purpose, certifies that the proposed law —
(a) does not affect the substance of any provision to be altered by it; or
(b) is designed to correct a self-evident error or omission; or
(c) is merely incidental to or consequential on some other alteration of this Constitution or of any other law,
and such a law may be made in the same way as Acts of the Parliament.

(7) The Supreme Court may, on the application of any person made within four weeks after the date of a certificate under Subsection (6) or such further time as a Judge, on application made within that period, considers reasonable in the particular circumstances, disallow the certificate, but otherwise the certificate is conclusive.

STRICT COMPLIANCE MANDATORY

Held

Compliance with s.14 is mandatory notwithstanding the fact that the proposed law is only intended to amend a provision of an Organic Law which might have been made by an ordinary Act of the Parliament. Failure to comply renders the law invalid.
S.C.R. No 2 of 1982; Re Organic Law [1982] PNGLR 214; see Kidu C.J. at pp.219, 220, Kearney Dep.C.J. at pp.222–224.

Referred to

by Williams J. in *In re Moresby North East Election Petition* [1977] PNGLR 429 at p.440;

per Curiam in *S.C.R. No 2 of 1982; Re Organic Law* [1982] PNGLR 214 at p.217.

15. — URGENT ALTERATIONS.

(1) The provisions of this section cease to have effect at the first moment of the fourth anniversary of Independence Day.

(2) Subject to Subsection (5), the requirements of Section 14(2) (*making of alterations to the Constitution and Organic Laws*) may be waived, on the ground of urgency, by the Parliament on a division in accordance with the Standing Orders of the Parliament by a two-thirds absolute majority vote.

(3) The requirements of Section 14(2) (*making of alterations to the Constitution and Organic Laws*) shall not be waived under Subsection (2) unless —
- (a) at least four days' notice of the intention in accordance with Standing Orders of the Parliament to invoke Subsection (2) has been given; and
- (b) the proposed law has been circulated, in accordance with the Standing Orders of the Parliament, to all members of the Parliament and published in full by the Speaker in the National Gazette at least four days before the motion to invoke Subsection (2) is moved; and
- (c) the opportunities for debate referred to in Section 14(1) (making of alterations to the Constitution and Organic Laws) have been separated in time by at least two weeks, but not necessarily during different meetings of the Parliament.

(4) Amendments to a proposed law to amend this Constitution or a proposed Organic Law to which this section applies shall not be moved unless they have been circulated to members of the Parliament before the end of the first debate on the matter.

(5) This section does not apply to proposed laws to alter the following provisions of this Constitution, or Organic Laws made for the purposes of any such provision:—
- (a) this section;
- (b) the Preamble;

(c) Division II.2. (*constitutional laws*);
(d) Division III.1. (*National Goals and Directive Principles*);
(e) Division III.2. (*leadership code*);
(f) Division III.3. (*basic rights*);
(g) Division III.5 (*basic social obligations*);
(h) Part IV. (*citizenship*);
(i) Division VI.2. (*the National Parliament*);
(j) Division VI.3. (*special instances of the legislative power*);
(k) Division VI.5. (*the administration of justice*);
(ka) Part VIA. (*provincial government and local level government*); (*Added by Constitutional Amendment No.3. — Provincial Government (Consequential Amendments) s.1*)
(l) Division VII.2. (*the Public Services Commission*);
(m) Division VII.4. (*special provisions in relation to the Police Force*);
(n) Division VII.5. (*special provisions in relation to the Defence Force*);
(o) Part VIII. (*supervision and control*);
(p) Part IX. (*constitutional office-holders and constitutional institutions*);
(q) Part X. (*emergency powers*).

TRANSITION PROVISIONS SPENT

Comment

Section 15 ceased to have effect on the 16th September, 1979.

16. — INDIRECT ALTERATIONS.

(1) No Constitutional Law takes effect so as to affect the operation of any provision of such a law in force immediately before the commencement of the first-mentioned law unless it was made in the manner and form required for the alteration of that provision.

(2) For the avoidance of doubt, it is hereby declared that Subsection (1) extends to Schedule 1 (*Rules for Shortening and Interpretation of the Constitutional Laws*) in its application to any provision of this Constitution.

17. — "PRESCRIBED MAJORITY OF VOTES".

(1) Subject to this section, in relation to a proposed law to alter any provision of this Constitution the prescribed majority of votes for the purposes of Section 14 (*making of alterations to the Constitution and Organic Laws*) is the majority of votes prescribed by this Constitution in relation to that provision, or if no majority is prescribed a two-thirds absolute majority vote.

GENERALLY

Referred to

by Pritchard J. in *In re Moresby North East Election Petition* [1977] PNGLR 424 at p.446.

(2) For the purposes of Subsection (1) the prescribed majority of votes for this subsection, Sections 3, 6, 8, 20, 21, 23, 24, 26 to 31 (inclusive), 63, 68, 69, 73, 77 to 98 (inclusive), 101, 103, 104, 110, 117, 138, 139, 150, 156, 165, 167, 171, 184 to 187 (inclusive), 206, 248 to 252 (inclusive), 264 to 268 (inclusive), Sch.1.21, Sch.2.1 to Sch.2.14 (inclusive), Schedules 3, 4 and 5 is an absolute majority.

MATTER PERMITTED TO BE AMENDED BY AN ABSOLUTE MAJORITY

Comment

The matters which may be altered by an absolute majority include provisions relating to the national symbols; oaths of loyalty; rules of and aids for constitutional interpretation; adoption and form of the underlying law; criminal sanctions for breach of the constitution; leadership code; enforcement of the Basic Social Obligations; naturalization — the regaining of citizenship and the nationality of foundlings and children; Head of State and the Head of State's functions; Governor General — his appointment, functions and terms and conditions of office; membership and normal term of office of the parliament; certification of the making of laws; adherence to treaties; executive power and the national executive; Secretary to the N.E.C; the Law Officers; Acting Judges and Assistant Judges: seniority of judges; rules of court and court practice; visiting armed forces; vesting of rights and liability of the pre-Independence Government; oaths and declarations of office; National Gazette; provisional and transitional laws; Law Reform Commission.

(3) For the purposes of Subsection (1) the prescribed majority of votes for this subsection, Sections 35, 36, 50, 57, 105, 106, 109, 113, 125, 126, 155, 157, 160, 163, 217, 235, 239, 243, 244, 245 and 269 is a three-quarters absolute majority.

MATTERS REQUIRING A THREE-QUARTERS ABSOLUTE MAJORITY

Comment

The matters which may only be altered by a three-quarters absolute majority include provisions relating to the rights to life and freedom from inhuman treatment; right to vote and stand for office; enforcement of guaranteed rights and freedoms; general elections and by-elections; the Parliament's power of law making and its quorum; electorates and elections; form and independence of the National Judicial System; establishment of National and Supreme Courts; Ombudsman Commission; custody of Members of Parliament under Emergency Regulations; Parliamentary control of emergency powers and internment.

(4) Subject to this section, for the purpose of a proposed law to add a new provision to this Constitution the prescribed majority of votes is the same as the prescribed majority of votes that would be required to alter that provision if it was already enacted.

(5) Subject to Section 12(3) (*Organic Laws*), in relation to a proposed Organic Law the prescribed majority of votes is —
(a) in the case of a proposed Organic Law to alter a provision of an Organic Law — the same as the majority that would be required for the making of the provision proposed to be altered; and
(b) in any other case —
(i) the majority of votes (not being less than an absolute majority) prescribed by this Constitution for the making of the Organic Law; and
(ii) if no majority is prescribed, a two-thirds absolute majority.

GENERALLY

Referred to

by Kearney Dep. C.J. in *S.C.R. No 2 of 1982; Re Organic Law* [1982] PNGLR 214 at p.224.

(6) Where, by virtue of the operation of the preceding provisions of this section, there are different prescribed majorities in relation to different provisions of a proposed law, the prescribed majority of votes in relation to the law as a whole is the greatest of those majorities.

(7) Nothing in this section provents different majorities being prescribed in respect of different aspects or subject-matters of a provision.

(8) No Organic Law may require a majority of votes for the alteration of a provision of an Organic Law greater than that by which the first-mentioned law was made.

(9) Notwithstanding anything in this section, until 16 September, 1980 —
(a) for the purpose of a proposed law to add a new provision to this Constitution, the prescribed majority of votes is an absolute majority; and
(b) for the purpose of making an Organic law for which there was provision in this Constitution when adopted the prescribed majority of votes is an absolute majority.

TRANSITION PROVISION SPENT

Comment

Section 17(9) ceased to have effect on the 16th September, 1980.

18. — ORIGINAL INTERPRETATIVE JURISDICTION OF THE SUPREME COURT.

(1) Subject to this Constitution, the Supreme Court has original jurisdiction, to the exclusion of other courts, as to any question relating to the interpretation or application of any provision of a Constitutional Law.

C.P.C. Report Ch.8 p.13

E. *RESOLUTION OF CONSTITUTIONAL QUESTION*

133. The Constitution will be the supreme law of this country. All other laws and regulations will have to conform to its provisions. The Constitution we recommend will establish a number of institutions and will define their powers. It is inevitable that doubts will arise as to the precise scope of these powers and of the functions of these bodies, especially as to the respective powers and functions of two or more institutions. [p.14] Furthermore, we have recommended that the Constitution lay down a number of prescriptions and stipulations (for example, the National Goals and Directive Principles, and the Leadership Code) and safeguards for individuals (for example, through the human rights provisions in Chapter 5).

134. In order to ensure that the Constitution really is supreme, we believe it is necessary to provide machinery for the enforcement of its provisions and to resolve disputes arising under it.

135. It is of course possible to dispense with any special machinery. Under such a system it is assumed that each organ and institution of government knows its powers and the limitations on it, and can be relied on to stay within these limitations. Sometimes, although the machinery for enforcement is not dispensed with altogether, no enforcement provisions are made in respect of certain chapters or sections. It is not unusual that even though the legislative powers of Parliament are restricted in the Constitution, it is not possible to challenge a law passed by it on the ground that the law goes beyond the legislative powers vested in it.

136. The absence of special enforcement machinery is sometimes justified by the argument that the Constitution sets up several co-ordinate branches of government — the legislature, the executive and the judiciary — and that it is inconsistent with the theory of separation of powers that one branch should be told by another what it may or may not do. This line of argument does not require that there be no enforcement machinery at all, but that the enforcement machinery is self-administered. Thus, while courts cannot question the constitutionality of legislation, a legislature may set up a committee of its own to review legislative bills for constitutionality before enacting them; or the administration may set up a tribunal to resolve complaints against administrative decisions.

137. Another argument is also sometimes presented in favour of dispensing with enforcement machinery. It is said that the best guarantee of the supremacy of the Constitution lies in the vigilance of the people who, acting as an electorate, and through pressure groups, keep a check on state institutions. If this task is transferred to a specific institution, especially the courts, the political process is weakened, and the way is opened ultimately to greater arbitrariness.

138. We consider that these arguments are important, although we cannot agree that they are fully applicable to our situation. Our constitutional provisions are not based on a theory of absolute separation of powers. It is our belief that interaction between different state institutions can be beneficial. We do not consider that the presence of an enforcement machinery need necessarily weaken the political process. Countries which have been able successfully to dispense with an enforcement machinery are either those in which the political system has evolved gradually over the course of centuries, or those which have a clear and dominant ideology.

139. Our constitutional proposals represent in many ways a radical departure from the system under which our country has been governed until now. Given the immediacy of the numerous tasks that face us, it is scarcely open to us to permit a slow and unplanned evolution of our constitutional system. Our proposals envisage the establishment of numerous new institutions and a significant redistribution and devolution of power. There will be a new balance between institutions. We hope that the new Constitution will help to change the old ways and habits of doing things.

140. It is not our opinion that all of these changes and innovations can take place spontaneously. Also, it will be several years before the people will have a full grasp of the new constitutional system and as they have been suppressed over decades of colonialism, they may be afraid to stand up for their constitutional rights. Moreover, we have noticed a tendency in many parts of the world towards the establishment of a machinery to ensure the enforcement of the Constitution. We have given careful thought to this question, and have recommended elsewhere in this Report various devices to ensure both the implementation and the enforcement of the Constitution.

141. We have proposed in preceding chapters that several institutions in the country have a general responsibility to see to it that the Constitution is respected. Both the Prime Minister and the National Parliament should, we believe, have important roles in this respect. Political parties and other pressure groups and educational institutions have both an interest and an obligation to ensure that the Constitution is not flouted. We do not under-estimate the importance of these institutions, and indeed wish to state that in our opinion the specialised institutions and procedures we recommend will be truly effective only if they are supported by these general institutions and public opinion. It is, however, also our view [p.15] that it is necessary to provide for bodies especially charged with enforcement of the Constitution through the resolution of disputes.

142. One of the commonest ways to enforce the Constitution and resolve disputes is through the jurisdiction of the courts. The courts are given the power to interpret the Constitution and their rulings are authoritive and binding on all other institutions. We have given careful thought to the advantages and disadvantages of a primary reliance on courts for the settlement of constitutional disputes.

143. We believe, the main advantages of judicial review in regard to constitutional questions are as follows —

> It is the normal function of the courts to resolve disputes in accordance with law. It is a task for which they have pre-eminently the qualification and the expertise. The Constitution is law — in fact supreme law. It is therefore logical that the courts should be assigned the task of constitutional dispute settlement.
>
> Courts which have adequate constitutional protection are generally impartial, serving no narrow political or regional interests. The court procedures ensure a fair hearing for all sides, and in view of our proposals for the Public Solicitor, access to courts should be comparatively easy. Courts enjoy respect and prestige in our country, and their decisions are unlikely to be ignored or challenged.
>
> Whilst it is true that certain aspects of a country's Constitution, such as those concerning the internal procedures of the legislature and the executive, are best left to be enforced by those bodies themselves, there are many other provisions in most Constitutions in respect of which judicial interpretation is clearly the most appropriate means of dispute resolution and enforcement.

144. The principal disadvantages of giving the main responsibility to the judiciary seem to be the following —

> The courts tend to be formalistic and legalistic. While it is true that the Constitution is law, it is a special kind of law. All too often the courts approach the Constitution as if it were like ordinary law. They adopt a literal approach and sacrifice the spirit for the letter of the Constitution. By failing to recognise the dynamic character of a Constitution, the courts have often introduced unnecessary rigidities.
>
> On the other hand, judges, like other people, are not free of their biases and emotions. This situation is particularly difficult where the judiciary is predominantly expatriate, as it is likely to remain in our country for some years to come.
>
> Another disadvantage, especially where the formal amendment of the Constitution is very difficult, (as in Australia for example, where a referendum is needed to amend the Constitution) is that the courts become the final arbiters of the Constitution. In this situation the powers of other institutions which express more directly and clearly the wishes of the people may be weakened.
>
> Finally it is argued that courts have a limited capacity to effect compromises. In many constitutional controversies, especially as between various organs of the state, an authoritative decision in favour of one or the other party may precipitate a more acute crisis, whereas a compromise solution might have satisfied all parties. Also, the interference by the courts in what is often best left to the political process, can aggravate politically difficult situations. And by entering these contentious areas, the role and functions of the courts themselves become controversial. Those who believe that the courts play an important social role through their functions or ordinary adjudication are afraid that their involvement in political disputes — for such are many constitutional cases — may do serious damage to that social role.

145. As we have indicated in earlier chapters, we have adopted a selective approach towards the role of courts and other judicial bodies in relation to constitutional issues. We consider that there are areas where the safeguards of the judicial process and the independence of the judiciary are important assets and have recommended that courts, and in particular the Supreme Court, be used in those instances. In other areas we are concerned that the courts could introduce unnecessary rigidities or that their procedures would not permit acceptable compromises, and have accordingly sought alternative devices and methods. [p.16]

146. However, in relation to those chapters or parts of the Constitution where we do not make explicit reference to the method of resolving disputes, we recommend in this Part that the Supreme Court have exclusive original jurisdiction. We have recommended that except in regard to matters in which the human rights provisions of the Constitution are involved, full responsibility for such judicial review should be vested in the Supreme Court, which should have exclusive jurisdiction to decide all constitutional questions apart from those which, under the Constitution, are to be (or may be) resolved by another body.

147. We recommend that whenever, in proceedings before a court other than the Supreme Court, a justiciable constitutional issue other than one concerning the human rights provisions of the Constitution, arises, that court shall refer the issue to the Supreme Court for determination. Once the Supreme Court has decided the constitutional issue, the court which was originally dealing with the case must determine it in accordance with the ruling of the Supreme Court.

148. We consider that the new Supreme Court, (which we have recommended in Part A of this chapter should comprise three judges), is the appropriate body to be given this primary responsibility for deciding constitutional issues because the Constitution will be the supreme law of our country and judicial decisions to enforce and interpret it should surely be made by our highest court. As a general rule, we do not think it would be wise to give this heavy responsibility to a single judge or magistrate. In any event, the decision of a single member of the judiciary on such major questions as are likely to arise in relation to the Constitution would almost certainly be appealed against by one or other of the parties to the particular proceedings.

149. As, under our proposals, the courts, and in particular the Supreme Court, will play a considerable role in constitutional dispute settlement, we have made certain recommendations to ensure that the courts adopt a liberal approach in interpretation. In Chapter 2 we have recommended that the Constitution state explicitly that the courts should be guided by the National Goals and Directive Principles of Policy so that whenever there are ambiguities, an interpretation which favours these goals and principles should be adopted as against an alternative one. In our recommendations on human rights we have proposed that access to courts should not be excluded on the technical grounds of the standing of the person seeking an order from the court or the length of time which has elapsed since the cause of action arose.

RECOMMENDATIONS. [p.30]

E. *RESOLUTION OF CONSTITUTIONAL QUESTIONS*

Original Jurisdiction of Supreme Court

81. (1) The Supreme Court shall, except as otherwise provided or allowed in the Constitution, have original jurisdiction, to the exclusion of all other courts, to determine any matter concerning any provision of the Constitution.

(2) Without limiting the generality of clause (1) above, the jurisdiction conferred upon the Supreme Court by that clause shall include power to determine any matter —
(a) relating to the enforcement or interpretation of any provision of the Constitution; and
(b) where any question arises as to whether any law has been made or action taken in excess of the powers conferred by the Constitution upon the National Parliament or any other authority or person. [p.31]

(3) Where any issue relating to any matter or question referred to in clause (1) or (2) above arises in proceedings in any court other than the Supreme Court, that court shall stay the proceedings and refer the issue to the Supreme Court for determination; and the court in which the issue arose shall dispose of the case in accordance with the decision of the Supreme Court.

Note: Specific provision is made in recommendations contained in other chapters, such as Chapter 2, 'National Goals and Directive Principles', Chapter 3, 'The Leadership Code', Chapter 5, 'Human Rights and Obligations and Emergency Powers', Chapter 6, 'The Legislature' and Chapter 7, 'The Executive' for certain constitutional provisions to be either non justiciable or determined by a court or other judicial body other than the Supreme Court. Special provision has been made in Chapter 10, 'Provincial Government' for the resolution of disputes between central government and provincial governments.

IMPLIED POWER TO HOLD STATUTE LAW INVALID

Comment

Section 18(1) does not expressly confer jurisdiction upon the Supreme Court to hold statutes invalid (cf s.19). The Supreme Court has, however, not hesitated to exercise such power. Although rarely directly discussed by the court many precedents for the exercise of this power now exist. See for example: *Constitutional Reference No 3 of 1978; Re Intergroup Fighting Act 1977* [1978] PNGLR 421; *S.C.R. No 1 of 1981; Re Inter-Group Fighting Act 1977* [1981] PNGLR 151 and *S.C.R. No 2 of 1982; Re Organic Law* [1982] PNGLR 214.

'SUBJECT TO THIS CONSTITUTION'

Held

Because s.18(1) is expressed to be subject to the Constitution and because under s.57(1) and s.22 it was envisaged that certain constitutional questions were within the jurisdiction of both the

National and Supreme Courts there is no requirement to refer to the Supreme Court any question so arising.
The State v Peter Painke (No 2) [1977] PNGLR 141; see Frost C.J. at p.145; see also cases referred to under this heading under s.18(2).

STANDING TO INVOKE JURISDICTION UNDER SECTION 18(1)

Held

Petitioner (the then leader of the Opposition) had standing under s.18(1) to apply to the Supreme Court for a determination of the constitutional validity of the *Defence Force (Presence Abroad) Act* 1980 and of the act of sending members of the Papua New Guinea Defence Force to Vanuatu for peace keeping purposes.
S.C.R. No 4 of 1980; Re petition of M.T. Somare [1981] PNGLR 265; see Kidu C.J. at pp.273, 274 (below), Kapi J. at pp.285–296 (below), Miles J. at pp.300–311; but see also Kearney Dep.C.J. (dissenting) at pp.275, 276, Greville Smith J. at pp.279–284.

per Kidu C.J.

In my view, in cases where the constitutionality or otherwise of an Act of the National Parliament arises, locus standi should not be restricted to any particular group.

The Constitution of this country provides that all power belongs to the people. These powers are then given to three bodies — the National Parliament (legislative power), the Executive (the executive power) and the Judicial System (the judicial power). These powers are given with the clear understanding that they be used properly and constitutionally .... The People, depository of all powers in Papua New Guinea, have, through the Constitution, directed that the Parliament make laws which comply with the Constitution. If the legislative power is exercised contrary to the Constitution, why should not the People come to this court and complain? After all it is their power and they are, in my view, entitled to complain to the Supreme Court, in whom their power to determine the constitutionality or otherwise of an Act of the Parliament, is vested. As a beneficiary in trust is entitled to invoke the powers of the courts to ensure that the trustees act in their interest so should the People whose legislative power the Parliament exercises, complain to this court if they think the Legislature acts contrary to the Constitution through which their power has been given to it.
S.C.R. No 4 of 1980; Re petition of M.T. Somare [1981] PNGLR 265 at p.273; see also Kapi J. at pp.285–296 (below), Miles J. at pp.300–311; but see also Kearney Dep.C.J. (dissenting) at pp.275, 276 (below), Greville Smith J. at pp.279–284.

per Kapi J.

Having regard to all the matters I have discussed, I would formulate a rule that would draw a line between those who can and those who cannot have standing. At the same time, the modern view on locus standi is not restrictive as is the common law. It must have a much wider conception as has been found in the Canadian cases dealing with constitutional cases.

A general principle that would suit the above description is the new English rule on locus standi. The English rule on locus standi was a result of much study by the English Law Commission. This rule was recommended by the Law Commission in its report on remedies in administrative law in 1975. The new rule would be that the applicant must have sufficient interest in the matter.

As to what is sufficient interest, I would adopt the objective test laid down by Lord Denning in *R v Inland Revenue Commissioners; ex parte National Federation of Self-Employed and Small Businesses Ltd.* (1980) 2 A11 E.R. 378. It is not possible to lay down a workable definition for all cases because each case is different. I would leave it to courts to develop the application of the rule in individual cases ....

However, I consider that standing given to any citizen should be at the discretion of the court. In exercising this discretion the court should consider whether the applicant has exhausted other means of achieving the same thing. In this case the Leader of the Opposition opposed the motion and the Act but was unsuccessful in the Parliament. He also exhausted the means of getting this question referred under s.19 of the Constitution. His request to the Ombudsman Commission to refer the question was unsuccessful. There

is no suggestion that other authorities will refer the question. I am not suggesting that a citizen's right to complain depends on whether or not he has tried other means. Rather, if he does this, this is an indication that he is genuinely concerned with the matter. A person who simply comes straight to the court as a delaying tactic or for reasons other than that he is genuinely concerned with the matter should not be heard.
S.C.R. No 4 of 1980; Re petition of M.T. Somare [1981] PNGLR 165 at pp.295, 296; see also Kidu C.J. at pp.273, 274 (above), Miles J. at pp.300–311; but see also Kearney Dep. C.J. (dissenting) at pp.275, 276 (below), Greville Smith J. at pp.279–284.

per Kearney Dep.C.J. (dissenting)

The Constitution draws the necessary balance between the need to protect the rights and freedoms of the individuals as enshrined in the Constitution, and the law-making power of the Parliament; that indeed is a major function of any written Constitution. However, I consider that it also deals explicitly with the circumstances in which constitutional challenge to laws may be made, and with the persons and bodies who may institute such challenge . . . . [T]he Constitution authorizes certain bodies which, like the applicant in this case, are not themselves threatened or affected by a particular law, to apply to have that law declared invalid. That standing is given by the Constitution s.19(3). Applying the Constitution s.24(1) as an aid to interpretation, it is clear from pars. 150–154 on pages 8/16–8/17 of the Final Report of the Constitutional Planning Committee that the sole thrust of the Constitution s.19(3) is precisely to the question of standing to apply to have a law declared invalid, in these circumstances. I respectfully agree with the views expressed by Prentice Dep.C.J. (as he then was) and Williams J. in *Mopio v The Speaker* [1977] PNGLR 420 at p.423 as to the exclusive nature of Constitution s.19(3). That is, s.19(3) lists exhaustively those bodies which may apply as of right to the Court for a binding advisory opinion on constitutional issues. There are almost 50 such bodies so listed, many of them independent of the government of the day. The result is a law of automatic standing to attack the validity of laws, which is more liberal than that of any other democracy.

It is vital to note that because of the terms of the Constitution s.19(2), there is no difference in nature or in legal effect between an 'advisory opinion' under the Constitution s.19(1) as to the validity of an existing law, and a 'declaration' as to the validity of an existing law. Both involve a binding judicial declaration of the legal status of the law in question.

As the Constitution s.19(3) lists explicitly and exhaustively those offices and bodies which can apply as of right to have tested the validity of a law, and the office of Leader of the Opposition does not appear on that list, I consider that Mr. Somare as holder of that office lacks the necessary standing to bring these proceedings as of right.
S.C.R. No 4 of 1980; Re petition of M.T. Somare [1981] PNGLR 265 at pp.275, 276; see also Greville Smith J. (also dissenting) at pp.279–284; but see also Kidu C.J. at pp.273, 274 (above), Kapi J. at pp.285–296 (above), Miles J. at pp.300–311.

PRINCIPLES OF INTERPRETATION TO BE APPLIED

per Kearney J.

The process of statutory interpretation is essentially intuitive and subjective, in the absence of rules consistently applied. The Act is a Constitutional Law and thus subject to the general principles of interpretation set out in Constitution ss.10, 25(3), 63(3) and Basic Social Obligation (a), and 158(2); and to the more specific canons in Constitution ss.24, 109(4) when read with 12, and Sch.1.5. In my opinion these provisions amount to a direction to the Court that in carrying out its functions under Constitution s.18(1) the words actually used in the Act do not have to be strictly adhered to but are to be construed with the assistance of the materials referred to in Constitution s.24, so as best to attain what Parliament intended. When Constitution ss.109(4) and 158(2) are themselves interpreted with the aid of s.24, this view is fortified: there are several references in Chapter 8 of the Report of the Constitutional Planning Committee which point against the Court taking a 'narrowly legalistic' or 'literal' approach, and thus sacrificing the 'spirit for the letter of the Constitution'. The 'dynamic character' of the Constitution is emphasized; in interpreting the laws, the judges are urged to use 'judicial ingenuity' in appropriate cases, to do justice. One consequence of this approach to interpretation is that the Court should not fail to give

a provision the effect it considers the Parliament intended, by applying a literal or 'plain meaning' test nor should it attribute to the legislature an intention to produce a capricious or unjust result. The search throughout is for the intention of Parliament, a process which remains, formally at least, one of interpretation and not of legislation, and one in which the best guide remains the provisions of the Act itself.
The State v The Independent Tribunal; Ex Parte Sasakila [1976] PNGLR 491 at pp.506, 507.

Referred to

by Prentice Dep.C.J. (dissenting) in *Peter v South Pacific Brewery Ltd.* [1976] PNGLR 537 at pp.554–559 (liberal approach to be preferred);

by Wilson J. in *P.L.A.R. No 1 of 1980* [1980] PNGLR 326 at p.335 (the 'literal approach' to statutory interpretation decisively rejected by the Supreme Court: extracts of this judgment appear under s.158(2); see also Andrew J. at p.347.

GENERALLY

Referred to

by Prentice C.J. in *In re Moresby North East Election Petition* [1977] PNGLR 429 at p.432; see also Pritchard J. at p.443 (s.18(1) and s.155(2)(b) combined permit in exceptional cases the Supreme Court to entertain interlocutory applications concerning constitutional matters pending in the National Court).

(2) Subject to this Constitution, where any question relating to the interpretation or application of any provision of a Constitutional Law arises in any courts or tribunal other than the Supreme Court, the court or tribunal, shall, unless the question is trivial, vexatious or irrelevant, refer the matter to the Supreme Court, and take whatever other action (including the adjournment of proceedings) is appropriate.

'SUBJECT TO THIS CONSTITUTION'

Held

As s.18(2) is expressed to be subject to the Constitution and as s.42(5) authorizes and requires the National Court to hear and determine complaints that a person has been unlawfully detained; accordingly the National Court was not bound to refer such complaints to the Supreme Court.
Re s.42 of the Constitution and Jacob Hendrich Prai [1979] PNGLR 42; see Greville Smith J. at pp.45, 46.

Held

The Constitution gives the National Court jurisdiction to interpret and apply constitutional provisions in the context of protection and enforcement of fundamental rights under Part 3, Division 3, Sub-Division D of the Constitution. Section 18 is subject to the other provisions of the Constitution. The National Court is not obliged to refer such questions to the Supreme Court.
In Re Organic Law on National Elections [1982] PNGLR 289; see Kapi Dep.C.J. at p.290.

Referred to

by O'Meally A.J. in *The State v Kwambol Embogol* (1977 Unreported) N91 at p.6 (s.18 subject to express power of National Court to make orders under s.23);

by Miles J. in *Ready Mixed Concrete Pty Ltd v P.N.G.* [1981] PNGLR 396 at p.409;

See also cases referred to under this heading under s.18(1).

AS TO QUESTIONS WHICH ARE TRIVIAL, VEXATIOUS OR IRRELEVANT

Held

The question as to whether the *Defamation Act* 1963 conflicts with s.46 (Freedom of Expression) was 'vexatious' and possibly 'trivial' and did not warrant referral to the Supreme Court.
Cory v Blyth (No1) [1976] PNGLR 274; see Raine J. at p.297; note however that Kapi J. in *Hetura Paz Development Co Pty Ltd v Niugini Nuis Pty Ltd* [1982] PNGLR 250 at p.254 expressed doubt as to whether the law of defamation is constitutional.

Held

The question whether the *District Courts Act* (being a pre-Independence Act of the Parliament adopted under Sch.2.6) should be referred to as the '*District Courts Act* 1975' (the Act having in that year been adopted) or as the *District Courts Act* 1963 was trivial and should not have been referred to the Supreme Court.
Peter v South Pacific Brewery Ltd [1976] PNGLR 537; see Frost C.J. at p.551, Prentice Dep.C.J. at p.551, Kearney J. at p.561.

Held

A question as to the sufficiency of a complaint or charge is trival and should not be referred to the Supreme Court.
The State v John Rumet Kaputin (No1) [1979] PNGLR 532; per Curiam (Prentice C.J., Saldanha and Wilson J.J.) at p.534.

AS TO HYPOTHETICAL QUESTIONS

Held

A court may not refer hypothetical questions to the Supreme Court. Only those authorities referred to in s.19 of the Constitution are entitled to refer hypothetical questions.
S.C.R. No 5 of 1982; Hugo Berghauser and ors v Joseph Aoae [1982] PNGLR 379; see per Curiam (Kidu C.J., Kapi Dep.C.J. Andrew J.) at p.383.

per Curiam (Kidu C.J., Kapi Dep.C.J., Bredmeyer J.)

> We do not consider s.18(2) allows hypothetical questions to be referred by lower tribunals to the Supreme Court. This situation is within the ambit .... of s.19.
> We are of the opinion that a question which is referred to the Supreme Court must arise out of a factual situation established by the lower court or tribunal ....
> In constitutional matters referred under s.18 of the Constitution, it is our view that all findings of facts necessary for interpretation or application of a Constitutional Law must be made by the Court or tribunal before making the reference.
> *S.C.R. No 3 of 1982; Re ss.57 and 155(4) of the Constitution* [1982] PNGLR 405 at pp.407–408.

REFERRAL TO PRECLUDE FURTHER ACTION BY REFERRING COURT

per Kidu C.J.

> When a Judge, a Magistrate or a Tribunal finds it necessary to refer a Constitutional question to [the Supreme Court] the proper procedure, in my view, is to defer making any order disposing of the case and refer the question to [the Supreme] Court. The final disposition of the case should await the decision of [the Supreme] Court.

S.C.R. No 2 of 1981; In re s.19(1)(f) of the Criminal Code [1982] PNGLR 150 at p.153; see also Kearney Dep.C.J. at p.159, Greville Smith J. at pp.163–164 and Kapi J. at p.173.

AS TO COMMENCEMENT IN SUPREME COURT

Held

Proceedings become 'pending' in the Supreme Court by operation of law whenever any question relating to the interpretation or application of any provision of the Constitution arises and when the court in which it arises is satisfied that the question is not trivial, vexatious or irrelevant. Once that stage is reached the proceedings enter a pipeline that can only lead to the Supreme Court. (Rejecting a submission of no case to answer on the grounds that at the time an alleged contempt was committed no proceedings were pending in the Supreme Court).
Re Rooney No1 [1979] PNGLR 403; see Raine Dep.C.J. at p.407 (Saldanha, Wilson and Greville Smith J.J. agreeing, Kearney J. (dissenting) at p.414).

GENERALLY

Referred to

by Kearney J. in *Cory v Blyth (No 4)* [1976] PNGLR 525 at p.527;

by Kearney J. in *The State v The Independent Tribunal; Ex Parte Sasakila* [1976] PNGLR 491 at p.506;

by Pritchard J. in *In re Moresby North East Election Petition* [1977] PNGLR 429 at p.443;

per Curiam (Kidu C.J., Kearney Dep.C.J., Greville Smith, Andrew, Miles JJ.) in *In re Joseph Auna* [1980] PNGLR 500 at p.502;

by Kearney J. in *Re Rooney (No 2)* [1979] PNGLR 448 at p.484;

by Kearney Dep.C.J. in *S.C.R. No 2 of 1980; Re s.14(2) of the Summary Offences Act* [1981] PNGLR 50 at p.52; see also Miles J. at p.55;

per Curiam (Kidu C.J., Kapi Dep.C.J., Andrew J.) in *S.C.R. No 5 of 1982; Hugo Berghauser and ors v Joseph Aoae* [1982] PNGLR 379 at p.383 (may not refer hypothetical question under s.18(2)).

19. — SPECIAL REFERENCES TO THE SUPREME COURT.

(1) Subject to Subsection (4), the Supreme Court shall, on application by an authority referred to in Subsection (3), give its opinion on any question relating to the interpretation or application of any provision of a Constitutional Law, including (but without limiting the generality of that expression) any question as to the validity of a law or proposed law.

C.P.C. Report Ch.8 p.16

Advisory Opinions

150. A common device to get round the technical rules which restrict access to courts (as well as for other objectives) is to vest the jurisdiction to give an advisory opinion on constitutional issues in the courts. Under such a procedure specified bodies are authorised to refer a matter to the court for its opinion. It is not always necessary

that a dispute should have arisen; an institution may wish to have an authoritative ruling on a constitutional point before embarking on a particular piece of legislation or a certain policy. It is flexible in that a party or parties can define clearly and precisely the issues on which they need a ruling, and yet the ruling is, strictly speaking, not binding.

151. While this procedure has these advantages, it has been criticised on the ground that in view of the crucial importance of the facts of a case a court performs its functions best when it has an actual and specific dispute before it. It is also said that if such a procedure exists, political and administrative institutions are tempted to avoid their own responsibilities of decision-making by referring contentious issues to courts. It is further argued that courts may be caused embarrassment under such a procedure if, for example, a case is brought to court under its ordinary jurisdiction on a point which it has already given an advisory opinion.

152. Experience in countries which do permit judicial advisory opinions shows that such criticisms are not justified. In any case, we consider that the advantages outweigh the possible disadvantages and we recommend that provision be made for the Supreme Court to give an advisory opinion on any matter concerning any provision of the Constitution, including its implementation and enforcement.

153. We envisage advisory opinions as serving two aims. An advisory opinion will help an institution charged with the enforcement of a constitutional provision or the executive to establish what the law on a particular constitutional point is. It should also help to resolve a dispute about what the constitutional law is on a particular issue before the dispute becomes aggravated and the parties to it take strong and inflexible positions. It is important, however, to regard the advisory opinion as a rather special procedure to be resorted to only in exceptional circumstances.

154. Having given careful thought to who should be able to seek a judicial opinion, and on [p.17] what matters, we consider that only the following institutions should be empowered to seek advisory opinions —

- the First Parliamentary Committee (as the Permanent Parliamentary Committee charged with responsibility for constitutional affairs);
- the National Executive Council;
- the body charged with special responsibility in relation to the resolution of central-provincial government disputes; and
- the body responsible for recommending changes in existing legislation to achieve conformity with the national goals and directive principles and the human rights and obligations incorporated in the Constitution.

155. We recommend that this constitutional advisory jurisdiction be exercised only by the Supreme Court, as the court which has exclusive jurisdiction in regard to most constitutional matters. Advisory opinions given by that court should have considerable weight.

RECOMMENDATIONS [p.31]

Advisory Jurisdiction

82. (1) Except as otherwise provided by the Constitution, and subject to clause (2) below, the Supreme Court shall have exclusive jurisdiction to give an advisory opinion on any matter concerning any provision of the Constitution; including its implementation and enforcement.

(2) The following bodies, only, shall be entitled to seek an advisory opinion of the Supreme Court under clause (1) above —

(a) the National Executive Council;

(b) the First Parliamentary Committee;

(c) the body to be established in accordance with the recommendations in Chapter 10, 'Provincial Government' concerning the resolution of disputes between the central government and any provincial government;

(d) the body responsible for recommending changes in existing legislation to achieve conformity with the national goals and directive principles, and human rights and obligations, incorporated in the Constitution.

ANY QUESTION RELATING TO THE INTERPRETATION OR APPLICATION OF ANY PROVISION OF A CONSTITUTIONAL LAW.

per Kapi J.

The Principal Legal Advisor has referred a question for determination by this court under s.19 of the Constitution.

A preliminary question has arisen as to whether or not the question referred involves 'any question relating to the interpretation or application of any provision of a constitutional law'. The question referred is as follows:

> ... are the electoral boundaries for the 1982 elections as depicted in the maps and descriptions attached to the 1977 report of the Boundaries Commission or are they as intended by the 1977 report and depicted in maps to be produced before the Supreme Court ....

The preliminary issue raises the proper meaning to be given to the words 'interpretation' and 'application' in s.19 of the Constitution.

'Interpretation' of a constitutional law may arise in one of two ways under s.19 of the Constitution. A provision of the constitutional law may be referred to the Supreme Court for the court to explain the effect of, or the meaning of, either a particular word or words or the whole provision or provisions without any application to any particular issue raised by facts found or assumed, or without any application to any statutory provision. Alternatively, 'interpretation' of a constitutional law may arise in the application of a provision of the constitutional law provisions to an issue raised by facts found or assumed or to a provision of another statute. The question to ask here is whether the Reference raises any question of 'interpretation' of a word or words or provision of a relevant constitutional law. The issue raised by the Reference involves the intention of the Parliament. It is clear from the issue raised by the Reference that it does not involve an 'interpretation' of any constitutional law.

The term 'application' involves the consideration of a constitutional law provision in relation to an issue raised by facts found or assumed, or a provision of a statute or a proposed statute. An 'application' of a constitutional law provision necessarily involves the 'interpretation' of the same. Whether or not a question raised in a Reference involves an 'application' of a constitutional law under s.19 of the Constitution depends on whether a constitutional law provision has any relevance to the issue raised in the Reference. Unless a constitutional law provision is brought to bear upon the issue raised in the Reference there can be no 'application' of the Constitution. I am of the opinion that an 'interpretation' or an 'application', or both, of a constitutional law provision is involved when those constitutional law provisions are brought to bear upon the issue raised in the Reference. This view is reinforced by the C.P.C. Report, paragraph 153, p.8/16;

> We envisage advisory opinions as serving two aims. An advisory opinion will help an institution charged with the enforcement of a constitutional provision or the executive to establish what the law *on a particular constitutional point is*. I should also help to resolve a dispute about *what the constitutional law is on a particular issue* before the dispute becomes aggravated and the parties to it take strong and inflexible positions. It is important, however, to regard the advisory opinion as a rather special procedure to be resorted to only in exceptional circumstances (emphasis mine).

Having regard to the issue raised in this Reference, it is dealing with what the Parliament intended. I can find no constitutional law provision which bears on this particular issue. In other words there is no constitutional provision which can resolve the issue raised in the Reference.

I find that the question referred in the Reference does not involve an 'interpretation' or 'application' of a provision of a constitutional law, and therefore cannot be dealt with under s.19 of the Constitution.

S.C.R. No 2 of 1981; Re s.19 of the Constitution [1981] PNGLR 518 at pp.521–523; see also Kidu C.J. at pp.519–521 and Miles J. at pp.527–530.

MAY REFER HYPOTHETICAL QUESTIONS

per Curiam (Kidu C.J., Kapi Dep.C.J., Andrew J.)

The right to refer [hypothetical] questions is given under s.19 of the Constitution. Only those authorities referred to under this provision can refer hypothetical questions.

S.C.R. No 5 of 1982; Hugo Berghauser and ors v Joseph Aoae [1982] PNGLR 379 at p.383.

Referred to

per Curiam (Kidu C.J., Kapi Dep.C.J., Bredmeyer. J.) in *S.C.R. No 3 of 1982; Re ss.57 and 155(4) of the Constitution* [1982] PNGLR 405 at pp.407–408; (see extract under s.18(2)).

(2) An opinion given under Subsection (1) has the same binding effect as any other decision of the Supreme Court.

(3) The following authorities only are entitled to make application under Subsection (1):—

(a) the Parliament; and
(b) the Head of State, acting with, and in accordance with, the advice of the National Executive Council; and
(c) the Law Officers of Papua New Guinea; and
(d) the Law Reform Commission; and
(e) the Ombudsman Commission; and
(ea) a provincial legislature; and
(eb) a provincial executive; and
(ec) the council established in accordance with Section 187H(2) (*inter-governmental relations*) and any other body established by a Constitutional Law or an Act of the Parliament specifically for the settlement of disputes between the National Government, or between provincial governments; and (*Sub sections 19(3)(ea), (eb) and (ec) added by Constitutional Amendment No.3. — Provincial Government (Consequential Amendments) s.2*)
(f) the Speaker, in accordance with Section 137(3) (*Acts of Indemnity*).

SPECIFIC PURPOSE ONLY: DOES NOT COVER THE FIELD OF STANDING IN PUBLIC INTEREST SUITS

Held

Section 19(3) does not prevent or bar applications for rulings on the constitutionality or otherwise of Acts of Parliament by way of public interest suits under s.18.
S.C.R. No 4 of 1980; Re petition of M.T. Somare [1981] PNGLR 265 (see detailed discussion under s.18(1) above).

per Kidu C.J.

Section 19 empowers the Supreme Court to give advisory opinions when requested by 'authorities' enumerated in s.19(3) thereof. It is a special provision included in the Constitution for a specific purpose — to enable the court to give *advisory opinions*. It is not meant to cover the field in relation to public interest constitutional questions.
S.C.R. No 4 of 1980; Re petition of M.T. Somare [1981] PNGLR 265 at p.268; see also Kapi J. at p.287, Miles J. at pp.300–302; but see also Kearney Dep.C.J. (dissenting) at pp.275,276, Greville Smith J. at pp.281–284.

per Kearney Dep.C.J. (dissenting)

The Constitution authorizes certain bodies which, like the applicant in this case, are not themselves threatened or affected by a particular law, to apply to have that law declared invalid. That standing is given by Constitution s.19(3). Applying Constitution s.24(1) as an aid to interpretation, it is clear from paragraphs 150–154 on pages 8/16–8/17 of the Final Report of the Constitutional Planning Committee that the sole thrust of Constitution s.19(3) is precisely to the question of standing to apply to have a law declared invalid, in these circumstances. I respectfully agree with the views expressed by Prentice Dep.C.J. (as he then was) and Williams J. in *Mopio v The Speaker* [1977] PNGLR 420, as to the exclusive nature of Constitution s.19(3). That is, s.19(3) lists exhaustively those bodies

which may apply as of right to the Court for a binding advisory opinion on constitution issues.
S.C.R. No 4 of 1980; Re petition of M.T. Somare [1981] PNGLR 265 at pp.275, 276; see also Greville Smith J. (also dissenting) at pp.281–284, but see Kidu C.J. at p.268 (above), Kapi J. at p.287, Miles J. at pp.300–302.

Referred to

per Curiam (Frost C.J., Prentice Dep.C.J., Williams J.) in *James Eki Mopio v The Speaker of the National Parliament* [1977] PNGLR 420 at p.423 (only a designated authority may make an application in the form of a reference for the interpretation of the Constitution);

by Pritchard J. in *Constitutional Reference No1 of 1978 (s.19)* [1978] PNGLR 345 at p.371 (power to make applications is included in the powers and functions of the Public Solicitor) and at p.374 (as a responsibility of the Ombudsman Commission).

(4) Subject to any Act of the Parliament, the Rules of Court of the Supreme Court may make provision in respect of matters relating to the jurisdiction of the Supreme Court under this section, and in particular as to —

(a) the form and contents of questions to be decided by the Court; and
(b) the provision of counsel adequate to enable full argument before the Court of any question; and
(c) cases and circumstances in which the Court may decline to give an opinion.

per Miles J.

The Supreme Court is given wide powers under s.19(4) to make rules as to the cases and circumstances in which it may decline to give an opinion. It may decline to do so if in its opinion the question is trivial, vexatious, hypothetical or unlikely to have any immediate relevance to the circumstances of Papua New Guinea: *Supreme Court Rules* 1977, r.12.
S.C.R. No 4 of 1980; Re petition of M.T. Somare [1981] PNGLR 265 at p.301.

(5) In this section, "proposed law" means a law that has been formally placed before the relevant law-making body.

per Bredmeyer J.

Section 19 could be used by the State to ascertain the Constitutional validity of any new rules drafted to regulate the conditions of detainees held in the Maximum Security Block, B Division, of Bomana Central Corrective Institution.
Amaiu v Commissioner for C.I.S. and the State (1983 Unreported) N417 at p.51.

Division 3. — Adoption, Reception and Development of Certain Laws.

20. — UNDERLYING LAW AND PRE-INDEPENDENCE STATUTES.

(1) An Act of Parliament shall —

(a) declare the underlying law of Papua New Guinea; and
(b) provide for the development of the underlying law of Papua New Guinea.

NOT SELF EXECUTING

Comment

No Act has yet been passed.

GENERALLY

Referred to

by Greville Smith J. in *S.C.R. No 1 of 1980; Re s.22A(b) of Police Offences Act (Papua)* [1981] PNGLR 28 at pp.31–32;

by Bredmeyer J. in *Aundak Kapil v The State* (1983 Unreported) N435 at p.12.

(2) Until such time as an Act of Parliament provides otherwise —
(a) the underlying law of Papua New Guinea shall be as prescribed in Schedule 2 (*adoption, etc., of certain laws*); and
(b) the manner of development of the underlying law shall be as prescribed by Schedule 2 (*adoption, etc., of certain laws*).

GENERALLY

Referred to

by Frost C.J. in *Mauga Logging Company Pty Ltd v South Pacific Oil Palm Pty Ltd (No 1)* [1977] PNGLR 80 at p.83;

by Prentice Dep.C.J. in *Reference No 1 of 1977* [1977] PNGLR 362 at p.374;

by Kearney J. in *The State v Allan Woila* [1978] PNGLR 99 at p.100 (note misprint in report: s.20(2)(a) is misprinted in line 13 as s.2(2)(a));

by Wilson J. (dissenting) in *Premdas v Independent State of Papua New Guinea* [1979] PNGLR329 at p.376 (as link in argument that judicial and administrative proceedings to which the principles of natural justice would have applied immediately before Independence Day under the Common law are expressly made subject to those principles by the Constitution);

by Andrew J. in *P.L.A.R. No 1 of 1980* [1980] PNGLR 326 at p.344;

by Greville Smith J. in *S.C.R. No 1 of 1980; Re s.22A(b) of Police Offences Act (Papua)* [1981] PNGLR 28 at pp.31, 32;

by Greville Smith J. in *Avia Aihi v The State* [1981] PNGLR 81 at p.95;

by Narakobi J. in *State v Luku Wapulae and ors* (1980 Unreported) N233 at p.17;

by Kidu C.J. in *S.C.R. No 4 of 1980; Re petition of M.T. Somare* [1981] PNGLR 265 at p.271; see also Greville Smith J. at p.278 and Miles J. at p.302;

by Greville Smith J. in *S.C.R. No 2 of 1981; s.19(1)(f) of the Criminal Code* [1982] PNGLR 150 at p.164;

by Greville Smith J. in *Placer Holdings Pty Ltd v The Independent State of Papua New Guinea* (1982 Unreported) SC219 at p.4;

by Kapi Dep.C.J. in *Re James Allan Sannaga: Peter Timereke v Duncan Ferrie and anor* (1983 Unreported) SC255 at p.26;

by Kidu C.J. in *State v Paul Pokolo* (1983 Unreported) N404 at p.7;

by Kaputin J. in *State v Hane* (1983 Unreported) N442 at p.8.

Note: for substantive discussion of the underlying law provisions see under Sch. 2.

(3) Certain pre-Independence statutes are adopted and shall be adopted, as Acts of Parliament and subordinate enactments of Papua New Guinea, as prescribed by Schedule 2 (*adoption, etc., of certain laws*).

ACHIEVEMENT OF AUTOCHTHONOUS STATUS

per Frost C.J.

Before turning to the relevant provisions of the Constitution, it is important to note the legal arrangements which were made to ensure that all laws in the country must stem from its autochthonous or 'home-grown' Constitution. Constitution, s.24. Report of the Constitutional Planning Committee, Chapter 15, par. 14. The first step was the enactment by the pre-Independence House of Assembly of the *Laws Repeal Act* 1975 which came into operation immediately prior to the expiry of Independence Day, 15th September, 1975. The purpose of that Act, which was achieved by one simple section and without reference to particular enactments, was the repeal in bulk, as it were, of all the legislation and subordinate legislation of Papua New Guinea, and any other country applying to Papua New Guinea immediately before the commencement of the Act. It was then by force of s.20(3) and Sch.2.6 of the Constitution, which came into effect on 16th September, 1975, that all pre-Independence laws, which means for the purposes of this case all laws repealed by the *Laws Repeal Act* 1975, were adopted as Acts of the Parliament, and were brought into application to the extent to which they applied immediately before Independence Day. Just as the repeal was of the legislation in its entirety, so also was the adoption of that legislation under the Constitution and, of course, the *District Courts Act* was included in that adoption. Further, as the provision contained in Sch.2.6 is expressly made subject to any Constitutional law, it is clear that the adopted laws are subject to the same constitutional limitations as an Act of Parliament.
Peter v South Pacific Brewery Ltd [1976] PNGLR 537 at pp.540,541.

GENERALLY

Referred to

by Raine J. in *Cory v Blyth* [1976] PNGLR 274 at p.278;

by Greville Smith J. in *S.C.R. No 4 of 1980; Re petition of M.T. Somare* [1981] PNGLR 265 at p.278.

21. — PURPOSE OF SCHEDULE 2.

(1) The purpose of Schedule 2 (*adoption, etc., of certain laws*) and of the Act of the Parliament referred to in Section 20 (*underlying law and pre-Independence statutes*) is to assist in the development of

our indigenous jurisprudence, adapted to the changing circumstances of Papua New Guinea.

(2) For the purpose set out in Subsection (1), a Law Reform Commission shall be established in accordance with Schedule 2 (*adoption, etc., of certain laws*), and certain special responsibilities are imposed by that Schedule on the National Judicial System (and in particular on the Supreme Court and the National Court) and on the Law Reform Commission.

(*See: Law Reform Commission Act* Ch.18)

SPECIAL RESPONSIBILITY OF SUPREME COURT SHOULD BE ACCEPTED

per Wilson J.

It is clear, therefore, that the Supreme Court has (and should accept) a special responsibility to 'assist in the development of our indigenous jurisprudence, adapted to the changing circumstances of Papua New Guinea'.
P.L.A.R. No 1 of 1980 [1980] PNGLR 326 at p.334; see also Andrew J. at p.344.

Referred to

by Greville Smith J. in *S.C.R. No 1 of 1980; Re s.22A(b) of Police Offences Act (Papua)* [1981] PNGLR 28 at p.32;

by Kidu C.J. in *S.C.R. No 4 of 1980; Re petition of M.T. Somare* [1981] PNGLR 265 at p.271.

22. — ENFORCEMENT OF THE CONSTITUTION.

The provisions of this Constitution that recognize rights of individuals (including corporations and associations) as well as those that confer powers or impose duties on public authorities, shall not be left without effect because of the lack of supporting, machinery or procedural laws, but the lack shall, as far as practicable, be supplied by the National Court in the light of the National Goals and Directive Principles, and by way of analogy from other laws, general principles of justice and generally-accepted doctrine.

APPLICATIONS

Held

An accused may sit near his counsel. The Court has a duty, stemming from ss. 22 and 57 to see that court architecture does not render ineffective the exercise of the constitutional right of an accused to effective legal representation.
The State v Allan Woila (No 2) [1978] PNGLR 113; see Kearney J. at p.117.

Held

Section 30 of the *Corrective Institutions Act* 1957 which provided that there was not appeal from a finding or sentence made in respect of corrective institution and police lock-up offences was inconsistent with s.37(15) of the Constitution and invalid.

Pursuant to ss.22 and 185 of the Constitution and Supreme Court accordingly ordered that,

pending legislation to correct the situation, appeals would lie to the National Court and that such appeals would be governed as if made in accordance with the *Local Courts Act* and the rules made thereunder. The lack of a court record of evidence should be cured by the provision of a report by the magistrate on the one hand, and evidence by affidavit on the appellants' behalf on the other.
Constitutional Reference No 2 of 1978; Re Corrective Institutions Act 1957 [1978] PNGLR 404.

Held

Assuming, arguendo, (in the course of or for the purpose of argument) that Div.I Part XVIII of the *Organic Law on National Elections* is invalid, then the National Court would nevertheless have a duty to provide the necessary procedures to ensure that a citizen might stand for Parliament and not have his right to be elected defeated by an ineligible candidate; and, in exercising that function the Court may apply those statutory provisions as appropriate to safeguard and enforce those rights.
In re Moresby North East Election Petition [1977] PNGLR 429; see Prentice Dep.C.J. at pp.436, 437.

CONFLICT BETWEEN ENFORCEMENT AND NON-JUSTICIABILITY

Held

The general provisions of s.22 must give way to the particular provision of s.134 (proceedings of Parliament to be non-justiciable) and the Court accordingly lacked jurisdiction to entertain proceedings which sought to set aside the appointment of the Prime Minister.
James Eki Mopio v The Speaker of the National Parliament [1977] PNGLR 420; Frost C.J., Prentice Dep.C.J. and William J. at p.423.

Referred to

by Frost C.J. in *The State v The Independent Tribunal; Ex Parte Sasakila* [1976] PNGLR 491 at pp.499–502 (as to the need to achieve a proper balance between the right of the citizen to the protection of the law with the right to immunity to judicial review afforded the Head of State by the non-justiciability provision); see also Kearney J. at p.507.

NOT TO APPLY WHEN OTHER MEANS OF VINDICATING THE RIGHT EXIST

Held

Where the constitution provides other express sanctions and remedies for breach of a Constitutional provision there is no room for the application of s.22 (quaere, where if such sanctions prove to be inadequate, s.22 may be used to fill the 'gap'). Thus s.22 can not be applied so as to require an admission obtained in breach of s.42(2) of the Constitution to be excluded from evidence in a trial.
Reference No 1 of 1977 [1977] PNGLR 362; see Frost C.J. at p.366, Prentice Dep.C.J. at pp.377, 380, Williams J. at p.382, Kearney J. at p.383.

per Williams J.

> It is said in the argument advanced in favour of the affirmative case that the provisions of s.22 are relevant to this case in that the sanctions imposed by s.42(2) would be left without effect unless this Court were to answer the question raised in the affirmative. In effect the Court is asked to fill a gap which, it is said, exists.
>
> However, I can see no room for the application of s.22 of the Constitution. I do not think that it can be said that the rights conferred and the duties impliedly imposed by s.42(2) are left without effect, within the meaning of that term in s.22, for the simple reason that sanctions and remedies are provided for in s.23 and s.57. Whether or not these go as far as those propounding the affirmative case would like, seems to me to be beside the point. Section 22 appears to me to be concerned with a case in which the right conferred or the duty imposed may be completely hollow without some means to back it up. The kind of case presently under consideration does not fall within that category.
>
> An affirmative answer to the question raised by this reference would, it seems to me,

have the effect of adding to the sanctions already provided in the Constitution. The further sanction sought would be a mandatory one applying in all cases irrespective of the circumstances surrounding a particular case. This seems to me to be quite contrary to the intention of the framers of the Constitution. Reference to the Final Report of the Constitutional Planning Committee (in particular pages 5/1/18 and 5/1/19) shows that a careful and deliberate decision was made to leave the enforcement of the human rights provisions to the discretion of the Courts.

As was said by Mr Kidu in argument before the Court, an affirmative answer to the question raised would amount to a legislative act on the part of the Court, the effect of which would be to add a further sanction which the Parliament, as the law making body, did not itself see fit to make and one which, as I have said would be contrary to the intention of the framers of the Constitution.

Reference No 1 of 1977 [1977] PNGLR 362 at p.382; see also Frost C.J. at p.336, Prentice Dep.C.J. at pp.377, 380, Kearney J. at p.383.

per Prentice Dep.C.J.

But the Constitution is ambulatory, in the sense that it will continue to exist to cover the conditions of society that develop through the decades. If situations develop in this country as they did apparently in the United States of America such as to militate against the enjoyment of Constitutional Rights, and the sanctions that already exist in s.23 prove inadequate to the times, I would not take the decision of this Court now along the lines I suggest, to preclude the possibility that our successors in this Court might feel free then to discover a 'gap' or 'lack' which required the devising of further supporting machinery or procedural laws under s.22.

Reference No 1 of 1977 [1977] PNGLR 362 at p.380; see Frost C.J. at p.366, Prentice Dep.C.J. at p.377, William J. at p.382, Kearney J. at p.383.

GENERALLY

Referred to

by Frost C.J. in *The State v Peter Painke (No 2)* [1977] PNGLR 141 at p.145 (National Court has jurisdiction to enforce s.22 and need not refer such constitutional questions to the Supreme Court pursuant to s.18(2);

by Kearney J. in *The Government of P.N.G. and Davis v Barker* [1977] PNGLR 386 at p.398;

by Greville Smith J. in *Re s.42 of the Constitution and Jacob Hendrich Prai* [1979] PNGLR 42 at pp.45,46 (National Court has jurisdiction to enforce s.22 and need not refer such constitutional questions to the Supreme Court pursuant to s.18(2));

by Prentice C.J. in *Premdas v Independent State of Papua New Guinea* [1979] PNGLR 329 at pp.336,337 ('ouster clause' cannot operate to prevent enforcement of the Constitution); see also Andrew J. at p.401;

by Miles J. in *S.C.R. No 4 of 1980; Re petition of M.T. Somare* [1981] PNGLR 265 at p.311;

by Miles J. in *S.C.R. No 2 of 1981; Re s.19 of the Constitution* [1981] PNGLR 518 at p.530.

23. — SANCTIONS.

(1) Where any provision of a Constitutional Law prohibits or restricts an act, or imposes a duty, then unless a Constitutional Law or an Act of the Parliament provides for the enforcement of that provision the National Court may —

(a) impose a sentence of imprisonment for a period not exceeding 10 years or a fine not exceeding K10,000.00; or

(b) in the absence of any other equally effective remedy under the laws of Papua New Guinea, order the making of compensation by a person (including a government body) who is in default, or both, for a breach of the prohibition, restriction or duty, and may make such further order in the circumstances as it thinks proper.

(2) Where a provision of a Constitutional Law prohibits or restricts an act or imposes a duty, the National Court may, if it thinks it proper to do so, make any order that it thinks proper for preventing or remedying a breach of the prohibition, restriction or duty, and Subsection (1) applies to a failure to comply with the order as if it were a breach of a provision of this Constitution.

(3) Where the National Court considers it proper to do so, it may include in an order under Subsection (2) an anticipatory order under Subsection (1).

DOES NOT CONFER STANDING

Held

Section 23(2) does not confer standing. It is directed only to making effective the remedial processes of the Court.
S.C.R. No 4 of 1980; Re petition by M.T. Somare [1981] PNGLR 265; see Kidu C.J. at p.267, Kearney Dep.C.J. at p.274; but see Kapi J. at pp.286, 287.

DOES NOT AUTHORIZE THE COURT TO PUNISH THE PARLIAMENT OR PREVENT IT MAKING LAWS

per Kidu C.J.

It could be said that Parliament is under a duty to act within the ambit of powers conferred on it by the Constitution. If it does not, can it be sent to jail for 10 years or fined K10,000 or ordered to pay compensation? To me it seems that using s.23 to punish or penalise Parliament is not what the provision was intended to do. Although the court has power to rule acts of the Parliament unconstitutional, it has no power to penalise it, nor does it have power to order it to pay compensation. (See s.115 of the Constitution). It has no power either to stop the Parliament from making laws. The Court has power only to determine whether a law made by Parliament is constitutional or unconstitutional.
S.C.R. No 4 of 1980; Re petition by M.T. Somare [1981] PNGLR 265 at p.267; see also Miles J. at p.299.

AS TO APPLICATION WHEN OTHER PROVISIONS OF THE CONSTITUTION ALSO APPLY

per Frost C.J.

It is appropriate now to consider the legal relationships which arise under the Constitution, s.42(2). (The position is the same in the case of any of the fundamental or qualified rights). At the hearing there was no discussion of the jurisprudential implications of s.42(2), but it was agreed by all counsel that the provision gave rise to a legal duty upon a person who arrests or detains another, to comply with s.42(2). When read together with Subdivision D — Enforcement, in my opinion it is sufficient to note that a bundle of legally enforceable rights and duties does emerge. See Salmond on *Jurisprudence*, 12th ed., ss.39 and 40. The right is vested in a determinate class of persons, that is persons arrested or detained, and is enforceable by the legal processes instituted under s.57 for a protective order in the case of actual, imminent or reasonably probable infringement, and additionally under s.58 for compensation to be awarded as against the person who committed, or is responsible for, any infringement. The duty is owed by the person who arrests or detains, and is enforceable against him, in the case of infringement, under each provision. Of course the wide jurisdiction to make protective orders is not confined to orders as against the person who commits the infringement.

From this analysis of the Constitional provision and having regard to the provisions for enforcement to be found in Subdivision D—Enforcement, in my opinion an issue emerges as to whether s.23 has any application in respect of the enforcement of the rights and freedoms, including s.42(2). See Pearce, *Statutory Interpretation*, p.36. But as the issue was not argued, and, in my opinion the reference can be answered without deciding it, that issue should be left for later decision.
Reference No 1 of 1977 [1977] PNGLR 362 at p.368; see also Prentice Dep.C.J. at p.378 (below), William J. at p.381 (below), Pritchard J. at p.384 (below).

per Prentice Dep.C.J.

It is conceivable that an argument could be erected to the effect that ss.57 and 58 make provision for 'enforcement otherwise', as envisaged by s.23; and that s.23 is not therefore applicable to the protection of rights. Another view (in relation to which s.57(6) is relevant) would have it that both s.23 and ss.57, 58 are so available. The latter view would see ss.57, 58 as providing for the protection of rights directly; and s.23 as providing for such protection indirectly by the enforcement (by sanctions) of co-relative duties to provide such rights — making two sides of the one coin. In this reference, as I mentioned above, all counsel seemed to assume the latter view. The question therefore of whether the method of enforcement of rights ought to be regarded as provided for exclusively by ss.22, 57 and 58; or whether s.23 should also be taken to be available to protect them indirectly through enforcement of duties impliedly laid on citizens and authorities by the provision for and definition of rights, was not argued — and may be left for the future.
Reference No 1 of 1977 [1977] PNGLR 362 at p.378; see also Frost C.J. at p.368 (above) Williams J. at p.381 (below) Pritchard J. at p.384 (below).

per Williams J.

The Chief Justice in his judgment appears to entertain some doubt as to whether the provisions of s.23 are available following a breach of duty impliedly imposed by s.42(2). This was not raised in argument on the hearing of the reference; indeed the arguments assumed that the sanctions imposed by the section would be available. In the absence of any argument to the contrary I am disposed to assume that the section does have application. In any event, I think that the question raised in the reference may be disposed of having regard to the provisions of s.57 alone.
Reference No 1 of 1977 [1977] PNGLR 362 at p.381; see also Frost C.J. at p.368 (above), Prentice Dep.C.J. at p.378 (above), Pritchard J. at p.384 (below).

per Pritchard J.

I had been in the process of completing a draft judgment reaching the same conclusion but dealing with the matter in a different way to that of the judgments of the Chief Justice and Deputy Chief Justice. By this I mean I was intending to suggest guidelines of procedure by which the penal sanctions of s.23 of the Constitution should be implemented.

However, as has been pointed out, an issue may well arise as to whether s.23 applies at all to an infringement of the Basic Rights provisions of the Constitution, although at the hearing of this Reference, all concerned appeared to assume that it did. The problem therefore must be left for later decision. My researches at least prompt me to make two observations. Firstly, there is not only the individual's entitlement to his Constitutional freedoms to protect, there is a matter of public interest equally involved. Secondly, s.23, whatever its scope, contains such heavy maximum penalties that I believe the precise extent of its application should be a matter for legislative action rather than for a judge of this Court to attempt its definition.
Reference No 1 of 1977 [1977] PNGLR 362 at p.384; see also Frost C.J. at p.368 (above), Prentice Dep.C.J. at p.378 (above), Williams J. at p.381 (above).

GENERALLY

Referred to

per Curiam (Frost C.J., Prentice Dep.C.J., Raine, Saldanha, Kearney JJ.) in *Reference No 3 of 1976* [1976] PNGLR 242 at p.247;

per Curiam (Frost C.J., Prentice Dep.C.J., William J.) in *James Eki Mopio v The Speaker of the National Parliament* [1977] PNGLR 420 at p.422;

per Wilson J. in *Re Rooney (No 2)* [1979] PNGLR 448 at p.502 (not necessary to decide whether the giving of directions to the Supreme Court in respect of judicial functions was only punishable under s.23).

24. — USE OF CERTAIN MATERIALS AS AIDS TO INTERPRETATION.

(1) The official records of debates and of votes and proceedings —
- (a) in the pre-Independence House of Assembly on the report of the Constitutional Planning Committee; and
- (b) in the Constituent Assembly on the draft of this Constitution,

together with that report and any other documents or papers tabled for the purposes of or in connexion with those debates, may be used, so far as they are relevant, as aids to interpretation where any question relating to the interpretation or application of any provision of a Constitutional Law arises.

Comment

The C.P.C. Report has often been referred to by the judges as an aid to interpretation of the Constitution. There are, however, significant and unresolved differences between the approaches chosen by those judges who favour doing so as an inevitable practice and those who turn to aids to interpretation only if the plain and ordinary meaning of the words used in the Constitution is unclear, ambiguous or cannot be immediately apprehended. Examples of the two approaches appear below. Of these views, that of Kearney J. would seem most in keeping with the intention of the framers of the Constitution.

Note in this regard that in *P.L.A.R. No 1 of 1980* [1980] PNGLR 326 the literalist approach to statutory interpretation was decisively rejected by the Supreme Court.

per Kearney J.

> The process of statutory interpretation is essentially intuitive and subjective, in the absence of rules consistently applied. The Act is a Constitutional Law and thus subject to the general principles of interpretation set out in Constitution ss.10, 25(3), 63(3) and Basic Social Obligation (a), and 158(2); and to the more specific canons in Constitution ss.24, 109(4) when read with 12, and Sch.1.5. In my opinion these provisions amount to a direction to the Court that in carrying out its functions under Constitution s.18(1) the words actually used in the Act do not have to be strictly adhered to but are to be construed with the assistance of the materials referred to in Constitution s.24, so as best to attain what Parliament intended. When Constitution ss.109(4) and 158(2) are themselves interpreted with the aid of s.24, this view is fortified: there are several references in Chapter 8 of the Report of the Constitutional Planning Committee which point against the Court taking a 'narrowly legalistic' or 'literal' approach, and thus sacrificing the 'spirit for the letter of the Constitution'. The 'dynamic character' of the Constitution is emphasized; in interpreting the laws the judges are urged to use 'judicial ingenuity' in appropriate cases, to do justice. One consequence of this approach to interpretation is that the Court should not fail to give a provision the effect it considers the Parliament intended, by applying a literal or 'plain

meaning' test nor should it attribute to the legislature an intention to produce a capricious or unjust result. The search throughout is for the intention of Parliament, a process which remains, formally at least, one of interpretation and not of legislation, and one in which the best guide remains the provisions of the Act itself.
The State v The Independent Tribunal; Ex Parte Sasakila [1976] PNGLR 491 at pp.506-507.

Kearney J.'s judgment may, however, be contrasted with that of Wilson J.:

per Wilson J.

As, on the authorities and having regard to the Constitution itself, there can be no doubt as to the interpretation or application of any of the provisions of the Constitution to which reference will be made, I find it unnecessary (indeed I think it inappropriate) to use the final report of the pre-Independence Constitutional Planning Committee dated 13th August, 1974, and presented to the pre-Independence House of Assembly on 16th August, 1974, as an 'aid to interpretation' (see s.24 of the Constitution).
Premdas v Independent State of Papua New Guinea [1979] PNGLR 329 at p.376;

GENERALLY

Referred to

by Frost C.J. in *Reference No 2 of 1976* [1976] PNGLR 228 at p.232;

by Frost C.J. in *The State v The Independent Tribunal; Ex parte Sasakila* [1976] PNGLR 491 at p.496;

by Prentice Dep.C.J. in *Peter v South Pacific Brewery Ltd* [1976] PNGLR 537 at pp.554, 555;

by Frost C.J. in *Reference No 1 of 1977* [1977] PNGLR 362 at p.376 (C.P.C. Report dispelling doubt as to the interpretation of s.57 of the Constitution);

by Wilson J. in *Constitutional Reference No 1 of 1978 (s.19)* [1978] PNGLR 345 at p.359; (C.P.C. Report referred to to illustrate the functions and jurisdiction of the Ombudsman Commission); see also Pritchard J. at pp.377-384;

by Prentice C.J. in *Premdas v Independent State of Papua New Guinea* [1979] PNGLR 329 at p.340 (C.P.C. Report referred to as aiding the conclusion that the provisions as to 'rights' in the Constitution are, in the case of non-citizens, to be interpreted as subject to any restrictions imposed by law), but see Saldanha J. at p.376;

by Saldanha J. in *Re Rooney (No 2)* [1979] PNGLR 448 at p.472 (C.P.C. Report used to clarify the meaning of the constitutional provisions regarding freedom of expression);

by Kapi J. in *Minister for Lands v Frame* [1980] PNGLR 433 at p.467 and at p.473 (C.P.C. Report referred to to illuminate the relationship between ss.68(4) and 55 of the Constitution and the construction to be given to s.53);

by Kearney Dep.C.J. in *S.C.R. No 4 of 1980; Re petition of M.T. Somare* [1981] PNGLR 265 at p.275; see also Greville Smith J. at p.283;

by Kaputin J. in *S.C.R. No 2 of 1982; Re Opai Kunangel Amin* (1982 Unreported) SC231 at p.16;

by Bredmeyer J. in *Public Employees Association of Papua New Guinea v Public Service Commission* (1983 Unreported) SC253 at p.9.

(2) An Act of the Parliament may make provision for the manner of proof of the records and documents referred to in Subsection (1).

(*See: Constitutional Documents (Manner of Proof) Act* Ch.5.)

(3) In Subsection (1), "the report of the Constitutional Planning Committee" means the Final Report of the pre-Independence Constitutional Planning Committee dated 13 August 1974 and presented to the pre-Independence House of Assembly on 16 August 1974.

PART III. — BASIC PRINCIPLES OF GOVERNMENT.
Division 1. — National Goals and Directive Principles.

25. — IMPLEMENTATION OF THE NATIONAL GOALS AND DIRECTIVE PRINCIPLES.

(1) Except to the extent provided in Subsections (3) and (4), the National Goals and Directive Principles are non-justiciable.

(2) Nevertheless, it is the duty of all governmental bodies to apply and give effect to them as far as lies within their respective powers.

C.P.C. Report Ch.2 p.15

Implementation Of The Goals And Principles

121. We are well aware that it is one thing to establish inspiring goals for the nation, and sound principles to guide the government and our people in seeking to achieve those goals, yet quite another for effective steps to be taken which are directed towards achieving those goals. Clearly the Government of the day, as well as the people themselves, must be committed to taking the necessary action, much of which will be difficult, since it means confronting powerful vested interests and reducing their dominant position. We have had clear evidence of this in the course of our work. We fully realize that no Constitution can supply the necessary political will to ensure that all activities of the State and its institutions are directed towards the achievement of the goals of the nation, as we have recommended in this Chapter. That is something which only the people and the leaders can provide. As we make clear in Chapter 3, 'The Leadership Code', we believe a heavy responsibility rests with our leaders in this regard, as they are in the best position to see clearly the way ahead, and it is they who make the crucial decisions which set the nation on its course.

122. It is possible, however, for a Constitution to contribute to the direction taken by the people and their government. To the extent that this is practicable, we have tried, in our recommendations, to facilitate the implementation of the Directive Principles in this Chapter, which, in turn, are aimed at promoting the achievement of the National Goals. Thus, our recommendation that all activities of the State and its institutions should be based on the Directive Principles and directed towards achieving the National Goals is designed to help to reorient the thinking and attitudes of everyone who is a member of an elected body or who works in a government department, institution or authority; and to redirect the policies of those bodies towards the Goals.

123. Such a reorientation cannot be achieved overnight. The slowness with which the Eight Aims are being accepted and acted upon is some evidence of this. However, we believe that if both the people and the leaders work together to follow the Directive Principles, keeping the Goals steadily in view, there is good reason to be optimistic about the extent to which our objectives will be achieved.

124. Naturally, it will not always be possible to proceed in a straight line towards the achievement of the goals. There will be times of stress and difficulty when short-term measures to deal with particular situations will be necessary. However, everyone should still [p.16] be able to keep the goals and principles in mind, and endeavour to take fresh steps towards implementing them as soon as circumstances permit.

125. Our third recommendation is more specific than is Recommendation 2 (to which we have just referred). It is mainly directed to the courts and other tribunals which decide cases involving different interests. We propose that, like other institutions of government, they be guided in carrying out their functions by the National Goals and Directive Principles.

126. By this we mean that the courts and other tribunals should, in interpreting the law, in the procedures they adopt for the hearing of cases, and in other aspects of their work, try to give effect to the goals and principles. In some cases this will not be possible. If, for example, an Act of Parliament has been passed which clearly cuts across a particular goal or principle, a court may be unable conscientiously to give any other reasonable interpretation of the provisions of the Act than that it conflicts with the goal or principle, but is nevertheless a valid law. However, where the meaning of a particular law or rule of law is unclear or ambiguous, the courts should give an interpretation which is consistent with the goals and principles, not contrary to them.

127. The Committee appreciates that cases will almost certainly arise in which there will appear to be conflict between, for example, a human rights provision in the Constitution and a directive principle. In such a case, giving a proper interpretation of the provision in question will not be an easy matter, but we do not see the duty of the court in such a case as being significantly different from that where a provision in an Act of Parliament appears to be contrary to a common law principle of 'public policy'.

128. We have recommended also that the Government (and here we mean all levels of government — national, provincial and local) and all institutions of government (including the universities and other educational or statutory bodies) should make specific reference to the goals and principles indicating their relevance to national policies and programmes such as the Development Plan and the Budget. Already this is being done to some extent in relation to the Eight Aims.

129. In a note to this Recommendation we refer to a Recommendation we have made in Chapter 5, 'Human Rights and Obligations, and Emergency Powers', for the establishment of a body to review all existing legislation and policies with a view to bringing them into line with the National Goals and Directive Principles as well as with the Human Rights and Obligations recommended in that Chapter for inclusion in the Constitution. We propose in that Chapter that this body should be the Law Reform Commission, the establishment of which Cabinet has recently approved, or a special committee comprising Papua New Guinean public servants, and perhaps politicians also, with appropriate skilled staff and possibly outside consultants.

RECOMMENDATIONS [p.25]

Implementation Of The Goals And Principles

All activities of the State and its institutions should be based on the directive principles and directed towards achieving the National Goals set out in this Chapter.

The goals and principles as a guide in judicial interpretation.

(1) All courts and other adjudicatory tribunals shall be guided in the exercise of their functions by the National Goals and Directive Principles.
(2) Except to the extent provided for in this recommendation, the National Goals and Directive Principles shall not be directly justiciable. However, these goals and principles should not be regarded by any court, other adjudicatory tribunal or institution of government as being of less weight than other directly justiciable provisions.
(3) Government (including institutions of Government) should make specific reference to the National Goals and Directive Principles indicating their relevance to national policies and programmes such as the Development Plan and the Budget.

Note: (i) To exemplify the manner in which Clause (1) of this recommendation is intended to be applied as an aid to interpretation, we envisage that where the meaning of a constitutional provision is in question, or there is doubt as to the constitutional validity of any law or administrative action, or there is ambiguity in any law, or no particular law or principle of law appears to apply to the circumstances involved in any matter before a court, the court will give an interpretation which is consistent with the National Goals and Directive Principles rather than an alternative interpretation.

(ii) In part 1 of Chapter 5, Human Rights and Obligations, the Committee has recommended that the proposed Law Reform Commission, or another body comprising Papua New Guinean public servants, and possibly politicians also, with appropriate skilled staff, and outside consultants (if needed) be established to review all existing legislation and policies with a view to achieving their conformity with the National Goals and Directive Principles in this chapter and the Human Rights and Obligations in Chapter 5.

INDIRECT JUSTICIABILITY

Comment

Assuming (see definition of 'Constitutional Law' in Sch.1.2) that the National Goals and Directive Principles are Constitutional Laws then those Goals ought to play a significant part in the shaping of the underlying law under Sch.2 not only by direct reference (see Sch.2.3(1)(a)) but also as a measure against which both custom (see Sch. 2.1(2)) and the common law (see Sch 2.2(1)(a)) must be tested, and, to the extent inconsistent therewith, rejected.

(3) Where any law, or any power conferred by any law (whether the power be of a legislative, judicial, executive, administrative or other kind), can reasonably be understood, applied, exercised or enforced, without failing to give effect to the intention of the Parliament or to this Constitution, in such a way as to give effect to the National Goals and Directive Principles, or at least not to derogate them, it is to be understood, applied or exercised, and shall be enforced, in that way.

AS TO TESTAMENTARY DISPOSITIONS

Held

Section 43 of the *Wills, Probate and Administration Act* 1967 should be construed widely to the effect that any or several defects, informalities or non-compliance with statutory requirements shall not invalidate a document proved to be intended to operate as a last will and testament. This construction is justified, inter alia, by reference to ss.109(4) and 25(3) of the Constitution and the National Goals and Directive Principles, National Goal No 2.
Public Curator of Papua New Guinea v Public Trustee of New Zealand [1976] PNGLR 427; see Prentice Dep.C.J. at p.431 (below).

per Prentice Dep.C.J.

> Under National Goal No 2, that calling for Equality and Participation, the Constitution enacts as a directive, the 'equalization of services in all parts of the country, and for every citizen to have equal access to legal processes and all services, governmental and otherwise, that are required for the fulfulment of his or her real needs and aspirations ....'
> Section 25 of the Constitution directs that:
> 25. (3) Where any law, or any power conferred by any law (whether the power be of a legislative, judicial, executive, administrative or other kind), can reasonably be understood, applied, exercised or enforced, without failing to give effect to the intention of the Parliament or to this Constitution, *in such a way as to give effect to the National Goals and Directive Principles, or at least not to derogate them*, it is to be understood, applied or exercised, and shall be enforced, in that way ....
> ([emphasis] mine)
> The desire to make proper testamentary disposition of his property comes within the legitimate needs and aspirations of citizens. Equalization of access to the legal processes and services necessary to achieve these needs and aspirations, including (I conceive) the drafting and making of effective wills of which probate can be granted by the Court is a declared aim. The legislators would have been fully seized of the difficulties put in the way of an intending willmaker by the geography, isolation, lack of easy and the cost of, travel facilities, the fewness of lawyers, prevailing in Papua New Guinea. They have intended I think, to provide that the ability to make a valid will without rigid compliance with formalities should be more widely available.
> For each and all the above reasons I consider a wide rather than a restricted interpretation of s.43 (*of the Wills, Probate and Administration Act* 1967), to be called for.
> *Public Curator of Papua New Guinea v Public Trustee of New Zealand* [1976] PNGLR 427 at p.431.

Referred to

by Kidu C.J. (Andrew J. concurring) in *Re James Allan Sannga: Peter Timereke v Duncan Ferrie and anor* (1983 Unreported) SC255 at p.15; see also Kapi Dep.C.J. at pp.30–34.

GENERALLY

Referred to

by Prentice Dep.C.J. in *Peter v South Pacific Brewery Ltd* [1976] PNGLR 537 at p.555;

by Prentice Dep.C.J. in *Reference No 1 of 1977* [1977] PNGLR 362 at pp.373, 374;

by Kearney J. in *The State v The Independent Tribunal; Ex Parte Sasakila* [1976] PNGLR 491 at p.507;

by Andrew J. in *Premdas v Independent State of Papua New Guinea* [1979] PNGLR 329 at pp.396, 401 (National Goals and Directive Principles applied as of assistance in the interpretation of s.155(4) of the Constitution: no right of review of an administrative decision to deport a non-national); see also Prentice C.J. at p.341.

(4) Subsection (1) does not apply to the jurisdiction of the Ombudsman Commission or of any other body prescribed for the purposes of Division III.2 (*leadership code*), which shall take the National Goals and Directive Principles fully into account in all cases as appropriate.

GENERALLY

Referred to

by Pritchard J. in *Constitutional Reference No 1 of 1978 (s.19)* [1978] PNGLR 345 at p.374.

Division 2. — Leadership Code.

26. — APPLICATION OF DIVISION 2.

(1) The provisions of this Division apply to and in relation to —
  (a) the Prime Minister, the Deputy Prime Minister and the other Ministers; and
  (b) the Leader and Deputy Leader of the Opposition; and
  (c) all other members of the Parliament; and
  (d) heads of provincial executives; and (*Amended by Constitutional Amendment No.3. — Provincial Government (Consequential Amendments) s.3*)
  (e) all constitutional office-holders within the meaning of Section 221 (*definitions*); and
  (f) all heads of Departments of the National Public Service; and
  (g) all heads of or members of the boards or other controlling bodies of statutory authorities; and
  (h) the Commissioner of Police; and
  (i) the Commander of Defence Force; and
  (j) all ambassadors and other senior diplomatic and consular officials prescribed by an Organic Law or an Act of the Parliament; and
  (k) the public trustee; and
  (l) the personal staff of the Governor-General, the Ministers and the Leader and Deputy Leader of the Opposition; and
  (m) executive officers of registered political parties as defined by Section 128 ("*registered political party*"); and

(n) persons holding such public offices as are declared under Subsection (3) to be offices to and in relation to which this Division applies.

C.P.C. Report Ch.3 p.1

The Leadership Code

Quality of Leadership

1. The success of a nation, we believe, depends ultimately on its people and their leaders. No amount of careful planning in governmental institutions or scientific disciplines will achieve liberation and fulfilment of the citizens of our country unless the leaders — those who hold official positions of power, authority or influence — have bold vision, work hard and are resolutely dedicated to the service of their people.

2. Our notion of a 'leader' is not confined to the Ministers, the Speaker, the Leader of the Opposition and other members of the National Parliament, since they are not the only people who hold official positions of significant power, authority or influence in our country. Senior public servants, senior Police and Defence Force officers, constitutional office-holders (including judges and magistrates), senior officers of statutory bodies and boards, government nominated directors and general managers of corporations, members of provincial assemblies and senior officers employed by provincial governments, senior staff of Ministers and Opposition leaders, members of the Advisory committee on Citizenship Matters, and presidents, chairmen and mayors of local bodies exercising governmental functions (e.g. local government councils and associations such as Warakarai na Gunan and Greater Toma 'Council'), senior administrative officers of these bodies, academic and senior administrative staff of tertiary institutions, office-holders of registered industrial organizations, ambassadors, high commissioners and senior diplomatic officers, and office-holders at the national level of registered political parties — all of these people, we believe, should be regarded as leaders for the purposes of this Chapter.

RECOMMENDATIONS [p.13]

Definition of 'Leader'

2. For the purposes of the Leadership Code, the following are 'Leaders' —

- the Prime Minister, Deputy Prime Minister and other Ministers;
- the Leader and Deputy Leader of the Opposition;
- the Speaker, Deputy Speaker and other members of the National Parliament;
- senior public servants above a specified level or holding specified positions;
- senior members of the Parliamentary Service holding specified positions;
- members of statutory corporations and boards, and officers of those corporations and boards above a specified level or holding a specified position;
- government nominated chairmen, managing directors, directors and general managers of corporations in which the Government has an equity holding;
- members of provincial assemblies, and senior officers above a specified level or holding a specified position employed directly by provincial governments;
- constitutional and statutory office-holders, and senior public officers subject to their direction and control who hold specified positions;
- officer-holders (sic) at national level of registered political parties;
- academic and specified senior administrative staff at tertiary institutions;
- specified office-holders of registered industrial organizations;
- specified senior staff of ministers and of the Leader and Deputy Leader of the Opposition;
- ambassadors, high commissioners, and senior officers of Papua New Guinean missions abroad holding specified positions;
- presidents, chairmen and mayors of recognized local bodies exercising governmental functions;
- senior police and Defence Force Officers above a specified level or holding specified positions;
- members of the Advisory Committee on Citizenship Matters; and
- other specified office-holders.

Note: (i) The Committee recommends that the level in the Public Service at and above which office-holders should be categorised as 'leaders' for the purposes of this code be 'Chief of Division' or its equivalent. This should be done by law.

(ii) The specification of particular office-holders as leaders under this recommendation shall be made by law only after full consultation with the Public Service Commission and the Ombudsman Commission. The Committee recommends that the Ombudsman Commission have the power set out in Recommendation 4 below to specify by gazettal particular office-holders and positions for the purposes of this Code, as those of 'leaders'.

AS TO ACTING AND TEMPORARY APPOINTMENTS

per Curiam (Prentice C.J., Saldanha, Andrew JJ.)

Section 26(1)(f) of the Constitution provides that the provisions of the Leadership Code apply to 'all heads of Departments of the National Public Service'. Here 'head' is spelt with a small 'h' and 'Departments' with a capital 'D'. On the other hand the term 'Departmental Head' is used throughout the Act with capitals 'D' and 'H' for the spelling of 'Departmental' and 'Head' respectively. Obviously the use of the small 'h' in spelling 'head' and the retention of the capital 'D' for 'Departments' in s.26(1)(f) of the Constitution suggests that the word 'head' was meant to encompass the de facto head, the man at the pinnacle or apex of the Department, be he acting, temporary or substantive. A look at the description of the persons in s.26 of the Constitution who are subject to the Leadership Code shows clearly that they are all persons of power and influence. They are persons who are open to the temptation to abuse their powers for oppression of others or for personal gain to themselves, and are more exposed to bribery and corruption....

A leader has a duty not to place himself in a position in which he could have a conflict of interests or might be compromised when discharging his duties, not to demean his office or position, not to allow his public official or personal integrity to be called into question, not to endanger or diminish respect for and confidence in the integrity of government and not to use his office for personal gain. And in this connection we consider that the Constitution, insofar as it seeks to preserve the people of Papua New Guinea from misconduct by it leaders, should not be Considered a 'penal' statute. In requiring a higher standard of behaviour from its leaders than from ordinary citizens, it should not be considered as 'penalising' or 'punishing' a leader; but as ensuring in the interests of the safety of the people that only persons who are prepared to accept added restrictions on their personal behaviour should become leaders. No citizen *need* become a 'leader'.

In interpreting s.26(1)(f) of the Constitution one must have regard to the intention and spirit of the Leadership Code and the mischief that is aimed at.

Looked at in this light it makes no difference whether a Departmental Head is one that is acting, temporary or substantive.

Constitutional Reference No 1 of 1978 (s.18) [1978] PNGLR 460 at pp.463, 464.

LEADERSHIP CODE CANNOT APPLY TO A PERSON WHO HAS CEASED TO HOLD OFFICE

per Curiam (Kidu C.J., Kearney Dep.C.J., Greville Smith, Andrew, Miles JJ.)

We are of opinion that the Leadership Code is directed to persons actually holding an office as specified in s.26 of the Constitution; and that, as the Tribunal put it in this case, 'the entire thrust of the legislation is directed towards removing a person who is considered, after due enquiry, to be unworthy of continuing in office'. All the provisions of the Constitution and the Organic Law are consistent with, and support, that conclusion. Once the primary purpose of the legislation is clear, it is not anomalous that a person, having ceased to hold any of the designated offices, becomes immune from proceedings under the Leadership Code in respect of any alleged misconduct in office, during the time he held office. The purpose is to prevent continuance in office of unworthy people; and thus it is, that a person holding a leadership office may be proceeded against in respect of alleged misconduct in leadership office which he had formerly held; and, if found guilty, dismissed from his current office.

Section 35 of the Organic Law is an example of an offence which may be committed by a person no longer subject to the Leadership Code; the creation of such offences is founded upon s.28(1)(e) of the Constitution.

It is to be noted that s.28(1)(h) of the Constitution provides that an Organic Law may make any other provision that is necessary or convenient for attaining the objects of this Division.

Yet nowhere in the Organic Law is there any suggestion, that a leader who has left office remains subject to the Code in respect of any misconduct in office. The only specific provision dealing with such persons is s.35.

The major punishment, for a person found guilty of misconduct in office, and a matter which must be considered by the Tribunal following such a finding, is dismissal from office; s.28(1)(g)(ii) of the Constitution. The inference is irresistible that the person the subject of the inquiry must be the holder of an office subject to the Code, at the time the Tribunal makes its decision....

It is true, on the view we take, that in the absence of legislative provision under s.26(3) of the Constitution, which may well be impracticable, a leader who resigns from office before a finding of misconduct in office is made, is not subject to the disqualifications on dismissal which flow from s.31(1) of the Constitution. By itself, however, that anomaly is not sufficient to change the otherwise consistent thrust of the legislation. It is clear from the view we take that if any such leader assumed another leadership office, any proved misconduct in his earlier office could result in his being dismissed from his later leadership office.

The definition of 'person to whom this law applies' in s.1 of the Organic Law carries a clear connotation that it refers only to current office holders; and later provisions of the Organic Law referring to such persons all clearly contemplate that they are in office, and are quite inconsistent with any view that the phrase embraces persons who have ceased to hold office.

In re Joseph Auna [1980] PNGLR 500 at pp.504,505; see also *S.C.R. No 2 of 1982; Re Opai Kunangel Amin* (1982 Unreported) SC231.

GENERALLY

Referred to

by Pritchard J. in *Constitutional Reference No 1 of 1978 (s.19)* [1978] PNGLR 345 at p.374.

(2) This Division applies to and in relation to a person referred to in Subsection (1) not only in the office referred to in that subsection but also in any other office or position that he holds under any law by virtue of that office.

(3) An Organic Law or an Act of the Parliament may declare any public office (including an office in a provincial government or a local government body) to be an office to and in relation to which this Division applies.
(*Amended by Constitutional Amendment No. 3. — Provincial Government (Consequential Amendments) s.3*)

GENERALLY

Referred to

per Curiam (Kidu C.J., Kearney Dep.C.J., Greville Smith, Andrew, Miles JJ.) in *In Re Joseph Auna* [1980] PNGLR 500 at p.505.

(4) In the event of doubt as to whether a person is a person to whom this Division applies, the decision of the Ombudsman Commission is final.

GENERALLY

Referred to

per Curiam (Prentice C.J., Saldanha, Andrew JJ.) in *Constitutional Reference No 1 of 1978 (s.18)* [1978] PNGLR 460 at p.464.

27. — RESPONSIBILITIES OF OFFICE.

(1) A person to whom this Division applies has a duty to conduct himself in such a way, both in his public or official life and his private life, and in his associations with other persons, as not —

(a) to place himself in a position in which he has or could have a conflict of interests or might be compromised when discharging his public or official duties; or

(b) to demean his office or position; or

(c) to allow his public or official integrity, or his personal integrity, to be called into question; or

(d) to endanger or diminish respect for and confidence in the integrity of government in Papua New Guinea.

(2) In particular, a person to whom this Division applies shall not use his office for personal gain or enter into any transaction or engage in any enterprise or activity that might be expected to give rise to doubt in the public mind as to whether he is carrying out or has carried out the duty imposed by Subsection (1).

(3) It is the further duty of a person to whom this Division applies —

(a) to ensure, as far as is within his lawful power, that his spouse and children and any other persons for whom he is responsible (whether morally, legally or by usage), including nominees, trustees and agents, do not conduct themselves in a way that might be expected to give rise to doubt in the public mind as to his complying with his duties under this section; and

(b) if necessary, to publicly disassociate himself from any activity or enterprise of any of his associates, or of a person referred to in paragraph (a), that might be expected to give rise to such a doubt.

(4) The Ombudsman Commission or other authority prescribed for the purpose under Section 28 (*further provisions*) may, subject to this Division and to any Organic Law made for the the purposes of this Division, give directions, either generally or in a particular case, to ensure the attainment of the objects of this section.

(5) A person to whom this Division applies who —

(a) is convicted of an offence in respect of his office or position or in relation to the performance of his functions or duties; or

(b) fails to comply with a direction under Subsection (4) or otherwise fails to carry out the obligations imposed by Subsections (1), (2) and (3),

is guilty of misconduct in office.

C.P.C. Report Ch.3 p.1

3. Our 'leaders', as we have defined them, have a different role from others such as those who have responsible positions in private enterprise. Persons who hold office in private concerns as such are not the servants of the people of the nation.

4. In his public office, a leader's first responsibility is to the people he (or she) represents or on whose behalf he is working. This responsibility must override self interest. A leader's first loyalty must be to his office, not to

himself. Such priority of loyalties might in fact mean some personal loss of opportunity or benefit, but this personal and official responsibility of a leader is assumed when he takes office, and it continues throughout his entire tenure of office.

5. A leader's loyalty to his office must spring from his genuine concern for his country. It is always expected of a patriot that he will put his country's interests before his own. In the event of any conflict of interests, the interests of the people he serves must prevail over his own personal interest. The higher the office held in the state, the more serious the office-holder's responsibility. The greater the power, the greater the obligations of the person holding the powerful position. The power he holds is not meant to be for his own honour and fame; much less is it for his own material aggrandizement. The power he holds is for the betterment of the citizens of Papua New Guinea.

6. If the leader were to use his power for purposes other than the betterment of the citizens, he would be abusing it, and he would thereby be demonstrating his unworthiness of his high office. In short, his high office and all that it legitimately brings with it is never meant for the office-holder's material enrichment; it is meant to be used in the service of the citizens of the state and for their betterment. Apart from its citizens, the nation state is nothing. The state exists for them, and the leaders and bearers of high office are meant to serve the citizens as a whole, who make the nation what it is and what it is destined to become.

7. The members of the National Parliament are the elected representatives of all people of Papua New Guinea. They have been given their high position to represent the interests of their people, and not for their own special interests. What applies to the ordinary member of parliament is even more applicable to those who hold ministerial office in the nation state. The Ministers of the nation hold high office and wide powers so that they may be better equipped to serve the people of their nation.

8. What we have said of members of the National Parliament and Ministers applies also to elected members of the Provincial Assemblies (which, in Chapter 10, 'Provincial Government', we propose should be established) and to presidents and equivalent leaders of recognized local bodies exercising governmental functions (such as Warakarai na Gunan, Greater Toma 'Council' and Kabisawali Peoples' Government). Senior public servants and other officials are in a similar position. Though they have not been elected, their role as public servants or persons being paid from public funds is to serve the public. Office-holders of registered industrial organizations [p.2] and national office-holders of registered political parties hold influential positions of trust on behalf of or in relation to large numbers of Papua New Guineans, too.

9. We must presume that people who have won or have been appointed to high office are where they are because of their talents, their energy and personal character. These same talents and personal characteristics that the leader possesses are, as it were, instruments fitting him for his office. Those who have given the leader his high position can properly expect that these talents will be put to the best service of the people and their improvement, and will not be used to further the leader's own personal advantage.

10. The holders of responsible positions, the leaders, because of the positions they hold are very often in the public eye. How they conduct themselves is observed by many. For their part the people naturally expect great things of their leaders, who can set the tone for the whole nation and make a positive contribution to the national morale. For without being able to formalize their sentiments the citizens like to see embodied in their leaders all that is best in the nation; and they like to have leaders worthy of identifying themselves with. To this deep and traditional feeling, the leaders of the country must respond positively and truly. By doing so they will build up the confidence of the people, and give the nation additional solidarity, so that the citizens, inspired by the high standards set by their elected representatives and officials, can feel one with their leaders in contributing to and consolidating the national ethos.

11. No-one can do more to set the tone and style of the nation than the leaders. Contrariwise, no-one in the nation can do more to lower the standards than the leaders. Leaders are expected to demonstrate their leadership both by listening to the people, and by speaking to and for them. More importantly, they are meant to give leadership in action. Both by inaction and improper action, the leaders can betray the people's confidence in them. What the leaders do and how they are seen to do it; these are things that can legitimize them in the eyes of the people and set the standards for the nation.

12. Our government is government for the people and the more it represents the felt needs and aspirations of the people, the more it identifies with them and becomes their government. In this, as we have said, the role of our leaders is crucial.

The Leadership Code — underlying considerations

13. Experience in many countries has shown that constitutional provisions and declarations have little effect by themselves. We believe that perhaps the single most important factor in determining the direction of national development is the quality of leadership. If Papua New Guinea is to have any chance of implementing its national goals and directive principles, it must ensure that its leadership has a genuine commitment to these goals.

14. We believe also, as do our people, that it is necessary to take positive steps to ensure that our leaders do not use their position in ways that threaten these goals; for example, by accumulating personal wealth, by collaborating with foreign or national businessman, or by accepting bribes.

15. We recognize that we leaders, like all other people, have our strengths and weaknesses. And it is with full awareness of our human frailities (sic) that we have concluded that clear rules strictly enforced, are required to try to ensure the integrity of politicians at all levels, and of other leaders (as we have defined them) also. The Chief Minister's recent statement to the House of Assembly, in which he expressed serious concern about the problem of corruption in government, and announced the Government's intention to take immediate action to prevent corruption from becoming what he described as a 'disease' in this country, adds weight to this view. We welcome and fully support the initiative which the Government is taking to deal with the particular matter of gifts to leaders, which is an important aspect of the total problem of ensuring the integrity of our leaders.

16. Our proposals are designed to meet this need for positive action to be taken so that leaders will not be in a position where their private interests conflict with their public responsibilities. The personal interests of our leaders must not become identified with elements outside or within Papua New Guinea whose interests are an obstacle to the development of a genuinely just, honest and egalitarian society in this country.

17. There are various ways of regulating the conduct of leaders. Some of these are already incorporated in the Parliamentary Integrity Ordinance, and also in a proposed (but not officially released) Ministerial Code of Conduct. We have decided that these provisions should be extended to cover all leaders (as we have defined them), as we feel that to limit it to national politicians — would be to deal with only part of the problem of maintaining integrity in public life. The available evidence both within Papua New Guinea and abroad indicates clearly [p.3] that senior government officials, members of provincial governments and other categories of people whom we propose should be included in the definition are often just as much exposed to the temptations of corruption as are national parliamentarians. The Chief Minister's disclosure that a valuable diamond was recently offered to a senior official clearly demonstrates the nature of this problem.

18. Our proposals also involve greater restrictions on leaders' business activities than are included in either the Parliamentary Integrity Ordinance or the proposed Ministerial Code. This is because, after full consideration of this matter, we believe it is essential in the interests of our people to introduce these more stringent provisions. Our reasoning is given below and also later in this Chapter.

19. The proposed Leadership Code gives strong emphasis to firmly restricting leaders in their dealings with foreign controlled enterprises. We believe that experience both here and in other countries shows that involvement of leaders with foreign controlled corporations including the giant multi-national corporations, can lead to much corruption. These companies and other enterprises are in a position to offer tempting gifts and other favours, apparently with no strings attached, but in reality with the object of compromising the leader's own position, so that when negotiations or other dealings between the enterprise and the level of government at which the particular leader is working, take place, that leader will not be able to take an objective stand on behalf of his people. A similar danger exists if the leader has shares or some other beneficial interest in the foreign enterprise.

20. We have not, however, laid down such strict limitations in respect of local business enterprises, except in relation to Ministers, constitutional office-holders, senior public servants and members and senior officers of statutory authorities. Our reasoning has been that we believe some leaders should be in a position to help promote business activity among Papua New Guineans by their own example. We also feel that there is, at this stage of our development, significantly greater danger of corruption if leaders are involved in foreign controlled enterprises than if they have interests in Papua New Guinean enterprises. At a later date, it may of course become necessary to place stricter limitations on leaders' activities in this respect also — but that is something for the future.

21. It has been argued that our Committee could be bringing in measures that might not be suitable at our present stage of development and that they could result in the opposite of our aims being achieved. It is said that, in practical terms, there may be two opposing dangers; that the ideals we put forward for ourselves become a dead letter, so that we fall into disrepute because of the gap between what we preach and what we practice; or, on the other hand, that we make it impossible for many of our present leaders to pursue the path of leadership, forcing the people to turn to new leaders who might not be their natural choice, and who could even be less sincere and dedicated than the others.

22. We appreciate these anxieties but are convinced that it is not too early to make a start in establishing that high standards of personal conduct and integrity are required of our leaders. Our county needs men and women who have the courage of their convictions to take stands when vital principles are at stake. We need leaders who will not compromise the long term interests of our people for short term advantages to themselves. If our leaders were to be personally involved with foreign business interests, for example, it would surely be impossible for them in their official capacity to deal with those interests objectively for the benefit of Papua New Guinea as a whole.

23. Corruption in public life is, of course, a world wide problem which has reached very serious proportions in a substantial number of countries — developing and industrialized alike.

24. The scandal of 'Watergate' in the United States has highlighted the extent to which bribery, electronic eavesdropping, false smear campaigns, and other gross abuses of political power have infected the whole American political system. In Britain, too, deep seated corruption at local government level has recently been exposed.

25. In the past, many politicians and members of the public alike around the world have responded to this problem mainly by preaching, not suggesting or initiating any positive steps to remedy it. Others have simply shrugged their shoulders and resigned themselves to accepting the situation in the belief that nothing can be done about it.

26. However, recent developments in other countries show how much can be done once the public becomes fully aware of the magnitude of the problem of corruption. In the United States, where corruption in public life has been widespread for decades, tough new anti-corruption measures are being taken in legislatures in many parts of the country, leading public figures have been put on trial, and a number convicted and jailed. Prominent, long-serving politicians of doubtful integrity have lost public support, and a number of those who have had to face the [p.4] electors at the polls have been defeated.

27. A number of new Commonwealth States have taken firm action too. In 1973, Jamaica passed a new law concerning members of parliament along very similar lines to our own Parliamentary Integrity Ordinance. The Constitutional Commission of Trinidad and Tobago has recommended that similar provision be made in that country's new Constitution.

28. Tanzania introduced a stringent leadership code covering parliamentarians and a large number of officials at all levels, in 1967, and last year passed a new law to establish a Leadership Committee to enforce the Code more effectively than had previously been possible. Zambia adopted a similar code last year after establishing a special enforcement body called the Leadership Committee in its 1973 Constitution.

29. We do not suggest that it will be easy to make the proposed Leadership Code fully effective. But we do believe that if the political will is behind it, it can be made a potent force in maintaining public confidence in our leaders at all levels.

30. We wish to avoid misunderstanding. We are not proposing a code of conduct to divorce our leaders from every field of business activity or professional interest. In fact, no leader is worth his name if he is not in tune and in touch with the social and economic concerns of his people. But a leader should not place himself in a position where he may well have a conflict of interest due to his shareholdings or business activities, nor should he use his position to gain rewards or benefits which he would be unlikely to obtain if he were not in a position of leadership.

Referred to

per Curiam (Prentice C.J., Saldanha, Andrews JJ.) in *Constitutional Reference No 1 of 1978 (s.18)* [1978] PNGLR 460 at p.463;

per Curiam (Kidu C.J., Kearney Dep. C.J., Greville Smith, Andrew, Miles JJ.) in *In re Joseph Auna* [1980] PNGLR 500 at pp.501, 502;

by the Leadership Tribunal in *In the matter of the Hon. Michael Pondros MP* (1983 Unreported) N425 at pp.27–28.

28. — FURTHER PROVISIONS.

(1) For the purposes of this Division, an Organic Law —

(a) may give to the Ombudsman Commission or some other authority any powers that are necessary or convenient for attaining the objects of this Division and of the Organic Law; and

(b) shall make provision for the disclosure to the Ombudsman Commissioner or some other authority of the personal and business incomes and financial affairs of persons to whom this Division applies, and of their families and associates, and in particular of interests in contracts with governmental bodies and of directorships and similar offices held by them (including powers to nominate directors, trustees or agents, or similar officers); and

(c) shall empower the Ombudsman Commission or some other authority to require a person to whom this Division applies to dispose of, or place under the control of the public trustee, any assets or income where this seems to be desirable for attaining the objects of this Division; and

(d) may prescribe specific acts that constitute misconduct in office; and

(e) may create offences (including offences by persons to whom this Division applies and offences by other persons); and

(f) shall provide for the investigation by the Ombudsman Commission or some other authority of cases of alleged or suspected misconduct in office, and confer on the Commission or authority any powers that are necessary or convenient for that purpose; and

(g) shall establish independent tribunals that —

(i) shall investigate and determine any cases of alleged or suspected misconduct in office referred to them in accordance with the Organic Law; and

(ii) are required, subject to Subsection (1A), to recommend to the appropriate authority that a person found guilty of misconduct in office be dismissed from office or position; and (*added by Constitutional Amendment No.4. — Leadership Code*)

(h) may make any other provision that is necessary or convenient for attaining the objects of this Division.

(1A) An Organic Law may provide that where the independent tribunal referred to in Subsection (1)(g) finds that —

(a) there was no serious culpability on the part of a person found guilty of misconduct in office; and

(b) public policy and the public good do not require dismissal,

it may recommend to the appropriate authority that some other penalty provided for by law be imposed. (*Added by Constitutional Amendment No. 4. — Leadership Code*).

(*See: Organic Law on the Ombudsman Commission* Ch.1)
(*See: Organic Law on the Duties and Responsibilities of Leadership* Ch.1)
(*See: Leadership Code (Alternative Penalties) Act* Ch.1A)

C.P.C Report Ch.3 p.4

Supervision and enforcement of the Code

35. We intend the Leadership Code to be more than mere directives. It should be morally and legally binding on 'leaders', and firmly enforced. It is for this reason that we have recommended that a particular, independent institution of government, the Ombudsman Commission (which in Chapter 11 we propose should be established) ought to have responsibility for overseeing the Code and seeing to it that leaders comply with its provisions. We have preferred not to recommend the establishment of a separate institution to carry out this role as we are opposed to any unnecessary multiplication of institutions of government. It is our firm view that the Ombudsman Commission is particularly well suited to carrying out this role as its members should be people who themselves have complete integrity, and its procedures and [p.5] powers can readily be adapted to this purpose. Experience in other countries has shown that ombudsmen quite frequently come upon instances of corruption in the course of their investigations into administrative malpractices, so that we would anticipate that this additional role will mesh in quite well with its general jurisdiction.

36. We believe, most strongly, that the effectiveness of many of our proposals depends heavily on the acceptance of the Leadership Code which we propose. The Code is among our most fundamental recommendations, and as such, it should be entrenched in the Constitution, as a schedule to it. We have not, however, proposed that the Code be unduly difficult to change, as we recognize that it will be necessary to make changes to it in accordance with experience of its practical operation.

37. If it is included in the Constition, the Code's main provisions should become widely known, and this, in itself, should help to make it more effective, because people will be aware of the type of activities of leaders which are against the rules in the Code.

38. If a leader commits a breach of the Code he should automatically lose his office unless there are extenuating circumstances which justify a lesser punishment. A breach of the Code may also involve an offence under the Criminal Code or another law. For example, bribery is already an offence under the Criminal Code, and the Chief Minister is proposing to introduce legislation to make the acceptance of any gift from a company or investor valued at more than a certain amount, a criminal offence. We have made it clear that the provisions of the Leadership Code do not of themselves affect any offences under existing law, though we believe that the *Parliamentary Integrity Ordinance* 1971 should be repealed and replaced by new legislation which provides the machinery for the effective enforcement of the Leadership Code. (The Parliamentary Integrity Committee provided for under that Ordinance would be replaced by the Ombudsman Commission, under a separate Act dealing with that Commission.) We deal in detail with enforcement of the Code at the end of this chapter.

Annual Declaration

39. Our recommendation that each leader should disclose to the Ombudsman Commission various financial particulars concerning himself and his immediate family, each year, accords with our recommendation that the Leadership Code should be enforceable. Unless leaders declare their assets, liabilities, and business activities, the Ombudsman Commission will not be in a position to know whether they are living up to what is expected of them. Information is to be disclosed to and received by the Commission on the basis of confidentiality. However, such information would be able to be used in disciplinary or criminal proceedings if it were relevant.

40. This recommendation is virtually the same as a provision in the Parliamentary Integrity Ordinance, though its scope is much wider because it applies to leaders generally, not just to parliamentarians.

Bribery and misapplication of funds

41. Bribery takes many forms, some being much more obvious than others. We have mentioned earlier a clear example of attempted bribery which was disclosed by the Chief Minister at the June/July meeting of the House of Assembly. Other forms of bribery are more subtle — for example apparent generosity in offers of trips overseas, expensive dinners, free services such as the use of cars, etc. The fact that all of these forms of bribery are already being used in Papua New Guinea highlights the immediate danger to our society that this form of corruption presents.

42. If a leader was found to have accepted a bribe he would not only be likely to lose his office — he could be convicted of a serious offence under the Criminal Code and sentenced to imprisonment for a number of years.

43. The misapplication of funds is another very serious offence which is all too common at present not only in government but in co-operatives and private enterprise as well. We see a need for our leaders to set an example to others, both inside and outside government service, in the proper use of government funds, and therefore recommend the inclusion of this rule in the Code.

44. These recommendations are similar to sections 36 and 37 of the *Parliamentary Integrity Ordinance*, though of course those provisions apply only to parliamentarians. Those sections, however, make breach of them a criminal offence.

Interests in government contracts

45. It is clear that if a leader has an interest in a government contract this potentially [p.6] involves a conflict of interest, especially if the leader is in a position of considerable influence. The greater his interest in the contract, the greater is the conflict between his private interest and his public duty. A leader's interest in a government contract could be direct, through, for example, a small firm of which the leader and his family may be the major partners, or relatively indirect, through a shareholding held by the leader or a member of his family. In either case, we believe the principle is the same.

46. We recognize, however, that there are some situations where a leader's interest in such a contract is insignificant, or the nature of the particular contract is such that the leader's interest should be acceptable. In particular, we do not wish to prevent leaders from being involved in wholly Papua New Guinean owned enterprises which assist substantial numbers of our people to more fully participate in their own development and which have interests in government contracts which are merely incidental to their main activities. We think there is an important distinction to be made between enterprises in which a leader is primarily obtaining benefits for

himself and his own family, and enterprises in which the leader is assisting the people of his area to engage in commercial activities which actively involve and will directly benefit many of those people. We have in mind groups such as the Hiri Development Association, Kabisawali Village Development Corporation, the Bena Association and the New Guinea Development Corporation.

47. We appreciate that it is extremely difficult to lay down hard and fast rules to distinguish between these different types of enterprise, and propose that it should be a function of the Ombudsman Commission from time to time to make rules and publish guidelines laying down criteria by means of which these distinctions can be drawn. We also recommend that the Commission be empowered to grant exemptions from the general prohibition of leaders having an interest in a government contract, in particular, cases where that interest is of little practical consequence.

Shares in foreign companies or partnerships with foreign citizens

48. As we have already emphasized, we believe that our leaders should not compromise their position in relation to business enterprises with which they must deal in their capacity as leaders. We are only too well aware of the experience elsewhere, especially in developing countries, where foreign corporations have dictated the nature and pace of development within the country, through indirect control of the economy. There is no more effective way for foreigners to control our resources than to silence our leaders by enticing them into partnerships or the acceptance of shareholdings in their businesses. Our leaders must, we believe, resist this temptation if they are going to be true spokesmen and representatives of ordinary people.

49. Whilst we recognize that the danger to which we refer is not confined to foreign controlled enterprises, we believe that at this stage of our country's development, where foreign companies and firms control virtually the whole of our economy, these enterprises are the ones which should be singled out.

50. To give a concrete example of the type of situation with which we are concerned, suppose a substantial number of the Members of the House of Assembly hold shares in a particular foreign controlled company. It then becomes an issue in the House as to whether the agreement between that company and the Government should be changed to make it more favourable to the Government and the people, in the light of new circumstances which were not foreseen at the time the original agreement was made. Clearly all of the Members of the House who hold shares in the company would be faced with a conflict of interests as between their own personal interest which would be best served by voting against any change in the agreement, and the interest of the people as a whole. We believe that such a situation should not be allowed to arise, as it puts it risk the interests of the nation.

51. We realize that it will be a difficult matter to determine in a particular case, whether a company is in fact subject to effective foreign control, but we believe it is essential that this distinction be drawn, if necessary, by declaring under an Act, from time to time, particular companies as being effectively foreign controlled. Our recommendation gives a general indication of our thinking in this regard.

52. This general prohibition of leaders holding any shares in a foreign controlled company or being involved in partnership with foreign citizens may be thought by some to be hard, but we believe it is essential if our national integrity is to be maintained. At this stage in our development, it should be easier to implement this and other similar measures than it will be later on when more of our leaders have a vested interest to protect. Summing up our reasons for making this and other related recommendations, we believe it is vital that our leaders' sense of judgement of what is in the best interests of our people should not be impaired by their having beneficial interests in foreign corporations which are concerned with making good profits for their shareholders not with achieving Papua New Guinea's nation goals. Our [p.7] leaders' first responsibility is to the citizens of Papua New Guinea. Having beneficial interests in foreign corporations, we believe would place our leaders in the position where they are faced with a conflict of interests, and human nature being what it is, this would be likely to result in compromises or, worse still, preference being given to immediate personal benefits at the cost of the long-term interests of our country.

Leaders not to accept loans, etc. from foreign controlled companies or firms

53. For similar reasons to those which underlie our recommendation that leaders should not hold shares in foreign controlled companies or be partners in foreign controlled firms, we recommend that leaders should not accept any loan other than a normal bank loan, hold any franchise or accept any other benefit or advantage from a company or firm which is effectively controlled by foreign citizens. We do not believe our leaders should be obligated to foreign citizens or enterprises in this way, as such an obligation is likely to undermine their independence as leaders.

54. We recognize, however, that provision should be made for exceptions to this general rule. One such exception would be hire purchase agreements (though we have not provided for this specifically, preferring to leave the matter in the hands of the Ombudsman Commission which we propose should be empowered to make rules, publish guidelines and grant specific exemptions in particular cases, subject to such conditions as he (sic) considers necessary). In exercising these powers, the Commission should, we believe, take full account of potential conflicts of interest, and of the need to ensure that leaders do not use their position to gain advantages of this kind.

Outside benefits not to be accepted

55. We view with concern the growing practive, particularly among overseas businessmen, of giving or attempting to give favours, 'gestures of appreciation' and other forms of gift to our leaders in decision making positions, in order to obtain from thise leaders favourable consideration in their business dealings with the Government. The Chief Minister has indicated his awareness of this situation and, as we have mentioned earlier, has made a strong statement to the House of Assembly expressing his view that there is an urgent need for legislation to prohibit this type of activity and impose heavy penalties for those who indulge in it. We fully support the Chief Minister's stand in this matter.

56. We propose that there be provision in the Leadership Code prohibiting all leaders, their spouses and children from asking for, accepting or in any way obtaining any benefit other than the salary, allowances, etc. attached to the leader's office. We recommend that the Ombudsman Commission be given power to make rules or publish guidelines setting out the types of benefit which it is permissible for leaders and their families to accept, such as very small gifts of little value. We further recommend that if a leader is in doubt as to whether or not he should accept a particular benefit being offered to him, he should refer the matter to the Commission for a ruling.

Official information

57. The use of official information of which a leader becomes aware in the course of his duties is obviously an important matter. As experience in other countries clearly shows, it can be the means by which leaders acquire very significant advantages for themselves and their friends. Corruption of major proportions can develop rapidly if official information is used for personal gain, either directly or indirectly. Simply publishing official information prematurely, through the media can be a serious abuse of an official position, and we propose that this practice also, be prohibited under the Code.

58. While we are concerned that generally our citizens should have ready access to official information, this does not mean that there are not a number of circumstances in which the Government or an institution of government, should not, in the public interest, withhold certain information from the public, at least for a certain time. Matters concerning the Budget and negotiations with other countries are clear examples of this kind of situation.

Certain assets to be disposed of

59. A leader and his family who hold assets or other interests which, under the Code they are not entitled to retain, should, we recommend, dispose of those assets or interests within six months of the date when —

- the Leadership Code comes into force; or
- he takes office; or
- he is directed by the Ombudsman Commission to dispose of the particular assets. [p.8]

We recognize however, that it may not always be possible for a leader to dispose of large assets within that period. Accordingly, our recommendation is that the Commission be empowered to grant an extension of time of up to three months to enable a leader or a member of his family to sell a particular asset or interest if there are special circumstances which justify this action.

60. We also propose that the Ombudsman Commission be notified of the disposal of any asset in accordance with an obligation which a leader or a member of his family has under the Code. This rule will enable the Commission to check that the person concerned has in fact complied with the requirements of the Code.

Disclosure of interest before debate or discussion

61. In the ***Parliamentary Integrity Ordinance*** there is a provision which requires a Member of the House of Assembly to disclose any financial interest which he has in any matter on which he wishes to speak in the House, or in a committee of the House. We consider this to be an important rule which should be adapted for incorporation in the Code so that it applies to all leaders. A recommendation has been made accordingly.

62. An important effect of this rule will be to enable members of parliament, members of provincial assemblies, etc. to better assess the weight which they should give to speeches made by their colleagues. Obviously if a member of parliament has a financial interest in particular matter (sic), and he speaks in such way as to be effectively supporting his own interest, his speech will be given far less weight by his colleagues than would otherwise be the case and, we believe, rightly so.

63. We have further recommended that the Speaker or other person presiding should be entitled to direct that the person who has a financial interest in the particular matter should not vote on it.

Effect of breach of the Code

Effect of breach of the Code

64. We recommend that when a tribunal which hears charges of breaches of the Code (which we describe later in this chapter) decides that a leader has committed a breach, that leader should automatically lose his office unless the tribunal decides that there are extenuating circumstances which are such that loss of office by the leader would be too harsh a punishment. If a tribunal does find extenuating circumstances in a particular case, we recommend that it should be able to impose a punishment such as a fine, or a reprimand or require the offender to enter into a bond to be of good behaviour for a certain length of time. The tribunal should also, we believe, be able to recommend demotion of a leader who is a public officer (a person who is employed by a government or semi government body).

Reimbursement of accountancy fees relating to declarations

65. Leaders should not be out of pocket in respect of the cost of preparing their annual declaration, and we have recommended that they be able to claim from the Government all reasonable accountancy fees which they have incurred for this purpose.

ADDITIONAL LIMITATIONS UPON MINISTERS

66. As leaders who are responsible for the governing of the country at national level, ministers hold positions of very considerable responsibility and influence. It is essential that they give the highest priority to their ministerial duties and minimize their private interests. Any private interest which could conflict with the minister's public duty should be disposed of.

67. Because it would be unduly cumbersome to make detailed provision for restrictions on the private interests of ministers in legislation, we propose that the Ombudsman Commission be given power, after consultation with the Prime Minister, to publish general guidelines concerning the extent to which ministers may properly be invovled in outside interests. We further recommend that the Commission have power to give specific directions to ministers to withdraw from a particular interest if the Commission, in its discretion, considers that interest is or could be in conflict with his public duty. (We envisage that before giving a specific direction to a minister, the Commission would first notify the Prime Minister of its intention. The Prime Minister could then speak with the minister before he was given the direction.)

68. Such a conflict between a minister's public duty and his private interest could arise from the fact that his private business interest involves him in spending a considerable part of his time supervising any employees he may have, or in carrying out other work associated with that business. Certain business interests obviously should not be held by ministers [p.9] holding particular portfolios in which policy decisions concerning those types of business must be made either by the minister himself or by the National Executive Council on the submission of that minister.

69. In relation to ministers, the issue of the extent of the conflict between public duty and private interest goes further than that, however, as the National Executive Council will have responsibility for making decisions concerning all aspects of the life of the country. Just where the line should be drawn is not an easy matter to determine. However, we believe that our recommendation concerning the Ombudsman Commission's role of establishing guidelines, and if necessary, giving directions concerning individual ministers is the most satisfactory way of handling this problem of differentiating between acceptable and unacceptable degrees of involvement in private business, professional or other activities which provide income or other material benefits for ministers or for the wife, husband or child of a minister.

Ministers not to hold directorships

70. We believe a minister should not, as a general rule, he eligible to be a director of any company. Holding a directorship of a company would be quite likely to involve a minister in conflict between his public duty and his private interest as companies are usually involved in business activities on a larger scale than are individuals and firms, and tend to have a more direct and continuous involvement with governments. Our recommendation is that a minister, his spouse or one of his children must not hold a directorship except if it is either an honorary one or is a directorship in a small family company in which more than half of the voting rights are effectively held within the minister's immediate family.

71. To ensure that a directorship of this kind is held by a minister or a member of his family only in circumstances which justify this, we recommend that the approval of the Ombudsman Commission be required if a minister, his spouse or his child wishes to accept or retain such a directorship.

72. Somewhat similar provision in respect of the holding of directorships by ministers is made in both the *Parliamentary Integrity Ordinance* and the proposed Ministerial Code. A provision of this kind was also included in the Ministerial Code of Conduct which applied, for a number of years, firstly to Ministerial Members and then to Ministers. (The Ministerial Code of Conduct was discontinued in May 1973 at a time when a number of powers and functions were being transferred from the Australian Government to the Papua New Guinea Government.)

73. Our recommended provision concerning family companies is, however, more limited than those. This has been done in accordance with our view that there should be firm restrictions on the involvement of ministers and their families in private interests. We consider that to allow ministers to retain interests in companies controlled by others would be to allow so much latitude that the provision would have little significance.

74. We have made special provision for government nominees on the boards of directors of corporate bodies. These people should, we propose, be obliged to pay to the government any fee or other benefit they receive from the company of which they are board members.

75. As we have said earlier, our people wish to see their leaders set an example in the way in which they conduct themselves. We also believe that ministers should take particular care to ensure that they do not put themselves into any situation in which they might say or do something which could endanger the security of the country. There have been a number of examples of ministers in other countries becoming involved in situations which proved to be dangerous to the interests of their country. Papua New Guinea's security and its national interest should not be put at risk in this way. We have recommended accordingly.

ADDITIONAL LIMITATIONS UPON CONSTITUTIONAL OFFICE-HOLDERS AND SPECIFIED OFFICE-HOLDERS

76. Not only ministers are in positions of great responsibility and influence. We believe that constitutional office-holders, departmental heads and other senior public servants, statutory office-holders and certain senior officers who work under them hold positions of such importance that they, also, should be subject to restrictions additional to those which apply to leaders generally. These people hold high office and have a significant influence upon top level decisions. If they are to carry out their work capably they should concentrate fully upon it, and not be diverted by having other business interests or employment. [p.10]

77. We have recommended in Chapter 14, 'General', that a person should be disqualified from becoming (or being) a constitutional office-holder if he —

- is involved in the management of a business for profit;
- holds any other office or is engaged in a business, trade or profession;
- buys, rents or hires, accepts as a gift, or holds government property, except in accordance with the terms of his employment,
  provided that, subject to the Code, he may buy or rent government land in the same way as any citizen may do.

78. We recommend that these restrictions should apply under the Leadership Code to constitutional office-holders, and to specified office-holders also, as their position in this regard is very similar to that of constitutional office-holders.

79. Without these limitations on the activities of specified office-holders as well as constitutional office-holders, we consider there is a real danger that some of them may exploit their position in order to obtain advantages for themselves in their private business or employment — advantages which they would be unlikely to obtain if they did not hold such senior positions.

Restrictions on remuneration, gain or profit

80. For similar reasons to those we have just expressed, we believe there should be restrictions on the sources from which constitutional office-holders and specified office-holders should be able to obtain income. We propose that these be limited to —

- monies payable to the office-holder in respect of the office he holds;
- interest on money deposited in a bank or government financial institution;
- interest on government bonds; and
- subject to the Constitution (including this Code) gains made from land owned or occupied by the officer-holder.

81. We are aware that the fourth of these permitted sources of income is very wide compared with the others, and that it could be used to significantly reduce the effectiveness of this provision. However, we have given the Ombudsman Commission general responsibility for supervising the administration and enforcement of the Code and the power to publish guidelines designed to ensure that the Code is fully implemented and made effective. We envisage that if the Commission finds that unreasonable advantage is being taken of this provision by constitutional and specified office-holders contrary to the spirit of the Code, the Commission might either recommend that the Code be amended appropriately, or alternatively, it might make rules or publish guidelines which would close this loophole. Similarly, if the wives or children of constitutional or specified office-holders, with significant assistance from their husbands, become heavily involved in, for instance, business enterprises, there may need to be provision made for some restrictions to be placed on the 'outside' activities of these family members. Initially we think this is unnecessary.

Limitation on acceptance of directorship or consultancy of a foreign company

82. We are concerned to avoid the situation where a person who holds a senior position in a government department or in a statutory authority abuses that position to assist foreign controlled corporations generally, or a particular foreign corporation with which he may form an unofficial relationship, with a view to his being appointed as a member of the board of directors of such a corporation or as a paid consultant to it. Whilst no impropriety is necessarily involved in such an appointment, the possibility of it being a reward for past favours is always present. In any event it does not give a good impression. Such appointments also mean, of course, that the office-holder is able to assist the comp any concerned quite considerably through his contacts with senior public servants and possibly with ministers also. We recommend that these office-holders should not be allowed to accept a directorship of or paid consultancy to any company effectively controlled by foreign interests (whether or not it is incorporated in Papua New Guinea) until three years have expired after the office-holder left his public office. [p.11]

83. We intend this provision to apply to companies which are carrying on business in Papua New Guinea or have a significant interest in such a company, though we have not spelt this out in our recommendation. Breach of this rule would result in the former office-holder being fined or punished in such other manner (other than by imprisonment) as the tribunal which hears the case, in accordance with the Constitution and any law, thinks fit.

Special provision in respect of non-citizens

84. We recognize that non-citizens are in a somewhat different position from citizens who hold office as leaders. Many foreign citizens will eventually return to their own country and we appreciate their wish to make provision by investment for the time when they do return home. However, we consider that they should not be able to invest in a foreign controlled corporation which carries on business in Papua New Guinea or has a significant interest in such a corporation, otherwise these people would be likely to be faced with a conflict of interests which, in principle, we believe should be avoided by citizens and non-citizens alike.

85. The committee appreciates that it is a difficult matter to draw a clear distinction between corporations which have a significant interest in an enterprise which is operating in Papua New Guinea and those which do not have such an interest. However, we believe that it is possible for a meaningful distinction of this kind to be made. It should be done in ordinary legislation.

Code not to affect provisions of Criminal Code and other laws

86. We do not intend that the provisions of the Code should limit the effect of any provisions of the Criminal Code or any other law concerning offences similar to the breaches of the Leadership Code. It is additional to existing legislation. However, we envisage that the *Parliamentary Integrity Ordinance* 1971 would be repealed and replaced by an Act which provides the necessary machinery to enable the Code to be adequately enforced.

ENFORCEMENT OF THE CODE

Powers of the Ombudsman Commission in relation to enforcement of the Code

87. The Ombudsman Commission has been given responsibility for the supervision and enforcement of the Code under the terms of our recommendations in this Chapter. We consider that in the interests of flexibility and the overall effectiveness of the Code, the Commission should be given power to make rules and publish guidelines concerning the conduct, financial and business affairs of leaders, their spouses and children, and to make provision in those rules and guidelines for exemptions from the provisions of the Code where such exemptions are permitted by the Code.

88. The Commisssion should be in a good position to make these detailed rules and guidelines in the light of experience with the problems associated with the operation of the Code. Of course if, for example, the Commission felt that there was a major loophole in the provisions of the Code which was enabling leaders to circumvent restrictions on their business or professional activities, the Commission could recommend to the Prime Minister and the National Executive Council that the Code be amended accordingly.

89. To ensure that there is adequate political direction and involvement in relation to these rules and guidelines prior to their being made or published, we have recommended that before making or publishing them the Commission consult the Prime Minister, and the Chairman and Deputy Chairman of the First Parliamentary Committee, all of whom will be concerned with the functioning of the Leadership Code and of the Commission itself.

90. These rules and guidelines should be subject to disallowance by parliament in the same way as we have recommended that other rules made by the Commission, and regulations and statutory rules generally, should be able to be disallowed.

91. We recommend also, for similar reasons, that the Commission should be able, subject to the Constitution and in accordance with law, to specify by proclamation in the Government Gazette, office-holders who would then be designated 'leaders' for the purposes of the Code. Clearly, the task of identifying which particular positions should be designed as leadership positions is not one which can be satisfactorily done at a particular point of time and then left unchanged for a substantial period. New positions in government departments and in statutory bodies are constantly being created and old positions abolished. We feel that our recommendation provides for a continous review of the situation to be maintained, and that this should improve the effectiveness of the Code.

92. The Commission should also have power to give a direction to any leader to dispose of a particular asset or interest which, in the opinion of the Commission, he holds contrary to a [p.12] provision of the Code.

93. The maximum period of time within which a leader is to be required to dispose of a specified asset or interest should be six months, but we have provided for the Commission to be able to extend that period by up to three months in special cases, such as where a leader has difficulty in finding a buyer for a particular asset which does not have a ready market.

Tribunals to hear charges of breach of the Code

94. We have given full consideration to the question as to the kind of tribunal best suited to dealing with alleged breaches of the Code, and have decided that although all members of the tribunal should be drawn from the judiciary, the tribunal should be separate from an ordinary court. We feel that breaches of the Code are disciplinary offences rather than criminal offences (though some breaches would also constitute criminal offences and be dealt with as such).

95. We also consider that it would be inappropriate for alleged breaches of the Code to be dealt with by a single judge or magistrate as this would be placing an unduly onerous responsibility on a single person. Our recommendation is that in the case of a leader other than the Prime Minister or another minister, or the Chief Justice or another judge of the National Court, or any other constitutional or specified office-holder, the tribunal by which the charge should be heard should comprise a judge of the National Court and two senior magistrates appointed by the Judicial and Legal Service Commission. In the case of a minister or a constitutional or specified office-holder, we recommend that the tribunal consist of three National Court judges appointed by the Judicial and Legal Service Commission.

96. These tribunals should have all necessary powers and authority to conduct the hearing, summon witnesses, take evidence, make decisions and otherwise function as judicial bodies. We envisage that they may adopt procedures which are somewhat more informal than those of a court, but that there will be adequate protection of the rights of those charged with a breach of the Code.

97. As to the effect of a decision by one of these tribunals that a leader has committed a breach of the Code, we recommend that the leader should automatically be deprived of his office unless the tribunal is satisfied that there are extenuating circumstances which justify the tribunal imposing an alternative penalty, such as imposing a fine of up to a specified maximum sum (provided for by law), demoting the leader (if he is a public officer) reprimanding him, placing him on a bond to be of good behaviour for a certain period or such other punishment as may be laid down by law.

The right of citizens to make complaints of breaches of the Code

98. If the Code is to be adequately enforced much will depend on the readiness and ability of citizens to make complaints about activities of leaders which they believe to be breaches of the Code. We propose that the investigation of complaints should be facilitated, and have accordingly recommended that these complaints may be directed not only to the Ombudsman Commission itself but to any government department, statutory authority or government officer.

99. Whenever a complaint (other than one which is clearly frivolous or annoying) concerning a leader is received by a department, statutory authority or officer, the department, authority or officer who receives the complaint must forward it immediately to the Commission either himself or through his superior officer, so that it can be investigated. When forwarding the complaint, full details of it should be supplied to the Commission.

NOT SELF-EXECUTING

Held

Section 28(1)(g) of the Constitution is not self-executing and in the absence of a valid Organic Law which is authorized by the Constitution no recommendation for dismissal can be effective. *The State v The Independent Tribunal; Ex Parte Sasakila* [1976] PNGLR 491; see Frost C.J. at p.498, Saldanha J. at p.504.

GENERALLY

Referred to

per Curiam (Kidu C.J., Kearney Dep. C.J., Greville Smith, Andrew, Miles JJ.) in *In Re Joseph Auna* [1980] PNGLR 500 at pp.504, 505;

by Gajewicz J. in *S.C.R. No 2 of 1982; Re Opai Kunangel Amin* (1982 Unreported) SC231 at pp.33, 34, 45, 46.

(2) Where an independent tribunal referred to in Subsection (1)(g) makes a recommendation to the appropriate authority in accordance with that paragraph or with Subsection (1A), the appropriate authority shall act in accordance with the recommendation. (*Replaced by Constitutional Amendment No. 4 —. Leadership Code*)

'RECOMMENDATION' TO HEAD OF STATE JUSTICIABLE

per Frost C.J.

I think it has to be accepted that, so far as s.28(2) and (3) are concerned the provision for the Head of State and the appropriate authority respectively, as the person and body to whom any recommendations are to be made, and the consequent obligations to take action accordingly, are to be taken as self-executing. Now there would appear to be no reason why an order for dismissal implementing an invalid recommendation should be free from attack in the ordinary way if made by an appointing authority who is not the Head of State. So a leader to whom s.28(3) applies, who is found guilty of an act of misconduct, could succeed in those circumstances in having the order for dismissal set aside. But if the word 'advice' in s.28(2) is given its constitutional meaning as provided in s.86(4), and the recommendations acted on by the Head of State are not justiciable, a leader to whom that subsection applies, if found guilty of the same act of misconduct in office, would be left with no redress if the recommendation were invalid.

To adopt an interpretation which produces such a discriminatory result would not, in my opinion, be to accord the provisions of s.28(2) their fair and liberal meaning as required under the Constitution, Sch.1.5(2). A further pointer to the justiciability of recommendations upon which the Head of State must act under s.28(2) arises from the provision in s.28(5) that proceedings under sub-s.(1)(g), whilst not judicial proceedings, are subject to the principles of natural justice. (The precise implications of the proceedings not being judicial were not argued. The provision may be sufficient to exclude the National Court's power of review under Constitution, s.155(3)(a)). The provision bringing in the principles of natural justice would be quite ineffective unless an order for dismissal or other penalty could be impugned and set aside in the case, for example, of a leader who, in his absence and without any opportunity of being heard, and thus in breach of the principles of natural justice, was found guilty of misconduct in office. The remedy could be found in the Court's inherent power to grant relief — Constitution, s.155(4).

Section 28(5) is therefore a strong indication that a recommendation is not finally conclusive against a leader but is justiciable, and that proceedings may be brought to set aside an order made either by the Head of State or other appointing authority pursuant to a recommendation alleged to be invalid.

In an endeavour to find a solution I do not consider that this Court should proceed to cut down the force of the meaning of non-justiciability. The answer, I consider, is to be found by looking at the purpose of s.86(4). That provision is certainly to be given the plenary operation of putting beyond the scrutiny of the Courts the question of what advice (if any) is given by the National Executive Council to the Head of State. But the provision seems inappropriate to the proceedings of an independent Tribunal which acts judicially, conducts its hearings in public, and makes public its decision supported by reasons.

The conclusion I have come to is that so far as the obligation of the Head of State to act on the recommendation of such a Tribunal is concerned, special and exclusive provision is made for that subject-matter in s.28, and the general provisions of s.86, except possibly

sub-s.(3) which is concerned with the form of instruments, have no application. The terms of the order of dismissal which recite merely the receipt of a recommendation from the appropriate Tribunal without the use of the term 'advice' indicates that the draftsman probably took the same view. The order is thus not saved from invalidity.
The State v The Independent Tribunal; Ex Parte Sasakila [1976] PNGLR 491 at pp.500, 501; see also Kearney J. at p.505.

COMMENT

Since the decision in *Sasakila's Case* s.28(2) of the Constitution was amended by Constitutional Amendment No 4 — Leadership Code. Nothing in the amendment would however appear to affect the conclusions reached by the Supreme Court in *Sasakila's Case*.

(3) For the purposes of Subsections (1)(g), (1A) and (2), "the appropriate authority" —
- (a) in relation to —
  - (i) a person holding an office referred to in Section 26(1)(a), (b), (c) or (d) (*application of Division 2*); or
  - (ii) a person holding an elective office that is declared under Section 26(3) to be an office to and in relation to which this Division applies,

  means the Head of State; and
- (b) in relation to a person holding any other office to which this Division applies — means the appropriate appointing authority. (*Replaced by Constitutional Amendment No. 4. — Leadership Code*).

(4) An Organic Law may provide for the suspension from office of a person to whom this Division applies pending the investigation of any case of alleged or suspected misconduct in office by him.

(*See: Organic Law on the Duties and Responsibilities of Leadership, Ch.1*)

AS TO THE EFFECT OF SUSPENSION UPON RIGHT TO RESIGN

per Kapi Dep.C.J.

In any case I consider that suspensioin under s.28 of the Organic Law is limited. A person who is alleged to have committed misconduct in office is '*suspended from duty*'. Mr Roddenby has submitted that the word 'duty' is to be read as synonymous with the word 'office'. I do not consider that the word 'duty' has been used to mean 'office'. It is to be noted that both these words are used in s.28. They convey a different meaning. The word 'office' has a broader meaning than the word 'duty'. The word 'office' is used to mean the position which is occupied by the office-holder. This includes the 'duty' or 'duties' to be performed by virtue of the office. The word 'duty' is used to mean the functions and the proper actions which the law authorizes to be performed in the office. See *Canadian Pacific Tobacco Co. Limited v Stapleton* (1952) 86 CLR 1 per Dixon C.J. at p.6.

Consequently if an officer is suspended from duty, he is only suspended from the *performance of the duties* but he is still an occupant or office-holder of the position. This is to be contrasted with suspension of a Constitutional Officer-Holder from *office* under s.9 of the *Organic Law on the Guarantee of the Rights and Independence of the Constitutional Office-Holders*. See also suspension of the Prime Minister from office under s.142(6) of the Constitution. It appears to me that s.28 of the Organic Law simply suspends the leader from performing the duties and functions assigned to him by virtue of his office. Such a suspension also affects the salary because salary is connected to the performance of duties and functions. Such a suspension does not in any way affect the position or office occupied by a Member of the Parliament. Thus the right of a Member to resign from the seat is not affected.

Mr Roddenby has submitted that such a narrow interpretation of the word 'duty' under s.28 of the Organic Law would be contrary to s.28(4) of the Constitution. He submitted that it is a rule of interpretation that as far as possible provisions of the Constitution should be construed so as to be in harmony with each other. He made this submission to support his earlier contention that the word 'duty' should be interpreted to mean 'office'. However, I do not consider that the narrow interpretation of the word 'duty' under s.28 of the Organic Law is inconsistent with s.28(4) of the Constitution. Section 28(4) of the Constitution can be best described as delegation of power to the Organic Law to make provisions for suspension of persons pending investigation of misconduct in office. It does not set out the exact particulars of suspension to be provided for by the Organic Law. For instance it gives no guidance as to type of suspension, length, when it should begin to run, whether suspended officer should be on full pay, etc . . . These are matters left to be included in the provisions of the Organic Law. Suspension from performance of duty is within the powers given by s.28(4) of the Constitution.

I have concluded, therefore, that resignation by a Member of Parliament can not be affected by suspension from duty. It follows, therefore, that Mr. Kunangel has effectively resigned as Member of the Parliament.

On the authority of *In re Joseph Auna* [1980] PNGLR 500 as Mr. Kunangel is no longer a leader, the Tribunal can have no jurisdiction to deal with him.

S.C.R. No 2 of 1982; Re Opai Kunangel Amin (1982 Unreported) SC231 at pp.8, 9; see also Bredmeyer J. at p.12, Kaputin J. (dissenting) at pp.13A, 14, 18, 19, 24, Gajewicz J. at p.32.

GENERALLY

Referred to

per Curiam (Kidu C.J., Kearney Dep.C.J., Greville Smith, Andrew, Miles JJ.) in *In re Joseph Auna* [1980] PNGLR 500 at p.504.

(5) Proceedings under Subsection (1)(g) are not judicial proceedings but are subject to the principles of natural justice, and —
   (a) no such proceedings are a bar to any other proceedings provided for by law; and
   (b) no other proceedings provided for by law are a bar to proceedings under that paragraph.

(*See: Organic Law on the Duties and Responsibilities of Leadership* Ch.1)

GENERALLY

Referred to

by Frost C.J. in *The State v The Independent Tribunal; Ex Parte Sasakila* [1976] PNGLR 491 at pp.499, 501;

by Prentice C.J. in *Premdas v Independent State of Papua New Guinea* [1979] PNGLR 329 at p.342; see also Wilson J. at p.376;

by Miles J. in *Iambakey Okuk v Fallscheer* [1980] PNGLR 274 at p.291.

29. — PROSECUTION OF MISCONDUCT IN OFFICE.

(1) Where the Ombudsman Commission or other authority referred to in Section 28(1)(f) (*further provisions*) is satisfied that there is a

prima facie case that a person has been guilty of misconduct in office, it shall refer the matter to the Public Prosecutor for prosecution before a tribunal established under Section 28(1)(g) (*further provisions*).

GENERALLY

Referred to

per Curiam (Kidu C.J., Kearney Dep.C.J., Greville Smith, Andrew, Miles JJ.) in *In Re Joseph Auna* [1980] PNGLR 500 at p.505.

(2) If the Public Prosecutor fails to prosecute the matter within a reasonable period, the Commission may prosecute it in his stead.

30. — OTHER AUTHORITY.

Where another authority is prescribed under Section 28 (*further provisions*) that authority —

(a) shall be composed of a person or persons who are declared under Section 221(1) (*definitions*) to be a constitutional office-holder; and

(b) is not subject to direction or control by any person or authority.

31. — DISQUALIFICATIONS ON DISMISSAL.

(1) A person who has been dismissed from office under this Division for misconduct in office is not eligible —

(a) to election to any elective public office; or

(b) for appointment as Head of State or as a nominated member of the Parliament; or

(c) for appointment to a provincial legislature or provincial executive (including the office of head of a provincial executive), or to a local government body, (*replaced by Constitutional Amendment No. 3. — Provincial Government (Consequential Amendments), s.4*)

for a period of three years after the date of his dismissal.

CONSEQUENCES MAY BE AVOIDED BY PRIOR RESIGNATION BUT LIABILITY REVIVES IF FURTHER LEADERSHIP CODE OFFICE ACCEPTED

per Curiam (Kidu C.J., Kearney Dep.C.J., Greville Smith, Andrew, Miles JJ.)

It is true, on the view we take, that in the absence of legislative provision under s.26(3) of the Constitution, which may well be impracticable, a leader who resigns from office before a finding of misconduct in office is made, is not subject to the disqualifications on dismissal which flow from s.31(1) of the Constitution. By itself, however, that anomaly is not sufficient to change the otherwise consistent thrust of the legislation. It is clear from the view we take that if any such leader assumed another leadership office, any proved misconduct in his earlier office could result in his being dismissed from his latter leadership office.

The definition of 'person to whom this law applies' in s.1 of the Organic Law carries a clear connotation that it refers only to current office holders; and later provisions of the Organic Law referring to such persons all clearly contemplate that they are in office, and are quite inconsistent with any view that the phrase embraces persons who have ceased to hold office.

The reference to suspension from duty in s.28 of the Organic Law, points to a person currently in office.
In Re Joseph Auna [1980] PNGLR 500 at p.505.

GENERALLY

Referred to

by Pritchard J. in *Constitutional Reference No 1 of 1978 (s.18)* [1978] PNGLR 345 at p.374;

per Curiam (Kidu C.J., Kearney Dep.C.J., Greville Smith, Andrew, Miles JJ.) in *In Re Joseph Auna* [1980] PNGLR 500 at p.505.

(2) In the event of doubt as to whether an office or position is an office or position to which Subsection (1)(a), (b) or (c) applies, the decision of the Ombudsman Commission is final.

Division 3. — Basic Rights.

Subdivision A. — Introductory.

32. — RIGHT TO FREEDOM.

(1) Freedom based on law consists in the least amount of restriction on the activities of individuals that is consistent with the maintenance and development of Papua New Guinea and of society in accordance with this Constitution and, in particular, with the National Goals and Directive Principles and the Basic Social Obligations.

INTRODUCTION

Comment

The Human Rights Bill in the Papua New Guinea Constitution, Division 3 — Basic Rights, is divided into four sub-divisions:—
A — Introductory
B — Fundamental Rights
C — Qualified Rights
D — Enforcement

Sub-Division C — Qualified Rights is in turn divided into three parts
— General
— Rights of all Persons
— Special Rights of Citizens

For a general account of Division 3 see Goldring J., *The Constitution of Papua New Guinea*, Chapter 14, Human Rights pp.212–247.

In this Division cross references have been provided, where relevant, to the *Universal Declaration of Human Rights*, the *International Covenant of Economic Social and Cultural*

Rights, the *International Covenant of Civil and Political Rights* and the *European Convention for the Protection of Human Rights and Fundamental Freedoms*.

Miles J. In *S.C.R. No 1 of 1981; Re Inter-Group Fighting Act 1977* [1981] PNGLR 151 at p.170 made the following observation on the relationship between the Constitution, the C.P.C. Report, the *Universal Declaration of Human Rights*, the *International Covenant on Civil and Political Rights*, and the *European Convention on Human Rights*:—

> The Constitution avoids the concise and sweeping provisions of the *Universal Declaration of Human Rights* that 'Everyone has the right to life liberty and the security of person' (Art. 3) and 'No one shall be subjected to arbitrary arrest detention or exile' (Art. 9). The Constitutional Planning Committee recommended avoiding such an approach, taking the view that constitutional freedoms would be more effectively guaranteed if their definition were made 'as specific and as clear as possible so that the room for argument as to the meaning of particular provisions is minimised'. The Committee considered that the detailed provisions previously in force in this country as the *Human Rights Act* 1971 had been found quite suitable for Papua New Guinea. In reaching this conclusion the Committee rejected the simpler, more sweeping approach of the Universal Declaration which is repeated for instance in Art. 9.1 of the *International Covenant on Civil and Political Rights* 1966 and in s.20 of the abortive *Australian Human Rights Bill* 1973. The Papua New Guinea approach is similar to that of the *European Convention on Human Rights* where 'two lines of the Universal Declaration are expanded to nearly a page . . . when one uses the method of detailed definition' (A.H. Robertson, *Human Rights in Europe*, Manchester 1977, p.50). Two results follow. One is that it is easy in examining the detailed provisions of the Constitution to lose sight of the original aim as expressed by the Constitutional Planning Committee, namely to give effect to the purposes of the Universal Declaration. The other is that in interpreting and giving effect to these more or less precisely defined rights and freedoms the court is left, as the Constitutional Planning Committee intended it should be left, with less room to manoeuvre.

Cross references to the Constitutions of the United States of America and of India are also made because the decisions of the Supreme Courts of these countries may be of general assistance in the interpretation of the Papua New Guinean Constitution.

Reference is also made to some decisions of the *European Commission of Human Rights* and the *European Court of Human Rights*. A good working knowledge of the European Convention, which has many drafting similarities to the human rights provisions in the Papua New Guinean Constitution can be had by consulting F.G. Jacobs *The European Convention of Human Rights* (1975), copies of which are in the UPNG Law Library. A more up to date work is C.C. Morrison, Jr *The Dynamics of Development in the European Human Rights Convention System* (1981), also in the UPNG Law Library.

C.P.C. Report Ch.5 Part 1 p.1

'Human rights' — the historical background

1. The idea of human rights has developed over centuries in various countries of the world, largely as a result of the oppression of citizens by dictatorial governments and entrenched private groups. The 'rights of man' became a slogan in struggles against injustices and indignities perpetrated by such governments and groups. In these struggles, attempts were made to set down the minimum rights that could be demanded by all citizens, by the very fact of being human, of the government that rules them.

2. In the late seventeenth century these ideas began to be incorporated in constitutional documents. In England, after the 'Glorious Revolution' of 1688, the *Bill of Rights* of 1689 was adopted to preserve the people of the country from the re-emergence of arbitrary royal rule. The *Bill of Rights* set out what were described as 'the ancient rights and liberties' of the people, which included freedom of election of members of parliament, freedom of speech and debate in parliament, freedom from cruel or unusual punishments, from excessive fines or demands for excessive bail, and the right to trial by jury.

3. The American revolutionaries included in their *Declaration of Independence* in 1776 a claim to 'certain inalienable rights' including 'life, liberty and the pursuit of happiness'. They incorporated in their Constitution defined rights to freedom of speech and the press, to a speedy and public trial by an impartial jury, the right to free exercise of religion, and the right of people to be 'secure in their persons, houses, papers and effects against unreasonable searches and seizures'. Certain important additional rights were added by amendments to the Constitution in the 1860's after the Civil War. These included the prohibition of slavery, and the protection from deprivation, without due process of law, of every person's life, liberty and property. Another of these amendments prohibited the denial to any person in the United States, of the equal protection of the laws.

4. In 1789, the French revolutionaries, having disposed of their king, laid down in the *Declaration of the Rights of Man*, the rights which they said had been denied ordinary Frenchmen under the kings. They declared that men are born and remain free and equal in rights; those rights being 'liberty, property, security and resistance to oppression'. They listed in particular, freedom of speech, of the press, of religion, and freedom from arbitrary arrest.

5. Other European States, such as Sweden in 1809, and Holland in 1815 included clear statements of human rights in their constitution not long after the French Revolution, and since then many other countries in all parts of the world have given recognition to basic human rights in their constitutions and other laws.

International recognition of human rights

6. In the past, ideas about which are the most important human rights and freedoms have varied between people of different countries at a particular time, and between people of different generations in a single country. However, since the establishment of the United Nations Organisation, there has been general agreement internationally that there are a number of basic rights and freedoms which all people everywhere are entitled to have recognised.

These include —

- the right to live;
- the right not to be tortured, or made a slave;
- the right not to be imprisoned without a fair trial in court;
- the right not to be subjected to arbitrary interference with privacy, family, home or communications;
- the right to freedom of thought, conscience and religion;
- the right to speak freely, to join an association, and to hold public meetings;
- the right to take part in the government of his country, directly or through freely chosen representatives; [p.2]
- the right not to be arbitrarily deprived of one's property;
- the right to work, to free choice of employment and to just and favourable conditions of employment;
- the right to a standard of living adequate for the health and well being of each person and his family;
- the right to an education.

These and a number of other rights and freedoms have been set out in the *Universal Declaration of Human Rights*, which was adopted without dissent by the United Nations in 1948. The Declaration recognizes that the rights and freedoms it sets out are not unlimited — that the protection of the human rights of individuals and groups must be balanced against the interests of the people of a country as a whole, and against the rights and freedoms of other individuals and groups. It also recognizes that as well as having rights, all people have duties to the community in which they live, and must exercise their rights responsibly.

7. There are certain aspects of the Declaration, however, which to a significant degree limit its application to the domestic laws of states, and particularly those of emerging countries such as our own. Firstly, it makes no reference to the universally recognized distinction between the rights of the citizens of a country as opposed to those of foreign citizens within that country. This distinction is of great importance, as all countries give greater rights and privileges to their own citizens than to aliens, as we have pointed out in Chapter 4 'Citizenship'.

8. Secondly, at the time the Declaration was made very few of the Third World countries were independent, and their particular circumstances were not sufficiently taken into account when the Declaration was drafted. The Declaration should be seen against the background of World War II in the aftermath of which it was conceived and adopted.

Effect of the Universal Declaration of Human Rights

9. The *Universal Declaration of Human Rights* as such cannot be enforced by action in a court. Though it is true that some of its provisions set out accepted principles of international law, others simply represent basic humanitarian ideas, while a third category of rights is an attempt to establish new rules for the benefit of people throughout the world. Its main purpose has been to set a common standard of achievement for all peoples and all nations, so that individuals and institutions everywhere will 'strive, by teaching and education, to promote respect for these rights and freedoms, and by progressive measures, national and international, to secure their universal and effective recognition and observances'. It is therefore more a set of objectives than a document to which detailed reference can be made in relation to enforceable human rights provisions in constitutional documents.

10. We are only too well aware that the United Nations Organization is still far from achieving this purpose — that in a large number of countries many of the rights and freedoms set out in the Universal Declaration cannot be exercised by the vast majority of the citizens. This is so in both developed and developing countries. In a number of countries, basic human rights such as freedom from arbitrary arrest and imprisonment, freedom of expression and assembly, and protection from inhuman treatment are flagrantly disregarded by autocratic governments whose main concern is to entrench themselves in power.

11. In many new States however, well intentioned governments are simply unable to ensure that all of their citizens have enough food and clothing and reasonable shelter, since they do not have the resources to provide these necessities for all. In our own country, it will be a number of years yet before our government is able to provide education for all school-age children.

12. In framing our recommendations in Chapter 2 'National Goals and Directive Principles', we have taken full account of the need to give impetus to the achievement of economic, social and cultural goals such as the provision of an adequate standard of living for every family, education for all children and the opportunity to fully participate in all aspects of the life of the community and the nation. We do not feel that it is appropriate to deal with these matters in this chapter, as it is not possible to enforce this type of right in the same way as those which we have included here.

Enforceable Human Rights provisions in the constitutions of nations

13. Today the majority of the nations of the world have incorporated in their constitutions many of the basic human rights which have come to be recognized internationally, and are included in such historic documents as the *Universal Declaration of Human Rights.* [p.3]

14. Not all of these constitutional declarations of fundamental rights are enforceable, however. It has been said that some are more impressive in terms of literary style than in practical enforceability. A number of countries with a totalitarian system of government nevertheless have a ringing declaration of basic rights and freedoms included in their constitutions. On the other hand, the new states of the Commonwealth of Nations which have obtained their independence after the end of World War II, with few exceptions have included in their constitution human rights provisions which are legally enforceable ('justiciable'). India and Pakistan in the 1940s, Malaysia in the 1950s, Nigeria, Kenya, Zambia, Western Samoa and Nauru in the 1960s, and Fiji in 1970 — all have (or have had) similar constitutional provisions for the protection of civil and political rights, which can be enforced by a court order.

15. Although many of these new Commonwealth states have, in their short lifetimes, experienced considerable political change involving constitutional amendments of substantial character, in only one case has the 'bill of rights' disappeared from the current constitution (Malawi). Even under military government the fundamental rights provisions of the constitution may be excluded from the suspension of parts of the constitution, as in Nigeria (although such provisions can no longer prevail over inconsistent laws).

16. Among those countries which do not have any fundamental rights or freedoms included in their constitution there are many which recognise them in their ordinary laws or have accepted them under international agreements. Canada, for example, passed a *Bill of Rights* as an ordinary Act of Parliament, in 1960, and Britain which does not have a formal written constitution, has adopted a justiciable international bill of rights of becoming a party to the *European Convention on Human Rights* of 1950. Australia too, is at present considering a *Human Rights Bill*, which was introduced into parliament late last year.

Human Rights in Papua New Guinea

17. We Papua New Guineans are all too familiar with authoritian governments, having been ruled by them for almost ninety years. The last years of colonial rule have, of course, been enlightened by world standards, but in earlier times the basic rights and dignity of our people were frequently suppressed or ignored.

18. It is true, of course, that the English common law and Australian statute law which we have inherited does at least theoretically, provide substantial protection of human rights such as protection from the intentional deprivation of one's life, freedom from arbitrary arrest, the right to a fair trial, freedom from arbitrary search of one's person or property, but until recently discriminatory local legislation and the lack of access to independent legal advice prevented our people from effectively asserting their rights. The situation was not improved by the fact that in most cases they were obliged to make any claim of breach of a right or freedom to a person who could not be completely impartial as he was an administrator as well as a magistrate. Even today most of our people are not aware of many of their rights, and are therefore unable to stand up for those rights.

19. However, Papua New Guinea does now have a specific law which provides protection of human rights similar to that which we have described above — the *Human Rights Ordinance* 1971. It was introduced into the House of Assembly by a private member of the House, the Rev. Percy Chatterton, MHA, soon after the enactment of the controversial *Public Order Ordinance* 1970. That law allowed the Government ('the Administration' at that time) to restrict processions and public meetings, and included a number of new offences relating to demonstrations and other forms of civil disobedience. It gave rise to much strong criticism to the effect that it unjustifiably limited basic democratic freedoms, and that it was an attempt to suppress the efforts of Papua New Guineans seeking to recover land rights on the Gazelle Peninsular. Thus, the *Human Rights Ordinance* may be seen as a reassertion of the basic democratic freedoms in the light of a move by the Administration to impose significant restrictions upon the fundamental rights and freedoms of Papua New Guineans.

The Human Rights Ordinance 1971

20. The *Human Rights Ordinance* protects a total of eleven rights and freedoms, most of which are protected by similar provisions in the constitutions of new Commonwealth states such as those mentioned above. It is in fact based on the human rights provisions of the Constitution of Nauru, which are themselves similar to those of Nigeria.

21. These rights and freedoms are —

(1) the right to life;
(2) the right to personal liberty; [p.4]
(3) freedom from slavery and forced labour;
(4) freedom from inhuman treatment;
(5) the right to protection of property;
(6) the right to protection from arbitrary search and entry on premises;
(7) protection of law to ensure no imprisonment except on a proper charge and after a fair trial;
(8) freedom of thought, conscience and religion;
(9) freedom of speech and the right to publish;
(10) freedom of peaceful assembly and association; and
(11) freedom of choice of employment.

22. Under the Ordinance, all of these rights are enforceable by the Full Court of the Supreme Court, which may act upon the complaint of a person who claims his rights or freedoms have been denied, or on an application by the Public Solicitor or the Secretary for Law on behalf of such a person. The Full Court may then make whatever order it thinks is appropriate in the circumstances of the case.

Incorporation of human rights and freedoms in the Constitution

23. The submissions we have received from our people in various parts of the country make it clear that the protection of human rights in an independent Papua New Guinea is widely regarded as a matter of high priority. The views expressed to us have been heavily in favour of incorporating the substance of the provisions of the *Human Rights Ordinance* in our Constitution and of making these provisions legally enforceable in the same way as they are under the *Human Rights Ordinance*.

24. In recommending the inclusion of the eleven rights and freedoms in the Ordinance, with certain modifications, and the addition of four further rights and freedoms we have given due weight to the main arguments against taking this course.

These seem to be —

A number of British and Australian politicians, lawyers and political writers have for many years argued that there is no need to set out the basic human rights in a Commonwealth country's constitution, because these rights are protected anyway if there are independent judges who apply the rules of law which have been developed in England over hundreds of years (the common law). These people argue that because not many of the countries which have human rights and freedoms set out in their constitution (and as we have said, most countries in the world do) have succeeded in adequately protecting these rights and freedoms, putting these rights into the constitution doesn't really achieve anything.

There is little to be gained by putting human rights and freedoms in the Constitution because, in times of crisis, when they are most threatened, the Executive is likely to override them by using emergency powers. This has been the experience of a number of states in recent years.

Writing human rights into the Constitution may tend to over-emphasize the rights of individuals. The people of this country have not only rights, but duties as members of their new nation. Having individual rights included in the fundamental law of the country could embarrass the government in the future if it wants to emphasize the duties of individuals. It could also make it more difficult for the government to make sweeping economic changes in the interests of the majority but to the detriment of a privileged minority.

25. We believe that there are counter arguments which outweigh these arguments.

These are —

Although many basic human rights are already set out in Papua New Guinea's *Human Rights Ordinance*, this is only an ordinary law. It can be changed at any time if the government of the day passes a new law in the normal way — that is by [p.5] obtaining the agreement of a majority of the members of the House of Assembly who are present in the House at the time when a vote on the new law is taken. If these rights are included in the Constitution they would be harder for a government to change, and ought therefore to be better protected.

Government ministers, members of the House of Assembly and ordinary people would be more conscious of the effect of new policies or laws on basic human rights, especially if the part of the Constitution in which the rights are set out becomes widely known. This should make it less likely that policies or laws which cut across these human rights would be accepted either in Cabinet or in the House of Assembly.

In framing the provisions for inclusion in the Constitution, full account can be taken of the need to allow for future programmes on which the Government of the day may well wish to embark in the interests of the great majority of the people. The experience of other new States with constitutional 'bills of rights' is likely to be of great assistance in this respect.

The rights and freedoms for inclusion in the Constitution

26. We recommend that all eleven rights and freedoms set out in the *Human Rights Ordinance* be included in the Constitution, with a number of important modifications (which we set out below). In addition, four new rights and freedoms should be included, namely —

- freedom of movement;
- the right to privacy;
- the right to stand for election and to vote; and
- freedom of information.

The modifications to the *Human Rights Ordinance* provisions which we recommend fall into four main categories — two of which broaden the scope of the rights and freedoms protected under the Ordinance, whilst the other two involve adding further qualifications to them:

Firstly we propose the addition of a number of provisions under the head 'Provisions to secure protection of law' to give additional rights and protection to individuals. These include the right to appeal in accordance with a law which sets out permissible grounds of appeal; the right to be treated with humanity and respect whilst in a corrective institution; and the need for young persons to be kept apart from adult prisoners in corrective institutions.

Secondly, our recommended provisions would make far more meaningful the protection of the freedom of choice of employment — by narrowing the scope of the exception clauses in the Ordinance.

Thirdly, we propose qualifying a number of rights to take account of the distinction between the respective rights of citizens and of non-citizens in accordance with the philosophy which underlies our recommendations on citizenship. (When the Ordinance came into force there were of course no Papua New Guinea citizens so that this distinction could not be made). Thus we recommend that some of these *constitutional* rights be made exclusive to citizens (for example, the right to stand for election to public office and to vote, freedom of movement, freedom of information, and protection of property). We do not necessarily suggest that non-citizens be left without any protection in respect of these rights and freedoms. We simply wish to ensure that parliament has an unrestricted power to pass appropriate legislation in regard to non-citizens' rights in these areas in the same way as the parliaments of many other countries, including Britain and New Zealand for example, are empowered to do. Our reasoning is set out in detail below in relation to the particular rights and freedoms mentioned above.

In respect of certain other rights and freedoms, such as freedom of speech, freedom of assembly and association, and freedom of choice of employment, non-citizens as well as citizens are to be given protection, but allowance has been made for parliament to pass a law which specifically limits these freedoms insofar as non-citizens are concerned *provided* that law is 'reasonably justifiable in a democratic society.' (The choice of the clause 'reasonably justifiable in a democratic society' is explained below).

We wish to stress that we have recommended that eight of the most fundamental [p.6] human rights and freedoms, namely —

the right to life;
the right to personal liberty;
freedom from inhuman treatment;
freedom from forced labour;
the right to protection from arbitrary search and entry to premises;
the right to protection of law;
freedom of conscience, thought and religion; and
the right to privacy;

should apply equally to citizens and non-citizens, and that we consider the limitations upon the rights and freedoms of non-citizens which we have allowed for should, if they are imposed in the interests of our citizens, be brought into effect in a reasonable manner, on the basis of specified principles.

Finally, we have added further qualifications to a number of rights, particularly the right to protection from arbitrary deprivation of property, to ensure that the Government of the day is not unreasonably restricted in the measures it may take in relation to these rights in the interests of the community as a whole. These additional qualifications have been found necessary in a number of other developing countries, and we have drawn upon their experience in this regard.

Exceptions: 'Reasonably justifiable in a democratic society'

27. We recommend that this phrase, which is used in the *Human Rights Ordinance* in relation to exceptions to the rights and freedoms enunciated in that law, be retained. Whilst it is true that it presents judges with difficult problems of interpretation, since deciding the precise boundaries of democracy may perhaps be said to be more a matter for political philosphers rather than for lawyers, it has several advantages.

It provides flexibility which is essential in relation to many of the rights and freedoms protected, since much depends on particular circumstances, and in a new nation such as Papua New Guinea we believe it is essential to make adequate provision to enable the legislature and the executive to take appropriate action in situations which it is difficult to foresee at present.

Furthermore, by using the word 'justifiable' rather than 'necessary' or 'required' as in some other constitutional bills of right, the courts will not be obliged to substitute their own view of the way in which the legislature or the executive ought to have dealt with the particular situation. The courts will simply have to decide whether the legislation or administrative action in question is *justifiable* in a democratic society.

Finally, the fact that the same words have been used in a number of other constitutions in Commonwealth countries, means that the interpretation given to these words by judges in countries comparable with Papua New Guinea can be taken into account by our judges when they are required to make decisions as to whether or not a particular law or administrative action falls within the exception clause.

28. As a safeguard against these exception clauses being used by the Government of the day to undermine the general principles laid down in respect of particular rights and freedoms to be protected, we have made provision in Recommendation 18 for a law of this kind to be effective only during a State of Emergency or if it is passed by a three-fifths majority of the total membership of the Parliament.

29. Not all of the rights and freedoms we have recommended for inclusion in the Constitution are qualified by these broad exception clauses. Some are qualified only by certain specific exceptions, e.g. the right to life, and to personal liberty, the right to protection of law, and protection from forced labour. One right — that of protection from inhuman treatment — is not qualified at all.

30. It is, of course, implicit in our recommendations that the *Human Rights Ordinance* should be repealed as from the date on which the Constitution comes into force. [p.7]

The form in which the rights and freedoms are expressed

31. We have considered with care the question as to whether the form in which the human rights and freedoms are set out in the Ordinance should be retained, or whether it would be preferable to take the course which Canada in its *Bill of Rights* of 1960, and Trinidad and Tobago in its 1962 Constitution took, namely to set out the rights and freedoms simply and briefly, leaving the qualifications to them unstated.

32. We believe it is significant that almost all of the new Commonwealth states which have incorporated specific fundamental rights provisions in their constitutions have preferred to set out in detail the qualifications to those rights as has been done in the *Human Rights Ordinance* and as we propose should be done in respect of the constitutional provisions we have recommended.

33. The Constitution Commission of Trinidad and Tobago, which reported to the Governor General of that country in January 1974, after spending two and a half years reviewing the Trinidad Constitution, strongly recommended that the new constitution follow the pattern which we have proposed.

It said, at page 19 of its Report, that the effect of the unqualified statement of fundamental rights and freedoms set out in the 1962 Constitution was indeed to produce a brief and apparently simple statement of rights and freedoms. But the brevity and apparent simplicity were misleading. Many people were shocked to find out that rights and freedoms set out in absolute terms were subject to important limitations the extent of which was nowhere defined. This led some people to wonder, perhaps cynically, whether there was any meaning to these rights and freedoms at all.

34. 'We are convinced', the Commissioners said, 'that it is wrong to set out rights and freedoms in absolute terms, defining them as fundamental, and then to provide that parliament may pass laws expressly declaring that they shall have effect notwithstanding those rights and freedoms. The concept may well be seriously questioned if parliament finds it necessary or prudent to pass such laws with any frequency. Indeed, the position in our view is made worse when some of them, far from being restrictive, are plainly beneficial in that they make available social and economic advantages never before enjoyed'. The Commissioners concluded: 'we think, therefore, that it is better to define the rights and freedoms not in absolute but in qualified terms so that everyone should know and understand that they are limited in scope'.

35. Trinidad and Tobago having had experience with the short unqualified manner of stating fundamental rights and freedoms, and found it unsatisfactory, whilst many other States, including Papua New Guinea, have found the detailed form which we propose quite suitable, we believe our decision in this regard is well founded. It is also consistent with the approach we have adopted throughout our proposals, namely to try to make our recommendations as specific and clear as possible, so that the room for argument as to the meaning of particular provisions is minimised.

36. The history of Australia's Constitution shows how apparently simple, straightforward constitutional provisions can be the source of much litigation. We need only mention Section 92 which provides that 'Trade, commerce and intercourse between the States shall be absolutely free'. Over the seventy three years since Federation there have probably been more High Court cases concerning the meaning of this section than there have in relation to any other single section of the Constitution.

GENERALLY

Referred to

by Prentice Dep.C.J. in *Peter v South Pacific Brewery* [1976] PNGLR 537 at p.556;

by Prentice Dep.C.J. in *Reference No 1 of 1977* [1977] PNGLR 362 at p.376;

by Narakobi A.J. in *Tabo Sipo v Meli* (1980 Unreported) N240 at p.5.

(2) Every person has the right to freedom based on law, and accordingly has a legal right to do anything that —
(a) does not injure or interfere with the rights and freedoms of others; and
(b) is not prohibited by law,
and no person —
(c) is obliged to do anything that is not required by law; and
(d) may be prevented from doing anything that complies with the provisions of paragraphs (a) and (b).

GENERALLY

Referred to

by Quinlivan A.J. in *Marben v Gesa* (1981 Unreported) N314(M) at p.7;

by Pratt J. in *State v Kuya* (1983 Unreported) N431 at pp.8–12 (in relation to the effect of s. 32(2) on an accused person participating in an identification parade. In situations where an accused knows it is up to him or her whether or not to participate in a parade and participates, or feels obliged to participate but would rather not do so, and does not advise the police of his or her reluctance, then at a later time they may not rely on s.32(2) to challenge the admissibility of any evidence of the identification parade. His Honour was not prepared to rule that the police must advise an accused that he or she has an option to participate in an identification parade and that in the absence of such advice a court may refuse to admit such evidence).

(3) This section is not intended to reflect on the extra-legal existence, nature or effect of social, civic, family or religious obligations, or other obligations of an extra-legal nature, or to prevent such obligations being given effect to by law.

33. — OTHER RIGHTS AND FREEDOMS, ETC.

Nothing in this Division derogates the rights and freedoms of the individual under any other law and, in particular, an Organic Law or an Act of the Parliament may provide further guarantees of rights and freedoms and may further restrict the limitations that may be placed on, or on the exercise of, any right or freedom (including the limitations that may be imposed under Section 38 (*general qualifications on qualified rights*).

per Frost C.J.

This brings me to Pt III, Div 3 — Basic Rights. In Subdivision A — Introductory, s.33, there is included a provision for the future enactment of other guarantees of rights and freedoms and further restriction of the limitations to be placed on any right or freedom, thus taking full account of the need to allow for future programmes extending the present range of basic rights (Final Report of the C.P.C 5/1/4–5, par. 25).
Reference No 1 of 1977 [1977] PNGLR 362 at p.366.

34.— APPLICATION OF DIVISION 3.

Subject to this Constitution, each provision of this Division applies, as far as may be —

- (a) as between individuals as well as between governmental bodies and individuals; and
- (b) to and in relation to corporations and associations (other than governmental bodies) in the same way as it applies to and in relation to individuals,

except where, or to the extent that, the contrary intention appears in this Constitution.

Subdivision B. — Fundamental Rights.

35.— RIGHT TO LIFE.

(1) No person shall be deprived of his life intentionally except —

- (a) in execution of a sentence of a court following his conviction of an offence for which the penalty of death is prescribed by law; or
- (b) as the result of the use of force to such an extent as is reasonable in the circumstances of the case and is permitted by any other law —
  - (i) for the defence of any person from violence; or
  - (ii) in order to effect a lawful arrest or to prevent the escape of a person lawfully detained; or
  - (iii) for the purpose of suppressing a riot, an insurrection or a mutiny; or
  - (iv) in order to prevent him from committing an offence; or
  - (v) for the purpose of suppressing piracy or terrorism or similar acts; or
- (c) as the result of a lawful act of war.

C.P.C. Report Ch.5 Part 1 p.9

1. *THE RIGHT TO LIFE*

38. The first and most basic human right is that to life itself. Our recommended provision is almost identical with that in the *Human Rights Ordinance*. No-one is to be deprived of his life intentionally, except under the sentence of a court for an offence which carries the death penalty. Certain exceptions to this principle are provided for. If death results from defending a person from violence or in the course of carrying out a lawful arrest, or from preventing the escape of a person who has been lawfully imprisoned, the provision does not apply. Nor does it apply to a situation where death occurs in the course of suppressing a riot, or preventing a person from committing a criminal offence or if it is due to a lawful act of war. However, the person who caused the death could still be punished under the criminal law in any of these circumstances.

RECOMMENDATIONS [p.21]

Protection of right to life

1. (1) No person shall be deprived of his life intentionally, except in execution of a sentence of a court following his conviction of an offence for which the penalty of deprivation of life is prescribed by law.

(2) Without prejudice to any liability for a contravention of any other law with respect to the use of force in such cases as are hereinafter mentioned, a person shall not be regarded as having been deprived of his life in contravention of this section, if he dies as the result of the use of force to such an extent as is reasonably justifiable in the circumstances of the case:
(a) for the defence of any person from violence;
(b) in order to effect a lawful arrest or to prevent the escape of a person lawfully detained;
(c) for the purpose of suppressing a riot, insurrection or mutiny; or
(d) in order to prevent the commission by that person of a criminal offence;
or if he dies as a result of a lawful act of war.

CROSS REFERENCE

Universal Declaration of Human Rights: Article 3; *International Covenant on Civil and Political Rights:* Article 6; *European Convention on Human Rights:* Article 2; *Constitution of India:* Section 21.

GENERALLY

Referred to

by Frost C.J. in *Reference No 1 of 1977* [1977] PNGLR 362 at p.366 (this section not imposing a duty on any particular person);

by Narakobi A.J. in *The State v Wapulae and others* (1980 Unreported) N233 at pp.14, 18;

by Narakobi A.J. in *Tabo Sipo v Meli* (1980 Unreported) N240 at p.5;

by Kidu C.J. in *Avia Aihi v The State (No 3)* [1982] PNGLR 92 at p.99;

by Bredmeyer J. in *Aundak Kapil v The Independent State of Papua New Guinea* (1983 Unreported) N435 at pp.11, 16 (the custom of sanctioning non-payment of customary compensation by the killing or attempted killing of a member of the debtor clan offends against the Constitution and the general principles of humanity).

(2) Nothing in Subsection (1)(b) relieves any person from any liability at law in respect of the killing of another.

36. — FREEDOM FROM INHUMAN TREATMENT

(1) No person shall be submitted to torture (whether physical or mental), or to treatment or punishment that is cruel or otherwise inhuman, or is inconsistent with respect for the inherent dignity of the human person.

C.P.C. Report Ch.5 Part 1 p.9

4. *PROTECTION FROM INHUMAN TREATMENT*

44. We recommend that the section in the Ordinance which prohibits torture and treatment or punishment that is cruel, inhuman or degrading, be incorporated in this chapter of the Constitution. Some of our people are well aware of instances of torture and other inhuman treatment which has been meted out by successive colonial administrations, and in traditional society also. We firmly believe that these practices should be specifically outlawed in the Constitution.

RECOMENDATIONS [p.23]

Protection from inhuman treatment

4. No person shall be subjected to torture or to treatment or punishment that is cruel, inhuman or degrading.

CROSS REFERENCE

Universal Declaration of Human Rights: Article 5; *International Covenant on Civil and Political Rights:* Article 7; *Constitution of the United States of America* Am. VIII.

GENERALLY

Referred to

by Kidu C.J. in *Re Heni Pauta and Kenneth Susuve (No 1)* [1982] PNGLR 7 at p.14;

by Kidu C.J. in *Re Heni Pauta and Kenneth Susuve (No 2)* (1982 Unreported) N368 at p.9 (beating of persons on remand by prison warders);

by Bredmeyer J. in *Amaiu v Commissioner of Corrective Institutions and the State* (1983 Unreported) N417 at pp.19, 32–40 (in relation to the validity of a law which stipulated how a detainee could obtain release from the Maximum Security Block, B. Division, at Bomana Central Corrective Institution. There was evidence that conditions were such as to lead to serious mental illness. 'I consider for the law on the subject to be humane and not cruel, harsh or oppressive the medical officer should have some say in the release of a person from B Division'. His Honour found that the following matters which occurred in B Division cumulatively involved infringements of fundamental rights in that they were cruel, harsh, oppressive and did not respect the inherent dignity of the human person: the presence of a strict no-talking rule; detainees served food whilst holding night-soil bucket; showers turned off whilst detainees still had soap on their bodies; forcing detainees to get drinking water from Asian toilet; total ban on sports; total ban on visitors; warder swearing at detainees; detainees given 'joke' mohawk type haircuts; total ban on newspapers; total ban on radios; no lids to toilets at night; absence of string to tie up mosquito net. His Honour, however, noted that 'a detainee has no constitutional rights to visitors, to play sports, to have a newspaper, magazine and a radio . . . a prisoner has a constitutional right to be treated in a way which is not cruel, inhuman . . . and which respects the inherent dignity of the human person'. His Honour's finding, therefore, turns on the unintelligent exercise of the Commissioner's discretion in relation to depriving prisoners of *all* privileges.).

DEFINITION OF TORTURE

Comment

The *Declaration of the United Nations General Assembly* 9th December 1975 on the protection of all persons from torture and other cruel, inhuman or degrading treatment or punishment; Article 1 defines 'torture' as meaning:—

> any act by which severe pain or suffering, whether physical or mental, is intentionally inflicted by or at the instigation of a public official on a person for such purposes as obtaining from him or a third person information or confession, punishing him for an act he has committed or is suspected of having committed, or intimidating him or other

persons. It does not include pain or suffering arising from, inherent in or incidental to, lawful sanctions to the extent consistent with the Standard Minimum Rules for the Treatment of Prisoners. Torture constitutes an aggravated form of cruel, inhuman or degrading treatment or punishment.

(2) The killing of a person in circumstances in which Section 35(1)*(a)* (*right to life*) [applies] does not, of itself, contravene Subsection (1), although the manner or the circumstances of the killing may contravene it.

37. — PROTECTION OF THE LAW.

(1) Every person has the right to the full protection of the law, and the succeeding provisions of this section are intended to ensure that that right is fully available, especially to persons in custody or charged with offences.

C.P.C. Report Ch.5 Part 1 p.10

6. *PROTECTION OF LAW*

48. This is the equivalent of the 'due process' provision in the United States Constitution. We recommend the inclusion of this provision of the Ordinance subject to certain modifications in the light of the two and a half years' experience of the operation of the Ordinance which we have had.

49. In essence, this provision ensures that a person can only be convicted of an offence which is set out in a written law; that if charged with an offence he will be given a fair, public hearing within a reasonable time by an independent and impartial tribunal; that he will be able to obtain the assistance of an interpreter and, if this is practicable, the advice of and representation by a lawyer (including an officer of the Public Solicitor's office if the person concerned cannot afford to pay the fees of a private lawyer, and the case is one which justifies the granting of legal assistance by the Public Solicitor).

50. The recommendation specifically provides that a person should be presumed innocent until he is proved guilty according to law, that no person should be compelled to be a witness against himself, and that no person can be tried for an offence of which he has already been convicted, acquitted or pardoned. These provisions are already included in the Ordinance. However, we recommend a number of additional protections of the individual which we believe are important if Papua New Guinea's system for administering justice is to be one which in fact dispenses justice. These include safeguarding the right of every person convicted of an offence to an appeal to a higher court or tribunal; ensuring that people who are deprived of their liberty are treated with humanity; that juveniles who are under 16 years of age are not held in the same part of a corrective institution as are adult prisoners (some of whom would be hardened criminals); and that a person convicted of an offence should not be sent to an institution away from the area in which his relatives live, except for good reason.

RECOMMENDATIONS [p.23]

Provision to secure protection of law

6. (1) No person shall be convicted of an offence which is not defined by and the penalty [p.24] for which is not prescribed by written law.
Note: To the extent that inadequate provision at present exists in written law in relation to contempt of court the Committee recommends that early attention be given to rectifying this situation.

(2) A person charged with an offence shall, unless the charge is withdrawn, be afforded a fair hearing within a reasonable time, by an independent and impartial court established by law.

(3) A person charged with an offence —

(a) shall be presumed innocent until proved guilty according to law, *provided that* a law may place upon a person charged with an offence the burden of proving particular facts;

(b) shall be informed promptly in a language which he understands, and in detail of the nature of the offence with which he is charged;

(c) shall be given adequate time and facilities for the preparation of his defence;
(d) shall be permitted to have without payment the assistance of an interpreter if he cannot understand or speak the language used at the trial of the charge;
(e) shall be permitted to defend himself before the court in person or, at his own expense, by a legal representative of his own choice, or if he is a person in need, by the Public Solicitor, or another legal representative assigned to him in a case where in the opinion of the court the interests of justice so require, (and without payment by him in any such case if he does not, in the opinion of the Public Solicitor or of the court, as the case may be, have sufficient means to pay any part of the costs involved);
(f) shall be afforded facilities to examine in person or by his legal representative the witnesses called before the court by the prosecution, and to obtain the attendance and carry out the examination of witnesses and to testify before the court on his own behalf, on the same conditions as those applying to witnesses called by the prosecution, and, except with his own consent, the trial shall not take place in his absence unless he so conducts himself as to render the continuance of the proceedings in his presence impracticable and the court orders him to be removed and the trial to proceed in his absence, *provided that* provision may be made by law for a charge that a person has committed an offence the maximum penalty for which does not include imprisonment, (except in default of payment of a fine), to be heard summarily in his absence if it is established that the person has been duly served with a summons in respect of the alleged offence; and
(g) nothing in paragraph (f) above shall invalidate a law which imposes reasonable conditions which must be satisfied if witnesses called to testify on behalf of a person charged with an offence are to be paid their expenses out of public funds.

(4) No person shall be convicted of an offence on account of any act or omission that did not, at the time when it took place, constitute an offence, and no penalty shall be imposed for an offence that is more severe in degree or description than the maximum penalty that might have been imposed for the offence at the time when it was committed.

(5) No person who shows that he has been tried by a competent court for an offence and has been convicted or acquitted shall again be tried for that offence, or for any other offence of which he could have been convicted at the trial for that offence, except upon the order of a superior court made in the course of appeal, or review proceedings relating to the conviction or acquittal.

(6) No person shall be tried for an offence for which he has been pardoned.

(7) Every person who is tried for an offence shall have the right to give evidence at his trial.

(8) No person shall be compelled in the trial of an offence to be a witness against himself. [p.25]

(9) A determination of the existence or extent of a civil right or obligation shall not be made except by an independent and impartial court or other authority prescribed by law or agreed upon by the parties, and proceedings for such a determination shall be fairly heard within a reasonable time.

(10) Except with the agreement of the parties, or, by order of the court in the interests of national security, proceedings in any jurisdiction of a court and proceedings for the determination of the existence or extent of any civil right or obligation before any other authority, including the announcement of the decision of the court or other authority, shall be held in public.

(11) Nothing in clause (10) of this recommendation prevents a court or other authority from excluding from the hearing of the proceedings persons, other than the parties and their legal representatives, to such an extent as the court or other authority —
(a) is by law empowered to do and considers necessary or expedient in the interests of public welfare or in circumstances where publicity would prejudice the interests of justice, the welfare of minors or the protection of the private lives of persons concerned in the proceedings; or
(b) is by law empowered or required to do in the interests of defence, public safety or public order.

(12) In the event that the trial of a person in the National Court is not commenced within four months of the date on which he was committed for trial, a detailed report concerning the case shall be made to the Minister responsible for justice by the Chief Justice.

(13) Every person convicted of an offence (including an offence as a detainee) shall be entitled to have his conviction and sentence reviewed by a higher court or tribunal according to law.

(14) When a person has by a final decision been convicted of a criminal offence and subsequently his conviction has been reversed or he has been pardoned on the ground that a new or newly discovered fact shows conclusively that there has been a miscarriage of justice, the person who has suffered punishment as a result of such conviction shall be compensated according to law, unless it is proved that the non-disclosure of the unknown fact in time is wholly or partly attributable to him.

(15) No person shall be deprived by law of a right of appeal against his conviction or sentence by any court if at the commencement of that law, either the time for appealing against his conviction or sentence has not expired, or he has lodged an appeal which has not been determined.

(16) All persons deprived of their liberty shall be treated with humanity and with respect for the inherent dignity of the human person.

(17) Accused persons shall be segregated from convicted persons and shall be subject to separate treatment appropriate to their status as unconvicted persons.

(18) Accused persons who are under the age of 16 years shall be separated from other persons in custody.

(19) Offenders who are under the age of 16 years shall be segregated from other persons in custody and be accorded treatment appropriate to their age and legal status.

(20) An offender shall not be transferred to an area away from that in which his relatives reside except for good cause (particularly in terms of security). Where such a transfer is made, the reason for so doing shall be endorsed on the file of the offender.

(21) Notwithstanding the above clauses of this recommendation, the powers of, and procedure in 'village courts' as defined in the *Village Courts Act*, 1974, or in an Act establishing courts similar to those courts or amending the *Village Courts Act* 1974 shall not be invalid insofar as they are in accordance with the provisions of that Act or similar legislation and are not contrary to priciples of natural justice.

Note: (i) The constitutional provision which ensures the validity of the powers and procedures of village courts in accordance with clause (21) above [p.26] should allow for some flexibility in the powers and procedures of these courts conferred by legislation in the future, but should require that those powers and procedures accord with principles of natural justice.

(ii) In clause (20) of this recommendation an 'area' is intended to be defined broadly, and may icnlude a province in some circumstances.

CROSS REFERENCE

Universal Declaration of Human Rights: Article 6; *Constitution of the United States* Am. V.

AS TO APPLICATION OF U.S. ANALOGIES

per Frost C.J.

Further, I am quite clear on this, that having regard to the homegrown nature of the Constitution, no intention is shown that the notion of due process, developed in detail to meet United States conditions, should be introduced into the Papua New Guinea Constitution. It is true that the Committee refers to the 'due process' as provided in the United States Constitution, and states that s.37 — Protection of the Law — is 'the equivalent' of that provision. Report 5/1/10 para. 48. This indicates to me that s.37 deals with similar subject matter but not necessarily in the same terms.
Reference No 1 of 1977 [1977] PNGLR 362 at pp.372–3.

GENERALLY

per Bredmeyer J.

Section 37(1) means that if some aspect of the prisoners treatment in B Division is not regulated by a law then the section has been breached (at p.2).

I consider that there is a complete hierarchy of laws established and the orders and general instructions must comply with the Act and the Regulations. If the Commissioner issued an order which was inconsistent with the Act or Regulations, his order would be invalid. 'It would be invalid in the sense of ultra vires the Act and the Regulations but it would also be constitutionally invalid under s.37(1) (at p.6).

For the OIC of B Division to impose his own form of special punishment for misconduct in B Division, or for detainees who come to B Division with bad reputations as troublemakers elsewhere, is ultra vires the Act and the Regulations, which as I have said, only allow for three forms of punishment. It is also ultra vires s.37(1) of the Constitution because it is a form of punishment not regulated by law (at p.15).

In terms of s.37(1) of the Constitution there is no law governing how a person gets out of B Division. ...

This administrative practice of occasional review of some detainees is inadequate and contravenes s.37(1) of the Constitution. There must be a law providing for the periodic review of each prisoner's confinement in B Division (at p.19).
Amaiu v Commissioner of Corrective Institutions and the State (1983 Unreported) N417 at pp.2, 6, 15, 19; see also at p.51.

per Kidu C.J.

This right emphasises two things; firstly, no person in Papua New Guinea can be convicted of an offence which is not specifically prescribed by a written law; secondly, that for a person to be convicted of an offence the second criteria or condition is that the penalty for that offence must also be prescribed by a written law. Now s.19 of the *Local Courts Act* neither prescribed any offence nor does it prescribe a penalty of any offence. This reinforces my view that s.19 of the *Local Courts Act* is merely a restriction of jurisdiction provision and nothing else.
Kamda v Maima (1983 Unreported) N403(M) at pp.11–12.

Referred to

by Prentice Dep.C.J. in *Reference No 1 of 1977* [1977] PNGLR 362 at p.374;

by Prentice Dep.C.J. in *Government of PNG and Davis v Baker* [1977] PNGLR 386 at p.398;

by Pritchard J. in *Constitutional Reference No 1 of 1978* [1978] PNGLR 345 at p.383;

by Wilson J. in *Eiserman v Nanatsi* [1978] PNGLR 457, at p.458;

by Wilson J. in *Mathias Evertz v The State* [1979] PNGLR 174 at p.175 (in relation to an application for legal aid);

by Miles J. in *Ready Mix Concrete Pty Ltd v PNG* [1981] PNGLR 396 at p.410 (the issue of whether declaratory orders may be sought to determine whether a person is guilty of a criminal offence discussed);

by Bredmeyer J. in *Aundak Kupil v The Independent State of Papua New Guinea* (1983 Unreported) N435 at pp.11, 16 (the custom of sanctioning the non-payment of customary compensation by the killing or attempted killing of a member of a clan which owes compensation offends against the Constitution and the general principles of humanity).

(2) Except, subject to any Act of the Parliament to the contrary, in the case of the offence commonly known as contempt of court, nobody may be convicted of an offence that is not defined by, and the penalty for which is not prescribed by, a written law.

AS TO MEANING OF 'OFFENCE': WHETHER THE GROUP PENALTY PROVISONS OF THE INTER GROUP FIGHTING ACT PROVIDED FOR THE CONVICTION OF A PERSON FOR AN 'OFFENCE' NOT DEFINED BY LAW —

per Kidu C.J., Greville Smith and Andrew JJ.

The word 'offence' has no technical meaning in English Law ... nor in our view in the law of this country ...

In our opinion an 'offence' in the context of these provisions is any act or omission, whether by himself or someone else (we have in mind offences of vicarious liability) or any condition (we have in mind 'status' offences) in consequence of which a person may be, after proceedings and a finding against him, imprisoned, either immediately or upon non-payment of a fine or penalty. In our view such an adverse finding is a 'conviction', an adjudication that the 'offence' has been committed, and the body that makes that adjudication is a 'court', that is, a tribunal that exercises jurisdiction over persons by reason of the sanction of the law ...

In our view the combined effect of the provisions contained in ss.16, 17 and 20 of the Act is to provide for the conviction of a person for an offence that is not defined by a written law within the meaning of s.37(2) of the Constitution, without compliance with s.37(4)(b) of the Constitution, for an 'act' that did not at the time when it took place constitute an offence (being formulated in the magistrate's mind, during the hearing, whether expressed by him in some form or not, as the criterion upon which he should

decide under ss.16 and 17 whether a penalty should be imposed) and for the imprisonment of the person concerned, in the execution of a sentence of a court which is invalid by reason of the foregoing.
S.C.R. No 1 of 1981, Re Inter-Group Fighting Act 1977 [1981] PNGLR 151 at pp.153–156; see also Pratt J. at p.160 and Miles J. (dissenting) at pp.173, 175.

WHETHER THE CRIMINAL CODE'S PROVISION ON INCEST TAKES EFFECT IN DIFFERENT CUSTOMARY SOCIETIES AND VILLAGES, DIFFERENTIALLY.

per Prentice C.J.

... such an enquiry, or endless series of enquiries, would I think be contrary to the spirit and indeed the letter of s.37(2), of the Constitution that a person may not be convicted of an offence that is not *defined* by ... a written law. There would result anything but 'definition'. I do not conceive that 'crimes', as understood by the Constitution and the *Criminal Code*, can be constructed by the incrustation of unwritten (variable) custom upon the pillars of the Criminal Code.
Sanguma Wauta v The State [1978] PNGLR 326 at p.333.

AS TO SECTION 37(2) AND POWER TO IMPOSE PENALTIES UNDER THE CRIMINAL CODE.

per Kapi J.

To make an order by way of penalty contrary to the provisions of the Criminal Code would be contrary to s.37(2) of the Constitution ... To interpret s.155(4) of the Constitution in such a way as to give the court the power to determine penalty other than those provided would be in conflict with the provision of s.37(2) of the Constitution. I do not think the framers of our Constitution intended this.
S.C.R. No 2 of 1981, in the matter of s.19(1)(f) of the Criminal Code [1982] PNGLR 150 at p.173; see also Kidu C.J. at pp.153–155, Kearney Dep.C.J. at pp.158–159, Greville Smith J. at pp.162–167, Pratt J. at pp.176–177.

Referred to

by Kapi Dep.C.J. in *In the Matter of the State v Sunu and Ors* (1983 Unreported) SC269 at p.4.

GENERALLY

Referred to

by Greville Smith J. in *The State v John Rumet Kaputin (No 2)* [1979] PNGLR 544 at pp.546–547;

by Wilson J. in *Re Rooney (No 2)* [1979] PNGLR 448 at p.503;

by Quinlivan A.J. in *Kaupa v Police at Hutjena* (1981 Unreported) N320(M) at p.6;

by Quinlivan A.J. in *In Re Emmanual Lavaki* (1981 Unreported) N324(M) at p.1;

by Quinlivan A.J. in *Dai v Manda* (1981 Unreported) N324(M) at p.4;

by Kidu C.J. in *Kamda v Maima* (1982 Unreported) N403(M) at pp.11, 12.

(3) A person charged with an offence shall, unless the charge is withdrawn, be afforded a fair hearing within a reasonable time, by an independent and impartial court.

CROSS REFERENCE

Universal Declaration of Human Rights: Article 10; *European Convention on Human Rights*: Article 6(1); *Constitution of the United States* Am. VI.

DOES NOT APPLY TO DISCIPLINARY OFFENCES

Held

Not withstanding that s.85 of the *Public Service Act* deems the taking part, by a public servant, in a strike which interferes with the carrying on of any part of the public services to be 'an illegal action against the peace and good order of the country' and further provides for the summar dismissal of such strikers, s.85 creates a mere disciplinary offence.

Disciplinary offences are not criminal offences and there is no need in the case of disciplinary offences to afford a fair hearing within a reasonable time by an independent court because s.37(3) applies only to offences in the nature of criminal offences. To fall within this category an offence must

(a) be an act against the State and society;
(b) lead to criminal proceedings;
(c) result in a liability for penalty, if convicted, of a fine or imprisonment.

Public Employees Association of Papua New Guinea v Public Service Commission (1983 Unreported) SC253; see Kidu C.J. and Pratt J. at pp.2–6; see also Bredmeyer J. at pp.8–12 (adding the caveat that even if disciplinary offences could properly be characterised as criminal in nature s.159(3) of the Constitution expressly authorizes the Public Service Commission to hear and determine all such matters notwithstanding that the Commission may not be impartial).

Comment

The conclusion reached in the *Public Employees Case* (1983 Unreported) SC253 that s.37(3) guarantees a fair hearing only in proceedings in which conviction renders the defendant liable to a fine or imprisonment, is liable to produce inconsistent results. Traditionally, criminal punishments have also included corporal chastisement and even the death penalty. In other societies criminal wrongdoing can be punished by withdrawal of civil rights or banishment. To not afford the protection of s.37(3) to offences punishable by such measures is, in our opinion, an unjustifiably narrow construction.

Referred to

by Andrew J. in *Sudi Yaku v Commissioner for Police; ex parte The State* [1980] PNGLR 25 at p.32;

by Kapi J. in *P.E.A. and Liosi v Public Service Commission* (1983 Unreported) N405 at p.4 (disciplinary offences under the *Public Service Act* not affected by s.37(3)).

AS TO THE SEPARATION OF THE INVESTIGATORY AND JUDICIAL FUNCTION

per Pratt J.

> Once it is appreciated that what is being dealt with by the magistrate under s.17 is an offence under s.16, then in my view the essential weakness of the State's position is revealed. The opening words of s.17 read: 'Where in the opinion of *the* magistrate . . .'. It seems unarguable to me that the definite article appearing before 'magistrate' can only refer to the magistrate who conducts the enquiry under s.15 and comes to a view and thereby issues a notice to show cause under s.16. He is thus in the position of making enquiry, bringing the accusation and then acting as judge in the cause. Indeed because the allegation stems from his very own enquiries and because it is his own opinion which is being placed in question, the conclusion is irresistable that he is being directed to act as both accuser and judge. The prohibition against such a situation being permitted in the common

> law is one of the cornerstones of our criminal jurisprudence enshrined in s.37(3) of the Constitution which asserts that the person charged with an offence shall 'be afforded a fair hearing . . . by an independent and impartial court'. Having been charged with an offence, the individual is entitled to the protections set forth in s.37 of the Constitution and more particularly s.37(3). What has been omitted from the Act is a transitional section leading from the stage arrived at following investigation under s.15 plus the issue of a summons or notice to show cause under s.16, and the time when he is actually called upon in front of the magistrate to explain why a penalty should not be imposed. Before the provisions of s.17 can be successfully invoked, the person summonsed must be given the opportunity to hear the allegations made against him, not from the magistrate, but from those who can give first-hand knowledge which forms the basis of such allegations. He must be given the opportunity to question those persons and such proceedings must be taken before a magistrate who has not been involved in any way with the enquiry and formulation of the summons under ss.15 and 16 of the Act.
> *S.C.R. No 1 of 1981; Re Inter Group Fighting Act 1977* [1981] PNGLR 151 at pp.160, 161.

REQUIRES A FAIR HEARING OF ANY CHARGE LAID

Comment

It would appear from the dicta of Kearney Dep.C.J. in *S.C.R. No 1A of 1981; Re Motor Traffic Act* [1982] PNGLR 122 at pp.131–134, that s.37(3) requires a defendant to plead to an information, before a finding of guilty can be determined. It is only where a person consents to a trial proceeding in his absence, or where the offence has a maximum penalty which does not include imprisonment (except in default of a fine), that an information can be determined summarily in the absence of the defendant.
See also *Peter v South Pacific Brewery* [1976] PNGLR 537 and annotations under s.37(5).

AS TO WHETHER A PROPOSAL TO AMEND AN INDICTMENT COULD AMOUNT TO A REFUSAL TO AFFORD A FAIR HEARING WITHIN A REASONABLE TIME.

per Prentice Dep.C.J.

[referring to a similar provision, s.16(2) of the Pre-independence *Human Rights Act*.]

> The section is concerned with two elements, the securing of a fair hearing and the avoidance of delay therein. As I see it, the granting of an amendment would neither affect the fairness of the hearing of that charge being preferred, nor extend its determination by an unreasonable time.
> *The State v Tanedo* [1975] PNGLR 395 at p.416.

(*Note*: The *Human Rights Act* was repealed at Independence, however the Court expressed the opinion that its decision on s.16(2) of the Act would be adhered to on reference to the terms of s.37(3) of the Constitution).

AS TO SECTION 37(3) AND THE DISCRETION OF A PROSECUTOR TO WITHDRAW AN INDICTMENT AFTER TRIAL HAS COMMENCED.

Comment

In *The State v Sakai* (1982 unreported) N391 the prosecution ran into evidentiary problems and the State Prosecutor proposed to file a nolle prosequi. McDermott J. on the facts did not consider the crime had been properly investigated nor that the accused was in a double jeopardy situation. The nolle prosequi was accepted. McDermott J. cited Frost S.P.J. in *R v Arbia Tambule* [1974] PNGLR 250 at p.253, which was a case on s.16(2) of the *Human Rights Ordinance* — an equivalent provision to s.37(3).
In that case Frost S.P.J., as he then was, said (at p.253):

> But, in my opinion, if a charge is not withdrawn and the hearing commences, the accused's right to a fair hearing becomes the paramount consideration. Thus if a fair hearing requires

> upon the evidence a determination of the merits of the case in favour of the accused, that right cannot be defeated by permitting the Crown at that stage to withdraw the charge, and more particularly if the nature of the withdrawal does not prelude further proceedings. For the Crown to enter a nolle prosequl in circumstances similar to those of this case has been siad to be unfair .... The reason must be that it is tantamount to the accused being placed in double jeopardy which, of course, does not strictly attach until the final verdict.

Whether or not the court will accept a nolle prosequi after the trial has commenced — that is after arraignment — depends upon the issue of fairness to the accused. In *Sakai's* case, on the facts, it was decided that it was not unfair in the circumstances to accept the nolle prosequi.

AS TO WHETHER THE POSTPONEMENT OF TRIAL CAN AMOUNT TO A DENIAL OF THE RIGHT TO BE AFFORDED A FAIR HEARING WITHIN A REASONABLE TIME.

per O'Leary A.J.

> ... it is now some 14–16 months since the alleged offence was committed; 11 months since the accused was committed for trial; and six months since the case first came before the Court for trial. In those circumstances, I thought that to postpone the trial any longer would be ... to deny to the accused his right 'to be afforded a fair hearing within a reasonable time' as guaranteed by the Constitution. Although he has been on bail throughout, I thought the accused had already been under the cloud of the charge for far too long, and to allow that position to continue any longer would be to do a substantial injustice to him.
> *The State v Peter Painke (No 1)* [1976] PNGLR 210 at p.212.

ON THE RIGHT OF THE STATE TO PRESENT A FRESH INDICTMENT FOLLOWING A BREACH OF SECTION 37(3).

per O'Leary A.J.

> ... I did not think that at the time the nolle prosequi was presented in this case any question arose under s.37(3) of the Constitution. It may well be that the affording of a 'fair trial' to an accused person carries with it a right once the trial has commenced to have a verdict on the trial to the exclusion of any right in the State to withdraw or discontinue those proceedings. But I do not think the section confers any right on an accused person *before* the trial has commenced to demand a trial to the exclusion of the right of the State to withdraw the charge or not to proceed further with it. The section itself clearly contemplates a withdrawal of a charge and s.534 of the Code clearly confers on the Secretary for Law or a State Prosecutor the right to take steps not to proceed further with an indictment. I do not think s.37(3) of the Constitution in any way cuts down or delimits that right, at least up to the time that the trial commences.
> *The State v Peter Painke (No 1)* [1976] PNGLR 210 at p.214.

per Frost C.J.

[following the decision of O'Leary A.J. in *The State v Peter Painke (No 1)* (See above) a new indictment was presented before Frost C.J.]

> I am now to rule upon an application made by counsel for the accused that the accused be discharged. The application is made on two grounds. The first is based on the Constitution s.37(3) which, so far as is relevant, provides that a person charged with an offence shall, unless the charge is withdrawn, be afforded a fair hearing within a reasonable time. The second ground is that in all the circumstances the presentment of the indictment is an abuse of the process of the Court.
>
> The history of the case is that on 27th June, 1975 the accused was committed for trial on a charge of stealing as a public servant, alleged to have been committed between 30th January and 3rd March, 1975. That charge was not disposed of until 24th May, 1976 when the indictment was called on before O'Leary A.J. In the interval the indictment had been presented to the National Court, but at three successive sittings adjournments had been granted on the application of the State prosecutor. Another such application was then

made before O'Leary A.J. and was refused. The view taken by the learned judge was that because of the long delays, before and after committal, to postpone the trial any longer would be a breach of the accused's rights under s.37(3). Even although he had been on bail throughout, his Honour said 'the accused had already had already been under the cloud of the charge for far too long, and to allow that position to continue any longer would be to do a substantial injustice to him.' ... The State Prosecutor then proposed to present a nolle prosequi under the Criminal Code s.539. This course was objected to by counsel for the accused on the ground that to present a nolle prosequi would be a abuse of the process of the Court, but the learned judge held that no impropriety was involved at that stage. The view taken by His Honour was that the question whether there was any abuse of the process of the Court could only be determined if and when any further indictment was presented, and depended upon a consideration of the precise terms of that indictment. On that charge the accused was accordingly discharged.

It will be noted that under the present indictment the different offence of fraudulent false accounting is charged. Almost a year has elapsed since the last hearing. It is now more than one year and ten months from the date of committal, a very long delay having regard to the standard adopted under the Constitution, s.37(4), of trials being heard within 4 months of committal. .....

In my opinion the application is soundly based on the second ground and I would uphold it and stay the indictment.

So far as the argument upon s.37(3) is concerned, what did emerge is some possible difficulty in its application. The section is wide enough to cover offences triable summarily and also upon indictment after committal. But what if the offence stated in a long-standing charge is amended in some material particular immediately before the trial, or a different offence substituted? Counsel for the accused argued that that section refers to a hearing consequent upon the original charge, presumably irrespective of any amendment or change in the offence, an interpretation analogous to the effect of the Constitution, s.37(14). That section is expressed in the broad terms that a detailed report is required to be made in the event merely that the trial of a person is not commenced within four months of committal. The interpretation however submitted by the Public Prosecutor was that, on the plain meaning of the section the rights thereby conferred are to be restricted to an operation in respect of a specific charge. These arguments can be left until the matter is necessary for decision.

The State v Peter Painke (No 2) [1977] PNGLR 141 at pp.143–148.

AS TO INCOMPETENT COUNSEL

Comment

One interesting question not yet addressed by a Papua New Guinean court is whether the incompetence of counsel can amount to a breach of the Constitution's guarantee of a fair trial. Section 37(3) requires an accused to be accorded a fair hearing. Some support for the argument that a fair trial cannot be had if counsel is manifestly incompetent can be read into the judgment of the Supreme Court in *Busina Tabe v The State* (1983 Unreported) SC260. In that case a verdict was set aside after the Supreme Court heard evidence that a pair of inexperienced prosecution and defence lawyers had each failed to place before the trial judge cogent and available evidence probative of the innocence of the accused.

Although the Court did not take the opportunity to refer to the Constitution it is submitted that s.37(3) provides justification for the decision. It is submitted that s.37(3) authorises the National and Supreme Courts to declare to be a nullity any trial in which it can be shown that counsels' incompetence has caused real detriment to the defendant's chances of aquittal. Of course, as losing clients often unfairly blame their lawyers for their conviction, courts should be slow to accept this form of submission, but, in principle, it seems only fair that a person whose trial has miscarried because of the negligence of counsel should at least be entitled to a fair retrial.

GENERALLY

Referred to

by Frost C.J. (dissenting) in *Nai'u Limagwe and ors v The State* [1976] PNGLR 382 at p.395;

by Kearney J. in *The State v Allan Woila (No 2)* [1978] PNGLR 113 at p.115 (to place an accused person in the dock is not in accord with the principle that he is presumed innocent until he is proved guilty);

by Andrew J. in *The State v Atu Kote* [1978] PNGLR 212 at p.213 (application for speedy trial where accused pleaded guilty and prosecution sought to call him to give evidence on the trial of a co-accused which trial prosecution sought to stand-over);

by Greville Smith J. in *Re s.42 of the Constitution and Jacob Hendrick Prai* [1979] PNGLR 42 at pp.45, 46 (mentioned in relation to *The State v Peter Painke (No 2)* [1977] PNGLR 141 at p.145);

by Wilson J. in *Mathias Evertz v The State* [1979] PNGLR 174 at p.175 (in relation to an application for legal aid);

by Kearney J. in *Re Rooney (No 1)* [1979] PNGLR 403 at p.413;

by Kearney J. in *The State v John Rumet Kaputin* [1979] PNGLR 532 at p.535;

by Kearney J. in *S.C.R. No 1 of 1981; Re Inter-Group Fighting Act 1977* [1981] PNGLR 151 at p.154;

by Quinlivan A.J. in *Kaupa v Police at Hutjena* (1981 Unreported) N320(M) at pp.3, 5, 6;

by Quinlivan A.J. in *Dai v Manda* (1981 Unreported) N342(M) at p.4;

by Pratt J. (Kapi Dep.C.J. and Bredmeyer J. concurring) in *The State v The Principal Magistrate District Court Port Moresby; Ex parte the Public Prosecutor* (1983 Unreported) SC243 at p.19.

(4) A person charged with an offence —
(a) shall be presumed innocent until proved guilty according to law, but a law may place upon a person charged with an offence the burden of proving particular facts which are, or would with the exercise of reasonable care be, peculiarly within his knowledge; and

CROSS REFERENCE

Universal Declaration of Human Rights: Article 11(1); *International Covenant on Civil and Political Rights* 1966: Article 14.2; *European Convention on Human Rights*: Article 6(2)(3); *Constitution of the United States of America* Am. VI.

OVERVIEW

Comment

In a paper in the 1984 *Melanesian Law Journal* Mr John Kaburise of the Faculty of Law, University of Papua New Guinea made the following observations on s.37(4)(a) of the Constitution:

> Eight judges have had occasion in four different references to the Supreme Court between 1978 and 1982, to grapple with the meaning and scope of s.37(4)(a) of the Papua New Guinea Constitution, in particular with the effect of the proviso thereto. The result unfortunately is a maze of confusing expositions of the meaning of the section. I have endeavoured to isolate these and the outcome is that the Supreme Court has given three (3) differing interpretations of the section.

Briefly stated, the three approaches are:

(1) Saldhana J.'s view (expressed in *Constitutional Reference No. 3 of 1978; Re Inter-Group Fighting Act 1977* [1978] PNGLR 421) that *no matter*, whether a constituent element of the offence or in the nature of a defence thereto, should be required to be proved by the accused unless such matter is a 'fact which (is), or would with the exercise of reasonable care be, peculiarly within (the accused's) knowledge';

(2) Chief Justice Prentice's view (first outlined in *Constitutional Reference No. 3 of 1978*, and given a clearer exposition by Greville-Smith J. in *S.C.R. No. 1 of 1978; Re s.22A(b) of Police Offences Act (Papua)* [1981] PNGLR 28), that the proviso only prevents Parliament from calling upon the accused person to prove a constituent element of any offence unless the facts relating to that element are, or within such accused person's knowledge. According to this view, other matters which do not form constituent elements of an offence fall outside the scope of the proviso to s.37(4)(a) of the Constitution, and are governed *exclusively* by English common law by operation of Sch. 2.2 of the Papua New Guinea Constitution;

(3) Miles J.'s view, that only the constituent ingredients of offences are governed by the proviso to s.37(4)(a), with the result that any other matters that do not involve proof of constituent elements of an offence fall outside the scope of the constitutional provision. With regards to matters falling outside the scope of the proviso to s.37(4)(a), this view holds that Parliament's competence to place the burden of proof on an accused person is not limited to the exceptions recognized by English common law. Indeed Kapi J. gave an indication of the breadth of this view when he said:

> The expression 'according to law' in s.37(4)(a) ... simply means 'according to the laws of Papua New Guinea'. One has to go to these laws, which are set out under s.9 of the Constitution. (*S.C.R. 1A of 1981; Re Motor Traffic Act* [1982] PNGLR 122 at p.138)

... It will be noticed that according to this view, the accused is exposed to greater incidence of the burden of proof than under either of the other two views outlined above.

In his paper Mr Kaburise goes on to argue that in his opinion the interpretation of Saldanha J. best accords with the intention of the framers of the Constitution. We agree with this broad conclusion but note that in our opinion Prentice C.J.'s views are in fact closer to those of Miles J. than to those of Greville Smith J.

HISTORY

per Miles J.

The history of s.37(4)(a) of the Constitution was traced by Saldhana J. in *Constitutional Reference No 3 of 1978; Re Inter-Group Fighting Act 1977* [1978] PNGLR 421 at p.428 in the following passage:

> The history of s.37(4)(a) of the Constitution is as follows. It started with the *Human Rights Act*, 1971, s.16(3)(a) of which provided that:
>
> '16(3) A person charged with an offence —
>
> (a) shall be presumed innocent until proved guilty according to law.'
>
> The Final Report of the Constitutional Planning Commitee Pt. 1 at p.5/1/24 par. 6(3)(a) recommended that the following provision should be incorporated in the Constitution, that:
>
> '6(3) A person charged with an offence —
>
> (a) shall be presumed innocent until proved guilty according to law, provided that a law may place upon a person charged with an offence the burden of proving particular facts.'
>
> The provision ultimately incorporated in s.37(4)(a) of the Constitution is in the following terms:
>
> '37(4) A person charged with an offence —
>
> (a) shall be presumed innocent until proved guilty according to law but a law may place upon a person charged with an offence the burden of proving

particular facts which are, or would with the exercise of reasonable care be, peculiarly within his knowledge.'

It will be noticed how the *Human Rights Act* provided for just the presumption of innocence, that the Constitutional Planning Committee elaborated on that by recommending that a proviso should be added to the effect that the burden of proving particular facts should be placed on the accused and s.37(4)(a) of the Constitution narrowed down the proviso by allowing this burden to be placed upon the accused only in cases where particular facts were peculiarly within his knowledge. It is necessary therefore to be strict in the interpretation of s.37(4)(a) of the Constitution and particularly careful not to assume that there are facts peculiarly within the knowledge of the accused when this may not be so.

(*Note*: the other judges of the Court, Prentice C.J. and Andrew J., did not appear to disagree with this analysis of the background and effect of s.37(4)(a).)
S.C.R. No 1 of 1980; Re s.22A(b) of Police Offences Act (Papua) [1981] PNGLR 28 at pp.41–42.

JUDGES REPORT 1979

Comment

The Special Report on the Developing State of Lawlessness by the Judges to the Parliament of Papua New Guinea, July 1979, at para. 4 stated in relation to s.37(4)(a):—

Parliament may consider that new, or more drastic laws are necessary. If this be so, we would respectfully draw its attention to the form in which s.37(4)(a) of the Constitution was recommended to the Constituent Assembly by the C.P.C., which form having been altered to the existing form resulted in a ruling of invalidity of s.11 of the *Tribal Fighting Act* (an Act which looked as though it was being very effective — because of its sanctions). Section 37(4)(a) as recommended by the C.P.C originally read:

> Shall be presumed innocent until proved guilty according to law, provided that a law may place upon a person charged with an offence the burden of proving particular facts.

It will be noted that as ultimately adopted, that particular section of the Constitution went on to include the further words 'which are, or would with the exercise of reasonable care be, peculiarly within his knowledge.'

During 1979 the Government drafted an amending bill to put into effect the suggestion of the Judges. The bill lapsed on the floor of Parliament for want of quorum.

'CHARGED'

Comment

Although not defined in the Constitution the term 'charge' appears in the *Arrest Act* s.18. In that context a 'charge' is a formal allegation made, generally, by the police alleging that an offence has been committed. Again, generally, a 'charge' is laid following a person being taken into custody and the entry of the name of the person, and the offence alleged into a permenant registrar of arrests. Support for this view is found in the 1964 Judges Rules, Rule 3, and in the Administrative Directions published with those rules.

In the *Practice Note* [1964] 1 All E.R. 237 at p.240 *Administrative Directions on Interrogations and the Taking of Statements*, Administrative Direction 6 states:—

As soon as a charge is accepted by the appropriate police office the accused person should be given a written notice containing a copy of the entry in the charge sheet or book, giving particulars of the offence with which he is charged.

See also Kidu C.J. in *S.C.R. No 1 of 1981; Re Inter-Group Fighting Act 1977* [1981] PNGLR 151 at pp.153–4.

PRESUMPTION OF INNOCENCE

Note: for further annotations concerning the term 'offence' see under s.37(3).

Referred to

by Kidu C.J., Greville Smith and Andrew JJ. in *S.C.R. No 1 of 1981; Re Inter-Group Fighting Act 1977* [1981] PNGLR 151 at pp.153, 154;

by Kapi Dep.C.J. in *P.E.A. and Liosi v P.S.C.* (1983 Unreported) N405 at p.3.

per Wilson J.

One of the fundamental rights so guaranteed is the right of every person to the full protection of the law (s.37). Under s.37(4)(a) any person (whether he be a national of Papua New Guinea or not) when charged in Papua New Guinea with an offence 'shall be presumed innocent until proved guilty according to law'. It will be seen therefore that, at Independence, Papua New Guinea had enshrined into its Constitution this basic presumption, which, incidentally, is at the foundation of those legal systems that are based on the notion of British justice.
Eiserman v Nanatsi (1978) PNGLR 457 at p.458.

per Miles J.

The presumption of innocence is not confined to legal systems derived from the English model. In recent decades there have been efforts to have it incorporated into the international law of mankind. Provisions aimed at guaranteeing the presumption of innocence first appeared in the *Universal Declaration of Human Rights* adopted by the United Nations on 10th December, 1948, and were expressed in the following terms:

'Article 11.

1. Everyone charged with a penal offence has the right to be presumed innocent until proved guilty according to law in a public trial at which he has had all the guarantees necessary for his defence.'

In 1966 there was a further development in this area when the *International Covenant on Civil and Political Rights* was opened for signature. Nations who become signatories to the Covenant undertake to ratify it and to give effect to it within their respective domestic legal systems. Article 14.2 of the Covenant is in terms practically identical to those of art. 11(1) of the *Universal Declaration of Human Rights* set out above.

In 1971 when the then Territory of Papua and New Guinea was not self-governing, and when the metropolitan power. Australia, was not a signatory to the International Covenant, the Legislative Assembly passed the then *Human Rights Ordinance*. It is said that this was in response to government plans to enact laws to restrict the right of free speech and assembly. The provisions of s.16(3)(a) of the Ordinance of followed those of art. 14.2 of the International Covenant. Then upon Independence, as has already been pointed out, the Constitution went further, to secure in s.37(4)(a) a constitutional guarantee of the right therein provided for, namely the presumption of innocence until proven guilty according to law, I understand that the Independent State of Papua New Guinea has not become a signatory to the *International Covenant on Civil and Political Rights*, and perhaps that would serve little purpose as many of the rights recognized by the International Covenant appear to be guaranteed by the Constitution. The constitutional guarantee of the presumption of innocence however is expressed to be subject to a proviso, which is absent from the International Covenant.
S.C.R. No 1 of 1980; Re s.22A(b) of Police Offences Act (Papua) [1981] PNGLR 28 at pp.43–44; but see also Greville Smith J. at pp.38–39 (below).

per Greville Smith J.

In my opinion, as a result of s.37(4)(a) the law in Papua New Guinea relating to the proof of guilt in criminal cases is that the onus is on the prosecution to prove each element of the offence charged beyond reasonable doubt, subject to the following exceptions; namely:

'(a) In the case of a defence of insanity, where there is a presumption of sound mind until the contrary is proved.

(b) Where an enactment prohibits the doing of an act save in specified circumstances, or by persons of specified classes, or with special qualification or with the licence or persuasion of specified authorities, then oncethe prosecutor has proved beyond reasonable doubt the doing of the act the burden is on the person charged to bring himself within the exception or proviso, that is, to prove that he was entitled to do the prohibited act, independently of whether the facts he must prov e to do so are, or would with the exercise of reasonable care be, peculiarly within his knowledge.

(c) In the case of an enactment which places upon the person charged the burden of providing particular facts which are, or would with the exercise of reasonable care be, peculiarly within his knowledge.'

In the case of each exception the burden that rests on the accused is the legal, or as it is sometimes called the persuasive burden, not an evidentiary burden, and it is a burden of satisfying the court on a balance of probabilities, of persuading the court, on the probabilities, of the matter alleged by way of defence.
S.C.R. No 1 of 1980; Re s.22A(b) of Police Offences Act (Papua) [1981] PNGLR 28 at pp.38–39; but see also Miles J. at pp.43–44 (above).

per Frost C.J. (dissenting)

. . . the effect of a plea of not guilty has under the [Criminal] Code the same breadth of meaning as at common law, which is to render it 'incumbent upon the prosecution to prove every fact and circumstance constituting the offence charged in the indictment'. . . . This rule is enshrined in its full force in the Constitution which preserves as a fundamental right that a person shall be presumed innocent until proved guilty, s.37(4)(a).
Nai'u Limagwe and Others v The State [1976] PNGLR 382 at p.391.

Held

The right to the presumption of innocence in s.37(4)(a) casts upon the prosecution the burden of proving a number of essential ingredients. Absence of proof of an essential ingredient of an offence cannot be cured by an admission by the accused, where the ingredient is not an act of, or within the knowledge of the accused. *Surujpaul v R* (1958) 3 ALL ER 300 followed and applied.
Eiserman v Nanatsi [1978] PNGLR 457; see Wilson J. at pp.458, 459.

per Kearney Dep.C.J.

The 'no case' practice serves a separate and essential purpose: it is a procedural reinforcement to the presumption of innocence in the Constitution s.37(4)(a), and to the accused's right to silence in Constitution s.37(10). These citizens rights entail that the State must make out its case by the evidence *it* adduces; it cannot rely on making good any defects in its own case, by cross-examination of the accused or his witnesses.
The State v Kuriday (1981 Unreported) N300 at p.2.

Referred to

by Kidu C.J. in *In the Matter of the State v Pep* (1983 Unreported) SC261 at p.18 (trial judge should not consider whether or not the State has discharged its onus of proving its case beyond reasonable doubt until the end of the proceedings); see also Pratt J. at p.4;

by Kidu C.J. in *The State v Puri and Maip* (1983 Unreported) N400 at pp.11, 12 (following *State v Pep* (above));

by Kidu C.J. in *Kamda v Maima* (1983 Unreported) N403(M) at p.3.

per Kidu C.J.

A person charged with an offence is guaranteed two rights by s.37(4)(a): first, the right to be presumed innocent of the charge . . .
S.C.R. No 1A of 1981; Re Motor Traffic Act [1982] PNGLR 122 at p.127.

UNTIL PROVED GUILTY

per Greville Smith J.

The effect of the provisions contained in s.19AC(2)(iii) of the *Motor Traffic Act*, 138A(1)(b) of the *District Courts Act* and s.138A(1)(c) of the *Local Courts Act* would be to dispense with the proof of guilt required by the provisions of s.37(4)(a) of the Constitution and such provisions are therefore in my view unconstitutional and nullities.
S.C.R. No 1A of 1981; Re Motor Traffic Act [1982] PNGLR 122 at p.137; see also Kidu C.J. at p.127.

per Kidu C.J.

. . . a person charged with an offence is guaranteed two rights by s.37(4)(a): first the right to be presumed innocent of the charge; and second, the right to have the charge against him proved according to law.
S.C.R. No 1A of 1981; Re Motor Traffic Act [1982] PNGLR 122 at p.127; see also Greville Smith J. at p.137.

ACCORDING TO LAW

per Kearney Dep.C.J.

In my opinion the phrase 'according to law' refers to the whole body of law in the country, as exhaustively defined in the *Constitution*, s.9; it includes both the statute law and the underlying law.
S.C.R. No 2 of 1980; Re s.14(2) of the Summary Offences Act [1981] PNGLR 50 at p.53; Andrew and Miles JJ. agreeing.

AS TO STANDARD OF PROOF: A MATTER OF UNDERLYING LAW OR DERIVED FROM SECTION 37(4)(a)

per Greville Smith J.

In my opinion, as a result of s.37(4)(a) the law in Papua New Guinea relating to the proof of guilt in criminal cases is that the onus is on the prosecution to prove each element of the offence charged beyond reasonable doubt, . . . [following an examination of English case-law seeking to found s.37(4)(a) in *Woolmington's Case* and in *Turner* (1816) 5 M & S 206].
S.C.R. No 1 of 1980; Re s. 22A(b) of the Police Offences Act (Papua) [1981] PNGLR 28 at pp.38–9.

per Kidu C.J.

The proviso to s.37(4)(a) is not relevant in this Reference. However, if it were, I would hold that it would make no difference to my view that a person charged with an offence is guaranteed two rights by s.37(4)(a): first, the right to be presumed innocent of the charge; and second, the right to have the charge against him proved according to law.
S.C.R. No 1A of 1981; Re Motor Traffic Act [1982] PNGLR 122 at p.127; see also Greville Smith J. at pp.136–138; but see also Kearney Dep.C.J. at p.136 (below), Kapi J. at pp.138, 139 (below), Andrew J. at p.138.

per Kearney Dep.C.J.

With great respect, I do not agree with the effect of s.37(4)(a) as set out by Greville Smith J. in *S.C.R. No 1 of 1980* [1981] PNGLR 28 quoted by the Chief Justice at page 127. Had the Constitution intended directly to entrench by s.37(4)(a) the concept of presumption of innocence as it stood in the common law of England on 16th September 1975, it surely would have clearly so stated. The term 'law' is defined in Constitution Sch. 1.2(1) as *including* the underlying law; and both Andrew and Miles JJ. in *S.C.R. No 1 of 1980* (supra) construed the word 'law' in s.37(4)(a) as encompassing all the laws of the

country including the underlying law, and thus do not accept the approach of Greville Smith J. For myself, I adhere to the meaning of the phrase 'according to law' I set out in *S.C.R. No. 2 of 1980; Re s.14(2) of the Offences Act* [1981] PNGLR 50, quoted by the Chief Justice at p.128. In that judgment, both Andrew and Miles JJ. appear also to adopt that view of s.37(4)(a). It seems to me, with respect, that it is quite competent for Parliament to make laws on matters which are relevant to proof of guilt, such as the mode and standard of proof in criminal cases, provided those laws fall within its law-making competence and do not invade matters exclusively within the competence of other arms or organs of government, and are otherwise consonant with the Constitution. I might add that as a result of countless decisions over the last 6 years, I think it is now clearly part of the underlying law of this country, appropriate to its circumstances, that guilt must be proved beyond reasonable doubt. The underlying law is shaped as much by the way it is practised as by judical dicta.
S.C.R. No 1A of 1981; Re Motor Traffic Act [1982] PNGLR 122 at p.136; see also Kapi J. at pp.138, 139 (below), Andrew J. at p.138; but see also Kidu C.J. at p.127 (above), Greville Smith J. at pp.136–138.

per Kapi J.

In relation to the question of the proper effect of the adaptation of the common law principle of presumption of innocence through s.37(4)(a) of the Constitution, I adopt the reasoning of the Deputy Chief Justice. The expression 'according to law' in s.37(4)(a) does not adopt any particular principle of law. it simply means 'according to the laws of Papua New Guinea'. One has to go to these laws, which are set out under s.9 of the Constitution. The relevant provision in this case in s.9(f) — *underlying law*. Strictly speaking, underlying law is different from the common law of England. Common law embodies the principles which apply in England. Underlying law embodies the principles established under Sch.2 of the Constitution; so it includes adoption of custom under Sch.2.1, adoption of common law principles under Sch.2.2, creation of new principles under Sch.2.3 and the development of these principles under Sch.2.4. See also my judgment in *S.C.R. No. 4 of 1980; Re petition of M.T. Somare* [1981] PNGLR 265 at p.284, the first Vanuatu judgement. Section 9(f) and s.37(4)(a) (in this particular context) speak of underlying law as processed and established under Sch.2 of the Constitution and not of the raw principles of the common law of England.

The proper view is that the presumption of innocence is applied in Papua New Guinea as a part of the underlying law through Sch.2.2 of the Constitution. The principle is therefore subject to:

(a) any change by the Constitution or an Act of the Parliament in the future; and
(b) change in the circumstances of the country which may cause the principle to be altered from time to time by a process of the development of the underlying law according to Sch.2.4.

S.C.R. No 1A of 1981: Re Motor Traffic Act [1982] PNGLR 122 at pp.138, 139; see also Kearney Dep.C.J. at p.128 (above), Andrew J. at p.138; but see Kidu C.J. at p.127 (above), Greville Smith J. at pp.136–138.

AS TO SECTION 37(4)(a) AND SECTION 11(3) OF THE INTER-GROUP FIGHTING ACT AND AS TO THE EXPRESSION 'PECULIARLY WITHIN HIS KNOWLEDGE'

Note: Section 11(3) *Inter-Group Fighting Act* provided:
A person charged with an offence against this section is guilty of that offence unless he proves to the satisfaction of the court, that he did not take part in the actual fighting.

per Saldanha J.

I cannot see how the fact whether an accused person, charged with taking part in an inter-group fight, did or did not take part in the actual fighting is a fact peculiarly within his knowledge. Dozens if not hundreds of warriors on his side would know whether or not he had been actually fighting. I agree that it might be difficult to prove that he had been actually fighting. But in order to secure a conviction it is not necessary to prove that a person had been actually fighting. It is all the more odd therefore that an accused person by proving that he did not take part in the actual fighting should be able to secure an acquittal.

In my view s.11(3) is invalid because it places upon an accused person the onus of

proving that he did not take part in the actual fighting when that particular fact is not peculiarly within his knowledge.
Constitutional Reference No 3 of 1978; Re Inter-Group Fighting Act 1977 [1978] PNGLR 421 at p.431; see also Andrew J. at p.435 (below) and Prentice C.J. (dissenting) at pp.426, 427 (below).

per Andrew J.

In my opinion the situation of taking part in the actual fighting of an inter-group fight is not a matter peculiarly within a defendant's knowledge. It is true that there are great difficulties of proof in identifying who actually took part in the fighting and a defendant may well know what part he took but this does not, to my mind, mean that it is peculiarly within his knowledge. A tribal fight takes place in the open; those who are charged are normally arrested in groups and the basis of the arrest is often evidence in the form of weapons they are carrying and/or evidence of participation from the police. These are general matters which in the normal course will subsequently have to be proved in court but I cannot see that they are matters *peculiarly* within the defendant's knowledge. One's partaking in the fight would in the normal course be a matter known to many people, including friend, foe and others.

In my view one guide in attempting to understand the intention of s.37(4)(a) of the Constitution in introducing the common law concept of peculiar knowledge is the history of the concept and its present meaning in the common law. I take its present meaning to be that outlined in *R. v Edwards* [1974] 2 All E.R. 1085 that it does not furnish any working rule. The phrase has, however, been connected with and limited to offences arising under enactments which prohibit the doing of an act save in specified circumstances such as in the case of *R. v Oliver* [1944] K.B. 68. Thus it has found some usage in the common law in the areas of certificates, prescriptions and licences.

The narrowness of its application in the past in the common law must be construed in the context of the whole of s.37(4)(a). The importance of the section is seen by the fact that it is contained in Division 3 (Basic Rights) of the Constitution and in Sub-division B thereof (Fundamental Rights). The presumption of innocence until proof of guilt according to law is therefore a basic and fundamental right and the proviso in the remainder of the section shows that this right may only be varied in exceptional circumstances.
Constitutional Reference No 3 of 1978; Re Inter-Group Fighting Act 1977 [1978] PNGLR 421 at p.435; see also Saldanha J. at p.431 (above) and Prentice C.J. (dissenting) at pp.426, 427 (below).

per Prentice C.J. (dissenting)

From our own knowledge, the facts in a tribal fight in which many hundreds may be involved on each side, moving across a wide and perhaps lengthy stretch of country, must be multifarious and confused. It is well known that with the object of not being identified by photography and singled out for prosecution, for example, tribal fighters are wearing balaclavas and other clothing to disguise themselves. It seems to me that the question of whether a particular villager *took part in the actual fighting* in a tribal encounter, instead of merely being present through being caught up innocently when a fight swept past where he was standing, or being present in the positive attempt to restrain or stop a fight in his capacity as a leader, peace officer or village court magistrate; would frequently be a matter both difficult of ascertainment by outsiders on the one hand, and distinctively, specially, particularly, (peculiarly), within *his* own knowledge on the other.

I am of the opinion that s.11(3) of the *Inter-Group Fighting Act* has done no more than take advantage of the exception allowed for in s.37(4)(a) of the Constitution, and has legitimately placed the burden of proving exculpatory matter peculiarly within his own knowledge, upon the accused. The prosecution must prove (a) a declaration that the provisions of the Act apply to the area at the particular time, (b) the existence of an unlawful assembly (s.10(1)), (c) that a member of the unlawful assembly assaulted or attempted to assault or commenced to fight with a member of another group of persons, (d) that the defendant took part in the *unlawful assembly*. If the defendant proves that he took no part in the *actual fighting*, his culpability under s.11 is excluded though he may remain liable to conviction under s.10 and to sentence for a lesser penalty. *Constitutional Reference No 3 of 1978; Re Inter-Group Fighting Act 1977* [1978] PNGLR 421 at pp.426,427; but see Saldanha J. at p.431 (above) and Andrew J. at p.435 (above).

SECTION 37(4)(a) AND SECTION 22A(b) POLICE OFFENCES ACT (PAPUA)

Note: Section 22A of the *Police Offences Act* 1912 (Papua) provided;

22A. A person who obtains any chattel, money or valuable security by passing a cheque which is not paid on presentation, or who passes any such cheque in payment or part-payment for services rendered or to be rendered to himself or to any other person, or partly in such payment or part-payment and partly for some other purpose, shall, notwithstanding that there may have been some funds to the credit of the account on which the cheque was drawn at the time it was passed, be guilty of an offence, unless he proves —

(a) that he had reasonable grounds for believing that the cheque would be paid in full on presentation; and

(b) that he had no intent to defraud.

Penalty: Imprisonment for twelve months.

per Miles J., (Andrew J. concurring)

It is sufficient for the purpose of answering the question in the reference to decide that a person charged under s.22A of the *Police Offences Act (Papua)* 1912 (repealed) who wishes to raise the particular defence available under that section caries the burden of proving a particular fact, namely the lack of intention to defraud, which fact is peculiarly within the knowledge of the person charged. For that reason apart from any other, the section is not unconstitutional given the provisions of s.37(4)(a) of the Constitution and the question posed in the reference may be answered in the negative [at p.42.]

[Miles J. went on to discuss the separate but important issue that the proviso in the prosecution carries an onus.]

However, a further argument was raised by Ms. Pert for the principal legal adviser to the National Executive that the provisions of s.22A are such that they do not offend against s.37(4)(a) regardless of whether or not they require proof of facts peculiarly within the knowledge of the defendant. In other words, so it is submitted, the Court would not on a proper construction of s.22A as a whole, find it to be a law which removes the presumption of innocence until proven guilty according to law. ....

This Court is bound under Sch. 1.16 to give the provisions of the Constitution their fair and liberal meaning, when determining what it was that the makers of the Constitution intended. It would not be a fair and liberal interpretation of the proviso to s.37(4) to say that it is mere surplusage, that it merely makes explicit what was implied in any event without the proviso. The history of the section as outlined by Saldhana J. in *Constitutional Reference No 3 of 1978* [1978] PNGLR 421 at p.428 is sufficient answer to that.

A literal interpretation of the proviso to s.37(4)(a) of the Constitution would yield results which the makers of the Constitution could hardly have intended. Suppose that a law established a curfew and provided that any person found in a public place between sunset and sunrise is quilty of an offence. (Leave aside possible constitutional objections under Constitution ss.47 and 52.) Suppose further that the harshness of this hypothetical curfew law were reduced by a proviso that a person should not be guilty of the offence if he proved that the date on which he was found in the public place was a date on which the operation of that law was suspended by the Minister. The fact of the suspension would not be a matter peculiarly within the knowledge of the person charged. Yet it would be strange indeed if s.37(4)(a) — which is part of a section broadly intended to confer an unqualified right to protection of the law for all people — were to allow the legislation in its absolute form but to strike it down where it provided for a defence on the ground that the defence involved the proof of a fact not peculiarly within the knowledge of the person charged.

The way out of this impasse may be found by given proper weight to the words 'offence ... according to law' as they appear in s.37(4)(a). The word 'law' here encompasses all the laws of Papua New Guinea as set out in the Constitution, s.9 and includes the underlying law. As already indicated, it is a principle of the underlying law that the presumption of innocence continues until a court is satisfied beyond reasonable doubt of the guilt of the accused. The court must be so satisfied in relation to all those elements or matters which go to constituting the offence charged. The effect of s.37(2) of the Constitution, is that every offence (except contempt of court) must be defined by a written law. Thus a person is presumed innocent until the prosecution has proved against him beyond reasonable doubt the elements of the offence as defined in a written law. If the proviso to s.37(4)(a) is taken to apply only to the essential ingredients or elements or the offence as they are defined and required to be proved according to law, the difficulty arising from the hypothetical curfew law just mentioned may be avoided.

The offence is defined without reference to a date: to provide that the accused may prove that the event occurred on a particular date and thus escape a finding of guilt does not place upon him an onus of proving a 'particular fact' which has any relation to the elements of the offence to be proved 'according to law'. Where the offence is defined without reference to the matter on which the accused bears an onus, there will simply be no room for the application of the proviso to s.37(4)(a).

Similarly in the present case under s.22A of the *Police Offences Act (Papua)* 1912, the offence contains a number of elements but an intent to defraud is not one of them. The offence may be proved without any consideration of whether the defendant possessed an intent to defraud or not. The defence provided for, namely a lack of intention to defraud, introduces new matter altogether unrelated to the elements of the offence, proof of which will enable the defendant to aovid a finding of guilt. The provision of such a defence does not affect the presumption of innocence having regard to what the prosecution is required to prove in order to establish the offence as defined.

S.C.R. No 1 of 1980: Re s.22A(b) Police Offences Act (Papua) [1981] PNGLR 28 at pp.42, 46, 47; but see also Greville Smith J. at pp.31–39.

Comment

In *S.C.R. No 1 of 1980; Re s.22A(b) Police Offences Act (Papua)* [1981] PNGLR 28 Greville Smith J. came to the same conclusions as Miles and Andrew JJ. (above) but for reasons that have been the subject of severe criticism: see Kearney Dep.C.J. in *S.C.R. No 1A of 1981: Re Motor Traffic Act* [1982] PNGLR 122 at p.136.

AS TO SECTION 37(4)(a) AND SECTION 14(2) SUMMARY OFFENCES ACT

Note: the *Summary Offences Act* Section 14 provided;

14. VALUELESS CHEQUES

(1) A person who obtains, or pays for, any goods, money, valuable security, credit, benefit or advantage by passing a cheque which is not paid on presentation to the bank against which it is drawn is guilty of an offence.
Penalty: A fine not exceeding K400.00 or imprisonment for a term not exceeding one year.

(2) It is a defence to a charge for an offence against Sub-Section (1) if the person charged proves that he had reasonable grounds for believing that the cheque would be paid in full on presentation.

(3) The fact that at the time the cheque was passed there was some funds to the credit of the account against which the cheque was drawn is not, of itself, a defence to a charge of an offence against Sub-Section (1).

Held

The facts upon which a person bases his belief that a cheque which he passes will be paid in full by the bank when presented, are facts which are either peculiarly within the knowledge of the person passing the cheque, or would be with the exercise of reasonable care, within the meaning of s.37(4)(a) of the Constitution; whether or not these facts constitute reasonable grounds is a matter for determination by the court before whom the defence is raised, and the defendant may discharge such a burden of proof upon the balance of probabilities.

The phrase 'according to law' in s.37(4)(a) of the Constitution refers to the whole body of law in the country as exhaustively defined in s.9 of the Constitution; it includes both the Statute law and the underlying law.

It would be unconstitutional to place upon the accused the ultimate burden of establishing his innocence with respect to the elements of the offence charged.

S.C.R. No 2 of 1980; Re s.14(2) of the Summary Offences Act [1981] PNGLR 50; see Kearney Dep.C.J., Andrew and Miles JJ.

GENERALLY

per Kidu C.J.

[On appeal of the life sentence imposed for the wilful murder of an accused who was attending a view, in the eye of the court, Kidu C.J. referred to the rights in s.37(4)(a) and in other paragraphs of the sub-section, as follows:—]

> These rights are guaranteed for every person in Papua New Guinea, whether they are citizens or non-citizens. They cannot and should not be compromised. No person in this country must be allowed to take the law into his or her own hands. The Court must not permit people to kill with impunity, especially in cases where those who are accused of committing breaches of the law are in the custody of the Courts. People in such custody must be assured that they will be tried according to law. That one place where people should feel secure from arbitrary treatment is a court of Justice. The National Court of Justice is one such court.
>
> The people of Papua New Guinea (citizens and non-citizens) must be asured by this Court that when they are in breach of any law of this country, they will be guaranteed a fair trial according to the dictates of our Constitution.
>
> I hold no qualms in asserting the proposition that any person who kills another in the custody of the court deserves the maximum penalty, save those who are mentally unbalanced or who are provoked, legally speaking.
>
> The facts of this case very clearly show that this Court ought not to be swayed by emotional factors.
>
> I would order that this appeal be dismissed.
>
> *Avia Aihi v The State (No 3)* [1982] PNGLR 92 at p.99.

Referred to

by Prentice Dep.C.J. in *Reference No 1 of 1977* [1977] PNGLR 362 at p.378;

by Wilson J. in *Mathias Evertz v The State* [1979] PNGLR 174 at p.175 (in relation to an application for legal aid);

by Quinlivan A.J. in *Kaupa v Police at Hutjena* (1981 Unreported) N320(M) at pp.3–5;

by Miles J. in *Townsend v Oika* [1981] PNGLR 12 at p.26;

by Quinlivan A.J. in *Dai v Manda* (1980 Unreported) N342(M) at p.4;

by Kidu C.J. in *Ao v Vagi* (1982 Unreported) N357(M) at pp.3, 4;

by Kidu C.J. in *S.C.R. No 1A of 1981; Re Motor Traffic Act* [1982] PNGLR 122 at pp.127–129; and see also Kearney Dep.C.J. at pp.131, 136; Greville Smith J. at pp.136, 137, Kapi J. at pp.138, 139.

(b) shall be informed promptly in a language which he understands, and in detail, of the nature of the offence with which he is charged; and

CROSS REFERENCE

Constitution of the United States Am. VI

GENERALLY

Referred to

by Saldanha J. in *Prai v Officer of the Government of PNG* [1979] PNGLR 1 at p.2;

by Kidu C.J., Greville Smith and Andrew JJ. in *S.C.R. No 1 of 1981; Re Inter-Group Fighting Act 1977* [1981] PNGLR 151 at pp.153–156; for extracts of the judgment see under s.37(2);

by Andrew J. in *Gasika v The State* (1983 Unreported) SC245 at p.9 (police standing instructions which require a record of interview to be conducted in a language understood by the accused supplements s.37(4)(b)).

(c) shall be given adequate time and facilities for the preparation of his defence; and

GENERALLY

Referred to

by Kearney J. in *The State v Allan Woila (No 2)* [1978] PNGLR 113 at p.116;

by Saldanha J. in *Prai v Officer of the Government of PNG* [1979] PNGLR 1 at p.2.

(d) shall be permitted to have without payment the assistance of an interpreter if he cannot understand or speak the language used at the trial of the charge; and

GENERALLY

Referred to

by Saldanha J. in *Prai v Officer of Government of PNG* [1979] PNGLR 1 at p.3;

by Narakobi A.J. in *The State v Lakio Tambai* (1980 Unreported) N235 at p.5 (s.37(4)(d) used to help decide the question of whether the absence of the name of an interpreter on a Record of Interview should influence the weight to be given to the Record of Interview).

(e) shall be permitted to defend himself before the court in person or, at his own expense, by a legal representative of his own choice or if he is a person entitled to legal aid, by the Public Solicitor or another legal representative assigned to him in accordance with law; and

CROSS REFERENCE

Constitution of the United States Am. VI

AS TO THE RIGHT TO COUNSEL OF AN ACCUSED'S CHOICE

per Curiam (Kidu C.J., Greville Smith and Pratt JJ.)

... the right of an accused person cannot extend to a right to have counsel who is employed as a State prosecutor to defend him, or who is employed as an officer of the Public Solicitors Office if he is not entitled to legal aid, or the Public Solicitor himself instead of one of the Public Solicitor's Officer's if he is entitled to legal aid, or a particular officer of the Public Solicitor's Office, or a counsel who has by acceptance of a prior brief engaged himself so as to be unavailable at the time of the trial, or who, as in this case, is disqualified on ethical . . . and other grounds in respect of appearing as defence counsel in the trial in question. The aforestated exceptions are not exhaustive.

What an accused person is entitled to is to counsel of his choice but not necessarily his first choice. His choice is subject to all proper exceptions. One thing that the right conferred by the provision in question would do would be to prevent an accused person being against his will assigned by the State a defence counsel whom he did not want.
In Re Joseph Mavuk [1980] PNGLR 507 at pp.508, 509.

AS TO THE RIGHT OF AN ACCUSED TO SIT NEAR COUNSEL RATHER THAN IN THE DOCK

per Kearney J.

I consider that to make effective the rights of an accused under Constitution s.37, he must have free and unrestricted communication with his legal representative in court, during his trial . . . .

If I am wrong in this, and the question remains one of indulgence by the court, I consider that requests to sit near counsel should now be very freely granted in the interests of dispensing justice to the individual.
The State v Allan Woila (No 2) [1978] PNGLR 113 at p.117.

Referred to

by Pritchard J. in *Constitutional Reference No 1 of 1978 (s.19)* [1978] PNGLR 345 at p.371.

(f) shall be afforded facilities to examine in person or by his legal representative the witnesses called before the court by the prosecution, and to obtain the attendance and carry out the examination of witnesses and to testify before the court on his own behalf, on the same conditions as those applying to witnesses called by the prosecution.

CROSS REFERENCE

Constitution of the United States Am. VI.

Referred to

by Kearney J. in *The State v Allan Woila (No 2)* [1978] PNGLR 113 at p.116;

by Saldanha J. in *Prai v Officer of the Government of PNG* [1979] PNGLR 1 at p.3;

by Kearney J. in *Kiso v Manuamanun* (1981 Unreported) N359(M) at p.2.

(5) Except with his own consent, the trial shall not take place in his absence unless he so conducts himself as to render the continuance of the proceedings in his presence impracticable and the court orders him to be removed and the trial to proceed in his absence, but provision may be made by law for a charge that a person has committed an offence the maximum penalty for which does not include imprisonment, (except in default of payment of a fine), to be heard summarily in his absence if it is established that he has been duly served with a summons in respect of the alleged offence.

AS TO WHETHER THE HEARING OF AN OFFENCE IN THE ABSENCE OF AN ACCUSED UNDER THE DISTRICT COURTS ACT IS PERMITTED UNDER SECTION 37(5).

Note: Section 131 of the *District Courts Act* provided:

If, at the time and place appointed by a summons for hearing and determining an information of a simple offence, the defendant does not appear when called, and proof is made to the Court upon oath, or by deposition made as prescribed by s.55 of this Act of due service of the summons upon the defendant a reasonable time before the time appointed for his appearance, the court may either —

(a) proceed ex parte to hear and determine the case in the absence of the defendant; or
(b) upon oath being made before it, substantiating the matter of the information to its satisfaction, issue its warrant for the arrest of the defendant to bring him before a court to answer to the information and to be further dealt with according to law.

per Frost C.J. (Kearney J. in substantial agreement)

Section 37(5) can conveniently be divided into two parts. First, it prohibits the trial of a person taking place, except with his consent, in his absence unless he so conducts himself as to render the continuance of the proceedings in his presence impracticable, and the Court orders him to be removed. Secondly, it authorizes provision to be made by law for a charge that a person has committed an offence the maximum penalty for which does not include imprisonment (except in default of a fine), to be heard summarily in his absence if it has been established that he has been duly served with a summons in respect of the alleged offence .....

The Deputy Chief Justice seems to have reached the same answer as I have excepting that in his opinion the section should be read and construed in such a manner as to permit an ex parte hearing in the case of offences punishable by imprisonment if the defendant consents to the charge being heard in his absence. To enable a proper answer to be given I should refer to His Honour's addition of an enabling jurisdiction in the case of consent. I regret that I am unable to agree with that construction for a number of reasons. First, on the plain meaning of s.10 its only operation is to preserve that portion of the law which remains valid; no power is given to the Court to propound any additional provision, except as is necessarily involved and therefore impliedly permissible under the section by way of words of qualification to preserve that portion of the existing law which is not in excess of authority. This extension of jurisdiction may be passed off as judicial legislation, but in Papua New Guinea, as I have said, the legislative power is vested in Parliament — Constitution, s.100(1).

Secondly, can this Court be sure that the proposed extension of jurisdiction under *District Courts Act*, s.131, is, without further provision, for the 'peace, order or good government of Papua New Guinea or the welfare of the People'? There may be little risk of abuses creeping in under the present limited jurisdiction of the *District Courts Act*, but what if the Court's summary jurisdiction is increased to enable it to hear and determine indictable offences with power to impose terms of imprisonment up to 2 years, or 5 to 7 years as is the case in other developing countries? The line has to be drawn at some point, and that is the province of the National Parliament and not a judge. Safe-guards are required and the procedure should not be introduced until a statute is passed prescribing the manner of recording and the proof of consent.

Finally, I do not understand the Deputy Chief Justice to hold that the fundamental right secured by the Constitution, s.37(5), in effect that, except with his own consent a trial of a person charged with an offence shall not take place in his absence unless because of his misconduct at the trial, has a self executing operation under s.11, so as to support the proposed construction of s.131. It is sufficient to say that if that was the effect of the Constitution, s.37(5), it would have the over-riding and wholly undesirable effect of enabling the trial of an indictable offence under the Criminal Code in the absence of a defendant who consents.

Peter v South Pacific Brewery Ltd. [1976] PNGLR 527 at pp.539, 550, 551; but see Prentice Dep.C.J. (dissenting) at pp.556–560 (below).

per Prentice Dep.C.J. (dissenting)

... it is clear that the Legislature (in this case the Constituent Assembly), intended that:

1. Trials for offences involving the penalty of imprisonment *may* take place in the absence of an accused if he consents thereto;
2. District Courts should have power to conduct trials in the absence of an accused if notice be proved to have been given to him;
3. District Courts should have power to try a large range of offences for which the penalty is fine or imprisonment.

Some of the charges hitherto brought in courts of summary jurisdiction, alleged offences under income tax, pure food, restaurant licensing, sanitation, price control, misuse of water laws, and so on — laws of a regulatory nature. There is a large number also of the nature of traffic offences, such as driving without a licence or while under the influence of liquor, which carry the possible penalty of imprisonment. Many of these offences of this nature involve menace to the freedom and activities of other citizens who are entitled to the protection of the law. Clearly in a modern state imprisonment is a necessary sanction for the protection of other members of the community against, for example, repeated driving offences of a dangerous nature, or offences perhaps by executives or employees of powerful corporations, to whom fines, which could be expected to be paid by their corporations would not be a deterrent. But most of such offences would be well met by the imposition of fines; and in the hearing of charges relating thereto the accused would frequently not wish to be present. I ask myself is it consistent with the least restriction on the activities of accused individuals that a law should be so construed as to require their attendance on perhaps repeated adjournments of a court seized with the hearing of an offence perhaps comparatively trivial in the actual circumstances (e.g. for driving without a licence), merely because it (and query desirably) carries a possible penalty of imprisonment. The reverse side of the coin may be seen if one asks should a prosecutor or informant living at a remote part of the country have to suffer the disadvantage of expensively and inconveniently attending at perhaps repeated adjournments of a court perhaps located far away to ensure the attendance of the accused at the hearing and to obtain the prosecutor's rights to pursue legal process in which a possible imprisonment of the accused might (but would be unlikely to) result — if this result could be effected by a permissible interpretation otherwise of the law.

It seems to me manifestly clear that it is desirable not only in order to achieve the National Goals and Directives, but also to secure the basic rights of individuals, that certain classes of charges involving possible imprisonment, should be capable of being heard summarily in the absence of the defendant if he so consents — thus avoiding his arrest and compulsory attendances in court — even though potentially imprisonment could result .....

Section 131 *District Courts Act* is not invalid. The section is to be read and construed as follows:

> If at the time and place appointed by a summons for hearing and determining an information of a simple offence, the defendant does not appear when called, and proof is made to the court upon oath, or by deposition made as prescribed by s.55 of this Act of due service of the summons upon the defendant a reasonable time before the time appointed for his appearance, *and in the case of an offence punishable by imprisonment (otherwise than for default in payment of a fine) if the accused consents to the charge being heard in his absence*, the court may either:
> (a) proceed *ex parte* to hear and determine the case in the absence of the defendant; or
> (b) upon oath being made before it, substantiating the matter of the information to its satisfaction, issue its warrant for the arrest of the defendant.

Peter v South Pacific Brewery Ltd. [1976] PNGLR 537 at pp.556–560; but see Frost C.J. at pp.539, 550, 551 (above), Kearney J. at pp.560, 561.

SECTION 37(5) AND ON THE SPOT FINES

Comment

Section 38A(1)(c) of the *Local Courts Act*, s.138A(1)(b) of the *District Courts Act* and s.19AB(2)(e)(iii) of the *Motor Traffic Act* were all held to be unconstitutional because they contravened s.37(5) of the Constitution in *S.C.R. No 1A of 1981: Re Motor Traffic Act* [1982] PNGLR 122.

per Kidu C.J.

In my opinion the Constitution s.37(5), cannot be read in isolation from the preceding subsections of s.37 .... Section 37(5) of the Constitution is said to allow the provisions under reference. I cannot see how. It does not do away with the requirement to have a proper hearing. In my view s.37(5) merely allows provisions to be made allowing certain summary offences to be dealt with in the absence of a defendant. A summary hearing does not involve the relaxation of the Constitutional requirements of s.37(4)(a) that a criminal charge be proved beyond a reasonable doubt, subject only to the proviso contained in that subsection.
S.C.R. 1A of 1981; Re Motor Traffic Act [1982] PNGLR 122 at pp.126, 129; see also Kearney Dep.C.J. at pp.131, 134 and Greville Smith J. at p.137.

SECTION 37(5) ENVISAGES A TRIAL

per Greville Smith J.

Consistently with the provisions of s.37(4)(a) of the Constitution the provisions of s.37(5) envisage a trial (which in the broad sense includes proceedings at which the person charged pleads guilty) when it makes the primary provision that except with his own consent 'the trial' of a person charged with an offence shall not take place in his absence. It seems hardly necessary to define the word 'trial' in the context of s.37. However a 'trial' is the action or process of putting to proof, 'the formal examination of the matter in issue in a cause before a competent tribunal for the purposes of determining such issue' (*Websters' New International Dictionary*, Second Edition (1934) p.2705, 'trial' 1, 8).

'Trial is to find out by due examination the truth of the point in issue or question between the parties, whereupon judgment may be given'. — *Whartons Law Lexicon*, Fourteenth Edition (1938), p.1011).
S.C.R. No 1A of 1981; Re Motor Traffic Act [1982] PNGLR 122 at p.137.

(6) Nothing in Subsection (4)(f) invalidates a law which imposes reasonable conditions that must be satisfied if witnesses called to testify on behalf of a person charged with an offence are to be paid their expenses out of public funds.

(7) No person shall be convicted of an offence on account of any act that did not, at the time when it took place, constitute an offence, and no penalty shall be imposed for an offence that is more severe in degree or description than the maximum penalty that might have been imposed for the offence at the time when it was committed.

CROSS-REFERENCE

Universal Declaration of Human Rights: Article 11(2); *European Convention on Human Rights*: Article 7(1); *Constitution of India*: Section 20(1)

GENERALLY

per Williams J.

Ordinary logic suggests to me that a previous criminal responsibility should, in the absence of any specific statutory provision to the contrary, be governed by the law as it was at the time of the acts giving rise to the charge. Section 37(7) of the Constitution of Papua New Guinea seems to proceed on this basis in that it provides that no person shall be convicted of an offence on account of any act that did not, at the time when it took place, constitute an offence. The subsection then goes on to provide with respect to punishment. The subsection appears to recognize that substantive liability is to be determined by the law

in force at the time when the acts constituting the charge were done.
Nai'u Limagwe and others v The State [1976] PNGLR 382 at p.413; see also Frost C.J. at pp.406, 408.

Referred to

by Kidu C.J. in *S.C.R. No 1 of 1981; Re Inter-Group Fighting Act (1977)* [1981] PNGLR 151 at p.154; see also Miles J. (dissenting) at p.173.

(8) No person who shows that he has been tried by a competent court for an offence and has been convicted or acquitted shall again be tried for that offence or for any other offence of which he could have been convicted at the trial for that offence, except upon the order of a superior court made in the course of appeal or review proceedings relating to the conviction or acquittal.

CROSS REFERENCE

Constitution of the United States Am. V; *Constitution of India*: Section 20(2).

AS TO DISCIPLINARY PROCEEDINGS

Held

A member of the Police Force may be charged with a disciplinary offence under the *Police Force (Interim Arrangements) Act*, (now the *Police Force Act* Ch.65) notwithstanding that the matters alleged are identical to those which grounded the officer's earlier conviction for an offence under the Criminal Code. A disciplinary proceeding does not allege any 'offence' within the meaning of s.37(8) of the Constitution. The term offence as used in s.37(8) refers only to crimes, misdemeanors and simple offences.
Sudi Yaku v Commissioner of Police [1980] PNGLR 27; see Andrew J. at p.32.

GENERALLY

Referred to

by Kearney Dep.C.J. in *Apelis v Willy* (1981 Unreported) N348(M) at p.3;

by Pratt J. in *The State v Arazi: ex parte Gaius* (1981 Unreported) N322 at p.2;

by Pratt J. in *S.C.R. No 1 of 1981; Re Inter-Group Fighting Act (1977)* [1981] PNGLR 151 at p.157; see also Miles J. at p.174;

by Kearney Dep.C.J. in *S.C.R. No 2 of 1981; Re s.19(1)(f) at the Criminal Code of* [1982] PNGLR 150 at p.160.

(9) No person shall be tried for an offence for which he has been pardoned.

Comment

As to a so-called 'customary pardon' see Kidu C.J. in the *State v Paul Pokolo* (1983 Unreported) N404 at p.6.

(10) No person shall be compelled in the trial of an offence to be a witness against himself.

CROSS REFERENCE

Constitution of the United States: Am. V; *Constitution of India*: Section 20(3)

THE EXERCISE OF THE RIGHT TO SILENCE DOES NOT IMPUTE GUILT

Referred to

by Narokobi A.J. in *Tabo Sipo v Meli* (1980 Unreported) N240 at pp.3–5;

by Kearney Dep.C.J. in *The State v Tovue* (1981 Unreported) N288 at p.1;

by Andrew J. in *Pawa v The State* [1981] PNGLR 498 at pp.503–505.

SECTION 37(10) AND MIRANDA V ARIZONA

per Frost C.J.

In his third submission the Acting Public Solicitor relies upon s.37 which provides, as one of the fundamental rights, that 'no person shall be compelled in the trial of an offence to be a witness against himself'. It was submitted that the provision is very similar to the Fifth Amendment of the *Constitution of the United State of America* which is to the effect: 'No person shall ... be compelled in any criminal case to be a witness against himself'. That provision has been construed by the United States Supreme Court as according to each individual the privilege, at any stage before trial or at the trial, not to be compelled to incriminate himself. (*Miranda v Arizona* (1966) 384 U.S. 43). The principle is also deep-rooted in the common law, and provides one of the reasons for the rejection of a confession on the ground that it is involuntary. *Commissioners of Customs and Excise v Harz & Another* [1967] 1 A.C. 760, per Lord Reid at 820, *McDermott v The King* (1948) 76 C.L.R. 501, per Dixon J. (as he then was) at p.513. In the United States the law has been developed further, and the prosecution may not use statements, whether exculpatory or inculpatory, stemming from the custodial interrogation of the accused, unless it demonstrates the use of certain procedural safeguards effective to secure the privilege against self-incrimination. *Miranda v Arizona*. The measures go beyond the requirements of the Constitution and the common law in at least one respect, in that the unconditional right to the presence of an attorney is accorded.

It was also submitted that the Constitution s.37(10) imports the United States' Constitutional right under the *Fifth Amendment* of 'due process of law' which involves not only observance of proper Court procedure but also compliance with proper conduct on the part of those who enforce the law. This line of reasoning, I assume, provides ground for the submission that breach of Constitution s.42(2) constitutes improper conduct on the part of the persons making the arrest or effecting the detention and therefore lack of due process, leading to the rejection of any subsequent admission under Constitution s.37(10).

Now I was impressed with the inference made in the judgment of Mwendwa C.J. in *Republic v El Mann* [1969] E.A. 357 at p.361 (a case under a similar provision in the Kenya Constitution), that the words 'against himself' in the present context suggest the principle generally against self-incrimination. But reading Constitution s.37(10) as a whole I consider that the words 'in the trial of an offence', which are of technical significance under the *Criminal Code*, do limit the right to an immunity from being called as a witness on the floor of the Court. Taking into account the objects of the protection to be afforded, no reason emerges for the right being given any wider operation than the plain meaning of s.37(10) requires. This approach is in keeping with the aim of the Constitutional Planning Committee which was to entrench in the Constitution only basic rights, with full account being taken for extension in the future. The Constitution which the Committee proposed was one soundly based on the independence of the judiciary, the Rule of Law (Constitution s.57(2)(c)), and the principles of natural justice. Thus, for example, the Committee was content to recommend, in the context of the right to life, immunity from wilful murder only and to allow the necessary wider protection to be ensured under the *Criminal Code* (Report 5/1/9, par. 38).

Further, I am quite clear on this, that having regard to the homegrown nature of the Constitution, no intention is shown that the notion of due process, developed in detail to meet United States conditions, should be introduced into the Papua New Guinea Constitution. It is true that the Committee refers to the 'due process' as provided in the United States Constitution, and states that s.37 — Protection of the Law — is 'the equivalent' of that provision. Report 5/1/10, par. 48. This indicates to me that s.37 deals with similar subject matter but not necessarily in the same terms. Reading the Constitution as a whole, s.37(10) cannot be taken so far as to constitute an indirect method of enforcement of s.42(2), for which specific provision as to enforcement is made at least in Division 3.

Reference No 1 of 1977 [1977] PNGLR 362 at pp.371–373; see also Prentice Dep.C.J. at pp.375–380 (below) and Williams J. at p.383 (below).

per Prentice Dep.C.J.

Finally, it is urged that the provision of s.37(10) that 'No person shall be compelled in the trial of an offence to be a witness against himself'; requires as a corollary the reading of s.42(2) in such a fashion as to render confessional evidence received in breach of its terms, inadmissible against the person concerned. Analogy is sought in the history of the interpretation of the *Constitution of the United State of America* and in particular of its *Fifth Amendment* which states:

'No person should . . . be compelled in any criminal case to be a witness against himself' . . . .

Lastly, Mr Kapi asks this Court to consider the way in which the Supreme Court of the United States of America developed a doctrine and laid down ultimately the 'Miranda Rules'; and by analogy, to suit the circumstances of Papua New Guinea by making a ruling in the affirmative. Such a policy, it is submitted, may be built upon the requirement of s.37(10) that 'No person shall be compelled in the trial of an offence to be a witness against himself'.

Under our current code, a 'trial' does not commence until a person is called upon to plead following arraignment (s.569). The position in Papua New Guinea would therefore appear to be more akin to that existing in Kenya: s.21(7) of the Constitution of which country provides that 'No person who is tried for a criminal offence should be compelled to give evidence at his trial'. In considering the United States' cases, the High Court of Kenya came to the conclusion that s.21(7) had no reference to pre-trial procedures in that no ambiguity existed such as would allow it to be interpreted in the analogous U.S. sense (*Republic v El Mann* [1969] E.A. 357 at p.361). The first ten amendments to the United States Constitution having been proposed in 1789, were adopted in 1791. By the Miranda decision, 175 years later, rules were devised apparently in furtherance of a constitutional interpretation of the phrase in the *Fifth Amendment* '. . . in any criminal *case* to be a witness against himself', and of the 'due process' provision of the *Fourteenth Amendment*; to deal with the great abuses which it was thought had developed in investigatory processes, including forms of invasion of privacy, duress and torture. It was there thought apparently, that in the absence of sanctions in the Constitution itself, it was necessary in the attempt to achieve justice for the Court itself to devise sanctions in a form of severe restrictions on the admissibility of evidence. The situation in the United States of America in the early decades of this century provided a very different background to that obtaining in Papua New Guinea, at present — particularly when one contrasts the specific sanction provisions of our Constitution with the total lack of sanctions against those breaching civic rights in that of the United States of America.

I am unable to come to the conclusion that, in any case, the words of s.37(10) of our Constitution, referring as they do to the trial, not to the pre-trial period, are relevant to a consideration of whether evidence may be given of alleged admissions made by a person in arrest or detention.

For the above reasons, I would answer the question 'No'.

Before parting from the subject I would wish to add a few observations. In a recent paper delivered to the Hobart Judicial Conference in Australia (1977), after discussing possible legislative alterations to the law of evidence, Professor J.D. Heydon stated:

> The Escobedo-Miranda doctrine may be thought unsuitable in Australia. It leads to the exclusion of confessions made by the accused virtually spontaneously the moment the

police meet him as well as those produced by hours of questioning, *Orozco v Texas* 394 U.S. 324 (1969).

To those who have been practising many years in the Courts here, the situation in which a man or woman having committed a grave crime of violence, immediately runs to the nearest police station, makes an initial confession, and demands to be locked up for protection against instant pay-back killing — is most common, and part of the customary fabric of society. In circumstances of this kind as well as others, breaches of constitutional rights by police or administration officers may occur which may vary from a comparatively trivial one on the instant facts, to a grave infringement. To arrive at the conclusion that the Constitution requires *any* such breach to render inadmissible any confession subsequently obtained would it seems, be to make a decision unalterable except by Constitutional amendment. On the other hand such a law, as would produce that result (if it were desired) could be introduced as an amendment to the law of evidence.

Reference No 1 of 1977 [1977] PNGLR 362 at pp.375, 379–380; see also Frost C.J. at pp.171–173 (above) and Williams J. at p.383 (below).

per Williams J.

It was sought to derive further support for the affirmative case from the provisions of s.37(10) of the Constitution which simply provides that no person shall, in the trial of an offence, be a witness against himself. To my mind this provision is perfectly clear. In its literal terms it provides that a person cannot be called to give evidence *at his trial* as a witness against himself. In my view s.37(10) has no relevance to the questions presently under consideration. It is, I think, directed to situations such as those which may arise under provisions like s.251 of the *Customs Act* 1951 which provided that in every custom prosecution (except for an indictable offence or one directly punishable by imprisonment) the defendant shall be compellable to give evidence.

Reference No 1 of 1977 [1977] PNGLR 362 at p.383; see also Frost C.J. at pp.371–373 (above) and Prentice Dep.C.J. at pp.375–380 (above).

AS TO SECTION 37(10) AND THE ISSUE OF THE STANDARD OF PROOF ON VOIR DIRE

per Kearney J.

Finally, in 1976, in South Australia the Supreme Court (in Banco), also following *Wendo v The Queen* (1963) 109 CLR 559 held that the probabilities standard is to be applied: *R. v Stafford* (1976) 13 SASR 392.

From these authorities, I conclude that in the common law of Australia, the correct standard is the probabilities standard. In the United States the question of the correct standard had been much debated after *Jackson v Denno* (1964) 378 U.S. 368 until 1972 in *Lego v Twomey* 409 U.S. 477 the Supreme Court held by a majority of 4 to 3 that the prosecution was constitutionally required to prove the voluntariness of a confession only by a preponderance of the evidence, and not beyond reasonable doubt. The various States were, however, free to adopt a higher standard; as many in fact do — a list appears in *Wharton's Criminal Evidence* (13th Edition). The majority noted that it had been settled since 1961 that 'the exclusion of unreliable confessions is not the purpose that a voluntariness hearing is designed to serve .... The sole issue in such a hearing is whether a confession was coerced', 30 L.Ed. 2nd 618 at p.625. That rationale involves a rejection of the original 'reliability' basis of the common law rule, as expressed in *R. v Warickshall*, 168 E.R. 234 at p.235 and a founding upon the constitutional privilege against self-incrimination in the Fifth Amendment. A parallel provision to the Fifth Amendment appears at s.37(10) of our Constitution but may not apply to pre-trial interrogation as a separate exclusionary principle: *Reference No 1 of 1977* [1977] PNGLR 362. However, it would seem that reliability, the privilege against self-incrimination, and control by the courts of improper police practices, all now possibly under-pin the voluntary confession rule in our jurisprudence: see *R. v Toomey and Frost* [1969] Tas. S.R. 99.

The State v Allan Woila [1978] PNGLR 99 at pp.109,110.

AS TO THE EFFECT OF SECTION 37(10) ON A REQUEST BY COUNSEL THAT A 'NOT GUILTY' PLEA BE ENTERED, FOLLOWING A 'GUILTY' PLEA BY ACCUSED

per Prentice Dep.C.J.

Having refused to accede to counsel's requests, his Honour proceeded to ask three questions of each of the principals who had allegedly wounded the victim. This procedure has been heavily criticized on appeal. It is said that the questions were not asked in genuine inquiry as to whether the accused were stating they were guilty or not guilty. Objection is taken to the questions having been asked at all — there was no statutory basis for them, it is said, and they were in direct conflict with s.37(10) of the Constitution. The accused were given no freedom of choice in answering, the questions should have been objected to.

Section 37(10) of the Constitution provides that "No person shall be compelled in the trial for (sic) an offence to be a witness against himself". In my opinion, there is no room for its application to the circumstances being canvassed. It is of course essential that when persons of no education are being charged with offences the legal elements of which they may not comprehend, and arraigned through the medium of interpreters, the Court should inform itself assuredly that its arraignment and any consequent plea is understood by the accused and the Court. For this purpose it is sometimes necessary to put questions supplementary to those translated in the initial arraignment. In view of the unusual attitude taken by counsel herein in regard to the plea, his Honour was no doubt concerned to ascertain again and in more detail, that he was not mistaking the answers of the accused. I do not regard his additional questions as inapt for this purpose, and I do not appreciate how they can be interpreted as amounting to compulsion to give evidence. No doubt, if thereafter counsel had renewed his application, stated reasons and been allowed to substitute pleas of not guilty, the Court would have been requested to disregard any answers to the supplementary questions; or alternatively his Honour could have been asked to stand the trial over for hearing before another judge, if prejudice was thought to have occurred.
Nai'u Limagwe and Others v The State [1976] PNGLR 382 at p.405

AS TO SECTION 37(10) AND NO CASE TO ANSWER

per Kearney Dep.C.J.

... the 'no case' practice serves a separate and essential purpose: it is a procedural reinforcement to the presumption of innocence in the Constitution s.37(4)(a), and to the accused's right to silence in Constitution s.37(10). These citizens rights entail that the State must make out its case by the evidence *it* adduces; it cannot rely on making good any defects in its own case, by cross-examination of the accused or his witnesses.
The State v Kuriday (1981 Unreported) N300 at p.2.

(11) A determination of the existence or extent of a civil right or obligation on shall not be made except by an independent and impartial court or other authority prescribed by law or agreed upon by the parties, and proceedings for such a determination shall be fairly heard within a reasonable time.

CROSS REFERENCE

Universal Declaration of Human Rights: Article 10; *International Covenant on Civil and Political Rights*: Article 14; *European Convention on Human Rights*: Article 6(1).

PLEADING IMPLEMENTS THE RIGHT TO A FAIR HEARING

Held

Parties to litigation are bound to observe the *Rules of Court*, which embody much of the procedural law by which civil justice in the National Court is administered. The system set up by the Rules involves pleadings by the parties, the chief purpose of which is to elicit at their close and prior to trial, clearly and precisely, the real points at issue between the parties, so that they may prepare and present their cases for adjudication by the Court. Thus expense and delay are reduced, certainty and finality achieved on all matters in controversy, and the Court is made aware of the only issues before it. The system also assists in implementing Constitution s.37(11) — the right to a fair hearing — by ensuring that each party is not taken by surprise at trial as to material facts at issue, since the case can be decided only on the issues on the record.
Cory v Blyth (No 4) [1976] PNGLR 525; see Kearney J. at p.530.

'CIVIL RIGHTS AND OBLIGATIONS' MEAN THE RIGHTS AND OBLIGATIONS GIVEN BY THE CIVIL LAW

per Prentice C.J.

The question of whether a permit to enter Papua New Guinea confers upon an alien a 'civil right' which enjoys the protection of s.37(11) and (12) of the Constitution is a difficult one. The term 'civil right' is not defined. The phrase does appear in art. 6(1) of the *European Convention on Human Rights*, from which, a comparison would seem to indicate, the whole of our s.37 of the Constitution has been taken. In litigation in Europe the phrase has been taken to encompass rights given under the law — meaning in the private not public law fields (*Birdi v Secretary of State for Home Affairs* (1976) 92 LQR 34). Jacobs, *The European Convention on Human Rights* (1975), at p.77, suggests that there must be some pre-existing relationship under civil law, and that many kinds of administrative proceedings will not be covered by art. 6(1). In *Birdi's* case, decided 11th February, 1975, Lord Denning at p.8 of his judgment stated:

> We were also referred to article 6. It says that:
>
> 'In the determination of his civil rights and obligations or of any criminal charge against him, everyone is entitled to a fair and public hearing within a reasonable time by an independent and impartial tribunal established by law'.
>
> There is no infringement of that article here. The words 'civil rights and obligations' are used to denote the rights and obligations given by the civil law of the country. The article does not extend to administrative procedures, such as licences given by a licensing authority, nor to the permissions given to aliens to enter a country. Nor does it apply to the leave given or refusal made under the *Immigration Act* 1971.

That the grant of an entry permit amounts not to a 'civil right' but to a mere licence revocable at any time by executive act is supported by a number of cases based on comparable foreign statutory provisions. The starting point is the declaration of the Privy Council in *Attorney-General for the Dominion of Canada v Cain* [1906] AC 542 in reliance upon Vattel's *Law of Nations* that:

> One of the rights possessed by the supreme power in every State is the right to refuse to permit an alien to enter that State, to annex what conditions it pleases to the permission to enter it, and to expel or deport from the State, at pleasure, even a friendly alien, especially if it considers his presence in the State opposed to its peace, order, and good government, or to its social or material interests.

The decisions of *R. v Inspector of Leman Street Police Station: Ex parte Venicoff [1920] 3 KB 72, R. v Governor of Brixton Prison; Ex parte Soblen* [1963] 2 QB 243, and *Re Marles' Application* [1958] EA 153, illustrate that 'rights' were not in question when deportation of aliens was being considered, and that the procedures therein involved not judicial but administrative functions. In the latter case it was expressly stated by the Supreme Court of Kenya that 'Immigration is, and we think must always be, a jealously guarded privilege, and it would seem that the fact that it is a *privilege*, and *not a right* is often overlooked' (emphasis mine), (MacDuff J. at p.161). I am unable to see that if a permit to enter does not itself confer rights, that an alien can by entering upon a contract of employment convert a 'licence to remain' into a 'right to remain'. Such a process would surely make nonsense of the sovereign power of the people exercised through their Government, to allow entry of aliens to Papua New Guinea.

The sections of the Constitution which deal with rights, though containing provisions which are restricted to citizens only, may be thought to be far from explicit as to the extent to which guaranteed rights adhere to aliens in any event. Schedule 1.3 of the Constitution recites that recourse may be had to the preamble as an aid to interpretation in cases of doubt. And s.24 of the Constitution provides that the report of the Constitutional Planning Committee may be used as an aid to interpretation of any provision of a constitutional law.

The Commission's observations on the national goals and principles, as a guide to interpretation (C.P.C. 2/25), states on note (i):

> To exemplify the manner in which cl. (1) of this recommendation is intended to be applied as an aid to interpretation, we envisage that where the meaning of a constitutional provision is in question, or there is doubt as to the constitutional validity of any law or administrative action, or there is ambiguity in any law, or no particular law or principle of law appears to apply to the circumstances involved in any matter before a court, the court will give an interpretation which is consistent with the National Goals and Directive Principles rather than an alternative interpretation.

At page 5/1/12 par. 70 the Commission observed that:

> All countries, in the interests of their own citizens place restrictions on the entry of foreign citizens to their territory, and upon the period during which they may remain in the country, though of course some states are much more strict in this regard than are others. All countries also have legislation which provides for the deportation of foreign citizens in a range of circumstances which usually includes a number of situations besides that in which a foreign citizen is found guilty of a criminal offence. For example, under United Kingdom legislation a foreign citizen may be deported whenever the Home Secretary 'deems it conducive to the public good'.
>
> 71. We believe the right to limit the movement of foreign citizens is part of a country's sovereign rights, and should be retained as such. This is not to say that we consider that foreign citizens should be unreasonably restricted in regard to the parts of the country to which they may travel. We simply believe that the full power of Parliament to make appropriate laws to limit the movement of non-citizens in the interests of all Papua New Guinean citizens must be retained.

Section 25 of the Constitution provides in sub-s.(3) that:

> Where any law, or any power conferred by any law (whether the power be of a legislative, judicial, executive, administrative or other kind), can reasonably be understood, applied, exercised or enforced, without failing to give effect to the intention of the Parliament or to this Constitution, in such a way as to give effect to the National Goals and Directive Principles, or at least not to derogate them, it is to be understood, applied or exercised, and shall be enforced, in that way.

And sub-s.(4) states:

> Subsection (1) does not apply to the jurisdiction of the Ombudsman Commission or of any other body prescribed for the purposes of Division 111.2 (leadership code), which shall take the National Goals and Directive Principles fully into account in all cases as appropriate.

The declaratory acknowledgements as to 'Basic Rights' in the preamble to the Constitution assets (emphasis mine):

> We hereby acknowledge that, *subject to any restrictions imposed by Law on non-citizens*, all persons in our country are entitled to the fundamental rights and freedoms of the individual, that is to say ...

Having regard to the above interpretative injunctions, I form the opinion that the provisions of the Constitution as to 'rights' are *in the case of non-citizens*, to be interpreted 'subject to any restrictions imposed by law'; so that were the permit to enter to be considered 'a civil right', it would nevertheless be subject to restrictions imposed by law — and I do not apprehend that such a law (in the case of non-citizens) need comply with s.38(2) of the Constitution, the operation of which would catch measures applying to citizens as well as aliens or to citizens alone.

Premdas v The Independent State of Papua New Guinea [1979] PNGLR 329 at pp.339–341; see also Raine Dep.C.J. at pp.347–349 (generally agreeing with the Chief Justice), Wilson J. (dissenting) at pp.378, 379 (below) and Andrew J. at pp.396–398.

per Wilson J. (dissenting).

Is the Committee of Review an authority which is 'determining the existence or extent of a civil right or obligation'? To answer this question one must ascertain the meaning of the words 'civil right or obligation'. To ascertain the meaning of those words one needs to go no further than the Court of Appeal decision in *Birdi v Secretary of State for Home Affairs* (1976) 92 LQR 34 in which Lord Denning M.R. said:

The words 'civil rights and obligations' are used (in Article 6 of the *European Convention on Human Rights*) to denote the rights and obligations given by the civil law of the country. The Article does not extend to administrative procedures, such as licenses given by a licensing authority, nor to the permissions given to aliens to enter a country. Nor does it apply to the leave given or refusal made under the *Immigration Act*, 1971.

Applying that principle to the instant case (and remembering that, just as the United Kingdom has adhered to the Convention of which art.6 is but one part, so have the people of Papua New Guinea incorporated into their Constitution (in s.37(11) a provision in very similar terms); s.37(11) does not extend to administrative procedures such as the granting of entry permits to non-nationals or the revocation of such permits under the *Migration Act* 1963.

It follows that the Committee of Review is not an authority which is 'determining the existence or extend of a civil right or obligation'.

Premdas v The Independent State of Papua New Guinea [1979] PNGLR 329 at pp.378, 379; see also Prentice C.J. at pp.339–341 (above), Raine Dep.C.J. at pp.347–349 and Andrew J. at pp.396–398.

Referred to

by Wilson J. in *Re Rooney (No 2)* [1979] PNGLR 448 at p.492 (note the report contains a typographical error; it is clear from the text that section 37(11) is intended to be referred to rather than section 37(1)).

(12) Except with the agreement of the parties, or by order of the court in the interests of national security, proceedings in any jurisdiction of a court and proceedings for the determination of the existence or extent of any civil right or obligation before any other authority, including the announcement of the decision of the court or other authority, shall be held in public.

CROSS REFERENCE

Constitution of the United States: Am. VI.

GENERALLY

Comment

For text explaining the meaning of 'civil right or obligation' see annotations under s.37(11)

Referred to

by Kearney Dep.C.J. in *The State v Giddings* [1981] PNGLR 423 at p.429.

(13) Nothing in Subsection (12) prevents a court or other authority from excluding from the hearing of the proceedings before it persons, other than the parties and their legal representatives, to such an extent as the court or other authority —

(a) is by law empowered to do and considers necessary or expedient in the interests of public welfare or in circumstances where publicity would prejudice the interests of justice, the welfare of persons under voting age or the protection of the private lives of persons concerned in the proceedings; or

(b) is by law empowered or required to do in the interests of defence, public safety or public order.

(14) In the event that the trial of a person is not commenced within four months of the date on which he was committed for trial, a detailed report concerning the case shall be made by the Chief Justice to the Minister responsible for the National Legal Administration.

GENERALLY

Referred to

by Frost C.J. in *The State v Peter Painke (No 2)* [1977] PNGLR 141 at pp.143,146.

(15) Every person convicted of an offence is entitled to have his conviction and sentence reviewed by a higher court or tribunal according to law.

MEANING OF 'ACCORDING TO LAW' IN SECTION 37(15)

per Kidu C.J.

It was said that because s.37 appears in the part of the Constitution headed 'Sub Division B-Fundamental Rights', s.37(15) is an absolute right incapable of being cut down by any ordinary law. This would have been true except for the words 'according to law'. The argument that 'according to law' here means the review of the conviction and sentence must be according to principles such as fair hearing, hearing within a reasonable time and so forth seems to me to be unnecessarily restrictive of the meaning of the phrase 'according to law'.

The term 'law' is defined in Sch.1.2(1) as including the underlying law. It seems to me that the term 'law' as appearing in s.37(15) of the Constitution means any law applicable to or affecting s.37(15), if a liberal interpretation of s.35(15) is applied as dictated by Sch.1.5 of the Constitution which reads:

(1) Each Constitutional Law is intended to be read as a whole.
(2) All provisions of, and all words, expressions and propositions in, a Constitutional Law shall be given their fair and liberal meaning.

That the right guaranteed by s.37(15) can not be done away with by any Act is not open to dispute. Any Act which purports to do this will be quite clearly unconstitutional. See *Constitutional Reference No. 2 of 1978; In Re The Corrective Institutions Act 1957* [1978] PNGLR 404.

This is not such a case. Section 27 of the *Supreme Court Act* does not prohibit appeals; it merely regulates the right to appeal. In my opinion s.37(15) itself allows this to be done by subjecting the right to be '*according to law*'.

Avia Aihi v The State [1981] PNGLR 81 at p.85; see also Kearney Dep.C.J. at p.89, Greville Smith J. at p.94, Andrew J. at p.99; Kapi J. at p.106.

DISTINCTION BETWEEN REVIEW AND APPEAL

per Kidu C.J.

Counsel for the respondent submitted that what is guaranteed in s.37(15) is an entitlement to *review*, and not a right of *appeal*; that ss.21 and 27 of the *Supreme Court Act* relate to appeals and therefore s.37(15) of the Constitution does not affect them. It was argued that ss.21 and 27 of the Act were laws made under s.155(2)(c) of the constitution which provides that the Supreme Court 'has such other jurisdiction and powers as are conferred on it by this Constitution or any other law'. The Constitution gives power of review to the Supreme Court under s.155(2)(b) which says the Supreme Court has 'an inherent power to review all judicial acts of the National Court'. What was submitted by counsel for the respondent was the Constitution provides for two different things in s.37(15); it guarantees the right of review whereas s.37(16) relates to the right of appeal.

I consider that s.37(16) is not to be used to infer or draw a distinction between appeals and reviews. In my opinion what s.37(16) does is to ensure that when a person is convicted and sentenced and at the time of such conviction and sentence there existed a right of appeal he should not be deprived by any law of such a right. It does not in my view create a distinction between a right of appeal and a right of review. I consider that s.37(16) has no relevance to the present matter before this Court.
Avia Aihi v The State [1981] PNGLR 81 at p.86; see also Kearney Dep.C.J. at p.89 and Kapi J. at pp.105,106 (below).

per Kapi J.

Before I consider the merits of these submissions, I shall first consider a submission by counsel for the State, namely that s.37(15) of the Constitution is not applicable because it deals with a 'review' and not an 'appeal'. He tried to distinguish between the use of the word 'appeal' in s.37(16) and 'review' in s.37(15). In my view there is no difference between the use of the words 'appeal' and 'review' under s.37(15) and (16) of the Constitution. As far as this case is concerned these terms refer to the same process. The word 'appeal' is used when a person who is given the right to appeal is invoking the power of the appellate court to review a decision of a lower court. The word 'review' is used to describe the same process from the point of view of the appellate tribunal which is exercising the power to hear the appeal by the person appealing. As a matter of English language, you cannot say that the appellate tribunal is exercising a right of appeal or is appealing a decision of a lower court, nor can you say a person who is appealing is exercising their right to review, or is reviewing against a decision of a lower court. It follows that under s.37(15) you cannot say that every person convicted of an offence is entitled to have his conviction and sentence appealed by a higher court or tribunal, according to law. In the same way, you cannot say that under s.37(16) no person shall be deprived by law of a right of review against his conviction or sentence by any court that existed at the time of the conviction or sentence as the case may be. In so far as the use of the words 'appeal' and 'review' are concerned they are referring to the same process. However, the word 'review' is wide enough to include the power of the court to review any act of the National Court by way of prerogative writs. We are not concerned with this type of review in this case. In this case we are concerned with review by way of an appeal. As far as appeals from the National Court to the Supreme Court are concerned, the right of a person to appeal or extend time in which to appeal is provided for under the *Supreme Court Act*.
Avia Aihi v The State [1981] PNGLR 81 at pp.105,106; see also Kidu C.J. at p.86 (above) and Kearney Dep.C.J. at p.89 (agreeing with Kapi J.).

EFFECT OF LIMITATION BY STATUTE

per Kearney Dep.C.J.

The first argument is put on a basis of right, that the applicant has a right to have her application considered by this Court. The argument was directed to the scope of the basic right of a convicted person under the Constitution, s.37(15). I consider that that right is not unlimited; in its terms, it contains the seeds of its own limitation in the phrase 'according to law'. That phrase, in my opinion, means the same as it does in the Constitution, s.37(4)(a), that is, it refers to the whole of the law of the country, statute and underlying, as exhaustively defined in the Constitution, s.9.

A law which imposes time-limits on appeals, such as s.27 of the Act, is not rendered unconstitutional by the Constitution, s.37(15); it is a 'law' within the meaning of that word in the phrase 'according to law'. It is therefore not surprising that the Constitution itself should contemplate that there will be statutory time-limits on appeals; for example, in s.103(4).
Avia Aihi v The State [1981] PNGLR 81 at p.89.

EFFECT ON APPEALS UNDER SUPREME COURT ACT

per Kearney Dep.C.J.

I consider that both s.21 and s.27 of the Act [providing time limits in respect to appeals]

are founded on the Constitution, s.155(2)(c) and s.37(15). They regulate the rights of individuals in a certain respect, namely the right to appeal in criminal cases; and confer correlative appellate jurisdiction on this Court to entertain such appeals, so regulated. They do not purport to be exhaustive of appellate power.
Avia Aihi v The State [1981] PNGLR 81 at p.90.

AVENUE AVAILABLE WHEN SECTION 37(15) RIGHTS ARE TIME BARRED.

per Kearney Dep.C.J.

I consider that the applicant, a person affected by a judicial act of the National Court, lacking now any right to have that act reviewed, may yet ask this Court to exercise its inherent and discretionary power to review, under the Constitution s.155(2)(b); and the court may hear the appeal.
Avia Aihi v The State [1981] PNGLR 81 at p.93; for further detail see commentary under s.155(2) and (4).

AS TO WHETHER SECTION 30 OF THE CORRECTIVE INSTITUTIONS ACT 1957 CONTRAVENED SECTION 37(15).

Note: Section 30 *Corrective Institutions Act* provided:

There is no appeal from a finding or extension of sentence made or imposed under this Part [decisions on Corrective Institution offences by Visiting Justices].

Held

Section 30 must yield to s.37(15), and pending legislation, appeal is to lie from decisions under ss.26 and 27 of the *Corrective Institutions Act* to the National Court. Such appeals should be brought in accordance with the provisions of the *Local Courts Act* — recourse being had to a report from the presiding magistrate and affidavits when necessary.
Constitutional Reference No 2 of 1978; Re Corrective Institutions Act 1957 [1978] PNGLR 404 at p.410.

per Prentice C.J., Saldanha and Andrew JJ.

We are satisfied therefore that Pt.VI's provisions do not purport to authorize unconstitutionally the deprivation of liberty or power to punish in a body other than a 'court' (s.42, s.159 of the Constitution) — even if one were to assume that 'corrective institution offences' are to be included in the phrase 'criminal offences' as used in s.159.

That being so, decisions of the court authorized by the *Corrective Institutions Act* to deal with corrective institutions offences (both minor and aggravated) if resulting in convictions, must be subject to a right in the convicted person to have both conviction and sentence reviewed (s.37(15) of the Constitution). In the sense in which used here, it seems that 'review' is equivalent to 'appeal'. Section 30 of the *Corrective Institutions Act*, insofar as it purports to deny any such right of appeal must yield to s.37(15) and should therefore be ruled invalid (s.10 of the Constitution).
Constitutional Reference No 2 of 1978; Re Corrective Institutions Act 1957 [1978] PNGLR 404 at pp.408, 409.

Referred to

by Kearney J. in *Saki v The State* [1980] PNGLR 33 at p.34;

by Bredmeyer J. in *Amaiu v Commissioner of Corrective Institutions and The State* (1983 Unreported) N417 at p.5.

GENERALLY

Referred to

by Quinlivan A.J. in *Kaupa v Police at Hutjena* (1981 Unreported) N320(M) at p.6;

by Quinlivan A.J. in *Orabi v Tamean* (1981 Unreported) N323(M) at p.4;

by Quinlivan A.J. in *Dai v Manda (No 1)* (1981 Unreported) N342 at p.4; per Curiam (Kidu C.J., Kapi Dep.C.J., Bredmeyer J.) in *S.C.R. No 3 of 1982; Re ss.57 and 155(4) of the CONSTITUTION* [1982] PNGLR 405 at p.406 (as entrenching the right of a detainee to have access to the Public Solicitor for the purpose of giving instructions to institute or prosecute an appeal to a higher court);

by Kidu C.J. in *In the matter of the Organic Law on National Elections; Malipu Balakau v Paul Torato and anor* (1983 Unreported) SC256 at pp.2–4 (s.37(15) has no bearing upon the general power of the National Court and the Supreme Court to review the judicial acts of inferior courts pursuant to s.155 of the Constitution), see also Kapi Dep.C.J. at pp.16–19.

(16) No person shall be deprived by law of a right of appeal against his conviction or sentence by any court that existed at the time of the conviction or sentence, as the case may be.

GENERALLY

Comment

Refer to annotations on s.37(15) in respect of the distinction between review and appeal; see *Avia Aihi v The State* [1981] PNGLR 81, (Kidu C.J. at p.86, and Kapi J. pp.105,106; but see also under s.155(2)(b)).

Referred to

by Kidu C.J. in *In the Matter of the Organic Law on National Elections: Malipu Balakau v Paul Torato and anor* (1983 Unreported) SC256 at pp.2–4 (s.37(15) has no bearing upon the general power of the National or Supreme Court to review the judicial acts of inferior courts pursuant to s.155 of the Constitution); see also Kapi Dep.C.J. at pp.16–19.

(17) All persons deprived of their liberty shall be treated with humanity and with respect for the inherent dignity of the human person.

AS TO WHAT CONSTITUTES INHUMANE TREATMENT

Held

Where defendants were arrested in one province and taken on a two hour journey to another province, Frost C.J. held that this was 'against the spirit of the Constitution s.37(17), which provides that persons deprived of their liberty should be treated with humanity, that in the circumstances of this case the men should [not] have been taken so far a distance for their trial without any advance warning to their families'.
Yamore Memera and ors v Matthew Bisang [1976] PNGLR 419 at p.421.

Held

Kidu C.J. found that beatings administered to young detainees while on remand constituted a violation of s.37(17). The Chief Justice made orders to cease, and awarded damages.
Re Heni Pauta and Kenneth Susuve [1982] PNGLR 7.

Referred to

by Bredmeyer J. in *Amaiu v Commissioner of Corrective Institutions and The State* (1983 Unreported) N417 at p.3; (see also annotation for this case under s.36 of the Constitution).

(18) Accused persons shall be segregated from convicted persons and shall be subject to separate treatment appropriate to their status as unconvicted persons.

AS TO JUVENILE REMANDEES

Held

The National Court may order the transfer of a young remandee from B Division which accommodated juveniles . . .
Re Heni Pauta and Kenneth Susuve [1982] PNGLR 7; see Kidu C.J. at pp.14,15.

Referred to

by Narakobi A.J. in *The State v Lakio Tambai and ors* (1980 Unreported) N235 at p.3.

(19) Persons under voting age who are in custody in connexion with an offence or alleged offence shall be separated from other persons in custody and be accorded treatment appropriate to their age.

GENERALLY

Referred to

by Narakobi A.J. in *The State v Lakio Tambai and ors* (1980 Unreported) N235 at p.3;

by Kidu C.J. in *Re Heni Pauta and Kenneth Susuve* [1982] PNGLR 7 at p.14.

(20) An offender shall not be transferred to an area away from that in which his relatives reside except for reasons of security or other good cause and, if such a transfer is made, the reason for so doing shall be endorsed on the file of the offender.

(21) Nothing in this section —
(a) derogates Division III.4 (*principles of natural justice*); or
(b) affects the powers and procedures of village courts.

C.P.C. Report Ch.5 Part 1 p.10

51. We recognize that some of the rules for a fair trial which are laid down in this recommendation are not appropriate for hearings in the newly established village courts, as these rules have been developed under the English common law which we have inherited. We have therefore proposed that the powers and procedures of village courts as laid down in the recently passed *Village Courts Act* (or in similar legislation) should not be invalid to the extent that these conflict with the rules laid down here, unless those powers or procedures are against principles of natural justice. (One of these principles is the right to be heard, and another that the tribunal which hears a case should not biased in favour of one side).

per Saldanha J

It is possible that the principles of natural justice are part and parcel of the protection of the law guaranteed by s.37 of the Constitution by virtue of s.37(21)(a).
Premdas v The Independent State of Papua New Guinea [1979] PNGLR 329 at p.362; but see also annotations under s.59.

(22) Notwithstanding Subsection 21(b) the powers and procedures of village courts shall be exercised in accordance with the principles of natural justice.

GENERALLY

Referred to

by Saldanha J. in *Premdas v The Independent State of Papua New Guinea* [1979] PNGLR 329 at p.362; see also Wilson J. (dissenting) at p.376;

by Miles J. in *Iambakey Okuk v Fallscheer* [1980] PNGLR 274 at p.291.

Subdivision C. — Qualified Rights

General

38. GENERAL QUALIFICATIONS ON QUALIFIED RIGHTS.

(1) For the purposes of this Subdivision, a law that complies with the requirements of this section is a law that is made and certified in accordance with Subsection (2), and that —
- (a) regulates or restricts the exercise of a right or freedom referred to in this Subdivision to the extent that the regulation or restriction is necessary —
  - (i) taking account of the National Goals and Directive Principles and the Basic Social Obligations, for the purpose of giving effect to the public interest in —
    - (A) defence; or
    - (B) public safety; or
    - (C) public order; or
    - (D) public welfare; or
    - (E) public health (including animal and plant health); or
    - (F) the protection of children and persons under disability (whether legal or practical); or
    - (G) the development of underprivileged or less advanced groups or areas; or
  - (ii) in order to protect the exercise of the rights and freedoms of others; or

(b) makes reasonable provision for cases where the exercise of one such right may conflict with the exercise of another,

to the extent that the law is reasonably justifiable in a democratic society having a proper respect for the rights and dignity of mankind.

OVERVIEW

Comment

J. Goldring in his book *The Constitution of Papua New Guinea*, at p.223 states:

Only the rights to life, to freedom from cruel or inhuman treatment, and to protection of the law are expressed in absolute terms. All other rights guaranteed by the Constitution may be qualified or limited by a law which is passed by an absolute majority of the Parliament and certified accordingly by the Speaker under s.110 of the Constitution. Such a law must be expressed to be a law which does restrict a guaranteed right or freedom and must specify the right or freedom which it purports to restrict or modify (s.38(2)). It must, in accordance with s.38(1), be a law that:

(a) regulates or restricts the exercise of a right or freedom referred to in this Subdivision to the extent that the regulation or restriction is necessary —
  (i) taking account of the National Goals and Directive Principles and the Basic Social Obligations, for the purpose of giving effect to the public interest in —
    (A) defence; or
    (B) public safety; or
    (C) public order; or
    (D) public welfare; or
    (E) public health (including animal and plant health); or
    (F) the protection of children and persons under disability (whether legal or practical); or
    (G) the development of under-privileged or less advanced groups or areas; or
  (ii) in order to protect the exercise of the rights and freedoms of others; or
(b) makes reasonable provision for cases where the exercise of one such right may conflict with the exercise of another, to the extent that the law is reasonably justifiable in a democratic society having a proper respect for the rights and dignity of mankind.

However the terms of s.38 do not, in our opinion, warrant the conclusion that 'all other rights guaranteed by the Constitution may be qualified or limited' by a law passed in accordance with s.38.

Read naturally s.38 merely provides a complex criterion or test against which the form and content of other laws may be measured.

This yardstick is important because the Constitution expressly provides that many of the civil and political rights conferred in Sub-division C can be regulated or restricted by a law which takes that form.

There are, however, a number of provisions within Sub-division C that do not contain words permitting the regulation or restriction of specific rights. These include:—

Section 40, validity of emergency laws; s.41, proscribed acts; s.42, liberty of the person; s.50, right to vote and stand for public office; s.53, protection from unjust deprivation of property; s.54, special provision in relation to certain lands; s.55, equality of citizens; s.56, other rights and privileges of citizens.

It is submitted that the rights contained in these provisions can not be regulated or restricted by a law which complies with s.38 because these rights are not expressed as being subject to regulation or restriction at all by s.38. It is only those rights that contain a provision permitting regulation or restriction that may be regulated or restricted, and then only in accordance with s.38, because that is the form stipulated.

A further matter that has not been decided by the Supreme Court, is the extent to which s.38 applies to pre-Independence statutes. The approach of the courts has been to avoid invalidating pre-Independence statutes by construing them in such a way that they are not held to regulate or restrict subdivision C rights. [for detailed annotations see under s.38(2)].

GENERALLY

Referred to

by Raine J. in *Cory v Blyth* [1976] PNGLR 274 at p.278 (Section 38(1) and the *Defamation Act* considered: see under s.46);

by Frost C.J. in *Reference No. 1 of 1977* [1977] PNGLR 362 at p.366;

by Greville Smith J. in *Re s.42 of the Constitution and Jacob Hendrich Prai* [1979] PNGLR 42 at p.44;

by Prentice C.J. in *Premdas v The Independent State of Papua New Guinea* [1979] PNGLR 329 at p.340 (rights of non-citizens can be affected by laws not having the form of s.38);

by Kidu C.J. in *The State v Kosi and ors* (1981 Unreported) N306 at p.4 (whether the 'unlawful assembly' crimes defined in ss.61 and 62 of the Criminal Code 'regulate or restrict' rights under ss.45, 46, 47 and 52 of the Constitution. Held not to so regulate or restrict. 'Anything uttered in a meeting or rally that advocates violence or force or that defames is in my opinion outside the protection guaranteed by the Constitution.');

by Kapi Dep.C.J. in *Hetura Paz Development v Nuigini Nuis P/L* [1982] PNGLR 250 at pp.253,254 (Section 38 and the *Defamation Act* considered: see under s.46).

(2) For the purposes of Subsection (1), a law must —
  (a) be expressed to be a law that is made for that purpose; and
  (b) specify the right or freedom that it regulates or restricts; and
  (c) be made, and certified by the Speaker in his certificate under Section 110 (*certification as to making of laws*) to have been made, by an absolute majority.

AS TO WHETHER PRE-INDEPENDENCE STATUTES ARE TO BE DEEMED TO COMPLY WITH THE REQUIREMENTS OF SECTION 38.

Comment

It remains an open question as to whether pre-Independence statutes, adopted as Acts of the Parliament under Sch.2.6(2), should be read as if they comply with the terms of s.38. Sch.2.6(2) provides that such adopted Acts 'apply to the extent to which they applied . . . immediately before Independence . . .'.

Sch.2.6(2) is however expressly subject to any Constitutional Law and the Supreme Court in *Peter v South Pacific Breweries* [1976] PNGLR 573 held that adopted laws are subject to the same constitutional limitations as are Acts of Parliament.

As no pre-Independence statute takes the form required by s.38(2), strict application of the above principle would entail the invalidity of all such laws which would otherwise restrict or regulate the rights conferred under Sub-division C.

Alternatively it could be argued that it is more natural to read s.38(2) as applying only prospectively so that adopted laws are not affected retrospectively and thus do not need to comply with the 'form' requirements of s.38.

This question has never been squarely before the Courts. Only Raine J. in *Cory v Blyth* [1976] PNGLR 274 at p.278 has touched upon the matter and he was able to decide the issue in that case on different grounds without expressing an opinion upon the s.38 matter.

In the authors' view, although both alternatives can be plausibly argued, there is reason to prefer the view that no pre-Independence statute can affect a qualified right. In our opinion s.38(2) is best read as expressing the intention that the rights guaranteed under the Constitution in Sub-division C can be restricted *only* by the deliberate act of an absolute majority of the members of the post-Independence Parliament.

GENERALLY

Referred to

by Prentice C.J. in *Premdas v The Independent State of Papua New Guinea* [1979] PNGLR 329 at p.341 (restrictions imposed by law on non-citizens do not have to comply with s.38(2)).

(3) The burden of showing that a law is a law that complies with the requirements of Subsection (1) is on the party relying on its validity.

ONUS OF PROOF

per Kapi J.

Mr Donigi submitted that the State has the onus of proof that a law passed by the Parliament is within the limitation provided by s.50(2)of the Constitution. He submitted this by way of analogy from s.(38)3 of the Constitution. Mr Maino on the other hand submitted that the onus of proving the unconstitutionality of an Act is on the party alleging that it is unconstitutional. He relied on the opinion of three Judges in the *Vanuatu Case, S.C.R. 4 of 1980 (No. 2)* [1982] PNGLR 65.

The right to stand for elective public office comes under the provisions which deal with qualified rights. Under these provisions, there are a number of ways a right may be qualified. A right may be regulated or restricted by a law that makes 'reasonable provision' — see s.44(a) and s.47(a) of the Constitution. Or a law may regulate or restrict a right by imposing 'reasonable restrictions' — see s.46(1)(a) and s.47(a) of the Constitution. Or a law may regulate or restrict a right which is 'reasonably necessary' — see s.53(5)(f). Or a law may regulate or restrict a right which complies with all the requirements of s.38 of the Constitution.

Where a law is required to comply with the provisions of s.38, it must comply with all the requirements set out under s.38. One of the requirements under s.38 of the Constitution and perhaps the most important one is that, where a law regulates or restricts or makes reasonable provisions etc., such laws are to be 'to the extent that the law is reasonably justifiable in a democratic society having a proper regard for the rights and dignity of mankind'.

In my view it would be inconsistent with s.38(3) of the Constitution to suggest a different onus of proof on the requirement 'reasonably justifiable in a democratic society which has regard for the right and dignity of mankind' wherever it appears in the same sub-division. Whether the requirement of 'reasonably justifiable in a democratic society' appears under s.38 with other requirements or by itself as required under s.50(2) of the Constitution, in my opinion, the onus would be the same. Wherever this phrase has been used in this sub-division, no provision on the question of onus is included.

The answer in my view is quite simple; this is adequately covered under s.38(3) of the Constitution. This construction makes sense because all these provisions appear under the same sub-division. In my view, this construction is in line with the intention of the Constitutional Planning Committee. When the Constitutional Planning Committee made its recommendations on the right to stand for election to public office, it recommended that this right may be subject to reasonable restrictions. By Recommendation 13, sub-s.3, the Committee recommended:

> the burden of proving that a restriction referred to in Clause 1 above, is a reasonable restriction lies upon the person asserting that the restriction is reasonable.
>
> (See *C.P.C. Report*, p.5/1/28 to p.5/1/29, Recommendation 13).

As I have explained before the question of onus does not appear under s.50(2) of the Constitution because this is adequately dealt with under s.38(3).

Our Constitution in this regard has made plain what has been a conflict of views by the Justices in India regarding the question of onus relating to the restrictions on the fundamental rights. It appears that our Constitution adopted the view held by Meredith C.J. in the consideration of the Indian Constitution in *Brajnandan Sharma v Bihar* [1950] AIR Patna 322. This view has been subsequently contradicted by later decisions in India. See *S.I.S. Limited v Union of India* [1972] AIR Delhi 159. The view held by Meredith C.J.,

is endorsed by Dr. T.K.K. Iyer in his very informative book *Judicial Review of Reasonableness in Constitutional Law* at pp.93 to 99. I endorse the reasons given for this view.
S.C.R. No 2 of 1982; Re Organic Law [1982] PNGLR 214 at pp.237,238; see also Kidu C.J. at p.221.

39. — 'REASONABLY JUSTIFIABLE IN A DEMOCRATIC SOCIETY', ETC.

(1) The question, whether a law or act is reasonably justifiable in a democratic society having a proper regard for the rights and dignity of mankind, is to be determined in the light of the circumstances obtaining at the time when the decision on the question is made.

AS TO WHAT IS 'REASONABLY JUSTIFIABLE IN A DEMOCRATIC SOCIETY'

per Kearney Dep.C.J.

The constitution entrusts to this Court in many instances the decision whether a certain Act is 'reasonable'. In America and Australia, the reasonableness of an Act is for the legislature; once the end to be achieved is seen to be constitutionally legitimate, all means to achieve it which are not prohibited are constitutional. See e.g. *M'Culloch* v *Maryland* (1819) 4 Wheat 316 at p.321 and *Australian Communist Party* v *The Commonwealth* (1951) 83 CLR 1 at p.149 per Latham C.J. That is not the case in our body politic. What is 'reasonable' cannot be separated from questions of policy. In such a case the best this Court can do is to apply an objective test: 'Would a reasonable man necessarily consider the Act unreasonable?' The personal views of the Judges cannot be allowed to obtrude.
S.C.R. No 2 of 1982; Re Organic Law [1982] PNGLR 214 at p.227; see also Kidu C.J. at p.221, Greville Smith J. at p.232 and Andrews J. at p.233; but see also Kapi J. (below) at pp.235–237.

per Kapi J.

What is 'reasonably justifiable in a democratic society'? This phrase was borrowed from the pre-Independence *Human Rights Ordinance* 1971. I am not aware of any case in this jurisdiction which considered the meaning of this phrase.

It is clear from the Constitutional Planning Committee Report that this phrase was borrowed from the Constitutions of other Commonwealth Countries on Human Rights (See C.P.C. Report, p.5/1/6; para.27). The countries which have used this phrase or similar words are Zambia, Kenya, Nigeria, Uganda and Sierra Leone. Unfortunately, counsel did not refer the Court to any relevant judicial decisions in these countries.

It is extremely difficult to give any proper interpretation of the phrase. The Constitution itself avoided any definition of it. The only assistance the Constitution can offer is s.39(3) of the Constitution which sets out some of the materials to which the court may have regard to in deciding whether a law or thing is reasonably justifiable in a democratic society. Again, counsel did not take the Court through all the materials under this provision.

Within the context of s.50(2), of the Constitution the question which is posed by the use of this phrase is whether the regulation by the law which requires a deposit of K1,000 to qualify for nomination, having regard to the purpose for the deposit, has regard to the interest of all classes or groups of citizens in this country. It all boils down to the question of the reasonableness of the regulation of the exercise of the right by the law. What is the standard of the reasonableness to be applied? The courts in India have considered this question. The courts considered this in the context of Article 19 of the Constitution of India. The Constitution of India used the words 'reasonable restrictions'. In the case of *Madras* v *V.B. Row* AIR (1952) SC 196 at p.200 Patanjali Sastri C.J. said:

> It is important in this context to bear in mind the test of reasonableness, wherever prescribed, should be applied to each individual statute impugned and no abstract standard, or general pattern, or reasonableness, can be laid down as applicable to all cases. The nature of the right alleged to have been infringed, the underlying purpose of

the restrictions imposed, the extent and urgency of the evil sought to be remedied thereby, the disproportion of the imposition, the prevailing conditions at the time, should all enter into the judicial verdict. In evaluating such elusive factors and forming their own conception of what is reasonable in all circumstances of a given case, it is inevitable that the social philosophy and the scale of values of the judges participating in the decisions should play an important part, and the limit to their interference to the legislative judgment in such cases can only be dictated by their sense of responsibility and self restraint and the sobering reflection that the Constitution is meant not only for people of their way of thinking but for all, and that the majority of the elected representatives of the people have in authorizing the imposition of the restrictions considered them to be reasonable.

I would with respect adopt this passage to apply to the interpretation of what is reasonably justifiable in any given case. I note that this course has also been suggested by Donald Chalmers in an article entitled ***Human Rights and what is reasonably justifiable in a democratic society*** (1975) Vol. 3 No. 1 Melanesian Law Journal p.92. I find this approach is consistent with the approach given by the High Court of Uganda in *Uganda* v *Commissioner of Prisons; Ex-parte Matobu* (1966) EALR 514. The court was concerned with the consideration of the terms of s.30(5), of the Constitution of Uganda which is in the following terms:

30(5), Nothing contained in or under the authority of an Act of Parliament shall be held to be inconsistent with or in contravention of Articles 19, 24 or 29 of this Constitution to the extent that the Act authorized the taking during any period when Uganda is at war or any period when a declaration of state of public emergency under this Article is in force of measures that are *reasonably justifiable* for the purpose of dealing with the situation that exists during that period. (emphasis mine).

The court rejected a submission that it should apply an objective interpretation to the phrase 'reasonably justifiable' but in my view accepted an interpretation which falls in line with the test of reasonableness by Sastri C.J. in India. At p.543 of the (1966) East African Reports the court said the following:

Such measures must be reasonably justifiable for purposes of dealing with the situation which exists at any particular time and therefore whatever measures are adopted must depend upon how grave the situation is at any given time. (emphasis mine)

I also consider that the approach by the Nigerian cases would fall within the general test of reasonableness set out by Sastri C.J. In the Nigerian case of *Cheranci* v *Cheranci* (1960) NRNLR 24, the Court was concerned with a consideration of whether the provisions of the *Northern Region Children and Young Persons Law of 1958* was a law which was reasonably justifiable in a democratic society in the interest of public order, public defence etc. Bate J. at p.29 said:

'a restriction upon a fundamental human right must before it may be considered justifiable —

(a) be necessary in the interest in the public defence, public order, etc.; and
(b) must not be excessive or out of proportion to the object which it is sought to achieve'.

In another Nigerian case of *Dr. Chike Obi v DPP* (1961) Unreported F.S.C. 56, the court was concerned with the consideration of the provisions of the Criminal Code in relation to sedition. The Chief Justice Sir Adetokunbo Ademola said:

It seems to me that ... it must be justifiable in a democratic society to take reasonable precautions to preserve public order and this may involve the prohibition of acts which if unchecked and unrestrained might lead to disorder even though those Acts would not themselves do so directly.

(Case is referred to by Nwabueze in *Constitutional Law of the Nigerian Republic* — p.396).

The subjective approach to the interpretation of what is reasonably justifiable is confirmed by the provisions of s.39(1) of the *Constitution.*

S.C.R. No 2 of 1982; Re Organic Law [1982] PNGLR 214 at pp.235–237; but see Kearney Dep.C.J. (above) at p.227, Kidu C.J. at p.221, Greville Smith J. at p.232, Andrew J. at p.233.

GENERALLY

Referred to

by Narakobi A.J. in *Tabo Sipo* v *Meli* (1980 Unreported) N240 at p.6.

(2) A law shall not be declared not to be reasonably justifiable in a society having a proper regard for the rights and dignity of mankind except by the Supreme Court or the National Court, or any other court prescribed for the purpose by or under an Act of the Parliament, and unless the court is satisfied that the law was never so justifiable such a declaration operates as a repeal of the law as at the date of the declaration.

(3) For the purposes of determining whether or not any law, matter or thing is reasonably justified in a democratic society that has a proper regard for the rights and dignity of mankind, a court may have regard to —

(a) the provisions of this Constitution generally, and especially the National Goals and Directive Principles and the Basic Social Obligations; and

(b) the Charter of the United Nations; and

(c) the Universal Declaration of Human Rights and any other declaration, recommendation or decision of the General Assembly of the United Nations concerning human rights and fundamental freedoms; and

(d) the European Convention for the Protection of Human Rights and Fundamental Freedoms and the Protocols thereto, and any other international conventions, agreements or declarations concerning human rights and fundamental freedoms; and

(e) judgements, reports and opinions of the International Court of Justice, the European Commission of Human Rights, the European Court of Human Rights and other international courts and tribunals dealing with human rights and fundamental freedoms; and

(f) previous laws, practices and judicial decisions and opinions in the country; and

(g) laws, practices and judicial decisions and opinions in other countries; and

(h) the Final Report of the pre-Independence Constitutional Planing Committee dated 13 August 1974 and presented to the pre-Independence House of Assembly on 16 August 1974, as affected by decisions of that House on the report and by decisions of the Constituent Assembly on the draft of this Constitution; and

(i) declarations by the International Commission of Jurists and other similar organizations; and

(j) any other material that the court considers relevant.

AS TO THE TERM 'PROPER REGARD'

per Kearney Dep. C.J.

The 'proper regard' which characterizes such a society is, I think, for present purposes to be found mainly by an examination of our own Constitution, though the other matters listed in s.39(3) may also be regarded.
S.C.R. No 2 of 1982; Re Organic Law [1982] PNGLR 214 at p.230; see also Kapi J. at pp.235,236.

40. — VALIDITY OF EMERGENCY LAWS

Nothing in this Part invalidates an emergency law as defined in Part X (*emergency powers*), but nevertheless so far as is consistent with their purposes and terms all such laws shall be interpreted and applied so as not to affect or derogate a right or freedom referred to in this Division to an extent that is more than is reasonably necessary to deal with the emergency concerned and matters arising out of it, but only so far as is reasonably justifiable in a democratic society having a proper regard for the rights and dignity of mankind.

41. — PROSCRIBED ACTS

(1) Notwithstanding anything to the contrary in any other provision of any law, any act that is done under a valid law but in the particular case —
- (a) is harsh or oppressive; or
- (b) is not warranted by, or is disproportionate to, the requirements of the particular circumstances or of the particular case; or
- (c) is otherwise not, in the particular circumstances, reasonably justifiable in a democratic society having a proper regard for the rights and dignity of mankind, is an unlawful act.

CROSS REFERENCE

Constitution of the United States; Am. VIII (excessive bail and fines).

C.P.C. Report Ch.5 Part 1 p.20

120. We recommend that to provide a safeguard against abuse of or excessive use of a legal power provided for in this Part, any action which is excessive or oppressive in the actual circumstances of the case should be unlawful. Interpreting legislative provisions of this kind is not new to the courts.

DEPORTATION UNDER MIGRATION ACT AS A PROSCRIBED ACT

per Prentice C.J.

The court was informed by counsel for the Government that he was unable to discover any comparable provision in the constitutions of any of the countries of the world. And we know that this is the first occasion on which its aid has been sought in argument in this Court.

As I understand Mr Gawi's argument on this branch of his submissions, he relies upon subsections (a) and (b) of the section. The acts to which he addresses complaint are those of revocation of entry permit and making of a deportation order. He submits that such orders were harsh and oppressive, and not warranted by and disproportionate to the particular circumstances. The reasons he advances are that the applicant was acting under the directions of the Minister of the Department concerned, who himself alleges that he had the approval of the Prime Minister to engage the applicant, and that the applicant had done nothing to warrant deportation. It is material to consider, Mr Gawi says, that the applicant was not engaged under the *Ministerial Personal Staff Act* and was acting in an unpaid capacity. No significance is to be attached he says, to the fact the section appears in that subdivision (III.3.C) dealing with qualified rights; inferentially it can be prayed in aid of more basic rights as well.

I find difficulty in understanding why such a novel power should be restricted to the protection of qualified rights and not apply to basic and fundamental rights as well. Paragraph 120 of the C.P.C. report (at 5/1/20) insofar as it states 'We recommend that to provide a safeguard against abuse of or excessive use of illegal power provided for in this part' (human rights and obligations and emergency powers) 'any action which is excessive or oppressive in the actual circumstances of the case should be unlawful . . .', would appear to indicate an intention of general application — as does recommendation 19 (at 5/1/33). The body of s.41 itself contains no reference at all of its being restricted to the support of rights!

I consider that, giving s.41 a fair and liberal meaning as the court is instructed to do by Sch. 1.5(2) of the Constitution, it should be regarded as of general application. The criteria put forward in the section are clearly questions of fact. Both counsel concur in the submission that in assessing the quality of the relevant facts, the test should be an objective one. I feel that the test should be to question whether the Minister and the Committee acted as reasonable men in the circumstances, having regard to the policy of the act on the one hand and the various provisions of the Constitution on the other.

Assistance may be gained I believe, from an examination of the licensing (not migration cases) referred to by government counsel on this aspect, namely *Associated Provincial Picture Houses Ltd. v Wednesbury Corporation* [1948] 1 KB 223 and *Padfield v Minister of Agriculture, Fisheries and Food* [1968] AC 997. In the former case Lord Greene M.R. stated, the case being one where abuse of a discretionary power was alleged (at pp.228–230):

> When discretion of this kind is granted the law recognises certain principles upon which the discretion must be exercised, but within the four corners of those principles the discretion, in my opinion, is an absolute one and cannot be questioned in any court of law ... that the decision of the ... authority can be upset if it is proved to be unreasonable, really meant that it must be proved to be unreasonable in the sense that the court considers it to be a decision that no reasonable body could have come to. It is not what the court considers unreasonable, a different thing altogether.

In *Padfield's* case, Lord Reid sees the order of mandamus as running to the Minister under the Act in question, where the Minister by reason of having misconstrued the Act or for any other reason, so uses his discretion as to thwart or run counter to the policy and objects of the Act. There can be no such matter urged in the instant case.

There are five affidavits before the court, those of the applicant of 3rd and 4th July, that of the Minister Roy Evara of 22nd July, that of Secretary John Natera of 27th July, and that of Minister N.E. Olewale of 27th July.

The facts which emerge disclose a conflict between the desires of the Minister Mr. Evara and the instructions of the Prime Minister. The applicant apparently assumed the role of and described himself as, an 'executive officer' between the end of February and the 2nd of May. He issued instructions direct to the departmental staff — on 5th March for example he issued eleven minutes. He involved himself in another Department's affairs. He had access to classified material. He had not been subject to a security check, nor had he been required to take the oath of secrecy. It must be inferred I think that he became aware of the Prime Minister's letters requiring his dismissal from the office (though not from the private counsels of the Minister outside office hours). He continued to issue instructions. He was present in the office with access to files as late as 24th May and 6th June. His activities clearly affected staff work. It may be that he stayed on at the urging of Minister Evara, but when he did so against the express requirements of the Prime Minister, he as a politically aware academic must have known he was possibly exposing himself to executive action. He himself indicated in his submission to the Secretary of the Department of Foreign Affairs and Trade that he became associated with 'student political arm' at the University.

It is I think fair to say that a serious situation had arisen as a result of the applicant's access to confidential documents when not employed under the *Ministerial Personal Staff Act* 1972 and was still employed in the Department of Politics and Administrative Studies at the University; and that a serious staff and morale situation had arisen at the Department of Primary Industry because of his activities therein. In those circumstances it appears to me that the Minister acted reasonably and in accordance with the policy and intent of the *Migration Act 1963* and its 1975 amending Act which is entitled — 'An Act to amend the Migration Act 1963 as amended to date, to give the Government greater control over the entry into and stay in Papua New Guinea of non-nationals . . .'

Both the Minister and the Committee acted lawfully in my opinion. That I believe they could each have acted more advisedly and with greater *apparent* regard to fairness and proprieties — an end which no doubt would have been furthered by a public hearing at which the applicant was allowed to make personal representation — is not in my opinion, to the point. They had acted within well understood principles as to a sovereign state's maintaining control over the activities of aliens within its borders. I do not consider the revocation of entry permit and order for deportation to have been shown to be harsh or oppressive — even having regard to the professional contract which the applicant held. Nor do I regard it as unwarranted by or disproportionate to the requirements of the particular case. No doubt the problem could have been met by the withdrawal of the Minister's portfolio should he have continued to insist on the applicant's presence and advice in departmental affairs. That the state of concern about staff morale and security was met rather by the order to deport the applicant, is not I think a matter which comes to his assistance in invoking s.41.

I would answer question 3, 'No'. Having regard to my suggested answers to the foregoing questions, I would answer question 5, 'No'.

Premdas v The Independent State of Papua New Guinea [1979] PNGLR 329 at pp.343–346; see also Raine Dep.C.J. (below) at pp.349,350, Andrew J. (below) at pp.399,400 Saldanha J. (below) at pp.358,359.

per Raine Dep.C.J.

Question 3.

The answer to this requires an examination of s.41 of the Constitution which is set out in other judgments. The section is an unusual one, I have never had to consider it before. The Chief Justice in his judgment said that he understood Mr Gawi to rely on s.41(1)(a) and (b). This may well be correct. Whether it is or not, my notes do not assist me. I place some reliance on subsection (c). It reads:

or
(c) is otherwise or not, in the particular circumstances, reasonably justifiable in a democratic society having a proper regard for the rights and dignity of mankind . . . .

Although subsection (c) is an *alternative* reason for striking at certain acts; and rendering them unlawful, it seems to me that it gives guidance in construing the section as a whole. The circumstances here were most particular. I see a reasonable justification for the action taken, even in 'a democratic society'. I see nothing harsh, oppressive, or unwarranted in the circumstances.

A democracy does not permit those living within it to have, as, it were, absolute licence. An Executive decision might hurt, and here and elsewhere, as we all know, people grumble at some of the Executive decisions made from time to time. But how can it be said that 'the rights and dignity' of Dr Premdas have been infringed. He bears the onus, and I do not believe he has discharged it. It may be that I as a judge might have come to a different conclusion, but that is not to the point. I am unable to say that the Minister and the appellate Committee fell foul of the requirements of all or any of subsections (a), (b) and (c). I think I might have acted differently, that is, adopted different procedures, had I been in their place. But I am not, nor was I, in their place. My task, and that of my brethren, is to examine what the Minister and the Committee did, or, if you like, failed to do, as representatives of what is a completely sovereign state. I see no good reason to state that what they did constituted an illegality.

Few areas involving the intervention of the Executive can be more sensitive than the presence on a country's soil of aliens thought to be undesirable or even dangerous. It is an area where, I suppose, mistakes have and will be made. My position is that I am not persuaded here that a grave mistake, or mistake at all, was made by the senior people involved. Obviously there was, within Minister Evara's Department, a most serious clash of personalities. The Prime Minister's attitute was twice made very clear. The remedy was, to put it bluntly, seen to be surgery. As an Executive device I am not persuaded, on a balance of probabilities, (see s.41(2)) that the surgery was so drastic and so clearly wrong as to be manifestly unreasonable in the sense that nobody could reasonably come to such a decision, placed in the Minister's shoes, or those of the Committee.

I generally agree with what the Chief Justice and my brother Andrew have to say on the matter.

Premdas v The Independent State of Papua New Guinea [1979] PNGLR 329 at pp.349, 350; see also Prentice C.J. (above) at pp.343–346; Saldanha J. (below) at pp.358, 359 and Andrew J. (below) at pp.399, 400.

per Saldanha J.

The applicant maintains that having regard to the fact that his services were rendered free of charge, at the express invitation of the Minister and with the approval of the Prime Minister the revocation of his entry permit is harsh and oppressive or, alternatively, is not warranted by, or is disproportionate to, the requirements of the circumstances of his case. Mr Evara has sworn an affidavit deposing that the applicant's appointment had the approval of Miss Kekedo, the Acting Secretary of the Department, and of the Prime Minister. There have been no afidavits in reply either from Miss Kekedo or from the Prime Minister but the two letters from the Prime Minister to Mr. Evara would seem to suggest that the Prime Minister objected strongly to the physical presence of the applicant within the Department and the great latitude which had been allowed to the applicant. The applicant must have been aware of these letters but he chose to ignore the Prime Minister's wishes right up the eve of the service of the notice of revocation upon him. As a political scientist he should have known better.

According to Mr. Natera the applicant issued memoranda to various officers of the Department signed by him as 'executive officer' and his presence and activities had a disturbing influence and affected morale in the Department.

Miss Kekedo's letter to him dated 20th June, 1979, stated that the Minister had considered that his activities were 'disruptive and detrimental to the good government of this country'.

The applicant was Chairman of the Political and Administrative Studies Department at the University and the Committee of Review would appear to have taken the view that his dual rule as lecturer at the University and aide to the Minister could have led to a conflict of interest and a clash of loyalties.

The Prime Minister had told Mr. Evara on 18th April to terminate the applicant's services. By 8th May he appears to have been furious that Mr. Evara had not got rid of the applicant and that he still had access to confidential material. Of course, the Prime Minister could have dismissed Evara as Minister but as he had only recently formed a new Coalition Government consisting of the Pangu Party and the United Party and while he himself was a member of the Pangu Party Mr Evara was a member of the United Party, the Prime Minister may have had his difficulties. It might have been thought more politic to get rid of the applicant by revoking his entry permit. After all the decisions of Ministers are governed by policy and expediency and, the fact that this particular decision may have resulted in incidental, but not necessarily intentional, harshness to the applicant, is surely irrelevant.

Also in judging the Minister's act the test must be objective and not subjective. It is not a question of whether the court thinks the Minister's act was harsh and oppressive. The question is: did the Minister act within the scope of his responsibility for the good government of the country? .... I believe he did.

I am of the view that the Minister's decision cannot be challenged on this ground and I would answer question 3 'No'.

Premdas v The Independent State of Papua New Guinea [1979] PNGLR 329 at pp.358, 359; see also Prentice C.J. (above) at pp.343–346, Raine Dep.C.J. (above) at pp.349,350 and Andrew J. (below) at pp.399,400.

per Andrew J.

This section of the Constitution is perhaps unique in that there appears to be no parallel in any other Constitution of any of the countries of the world. It appears in the introductory part to the qualified rights section. However, the section is in wide terms and does not restrict itself to qualified rights. It may be that it applied also to fundamental rights but I find it is not necessary to decide that question here.

I turn to the facts in this case. Affidavit evidence has been placed before this Court. I do not set out their contents but in my view there is shown, on the balance of probabilities, that:

(a) a serious staff and morale situation had arisen at the Department of Primary Industry, because of Dr Premdas' interference in the affairs of that Department, and
(b) a serious situation had developed as a result of his access to confidential documents whilst not employed under the *Ministerial Personal Staff Act* 1972 and still employed at the University of Papua New Guinea.

The applicant would have to show that the Minister's decision was one which no reasonable body could have come to and that the Minister's discretion was not exercised in accordance with the policy and objects of the *Migration Act* 1963.

The amendment to the *Migration Act* 1975 stated in its title:

An Act to amend the *Migration Act* 1963 as amended to date, to give the Government *greater control* over the *entry into and stay in* Papua New Guinea of non-nationals . . .

(The emphasis is mine.)

In my view there is nothing to show that the Minister or Committee acted in any way contrary to the policy and objects of the *Migration Act 1963*. The applicant was advised of the nature and reasons for the proceedings. He was allowed to make written representations. I have held that the rules of natural justice do not apply and I have already indicated the undoubted intention of the Constitution to give the Sovereign State control over non-nationals with the country.

I do not find the actions of the Minister or the Committee to be harsh or oppressive nor do I think it was not warranted by, or disproportionate to, the requirements of the particular circumstances of the case. In my opinion the applicant was given greater consideration than would be granted in most other countries of the world.

I would answer question 3 as 'No'.

Premdas v The Independent State of Papua New Guinea [1979] PNGLR 329 at pp.399, 400; see also Prentice C.J. (above) at pp.343–346, Raine Dep.C.J. (above) at pp.349,350 and Saldanha J. (above) at pp.358,359.

AS TO ONUS

per Curiam (*Kapi Dep.C.J., Kaputin and McDermott JJ.*).

We note that counsel did not rely on s.41 of the Constitution in relation to the detention of the appellant (whilst awaiting deportation under the *Migration Act*). The onus is on the party alleging an act is unlawful. Prentice C.J. in the *Premdas* case [1979] PNGLR 329 at p.344 said:

The criteria put forward in the section are clearly questions of fact. Both counsel concur in the submission that, in assessing the quality of the relevant facts the test should be an objective one.

There is absolutely no evidence before this Court in relation to the question of the detention of the appellant. We find that there are no facts which give rise to the consideration of s.41 of the Constitution. We therefore refuse to grant the application to release the appellant from detention.

Perryman v Minister for Foreign Affairs and Trade [1982] PNGLR 339 at p.341.

APPLICATION OF SECTION 41 TO PREVENT ABUSIVE TREATMENT OF DETAINEES IN MAXIMUM SECURITY-B DIVISION.

Held

[*Note*: Section 41 was referred to in conjunction with ss.36, 37(1), and 37(17).]

That it is cruel, harsh and oppressive to incarcerate a prisoner in the high-security 'B Division' of Bomana Corrective Institution without providing, inter-alia, for a medical officer to see the prisoners and without providing for the medical officer to play a part in determining when prisoners ought be released from that Division.

'B Division' must therefore be closed until valid regulations for its operation are brought into effect by the Commissioner of Corrective Services. For detailed annotations of this decision see under s.36.

Amaiu v Commissioner of Corrective Institutions and the State (1983 Unreported) N417 (see Bredmeyer J. at p.19).

GENERALLY

Referred to

by Greville Smith J. in *Re s.42 of the Constitution and Jacob Hendrich Prai* [1979] PNGLR 42 at p.44.

GENERALLY

Referred to

by Prentice Dep.C.J. in *Peter v South Pacific Brewery Ltd* [1976] PNGLR 531 at p.556;

by Kapi J. in *PEA and Liosi* v *Public Service Commission* (1983 Unreported) N405 at pp.4, 5.

(2) The burden of showing that Subsection (1)(a), (b) or (c) applies in respect of an act is on the party alleging it, and may be discharged on the balance of probabilities.

GENERALLY

Referred to

by Raine Dep.C.J. in *Premdas* v *The Independent State of Papua New Guinea* [1979] PNGLR 329 at p.350 (see extract above under s.41(1)); see also Frost C.J. at pp.343–346 and Andrew J. at pp.399,400;

per Curiam (Kapi Dep.C.J., Kaputin and McDermott JJ.) in *Perryman* v *Minister for Foreign Affairs and Trade* [1982] PNGLR 339 at p.341 (see extract above under s.41(1)).

(3) Nothing in this section affects the operation of any other law under which an act may be held to be unlawful or invalid.

RIGHTS OF ALL PERSONS

42. — LIBERTY OF THE PERSON.

(1) No person shall be deprived of his personal liberty except —
- (a) in consequence of his unfitness to plead to a criminal charge; or
- (b) in the execution of the sentence or order of a court in respect of an offence of which he has been found guilty, or in the execution of the order of a court of record punishing him for contempt of itself or another court or tribunal; or
- (c) by reason of his failure to comply with the order of a court made to secure the fulfilment of an obligation (other than a contractual obligation) imposed upon him by law; or
- (d) upon reasonable suspicion of his having committed, or being about to commit, an offence; or
- (e) for the purpose of bringing him before a court in execution of the order of a court; or

(f) for the purpose of preventing the introduction or spread of a disease or suspected disease, whether of humans, animals or plants, or for normal purposes of quarantine; or

(g) for the purpose of preventing the unlawful entry of a person into Papua New Guinea, or for the purpose of effecting the expulsion, extradition or other lawful removal of a person from Papua New Guinea, or the taking of proceedings for any of those purposes; or

(h) in the case of a person who is, or is reasonably suspected of being of unsound mind —

(i) or addicted to drugs or alcohol, for the purpose of his care or treatment or the protection of the community, under an order of a court; or

(ii) for the purpose of taking prompt legal proceedings to obtain an order of a court of a type referred to in Subparagraph (i).

C.P.C. Report Ch.5 Part 1 p.9

2. *PROTECTION OF PERSONAL LIBERTY*

39. Again following closely the provisions of the *Human Rights Ordinance*, we recommend that the personal liberty of all people be safeguarded, subject to certain specific exceptions. No-one should be arrested or imprisoned except under a written law, in one or other of the circumstances set out in the recommendations. For example, a person can be arrested if he is reasonably suspected of having committed a crime. He can also be arrested or imprisoned under an order of court.

RECOMMENDATIONS [p.21]

Protection of personal liberty

2. (1) No person shall be deprived of his personal liberty, except as authorized by law in any of the following cases:—

(a) to a reasonable extent in the normal course of the education or discipline of a child, by his parent, guardian or other person into whose care he has been committed, or for his protection or the protection of others;

(b) in consequence of his unfitness to plead to a criminal charge;

(c) in execution of the sentence or order of a court in respect of a criminal offence of which he has been found guilty or in the execution of the order of a court of record punishing him for contempt of itself or of another court or tribunal;

(d) by reason of his failure to comply with the order of a court made to secure the fulfilment of any obligation other than a contractual obligation, imposed upon him by law;

(e) upon reasonable suspicion of his having committed, or being about to commit, an offence;

(f) for the purpose of bringing him before a court in execution of the order of a court;

(g) in the case of a person who has not attained voting age, under the order of a court or with the consent of his guardian, for the purpose of his education or welfare during any period ending not later than the date when he attains voting age;

(h) for the purpose of preventing the introduction or spread of a disease or a suspected disease, whether of humans, animals or plants, or for normal purposes of quarantine;

(i) in the case of a person who is, or is reasonably suspected to be of unsound mind, addicted to drugs or alcohol, or a vagrant, for the purposes of his care or treatment or the protection of the community (under the order of a court); and in the case of a person reasonably suspected to be of unsound mind, for the purpose of taking prompt legal proceedings to obtain such an order of a court;

(j) for the purpose of preventing the unlawful entry of a person into Papua New Guinea or for the purpose of effecting the expulsion, extradition or other lawful removal of a person from Papua New Guinea, or the taking of proceedings for any of these purposes. [p.22]

CROSS REFERENCES

Constitution of India: Section 21; *Constitution of the United States*: Am. V; *Universal Declaration of Human Rights*: Article 9; *European Convention on Human Rights*: Article 5(1).

MEANING OF 'PERSONAL LIBERTY'

Comment

This matter was dealt with in *Premdas v The Independent State of Papua New Guinea* [1979] PNGLR 329.

Raine Dep.C.J. at p.347 said:

> . . . s.42 clearly directs itself to the body of a man, if I might put it that way. It is aimed at situations where the authorities locked somebody up for no good reason, or, if there was good reason, kept him locked up without charging him, or trying him. There are a number of necessary and reasonable exceptions to the basic principle, none of which are peculiar to this country, namely, where for reasons of health, unsoundness of mind etc., it is essential to take people into custody in what would otherwise appear to be an arbitary way . . . .

Saldanha J., in the same case, at p.357 observed,

> Section 42(1) protects the right to personal liberty or the right not to be arrested, detained or imprisoned except by due process of law. The applicant has not been deprived of his personal liberty. The rights referred to in the other subsections of s.42 are the rights of persons under detention and other similar rights. As the applicant is not under detention the question whether any of these rights have been violated does not arise.

Andrew J. at p.398 stated,

> But s.42 of the Constitution is dealing only with the liberty of the subject and almost exclusively in relation to persons charged, convicted and sentenced few offences under the criminal law.

In India, however, the words 'personal liberty' have not been confined to detention and imprisonment. One of the leading cases in that jurisdiction was about the right of a subject to travel abroad-somewhat ironic in the circumstances of *Premdas*, which is about the right of a foreigner to stay in the country.

The Supreme Court of India took a different approach to interpreting the phrase 'personal liberty'.

In *Manaka Gandi v the Union of India* [1978] AIR 597 the petitioner's passport had been impounded by an order made 'in the public interest'. The petitioner applied to have the impoundig quashed and her passport returned. Part of the petitioner's case was based on Article 21 of the Indian Constitution which reads:—

> No person shall be deprived of his life or *personal liberty* except according to procedure established by law (emphasis added)

The Supreme Court quashed the order and directed the impounded passport to be returned to the petitioner. In the majority judgment Bhagwati J. at pp.621,622 said:

> It is indeed difficult to see on what principle we can refuse to give its plain natural meaning to the expression 'personal liberty' as used in Article 21 and read it in a narrow and restricted sense so as to exclude those attributes of personal liberty which are specifically dealt with in Article 19 (which permits reasonable restrictions to be imposed on the exercise of the fundamental rights). We do not think that this would be a correct way of interpreting the provisions of the Constitution conferring fundamental rights. The attempt of the court should be to expound the reach and ambit of the fundamental rights rather than attenuate their meaning and content by a process of judicial construction.

ON SECTION 42(1)(b) AND PART VI CORRECTIVE INSTITUTIONS ACT — VJ OFFENCES

per Curiam (Prentice C.J., Saldanha and Andrew JJ.)

We are satisfied therefore that Part VI's provisions do not purport to authorise unconstitionally the deprivation of liberty or power to punish in a body other than a 'court' (s.42, s.159 of the Constitution) — even if one were to assume that 'corrective institution offences' are to be included in the phrase 'criminal offences' as used in s.159.
Constitutional Reference No 2 of 1978; Re Corrective Institutions Act 1957 [1978] PNGLR 404, at p.408.

Referred to

per Curiam (Kidu C.J., Kapi Dep.C.J., Bredmeyer J.) in *S.C.R. No 3 of 1982; re ss.57 and 155(4) of the Constitution* [1982] PNGLR 405 at p.406 (Section 42 by implication guarantees the right of a detainee to have access to legal counsel if charged with a VJ offence under the *Corrective Institutions Act*).

THE INTER-GROUP FIGHTING ACT AND THE MEANING OF 'OBLIGATION IMPOSED ON HIM BY LAW'

per Pratt J.

The fourth ground of reference before the Court involves s.42 of the Constitution and s.20 of the Act. In relation to s.20, it should be noted that the magistrate referred to in the section need not necessarily be the same magistrate who acted under ss.15, 16 or 17. If I am incorrect in my reasoning that s.17 of the Act is invalid because it fails to comply with requirements set forth in the Constitution and that one of the basic reasons why I am in error is there has been no offence committed, no charge laid and no conviction recorded, then if there is no sentence or order of a court in respect of an offence of which a person has been found guilty obviously s.42(1)(b) of the Constitution has no application. It remains however to decide whether there has been a deprivation of liberty, either within or outside the terms of s.42(1)(c) which reads:

> No person shall be deprived of his personal liberty except ....
> (c) by reason of his failure to comply with the order of a court made to secure the fulfilment of an obligation (other than a contractual obligation) imposed upon him by law.

Counsel for the State maintains that a court order is properly made under s.17 in order to ensure payment of a penalty and thus an obligation to pay is imposed by law following on, and as a result of, the order. A failure to comply with such order permits a court to impose a penalty by way of deprivation of liberty. Because s.17(b) deals with a deprivation following the execution of a sentence or order in respect of an offence, and because the State's argument is based on the contention that no offence has been committed, it is clear that the State is forced to rely heavily on s.42(1)(c). The State argument is quite brief on this point. Counsel says:

> A court order is made under s.17 to ensure the payment of the penalty. The obligation to pay is imposed by law when the order is made. If the leader as representative of the group does not comply with this order within three months, he can be imprisoned. This procedure is covered by the exception established by s.42(1)(c), and therefore s.20 of the Act is not unconstitutional.

To that argument, counsel for the affirmative replies to the effect that s.42(1)(c) is not applicable to the circumstances of a case coming within the terms of s.16 of the Act and s.20, simply because what the magistrate is doing is not enforcing an obligation imposed by law but rather is enforcing an order made by another court. Putting it another way, Mr. Amet says that the wording of the section would have to read not as presently worded — 'imposed upon him by law' — but rather — 'imposed upon him by another court'. I think this interpretation has some merit, though I would not be prepared to concede that an order made by a magistrate under s.17 is an order of 'a court' at all within the meaning of that word as used in s.42 of the Constitution, irrespective of various sections in Pt. IV of the *Inter-Group Fighting Act* granting District Court powers to an enquiring magistrate. The very fact that the legislature has distinguished the magistrate's functions under s.15 of the

Act (see s.22) indicates that the 'proceedings' referred to in ss.23 and 24 must still be performed in a manner normaly expected in a court of law and not the inquisitorial procedure prescribed in ss.16 and 17 of the Act. However I do not think it is necessary to examine this aspect as there is a much clearer breach of s.42(1)(c) of the Constitution. To my mind, s.42(1)(c) is not directed to the type of situation created by Pt. IV of the *Inter-Group Fighting Act* but is directed to an entirely different set of circumstances. Perhaps one of the best examples of the type of legislation which this sub-section of the Constitution supports may be found in the *Deserted Wives and Children Act* 1951. By s.5 of that Act, an obligation is imposed on a husband to support his wife and children and a failure to so support them will lead to a court hearing and to an order against him to fulfil his obligations. Under s.12 of the Act the court may, upon complaint on oath, issue a warrant to apprehend a person to answer a complaint that he has failed to comply with the order and after due enquiry into such complaint may then 'enforce compliance with the order by the committal of the person summonsed or apprehended to prison' for a certain period of time. There is no offence of course created under the Act and were it not for s.42(1)(c) in the Constitution, it is clear to my mind that the apprehension and imprisonment of the erring husband would be unconstitutional. It certainly could not be supported under s.42(1)(b) because there has been no sentence imposed and no order in respect of an offence. Section 12 however does underline the fact that s.42(1)(c) does not envisage a committal to gaol without giving a person an opportunity to hear what is said against him before an impartial tribunal and to put his own case in reply. Putting one's case in reply is not merely restricted to producing one's own evidence — it is an essential part of one's case to be given the opportunity to test the evidence which has been adduced against the cause which you seek to support. If the State submissions are correct, of course none of this procedure would be available to a person committed to prison under s.20 of the *Inter-Group Fighting Act*.

Though there may possibly be an obligation placed on a leader by virtue of s.16 of the Act to ensure that groups do not fight or desist from fighting (and I do not decide the point), there is no provision for any court to make an order to carry out this obligation (as in the case of the defaulting husband already referred to). The only orders made are (1) to show cause why a penalty should not be imposed and (2) the penalty itself. That is, the order being imposed is not passed in the positive terms, 'I order you to stop the fight', because there is an obligation to do so imposed by inference under the *Inter-Group Fighting Act*, but it is an order relative to a failure to carry out the obligation itself but without any proper court hearing into the facts constituting either the existence of the obligation or the failure to perform. This essential step has been omitted, and it is precisely because of the omission that the legislation cannot gain support from s.42(1)(c). If there is an obligation imposed by law then there must first of all be a court order made ordering the enforcement of the obligation before any further proceedings can be taken. And the order must be made by a 'court' within the proper and ordinary meaning of that word which implies at the very least the application of the principles of natural justice, with the possible exception of courts set up under s.172(2) of the Constitution. What Pt. IV of the Act achieves is a final order by way of penalty without any proper hearing by a court as to whether or not the obligation vests in the first place, and when it does so find, then making an order on the party to meet his obligations or face the consequences. It is just as clear by implication that the deprivation of personal liberty following on a failure to comply with such order should only result after proper proof of such failure had been given with provision made for a proper hearing of the allegations that such failure to perform had occurred.
S.C.R. No 1 of 1981; Re Inter-Group Fighting Act (1977) [1981] PNGLR 151 at pp.166–168; see also Kidu C.J., Greville Smith and Andrew JJ. at pp.155,156; Miles J. (below) at pp.171, 172.

per Miles J.

In her argument supporting the constitutional validity of s.20 of the Act, Mrs. Daniels for the Principal Legal Adviser to the National Executive Council has expressly disclaimed any reliance upon any provision in the Constitution other than s.42(1)(c). This is as follows:—

(1) No person shall be deprived of his personal liberty except —
    (c) by reason of his failure to comply with the order of a court made to secure the fulfilment of an obligation (other than a contractual obligation) imposed upon him by law,

The major judgment of the court in this case is that s.20 of the Act does not fall within s.42(1)(c) of the Constitution. I agree with this conclusion.

Assuming that a determination of liability under s.17 of the Act is 'an order of a court', it is necessary before s.42(1)(c) of the Constitution can apply that the order be 'made to secure the fulfilment of an obligation (other than a contractual obligation) imposed upon him by law'. This constitutional provision is directed at authorizing imprisonment by way of attachment of the person for non-compliance with an order of a superior court in a civil case (over and above the power to imprison for contempt of court which is authorized by s.42(1)(b)). Attachment of the person is still a procedure available under the National Court Rules: O. 50, rr. 1 to 5. Section 91 of the *Matrimonial Causes Act* 1962 enables the National Court to enforce by attachment an order for payment of maintenance or costs or in respect of the custody of or access to children. A person may be liable to imprisonment for non-payment of a maintenance order made for instance under s.12 of the *Deserted Wives and Children Act* 1951, or s.63 of the *Child Welfare Act* 1961. Such orders to pay maintenance arise out of the obligation at law to maintain a spouse or child, an obligation which is not an obligation arising out of contract. Yet the enforcement of that obligation by court order and by imprisonment for noncompliance does not depend upon the person owing the obligation being charged and convicted of a criminal offence. It has been held elsewhere that where imprisonment is ordered by a court for the vindication of a civil right and may be avoided or ended by compliance, it is not in the nature of punishment for a criminal offence: *Folwell v Folwell* [1921] V.L.R. 229 cf.*Dyke v Whittleton* [1969] 2 NSWR 494.

Is an order made upon a group leader to pay a penalty under s.17 made to secure the fulfilment of an obligation (other than a contractual obligation) imposed upon him by law? The question may be answered affirmatively only by successfully identifying the obligation which the order seeks to enforce. It is very difficult to see what such an obligation might be. It might be suggested that by inference s.17(3) casts or recognizes an obligation on group leaders to keep out of an area where group fighting takes place and to do everything reasonably within their power to prevent inter-group fighting taking place. Wherever the onus of proof may lie, s.17(1) does not limit the matters which may be raised in support of or in opposition to a notice to show cause to the matters set out in s.17(3). What the criteria are for deciding whether or not a leader has 'failed to show cause or adequate cause' are not stated. The failure of a leader to keep out of an area or to prevent group fighting taking place does not of itself give rise to any sort of liability enforceable by legal action. It is not clear that the intention of the legislature is to impose a legal obligation upon a leader to keep out of an area where tribal fighting takes place and to do everything reasonably within his power to prevent group fighting taking place. It would have been relatively easy for the legislature to have laid down such an obligation in clear terms. It would also have been relatively easy for the legislature to have declared that the purpose of an order under s.17 was to secure the fulfilment of such an obligation. This was not done. The provisions of s.8 of the Constitution, Sch.1.5 and s.10 do not require such matters to be read into the Act; on the contrary the principle of the underlying law that the ambiguity or doubt is to be resolved in favour of the liberty of the person should be applied.

It was put briefly in the written submission on behalf of the Principal Legal Adviser that the obligation to pay the penalty for which liability arises under s.17(1) is 'imposed by law when the order is made' and that 'this procedure is covered by the exception established by s.42(1)(c)'. This submission is in my view unsound and confuses the present constitutional provisions in s.42(1)(c) with their counterpart in the *Human Rights Act* 1971. According to the provisions in s.11(1)(c) of the former Act (which were similar to those of the *European Convention on Human Rights*, Art.5(1)(b)) deprivation of liberty was authorized in two situations: the first in cases of failure to comply with an order of a court and the second in order to secure the fulfilment of any obligation imposed upon a person by law. The present constitutional provision is radically different: the authorization occurs only in pursuance of a court order and then only in the case of a court order which is of special type, that is one which is made to secure the fulfilment of an obligation (other than a contractual obligation) imposed upon the person by law and independently of the order itself. For reasons already given, an adjudication under s.17 of the *Inter-Group Fighting Act* is not such an order.

S.C.R. No 1 of 1981; re Inter-Group Fighting Act (1977) [1981] PNGLR 151 at pp.171,172; see also Kidu C.J. Greville Smith and Andrew JJ. at pp.155,156 and Pratt J. (above) at pp.166–168.

GENERALLY

Referred to

by Prentice C.J., Saldanha and Andrew JJ. in *Constitutional Reference No 2 of 1978; Re Corrective Institutions Act 1957* [1978] PNGLR 401 at p.405;

by Greville Smith J. in *Re s.42 of the Constitution and Jacob Hendrich Prai* [1979] PNGLR 42 at p.43 (Section 42(1)(g) referred to);

by Prentice C.J. in *Premdas v The Independent State of Papua New Guinea* [1979] PNGLR 329 at p.338;

by Narakobi J. in *Tabo Sipo v Meli* (1980 Unreported) N240 at p.5;

per Curiam (Kapi Dep.C.J., Kaputin and McDermott JJ.) in *Perryman* v *Minister of Foreign Affairs and Trade* [1982] PNGLR 339 at p.340, (Sections 42(1)(b), (d) and (g));

by Kapi Dep.C.J. in *The State v Kor* (1983 Unreported) N409 at p.4 (An accused person arrested on reasonable suspicion of his having committed an offence and held in custody for over a year pending trial, upon which he was acquitted does not have a claim for infringement of s.42(1)(d). Note: it is not certain why the application for damages made under s.58 was restricted to the right under s.42(1)(d). Section 37(3) would be a more appropriate right in which to found this type of action — see annotations to s.37(3).)

(2) A person who is arrested or detained —
- (a) Shall be informed promptly, in a language that he understands, of the reasons for his arrest or detention and of any charge against him; and
- (b) shall be permitted whenever practicable to communicate without delay and in private with a member of his family or a personal friend, and with a lawyer of his choice (including the Public Solicitor if he is entitled to legal aid); and
- (c) shall be given adequate opportunity to give instructions to a lawyer of his choice in the place in which he is detained,

and shall be informed immediately on his arrest of his rights under this subsection.

CROSS REFERENCE

Constitution of India: Section 22(1); *European Convention on Rights:* Article 5(2).

C.P.C. Report Ch.5 Part 1 p.9

40. Whenever a person is arrested or held, he must be informed promptly, in a language he understands, of the reasons for his arrest or detention, and given the opportunity, whenever practicable, to contact a member of his family or a personal friend, and to seek advice from a lawyer of his choice without delay. He should be able to speak with any of these people in private. He must be brought before a judge or magistrate as soon as is practicable after his arrest or detention, and may not be further held in custody in connection with the offence except by order of a judge or magistrate.

(2) (a) A person who is arrested or detained shall be informed promptly, in a language which he understands, of the reasons for his arrest or detention and of any charge against him, and shall be permitted whenever practicable, to communicate without delay and in private with a member of his family or a personal friend, and with a lawyer of his choice (including the Public Solicitor, if that person is entitled to legal aid), and to have adequate opportunity to give instructions to a lawyer of his choice in the place in which he is detained.

(b) A person who is arrested or detained shall be informed immediately upon his arrest of his rights under paragraph (a) of this clause.

WHETHER FAILURE TO COMPLY WITH ALL OR ANY OF THE PROVISIONS OF SECTION 42(2) FOR THAT REASON ALONE RENDERS SUBSEQUENT ADMISSIONS BY AN ACCUSED PERSON INADMISSIBLE AS EVIDENCE AT TRIAL

Held

Failure to comply with all or any provisions of s.42(2) does not for that reason alone render later admissions inadmissable in evidence at the accused's trial.
Reference No 1 of 1977 [1977] PNGLR 362; for extracts of the leading judgments see below.

per Frost C.J. (Kearney and Pritchard JJ. agreeing)

> However, I would add the following to the answer: but the National Court under Constitution s.57(1), in the course of a trial of an offence, has power and, according to the circumstances of the case, may be bound to make an order or declaration that admissions obtained in breach of the Constitution s.42(2) should be excluded from evidence in the trial.
> *Reference No 1 of 1977* [1977] PNGLR 362 at p.373; see also Prentice Dep.C.J. at pp.380–381 (below) and Wilson J. at p.383 (below).

per Prentice Dep.C.J.

I feel that in the present circumstances Constitutional Rights can be safeguarded by the courageous and firm exercise in appropriate circumstances, of the provisions of ss.22, 57, 58 and possibly of s.23. I have no doubt the National Court judges will exercise them. But the Constitution is ambulatory, in the sense that it will continue to exist to cover the conditions of society that develop through the decades. If situations develop in this country as they did apparently in the United States of America such as to militate against the enjoyment of Constitutional Rights, and the sanctions that already exist in s.23 prove inadequate to the times, I would not take the decision of this Court now along the lines I suggest, to preclude the possibility that our successors in this Court might well feel free then to discover a 'gap' or 'lack' which required the devising of further supporting machinery or procedural laws under s.22.

For the present I feel confident that the use of the sanctions already provided and in particular by the adding of 'breach of Constitutional Rights' to the category of factors which allow 'discretionary rejection', as set out in the much quoted Australian cases of the *King v Lee and others* (1950) 82 CLR 133 and *McDermott v The King*, (1948) 76 CLR 501 will prove adequate to ensure the enjoyment by the residents of this country of the rights so eloquently and firmly established for them by the striking document of 15th September, 1975 — the Constitution of the Independent State of Papua New Guinea.
Reference No 1 of 1977 [1977] PNGLR 362 at pp.380,381; see also Frost C.J. at p.373 (above) and Wilson J. at p.383 (below).

per Wilson J.

Upon the proper construction of all the relevant provisions of the Constitution confessional statements obtained following a breach of s.42(2) are not automatically excluded from being given in evidence at the trial of the person concerned. The Constitution has conferred upon the Courts a discretion to deal with this situation as in the case of any breach of fundamental rights conferred by the Constitution. The exercise of a judicial discretion necessarily involves a consideration of the facts surrounding a particular case. If in a particular case it appears that there has been a breach of s.42(2) then this is a matter for the trial judge to take into account together with all the circumstances of the case when exercising his discretion whether or not to admit evidence obtained following the breach.
Reference No 1 of 1977 [1977] PNGLR 362 at p.383; see also Frost C.J. at p.373 (above) and Prentice Dep.C.J. at pp.380,381 (above).

ON THE FAILURE TO PROVIDE FACILITIES TO COMMUNICATE WITH FAMILY, FRIEND OR LAWYER ETC.

per Prentice Dep.C.J.

The grounds of objection are that constitutional rights were not given the accused; no 'caution' was administered; a threat was made (s.86 *Evidence Act* 1975); and the accused was in such a state of health and fatigue as to render his answers to questions involuntary or such as not fairly to be used against him. There are other grounds which suggest that only some of the questions and answers were recorded, that some were incorrectly recorded, that alterations (presumably without accused's concurrence) were made and that one particular question (that now conveniently numbered 23) was neither asked of, nor read back to, the accused. I am of the opinion that these other grounds do not go to the question of voluntariness or admissibility, but are of the kind which would be decided by a jury if this were a jury trial (cf. The *Queen v Matheson, Cook and Manuel* [1969] SASR 53). However as a matter of practical convenience the evidence relating to these details has also been taken.

On the accused's own version of events, the interview at the police station occurred as a result of his going himself to the station on the morning of the 1st January to report what he understood to have happened the night before. On the police version it was had some 12 hours later at 9.00 p.m.

I consider the defence has failed to establish to the necessary degree (that is on the probabilities), that any state of illness or exhaustion existed in the accused such as would render it unfair for the record of interview to be used against him and would call for the exercise of the court's discretion against its admission in evidence (cf. *R. v Sykes and Campi (No 1)* [1969] VR 631). Other matters raised cause more concern, to my mind.

In the first place, the record itself contains no reference to the giving of any caution or warning that the accused had a right to remain silent and that any admissions made could be used in evidence. Constable Paia himself admits that no such warning was given. The giving of the usual caution is of course elementary to police procedure, is laid down in police instructions, and stipulated for by the various Judges' Rules of the past in the countries from which our Criminal Code and criminal procedure initially derive. It may be that Constable Paia on this occasion lost sight of the necessity for such a safeguard after he had given what he appears to have regarded as the 'Constitutional Rights' statement. One could understand (though not approve) his overlooking the normal caution, if the fact had been as the accused stated — that he, the accused, came to the station of his own volition to report. But Constable Paia, though his recollection is vague and unsatisfactory on the subject, suggests that he himself arrested the accused and proceeded to take a statement.

The record of interview, in translation from the Pisin, reveals the following exchange:

(Const.)

The Constitution of Papua New Guinea says I must now tell you about your rights. I must first tell you why I am arresting you. I am arresting you because I believe you killed a man by the name of Patrick Yawi. At the moment you have not been charged with any offence. You have the right to send a message or speak to a member of your family or a personal friend, or any lawyer you wish or to the Public Solicitor. If you get a lawyer he may come and see you wherever you are kept and you will be allowed to talk to him about this matter.

Q. Do you want to get a lawyer or the Public Solicitor in?

A. I know some lawyer but I don't know their house and telephone.

In evidence Constable Paia said that following this answer he proceeded directly to the next recorded question, namely:

Q. For the purpose of this record of interview I want to know the name of your small village, sub-province and province;

thence to its sequelae.

It would appear that the accused had been so treated as to comply with the requirement that an arrested person be 'informed immediately on his arrest of his Rights under this subsection' as required by s.42(2) of the Constitution — even if he had *not* then technically been arrested ... But, the defence submission proceeds, there was a breach of the provisions of s.42(2)(b) and (c), in that the accused had not 'been permitted wherever practicable to communicate without delay and in private with a member of his family or a personal friend, and with a lawyer of his choice ....', and had not been 'given adequate opportunity to give instructions to a lawyer of his choice in the place where he was detained'.

Now the Constitution makers' provisions in regard to rights are detailed and explicit. I desire specifically to prescind from any intention to add to the rights actually given, by any interpretive extension by me, and from any intention to introduce restrictions on the rights and duties of the police in the investigation of crime, beyond those stated in the laws of Papua New Guinea. However, it is I think, clear from the conjunction with (a), (b) and (c) of s.42(2), of the further provision as to *being informed* of his rights — that the Constitution envisages that something more practical and useful than a mere statement of rights *may* be called for to give effect to s.42(2) in any particular instance. In my view, the Court should not attempt to lay down a detailed guide for procedure which must be followed by the police in each case if they wish to ensure compliance with the Constitution; (though of course the police authorities themselves might as a matter of prudence, endeavour to produce for the members of the force some such assistance). I imagine the treatment necessary on the one hand, to accord constitutional rights to a man who had run miles across mountains, axe-in-hand, to a police post, to admit to a crime with the object of securing his own and his family's safety following a crime he said he had committed, would differ greatly on the other, from that necessary to ensure rights to a man arrested against his will who at the beginning protests his innocence. These are perhaps the extremes of the spectrum; many differing shades of colour will appear in the instances between. I feel that the question of whether constitutional rights have been given, will necessarily in each case, have to be answered on a consideration of its particular facts.

The accused here describes himself as 'Managing Director' of a business at Koki known as 'Lakatoi Artefacts'. This may seem perhaps rather a pretentious description of his occupation. But he speaks English, is urbanized, and is carrying on a business in the environment in which he was being questioned. The questioning was taking place in an office in Port Moresby, connected with a telephone. The telephone directory was nearby. It may be that the policeman was, in the circumstances of the degree of sophistication of the accused, and considering that this was the night of a public holiday — satisfied —

(a) that the accused's answer indicated that he did not wish to avail himself of his rights to communicate or give instructions; and
(b) that nothing further than the giving of information as to rights was therefore practicable or required.

However, I find myself with a feeling that in *the circumstances of this case* (I emphasize again my intention not to be making a rule of general precedent), something more by way of clarification was called for — that the accused should have at least been asked whether he wished to look at the directory, or to ring anyone in particular, and that facilities to do so should have been provided if he so required.

These two circumstances — the lack of adequate provision of constitutional rights and the failure to caution — convince me that I should exercise my discretion against admitting the record of interview herein into evidence (cf. *McDermott's* case (1948) 76 CLR 501 and *Cornelius'* case (1936) 55 CLR 235 at p.247, even were I convinced that it was voluntary in the common law sense and not induced by threat or promise (cf. *The King v Lee and Others* (1950) 82 CLR 133). I therefore do not consider it necessary to proceed to any conclusion on the question of the alleged threat. I find myself confirmed in this opinion by the admission of Constable Paia in evidence, that in one respect at least, the record of interview is inaccurate when it stated in question 35 that the accused had told the Constable that the deceased had died at the hospital.

I reject the tender of the record of interview.
The State v Joseph Maino [1977] PNGLR 216, at pp.218–221.

GENERALLY

Referred to

by Saldanha J. in *Prai v Officer of the Government of PNG* [1979] PNGLR 1 at p.1;

by Narakobi J. in *The State v Tanbai and ors* (1980 Unreported) N235 at p.3;

by Quinlivan A.J. in *Kaupa v Hutjena Police* (1981 Unreported) N320(M) at p.6;

by Quinlivan A.J. in *Dai v Manda (No1)* (1981 Unreported) N342(M) at p.4.

(3) A person who is arrested or detained —
  (a) for the purpose of being brought before a court in the execution of an order of a court; or
  (b) upon reasonable suspicion of his having committed, or being about to commit, an offence,

shall, unless he is released, be brought without delay before a court or a judicial officer and, in a case referred to in paragraph (b), shall not be further held in custody in connexion with the offence except by order of a court or judicial officer.

CROSS REFERENCE

Constitution of India: Section 22; *European Convention on Human Rights*: Article 5(3).

C.P.C. Report Ch.5 Part 1 p.22

(3) A person who has been arrested or detained in the circumstances referred to in paragraph (e) of clause (1) of this recommendation and has not been released, shall be brought before a judge or magistrate as soon as is practicable after the arrest or detention and shall not be further held in custody in connection with the offence except by order of a judge or magistrate.

(4) The necessity or desirability of interrogating the person concerned or other persons, or any administrative requirement or convenience, is not a good ground for failing to comply with Subsection (3), but exigencies of travel which in the circumstances are reasonable may, without derogating any other protection available to the person concerned, be such a ground.

C.P.C. Report Ch.5 Part 1 p.22

(4) The necessity or desirability of interrogating a person or other persons, or of obtaining evidence, or any administrative requirement or convenience, is not a good ground for delay in complying with clause (3) of this recommendation, but the exigencies of travel which in the circumstances are reasonable may be taken as such a good ground without derogating from other remedies which may be open to him.

(5) Where a complaint is made to the National Court or a Judge that a person is unlawfully or unreasonably detained —
  (a) the National Court or Judge shall inquire into the complaint and order the person concerned to be brought before it or him; and
  (b) unless the court or Judge is satisfied that the detention is lawful, and in the case of a person being detained on remand pending his trial does not constitute an unreasonable detention having regard, in particular, to its length, the Court or a Judge shall order his release either unconditionally or subject to such conditions as the Court or Judge thinks fit.

CROSS REFERENCE

European Convention on Human Rights: Article 5(4).

C.P.C. Report Ch.5 Part 1 p.22

(5) Where a complaint is made to the National Court or a judge of that court that a person is unlawfully or unreasonably detained, the National Court shall inquire into the complaint, and order the person to be brought before it. Unless satisfied that the detention is lawful and, in the case of a person being detained on remand pending his trial, does not constitute an unreasonable detention having regard, in particular, to the length of that detention, the court or a judge shall order his release either unconditionally or on such conditions as the court or judge thinks fit.

GENERALLY

per Curium (Kapi Dep.C.J., Kaputin, McDermott JJ.)

There are two parts to this provision. First the court has to be satisfied that the detention is lawful. We have already found that the detention is lawful under the *Migration Act*.

As we understand the submission of counsel he further relies on the second part of s.42(5)(b) in that the appellant Mr Perryman is detained unreasonably. In our opinion the second part of s.42(5)(b) of the Constitution only applies to persons arrested or detained on remand pending their trial. We therefore find that this does not assist the appellant. *Perryman v Minister for Foreign Affairs and Trade* [1982] PNGLR 334 at pp.340,341.

Comment

It is clear that in order to be successful on a s.42(5) application in respect of a detention that is otherwise lawful — and does not involve an offence — s.42(5) has to be used in conjunction with s.41 of the Constitution. Section 41 is subject to objective tests and the one of showing that an act falls within s.41 rests with the applicant. See *Perryman* v *Minister for Foreign Affairs and Trade* [1982] PNGLR 339 at pp.340,341.

GENERALLY

Referred to

by Greville Smith J. in *Re s.42 of the Constitution and Jacob Hendrich Prai* [1979] PNGLR 42 at pp.43–46 (in relation to an applicant deprived of liberty under the *Migration Act*);

by Kidu C.J. in *S.C.R. No 4 of 1980; Re petition of M.T. Somare* [1981] PNGLR 265 at p.267 (applications to be made to the National Court).

(6) A person arrested or detained for an offence (other than treason or wilful murder as defined by an Act of the Parliament) is entitled to bail at all times from arrest or detention to acquittal or conviction unless the interests of justice otherwise require.

(See: *Bail Act* Ch.340)

C.P.C. Report Ch.5 Part 1 p.9.

41. We recommend that two new provisions be added to those included in the *Human Rights Ordinance*. The first of these is to ensure that a person who is arrested or held for an offence other than treason or wilful murder, is treated as being entitled to bail at all times from his arrest until his conviction *unless* it is necessary, in the interests of justice, that he be held in custody pending his trial. The onus should be on the police to show why a person should not be granted bail rather than the other way about.

RECOMMENDATIONS

(6) Any person who is arrested or detained —
(a) for the purpose of being brought before a court in the execution of the order of a court; or
(b) upon reasonable suspicion of his having committed or being about to commit a criminal offence,

shall, unless he is released, be brought without delay before a court, a judge or a magistrate.

(7) Any person arrested or detained for an offence other than treason or wilful murder shall be entitled to bail at all times from arrest until conviction except where the interests of justice otherwise require. A court or person with the authority to grant bail shall, when bail is refused, and when requested by the person so refused or his representative, state the reason for such refusal in writing. Any person refused bail or his representative may apply to the National Court or the Supreme Court in a summary manner for his release.

(8) Any person who is unlawfully arrested or detained by any other person shall be entitled to compensation from that other person.

AS TO DISCRETION TO GRANT BAIL

per Andrew J.

The question has arisen in the interpretation of s.9(1) (of the *Bail Act* Ch.340) as to whether, if one or all of the criteria for refusing bail is shown, it then follows that bail must be refused.

In my judgement there is a discretion in every case ..... The use of the words in s.9(1) that the bail authority 'shall not refuse bail unless satisfied' illustrate prima facie one is entitled to bail. That is the intent of the Constitution and of the *Bail Act*. When one or more of the considerations in s.9(1) is shown to exist then there is a ground for refusing bail. The use of the word 'shall' does not mean, in my opinion, bail must as a matter of course be refused when those matters are proved. To read it this way would be contrary to the whole scheme and intent of the Constitution and the *Bail Act*. Whether or not bail is refused is a matter of discretion.
In the Matter of An Application for Bail: Keating v The Independent State of Papua New Guinea (1983 Unreported) SC257 at pp.15, 16; see also Kidu C.J. at pp.2–7 and Kapi Dep.C.J. at pp.10–12.

Referred to

by Wilson J. in *Paul Louis Kysely v The State* [1980] PNGLR 36 at p.37 (applicant starts with a heavy presumption in his favour; bail is not to be denied unless conditions established by ss.9(1)(a) to (g) of the Bail Act are established.)

NO CONSTITUTIONAL RIGHT TO BAIL PENDING APPEAL

Held

Admission to bail on an application pending appeal from a conviction by a lower court is discretionary and there is no right to bail under s.42(6) of the Constitution.
Logalio Piaro and anor v Kumbamung [1976] PNGLR 283; see Kearney J. at p.286.

Held

There is no constitutional right to bail in the case of appeals from the National Court to the Supreme Court.
Smedley v The State [1978] PNGLR 452; see Wilson J. at p.454.

AN APPLICANT HAS A CONSTITUTIONAL RIGHT TO BAIL DURING THE COURSE OF TRIAL

per Kearney Dep.C.J.

It is clear from Constitution s.42(6) that the applicant is entitled to bail during the course of his trial unless the interests of justice otherwise require. Some matters which are relevant to the interests of justice when considering bail during trial are set out in a *Practice Note* in England in 1974 [1974] 2 A11 ER 794.
Re Herman Kagl Diawo [1980] PNGLR 148 at p.151.

NO BAIL WHILST DETAINED UNDER MIGRATION ACT

Held

Section 42(6) applies only to persons arrested or detained for an offence.
Re s.42 of the Constitution and Jacob Hendrich Prai [1979] PNGLR 42; see Greville Smith J. at p.46.

Held

Section 42(6) does not apply to persons detained for the purposes of deportation.
Perryman v Minister for Foreign Affairs and Trade [1982] PNGLR 339; see per Curiam (Kapi Dep.C.J., Kaputin, McDermott JJ.) at p.341.

NO CONSTITUTIONAL RIGHT TO BAIL ON A CHARGE OF WILFUL MURDER

per Andrew J.

Because the constitutional entitlement to bail is removed in the case of wilful murder it follows, in my opinion, that the onus shifts to the applicant to establish he should be entitled to bail. By s.4 of the *Bail Act*, bail may only be granted in cases of wilful murder and murder, by the National Court or the Supreme Court ..... The *Bail Act* 1977 purports to abolish certain common law rules relating to bail .... and is accordingly a complete code dealing with the grant or refusal of bail ... [where it is not subject to s.42(6) of the Constitution].
In the matter of an Aplication for Bail: Keating v The Independent State of Papua New Guinea (1983 Unreported) SC257 at pp.14,15; see also Kidu C.J. at p.7 and Kapi Dep.C.J. at p.12.

Referred to

by Gajewicz J. in *Atingi v Joshiah* (1982 Unreported) N396 at pp.3,4 (applicant charged with wilful murder may be granted bail only if he shows special or exceptional circumstances: Note this view was expressly disapproved of by Kidu C.J. in *In the Matter of an Application for Bail: Keating v the Independent State of Papua New Guinea* (1983 Unreported) SC257 at p.7 and, by implication, by Kapi Dep. C.J. at pp. 10–12 and Andrew J. at pp. 14–16.)

(7) Where a person to whom Subsection (6) applies is refused bail —
   (a) the court or person refusing bail shall, on request by the person concerned or his representative, state in writing the reason for the refusal; and
   (b) the person or his representative may apply to the Supreme Court or the National Court in a summary manner for his release.

CROSS REFERENCE

Constitution of the United States: Am. VIII

(8) Subject to any other law, nothing in this section applies in respect of any reasonable act of the parent or guardian of a child, or a person into whose care a child has been committed, in the course of the education, discipline or upbringing of the child.

(9) Subject to any Constitutional Law or Act of the Parliament, nothing in this section applies in respect of a person who is in custody under the law of another country —
   (a) while in transit through the country; or
   (b) as permitted by or under an Act of the Parliament made for the purposes of Section 206 (*visiting forces*).

43. FREEDOM FROM FORCED LABOUR.

(1) No person shall be required to perform forced labour.
(2) In Subsection (1), "forced labour" does not include —
   (a) labour required by the sentence or order of a court; or
   (b) labour required of a person while in lawful custody, being labour that, although not required by the sentence or order of a court, is necessary for the hygiene of, or for the manintenance of, the place in which he is in custody; or
   (c) in the case of a person in custody for the purpose of his care, treatment, rehabilitation or welfare, labour reasonably required for that purpose; or
   (d) labour required of a member of a disciplined force in pursuance of his duties as such a member; or
   (e) subject to the approval of any local government body for the area in which he is required to work, labour reasonably required as part of reasonable and normal communal or other civic duties; or
   (f) labour of a reasonable amount and kind (including, in the case of compulsory military service, labour required as an alternative to such service in the case of a person who has conscientious objections to military service) that is required in the national interest by an Organic Law that complies with Section 38 (*general qualifications on qualified rights*).

CROSS REFERENCE

Constitution of India: Section 23(1); *European Convention on Human Rights:* Article 4.

C.P.C. Report Ch.5 Part 1 p.9

3. *PROTECTION FROM FORCED LABOUR*

43. This recommended provision is also very similar to a section of the *Human Rights Ordinance* (which we refer to below as 'the Ordinance'), though we have proposed that the use of the word 'slavery' in the Ordinance be dropped, as it is really encompassed by the words 'forced labour'. We propose that 'forced labour' be defined so as *not* to include —

* labour to be performed in a corrective institution under a court order;
* labour which a soldier or policeman is required to perform in the course of his duties, or which a conscientious objector to military service may reasonably be required by law to carry out; or

- labour reasonably required, with the approval of a recognised local authority exercising governmental functions in the area in which a person is required to work, as part of normal communal or civic obligations.

The last of these provisions would for example enable local authorities to continue to require people in their area to carry out road maintenance work.

RECOMMENDATIONS [p.22]

Protection from forced labour

3. (1) Subject to Recommendation 3 in Part 2 of this Chapter ('Emergency Powers'), no person shall be required to perform forced labour.
(2) In clause (1) of this recommendation 'forced labour' does not include:—
(a) labour required by the sentence or order of a court;
(b) labour required of a person while he is lawfully detained, being labour that, though not required by the sentence or order of a court, is reasonably necessary for the purposes of hygiene or for the maintenance of the place at which he is detained;
(c) in the case of a person detained for the purpose of his care, treatment, rehabilitation, education or welfare, is reasonably required for that purpose; [p.23]
(d) labour required of a member of a disciplined force in pursuance of his duties as such a member or in the case of a person who has conscientious objections to service in the armed forces, any reasonable labour required by law instead of that service; or
(e) subject to the approval of any local government council or other legally recognized governmental authority at the local level for the area in which he is required to work, labour reasonably required as part of reasonable and normal communal or other civic obligations.

AS TO THE ENFORCEMENT OF THE RIGHTS OF ALL PERSONS

per Frost C.J.

In the case of the Rights of All Persons, again the passive voice is used, in ss.42, 43, 44, but the other sections are in the form, e.g. 'Every person has the right to freedom of conscience', s.45. The form of these sections bears upon the applicability of s.23 — Sanctions, because generally in the rights and freedoms set out in Sub-divisions B and C there is no provision expressly imposing on any person a duty correlative to the right. *Reference No 1 of 1977* [1977] PNGLR 362 at p.366.

Referred to

by Narokobi A.J. in *Tabo Sipo v Meli* (1980 Unreported) N240 at p.5.

44. — FREEDOM FROM ARBITARY SEARCH AND ENTRY

No person shall be subjected to the search of his person or property or to entry of his premises, except to the extent that the exercise of that right is regulated or restricted by a law —

(a) that makes reasonable provision for a search or entry
   (i) under an order made by a court; or
   (ii) under a warrant for a search issued by a court or judicial officer on reasonable grounds, supported by oath or affirmation, particularly describing the purpose of the search; or
   (iii) that authorizes a public officer or government agent of Papua New Guinea or an officer of a body corporate established by law for a public purpose to enter, where necessary, on the premises of a person in order to inspect those premises or anything in or on them in relation to any rate or tax or in order to carry out work connected

with any property that is lawfully in or on those premises and belongs to the Government or any such body corporate; or

(iv) that authorizes the inspection of goods, premises, vehicles, ships or aircraft to ensure compliance with lawful requirements as to the entry of persons or importation of goods into Papua New Guinea or departure of persons or exportation of goods from Papua New Guinea or as to standards of safe construction, public safety, public health, permitted use or similar matters, or to secure compliance with the terms of a licence to engage in manufacture or trade; or

(v) for the purpose of inspecting or taking copies of documents relating to —

(A) the conduct of a business, trade, profession or industry in accordance with a law regulating the conduct of that business, trade, profession or industry; or

(B) the affairs of a company in accordance with a law relating to companies; or

(vi) for the purpose of inspecting goods or inspecting or taking copies of documents, in connexion with the collection, or the enforcement of payment of taxes or under a law prohibiting or restricting the importation of goods into Papua New Guinea or the exportation of goods from Papua New Guinea or

(b) that complies with Section 38 (*general qualifications on qualified rights*).

(See: *Search Act* Ch.341.)

CROSS REFERENCE

Constitution of the United States: Am. IV

C.P.C. Report Ch.5 Part 1 p.10

5. *PROTECTION FROM ARBITRARY SEARCH OR ENTRY*

45. Another fundamental personal freedom is that which involves protection from having one's person or property searched, or one's house or other premises entered by other people, without consent. We recommend that the provision in the *Ordinance* which safeguards this freedom, subject to certain exceptions (some of which are additional to those in the relevant section of the *Ordinance*) referred to below, be adopted for the Constitution. Constitution.

46. The exceptions include some which are specific and others which are very general. The specific exceptions which are at present included in the *Ordinance* allow for a law providing that a government officer or agent or an officer of a public authority may enter premises where it is reasonably necessary to inspect them in relation to a rate or tax, or to carry out any work on any property on the premises which is owned by the government or the authority. Allowance is also made for a person to be searched or have his house entered in accordance with a court order. To these we propose that certain additional exceptions be added such as provision for a law to give authority, under a warrant for a search issued by a judge or magistrate on reasonable grounds, describing the purpose of the search.

47. The general exceptions allow for laws to be passed which make provision which is 'reasonably justifiable in a democratic society in the interests of defence, public safety, public order, public health or public welfare, or to protect the rights or freedoms of other persons'.

RECOMMENDATIONS [p.23]

Protection against arbitrary search or entry

5. (1) No person shall without his consent be subject to the search of his person or property or the entry to his house or other premises by other persons.

(2) Nothing contained in or done under the authority of any law shall be held to be inconsistent with or in contravention of clause (1) above to the extent that the law makes provision for a search or entry —

(a) under an order made by a court;

(b) under a warrant for a search issued by a court or judicial officer on reasonable grounds, supported by oath or affirmation, particularly describing the purpose of the search;

(c) that authorizes a public officer or government agent of Papua New Guinea or an officer of a body corporate established by law for a public purpose, to enter, where reasonably necessary, on the premises of a person in order to inspect those premises or any thing in or on them in relation to any rate or tax or in order to carry out work connected with any property that is lawfully in or on those premises and belongs to the Government or any such body corporate;

(d) pursuant to a law that authorizes the inspection of goods, premises, vehicles, ships or aircraft to ensure compliance with lawful requirements as to the entry of persons or importation of goods into Papua New Guinea or the departure of persons or exportation of goods from Papua New Guinea or as to standards of safe construction, public safety, public health, permitted use or similar matters, or to secure compliance with the terms of a licence to engage in manufacture or trade;

(e) for the purpose of inspecting or taking copies of documents relating to —

(i) the conduct of a business, trade, profession or industry pursuant to a law regulating the conduct of that business, trade, profession or industry; or

(ii) the affairs of a company pursuant to a law relating to companies;

(f) for the purpose of inspecting goods, or inspecting or taking copies of documents, in connexion with the collection, or the enforcement of payment, of taxes or pursuant to a law prohibiting or restricting the importation of goods into Papua New Guinea or the exportation of goods from Papua New Guinea; or

(g) that is reasonably justifiable in a democratic society in the interests of defence, public safety, public order, public health or public welfare; or for protecting the rights or freedoms (whether under the Constitution or otherwise) of other persons.

Note: As to the effect of a violation of this right in regard to the use of information or physical evidence thereby obtained, and in particular whether or not it should be admissible as evidence in court proceedings, the Committee recommends that the proposed Law Reform Commission should give early consideration to this issue.

GENERALLY

Referred to

by Frost C.J. in *Reference No 1 of 1977* [1977] PNGLR 362 at p.366; see also Prentice Dep. C.J. at p.377;

by Narakobi A.J. in *Tabo Sipo v Meli* (1980 Unreported) N240 at p.5;

by Kapi Dep.C.J. in *S.C.R. No 2 of 1982; Re Organic Law* [1982] PNGLR 214 at p.237.

45. FREEDOM OF CONSCIENCE, THOUGHT AND RELIGION

(1) Every person has the right to freedom of conscience, thought and religion and the practice of his religion and beliefs, including freedom to manifest and propogate his religion and beliefs in such a way as not to interfere with the freedom of others, except to the extent that the exercise of that right is regulated or restricted by a law that complies with Section 38 (*general qualifications on qualified rights*).

(2) No person shall be compelled to receive religious instruction or to take part in a religious ceremony or observance, but this does not

apply to the giving of religious instruction to a child with the consent of his parent or guardian or to the inclusion in a course of study of secular instruction concerning any religion or belief.

(3) No person is entitled to intervene unsolicited into the religious affairs of a person of a different belief, or to attempt to force his or any religion (or irreligion) on another, by harassment or otherwise.

(4) No person may be compelled to take an oath that is contrary to his religion or belief, or to take an oath in a manner or form that is contrary to his religion or belief.

(5) A reference in this section to religion includes a reference to the traditional religious beliefs and customs of the peoples of Papua New Guinea.

CROSS REFERENCE

Constitution of India: Section 25; *Constitution of the United States*: Am. 1; *Universal Declaration of Human Rights*: Article 18; *European Convention of Human Rights*: Article 9.

C.P.C. Report Ch.5 Part 1 p.10

7. *FREEDOM OF CONSCIENCE, THOUGHT AND RELIGION*

52. This right is widely regarded as a basic 'civil right'. Other such rights (which follow this one) are 'freedom of expression and publication' and 'freedom of assembly and association'. They are clearly fundamental to any democracy. Our recommendations concerning them follow the equivalent provisions in the Ordinance very closely.

53. All of these rights have some exceptions in common; they can all be qualified with the consent of the person concerned, and they can also be qualified in the interests of defence, public safety, public order, public health or public welfare, though as we have stated, a law [p.11] which is dependent upon this qualification for its validity must, in normal times, be passed by a three-fifths majority of the members of parliament. Again, these rights may be limited insofar as they are reasonably required for protecting the rights and freedoms of others. These limitations are not, however, valid (and therefore effective) unless they are 'reasonably justifiable in a democratic society'.

54. The freedom of conscience, thought and religion which we recommend gives every person in the country freedom either alone or with others, and both in public and in private, to practise his religion or belief in worship, teaching or observance. However we propose that no-one should be compelled at an educational institution to receive religious instruction in a religion other than his own.

55. We recommend certain specific qualifications on religious freedom. These include provisions in a law for the protection of the rights and freedoms of other persons from interference by people who follow another religion. They also allow for the provision of courses of instruction, in a place of education, which include the fundamental doctrines of Christianity, the doctrines of other world religions, and the ancient religious beliefs of our own peoples.

RECOMMENDATIONS [p.26]

Protection of Freedom of conscience, thought and religion

7. (1) Subject to clause (5) below, all persons have the right to freedom of conscience, thought and religion, including freedom to change their religion or belief, and freedom, either alone or in community with others, and in public or in private, to manifest and propagate their religion or beliefs in worship, teaching, practice and observance.

(2) Except with his consent, no person shall be hindered in the enjoyment of a right of freedom referred to in clause (1) above.

(3) Except with his consent, or if he is a minor, the consent of his parent or guardian, no person attending a place of education shall be required to receive religious instruction or to take part in or attend a religious ceremony or observance if that instruction, ceremony or observance relates to a religion other than his own religion or belief.

(4) No person shall be compelled to take any oath which is contrary to his religion or belief or to take any oath in a manner which is contrary to his religion or belief.

(5) Nothing contained in or done under the authority of any law shall be held to be inconsistent with, or in contravention of, this recommendation to the extent that that law makes provision which is reasonably justifiable in a democratic society —
(a) in the interests of defence, public safety, public order, public health, or public welfare;
(b) for protecting the rights and freedoms of other persons (whether or not they hold any religious beliefs) including the right to observe and practise religion without the unsolicited intervention of adherents of another religion; or
(c) for regulating the secular education provided in any place of education in the interests of persons receiving instruction in that place, and in particular, providing courses in religion which include the fundamental doctrines of Christianity, the doctrines of other world religions, and the ancient religious beliefs of the peoples of Papua New Guinea.

Note: References in this Chapter to religion and to beliefs include references to traditional religious beliefs of the peoples indigenous to Papua New Guinea.

GENERALLY

Referred to

by Frost C.J. in *Reference No 1 of 1977* [1977] PNGLR 362 at p.366;

by Narakobi A.J. in *Tabo Sipo v Meli* (1980 Unreported) N240 at p.5;

by Kidu C.J. in *The State v Kosi and ors* (1981 Unreported) N306 (the offence of unlawful assembly created under ss.61 and 62 of the *Criminal Code* does not infringe the constitutional guarantee of freedom of conscience, thought and religion.)

46. FREEDOM OF EXPRESSION

(1) Every person has the right to freedom of expression and publication, except to the extent that the exercise of that right is regulated or restricted by a law —
(a) that imposes reasonable restrictions on public office-holders;
(b) that imposes restrictions on non-citizens; or
(c) that complies with Section 38 (*general qualifications on qualified rights*).

(2) In Subsection (1), "freedom of expression and publication" includes —
(a) freedom to hold opinions, to receive ideas and information and to communicate ideas and information, whether to the public generally or to a person or class of persons; and
(b) freedom of the press and other mass communications media.

(3) Notwithstanding anything in this section, an Act of the Parliament may make reasonable provision for securing reasonable access to mass communications media for interested persons and associations —
(a) for the communication of ideas and information; and

(b) to allow rebuttal of false or misleading statements concerning their acts, ideas or beliefs,

and generally for enabling and encouraging freedom of expression.

CROSS REFERENCE

Constitution of the United States: Am.1; *Constitution of India*: Section 19(a); *Universal Declaration of Human Rights:* Article 19; *European Convention on Human Rights:* Article 10.

C.P.C. Report Ch.5, Part 1 p.11

8. *FREEDOM OF EXPRESSION*

56. One of the great principles on which democracy rests is the right to differ on any topic of discussion, be it social, economic, political, cultural or religious. People view any particular question or situation in different ways, and we firmly believe that they should have the right to express their own views, within very broad limits, on any particular matter.

57. Not only do we believe it to be essential that differences be freely expressed, but we also hope that the right to free speech will provide a basis for settling the inevitable differences between us which will continue to arise after independence, without resorting to force. We therefore believe that in principle every citizen should be free to criticise the policies of the Government of the day. The media have a particular responsibility in this regard, as unless those who wish to express independent opinions are reported in the media their effectiveness is likely to be much reduced, and the opportunity for meaningful debate of important public issues may be lost.

58. The formation and expression of public opinion is vital to the kind of participatory democracy we believe our people want. We hold that opposing views should be free to attract support, and to compete in a healthy atmosphere. Only then do we feel there is reason to hope that the activities of the government can be discussed freely and clearly understood. The views of the people can then have some effect on the policies of the government.

59. In framing our recommendations we have closely followed the equivalent provision in the *Ordinance* which makes particular reference to freedom of the press. Of course, 'freedom of the press' does not mean freedom without responsibility. In an emerging nation such as ours, we believe the media have a very important responsibility to report news accurately, and to give equal opportunities and facilities for the expression by citizens of opposing or differing views.

60. We have added certain additional qualifications to this right of free expression to enable legislation to be passed for the effective prevention of disclosure of information received in confidence (and here we have in mind official information particularly), and for reasonable restrictions to be placed upon the freedom of non-citizens to express their views publicly. The latter provision is necessary, we feel, because of the very considerable influence which outsiders are able and will for some years continue to be able to exercise on the formation of public opinion among our people. This influence can, of course, be beneficial, but it can also be detrimental, and as non-citizens bear no responsibility for the future development of the country, and often have their own vested interests to protect, we feel that our recommended qualification is essential. We would stress, however, that any law restricting the freedom of expression of non-citizens would have to be reasonably justifiable in a democratic society if it is to be valid. Reasonable restrictions on their freedom of expression could also be placed on constitutional office-holders, public servants, and members of the disciplined forces.

RECOMMENDATIONS [p.26]

Protection of freedom of expression

8. (1) Subject to clause (4) below, all persons have the right to freedom of expression and publication, that is to say, freedom to hold opinions, freedom to receive ideas and information, freedom to communicate ideas and information (whether the communication is to the public generally or to any class of persons) and freedom from interference with their correspondence.

(2) In clause (1) above 'freedom of expression and publication' includes freedom of the press and of other mass media of communication.

(3) Except with his consent, no person shall be hindered in the enjoyment of the rights referred to in clause (1) above.

(4) Nothing contained in or done under the authority of any law shall be held to be inconsistent with, or in contravention of, this recommendation to the extent that that law makes provision that is reasonably justifiable in a democratic society —

(a) in the interests of defence, public safety, public order, public health or public welfare;

(b) for the purpose of protecting the reputations, rights and freedoms of other persons or the private lives of persons concerned in legal proceedings, [p.27] preventing the disclosure of information received in confidence, or maintaining the authority and independence of the courts;
(c) for the purpose of regulating the technical administration or technical operation of telephony, telegraphy, posts, wireless, broadcasting or television or restricting the establishment or use of telephonic, telegraphic, wireless, broadcasting or television equipment or of postal services;
(d) imposing restrictions on constitutional office-holders, members of the public services and members of a disciplined force; or
(e) imposing restrictions on persons who are not citizens of Papua New Guinea.

AS TO DEFAMATION AND UNLAWFUL ASSEMBLY

Comment

The language of s.46(1) is wide and without apparent qualification. It ostensibly confers the right to an *absolute* freedom of speech to citizens unless and until the Parliament passes a law which complies with s.38 to restrict such freedom.

This section has, however, provoked inconsistent judicial responses. The most striking of those responses was that of Raine J. in *Cory v Blythe* [1976] PNGLR 274. In that case a defendant in an action for defamation brought under the pre-Independence *Defamation Act* 1962 applied to amend his defence by adding a pleading to the effect that the Act was inconsistent with s.46.

His Honour, in referring to the application as 'vexatious' and possibly 'trivial', said:

> I cannot see for a moment, until better instructed, that s.46 inhibits actions for defamation, and then absolutely. It is unimaginable that s.46 declares an open season on people who are defamed ...

[As to the relationship between pre-Independence laws and s.38 see annotations under that section]

A similar view was expressed by Kidu C.J. in *The State v Kosi and ors* (1981 Unreported) N306 whilst addressing the question of whether the unlawful assembly offences contained within the *Criminal Code* offended against s.46. At p.4 he said:

> Anything uttered in a meeting or rally that advocates violence or force or that defames is in my opinion outside the protection guaranteed by the Constitution.

However, in *Hetura Paz Development v Niugini Nius P/L* [1982] PNGLR 250. Kapi Dep.C.J. expressed himself more cautiously. At p.254 he said:

> In so far as [the Defamation] Act is dealing with the regulation or restriction of the right of all persons in the country, it must comply with the requirements in s.38 of the Constitution (s.41(1)(c) of the Constitution). An interesting issue which arises is whether the *Defamation Act* which applies to all persons complies with s.38 of the Constitution. This was not argued before me [in the interlocutory proceedings] but I understand it may be argued in the trial of the action.

In our opinion the more cautious view of Kapi Dep.C.J. is correct. We concur with Goldring's (*The Constitution of Papua New Guinea*, Law Book Company 1978) conclusions at pp.235,236 that it is 'certainly arguable that the freedom of expression conferred by s.46 does substantially affect the law of defamation, which is a very substantial restriction upon what a person may speak, write or otherwise publish.'

We would only add that it appears to us equally arguable that the *Criminal Code* is also subject to and limited by s.46.

CONTEMPT AND SECTION 46.

per Saldanha J.

[Note ss.160(2) and 163(2) expressly confer upon the National Court and the Supreme Court the power to 'punish the offences against [themselves] commonly known as 'contempt of court'.]

> Before considering whether or not the Minister is guilty of the charges brought against her it is necessary to decide what law is applicable. The Minister's counsel, Mr Priestley, urges us to adopt the American approach. He says that s.46 of the Constitution which provides for freedom of expression is similar to the American legislation on freedom of expression. He says that in the United States of America the concept of contempt of court is narrower than that in England and Australia. The question appears to be to what extent freedom of expression should be restricted by the law of contempt or, in other words, the

problem that arises is the need to strike a balance between the ideal in a democratic society to permit maximum freedom of expression with the need to safeguard the administration of justice from undue interference. I think it is too late in the day for this court to embark upon such speculations. These were matters proper for consideration by the Constitutional Planning Committee who made recommendations and the members of the Constituent Assembly who drew up the Constitution. We have no choice as to the law to be applied. Our duty is to find out what the law in our jurisdiction on this subject is and then to apply it.

Section 24 of the Constitution provides that the report of the Constitutional Planning Committee (in addition to other materials) may be used as an aid to the interpretation of any provision of a constitutional law. The recommendations regarding freedom of expression are contained at p.5/1/11 of the report. There is no suggestion that the American approach should be adopted, as is done in the recommendation at p.5/1/10 regarding protection of the law, which is to the effect that it 'is the equivalent of the 'due process' provision in the United States Constitution'.

The relevant part of Sch.2.2 of the Constitution provides as follows:

Adoption of a common law.

(1) Subject to this Part, the principles and rules that formed, immediately before Independence Day, the principles and rules of common law and equity in England are adopted, and shall be applied and enforced, as part of the underlying law, except if, and to the extent that —

(a) they are inconsistent with a Constitutional Law or a statute; or

(b) they are inapplicable or inappropriate to the circumstances of the country from time to time; or

(c) in their application to any particular matter they are inconsistent with custom as adopted by Part 1.

I see nothing in the English law on 'contempt' that is inconsistent with a constitutional law or statute or custom and nothing that makes it inapplicable or inappropriate to the circumstances of the country at the present time. I am of the view therefore that the law applicable in the proceedings before us is the English law on contempt of court. The statement of the law of England is set out in *Halsbury's Laws of England* (4th ed., vol.9) at pp.7, 8, and 21, in the following terms (omitting irrelevant parts):

> CONDUCT AMOUNTING TO CONTEMPT. In general terms, words spoken or otherwise published, or acts done, outside court which are intended or likely to interfere with or obstruct the fair administration of justice are punishable as criminal contempts of court. The commonest examples of such contempts are: (1) publications which are intended or likely to prejudice the fair trial or conduct of criminal or civil proceedings; (2) publications which prejudge issues in pending proceedings; (3) publications which scandalise, or otherwise lower the authority of, the court;
>
> 'TENDING' OR 'INTENDED' TO PREJUDICE. For a publication to amount to a contempt, it is not necessary that it should be shown actually to prejudice a fair trial or the conduct of the proceedings. The true test appears to be whether the publication is likely or tends to prejudice the trial or conduct of the action ....
>
> SCANDALISING THE COURT. Any act done or writing published which is calculated to bring a court or a judge into contempt, or to lower his authority, or to interfere with the due course of justice or the lawful process of the court, is a contempt of court ...

All three charges are alleged by the prosecution to be in relation to the Supreme Court. The first charge is laid on the sub judice basis, namely, on the ground that the statements and comments the Minister made in her letter to the Chief Justice dated 11th July, 1979, were made about proceedings pending before the Supreme Court. In the ruling delivered by the Deputy Chief Justice on the 'no case' submission made by Mr. Priestley — a ruling to which I subscribed - the Deputy Chief Justice gave reasons for his finding that the proceedings were pending before the Supreme Court and it is not necessary now for me to repeat them.

To show the necessity for the law of 'contempt' and to indicate the restraints within which it operates I can do no better than cite the following passage from the speech of Lord Morris of Borth-y-Gest in *Attorney-General v Times Newspapers Ltd* [1973] 3 All E.R. 54 at p.66:

[Editors' comment: This decision has been affected by subsequent decisions of the European Court of Human Rights.]

In an ordered community courts are established for the pacific settlement of disputes and for the maintenance of law and order. In the general interests of the community it is imperative that the authority of the courts should not be imperilled and that recourse to them should not be subject to unjustifiable intereference. When such unjustifiable interference is suppressed it is not because those charged with the responsibilities of administering justice are concerned for their own dignity: it is because the very structure of ordered life is at risk if the recognised courts of the land are so flouted that their authority wanes and is supplanted. But as the purpose and existence of courts of law is to preserve freedom within the law for all well disposed members of the community, it is manifest that the courts must never impose any limitations on free speech or free discussion or free criticism beyond those which are absolutely necessary. When therefore a court has to consider the propriety of some conduct or speech or writing decision will often depend on whether one aspect of the public interest definitely outweighs another aspect of the public interest. Certain aspects of the public interest will be relevant in deciding and assessing whether there has been contempt of court.

There is ample authority for the proposition that in order to be guilty of contempt of court regarding proceedings which are sub judice it is not necessary that there should be an intention to commit contempt of court. It is sufficient if the statements and comments made had a tendency to interfere with the course of justice or had a tendency to prejudice or embarrass the fair trial of the proceedings.

Re Rooney (No 2) [1979] PNGLR 448 at pp.472–474; see also Wilson J. at pp.503,504 (below).

per Wilson J.

Section 46 of the Constitution recognises the right to freedom of expression. Section 46 provides: [quoted in full] . . . This is an important provision in the Constitution which quite obviously limits the field of operation of the law of contempt. If what might otherwise have been regarded at common law as contempt of court may be characterised as the legitimate exercise of the right to freedom of expression, then in those circumstances the boundaries of the law of contempt are narrowed. However, because what the Minister did went much further than the legitimate exercise of her right to freedom of expression and because, in any event, the right to freedom of expression is qualified by the restrictions which the law of contempt as expressed in the Constitution itself imposes, I need consider no further the extent to which s.46 narrows the operation of the law of contempt. It does not afford any protection against contempt of court as found here.

I was surprised to hear Mr. Gregory, who appeared for the principal legal adviser to the National Executive, suggest by his submissions on the Constitutional questions that the Minister may have been guided by the fifth national goal and directive principle in the preamble to the Constitution which provides:

WE ACCORDINGLY CALL FOR —

(1) a fundamental re-orientation of our attitudes and the institutions of government, commerce, education and religion towards Papua New Guinean forms of participation, consultation, and consensus, and a continuous renewal of the responsiveness of these institutions to the needs and attitudes of the People; and

(2) particular emphasis in our economic development to be placed on small-scale artisan, service and business activity; and

(3) recognition that the cultural, commercial and ethnic diversity of our people is a positive strength, and for the fostering of a respect for, and appreciation of, traditional ways of life and culture, including language, in all their richness and variety, as well as for a willingness to apply these ways dynamically and creatively for the tasks of development; and

(4) traditional villages and communities to remain as viable units of Papua New Guinean society, and for active steps to be taken to improve their cultural, social, economic and ethical quality.

It is ironic that the Minister's letter of 11th July was couched in language more typical of 'foreign laws' and foreign influence than of 'Papua New Guinean forms of participation, consulation, and consensus'.

Re Rooney (No 2) [1979] PNGLR 448 at pp.503,504; see also Saldanha J. at pp.472–474 (above).

GENERALLY

Referred to

by Kearney J. in *Cory v Blyth (No 4)* [1976] PNGLR 525 at p.527;

by Narakobi A.J. in *Tabo Sipo v Meli* (1980 Unreported) N240 at p.5;

by Kidu C.J. in *The State v Kosi and ors* (1981 Unreported) N305 at p.4;

by Kapi J. in *S.C.R No 2 of 1982; Re Organic Law* [1982] PNGLR 214 at p.237.

47. FREEDOM OF ASSEMBLY AND ASSOCIATION

Every person has the right peacefully to assemble and associate and to form or belong to, or not to belong to, political parties, industrial organisations or other associations, except to the extent that the exercise of that right is regulated or restricted by a law —

(a) that makes reasonable provision in respect of the registration of all or any associations; or

(b) that imposes reasonable restrictions on public office-holders; or

(c) that imposes restrictions on non-citizens; or

(d) that complies with Section 38 (*general qualifications on qualified rights*).

CROSS REFERENCE

Universal Declaration of Human Rights: Article 20; *Constitution of India:* s.19(1)(b)(c); *Constitution of the United States*: Am.1; *European Convention on Human Rights:* Article 11.

C.P.C. Report Ch.5 Part 1 p.11

9. *FREEDOM OF ASSEMBLY AND ASSOCIATION*

61. We believe that if we guarantee freedom of expression it follows that we should also guarantee freedom of assembly and association. Our recommendation safeguards the right of every person to join a political party, a trade union or any other association or group. People of like mind, such as members of a political party, or with similar interests, such as trade unionists, should be able to join together to work for common purposes. [p.12]

62. For a government to arbitrarily restrict its citizens' fundamental human right of freedom of assembly and association would, we believe, be to indicate clearly an intention to turn away from democracy, as it is generally only through organized groups that consistent pressure can be effectively applied to a government by those who are critical of its policies.

63. We fully appreciate that there are likely to be times other than during a State of Emergency when the holding of a large public meeting might endanger public safety — for example, at a time when emotions are running high and there are serious divisions among the people in a particular city or other area of the country. The exception provisions in our recommendation allow for such situations, and establishing this constitutional right would not, therefore, prevent reasonable measures being taken to deal with these situations.

64. Our proposed section is based on the equivalent one in the Ordinance, but we have made special provision for the registration of political parties, industrial organisations and other associations or organisations, and for prohibiting any association from placing restrictions based on race or colour on the admission of members to an association. As in the case of the protection of freedom of expression, reasonably justifiable restrictions could also be placed on the freedom of assembly and association of constitutional office-holders, public servants, members of the disciplined forces, and non-citizens.

RECOMMENDATIONS [p.27]

Protection of freedom of assembly and association

9. (1) Subject to clause (3) below, all persons have the right to assemble and associate peaceably and to form or belong to political parties, industrial organisations or other associations.

(2) Except with his consent, no person shall be hindered in the enjoyment of a right referred to in clause (1) above.

(3) Nothing contained in or done under the authority of any law shall be held to be inconsistent with, or in contravention of, this recommendation to the extent that that law makes provision that is reasonably justifiable in a democratic society —
(a) in the interests of defence, public safety, public order, public health or public welfare;
(b) for protecting the rights and freedoms of other persons;
(c) for imposing restrictions upon constitutional office-holders, members of the public services and members of a disciplined force;
(d) for the registration of political parties, industrial organizations and other associations or organizations, (including churches and missions) in registers provided for by law, and for imposing reasonable conditions concerning the procedure for entry in such a register.
(e) for prohibiting any association from placing restrictions based on race or colour on the admission of members to the association; or
(f) imposing restrictions on persons who are not citizens of Papua New Guinea.

AS TO WHETHER SECTION 47 CONFERS A RIGHT TO STRIKE

per Kapi Dep.C.J.

Finally, I bought to counsel's attention the possibility of an argument that s.85 of the [*Public Services*] Act could be unconstitutional for being inconsistent with s.47 of the Constitution .... s.47 of the Constitution guarantees freedom of assembly and association. It is a freedom to persons to join political parties, unions and other organisations. The PEA is such an organisation. All members who have joined PEA have exercised the right given by s.47 of the Constitution. This right deals with
(a) the right to *assemble and associate*
(b) the *right to form* and;
(c) the *right to belong to or not to belong* to a political party, an industrial organisation or other forms or association.
That is as for as s.47 goes. It does not concern itself with the activities of a political party, an industrial organisation or other associations.
Public Employees Association and Liosi v Public Service Commission (1983 Unreported) N405 at p.5.

GENERALLY

Referred to

by Narakobi A.J. in *Tabo Sipo v Meli* (1980 Unreported) N240 at p.5;

by Miles J. in *S.C.R. No 1 of 1980; Re s.22A(b) of Police Offences Act (Papua)* [1981] PNGLR 28 at p.46;

by Kidu C.J. in *The State v Kosi and others* (1981 Unreported) N306 (the unlawful assembly provisions of the Criminal Code do not offend s.47: but see also heading *Comments* under s.46);

by Kapi Dep.C.J. in *S.C.R. No 2 of 1982; Re Organic Law* [1982] PNGLR 214 at p.237.

48. — FREEDOM OF EMPLOYMENT

(1) Every person has the right to freedom of choice of employment in any calling for which he has the qualifications (if any) lawfully required, except to the extent that that freedom is regulated or restricted voluntarily or by a law that complies with Section 38 (*general qualifications on qualified rights*), or a law that imposes restrictions on non-citizens.

(2) Subsection (1) does not prohibit reasonable action or provision for the encouragement of persons to join industrial organizations or for requiring membership of an industrial organization for any purpose.

CROSS REFERENCE

Universal Declaration of Human Rights: Article 23; *Constitution of India:* Section 19(1)(g).

C.P.C. Report Ch.5 Part 1 p.12

10. *FREEDOM OF EMPLOYMENT*

65. We believe that the principle that a person should be able to freely choose his employment is also important, and that it should be incorporated in the Constitution. However, it is obviously essential to draw a distinction between citizens and non-citizens in this regard, and this we have done. It has been government policy for a number of years now for preference to be given to Papua New Guineans in relation to employment opportunities both in the public and private sectors, and this policy should certainly continue. The role of non citizens is to work in positions for which there is no Papua New Guinean with the necessary skills available.

66. The qualifications of this freedom which are included in the *Ordinance* are so wide as to make the relevant provision virtually meaningless. We have therefore modified the exception clauses so that they provide for what we see as no more than reasonable qualifications of the basic right, but which provide the necessary flexibility to enable the Government of the day to give preference to underprivileged groups.

RECOMMENDATIONS [p.27]

Protection of freedom of employment

10. (1) Subject to clauses (3) and (4) below, all persons have the right to freedom of employment. For the purposes of this recommendation 'freedom of employment' means freedom of choice of employment, that is to say, each person shall have the right, in accordance with his own wishes, to practise any lawful profession or carry on any lawful trade or business.

(2) Except with his consent, no person shall be hindered in the enjoyment of the right referred to in clause (1) above, *provided that* this provision shall not be interpreted as meaning that reasonable activities of trade unions intended to persuade persons in employment to join them as members are unlawful.

(3) Nothing contained in or done under the authority of a law shall be held to be inconsistent with or in contravention of, this recommendation to the extent that that law imposes any disability or restriction or accords any privilege or advantage which, having regard to its nature and to special circumstances co ncerning the persons to whom it applies, is reasonable justifiable in a democratic society.

(4) Nothing contained in or done under the authority of a law shall be held to be inconsistent with, or in contravention of, this recommendation to the extent that that law makes provision that is reasonably justifiable in a democratic society —
(a) in the interests of defence, public safety, public health or public welfare;
(b) for the protection of minors or persons under a disability;
(c) for the protection of workmen; [p.28]
(d) for the regulation of industrial organizations or industrial relations or the prevention or settlement of industrial disputes;

(e) for establishing and maintaining standards of workmanship or production, for quality control or for the protection of industries;
(f) for prescribing and regulating the qualifications required for particular types of employment; or
(g) for restricting or prohibiting any person who is not a citizen of Papua New Guinea from practising any profession or from carrying on any occupation, trade or business.

AS TO THE NATURE OF THE RIGHT PROTECTED

per Prentice C.J.

The right guaranteed is to *choice* not to the practice of employment. The right to freedom of choice of employment is by the section expressly made subject to the exception of 'a law that imposes restrictions on non-citizens'.
Premdas v The Independent State of Papua New Guinea [1979] PNGLR 329 at p.339; see also Saldanha J. at p.357 (no right to employment conferred by the Constitution) and Andrew J. at p.399 (as to indirect infringement of the right to choice of employment: indirect infringements are not prohibited).

GENERALLY

Referred to

by Narakobi A.J. in *Tabo Šipo v Meli* (1980 Unreported) N240 at p.5.

49. — RIGHT TO PRIVACY

Every person has the right to reasonable privacy in respect of his private and family life, his communications with other persons and his personal papers and effects, except to the extent that the exercise of that right is regulated or restricted by a law that complies with Section 38 (*general qualifications on qualified rights*).

CROSS REFERENCE

Universal Declaration of Human Rights: Article 12; *European Convention on Human Rights:* Article 8; *Constitution of the United States*: Am.1V.

C.P.C. Report Ch.5 Part 1 p.13

12. *THE RIGHT TO PRIVACY*

73. Another new right which we recommend should be included in our constitutional Declaration of Fundamental Rights and Freedoms is the right to privacy in respect of one's family life, home, communications by telephone and correspondence. This right is, of course, closely linked with the right to freedom from arbitrary search and entry, and should be seen as complementary to it. The public controversy which occurred in 1972 in relation to the tapping of telephones highlighted the danger to democratic freedoms which the recording by police or other government officials, of private conversations can pose. We believe the constitutional provision which we recommend here will reinforce the *Private Communications (Telephone Tapping) Act* 1973, which was passed by the House of Assembly to limit much more strictly than previously official power to record telephone conversations.

74. We recognise that the interests of the community must be balanced against the right of individuals in regard to this, as well as other human rights and freedoms. Accordingly, we have recommended that the right to privacy be subject to the general exception clause which allows for a law to be passed which would otherwise be contrary to this provision if it is a law which is reasonably justifiable in a democratic society in the interests of defence, public safety, public order, etc; or for the protection of the rights and freedoms of other persons. As we have already stated, such a law would, however, need the support of three fifths of the members of the National Parliament, unless it was passed during a State of Emergency.

RECOMMENDATIONS [p.28]

Protection of right to privacy

12. (1) Every person shall be entitled to respect for his private and family life, his home, his communications by telephone and other electrical or electronic means, and his correspondence.

(2) Nothing in this recommendation shall invalidate any law insofar as the law is reasonably justifiable in a democratic society —
(a) in the interests of defence, public safety, public order, public health or public welfare; or
(b) for the protection of the rights and freedoms of other persons.

GENERALLY

Referred to

by Prentice C.J. in *Reference No 1 of 1977* [1977] PNGLR 329 at p.377;

by Narakobi A.J. in *Tabo Sipo v Meli* (1980 Unreported) N240 at p.5.

SPECIAL RIGHTS OF CITIZENS

50. — RIGHT TO VOTE AND STAND FOR PUBLIC OFFICE.

(1) Subject to the express limitations imposed by this Constitution, every citizen who is of full capacity and has reached voting age, other than a person who —
(a) is under sentence of death or imprisonment for a period of more than nine months; or
(b) has been convicted, within the period of three years next preceding the first day of the polling period for the election concerned, of an offence relating to elections that is prescribed by an Organic Law or an Act of the Parliament for the purposes of this paragraph,

has the right, and shall be given a reasonable opportunity —
(c) to take part in the conduct of public affairs, either directly or through freely chosen representatives; and
(d) to vote for, and to be elected to, elective public office at genuine, periodic, free elections; and
(e) to hold public office and to exercise public functions.

CROSS REFERENCE

Universal Declaration of Human Rights: Article 21

C.P.C Report Ch.5 Part 1 p.13

13. *THE RIGHT TO STAND FOR ELECTION TO PUBLIC OFFICE AND TO VOTE*

75. As we have indicated earlier, both in our 'Introduction' and in Chapter 2, 'National Goals and Directive Principles', one of the main themes which runs through the consitutional provisions we recommend is that of participation by our people in all aspects of the life of the country. We see as a major factor in ensuring that our people *are* able to be meaningfully involved in their own development the effective functioning of the system of elections, at all levels of government.

76. In Chapter 6 'The Legislature' we have made a number of recommendations designed to ensure that regular, fairly conducted elections are held throughout the country. However, we believe it is important to include among the fundamental rights safeguarded here, the right of every citizen to have the opportunity without unreasonable restriction, to take part in public affairs, either directly or through freely chosen representatives. Each citizen should be able to vote and be elected to public office, at genuine, periodic elections in which all adults are able to participate, and held by secret ballot. We have made special provision to allow for assistance to be give to voters who are illiterate or who for any other reason cannot complete their ballot paper without help.

77. To emphasize the need for more women to be involved in public life, we have specifically provided that women are entitled to hold public office and to exercise all public functions in accordance with law, on equal terms with men, without discrimination.

RECOMMENDATIONS [p.28]

The right to stand for election to public office and to vote

13. (1) Subject to the Constitution every Papua New Guinean citizen shall have the right and the opportunity, without unreasonable restrictions —
   (a) to take part in the conduct of public affairs, directly or through freely chosen representatives;
   (b) to vote and to be elected to public office at genuine periodic elections which shall be by universal adult suffrage and shall be held by secret ballot guaranteeing the free expression of the will of the electors, *provided that* provision may be made by law for reasonable assistance to be given to a voter in marking his ballot paper in any election if he is illiterate or is for any other reason unable to complete his ballot paper without assistance; or ... [p.29]
   (c) to hold public office and to exercise all public functions in accordance with law.

(2) Women are entitled to hold public office and to exercise all public functions in accordance with law, on equal terms with men, without any discrimination.

(3) The burden of proving that a restriction referred to in clause (1) above is a reasonable restriction lies upon the person asserting that the restriction is reasonable.

EXCESSIVE ELECTION DEPOSITS ARE UNCONSTITUTIONAL

Held

A regulating law under s.50(2) may regulate, but cannot prohibit the exercise of s.50(1) rights. Given the evidence before the Court of social and economic conditions applying in Papua New Guinea, a requirement for a K1000.00 deposit effectively denied a reasonable opportunity to stand for Parliament to the majority of eligible citizens. The requirement for parliamentary candidates to pay a K1000.00 deposit before standing for election cannot be said to be reasonably justifiable in terms of s.50(2) given the Constitution's manifest emphasis on free and equal participation by citizens (see also commentary under ss.50(2), 55 and 57 of the Constitution).
S.C.R. No 2 of 1982; Re Organic Law [1982] PNGLR 214; see Kidu C.J. at p.221, Kearney Dep. C.J. at pp.224–232, Greville Smith J. at p.232, Andrew J. at p.223, Kapi J. at pp.239,240.

NATIONAL COURT CANNOT EXTEND THE TIME FOR NOMINATION PRESCRIBED BY THE ORGANIC LAW ON NATIONAL ELECTIONS

Held

Notwithstanding that the applicant, an intending candidate, had been arrested by the police who then kept him in custody for several hours during which period the time for nomination prescribed under the *Organic Law on National Elections* expired, the Court had no power to extend the time for lodgement of nominations. An order to extend nomination time would not be ancillary to the rights guaranteed under s.50. Strict compliance with the *Organic Law on National Elections* was mandatory.
In re Organic Law on National Elections [1982] PNGLR 289; see Kapi Dep. C.J. at pp.290,291.

'SUBJECT TO THE EXPRESS LIMITATIONS IMPOSED BY THIS CONSTITUTION . . .'

per Andrew J.:

Section 103 is just such an express limitation. The two sections can quite easily be read together. In my opinion, it is not conceivable that Parliament in adopting the Constitution could have contemplated that a man could be a candidate and stand for national elections when it was known that when he came to take his seat, he would not be qualified. It must follow from s.103 of the Constitution that if the candidate is not twenty-five when he comes to take his seat, that he was not qualified to stand in the first place.
Okuk v Nilkare (1983 Unreported) N406 at p.6.

Comment

It would appear that a candidate may nominate for elections even thought he/she is not 25 years old at the time of nomination, providing at the time of 'taking' his/her seat he/she will be 25 years. If the candidate's 25th birthday falls before the return of the writ for elections then the nomination must be accepted.

GENERALLY

Referred to

per Curiam (Frost C.J., Prentice Dep. C.J., Williams J.) in *James Eki Mopio v The Speaker* [1977] PNGLR 420 at p.422;

by Narakobi A.J. in *Tabo Sipo v Meli* (1980 Unreported) N240 at p.5;

by Andrew J. in *Okuk v Nilkare* (1983 Unreported) N406 at p.6.

(2) The exercise of those rights may be regulated by a law that is reasonably justifiable for the purpose in a democratic society that has a proper regard for the rights and dignity of mankind.

(*See*: *Organic Law on National Elections* Ch.1)

AS TO THE MEANING OF THE EXPRESSION 'REASONABLY JUSTIFIABLE IN A DEMOCRATIC SOCIETY'

For detailed discussion see under s.38.

Referred to

by Kearney Dep.C.J. in *S.C.R. No. 2 of 1982; Re Organic Law* [1982] PNGLR 214 at p.227 (Court must apply an objective test to decide whether a particular matter is 'reasonably justifiable'), but see Kapi J. at pp.235–237 (contra).

APPLIED TO EXCESSIVE ELECTION DEPOSITS

Held

The *Organic Law on National Elections (Amendment) Act* 1981, by requiring a candidate for election to Parliament to validate his or her nomination with a deposit of K1000 is not a law which is 'reasonably justifiable' in terms of s.50(2) of the Constitution as it denies the majority of eligible citizens a reasonable opportunity to stand for election and is inconsistent with the Constitution's emphasis on free and equal participation by citizens in the electoral process.
S.C.R. No 2 of 1982; Re Organic Law [1982] PNGLR 214; see Kidu C.J. at p.221, Kearney Dep.C.J. at pp.224–232, Greville Smith J. at p.232, Andrew J. at p.223, Kapi J. at pp.239,240.

51. — RIGHT TO FREEDOM OF INFORMATION.

(1) Every citizen has the right of reasonable access to official documents, subject only to the need for such secrecy as is reasonably justifiable in a democratic society in respect of —

(a) matters relating to national security, defence or international relations of Papua New Guinea (including Papua New Guinea's relations with the Government of any other country or with any international organization); or

(b) records of meetings and decisions of the National Executive Council and of such executive bodies and elected governmental authorities as are prescribed by Organic Law or Act of the Parliament; or

(c) trade secrets, and privileged or confidential commercial or financial information obtained from a person or body; or

(d) parliamentary papers the subject of parliamentary privilege; or

(e) reports, official registers and memoranda prepared by governmental authorities or authorities established by government, prior to completion; or

(f) papers relating to lawful official activities for investigation and prosecution of crime; or

(g) the prevention, investigation and prosecution of crime; or

(h) the maintenance of personal privacy and security of the person; or

(i) matters contained in or related to reports prepared by, on behalf of or for the use of a governmental authority responsible for the regulation or supervision of financial institutions; or

(j) geological or geophysical information and data concerning wells and ore bodies.

C.P.C. Report Ch.5 Part 1 p.13

14. *FREEDOM OF INFORMATION*

78. For our citizens to be able to participate effectively in the public affairs of this country, it is essential that they have access to official information. Without information as to governmental activity a person cannot make a meaningful contribution to discussion of the issues involved in government policies and programmes. The degree to which citizens are able to fully participate in debate on the public affairs of the country will be a good measure of the extent to which our system of government is truly democratic.

79. Governments in many countries fail to communicate effectively to their people the actions they are taking or contemplating, and the problems which face them. Sometimes this is due to sheer inefficiency on the part of the government information office but sometimes it is a case of the government wanting to keep from the voters the truth about matters which might cause a loss of support for the government if they were widely known. [p.14]

80. In developing countries such as Papua New Guinea, it is an unfortunate fact that often foreign businessmen know far more about the actions and policies of the Government than do all but a select few of its own citizens. Thus these business interests are in a position to exercise influence on the government without any reaction from nationalist groups being felt by the Government until it is too late for it to take any positive action in response to such reaction.

81. We have therefore recommended that a further civil right — that of freedom of access to official documents — be included in the Constitution, subject to appropriate qualifications which take account of the need for such secrecy as is reasonably justifiable in a democratic society in respect of matters such as —

- those relating to national security and relations between Papua New Guinea and foreign states;
- national economic interests and the legitimate economic interests of communities and individuals;

- minutes of meetings and associated papers of the National Executive Council and of such other governmental authorities as are specified in a law;
- incomplete official reports and memoranda;
- parliamentary papers (not, for example, Hansard) which are privileged;
- the prevention, investigation and prosecution of crime; and
- maintaining privacy, the safety of individuals and decency.

82. From our own experience, we fully appreciate the need for confidentiality in the preparation of reports for government and parliament, but once a report is completed it should be readily available to the general public.

83. Our recommended provision is similar to part of a constitutional enactment, the *Freedom of the Press Act*, which has been in force in Sweden since 1912, and is part of the basic framework of the democratic freedom enjoyed by Swedish citizens. We have further recommended that provision be made by law to established procedures by which citizens may obtain ready access to official information. It is obviously important that not only the principle of publicity of official documents be firmly established but that the procedures adopted for making that principle effective be simple and widely known.

84. Our final proposal under this head is that as a step towards ensuring that official information is used responsibly by the press in the interests of Papua New Guinean citizens, the managing editor of any newspaper, magazine, etc., published in this country must be a citizen. Furthermore that person must accept responsibility for any breach of the law in a publication produced by the enterprise of which he is managing editor. Today in democratic states the threat to a free press and to a many-sided discussion of public affairs does not come only, or even primarily from the State authorities. Often, in even higher degree, it comes from other powerful forces in society, notably economic groups such as multi-national corporations. In many States, also, newspapers are owned by a few monopolistic groups. The South Pacific, including Australia, exemplifies this situation. Our proposal that the managing editor of a newspaper or magazine produced here be a citizen and take full responsibility for publications is designed to try to limit the influence of these powerful groups and to orient the press towards serving the best interests of our own people.

RECOMMENDATIONS [p.29]

Protection of freedom of information

14. (1) To further free interchange of opinion and general enlightenment, every Papua New Guinean citizen shall have free access to official documents, subject only to the following restrictions — the need for such secrecy as is reasonably justifiable in a democratic society in respect of —
(a) matters relating to national security and relations between Papua New Guinea and foreign States;
(b) national economic interests and the legitimate economic interests of communities and individuals;
(c) minutes of meetings and associated papers of the National Executive Council and of such other governmental authorities as are prescribed by law;
(d) parliamentary papers the subject of parliamentary privilege;
(e) reports, official registers and diaries prepared by governmental authorities or authorities established by government, prior to completion;
(f) memoranda or other notes prepared by a governmental authority to prepare or present a case or matter for decision, unless after the case or matter has been decided by the authority the matter is placed on permanent record;
(g) papers relating to lawful official activities for investigation, inspection, control or other supervision;
(h) prevention, investigation and presecution of crime;
(i) the maintenance of privacy, security of the person and decency.

(2) Provision shall be made by law to establish procedures by which citizens may obtain ready access to official information.
Note: In this Chapter 'official documents' means all documents kept by the national government or by a privincial government or local government authority, whether received or prepared by that authority. The term includes maps, drawings and pictures (including photographs).

(3) As a step towards ensuring that official information is used responsibly by the press in the interests of Papua New Guinean citizens it is recommended that the managing editor of any newspaper, magazines, or other similar publication which is published in Papua New Guinea shall be —
(a) a citizen; and
(b) the person responsible for any breach of the law in a publication produced by the corporation or other enterprise of which he is managing editor.

GENERALLY

Referred to

by Narakobi A.J. in *In the matter of the Adoption of Children Act 1968* (1980 Unreported) N221 (application by counsel to inspect welfare reports in an adoption case refused);

by Narakobi A.J. in *Tabo Sipo v Meli* (1980 Unreported) N240 at p.5;

by Kearney Dep.C.J. in *S.C.R. No 2 of 1982; Re Organic Law* [1982] PNGLR 214 at p.225 (the power to restrict can extend to prohibition but the power to regulate cannot).

(2) A law that complies with Section 38 (*general qualifications on qualified rights*) may regulate or restrict the right guaranteed by this section.

(3) Provision shall be made by law to establish procedures by which citizens may obtain ready access to official information.

(4) This section does not authorize —
 (a) withholding information or limiting the availability of records to the public except in accordance with its provisions; or
 (b) withholding information from the Parliament.

AS TO WHETHER IN THE ABSENCE OF A LAW MADE UNDER SECTION 51(3) THE RIGHT TO FREEDOM OF INFORMATION MAY BE ENFORCED.

COMMENT

Section 51(1) confers the right of reasonable access to official documents and s.51(3) directs that provision shall be made by law to establish procedures for citizens to obtain such access.

Because Parliament is yet to pass a law as directed by s.51(3) an interesting question arises as to whether the right can be enforced in the absence of such legislation.

An analogous problem was considered by the High Court of Australia in *Downey v Prior* (1960) 103 CLR 353. In that case s.219 of the *Local Government Act* 1919 (N.S.W.) provided: 'Any elector may at the council's office inspect books of account . . . as prescribed.' No method of inspection was subsequently prescribed. The High Court held that the prescription of a method was not essential to complete the right of inspection granted by the section. In the absence of a prescription the right could be exercised in any reasonable manner. A similar approach to the construction of ss.51(1) and (3) would, it is submitted, be appropriate in Papua New Guinea to implement the intention of this constitutional provision, and would accord with the intent of Constitution s.11(2).

52. — RIGHT TO FREEDOM OF MOVEMENT

(1) Subject to Subsection (3), no citizen may be deprived of the right to move freely throughout the country, to reside in any part of the country and to enter and leave the country, except in consequence of a law that provides for deprivation of personal liberty in accordance with Section 42 (*liberty of the person*).

(2) No citizen shall be expelled or deported from the country except by virtue of an order of a court made under a law in respect of the extradition of offenders, or alleged offenders, against the law of some other place.

(3) A law that complies with Section 38 (*general qualifications on qualified rights*) may regulate or restrict the exercise of the right referred to in Subsection (1), and in particular may regulate or restrict the freedom of movement of persons convicted of offences and of members of a disciplined force.

CROSS REFERENCE

Universal Declaration of Human Rights: Article 13; *Constitution of India:* Section 19(1)(d), (e); Fourth Protocol of September 16, 1963 to the *European Convention on Human Rights:* Article 2.

C.P.C. Report Ch.5 Part 1 p.12

11. *FREEDOM OF MOVEMENT*

67. This safeguard of the right to move is not provided by the *Ordinance*, but we believe it is vital in any free society. There has been much public discussion of this issue in Papua New Guinea in recent years, with resentment being expressed in some quarters concerning substantial numbers of people from other parts of the country congregating in particular towns or other areas. We fully recognise the seriousness of the problems involved, especially in urban areas, but we feel that the principle that all citizens should be free to move throughout the country, provided they respect the rights and interests of those in the places to which they go, is widely accepted among our people, and should be entrenched in the Constitution. People who live in areas where there is little opportunity for participation in the national economy should have the opportunity to move to another area to seek employment.

68. We also believe that the right of citizens to enter and leave the country freely is an important principle, and have provided for this. Specific provision should, however, be made to allow for legislation restricting a citizen's freedom to leave the country if he has not fulfilled a legal obligation. Our recommendation has been made accordingly.

69. We have recommended limiting the scope of this protection of freedom of movement to citizens, for much the same reasons as a number of other new Commonwealth states such as Nigeria and Kenya have done so. Although some states do extend this constitutional right to foreign citizens, they have almost invariably qualified it to allow legislation to be passed specifically limiting the freedom of movement of foreign citizens.

70. All countries, in the interests of their own citizens place restrictions on the entry of foreign citizens to their territory, and upon the period during which they may remain in the country, though of course some states are much more strict in this regard then are others. All countries also have legislation which provides for the deportation of foreign citizens in a range of circumstances which usually includes a number of situations besides that in which a foreign citizen is found guilty of a criminal offence. For example, under United Kingdom legislation a foreign citizen may be deported whenever the Home Secretary 'deems it conducive to the public good'. [p.13]

71. We believe the right to limit the movement of foreign citizens is part of a country's sovereign rights, and should be retained as such. This is not to say that we consider that foreign citizens should be unreasonably restricted in regard to the parts of the country to which they may travel. We simply believe that the full power of parliament to make appropriate laws to limit the movement of non-citizens in the interests of all Papua New Guinean citizens must be retained.

72. We further propose that provision be made to allow for reasonable limitations to be placed on the movement of public servants or members of a disciplined force.

RECOMMENDATIONS [p.28]

Protection of freedom of movement

11. (1) Subject to clauses (2) and (3) below no citizen shall be deprived of his freedom of movement. For the purposes of this recommendation that freedom means the right to move freely throughout Papua New Guinea, the right to reside in any part of Papua New Guinea, the right to enter Papua New Guinea, the right to leave Papua New Guinea, and immunity from explusion from Papua New Guinea.

(2) A restriction on a citizen's freedom of movement that is necessarily involved in lawful detention shall not be held to contravene this recommendation.

(3) Nothing in this recommendation shall invalidate any law by reason only that the law makes provision which is reasonably justifiable in a democratic society —
  (a) for the imposition of restrictions on the acquisition or use by any person of land or other property in Papua New Guinea;
  (b) for the removal of a citizen from Papua New Guinea to be tried outside Papua New Guinea for a criminal offence or to undergo imprisonment outside Papua New Guinea in execution of a sentence of a court (established for Papua New Guinea or for some other country) in respect of a criminal offence of which he has been convicted;
  (c) for the imposition of restrictions on the movement or residence of members of a public service or members of a disciplined force;
  (d) for the imposition of restrictions on the right of any person to leave Papua New Guinea that are reasonably required in order to secure the fulfilment of any obligation imposed on that person by law, or which is enforceable in legal proceedings; or
  (e) for the imposition of restrictions on the freedom of movement of any person that are reasonably required in the interests of defence, public safety, public order, public health, public welfare, or environmental conservation.

AS TO THE CONSTITUTIONAL VALIDITY OF THE VAGRANCY ACT.

Comment

In apparent reliance upon the power conferred by s.52(3) to make a law, complying with s.38, to 'regulate or restrict' the right to freedom of movement, Parliament has passed the *Vagrancy Act* Ch.268. That Act provides, inter alia, that a magistrate may order an indigent person to leave any part of Papua New Guinea where he is found unless he is native to the area or has employment etc.

The *Vagrancy Act* appears however not to fully comply with the formal requirements of s.38(3). It fails to bear the certificate of the Speaker indicating that it was passed by an absolute majority. More fundamentally, it is also arguable that as the majority of citizens possess little money and few are in full time employment, the effect of the *Vagrancy Act* is to effectively prohibit the majority of citizens from exercising their right to freedom of movement. Such a conclusion would suggest that the Act could be challenged as unconstitutional, either because it is 'not reasonably justifiable in a democratic society' or because it exceeds the power granted by s.52(3) to 'regulate or restrict' the right. However for the latter argument to succeed the Courts would need to hold that the words 'regulate or restrict' do not authorise the effective prohibition of the right. In this regard it should be noted that in *S.C.R. No 2 of 1982; Re Organic Law* [1982] PNGLR 214 at p.255, Kearney Dep.C.J. expressed the opinion that while the power to 'regulate' cannot extend to prohibition, the power to 'restrict' can.

GENERALLY

Referred to

by Miles J. in *S.C.R. No 1 of 1980; Re s.22A(b) of Police Offences Act (Papua)* [1981] PNGLR 28 at p.46;

by Narakobi A.J. in *Tabo Sipo v Meli* (1980 Unreported) N240 at p.5;

by Kidu C.J. in *The State v Kosi and ors* (1981 Unreported) N306 at p.4 (Sections 61 and 62 of the Criminal Code which create the offences of unlawful assembly etc. 'do not infringe on any constitutional right. They do not restrict or regulate any guaranteed rights. They operate only when those exercising such rights go beyond the protections afforded by .... s.52 of the Constitution'. See also *Comment* under s.46.)

53. — *PROTECTION FROM UNJUST DEPRIVATION OF PROPERTY*

(1) Subject to Subsection 54 (sic) (*special prevision in relation to certain lands*) and except as permitted by this section, possession may not be compulsorily taken of any property, and no interest in or right over property may be compulsorily acquired, except in accordance with an Organic Law or an Act of the Parliament, and unless —

(a) the property is required for —
  (i) a public purpose; or
  (ii) a reason that is reasonably justified in a democratic society that has a proper regard for the rights and dignity of mankind,

that is so declared and so described, for the purposes of this section, in an Organic Law or an Act of the Parliament; and

(b) the necessity for the taking of possession or acquisition for the attainment of that purpose or for that reason is such as to afford reasonable justification for the causing of any resultant hardship to any person affected.

CROSS REFERENCE

Universal Declaration of Human Rights: Article 17; *Constitution of India:* Sections 19(1)(f) and 25; First Protocol of March 20, 1952 to the *European Convention on Human Rights:* Article 1.

C.P.C. Report Ch.5 Part 1 p.14

15. *PROTECTION FROM DEPRIVATION OF PROPERTY*

85. In the days of the French and American Revolutions and throughout the nineteenth and much of the twentieth century, great stress was laid on property rights as being among the most fundamental of human rights. This was part of the political philosophy of laissez-faire which was dominant in the thinking of Western societies until quite recently.

86. With the emergence of many new states in which the vast majority of the people have relatively few property rights to protect, whilst a small number of privileged people, both non-citizens and citizens, own the bulk of rural and industrial property, nationalist governments in many countries have regarded it as essential that positive action be taken to redistribute wealth more equitably. To do so, however, has been a daunting task, and some of these countries, particularly new Commonwealth states, have found that constitutional provisions have limited their ability to acquire foreign owned property and have also been instrumental in obliging them to pay very substantial sums, on strict conditions, as compensation for the property they have acquired. This in turn has restricted the ability of the governments of these states to carry out programmes designed to achieve a fairer distribution of their resources and of the benefits obtained from their use. [p.15]

87. Countries of the Third World have become increasingly concerned by, and resentful of, the extent to which giant foreign corporations are dominating their economies and obtaining massive profits from operations in their countries. This situation was clearly evidenced at a reçent Special Meeting of the United Nations to consider the need to drastically change the present international economic order. We in Papua New Guinea are all too familiar with the extent and effects of the present foreign control of our economy, as we have indicated in Chapter 2. Our own people are, however, more fortunate than those in many other new states in that most still have their own land, their rights to which they rightly intend to protect most vigorously.

88. After very careful consideration we have decided to recommend that the constitutional protection of property interests should be limited to our own citizens. The interests of foreign citizens can be protected in a number of ways by the Government of the day — by legislation such as that proposed for the establishment of the National Investment and Development Corporation, by agreement between the government and particular enterprises, or by a general law concerning a certain type of property. Our aim is to give the Government of the day sufficient flexibility to deal with the acquisition of foreign owned property and payment for it in an appropriate way, according to the particular circumstances with which it is faced. We believe that this view is in line with the position taken by the great majority of countries of the Third World.

89. The *Land Acquisition Bill* 1974, which is at present before the House of Assembly, is a good example of the kind of legislation which we believe our government ought to be able to put forward without having the problem of a constitutional restriction on its legislative power. In such circumstances there are certain to be strong political pressures brought to bear on it by foreign interests, and these will undoubtedly limit the government's freedom of action in any event. International law may also have a bearing in some cases.

90. Apart from the limitation of its scope to Papua New Guinean citizens, the provision we recommend is somewhat similar to the equivalent section of the *Ordinance*. However, there are two other significant differences between the respective provisions. The first is that instead of using the phrase 'on just terms' in respect of the power to deprive a person of his property (which is identical to that used in s.51 (xxxxi) of the *Australian Constitution*) we have preferred to use the phrase 'in accordance with principles of justice'. This latter phrase we propose should be interpreted so as to give full weight to the National Goals and Directive Principles in the Constitution, to the national interest (and in particular to the expression of that interest by parliament) as well as to the interests of the person deprived of his property. The effect of this recommendation should be that the courts will not simply follow precedents from Australia in assessing whether or not laws providing for the payment of compensation for acquired property are valid but will give weight to the interests of the people of the country as a whole, and in particular, to parliament's interpretation of those interests, as well as to the interests of the individual concerned.

91. A further difference between our recommended provision and that in the *Ordinance* is that we have added a number of additional qualifications to the right to compensation for property acquired by the State. As mentioned above, we have done so in light of the experience of a number of other new states which have had cause to amend their equivalent human rights provisions to take account of circumstances which have arisen after Independence. It should be remembered that the *Human Rights Ordinance* can easily be amended, whereas to amend the constitutional provision we propose would require a special procedure, and the support of a two-thirds majority of the members of the National Parliament.

RECOMMENDATIONS [p. 29]

Protection from deprivation of property

15. (1) (a) Subject to clause (2) below, no citizen shall be deprived compulsorily of any property or interest in or right over such property except in accordance with law and principles of justice.
(b) In applying principles of justice under this clause a court shall, in addition to giving full weight to the National Goals and Directive Principles in the Constitution, have due regard for the national interest and in particular to the expression of that interest by the representatives of the people in Parliament, as well as to the interests of the person deprived of his property. [p. 30]

Note: The Committee envisages that appropriate provision will be made by law from time to time for the protection of the property rights and interests of foreign investors and other foreign citizens and for payment to be made to them in respect of their rights and interests in case of expropriation. The proposed government bill for the establishment of NIDA contains a guarantee of this kind to foreign investors.

(2) Nothing contained in or done under the authority of a law shall be held to be inconsistent with or in contravention of clause (1) of this recommendation to the extent that that law makes provision —
(a) for the deprivation of any property or of any interest in or right over property —
(i) the possession of which is declared by law to be unlawful, either absolutely or in certain circumstances or with certain exceptions;
(ii) in satisfaction of a rate, tax or due;
(iii) by way of penalty for a breach of the law or forfeiture in consequence of a breach of the law;
(iv) by way of taking a sample for the purposes of any law;
(v) as an incident of any deposit required to be made with the government of a reasonable number of copies of every book, magazine, newspaper or other printed work published in Papua New Guinea;
(vi) by way of requiring persons carrying on business in Papua New Guinea to deposit money with government or an agency of government for the purpose of controlling credit or investment in Papua New Guinea, or otherwise for the protection of people generally;
(vii) for the purpose of marketing property of that description in the common interests of the various persons otherwise entitled to dispose of that property;
(viii) for so long only as may be necessary for the purpose of an examination, investigation, trial or enquiry, or, in the case of land, the carrying out on the land —
(aa) of work of soil or forest conservation or the conservation of other natural resources;
(bb) of agricultural or other development or improvement which the owner or occupier of the land has been required and has without reasonable and lawful excuse refused or failed to carry out;
(ix) upon the attempted removal of the property in question out of or into Papua New Guinea in contravention of any law;
(x) where the property consists of an animal, upon its being found trespassing or straying;
(xi) for the purpose of its administration, care or custody on behalf of and for the benefit of the person entitled to the beneficial interest in it;
(xii) in terms of any law relating to abandoned, unoccupied, unutilised or underdeveloped land (other than customarily owned land) as defined in that law;
(xiii) in terms of any law relating to absent or non resident owners or occupiers as defined in such law, of any property other than customarily owned land;
(xiv) as a condition in connection with the granting of permission for the utilization of that or other property in any particular manner;

(xv) by way of the acquisition of the shares, or a class of shares in a body corporate on terms agreed to by the holders of not less than nine-tenths in value of those shares or that class of shares;
(xvi) where the property is any natural resource any rights occuring by virtue of any title or licence for the purpose or searching for, surveying or exploiting any natural resource —
(aa) upon failure to comply with any provision of such law relating to the title or licence or to the exercise of the rights accruing or to the development or exploitation of any natural resource; or [p.31]
(bb) in terms of any law vesting any such property or rights in the government;
(xvii) in terms of any law providing for the conversion of titles to land from freehold to leasehold and the imposition of any restriction on subdivision, assignment or sub-letting;
(xviii) in terms of any law relating to —
(aa) the forfeiture or confiscation of the property of a person who has left Papua New Guinea for the purpose, or apparent purpose, of defeating the ends of justice;
(bb) the imposition of a fine on, and the forfeiture or confiscation of the property of, a person who admits a contravention of any law relating to the imposition or collection of any duty or tax or to the prohibition or control of dealings or transactions in gold, currencies or securities;
(xix) as an incident of a lease, tenancy, mortgage, charge, bill of sale, pledge or contract;
(xx) in the execution of a judgement or order of a court;
(xxi) in circumstances where it is reasonably necessary so to do because the property is in a dangerous state or is potentially dangerous or is (or may be) injurious to the health of human beings, animals or plants; or
(xxii) in consequence of any law with respect to prescription or the limitation of actions; or
(b) for the taking of possession or acquisition of any of the following property:-
(i) property of a deceased person, a person of unsound mind or a minor, for the purpose of administering it for the benefit of the person entitled to the beneficial interest in the property;
(ii) property of a person adjudged bankrupt or insolvent or of a body corporate in liquidation, for the benefit of the creditors of the bankrupt or insolvent or body coroporate and, subject thereto, for the benefit of other persons entitled to the beneficial interest in the property;
(iii) property subject to a trust, for the purpose of vesting the property in persons appointed as trustees under the instrument creating the trust or by a court, or, by order of a court, for the purpose of giving effect to the trust; and
(iv) property held by a body corporate established by law for a public purpose;
(v) property for the purpose of vesting or administering that property.

AS TO THE NATURE OF AND ENTITLEMENT TO JUST COMPENSATION

Comment

The leading case on s.53 is *Minister for Lands v Frame* [1980] PNGLR 433. That case arose out of the compulsory aquisition of a coffee plantation owned by Frame. Frame was a naturalised citizen. Section 68(4) of the Constitution provides that for the first five years after Independence, only automatic citizens shall have the rights conferred by s.53. As the aquisition took place within that period, Frame could not rely upon s.53 and his right to compensation fell to be determined under the ordinary law, the *Lands Aquisition Act* 1974.

Following the compulsory aquisition of Frame's land the Minister determined that the compensation payable to Frame under the Act was K200,000.00. Frame appealed to the National Court (Raine A.C.J.) which upheld his appeal and substituted a determination of K290,000.00. The Minister then appealed to the Supreme Court which however, (Greville Smith and Miles JJ.; Kapi J. dissenting) confirmed the National Court's judgment.

Notwithstanding the manifestly obiter nature of the judgments, each member of the Supreme Court bench made detailed and considered comments upon the nature of s.53 rights and to the relationship between it and the *Lands Aquisition Act*. Extracts of those judgments appear below. Note that the relevant terms of the *Lands Aquisition Act* are set out in the National Court judgment at first instance, *Frame v Minister for Lands, Surveys and Environment* [1979] PNGLR 626 at pp.628-631.

per Greville Smith J.

It is not necessary, in my view, for the purposes of this judgment, to attempt to define the expression 'just compensation ...... on just terms', as it appears in the Constitution, any more than to attempt to define the expression 'just terms' in the now repealed *Human Rights Act*. The two expressions as so used may have the same meaning, or a closely analogous meaning, and the word 'compensation' in the former case may not have the same meaning as the word 'compensation' in the *Lands Acquisition Act*. Qualified by the word 'just', and in the context in which it appears, it may have a different meaning.

The effect of the foregoing can be compendiously put by saying that in my view saving of the suceeding provisions of Pt.III by s.16 from the operation of the provisions of s.14 of the *Human Rights Act* did not by implication or otherwise cut down or qualify the natural meaning of the word 'compensation' in the Act in any way which would assist the appellant's contentions.

It seems to me that the money 'value of the land taken from him', obtained by the procedures and subject to the terms laid down by the Act, might in some cases amount to 'just compensation ...... made on just terms' within the meaning of s. 53(2) of the Constitution and in some cases might not, depending in each case on all the circumstances and relevant considerations. If in a particular case involving an automatic citizen 'just compensation ..... on just terms' did not result, then in that case the operation of the Act would be overridden for the purposes of that case by the provisions of the Constitution. But the relevant provisions of the Act are not rendered invalid, or inapplicable in the first instance, or the meaning of their provisions changed by such a possibility.

Minister for Lands v Frame [1980] PNGLR 443 at p.444; see also Pratt J. at pp.482,483; 489-491 (below), but see also Kapi J. (dissenting) at pp.465-467 (below).

per Kapi J. (dissenting)

As I have pointed out earlier, this Act was adopted under Sch.2.6 of the Constitution. The Constitution adopted the Act in its original meaning, which has not changed. However, the Act is to be construed subject to the Constitution (s.10 of the Constitution). This is a general provision and must not be used to give blanket application of the provisions of the Constitution to any Act. The specific provisions of the Constitution dealing with the same subject matter must be closely examined.

Section 53 of the Constitution deals with compulsory acquisition and compensation. On compensation, s.53(2) provides that:

> ... just compensation must be made on just terms ... giving full weight to the National Goals and Directive Principles and having due regard to the national interest and to the expression of that interest by the Parliament, as well as to the person affected.

It is significant that s.53(7) restricts the application of s.53 to citizens only. The importance of the application of this section is contained in this sub-section. It applies to the recipient of compensation, namely the citizen. It is not a blanket application to all persons like s.14 of the *Human Rights Act*. Section 53(7) of the Constitution goes on to provide that power to compulsorily acquire property of a person who is not a citizen, and the protection of the rights of such persons, shall be provided for by an Act of the Parliament.

It is clear from this that the Government's power of compulsory acquisition, and the provisions of compensation for non citizens, is not to be found in the Constitution but in Acts of Parliament. The Constitution adopted two pre-Independence laws, which also apply to non citizens, being the *Land Act* 1962 and the *Lands Acquisition Act* 1974. In this case we are concerned with the *Lands Acquisition Act*.

While the Government intended to acquire land from expatriates only under the Act before Independence, many of these people have now become naturalized citizens after Independence. So that, after Independence, in acquiring alienated land under this Act, the Government, in some instances, will acquire land from naturalized citizens. The respondent in this case is a naturalized citizen. This is significant because there is clear discrimination between a non citizen and a citizen as far as protection from unjust deprivation of property is concerned.

Whether a person is a citizen or not, any claim for compensation under the Act must begin with the provisions of the Act, for it applies to all persons. The principle of assessing compensation is the same for all persons under the Act. When an amount of compensation is reached under the Act, that is as far as the Act can go. Where the claimant is a citizen, compensation calculated under the Act must be read subject to the provisions of the Constitution (s.10 and s.53 of the Constitution). Under s.53(2) of the Constitution the court can inquire further as to whether the amount of compensation reached under the Act is 'just compensation made on just terms'.

In the case of a claim for compensation by a non citizen, the claim must be calculated only by the scheme provided for calculation of compensation under the Act. This compensation is not subject to s.53(2) of the Constitution.

It can be said that compensation claimed by a citizen under the Act can be measured against the yardstick provided under s.53 of the Constitution, whereas in the case of a non citizen, he does not have such protection.

It could be said from this that compensation claimed by a citizen pursuant to the provisions of the Constitution may be different from compensation claimed by a non citizen pursuant to the Act alone.

It is now necessary to consider the effect of s.68(4) of the Constitution. Mr. Frame, the respondent, is not an automatic citizen but is a naturalized citizen. Section 68(4) of the Constitution must be considered as to whether it deprives Mr. Frame of the protection of the terms of s.53 of the Constitution or not. Counsel for the appellant submits that under s.68(4) of the Constitution, during the first five years after Independence, only automatic citizens may claim the protection provided for by s.53 of the Constitution. He submits that since Mr. Frame is a naturalized citizen and that his claim is made within the first five years after Independence, compensation under the Act is not subject to the provisions of s.53 of the Constitution.

Counsel for the respondent, on the other hand, submits that under s.68(4) of the Constitution, it would be competent for the Parliament to pass a law depriving non-automatic citizens of the right to compensation in respect of the land resumed. He submits that the Parliament has not passed such an Act. He further submits that the acquisition of Mr. Frame's land was made under the *Lands Acquisition Act* and that has only one meaning, and therefore s.68(4) of the Constitution has no relevance.

With respect, I do not think that the submissions made by counsel for the respondent are correct. Section 68(4) of the Constitution does not require that an Act of the Parliament should make special provision for non-automatic citizens whose land is acquired during the first five years after Independence. The sub-section quite clearly says that citizens other than automatic citizens shall not have less rights than those *accorded by law* to non citizens. The right of compensation by naturalised citizens in the first five years after Independence is the same as the rights given to non citizens by the law. As I have pointed out earlier, the rights of non citizens are provided for under the Act.

It is quite clear from these provisions of the Constitution that the protection given under s.53 of the Constitution was intended only for automatic citizens for the first five years after Independence. These provisions are consistent with the intentions of the founding fathers of our Constitution. They recognized that there was an element of control of the economy by foreigners and the impact of multinational corporations on this country before Independence, and their desire was for Papua New Guinean automatic citizens to take control of their own economy after Independence. (Final Report of the Constitutional Planning Committee dated 13th August, 1974. See 'Impact of Multi-national Corporations on Development' pars. 78-86 on pp.2/10 to 2/11; and see 'Protection from Deprivation of Property' pars.85-91 pp. 5/1/14 to 5/1/15.) (See s.24 of the Constitution).

It is necessary to consider the effect of s.55 of the Constitution in view of the fact that the rights that are conferred by virtue of s.68(4) seem to differentiate between classes of citizens under the Constitution; that is, the rights conferred by s.53 can only apply to automatic citizens, and not naturalized citizens, within five years after Independence. Section 55 of the Constitution provides that all citizens have the same rights, privileges, obligations and duties irrespective of race, tribe, etc. The question is whether s.55 of the Constitution overrides the provision of s.68(4). It appears that s.68(4) of the Constitution has an overriding effect over s.55 since s.68(4) reads: 'Notwithstanding anything in a Constitutional law ....' Section 55 therefore is to be read subject to the provisions of s.68(4) of the Constitution.

Having regard to all these considerations, I have come to the conclusion that naturalized citizens, for the first five years after Independence, do not have the protection in terms of s.53 of the Constitution by virtue of s.68(4) of the Constitution.

Minister for Lands v Frame [1980] PNGLR 433 at pp.465-467; but see Greville Smith J. at p.444 (above) and Pratt J. at pp.482,483; 489-491 (below).

per Pratt J.

To my mind, the appellant has overlooked the essential theme running through s.53 of the Constitution, namely that what the section does is *guarantee* certain rights to a citizen but it does not prohibit other classes of citizens or indeed other persons or corporations within the country from enjoying similar rights if they are granted by either the underlying law or Act of Parliament. What this amounts to is simply this. If an Act is directed at deprivation of property on terms which must be regarded as unjust or may be regarded as unjust by some, then such Act may well and properly do so. The non citizen could not complain because the Constitution did not provide him with any guarantees. However, in the case of a citizen, if the amount of compensation were proved to be unjust, then he could call upon the provisions of the Constitution to require the court to declare the Act or Regulation invalid. It has never been a part of the respondent's case that the legislature was prevented in any way, or inhibited in any way, from passing legislation which related to non citizens or naturalized citizens and specified that in such circumstances property may be acquired for any figure thought fit and proper by the legislature. If for example the *Lands Acquisition Act* declared that the government may acquire land from a non citizen or a naturalized citizen (within five years of Independence) for such amount as the Governor-General in Council may determine, then the respondent concedes that he would have no ground for complaint before the courts ....

Going then to the Debates, I think that the following passages are of assistance to the court in ascertaining what mischief was sought to be removed and what meaning should be given to the word 'compensation'. First, I refer to vol. 3, p.4347 of Hansard where the then Chief Minister, Mr. Somare says:

> I do not think my Government will expropriate property owned by an individual for this is not right. If we see that there is a national interest in a person's property, we will discuss the matter with him. I can assure all members that people will get fair compensation for their property.

A little earlier in Hansard at p.4289, we find the second reading speech of the Honourable the Minister for Lands. He said, inter alia:

> The second reason for special compensation machinery is that the *Lands Acquisition Bill* is aimed at correcting an imbalance of economic opportunity. This aim is in line with the eight-point plan. In determining the value of property, the Government cannot simply look at what is fair for Papua New Guineans to pay. Otherwise the price of properties will be beyond the reach of many Papua New Guinean groups. A country on the verge of Independence is entitled to prefer the rights and interests of its citizens to those of expatriates which were acquired during the colonial period. It is for this reason that s.14 of the '*Human Rights Act*' has been excluded.

As a clear indication of what mischief it was sought to remedy, the Minister said:

> It is perfectly clear that the Government is concerning itself with plantation land, and that land owned and controlled by expatriates. The Bill provides the Government with the power to acquire plantation land by compulsory process, where agreement with the owner cannot be reached.

If 'compensation' does not mean payment on just terms, then what does it mean? As I said earlier, no person prior to Independence was treated any differently from any other under the *Lands Acquisition Act*. All persons were deprived on 'just terms'. All persons were subject to payment in accordance with a definition of the word 'compensation' as it may then have been interpreted, if the call were made. Certainly the Act was for the benefit of non-overseas persons, but it did not specifically state that such benefit was to be at a financial sacrifice by any other group of persons.

Of course no amendment was made to the *Lands Acquisition Act* after the enactment of the Constitution and Organic laws following Independence on 16th September, 1975. What the Constitution has introduced however, is a guaranteed right of freedom from unjust deprivation of property to all citizens, but has refrained from guaranteeing such rights to non citizens and to naturalized citizens within five years of Independence (s.53). Once it is appreciated that the *Lands Acquisition Act* applies to all people, whether they be citizen or non citizen, then it is clear the term 'compensation' and indeed the amount of such compensation impliedly payable under the Act must be such as to comply with the requirements of the Constitution, irrespective of who is the recipient. There is no distinction made in the Act, there is no attempt at classification or division into various groups, depending on whether they be citizen or non citizen. The Act applies to all, and consequently whatever definition I arrive at for the term 'compensation', it must be a definition that applies to citizen and non citizen alike.

This approach, I think, gives the key to the solution of the problem faced by a court in endeavouring to re-define what was previously a well settled and clear interpretation of the term 'compensation', for in s.53 of the Constitution there is already an existing definition. Such compensation must by sub-s.2 be 'just compensation' made on 'just terms' but subject to certain important restrictions which clearly indicate that one can no longer interpret 'just terms' merely as just from the point of view of the person dispossessed. At arriving at a figure which the courts would regard as 'just compensation', the following guidelines are imposed:

1. Full weight must be given to the National Goals and Directive Principles.

2. Due regard must be given to the national interest.
3. Due regard must be given to the expression of the national interest by Parliament.
4. Due regard must be had to the person affected:
5. Terms shall not be deemed to be unjust merely because there is a 'fair provision for deferred payment, payment by instalments or compensation otherwise than in cash' (sub-s.3).

As regards point 1, the relevant part of the National Goals and Directive Principles, which would appear relevant for consideration by a court, are Goal Number 2(1) emphasizing equal opportunity; 2(3) an equitable distribution of incomes; and 2(6) the maximization of the number of citizens participating in every aspect of development. I also note that Goal 3(4) directed to national sovereignty and self-reliance is cast in terms that 'citizens and governmental bodies to have control of the bulk of economic enterprise and production'. Paragraph 7 of that third Goal states that economic development shall be 'by the use of skills and resources available in the country, either from citizens or the State and not in dependence on imported skills and resources'. In none of these goals does it state that such goals will be achieved by means of expropriation or force.

What may be regarded as 'the national interest and to the expression of that interest by the Parliament', may well be a little more difficult to define, but certainly within those phrases, bearing in mind the terms used in the National Goals, it is in the national interest that all citizens participate in the economic development of the country, despite the inescapable fact that the per capita income of citizens in this country is not great. However, I do not take a direction to observe the national interest requires an investigation by the court into the financial resources of any particular group in order to arrive at a just recompense. The court is called upon to administer a National Act with a view to the overall interest of the Nation, and it is the state of the Nation's resources and its commitments rather than one group of people in a small segment of the country which is the relevant area for examination. It is the country's ability to purchase that is in question, not an individual's, or a collection of individuals making up a clan or landholding group. It would also appear to be of equal importance to the national interest that in those areas where land shortage would be relieved by government acquisition of property which transferred to a number of citizens an area of land used and occupied by one non citizen, be he individual or company, then an alleviation of land shortage should be achieved. It is not my intention to engage the court in political or social debate. I merely observe these facts becaue it is obvious that where a land shortage exists, unhappiness and dissatisfaction must exist side by side, and such a state is not conducive to the national interest.

If the government of the day decided that it was in the national interest to expropriate certain properties of non citizens, there is undoubtedly a legal basis for such a result to be achieved. Not only however, is there nothing in the *Lands Acquisition Act* which distinguishes between a citizen and non citizen, but there is nothing in the Act which suggests that a power to expropriate is being sought although the factor chosen by the Governor-General in Council could theoretically lead to a result which was well nigh expropriation if the arguments of the appellant's counsel were accepted by the court.

During the Parliamentary Debate, reference was made to such terms as 'fair to both parties' or 'reasonable to both parties'. Indeed, the term 'reasonable' was one upon which Mr Morling spent some time during his submissions and it seems to me that that term is both adequate and apt for employment in an attempt to arrive at a new definition for the word 'compensation' .... In short, I consider the term 'compensation' to mean just compensation, in point of view both of the country as a whole and the person deprived of his property. Under the common law definition of compensation, the emphasis is laid on just terms for the individual deprived. It seems to me that in Papua New Guinea one must balance what is just for the landholder with what is just for the acquiring authority. Putting it another way, the compensation must be reasonable from the point of view of both parties when a balance is struck between their competing interests.

In establishing what are just terms for the giver and the receiver, the courts will obviously have to examine the evidence put forward on behalf of the acquiring authority in the light of the National Goals and Directive Principles and the national interest. Where of course a non citizen or a corporation is involved, then such regard will not be necessary where the legislation makes it clear that 'compensation' is not to be paid. In such circumstances, it would be advisable to avoid the use of the term 'compensation', and instead nominate some neutral term such as 'payment' or 'settlement'. It must be made quite clear in the legislation that such payment is being made in respect of acquisition from persons other than citizens, in order to avoid any breach of s.53 of the Constitution.

Minister for Lands v Frame [1980] PNGLR 433 at pp.482,483; 489-491; see also Greville Smith J. at p.444 (above), but see Kapi J. (dissenting) at pp.465-467 (above).

Referred to

by Prentice Dep. C.J. in *Reference No 1 of 1977* [1977] PNGLR 362 at p.377;

by Narakobi A.J. in *Tabo Sipo v Meli* (1980 Unreported) N240 at p.5.

THE ASSERTION OF A RIGHT TO POSSESSION IS NOT A 'COMPULSORY TAKING OF POSSESSION' UNDER SECTION 53

per Miles. J.

Before proceeding to consider the terms of the order it is necessary to consider a further and important matter raised in the submission of Ms. Doherty. The submission is that any order which has the effect of depriving the occupants of their right to possession amounts to a compulsory taking of property under s.53 of the Constitution, and the protective requirements of that section have not been met. The second half of the submission would seem to be quite correct, since according to the terms of s.53(2) possession may not be compulsorily taken of any property except in accordance with an Organic Law or Act of Parliament and unless certain other conditions are fulfilled. The applicant company in the present proceedings does not rely upon an Organic Law or Act of Parliament, nor do the conditions set out in s.53(1) appear to have been met. By s.53(4) a reference to the taking of possession of property is defined to include a reference to —

(a) the forfeiture;
(b) the extinction or determination (otherwise than by way of a reasonable provision for the limitation of actions or a reasonable law in the nature of prescription or adverse possession);

of any right or interest in property.

It has accordingly been submitted that an order having the effect of terminating the right of the occupants to be in possession of the land is a compulsory forefeiture, extinction or determination of a right or interest in property held by citizens and is prohibited by s.53. If the latter submission is correct it lies within the province of the National Court pursuant to the Constitution, s.57, to protect the freedom against unjust deprivation of property guaranteed by the Constitution, s.53.

There are a number of decisions in the National Court to the effect that it is not possible for this Court to exercise its jurisdiction under s.57(1) and (3) to make an order which is necessary for the protection of a constitutional right or freedom unless this Court both interprets and applies the relevant constitutional provision: e.g. *The State v Kwambol Embogol* (1977 Unreported) N91, *The State v Peter Painke (No. 2)* [1977] PNGLR 141 and *Re s.42 of the Constitution and Jacob Hendrich Prai* [1979] PNGLR 42. Conversely it seems to me that the jurisdiction may be exercised even though in the event the National Court may decide to refuse to make an order under s.57, for whatever reason. To put it another way, the jurisdiction encompasses not only a positive finding that the constitutional right or freedom is violated as a necessary step towards its enforcement and protection — it also extends to a negative finding that there is in the instant case no infringement of any constitutional threat of freedom. For these reasons I conclude that it is not necessary to refer the question now under consideration to the Supreme Court and I decline to take any steps pursuant to the Constitution, s.18(2).

The Constitution, s.53, carries the heading 'Protection from unjust deprivation of property'. The detailed provisions of the section itself vary markedly from the recommendations of the Constitutional Planning Committee. However Ch.5, pars. 85 to 91 of the Committee's Final Report (Pt. 1) make it clear that what the Committee was concerned with was the limitation on the power of government to redistribute wealth by means of the compulsory acquisition of property from citizens. In its final form in the legislation the provision as to acquisition of property was widened to include forfeiture, extinction or determination of any right or interest in property. The key word is 'compulsorily' which I think implies the exercise of some power conferred by statute on the State or an instrumentality of the State. In my view the section is not directed at the decision of a court which adjudicates declares or determines pre-existing rights. The word 'deprivation' in the heading sheds further light on the subject. A person is not deprived of property unless he is stripped of something to which he is entitled. The judgment of a court which determines that a person's claim to be entitled to possession is not recognized at law or is recognized only to a limited extent (for instance until the happening of some supervening event such as a contrary claim by someone with a better right) does not deprive a person of that interest. On the other hand the powers exercisable under legislation such as the *Land Acquisition Act* 1974 (to which the Constitutional Planning Committee referred) do have the effect of stripping a landowner of the land to which he is entitled, and of substituting that right to land with a right to compensation. Thus it is that s.53(2) provides for just compensation to be made by the expropriating authority. It is quite inapposite to consider the applicant company as being in any way an 'authority'. Its action in seeking to enforce its right to possession may not be characterized as an act of expropriation. For these reasons I conclude that s.53 of the Constitution is inapplicable to the present case.

It was submitted by Mr. Baulch for the company that s.53 does not apply to the circumstances of the present case because by virtue of s.53(5) the section does not apply, inter alia, to:

(c) any taking of possession or acquisition that was an incident of the grant or acceptance of, or of any interest in or right over, that property or any other property by the holder or any of his predecessors in title.

I have considerable difficulty in elucidating what is meant by this paragraph and if the matter had to be decided on this issue, I would have little hesitation in referring the question to the Supreme Court. However I have already decided that the Constitution, s.53, does not apply to the present case for the reason that the company's assertion of its right to possession is not a 'compulsory' taking of possession, and I decline to make any decision about the applicability of the Constitution, s.53(5)(c).

Ready Mixed Concrete Pty Ltd v PNG [1981] PNGLR 396 at pp.408-410.

(2) Subject to this section, just compensation must be made on just terms by the expropriating authority, giving full weight to the National Goals and Directive Principles and having due regard to the national interest and to the expression of that interest by the Parliament, as well as to the person affected.

CROSS REFERENCE

Constitution of the United States: Am.V.

GENERALLY

Referred to

by Raine A.C.J. in *Frame v Minister for Lands, Surveys and Environment* [1979] PNGLR 626 at p.628;

by Greville Smith J. in *Minister for Lands v Frame* [1980] PNGLR 433 at p.444 (see extract under s.53(1));

by Pratt J. in *Minister for Lands v Frame* [1980] PNGLR 433 at pp.489-491 (see extract under s.53(1));

by Kapi J. (dissenting) in *Minister for Lands v Frame* [1980] PNGLR 433 at pp.465-467 (see extract under s.53(1));

by Miles J. in *Ready Mixed Concrete Pty Ltd v PNG* [1981] PNGLR 396 at pp.408-410 (see extract under s.53(1)).

(3) For the purposes of Subsection (2), compensation shall not be deemed not to be just and on just terms solely by reason of a fair provision for deferred payment, payment by instalments or compensation otherwise than in cash.

(4) In this section, a reference to the taking of possession of property, or the acquisition of an interest in or right over property, includes a reference to —
   (a) the forfeiture; or
   (b) the extinction or determination (otherwise than by way of a reasonable provision for the limitation of actions or a reasonable law in the nature of prescription or adverse possession),

   of any right or interest in property.

(5) Nothing in the preceding provisions of this section prevents —
   (a) the taking of possession of property, or the acquisition of an interest in or right over property, that is authorized by any other provision of this Constitution; or
   (b) any taking of possession or acquisition —
      (i) in consequence of an offence or attempted offence against, or
      a breach or attempted breach of, or other failure to comply with a law; or
      (ii) in satisfaction of a debt or civil obligation; or
      (iii) subject to Subsection (6), where the property is or may be required as evidence in proceedings or possible proceedings before a court or tribunal,

      in accordance with a law that is reasonably justifiable in a democratic society that has a proper regard for the rights and dignity of mankind; or
   (c) any taking of possession or acquisition that was an incident of the grant or acceptance of, or of any interest in or right over, that property or any other property by the holder or any of his predecessors in title; or
   (d) any taking of possession or acquisition that is in accordance with custom; or
   (e) any taking of possession or acquisition of ownerless or abandoned property (other than customary land); or
   (f) any restriction on the use of or on dealing with property or any interest in or right over any property that is reasonably necessary for the preservation of the environment or of the national cultural inheritance.

GENERALLY

Referred to

by Miles J. in *Ready Mixed Concrete Pty Ltd v PNG* [1981] PNGLR 396 at pp.408-410;

by Kapi J. in *SCR No 2 of 1982; Re Organic Law* [1982] PNGLR 214 at p.237.

(6) Subsection (5)(b)(iii) does not authorize the retention of any property after the end of the period for which its retention is reasonably required for the purpose referred to in that paragraph.

(7) Nothing in the preceding provisions of this section applies to or in relation to the property of any person who is not a citizen and the power to compulsorily take possession of, or to acquire an interest in, or right over, the property of any such person shall be as provided for by an Act of the Parliament.

(*See: Lands Acquisition (Development Purposes) Act* Ch.192)

GENERALLY

Referred to:

by Pratt J. in *Minister for Lands v Frame* [1980] PNGLR 433 at p.481; see annotations under s.53(1).

54. — SPECIAL PROVISION IN RELATION TO CERTAIN LANDS

Nothing in Section 37 (*protection of the law*) or 53 (*protection for unjust deprivation of property*) invalidates a law that is reasonably justifiable in a democratic society that has a proper regard for human rights and that provides —

(a) for the recognition of the claimed title of Papua New Guinea to land where —
   (i) there is a genuine dispute as to whether the land was acquired validly or at all from the customary owners before Independence Day; and
   (ii) If the land were acquired compulsorily the acquisition would comply with Section 53(1) (*protection from unjust deprivation of property*); or

(b) for the settlement by extra-judicial means of disputes as to the ownership of customary land that appear not to be capable of being reasonably settled in practice by judicial means; or

(c) for the prohibition or regulation of the holding of certain interests in, or in relation to, some or all land by non-citizens.

GENERALLY

Referred to:

by Pratt J. in *Minister for Lands v Frame* [1980] PNGLR 433 at p.482.

55. — EQUALITY OF CITIZENS

(1) Subject to this Constitution, all cititzens have the same rights, privileges, obligations and duties irrespective of race, tribe, place of origin, political opinion, colour, creed, religion or sex.

AS TO WHETHER SUBSTANTIAL ELECTION DEPOSITS INDIRECTLY VIOLATE THE CONSTITUTIONAL PROHIBITION AGAINST DISCRIMINATION

per Kearney Dep. C.J.

I turn to the third question referred by the Commission which queries the validity of the requirement of a K1,000 deposit, on the basis that it discriminates between citizens on the basis of wealth, and thereby denies them the *equal right* to stand for election, guaranteed by the Constitution, s.55.

The Commission submits that it is aparent from the statistical material that per capita income — and thus ability to pay the deposit — is linked with 'place of origin', one of the qualities which cannot be used to base any distinction in rights. Whereas the average income in the North Solomons Province is over K2,000 per year, the average income in, for example, the Enga, Southern Highlands, West Sepik, Western and Gulf Provinces is less than K200 per year.

However, I do not think this submission is valid. Candidates stand for election in geographical constituencies *within* Provinces, and I see no scope for a 'place of origin' argument based on differences *between* Provinces.

Another quality which is not permitted to found any difference in rights under the Constitution s.55(2), is 'sex'. The statistical material shows that of eligible citizens employed in the private sector, for example, in 1977, only 4 percent were women. The Commission submits that in so far as the *effect* of the Act is to create an inequality of rights turning on sex, the law infringes the Constitution, s.55(1). I agree that what cannot be done directly, cannot be done indirectly; but I am not satisfied that the court has obtained sufficient relevant information concerning women and their access to cash, and I would accordingly not accede to this submission.

Upon reflection, I do not consider that the application of the Constitution, s.55, has been sufficiently argued before us to reach a safe conclusion on this submission; s.55 is a particularly difficult and subtle area. As the Act in question is unconstitutional for other reasons, it is unnecessary to pursue further the question whether it infringes s.55.
S.C.R. No 2 of 1982: Re Organic Law [1982] PNGLR 214 at p.232; see also Kapi J. at pp.240,241 (below).

per Kapi J.

Section 55 of the Constitution guarantees the equality of all citizens. We are concerned here with the equality of the right to stand for elective public office. However, the equality of all citizens on this right is qualified by the introductory words of s.55(1) '*subject to this Constitution*'. I discussed the meaning of the phrase '*subject to*' in the recent Bouraga Reference, *S.C.R. No. 1 of 1982; Re Bouraga* [1982] PNGLR 178.

This means that where other provisions of the Constitution or laws permitted to be made by other provisions of the Constitution may be considered to be contradictory to the concept of equality of citizens, those provisions of the Constitution or laws permitted to be made by other provisions of the Constitution shall prevail.

On the particular right with which we are concernecd, there is no Constitutional provision which may be said to be inconsistent with s.55. In fact s.50(1) gives every citizen equal right regardless of race, tribe, place of origin, political opinion, colour, creed or sex.

It is obvious that on the right to be elected to elective public office, s.55 takes the right no further than is provided for in s.50(1).

Section 55 of the Constitution is a general provision stating that all citizens have the same rights, privileges, obligations and duties. Whether it is permissible for a law to treat citizens differently regarding their rights, privileges, obligations and duties, is not dealt with by s.55. These are matters which are dealt with by other provisions. Where other provisions of the Constitution deal with inequalities or the exercise of those rights, etc., which in effect provide for inequalities between the citizens then s.55 must give way to those provisions. For example, see Rights and Privileges which may only be enjoyed by *automatic citizens*, s.68(3). See also s.68(4)(5)(6). As to regulation of the exercise of the right to be elected to elective public office, such law is permitted by s.50(2). Whether or not such law is valid is to be determined only by the limitations set by the terms of s.50(2). . . . .

Section 55 does not take the matter further as all these issues are dealt with by s.50(2) of the Constitution.
S.C.R. No 2 of 1982; Re Organic Law [1982] PNGLR 214 at pp. 240,241: see also Kearney Dep. C.J. at p.232 (above).

SECTION 55 AND THE DISCRETION ON SENTENCING TWO OFFENDERS

per Kapi J.

The police in expercising their discretion in the manner they did i.e. in charging Peter Sufo with lesser charges, have brought about an unfair application of the law in the case of the accused. All citizens are equal under s.55 of the Constitution and are entitled to the equal treatment and protection of law. The law should not be used so that people get different treatment by the law on the same facts as in this case. I believe that it is in the spirit of our Constitution that two people in the circumstances of this case should receive equal treatment or protection under the law. This is a factor which I take into consideration in sentence. Any punishment imposed by this court in this case should reflect the punishment that had been imposed on Peter Sufo in the circumstances of this case.
The State v Yomba Gende (1980 Unreported) N247 at p.5.

SECTION 55 AND 'BIG MEN'

per Kidu C.J.

Mr Donigi submitted that in Papua New Guinea 'big men' can speak in any forum. Mr Somare should be allowed to speak in this forum because he is such a man. If this is so, it goes against s.55(1) of the Constitution. ...

Section 55(3) does not apply because there is no operative pre-Independence law on the issue. Schedule 2.2 is not applicable.
S.C.R. No 4 of 1980: Re petition of M.T. Somare [1981] PNGLR 265 at p.271.

GENERALLY

Referred to

by Narakobi A.J. in *Tabo Sipo v Meli* (1980 Unreported) N240 at pp.4, 5, 7.

(2) Subsection (1) does not prevent the making of laws for the special benefit, welfare, protection or advancement of females, children and young persons, members of under-privileged or less advanced groups or residents of less advanced areas.

GENERALLY

Referred to

by Narakobi A.J. in *Tabo Sipo v Meli* (1980 Unreported) N240 at p.4;

by Kearney Dep.C.J. in *S.C.R. No 2 of 1982; Re Organic Law* [1982] PNGLR 214 at p.232;

by Andrew J. (dissenting) in *S.C.R. No 6 of 1981; State v O.I.C. of Wabag Corrective Institution* [1982] PNGLR 308 at pp. 317, 319.

(3) Subsection (1) does not affect the operation of a pre-Independence law.

GENERALLY

Referred to

by Narakobi A.J. in *Tabo Sipo v Meli* (1980 Unreported) N240 at pp. 4, 5;

by Kidu C.J. in *S.C.R. No 4 of 1980; Re petition of M.T. Somare* [1981] PNGLR 265 at p.271.

56. — OTHER RIGHTS AND PRIVILEGES OF CITIZENS

(1) Only citizens may —
  (a) vote in elections for, or hold, elective public offices; or
  (b) acquire freehold land

(See: *Land (Ownership of Freeholds) Act* Ch. 359)

(2) An Act of the Parliament may —
  (a) define the offices that are to be regarded as elective public offices; and
  (b) define the forms of ownership that are to be regarded as freehold; and
  (c) define the corporations that are to be regarded as citizens,
  for the purposes of Subsection (1).

(3) An Act of the Parliament may make further provision for rights and privileges to be reserved for citizens.

GENERALLY

Referred to

by Prentice Dep.C.J. in *Reference No 1 of 1977* [1977] PNGLR 362 at p.376;

by Narakobi A.J. in *Tabo Sipo v Meli* (1980 Unreported) N240 at p.5.

Subdivision D. — Enforcement.

57. — ENFORCEMENT OF GUARANTEED RIGHTS AND FREEDOMS

(1) A right or freedom referred to in this Division shall be protected by, and is enforceable in, the Supreme Court or the National Court or any other court prescribed for the purpose by an Act of the Parliament, either on its own initiative or on application by any person who has an interest in its protection and enforcement, or in the case of a person who is, in the opinion of the court, unable fully and freely to exercise his rights under this section by a person acting on his behalf, whether or not by his authority.

CROSS REFERENCE

Universal Declaration of Human Rights: Article 8; *European Human Rights Convention*: Article 5(5); *Constitution of India*; Section 32.

C.P.C Report Ch.5 Part 1 p.18

C. *GENERAL*

Enforcement of rights and freedoms

115. We have carefully weighed the arguments for and against the enforcement by the courts of the humans rights provisions we have recommended. In Part E of Chapter 8 'The Administration of Justice' we spell out what we believe are the main arguments for and against the judicial enforcement of constitutional provisions generally. The principal arguments in respect of this issue are similar.

Those who believe judges should not be involved in the enforcement of human rights generally argue firstly, that in deciding cases involving basic human rights the judges will often be concerned with matters which many people would say ought to be decided by members of the National Parliament rather than by a court. For example, the court may have to decide whether it is 'reasonably justifiable' for a law to be passed requiring all adult men in certain towns to hold a work permit or be prosecuted for vagrancy. Some people have spoken in the past of the 'need' for such a law.

It can be argued, further, that the task of both judges and government ministers in a [p.19] new nation such as Papua New Guinea is very difficult even if there are no enforceable human rights and freedoms set out in the Constitution. This is because ministers in such countries have the responsibilities of trying to bring together many different groups of people, some of whom are suspicious of one another, while at the same time trying to bring about rapid economic and social development. Unpopular decisions of courts can place extra strain on both judges and ministers and sometimes lead to serious friction between them. Giving judges the responsibility to decide cases about whether or not basic human rights included in the Constitution have been overridden may put too much strain on the relationship between ministers and judges, and perhaps lead to the judges becoming less independent of the Executive.

On the other hand it can be persuasively argued that if there is no power of enforcement of basic human rights their inclusion in the Constitution is of little value, as the Government and people and organizations who choose to do so, can ignore them. Under the *Human Rights Ordinance* the Full Court (three Supreme Court judges sitting together) has power to enforce the basic rights and freedoms mentioned earlier, and already that court has made an important decision that a particular right — that of being brought to trial within a reasonable time if one is charged with an offence — had been ignored, and the trial of the person concerned was ordered to take place immediately. The effect of enforceable human rights provisions in a Constitution is not limited to the decisions of courts — such provisions act as a deterrent to governments and parliaments which might otherwise disregard fundamental rights or at least give them insufficient consideration.

Secondly, in a country such as Papua New Guinea, where there are many fairly small groups, it is only by putting these rights and freedoms in the Constitution, and giving the courts power to decide whether or not they have been ignored and power to make orders to enforce them in individual cases, that these small groups can feel secure.

Thirdly, judges and magistrates at times have to make decisions which they know may be unpopular with the government in any event, but this is part of their role as independent members of the judiciary. Though the *Human Rights Ordinance* has been in force for only a relatively short period it has not given rise to any suggestion of conflict between the executive and the judiciary in relation to a decision of a court concerning the *Human Rights Ordinance* during that time.

116. *On balance*, we have concluded that the human rights provisions *should* be enforced by the courts. We have recommended that not only the Supreme Court, but the National Court and District (or Provincial) Courts should be able to decide such cases. Our purpose here is to ensure that the opportunity to raise human rights issues should not be stifled by being confined to the somewhat rarified atmosphere of the highest court in the land — the Supreme Court. People should be able to complain of a breach of a human right and have that complaint judicially decided without undue difficulty.

117. We have recommended the retention of the provisions of the *Ordinance* which allow the Secretary for Law or the Public Solicitor to bring an action in court for the protection or enforcement of a right or freedom set out in this part. However, we have not used the title Secretary for Law in case this should be changed in the future. We have simply referred to the most senior legal adviser to the Government.

Suspension of or derogation from human rights in the interests of defence, public safety, public order, public health or public welfare.

118. We are conscious that the exception provisions to the following effect — 'to the extent that the law makes provision —

(a) that is reasonably justifiable in a democratic society in the interests of defence, public safety, public order, public health or public welfare; or

(b) that is reasonably justifiable in a democratic society for protecting the rights or freedoms of other persons',

are very broad indeed and should be used by a government intent upon passing legislation which would otherwise be invalid, to pass numerous Acts contrary to the spirit of the recommendations contained in this Part simply by relying upon one or other of these exception clauses for its validity.

119. We recommend, in order to limit the use which may be made of these exception clauses, that a law may only be passed under one or other of them if either — [p.20]

(a) the relevant Act provides that it is only to have effect during a State of Emergency; or
(b) the bill for the Act is supported on its final reading by a three-fifths majority of the members of the National Parliament.

Action under valid law invalid if excessive or oppressive

120. We recommend that to provide a safeguard against abuse of or excessive use of a legal power provided for in this Part, any action which is excessive or oppressive in the actual circumstances of the case should be unlawful. Interpreting legislative provisions of this kind is not new to the courts.

Permanent Committee to review laws and policies for compliance with the Human Rights and Obligations and National Goals and Directive Principles set out in the Constitution

121. Although we have given a major role to the judiciary in the enforcement of the recommended human rights provisions of the Constitution we believe it is of considerable importance that we give the legislature a significant role in this regard also. Our proposal is that the Permanent Committee of the House responsible for justice or a sub-committee of that committee be responsible for ensuring that bills, regulations and government policies comply with the National Goals and Directive Principles set out in Chapter 2 and with the human rights and obligations provisions in this Part. The Committee should be able to make recommendations or move amendments for the alteration of bills and the disallowance of regulations where these are in conflict with either any provision of this Part or any of the National Goals and Directive Principles.

Transitional Provisions

122. We recommend that all current legislation and government policies should be carefully considered by either the proposed Law Reform Commission or a special committee comprising Papua New Guinean public servants, and perhaps politicians also, with appropriate skilled staff, and if needed, outside consultants. The Commission or committee should make recommendations from time to time, and make a final report within two years of its establishment, in regard to the repeal or amendment of legislation which is contrary to the proposed National Goals and Directive Principles. We also propose that this body recommend changes in policies of the Government, (and institutions of government) in order to achieve conformity with the Goals and Principles. This task is a vital one, as it is important that any pre-existing legislation or policies which are in conflict with these new constitutional provisions should be altered as soon as possible, in order that our people may immediately benefit from the standards set in the new Constitution.

Immediate implementation of Human Rights Provisions

123. We see no good reason why the human rights provisions should not come into force as soon as the Constitution becomes effective in the same manner as will almost all other provisions, although we realise that his will probably mean that some existing legislation will thereby be made invalid. However we consider that the fact that the *Human Rights Ordinance* has already been in force for almost three years, and most of the provisions we recommend follow closely those in that *Ordinance*, is of importance in this regard. The additional rights and freedoms which we propose would be included in the Constitution may possibly override parts of certain ordinances and regulations, but the most important of these could, we believe, be identified quickly. The proposed new advisory jurisdiction of the Supreme Court could be availded of in some instances where there is doubt as to the validity of a particular provision.

RECOMMENDATIONS [p.34]

Amendments to legislation and changes to policy concerning Human Rights and Obligations, National Goals and Directive Principles

23. The proposed Law Reform Commission (referred to in Chapter 8, 'The Administration of Justice') or a special committee comprising Papua New Guinean public servants, and perhaps politicians also, with appropriate skilled staff and, if needed, outside consultants, should give careful consideration to all current legislation and government policies with a view to making recommendations, over a period of approximately two years, for the repeal and amendment of legislation which is contrary to the National Goals and Directive Principles, or to the proposed constitutional provisions concerning Human Rights and Obligations. This body should also recommend changes in policies of the government, including the institutions of government, in order to achieve conformity with the National Goals and Directive Principles.

GENERALLY ON ENFORCEMENT OF THE RIGHTS AND FREEDOMS

per Frost C.J.

Provision for the enforcement of the rights and freedoms conferred in Div. 3 is set out in Subdivision D — Enforcement, which contains ss.57 and 58. Such a right or freedom is to be protected by and is enforceable in the Supreme Court and the National Court, and that protection is to be afforded either on the initiative of the Court, or on application by any person who has an interest in its protection and enforcement, or if unable to exercise his rights, by a person acting on his behalf (s.57). For the purposes of the section the Law Officers of Papua New Guinea and other defined persons have an interest in the protection and enforcement of the rights, but the subsection does not limit the persons or classes of persons who have such an interest (subs.(2)). Plainly a person who claims that his right is infringed is a person who has an interest in its protection and enforcement. If there were any doubt about this, it is dispelled by the Report of the Constitutional Planning Committee, which may be used, so far as it is relevant as an aid to interpretation of the Constitution (s.24(1)). Reference to that Report shows that the Committee based its recommendations on the pre-Independence *Human Rights Act* 1971, including the provision for enforcement of the fundamental rights and freedoms specified in the Act. In the Report it is expressly stated that the effect of the Act was to enable the Court to act on the complaint of a person who claims his rights or freedoms have been denied — Report 5/1/4, par.22, and that must be taken as the meaning to be given the recommendation for enforcement, which was basically adopted in the Constitution, s.57(1), (2) and (3). (Report 5/1/33).

A Court that has jurisdiction under s.57 is given the plenary power to make all such orders and declarations as are necessary and appropriate for the purposes of the section (subs. (3)), and further ancillary powers are added in subsections (4) and (5). That power must include the making of an order or declaration that a statement made by an accused person following non-compliance with s.42(2) be excluded from evidence, which is the most effective form of relief for any accused person. The jurisdiction and powers of the Courts under s.57, it is expressly provided, are in addition to, and not in derogation of, their jurisdiction and powers under any other provision of the Constitution (subs. (6)), which include of course the jurisdiction to award compensation under s.58. As that section is also expressed to be in addition to and not in derogation of s.57, (s.58(1)), the result presumably is that each section is to be given an independent operation. Whilst the requirement that the right or freedom shall be protected by the Court in s.57(1) would by its mandatory terms seem to be paramount, under s.58 there is an additional and independent entitlement, conferred upon a person whose rights or freedoms declared or protected by Div. 3 are infringed, to reasonable damages, and if the Court thinks proper exemplary damages (s.58(2)).

However, in the case of non-compliance with the Constitution, s.42(2), it may be thought inadequate for a Court to admit the accused's statement, and simply allow action to be taken under any other provision. In the ordinary case of a breach of s.42(2), particularly of sub-paragraphs (b) and (c), the Court may well feel bound to adopt the analogy of relief by way of *restitutio in integrum*, or restoration of the accused to the position as if s.42(2) had been complied with, taking into account the real possibility that the accused would have exercised his right to silence, and thus to exclude the admission under s.57. There is no reason why such an order should not be made in the course of a criminal proceeding before the National Court.

It is to be noted that the general omission, in the statement of the various rights and freedoms, of any definition of the persons under a correlative duty, is remedied under Subdivision D, for it is expressly provided that relief may be granted in cases of infringement under s.57, and damages may be awarded against any person who committed, or was responsible for, the infringement under s.58(3).

Reference No 1 of 1977 [1977] PNGLR 362 at pp.366–368.

ONUS OF PROOF AND PROOF OF MATTERS OF COMMON KNOWLEDGE IN CONSTITUTIONAL CASES

per Kearney Dep. C.J.

Mr. Donigi's submission on s.50(1) is that a K1000 nomination fee will deny in practice many eligible citizens their constitutional 'reasonable opportunity' to stand for election, because they lack the financial means to pay such a sum. Implicit in his argument is that the Court should set a standard for what is reasonable, followed by the assertion that a K1000 fee does not meet that standard.

To establish that contention Mr. Donigi tendered in evidence a large amount of statistical material and the Court heard testimony from the Director of the National Census, and from an officer from the Department of Labour and Industry, explaining calculations derived from this statistical material. Mr. Maino objected to the admission of all these materials; I deal first with that objection.

The question of the proof of facts, of information, which the Court requires to determine the constitutional validity of legislation, is one of considerable importance. In a constitutional case the Court must be satisfied of every fact the existence of which is necessary in law to provide a constitutional basis for the legislation. That is inherent in its duty of judicial review. These facts may be background facts, in the sense of information required by the Court to judge the validity of the Acts — see *Breen v Sneddon* (1961) 106 CLR 406 at p.411 per Dixon C.J. They could often be proved only with difficulty. What kind of evidence of such facts may be allowed? These are reference proceedings and so facts the proof of which might otherwise have already been established by judicial findings upon evidence adduced in the course of litigation between parties, before it reached this Court, are lacking. Even in cases between parties, there may be issues of general fact, not peculiar to those parties, relevant to the effect of an Act such as this, and thus to its constitutionality; see *Breen v Sneddon* (supra).

Historically, constitutional courts in some other countries do not appear to have coped particularly well with the problem of ascertaining such constitutional facts.

In Australia the High Court appears to require that such facts be ascertained solely upon materials within jucicial notice or proved by the parties according to the ordinary rules of evidence. See, for example, the refreshing of memory engaged in by the Court in *Ffrost v Stevenson* (1937) 58 CLR 528 at pp.549, 578 et seq.; and cf. *Uebergang v Wheat Board* (1980) 32 ALR 1. And see Mr. Brazil's article *The ascertainment of facts in Australian constitutional cases*, (1970-71) 4 F.L. Rev. 65, especially at pp.77,78. This approach was also adopted by the Privy Council; see *A-G for Alberta v A-G for Canada* [1939] AC 117 at p.130. See also Professor Lane's article *Facts in Constitutional Law*, (1963) 37 A.L.J. 108.

In the United States a broader approach is adpoted to matters treated as being within the scope of judicial notice. See the case review at (1937) 82 L.Ed. 1244, especially at p.1260. In other matters the parties may be required to introduce evidence. Other facts, outside the range of judicial notice may be the subject of judicial inquiry.

I consider that the statistical material tendered here is admissible, as dealing with matters of which judicial notice should be taken, for much the same reasons that prompted the United States Supreme Court to receive the materials in the 'Brandeis brief', in *Muller v Oregon* (1908) 208 US 412. In that case, to establish that long hours of work were dangerous for women because of their physical characteristics and that they merited special treatment (and thus a State law enacted under the police power limiting the working day of women should not be struck down by the Fourteenth Amendment) Mr. Louis Brandeis submitted a voluminous brief involving over ninety reports of committees, bureaus of statistics and so on, and economic reports on the general benefits of short hours. The Court accepted this material on the basis that it took 'judicial congizance of matters of general knowledge'; see p.431. So, I think, should this Court in constitutional cases.

There is another reason why a broader approach in constitutional cases to matters of which judicial notice should be taken, should be adopted than e.g. in Australia. The Constitution entrusts to this Court in many instances the decision whether a certain Act is 'reasonable'. In America and Australia, the reasonableness of an Act is for the legislature; once the end to be achieved is seen to be constitutionally legitimate, all means to achieve it which are not prohibited are constitutional. See e.g.*M'Culloch v Maryland*(1819) 4 Wheat 316 at p.321; 4 L.Ed. 579 at p.605 and *Australian Communist Party v The Commonwealth* (1951) 83 CLR 1 at p.149 per Latham C.J. That is not the case in our body politic. What is 'reasonable' cannot be separated from questions of policy. In such a case the best this Court can do is to apply an objective test: 'Would a reasonable man necessarily consider the Act unreasonable?' The personal views of the judges cannot be allowed to obtrude.

I should add that I think it very preferable that materials on which the Court is asked to rely as going to matters of general knowledge, be presented in open court in the manner adopted in this case, rather than it being left perhaps to the individual judge's private researches. See the article by Professor Nokes *The Limits of Judicial Notice* (1958) 74 LQR 59 from p.68. It is particularly appropriate to the system of the written brief increasingly and beneficially adopted in constitutional argument before this Court.

The guiding approach to the reception of such materials should, I think, be along the lines expressed by Dixon C.J. in *Commonwealth Freighters Pty Ltd v Sneddon* (1959) 102 CLR 280 at p.292:

> .... if a criterion of constitutional validity consists in matter of fact, *the fact must be ascertained by the court as best it can* when the court is called upon to pronounce validity.
> (emphasis mine)

If evidence is relevant to that task it should be admitted, and ways in which this is done should not be strictly limited. As Frankfurter J., dissenting, said in *Zorach v Clauson* (1952) 343 US 306 at p.322:

> When constitutional issues turn on facts, it is a strange procedure indeed not to permit the facts to be established.

I might briefly deal here with the question of the onus of proof. In general, the constitutional validity of an Act is assumed. It is questionable, I think, whether that assumption should be made, when the Act under constitutional attack depends, as here, for its validity upon some regulation or limitation of a Constitutional right. Be that as it may, in reference proceedings it seems to me that the nature of those proceedings is such that the referring authority must in general bear the onus of proving the unconstitutionality it queries, for there is not necessarily any adverse party. It is open whether the nature of the regulating law in s.50(2) is such that the onus of proof is as laid down in s.38(3), when the issue is whether s.50(2) is met.

I turn to the evidence, or rather to the conclusions which I consider are thereby established. The cogency of the statistical material is very high; there is, in fact, no possibility of its being disputed, it is beyond controversy. The statistics are comprehensive and suitable to the purpose at hand. That may be taken to be the minimum requirement for their admission cf. *Boardman v Duddington* (1959) 104 CLR 456 at pp.458,459, 471 and 474.

S.C.R. No 2 of 1982: Re Organic Law [1982] PNGLR 214 at pp.225-228.

WHETHER SECTION 22 OR SECTION 23 HAVE ANY APPLICATION IN RESPECT OF THE ENFORCEMENT OF THE RIGHTS AND FREEDOMS

per Frost C.J. (Kearney J. agreeing)

From this analysis of the Constitutional provision and having regard to the provisions for enforcement to be found in subdivision D–Enforcement, in my opinion an issue emerges as to whether s.23 has any application in respect of the enforcement of the rights and freedoms, including s.42(2). See Pearce, *Statutory Interpretation*, p.36. But as the issue was not argued, and, in my opinion the reference can be answered without deciding it, that issue should be left for later decision.

Reference No 1 of 1977 [1977] PNGLR 362 at p.368: see also Prentice Dep.C.J. at pp.378,379 (below), Williams J. at pp.381,382 (below) and Pritchard J. at p.384 (below).

per Prentice Dep.C.J.

It is conceivable that an argument could be erected to the effect that ss.57 and 58 make provision of 'enforcement otherwise', as envisaged by s.23; and that s.23 is not therefore applicable to the protection of rights. Another view (in relation to which s.57(6) is relevant) would have it that both s.23 and ss.57, 58 are so available. The latter view would see ss.57, 58 as providing for the protection of rights directly; and s.23 as providing for such protection indirectly by the enforcement (by sanctions) of co-relative duties to provide such rights — making two sides of the one coin. In this reference, as I mentioned above, all counsel seemed to assume the latter view. The question therefore of whether the method of enforcement of rights ought to be regarded as provided for exclusively by ss.22, 57 and 58; or whether s.23 should also be taken to be available to protect them indirectly through enforcement of duties impliedly laid on citizens and authorities by the provision for and definition of rights, was not argued — and may be left for the future.

Reference No 1 of 1977 [1977] PNGLR 362 at pp.378,379: see also Frost C.J. at p.368 (above), Williams J. at pp.381,382 (below) and Pritchard J. at p.384 (below).

per Williams J.

The Chief Justice in his judgment appears to entertain some doubt as to whether the provisions of s.23 are available following a breach of duty impliedly imposed by s.42(2). This was not raised in argument on the hearing of the reference; indeed the arguments assumed that the sanctions imposed by the section would be available. In the absence of any argument to the contrary I am disposed to assume that the section does have application. In any event, I think that the question raised in the reference may be disposed of having regard to the provisions of s.57 alone.

Sections 23 and 57 appear, at least to some extent, to overlap. But it emerges plainly from them that both the Supreme and National Courts are given wide discretionary powers to deal with a situation in which a right guaranteed under the provisions of Div. 3 of Pt. III of the Constitution has been denied. Amongst other things, compensation may be ordered to be paid to a person adversely affected, a traditional way in Papua New Guinea of redressing wrongs.

It is said in the argument advanced in favour of the affirmative case that the provisions of s.22 are relevant to this case in that the sanctions imposed by s.42(2) would be left without effect unless this Court were to answer the question raised in the affirmative. In effect the Court is asked to fill a gap which, it is said, exists.

However, I can see no room for the application of s.22 of the Constitution. I do not think that it can be said that the rights conferred and the duties impliedly imposed by s.42(2) are left without effect, within the meaning of that term in s.22, for the simple reason that sanctions and remedies are provided for in s.23 and s.57. Whether or not these go as far as those propounding the affirmative case would like, seems to me to be beside the point. Section 22 appears to me to be concerned with a case in which the right conferred or the duty imposed may be completely hollow without some means to back it up. The kind of case presently under consideration does not fall within that category.

Reference No 1 of 1977 [1977] PNGLR 362 at pp.381,382; see also Frost C.J. at p.368 (above), Prentice Dep.C.J. at pp.378-379 (above) and Pritchard J. at p.384 (below).

per Pritchard J.

However, as has been pointed out, an issue may well arise as to whether s.23 applies at all to an infringement of the Basic Rights provisions of the Constitution, although at the hearing of this Reference, all concerned appeared to assume that it did. The problem therefore must be left for later decision. My researches at least prompt me to make two observations. Firstly, there is not only the individual's entitlement to his Constitutional freedoms to protect, there is a matter of public interest equally involved. Secondly, s.23, whatever its scope, contains such heavy maximum penalties that I believe the precise extent of its application should be a matter for legislative action rather than for a judge of this Court to attempt its definition.

Reference No 1 of 1977 [1977] PNGLR 362 at p.384; see also Frost C.J. at p.368 (above), Prentice Dep.C.J. at pp.378-379 (above) and Williams J. at pp.381,382 (above).

WHETHER ANY QUESTION RELATING TO THE ENFORCEMENT OF RIGHTS SHOULD BE DEALT WITH BY THE SUPREME COURT OR THE NATIONAL COURT

per Frost C.J.

Whilst it is unnecessary to express any opinion on the first ground I should refer to the useful arguments raised by both counsel. If a breach of s.37(3) was proved, counsel for the accused sought an order pursuant to the Constitution, s.57(1) and (3) or s.22, enforcing the accused's Constitutional right. Section 18(1) of the Constitution confers exclusive jurisdiction on the Supreme Court as to any question relating to the interpretation or application of any Constitutional law. But both counsel agreed that as that section is expressed to be subject to the Constitution, and as under ss.57(1) and 22 it was envisaged that such a question fell within the jurisdiction of both the National Court and the Supreme Court, there was no requirement to refer to the Supreme Court any question relating to the application and interpretation of s.37(3). I consider this view to be correct. It does not seem to me possible for the National Court to exercise its jurisdiction under s.57(1) and (3) to make an order which is necessary for the protection of a Constitutional right or freedom

unless that Court both interprets and applies the relevant Constitutional provision. As to the case of *Mauga Logging Company Pty Ltd v South Pacific Oil Palm Development Pty Ltd* [1977] PNGLR 80, it was assumed there that the Court had jurisdiction, and the matter was not argued.
The State v Peter Painke (No 2) [1977] PNGLR 141 at pp.145,146

Comment
It is now clear that s.57 applications are ordinarily to be made in the National Court. This course is particularly appropriate if the matter involves the Court having to determine disputed matters of fact: see particularly Miles J. in *Ready Mixed Concrete v PNG* [1981] PNGLR 396 at p.408; see also *Re s.42. of the Constitution and Jacob Hendrich Prai* [1979] PNGLR 42 and *The State v Kwambol Embogol* (1977 Unreported) N91.

SECTION 57 POWERS ARE UNLIMITED AND PREVAIL AGAINST ANY EXCLUSION CLAUSE

per Prentice C.J.

However the Constitution specifically vests power in the National Court to enforce the Constitution under its ss.22, 57, and 58 (see s.166); and there is no provision for that power to be in any way invaded by an Act of Parliament. So far therefore as the enforcement of any provision of the Constitution or of any right granted by the Constitution *might* become involved, s.61AA [of the *Migration Act*] so far as it purports to bar any 'challenge' to a decision, could not prevail. It could not therefore operate to prevent the existance of rights sought to be declared as in this action, being ventilated and decided.
Premdas v The Independent State of Papua New Guinea [1979] PNGLR 329 at p.337; see also Saldanha J. at p.361 (below) and Andrew J. at p.401 (below).

per Saldanha J.

Under s.57(1) of the Constitution both the National Court and the Supreme Court have not only the right but the duty to protect and enforce the Constitutional rights and freedoms and s.155(4) confers upon both the National and the Supreme Courts powers to make orders in the nature of prerogative writs and such other orders as are necessary to do justice in the circumstances of a particular case. It follows that if there is no challenge on constitutional grounds there can be no appeal either from the decision if the Minister or the Committee of Review. But if there is a complaint that rights under the Constitution have been infringed the person aggrieved is entitled to come to the courts in order to enable them to inquire and ascertain whether he has any such rights and, if it is found that he does have such rights, the courts have a duty to give him relief if there has been an infringement of any of those rights.
Premdas v The Independent State of Papua New Guinea [1979] PNGLR 329 at p.361; see also Prentice C.J. at p.337 (above) and Andrew J. at p.401 (below).

per Andrew J.

The enforcement of the Constitution is vested in the National Court by ss.22, 57 and 58. These powers are unlimited. Section 61AA of the *Migration Act* 1963 excludes the court's jurisdiction in relation to appeals (which are statutory matters) and prerogative writ proceedings (which are review proceedings). This section however cannot limit the National Court's power to enforce any right guaranteed by the Constitution
Premdas v The Independent State of Papua New Guinea [1979] PNGLR 329 at p.401; see also Prentice C.J. at p.337 (above) and Saldanha J. at p.361 (above).

SECTION 57 AND SECTION 37 (15) WHEN OUT OF TIME ON APPEAL

per Kapi J.

The right of appeal given under the constitutional provision also has the benefit of other constitutional provisions as far as enforcement of this right is concerned. Counsel for the applicant submitted that, even though under s.27 of the *Supreme Court Act*, the applicant

is deprived of the right to appeal and the right to extend time, the applicant can enforce this right of appeal under s.57 of the Constitution. In my view s.57 of the Constitution does not assist the applicant. The right of appeal which may be enforced under ss.57 of the Constitution is the right of appeal which is *according to law*.
[*Note*: The only enforceable right of appeal under ss.57 and 37(15) is an appeal in accordance with the statute law. However although the applicant was out of time the Supreme Court decided to allow an application for leave to appeal to be made, using s.155(2)(b) of the Constitution.]
Avia Aihi v The State [1981] PNGLR 81 at p.106: see also annotations under ss.155(2) and 155(4).

GENERALLY

Referred to

by Prentice C.J. in *James Eki Mopio v The Speaker of the National Parliament* [1977] PNGLR 420 at p.422;

by Pritchard J. in *Constitutional Reference No 1 of 1978 (s.19)* [1978] PNGLR 345 at p.371;

by Prentice C.J. in *Premdas v The Independent State of Papua New Guinea* [1979] PNGLR 329 at p.336; see also Wilson J. (dissenting) at p.389;

by Pritchard J. in *The State v John Rumet Kaputin (No 1)* [1979] PNGLR 532 at p.535 (s.57 used to direct an early trial);

by Greville Smith J. in *Gaigo and ors v The Employers Federation* (1979 Unreported) N185 at pp.4, 5;

by Narakobi A.J. in *Reva Mase v The State* (1980 Unreported) N260 at p.3;

by Narakobi A.J. in *Ambi v Rabi and ors* (1980 Unreported) N279 at pp.4, 5;

by Kidu C.J. in *Avia Aihi v The State* [1981] PNGLR 81 at pp.83, 84; see also Kearney Dep.C.J. at p.90, Kapi J. at p.105;

by Kidu C.J. in *S.C.R. No 4 of 1980; Re petition of M.T. Somare* [1981] PNGLR 265 at p.267; see also Kapi J. at p. 297, Miles J. at pp.306, 315;

by Kapi Dep.C.J. in *In re Organic Law on National Elections* [1982] PNGLR 259 at p.290.

(2) For the purposes of this section —
(a) the Law Officers of Papua New Guinea; and
(b) any other persons prescribed for the purpose by an Act of the Parliament; and
(c) any other persons with an interest (whether personal or not) in the maintenance of the principles commonly known as the Rule of Law such that, in the opinion of the court concerned, they ought to be allowed to appear and be heard on the matter in question,

have an interest in the protection and enforcement of the rights and freedoms referred to in this Division, but this subsection does not limit the persons or classes of persons who have such an interest.

GENERALLY

Referred to

by Frost C.J. in *Reference No 1 of 1977* [1977] PNGLR 362 at pp.367, 372;

by Miles J. in *S.C.R. No 1 of 1981; Re Inter-Group Fighting Act 1977* [1981] PNGLR 151 at p.176;

by Greville Smith J. in *Gaigo and ors v Employers Federation* (1979 Unreported) N185 at p.5;

by Kearney Dep.C.J. in *S.C.R. No 4 of 1980; Re petition of M.T. Somare* [1981] PNGLR 265 at p.275; see also Miles J. at p.506.

(3) A court that has jurisdiction under Subsection (1) may make all such orders and declarations as are necessary or appropriate for the purposes of this section, and may make an order or declaration in relation to a statute at any time after it is made (whether or not it is in force).

ORDER FOR CLOSURE OF A JAIL — MAXIMUM SECURITY BLOCK — B DIVISION

Held

In order to ensure that prisoners' constitutional rights were not violated Bredmeyer J. ordered 'B' Division closed forthwith and to remain closed until new Regulations or Standing Orders were issued. All prisoners were to be transferred out of 'B' Division by 4 p.m. on the day of the Order and the facility was to remain closed until new regulations or standing orders describing how an inmate would be treated in, and how an inmate would get out of 'B' Division were made. Also ordered that all warders who had served more than one year in 'B' Division be barred from serving in the new 'B' Division when and if it re-opened, for a period of two years from the commencement of the new rules.
Amaiu v Commissioner of Corrective Institutions and the State (1983 Unreported) N417.

GENERALLY

Referred to

by Frost C.J. in *The State v Peter Painke (No 2)* [1977] PNGLR 141 at p.145;

by Frost C.J. in *Reference No 1 of 1977* [1977] PNGLR 362 at p.371;

by Narakobi A.J. in *Reva Mase v The State* (1980 Unreported) N260 at pp.3–5;

by Narakobi A.J. in *Ambi v Rabi and others* (1980 Unreported) N279 at p.3;

by Kidu C.J. in *Avia Aihi v The State* [1981] PNGLR 81 at p.86;

by Miles J. in *Ready Mixed Concrete v PNG* [1981] PNGLR 396 at p.408;

by Kapi Dep. C.J. in *In Re Organic Law on National Elections* [1982] PNGLR 289 at pp.290, 291 (does not confer power to extend the period of nomination under the *Organic Law on National Elections*).

(4) Any court, tribunal or authority may, on its own initiative or at the request of a person referred to in Subsection (1), adjourn, or otherwise delay a decision in, any proceedings before it in order to allow a question concerning the effect or application of this Division to be determined in accordance with Subsection (1).

GENERALLY

Referred to

by Frost C.J. in *Reference No 1 of 1977* [1977] PNGLR 362 at p.371.

(5) Relief under this section is not limited to cases of actual or imminent infringement of the guaranteed rights and freedoms, but may, if the court thinks it proper to do so, be given in cases in which there is a reasonable probability of infringement, or in which an action that a person reasonably desires to take is inhibited by the likelihood of, or a reasonable fear of, an infringement.

GENERALLY

Referred to

by Frost C.J. in *Reference No 1 of 1977* [1977] PNGLR 362 at p.371.

(6) The jurisdiction and powers of the courts under this section are in addition to, and not in derogation of, their jurisdiction and powers under any other provision of this Constitution.

GENERALLY

Referred to

by Prentice Dep.C.J. in *Reference No 1 of 1977* [1977] PNGLR 362 at p.378;

by Narakobi A.J. in *Ambi v Rabi and ors* (1980 Unreported) N279 at p.5.

58. — COMPENSATION.

(1) This section is in addition to, and not in derogation of, Section 57 (*enforcement of guaranteed rights and freedoms*).

(2) A person whose rights or freedoms declared or protected by this Division are infringed (including any infringement caused by a derogation of the restrictions specified in Part X.5 (*internment*) on the use of emergency powers in relation to internment) is entitled to reasonable damages and, if the court thinks it proper, exemplary damages in respect of the infringement.

C.P.C. Report Ch. 5 Part 1 p.9

42. We further recommend that if a person is unlawfully arrested or held by another, he should be entitled to compensation from that other person. This proposal, we believe, accords closely with the widespread custom which requires compensation to be paid where there has been a wrong done to an individual or group.

THE PLACEMENT OF BRACKETS IN SECTION 58(2)

per Kidu C.J.

> It seems that some copies of the Constitution have the closing bracket after 'internment' first appearing and not the second. The closing bracket should appear after the word 'internment' second appearing . . . The importance of where the closing bracket is placed is that if it is after the word 'internment' first appearing in s.58(2), it could be argued that the provision applies only in cases where infringement of rights occur during the use of emergency powers. I am satisfied, Counsel both agree, that the closing bracket should be after the word 'internment' second occurring in s.58(2). The effect of this view is that all persons have the right to apply for compensation for breach of guaranteed rights any time and not only during the use of emergency powers.
> *Re Heni Pauta and Kenneth Susuve* (*No 2*) (1982 Unreported) N337 at pp.1, 2.

Held

The principles to be applied in calculating compensation under s.58 follow the general law of damages.
Re Heni Pauta and Kenneth Susuve (No 2) (1982 Unreported) N337; see Kidu C.J. at pp.2-6.

Held

A prisoner whose constitutional rights had been infringed whilst detained in 'B' Division at Bomana Corrective Institution is entitled to damages, including exemplary damages. The total damages awarded to Amiau were made up of K100, for having to run 'doubled up'; K2850, for solitary confinment; K1624, for infringment of constitutional rights; K2000, exemplary damages; a total of K6574.00.
Amiau v Commissioner of Corrective Institutions and The State (1983 Unreported) N417; see Bredmeyer J. at pp.52-55.

GENERALLY

Referred to

by Frost C.J. in *Reference No 1 of 1977* [1977] PNGLR 362 at pp.367, 373; see also Prentice Dep.C.J. at pp.376, 378, 380;

by Prentice C.J. in *Premdas v The Independent State of Papua New Guinea* [1979] PNGLR 329 at p.337; see also Saldanha J. at p.360 and Andrew J. at p.401;

by Kidu C.J. in *S.C.R. No 4 of 1980; Re petition of M.T. Somare* [1981] PNGLR 265 at p.267;

by Kapi Dep.C.J. in *In Re Organic Law on National Elections* [1982] PNGLR 289 at p.291;

by Kapi Dep.C.J. in *The State v Kor* (1983 Unreported) N409; see also annotations under s.42(1).

(3) Subject to Subsections (4) and (5), damages may be awarded against any person who committed, or was responsible for, the infringement.

GENERALLY

Referred to

by Frost C.J. in *Reference No 1 of 1977* [1977] PNGLR 362 at p.368.

(4) Where the infringement was committed by a governmental body, damages may be awarded either —
 (a) subject to Subsection (5), against a person referred to in Subsection (3); or
 (b) against the governmental body to which any such person was responsible,

or against both, in which last case the court may apportion the damages between them.

GENERALLY

Referred to

by Narakobi A.J. in *Ambi v Rabi and ors* (1980 Unreported) N279 at p.5.

(5) Damages shall not be awarded against a person who was responsible to a governmental body in respect of the action giving rise to the infringement if —
 (a) the action was an action made unlawful only by Section 41(1) (*proscribed acts*); and
 (b) the action taken was genuinely believed by that person to be required by law,

but the burden of proof of the belief referred to in paragraph (b) is on the party alleging it.

GENERALLY

Referred to

by Narakobi A.J. in *Ambi v Rabi and ors* (1980 Unreported) N279 at p.5.

Division 4 — Principles of Natural Justice

59. — PRINCIPLES OF NATURAL JUSTICE.

(1) Subject to this Constitution and to any statute, the principles of natural justice are the rules of the underlying law known by that name developed for control of judicial and administrative proceedings.

THE CONSTITUTION AND NATURAL JUSTICE

Comment

The principles of natural justice form part of that body of law which applies in Papua New Guinea to control administrative and judicial proceedings. This area of the law is complex and much of it is far from settled. Three important aspects remain to be authoritatively determined. These are:

(a) what is the content of the rules of natural justice applying in Papua New Guinea,
(b) to what proceedings do these rules apply, and

(c) are the principles of natural justice constitutionally entrenched or can they be excluded by the legislature.

Content

Sections 59 and 60 of the Constitution are concerned, inter alia, with the content of the rules of natural justice. Section 59(1) states that the rules of natural justice '... are the rules of the underlying law known by that name ...'. Because custom would not appear to be relevant s.59(1) presumably refers to first, the common law of England adopted under Sch 2.2, and second, to the law as developed by the judiciary under Sch. 2. 3.

However, notwithstanding that s.60 directs the judges to develop an indigenous system of principles appropriate to Papua New Guinea, they have to date refrained from taking that step. Attention has been given almost exclusively to common law authorities.

The difficulty with this approach is that the common law rules concerning the content of natural justice are far from comfortably settled. There has been much confusing debate focused upon whether natural justice requires certain fixed standards to be met (right to be heard, right to an unbiased tribunal etc.) or whether there is no fixed content at all, the issue ultimately turning on what is fair in the particular circumstances. For the leading cases in this debate see *Re H.K. (An Infant)* [1967] 2 QB 617, per Lord Parker at p.630, *Pearlburg v Varty* [1972] 2 All ER 6, per Lord Pearson at p.17, *Maxwell v Department of Trade and Industry* [1971] Ch 338, per Lawton J. at p.398, *Dunlop v Woollahra Municipal Council* [1975] 2 NSWLR 447, per Wooton J. at p.568 and *Dixon v the Commonwealth* (1981) 55 FLR 34. No Papua New Guinean court has yet given extended consideration to these matters. Given the above it is submitted that s.59(2) should be read as a constitutional directive to the courts to ensure that, whatever content rules are finally settled upon as being appropriate to Papua New Guinea, there is at least a minimum content required: the duty to act fairly.

To what proceedings do the rules apply?

The Constitution gives no clear guidance as to which kind of proceedings the principles of natural justice ought apply. In the absence of more specific guidance, s.59 directs attention to the underlying law, that is, relevantly, the common law of England adopted under Sch.2.2 and the law as developed by the judiciary under Sch.2.3. No law has yet been developed under Sch.2.3. Attention has been directed at elucidating the common law.

Until the landmark case of *Ridge v Baldwin* [1964] AC 40 it had been thought that natural justice need only be accorded in judicial and quasi-judicial proceedings or in administrative proceedings in which the administrator was under a duty to act judicially. The distinction between judicial and non-judicial proceedings was for most purposes abandoned after *Ridge v Baldwin*, and following that case the criteria for determining whether or not natural justice was obligatory were stated by Lord Upjohn in *Durayappah v Fernando* [1967] 2 AC 337 at p.349 as follows:

> Outside the well-known classes of cases, no general rule can be laid down as to the application of the general principle in addition to the language of the provision. In their Lordship's opinion there are three matters which must always be borne in mind when considering whether the principle should be applied or not. These three matters are: first, what is the nature of the property, the office held, status enjoyed or services to be performed by the complainant of injustice. Secondly, in what circumstances or upon what occasions is the person claiming to be entitled to exercise the measure of control entitled to intervene. Thirdly, when a right to intervene is proved, what sanctions in fact is the latter entitled to impose upon the other. It is only upon a consideration of all these matters that the question of the application of the principle can properly be determined.

In Papua New Guinea the leading cases have been *Premdas v The Independent State of Papua New Guinea* [1979] PNGLR 329, *Fallscheer v Iambakey Okuk* [1980] PNGLR 101 and *Iambakey Okuk v Fallscheer* [1980] PNGLR 274. In each of these cases there has been little extended discussion of general principles and the majority of judges have preferred to rest their decisions upon narrow and situation-specific grounds. Of the judges who have considered the appropriate tests to apply, all but one have expressly or implicitly adopted the *Ridge v Baldwin* and *Durayappah* tests. The most detailed discussion of the issue was that of Greville Smith J. in *Fallscheer v Iambakey Okuk* at pp.110-123 who expressly adopted the *Durayappah* approach. Others to adopt a similar approach have been Wilson J. (at p.383) in *Premdas v The Independent State of Papua New Guinea* and Miles J. (at p.293, Pratt J. concurring) and Kapi J. (at p.288) in *Iambakey Okuk v Fallscheer*. Andrew J. who in *Premdas v The Independent State of Papua New Guinea* (at p.398) based his decision upon pre-*Ridge v Baldwin* criteria (the judicial/administrative dichotomy) obtained no support from his fellow judges and in *Iambakey Okuk v Fallscheer* appeared to abandon that analysis.

Even if it can be regarded as settled that the *Durayappah* factors have been adopted and apply in Papua New Guinea, no such certainty can be reached upon the question of whether the concept of 'legitimate expectations' applies. In England and Australia the concept of 'legitimate expectations' has accreted to the base of the *Ridge v Baldwin* and *Durayappah* tests. The concept was first articulated by Lord Denning in *Schmidt v Secretary of State for Home Affairs* [1969] 2 Ch. 149 who stated that an administrative body was bound, in proper cases, to give a person affected by its decisions an opportunity to make representations if that person possessed some legitimate expectation, although lacking any present right or interest in a matter.

Stephen J. of the High Court of Australia commented upon this development as follows:

> [T]he basis upon which the possession of a legitimate expectation gives rise to a right to be accorded natural justice ... stems, no doubt, from the same fertile source as has nourished the concept that those who possess rights and interests should not, in the absence of express enactment, be deprived of them by the exercise of an arbitary discretion and without observance of the rules of natural justice. *Salami v Minister for Immigration and Home Affairs (No 2)* 14 ALR 1 at p.14.

In *Premdas v The Independent State of Papua New Guinea* Wilson J. (dissenting at pp.379-388) held that the legitimate expectation principle applied as part of the law of Papua New Guinea but Saldanha J. held that the doctrine had not been sufficiently established as part of the common law of England at the date of reception for it to form any part of the law adopted under Sch.2.2.

Since *Premdas v The Independent State of Papua New Guinea* the question of the applicability of the legitimate expectation doctrine has not been further discussed and the question must be regarded as remaining open. It is submitted, however, whatever the substantive merits of the doctrine, it is unrealistic to read Lord Denning's repeated expositions of the doctrine as mere obiter dicta as submitted by Saldanha J. It is submitted that the better view as to the status of the doctrine is expressed by Wilson J.

Are the principles of natural justice entrenched?

The doctrine of ultimate Parliamentary supremacy is fundamental to the common law of England. Thus in England the courts have always acknowledged that express statutory language will displace the necessity to accord natural justice.

The doctrine of Parliamentary supremacy does not operate in Papua New Guinea. Instead the Constitution is legally supreme. It is thus possible to argue that the right to natural justice is entrenched by the Constitution. This question has again provoked divergent judicial responses.

In *Premdas v The Independent State of Papua New Guinea* Prentice C.J. argued vigorously that s.59 cannot be construed as conferring a constitutionally guaranteed right (at p.342), but Saldanha J. considered it 'possible that the principles of natural justice are part and parcel of the protection of the law guaranteed by s.37 of the Constitution by virtue of s.37(21)(a) ....' (at p.362) and Wilson J. held that the Constitution required observance of the principles of natural justice in, inter alia, all '[j]udicial and administrative proceedings to which the principles of natural justice applied immediately before Independence Day under the common law and equity in England as adopted as part of the underlying law' (at p.376). In *Iambakey Okuk v Fallscheer* Miles J. (with whom Pratt J. agreed) observed that the right to natural justice was 'to some extent recognised and made enforceable' by the Constitution. Although the matter is far from settled the preponderance of judicial opinion appears to support reading s.59 as entrenching the right to natural justice. It is submitted that there are strong textual reasons to support this conclusion. In this regard it is submitted that the placement of ss.59-62 in the same Part of the Constitution as contains the Leadership Code and the Basic Rights suggests that the principles of natural justice were regarded by those who framed the document as fundamental guarantees. To read s.59 as conferring a constitutionally guaranteed right would also, it is submitted, prevent s.62 from having to be read as mere surplusage.

Section 62 provides that acts done in 'deliberate judgment' are non-justiciable. An attractive reading, it is submitted, of ss.59 and 62 together would be to regard s.59 as entrenching the right to natural justice subject only to express exclusion by the Parliament enacting that a particular matter is to be non-justiciable as an act of 'deliberate judgment'. For completeness it should also be noted that in *Public Employees Association of Papua New Guinea v Public Service Commission* (1983 Unreported) SC253 Bredmeyer J. appeared to have regarded s.60 (rather than s.59) as conferring a constitutionally guaranteed right to natural justice; see annotations under s.60.

SECTION 59 AND THE UNDERLYING LAW

per Saldanha J.

It is possible that the principles of natural justice are part and parcel of the protection of the law guaranteed by s.37 of the Constitution by virtue of s.37(21)(a) which says that 'nothing in this section derogates Division 111.4 (*principles of natural justice*).' Section 59 of the Constitution says that 'the principles of natural justice are the rules of the underlying law known by that name developed for control of judicial and administrative proceedings.' I am not sure whether this means that the principles of natural justice are part of our law by virtue of Sch.2.2 of the Constitution whereby English common law (with certain limitations) has been made part of the underlying law in Papua New Guinea, for the reason that while in s.59 of the Constitution the word 'developed' is used in Sch.2.2 the word 'adopted' is used. It is likely that what is meant is that the principles of natural justice are the English rules of natural justice adopted under Sch.2.2 and developed under Sch.2.3 development, etc., of the underlying law and s.60 development of principles (of natural justice). Whatever s.59 may mean I am confident that the principles of natural justice in force in England as at Independence Day are part of our underlying law by virtue of Sch.2.2 of the Constitution.
Premdas v The Independent State of Papua New Guinea [1979] PNGLR 329 at p.362; see also Wilson J. (dissenting) at p.376, but see Prentice C.J. at p.342 (below).

per Prentice C.J.

Section 59 appears only to *define* the principles of natural justice for the purpose of construing the phrase in the application of the Constitution. Though s.59(1) refers to them as the 'rules of underlying law known by that name developed for control of judicial and administrative proceedings', it cannot in my opinion be read as an injunction that they shall as so described *be* applied in administrative proceedings. The only sections of the Constitution which *enjoin* their application appear to be s.28(5) — relating to Leadership Code proceedings, s.37(2) — relating to village court proceedings, and possibly s.37(11) in its requirement that proceedings involving civil rights shall be 'fairly heard'. I have already expressed my conclusion that no such civil right was here in question.
Premdas v The Independent State of Papua New Guinea [1979] PNGLR 329 at p.342; but see Saldanha J. at p.362 (above) and Wilson J. at pp.376-378.

SECTION 59 AND THE MIGRATION ACT

Held

The principles of natural justice do not apply in proceedings under the *Migration Act* 1963 because at common law decisions relating to the deportation of aliens are unexaminable. Accordingly a non-citizen has no right to be heard before a Committee of Review on an appeal against the revocation of an entry permit and an order for deportation.
Premdas v The Independent State of Papua New Guinea [1979] PNGLR 329; Prentice C.J., Raine Dep C.J., Saldanha and Andrew JJ.; Wilson J. dissenting (below).

per Wilson J. (dissenting)

There is no doubt in my mind from the material placed before this Court that the Committee of Review failed to act fairly and, therefore, conducted the proceedings before it in a manner contrary to the principles of natural justice. I so conclude having regard to 'the rules of the underlying law known as the principles of natural justice developed for the control of judicial and administrative proceedings' (see s.59 of the Constitution). I will make further reference later in this judgment to that section of the Constitution. The proceedings before the Committee of Review were conducted in a manner contrary to the principles of natural justice in that they were not held in public, in that Dr. Premdas was excluded from the hearing, in that the Committee of Review which was appointed to review the Minister's notice of revocation, being constituted of three other Ministers, was biased in that it might reasonably be apprehended or suspected by fair-minded persons that the

Committee might not resolve the question before it with a fair and unprejudiced mind (*R. v Watson; Ex parte Armstrong* (1976) 136 CLR 248) ... The decision of the Committee of Review upholding the revocation by the Minister of Dr Premdas' entry permit should be quashed in the exercise of the powers given under s.155(4) of the Constitution and an order should be made restraining the Minister from effecting the deportation of Dr Premdas until further order. If a properly constituted Committee of Review were to review the notice of revocation in accordance with the principles of natural justice and were to uphold the Minister's decision, then such an injunction could (and should) immediately be lifted.
Premdas v The Independent State of Papua New Guinea [1979] PNGLR 329 at pp.375, 389, 390.

Referred to

by Kapi J. in *Iambakey Okuk v Fallscheer* [1980] PNGLR 274 at p.281 (distinguishing the application of those common law rules which are said to exclude natural justice in immigration cases from those that apply in cases involving a dismissal from office.)

SECTION 59 AND DISMISSAL FROM OFFICE

Held

There is nothing in the *National Airline Commission Act* 1973 to exclude, either expressly or impliedly, the principles of natural justice. Such rules are part of the underlying law adopted under Sch.2.2(1) of the Constitution and are to some extent recognized and made enforceable by the Constitution.

In accordance with those principles, expounded in *Ridge v Baldwin* [1963] 2 WLR 935, the general manager of the National Airlines Commission, being a holder of a statutory office, has a right to be given reasons for his dismissal and an opportunity to be heard in his own defence before being removed from office under s.23(2) of the *National Airline Commission Act* 1973.
Iambakey Okuk v Fallscheer [1980] PNGLR 274; see also under Comment: The Constitution and Natural Justice (above).

per Kapi J.

In this case we are concerned with the principles of natural justice. These principles are set out under s.59 of the Constitution ...

These principles are the common law principles of natural justice as adopted under Sch. 2.2 of the Constitution or as developed under Sch.2.3 and s.60 of the Constitution. See the *Premdas Case*. It is only five years since the Constitution came into existence and this Court has yet to develop its own principles of natural justice. In considering these matters, the court has to look to see what the common law of England is on principles of natural justice.
Iambakey Okuk v Fallscheer [1980] PNGLR 274 at pp.279,280; see also Miles J. at p.292 (below).

per Miles J.

The use of language in s.59 and s.60 shows that the makers of the Constitution avoided a definition of what comprises the elements of natural justice. The provisions of Div. 4 provide a minimum requirement of acting fairly or 'in principle' being seen to act fairly. Otherwise the court has a duty to pay particular attention to the development of a system of natural justice and of administrative law 'specifically designed for Papua New Guinea, *taking special account* of the National Goals and Directive Principles and of the Basic Social Obligations and also of typically Papua New Guinean procedures and forms of organisation'.
Iambakey Okuk v Fallscheer [1980] PNGLR 274 at p.292; see also Kapi J. at pp.279,280 (above).

SECTION 59 AND INDUSTRIAL AWARDS

per Pritchard J.

> [The National Court has] a duty to enforce compliance with the award [of an Industrial Tribunal] unless it or part of it is clearly unlawful or is contrary to the principles of natural justice as referred to in s.59 of the Constitution.
> *Re Condon and National Airline Commission of Papua New Guinea* [1978] PNGLR 1 at p.14.

SECTION 59 AND ADMINISTRATIVE AND DISCIPLINARY TRIBUNALS — POLICE APPEALS TRIBUNAL

Held

A Police Appeal Tribunal hearing appeals under the *Police Force (Interim Arrangements) Act* 1973 must observe the principles of natural justice as stated in s.59 of the Constitution, but is not required either by the Act, or under adopted common law principles of natural justice to give reasons for its decisions.
Sausau v Police Commission and The State [1981] PNGLR 327; see Bredmeyer J. at pp.328-331.

SECTION 59 AND BIAS

per Bredmeyer J.

> All the courts in the judicial system of Papua New Guinea have a duty by s.60 of the Constitution to develop a system of natural justice which, by s.59, includes the 'duty to act fairly and in principle, to be seen to act fairly.' One of the principles of natural justice as developed by the courts in this country and elsewhere is that the judge or magistrate must be free of bias. The test is whether in all the circumstances a party or the public might reasonably suspect that the magistrate might not decide the question before him with a fair and unprejudiced mind. I have taken that test from the Australian case of *R. v Watson, Ex parte Armstrong* (1976) 136 CLR 248 at p.262.
> *Tara v Gugu* (1982 Unreported) N374(M) at p.3.

NATURAL JUSTICE AND WHETHER AN APPEAL COURT SHOULD SUBSTITUTE ITS OWN VERDICT OR SEND A MATTER BACK FOR RETRIAL

per Greville Smith J

> The submission that the judgment is so tainted that it should not be permitted to stand means, as I understand it, that the learned trial judge manifested such a disregard for fundamentals or such an absence of sound judgment, that certain consequences should follow, the first being that the underlying assumption upon which appeals ordinarily proceed, namely that the trial judge was on any point right unless shown to have been wrong, could not apply. In pursuance of this it was argued that as the learned trial judge's assessments of credibility, though on the specific record they might appear unimpeachable, could not be accepted by this court, and that as there had been at the trial substantial conflicts of evidence upon important points this court had nothing upon which to form its own view as to the sum that should have been awarded, either for the purpose of testing the learned trial judge's assessment of damages or of making an award of its own in substitution, so that the only proper course open was to order a new trial.
>
> Secondly, it was said that the error of the learned trial judge was such that whether justice had been done or not the appearance of justice having been done as required by s.59 of the Constitution was absent and that once again the situation could not be remedied by this court substituting its own verdict because this would involve reliance on the learned trial judge's findings as to credibility of witnesses.
>
> As to the first suggested consequence I am not satisfied that the error of the learned trial judge is of such a nature as necessarily to import error, or as to import probable error, where such error is not otherwise apparent, in other parts of his Honour's judgement or to

render those other parts unreliable. The onus is on the appellants and in my opinion in this respect that onus has not been discharged.

As to the second suggested consequence, that is a rather different matter and to my mind there is much to be said for clearing the air, so to speak, by a retrial. However, there are countervailing considerations. The respondent is resident outside the jurisdiction and may not be in a position to return for a retrial, or may not be able to afford a retrial, or may not be able again to assemble his witnesses. Or he may simply feel overborn by the prospect of still further litigation and just give up. I should think such a result of an order for retrial by no means unlikely. Over all, and after anxious consideration, I am not satisfied that the ends of justice or the appearance of justice having been done would be served by an order for a retrial.

Government of Papua New Guinea v Barker [1979] PNGLR 53 at pp.63,64.

NATURAL JUSTICE AND ACCESS TO WELFARE REPORTS

Held

Natural justice does not require that welfare reports prepared in an adoption matter be made available to counsel.

In the matter of the Adoption of Children Act 1968 (1980 Unreported) N221; see Narakobi A.J. at p.5.

NATURAL JUSTICE AND CORONER'S INQUESTS

Comment

In *The State v Jacob Toroken (Coroner)* (1981 Unreported) N281, a surgeon sought prohibition against a coroner's inquest in which the coroner had made a damaging finding against the surgeon. The surgeon was not called to give evidence. The finding was contained in a draft of the coroner's reasons which was leaked to the press, but which had not yet been formally handed down. The National Court (Quinlivan A.J.) was not required to decide whether there had been a breach of natural justice (see at pp.15-18), but granted prohibition on the basis that the inquest, by the action of the newspaper, had been aborted.

GENERALLY

Referred to

by Frost C.J. in *The Government of Papua New Guinea and Davis v Barker* [1977] PNGLR 386 at p.392; see also Prentice Dep.C.J. at p.398;

by Prentice Dep.C.J.in *Reference No 1 of 1977* [1977] PNGLR 362 at p.374;

by Wilson J. in *Re Fishermans Island* [1979] PNGLR 202 at p.233;

by Pratt J. in *S.C.R. No 1 of 1981; Re Inter-Group Fighting Act 1977* [1981] PNGLR 151 at p.162 (in relation to right to a fair hearing);

by Bredmeyer J. in *Aundak Kupil v The Independent State of Papua New Guinea* (1983 Unreported) N435 at p.58 (natural justice requires a plaintiff to give a defendent notice of a claim for interest under the *Judicial Proceedings (Interest on Debts and Damages) Act* Ch.52.).

(2) The minimum requirement of natural justice is the duty to act fairly and, in principle, to be seen to act fairly.

SECTION 59(2) AND LAND COURTS

per Kearney Dep. C.J.

A Local Land Court is required to observe the rules of natural justice, when conducting its hearing; that appears, a little indirectly, but very clearly, from s.59(b)(sic). The minimum requirement of those rules is set out in Constitution s.59(2): 'to act fairly and, in principle, to be seen to act fairly'. Failure to allow the disputing parties to put their respective cases in each others presence, is a breach of those rules. So was the failure to give notice of the place and time of hearing.
The State v Giddings [1981] PNGLR 423 at p.428.

SECTION 59(2) AND UNDUE JUDICIAL PARTICIPATION IN A CRIMINAL TRIAL

per Greville Smith J.

Counsel for the defence submitted that the trial had not been conducted, as required by s.59 of the Constitution, upon the principles of natural justice in that the court had not been seen to act fairly, one of the requirements of natural justice prescribed by sub-s.(2) of s.59. He said, and I quote, that 'the trial so far has been one fraught with difficulties which the court no doubt with the best intentions has sought to overcome' but that 'in so seeking the court may have given the impression to a detached observer and also to the accused that the court was not acting fairly'. He referred to the principle that justice must not only be done but must be seen to be done and said, rightly, that this meant not only through the eyes of the public and others but through the eyes of the accused. He said that though he was not submitting that the court was mistaken in any of the courses it had adopted, considered individually, when considered collectively its endeavours to ascertain the facts may well have given the impression that the court was not acting fairly and that the right of the accused to have proceedings conducted in a regular and therefore proper manner had been sacrified. He agreed, upon my query, that the court had observed in the formulation, substance and manner of asking of the questions it had asked the same restrictions as would have been proper to impose upon prosecuting counsel but said that as the effect of them overall was, as it had turned out, that they had brought to light material damaging to the accused they would have been likely to have given the impression that the court was helping the prosecution. He added that it had been evident that without the intervention of the court the prosecution would have been unable to establish a case, and that this must add to the impression that the court was acting in aid of the prosecution and therefore unfairly towards the accused, and tend to lose for the court the respect of the community, and to make the accused feel that he had not had a fair trial.

I rejected the motion for a declaration of mistrial, and my reason were follows. It seemed to me that counsel for the defence in his submissions had paid attention only to the second part of the maxim aforementioned and had overlooked the first, also the provision in s.59(2) of the Constitution which, in effect, requires a court to act fairly as well as to be seen to act fairly. A court is required to perform the sometimes difficult task of achieving both objectives. A criminal trial involves more than the interests of the accused person; it involves also the interests of the community and the justice and fairness called for are justice and fairness as between the accused and the community. This can best be served by the court having before it in the end as far as possible all relevant and admissible evidence. And I did not think that any number of individually unexceptionable attempts by a court to assist towards the realization of this ideal situation could ever properly be regarded as giving the appearance of unfairness to an accused, especially at a point not at the end of the trial but at the end only of the prosecution case and before the defence case, even where, as here, the net result at that point was a strengthening of the prosecution case.
The State v Birch [1978] PNGLR 79 at pp.92,93; (*Note*: the case-law relied on by Greville Smith J. may be found at pp.94-96 of the report).

Comment

In *Birch v The State* [1979] PNGLR 75 the decision of Greville Smith J. in *The State v Birch* [1978] PNGLR 79 (above) was the subject of an appeal.

The Supreme Court held that in criminal proceedings a trial judge has power to intervene (but not unduly) by asking questions and calling or recalling witnesses if he considers in his discretion that that course is necessary to the ascertainment of truth or in the interests of justice. In the circumstances of Papua New Guinea including difficulties of obtaining evidence from very young Papua New Guineans, the assistance of somewhat inexperienced prosecutors and inexpert evidence gatherers, and the absence of juries, it may be necessary for a judge to hold the balance between the interest of the State in enforcing the law and that of the accused in defending himself against a charge, by intervention of a rather more detailed and prolonged nature than would be called for or proper in other more sophisticated settings. The Supreme Court held that 186 questions asked by the trial judge, as compared to the prosecutor's 123 questions did not constitute an intervention that amounted to a miscarriage of justice.

GENERALLY

Referred to

by Frost C.J. in *The Government of Papua New Guinea and Davis v Barker* [1977] PNGLR 386 at p.392;

by Wilson J. in *Re Fishermans Island* [1979] PNGLR 202 at p.233;

by Quinlivan A.J. in *Dai v Manda (No 1)* (1981 Unreported) N342(M) at p.3.

60. — DEVELOPMENT OF PRINCIPLES.

In the development of the rules of the underlying law in accordance with Sch.2 (*Adoption, etc., of certain laws*) particular attention shall be given to the development of a system of principles of natural justice and of administrative law specifically designed for Papua New Guinea, taking special account of the National Goals and Directive Principles and of the Basic Social Obligations, and also of typically Papua New Guinean procedures and forms of organization.

OPERATES AS A CONSTITUTIONAL GUARANTEE

Held

Under s.60 of the Constitution a public servant charged with a disciplinary offence is entitled to the protection of all the principles of natural justice except that one (the right to a disinterested tribunal) which was necessarily excluded by the joint operation of s.159(3) of the Constitution and the *Public Service Act*.
Public Employees Association of Papua New Guinea v Public Services Commission (1983 Unreported) SC253; see Bredmeyer J. at p.12. (see also under *Comment: The Constitution and Natural Justice* under s.59(1)).

GENERALLY

per Miles J.

In any case involving a consideration of the rules of natural justice the court is bound under s.60 of the Constitution to take special account of typically Papua New Guinean procedures and forms of organization into account. We were not told of any such procedures or forms of organisation during the course of argument, nor am I with my imperfect knowledge and experience aware of any that would be relevant to the present case.
Iambakey Okuk v Fallscheer [1980] PNGLR 274 at p.292.

Referred to

by Kearney J. in *The State v The Independent Tribunal; Ex parte Sasakila* [1976] PNGLR 441 at pp.505, 507;

by Prentice Dep.C.J. in *The Government of Papua New Guinea and Davis v Barker* [1977] PNGLR 386 at p.398;

by Saldanha J. in *Premdas v the Independent State of Papua New Guinea* [1979] PNGLR 329 at p.362;

by Bredmeyer J. in *Tara v Gugu* (1982 Unreported) N374(M) at p.3.

61. — BASIC RIGHTS AND FREEDOMS

For the avoidance of doubt, it is hereby declared that nothing in the preceding provisions of this Division derogates any of the rights and freedoms provided for by Division 3 (*basic rights*).

GENERALLY

Referred to

by Miles J. in *Iambakey Okuk v Fallscheer* [1980] PNGLR 274 at p.292.

62. — DECISIONS IN "DELIBERATE JUDGEMENT"

(1) Where a law provides or allows for an act to be done in the "deliberate judgement" of a person, body or authority, the principles of natural justice apply only to the extent that the exercise of judgement must not be biased, arbitrary or capricious.

(2) Except —
(a) to the extent provided for by Subsection (1); and
(b) in accordance with Section 155(5) (*the National Judicial System*); and
(c) as provided by a Constitutional Law or an Act of the Parliament,

an act to which Subsection (1) applies is, to the extent to which it is done in the deliberate judgement of the person concerned non-justiciable.

GENERALLY

Comment

See under *Comment*: *The Constitution and Natural Justice* (above under s.59(1)).

Referred to

by Wilson J. in *Premdas v The Independent State of Papua New Guinea* [1979] PNGLR 329 at p.378; see also Prentice C.J. at pp.338, 342 (the Committee of Review under the *Migration Act* 1963 is not a body referred to in Section 62);

by Miles A.C.J. in *Iambakey Okuk v Fallscheer* [1980] PNGLR 274 at p.292 (a dismissal of the General Manager of the National Airline Commission under s.23(2) of the *National Airline Commission Act* 1973 is not done in the deliberate judgment of the Minister).

Division 5. — Basic Social Obligations

63. — ENFORCEMENT OF THE BASIC SOCIAL OBLIGATIONS

(1) Except to the extent provided in Subsections (3) and (4), the Basic Social Obligations are non-justiciable.

GENERALLY

Referred to

by Frost C.J. in *Reference No 1 of 1977* [1977] PNGLR 362 at p.365;

by Pritchard J. in *Constitutional Reference No 1 of 1978* [1978] PNGLR 345 at p.374.

(2) Nevertheless, it is the duty of all governmental bodies to encourage compliance with them as far as lies within their respective powers.

(3) Where any law, or any power conferred or duty imposed by any law (whether the power or duty be of a legislative, judicial, executive, administrative or other kind), can reasonably be understood, applied, exercised, complied with or enforced, without failing to give effect to the intention of the Parliament or this Constitution, in such a way as to enforce or encourage compliance with the Basic Social Obligations, or at least not to derogate them, it is to be understood, applied, exercised, complied with or enforced in that way.

GENERALLY

Referred to

by Kearney J. in *The State v The Independent Tribunal; Ex parte Sasakila* [1976] PNGLR 491 at p.506.

(4) Subsection (1) does not apply in the exercise of the jurisdiction of the Ombudsman Commission or other body prescribed for the purposes of Division III.2 (*leadership code*), which shall take the Basic Social Obligations fully into account in all cases as appropriate.

PART IV — CITIZENSHIP

Division 1. — Introductory

64. — DUAL CITIZENSHIP

(1) Notwithstanding the succeeding provisions of this Part but subject to Subsection (2), no person who has a real foreign citizenship may be or become a citizen, and the provisions of this Part shall be read subject to that prohibition.

(2) Subsection (1) does not apply to a person who has not yet reached the age of 19 years, provided that, before he reaches that age and in such manner as is prescribed by or under an Act of the Parliament, he renounces his other citizenship and makes the Declaration of Loyalty.

(3) A person who has a real foreign citizenship and fails to comply with Subsection (2) ceases to be a citizen of Papua New Guinea when he reaches the age of 19 years.

(4) For the purposes of this section, a person who —
(a) was, immediately before Independence Day, an Australian citizen or an Australian Protected Person by virtue of —
(i) birth in the former Territory of Papua; or
(ii) birth in the former Territory of New Guinea and registration under Section 11 of the *Australian Citizenship Act* 1948-1975 of Australia; and
(b) was never granted a right (whether revocable or not) to permanent residence in Australia,
has no real foreign citizenship.

(*See*: *Citizenship Act* Ch.12)

C.P.C. Report Ch.4 p.1

1. A citizen of Papua New Guinea should, we believe, be able to say proudly and surely that he or she belongs to Papua New Guinea. And, one of the main aims of this Report — upon which particular stress has been placed in the National Goals and Directive Principles proposed in Chapter 2, the Leadership Code in Chapter 3, and in our recommendation (in Chapter 7, 'The Executive') that the Constitution should explicitly state that power belongs to the people — is to ensure that Papua New Guinea also belongs to its citizens.

2. Papua New Guinea citizens will have certain rights (and obligations) that will be theirs alone. Only Papua New Guinean citizens will have the right to vote at elections, or to stand, for local government bodies, provincial assemblies and the National Parliament. They will have the *right* to be appointed to posts in government and private enterprise for which they are otherwise qualified. They will be eligible for services and other benefits the government may provide — in health, education, and economic development. They will receive protection from the Papua New Guinea Government when they travel abroad on its passports. And, in turn, they will owe their country certain *obligations* — to pay taxes, to uphold its laws, and to serve it in peace and in war.

3. Foreign citizens are likely to be invited for some time to come to lend their skills for limited periods to assist us in our country's development. But their rights should be limited while they are with us in Papua New Guinea, as ours are when we go abroad.

4. The recommendations made in this Chapter are vital to the definition of the identity of the Papua New Guinean nation. They have been prepared after careful consideration of the proposals put forward and questions raised in the many hundreds of oral and written submissions that the Committee has received from people in all parts of the country. They will have a profound effect in shaping not only our own and our children's future, but upon that of our children's descendants. We believe that our primary responsibility is to the future, and in particular to the future of the majority of this country's inhabitants, the indigenous people of Papua New Guinea. Their interests must be safeguarded above all.

5. Our overriding commitment to the indigenous people of Papua New Guinea does not spring from narrow self-interest, nor from any desire to distinguish between people on grounds of race or skin-colour. We have tried to make a frank and realistic assessment of our country's situation, and have held our assessment against the aspirations expressed in the National Goals and Directive Principles in Chapter 2 as well as the Human Rights and Obligations recommanded in Chapter 5 for inclusion in the Constitution.

6. We believe that it would be contrary to the spirit of those goals and principles, rights and obligations if we were to make recommendations that simply legitimated present vested interests. We are also convinced that it would be wrong if we sought to overcome present inequalities and injustices by recommending that there be a distinction between different classes of citizens — for example, indigenous and non-indigenous citizens — as has been done in Malaysia and Fiji. The opportunities for citizens should be equal.

7. Our recommendations have been made on the basis that a real opportunity must now be given to our indigenous people to obtain their full share of the benefits of this country's wealth. Up until now it has been foreigners, most of whom happen to be of different racial groups from us Papua New Guineans, who have taken the overwhelming bulk of these benefits. This redistribution of wealth would be made virtually impossible if we immediately made citizenship of our country freely available to foreign citizens who have lived here for some years during the colonial era.

8. We have recommended that many people who are not wholly descended from the indigenous inhabitants of this country should be treated, from the very beginning of our country's independence, as if they were — provided that they themselves have not cast off their identification with the indigenous people, nor been eligible for benefits available to foreign citizens but not to indigenous Papua New Guineas.

9. The distinctions we make in our recommendations between different groups of people who are partly descended from Papua New Guinea's indigenous inhabitants are based on the degree to which they have, in fact, been identified with the vast majority of the country's population. Even those who have qualified for certain advantages under colonial rule have been granted concessions in our recommendations regarding the time they need to wait until they become eligible for our country's citizenship. However, we emphatically reject the suggestion that [p.2] people who have enjoyed the privileges of foreign status under colonial rule should be able to enjoy the advantages of Papua New Guinean citizenship immediately and as of right. To allow them to do so would run counter to the spirit of our recommendations. It would represent a betrayal of the trust we hold on behalf of Papua New Guineans as a whole.

10. Those citizens of foreign countries who genuinely come to assist in the development of our country's rich natural and human resources will, we believe, be sympathetic towards our proposals. The Australian Government should also accept its responsibilities.

11. Citizens of foreign countries should be able to work here for limited periods and for specified purposes. They should help us to become self-reliant. If their desire to help us is sincerely held, they should not seek, nor should we too easily offer, rights to be exercised indefinitely by their descendants.

12. Our appreciation for the assistance of outsiders should not blind us to our people's longterm interests. These outsiders must not be allowed, either intentionally or unintentionally, to become obstacles to the advancement of our people. We believe the conditions for becoming a citizen of Papua New Guinea should protect the rights of the indigenous majority. These conditions should not serve as a blind for the entrenchment of a small, privileged minority of foreign origin, unduly rich in money and skills, which by its presence and its activities limits the opportunities open to the vast majority of our people.

13. We believe that the conditions set down for becoming a citizen of Papua New Guinea should —

- safeguard the longterm interests of the majority of our country's inhabitants;
- contribute to overcoming the present serious imbalance in the distribution of benefits and opportunities in our society; and
- preserve and enhance our people's sense of identity;
- enable the Government's present localization policy in employment and business activity to be fully implemented.

14. A weak citizenship law will help no one. It will not serve the interests of our indigenous people. It will not serve those of the foreigners among us, nor those of overseas investors. If they are realistic, they will derive no sense of security from a citizenship law that our people feel fails to safeguard their own and their decendants' future.

15. Today, many of our people curse the day when our forefathers sold their land (and ours) for an axe or glass beads. Let us do what we can to ensure that our successors do not curse us for compromising their birthright through a weak citizenship law. Those foreign citizens who really seek to help us or to share our lot will understand why we must be careful in admitting them to citizenship. They will prize our country's citizenship all the more for the value that they see we place upon it. Neither they nor we would welcome the suffering and anguish which would occur if weak proposals were accepted now only to be questioned later.

Single Citizenship

16. People in all parts of the country have expressed strong opposition to the idea of dual citizenship. The task of developing our country requires courage and commitment. Those who would enjoy the benefits of citizenship must share in its responsibilities. We do not believe that it is possible to be fully loyal to two countries at once. We recognize that foreign citizens may be able to contribute much to our country. But they do not need to become citizens to do so. To provide for dual citizenship would contribute nothing to our country. It would only confer additional benefits upon the privileged and mobile. Those who claim the rights of citizenship must be fully committed to staying with us to meet their obligations as citizens.

17. There are, however, certain situations in which the acquisition of a second citizenship is unavoidable. We shall deal with them below.

18. The citizenship laws of a number of other countries — including Australia — also make it difficult to implement the single citizenship principle in Papua New Guinea. Australian citizens, for example, cannot give up their citizenship rights completely. Although they may formally renounce their present citizenship rights in order to take up Papua New Guinean [p.3] citizenship, the way remains open to them to return to live in Australia and to easily regain their Australian citizenship. We have had to bear this fact in mind when making our recommendations as to the qualifications for naturalization.

Conclusion [p.12]

84. Our country stands on the threshhold of independence. The Papua New Guinea citizenship law will form part of the foundations of our country's freedom, independence and identity as a nation state. It is an essential part of those foundations because it states in law who the people are who belong to Papua New Guinea. These people will be the citizens of Papua New Guinea.

85. We believe that the objective of Papua New Guinea's citizenship law must be to restrict the rights and obligations of citizenship to those whose allegiance is to Papua New Guinea and to Papua New Guinea alone. The Constitution and other laws of our country must be designed to serve the needs of the citizens. The government must be their government, be responsive to their demands and act in their interests. When the government allows foreigners to enter Papua New Guinea to work and live here, or to operate business here, it should do so only because it believes this to be in the interests of the citizens, and not because the government feels that it has any obligation to help foreigners.

86. The recommendations made in this Chapter spell out who we believe should be entitled to become Papua New Guinean citizens as of right, and who should be eligible for naturalization. In arriving at these recommedations, we have borne in mind the need to ensure that those who seek to enjoy the privileges of citizenship will also accept its obligations.

87. The Committee has received many hundreds of written submissions on citizenship. In total, they have borne the names of thousands of people. Together with the thousands of verbal submissions made to us at the numerous public meetings we have held, they represent an attempt by our people to determine their own future; and, in particular, to define who should and who should not be able to claim a Papua New Guinea identity.

88. The people of Papua New Guinea have told us clearly and firmly that they do not believe that a person can be fully committed to more than one country. In making this point, they have frequently resorted to imagery; no man, it is said, can stand in more than one canoe.

89. The economic and social circumstances of our country have played a major part in shaping the recommendations contained in this Chapter. As we pointed out in our Second Interim Report, two-thirds of the developed section of our economy is controlled by Australian companies and individuals. Much of the remainder is controlled by other foreigners. Socially, our people have still not achieved full recognition as having equal status with foreigners.

90. The Australian citizenship law (and that of other countries too), has not made our task any easier. But, it has highlighted one of our problems. The knowledge that they can readily resume their Australian citizenship at any time may provide reassurance to people who do not have faith in Papua New Guinea, or who do not prize our country's citizenship as we do. However, to us, this same fact has only served as a reminder — of the difficulty of implementing the principle of single citizenship. We have therefore exercised the utmost care in our attempts to secure the rights of our Papua New Guinean people.

91. The rights of the indigenous people of Papua New Guinea must be paramount. We believe that opportunity must be equalized, by granting certain economic, political and social rights exclusively to those who really belong to this country. In making our recommendations accordingly, we are enabling long standing government policies of localization to continue to be fully effective for a few more years. We are not being racist, as some of our detractors would like to make out.

92. We have deliberated long and carefully the recommendations contained in this Chapter, and have sought to exercise our responsibility to the majority of our people, and their decendants, as best we can. We are concerned to protect, and to further, their interest. We have recommended that the place of birth of the grandparents of a person's grandparent, not his race, ethic origin or lifestyle, should determine who can and who cannot claim Papua New Guinean citizenship as of right. And, we have treated people with one or two foreign ancestors in exactly the same way as people with none — unless they have both in law and in fact, citizenship of another country which makes them eligible for privileges which have not been available to people identified as Papua New Guineans.

93. The Committee has also specifically declared its opposition to the creation of different [p.13] classes of citizenship. In principle all Papua New Guinean citizens should have equal rights and obligations. In making this recommendation, we have sought to eliminate race as a determinant of status in our society.

94. Yet it is common knowledge that race has been a major factor in defining who has had access to many rights and privileges, under colonial rule. A truly multi-racial society is one in which all citizens, regardless of race, have equal rights and duties in fact as well as in law. Those critics of our proposals who would label them 'racist' and seek to undermine them by attempting to contrast them with their own version of a 'multi-racial' society, should first ask themselves whether the rhetoric they employ masks a desire to entrench certain privileged interests after independence. We doubt whether many of these people are really ready to live in a society which embodies the values and aspirations set forth in the National Goals and Directive Principles we have recommended for inclusion in our country's Constitution.

95. We do not believe that our people want a multi-racial society such as that in some South American countries, for example, where social injustice is rife and the original inhabitants of the country are in a grossly inferior position. The Committee is not against multi-racialism, but it wants to see a multi-racial society based on equality and justice. We have a long way to go yet.

96. The submissions we have received show that our people are opposed to a weak citizenship law that would simply perpetuate the very substantial advantages presently enjoyed by a small minority of this country's inhabitants, most of whom have foreign citizenship rights. As the history of other recently independent States indicates, such a law would ultimately provide security for no-one. It would simply compromise the long term interests of us all. A realistic assessment will lead foreign investors and foreign citizens working in our country to the identical conclusion.

97. After C-Day, we will be able to ascertain more clearly than we can now exactly who is really committed to the future of our country, and who only appears to be. Among the residents who will not qualify for Papua New Guinean citizenship on C-Day, those who are really with us will be prepared to wait until they are eligible to apply. They will understand the problems we face in gaining control over our country's destiny, and in equalizing opportunity among all of our people. They will be prepared to stand beside us in good times and bad, and not to run. Foreign citizens will still be welcome in our country too — for purposes and periods of time that contribute to the long term welfare of the *citizens of Papua New Guinea.*

RECOMMENDATIONS [p.14]

SINGLE CITIZENSHIP: PRINCIPLE

1. In principle, Papua New Guinean citizens shall hold no other citizenship.
   Note: For the purposes of the recommendations in this Chapter, citizenship of the Commonwealth of Nations shall not be regarded as 'another citizenship'.

Division 2. — Acquisition of Citizenship

C.P.C. Report Ch.4 p.3

Acquisition of citizenship

19. The Committee proposes that there be three ways in which Papua New Guinean citizenship might be acquired:

- *automatically*, by legal definition alone;
- by *registration*, when a person's name is officially recorded in order to establish his or her citizenship; and
- by *naturalization*, when a foreign citizen is able to meet the conditions for becoming, and is then made, a citizen of the country which naturalizes (or grants citizenship status to) that person.

Automatic citizenship

20. The vast majority of the inhabitants of Papua New Guinea will become citizens of Papua New Guinea *as of right* when our recommendations come into force. They will *automatically* become Papua New Guineans. They will not have to do anything in order to become citizens. They will simply be *defined by law* as citizens.

21. Any person who was born in Papua New Guinea before the citizenship law comes into force (on what we call in this Chapter 'C-Day' shall be a citizen of Papua New Guinea if:
- he or she is not a 'real' citizen of a foreign country; and
- he or she has at least two indigenous grandparents.

22. For the purposes of this provision, persons who are Australian citizens by virtue only of their birth in Papua, and persons who are Australian Protected Persons, are regarded as holding no real foreign citizenship, *provided that* they have not been granted the right to reside in Australia. They must be, in effect, people who have always been identified with the indigenous inhabitants of Papua New Guinea. An indigenous grandparent is defined here as a grandparent all of whose own grandparents were born in Papua New Guinea or 'an adjacent area'. By 'an adjacent area', we mean Irian Jaya, the British Solomon Islands or the Torres Strait Islands.

23. There are persons in every village and clan in this country who are knowledgeable in local history and tradition. In cases of doubt, their assistance should be invaluable in determining whether or not the grandparents of a person's grandparents were born in Papua New Guinea or an adjacent area. And, our reference to 'an adjacent area' is deliberate. We make it in order to avoid trying to draw too fine a line between people for whom four generations ago, the boundaries drawn up for our country by the colonial powers had no meaning.

24. After C-Day, a child born in Papua New Guinea of a citizen parent should, we believe, become a citizen of Papua New Guinea automatically. So should the locally-born child of a person who would have become a Papua New Guinean citizen had he or she not died. However, should a child who becomes an automatic citizen of Papua New Guinea after C-Day for some reason hold a second citizenship, he or she must renounce it and swear allegiance to Papua New Guinea within one year of turning eighteen, or within such further period as the Minister responsible for citizenship matters allows.

Citizenship by registration

25. A few people who would otherwise be entitled to automatic citizenship will have been born overseas. They may thereby have acquired a foreign citizenship. This category of people would include some whose parents were or are only temporarily absent from Papua New Guinea at the time of their birth, and people whose parents have taken up permanent residence abroad.

26. We do not believe that children born abroad should be deprived of the right they would otherwise have had to claim Papua New Guinean citizenship. However, Papua New Guinea ought not to assume responsibility for, nor grant full citizenship rights to, the foreign-born offspring of its citizens without question. It seems only reasonable to us to require that their parents provide some indication that they actually want their children to be identified with Papua New Guinea. [p.4]

27. We therefore recommend that persons born outside Papua New Guinea before C-Day who would otherwise have been automatic citizens of Papua New Guinea should have to be registered as Papua New Guinean citizens within one year of C-Day. Those born after C-Day should be registered within one year of their birth. In accordance with our recommendation that no citizen of Papua New Guinea should in principle hold a second citizenship, both groups should be required to renounce any foreign citizenship they may have acquired by virtue of being born abroad within one year of becoming eighteen years of age (or such further period as the Minister responsible for citizenship matters allows). In the case of those persons who will be eighteen years of age or over at C-Day, the renunciation should be made within one year of C-Day.

28. Provision should also be made for a further category of people to become Papua New Guinean citizens by registration: children born before C-Day but aged less than eighteen years at C-Day, who have a foreign citizenship and at least one parent who is a citizen of Papua New Guinea. Like other children who have more than one citizenship, they should be required to renounce their foreign citizenship within one year of turning eighteen (or soon afterwards) if they wish to retain their rights as Papua New Guineans.

29. Under the recommendations made above, children born after C-Day of a citizen parent will automatically become citizens of Papua New Guinea if they are born in the country, and will be eligible for registration as Papua New Guinean citizens if born abroad. Persons aged more than eighteen years at C-Day who do not qualify for automatic citizenship or for citizenship by registration under the terms of the recommendations made above should, we believe, have to apply for naturalization if they wish to become Papua New Guinean citizens. Under

colonial rule, they had advantages open to them that were not available to those people who will qualify for automatic citizenship on C-Day. However, children with a citizen parent and foreign citizenship of their own and who will be aged less than eighteen years on the C-Day are in a different category. They have not grown up with all of the advantages enjoyed by foreigners under colonial rule, nor with the full rights of a citizen after C-Day. We do not recommend that these children should automatically become Papua New Guinean citizens. However, we do not think it reasonable, either, to deprive them of the opportunity children born after C-Day of a citizen parent will have of becoming Papua New Guinea citizens. We therefore recommend that parents who are themselves citizens of Papua New Guinea should be able to register such children as citizens on or after C-Day.

Naturalization

30. The recommendations that we have made above should enable the overwhelming majority of the people descended from the original inhabitants of Papua New Guinea to become automatic citizens on C-Day. A small number of these people will have to have their names registered in order to obtain the status of citizens. The children under eighteen years of both of these groups will have a similar right to Papua New Guinean citizenship as their parents. There is, however, a small minority of people in this country who may wish to become citizens of Papua New Guinea but will not qualify automatically under the preceding proposed rules. They include people of predominantly or exclusively foreign descent, as well as some people with two indigenous grandparents who have obtained a foreign citizenship or a right of residence in a foreign country in ways other than those provided for under the preceding recommendations. If these people wish to become citizens of Papua New Guinea, they will have to apply for naturalization. So will other foreign citizens whether they have lived in Papua New Guinea before C-Day, or come here afterwards.

31. The process of naturalization normally involves a person who is a citizen of one country (or the parent of that person) making a deliberate decision to apply for the citizenship of another country. Certain of the recommendations that we have made as to the conditions for naturalization apply to all foreign citizens, including people with two indigenous grandparents who seek to gain, and former citizens wishing to regain, Papua New Guinean citizenship. A small number of people who were born in Papua New Guinea and who do not hold a real foreign citizenship will also have to apply for naturalization if they wish to become citizens of our country.

65. — AUTOMATIC CITIZENSHIP ON INDEPENDENCE DAY

(1) A person born in the country before Independence Day who has two grand-parents who were born in the country or an adjacent area is a citizen.

(2) A person born outside the country before Independence Day who has two grand-parents born in the country is a citizen as from Independence Day if —
- (a) within one year after Independence Day or such longer period as the Minister responsible for citizenship matters allows in a particular case, application is made by him or on his behalf for registration as a citizen; and
- (b) the Province of the Republic of Indonesia known as Irian Jaya; of Loyalty —
  - (i) if he has not reached the age of 19 years — in accordance with Section 64(2) (*dual citizenship*); or
  - (ii) if he has reached the age of 19 years — at or before the time when the application is made.

(3) In Subsection (1), "adjacent area" means an area that immediately before Independence Day constituted —
- (a) the Solomon Islands; or
- (b) the Province of the Republic of Indonesia known as Irian Jaya; or
- (c) the islands in Torres Straits annexed to the then Colony of Queensland under Letters Patent of the United Kingdom of

Great Britain and Ireland bearing date the 10th day of October in the forty-second year of the reign of Her Majesty Queen Victoria (that is, 1978),

not forming on Independence Day part of the area of Papua New Guinea.

(4) Subsections (1) and (2) do not apply to a person who —
  (a) has a right (whether revocable or not) to permanent residence in Australia; or
  (b) is a naturalized Australian citizen; or
  (c) is registered as an Australian citizen under Section 11 of the *Australian Citizenship Act* 1948-1975 of Australia; or
  (d) is a citizen of a country other than Australia,

unless that person renounces his right to residence in Australia or his status as a citizen of Australia or of another country in accordance with Subsection (5).

(5) A person to whom Subsection (4) applies may, within the period of two months after Independence Day and in such manner as may be prescribed by or under an Act of the Parliament, renounce his right to permanent residence in Australia or his status as an Australian citizen or as a citizen of another country and make the Declaration of Loyalty.

(6) Where in his opinion it is just to do so, the Minister responsible for citizenship matters may in his deliberate judgement (but subject to Division 4 (*Citizenship Advisory Committee*)), extend the period of two months referred to in Subsection (4), but unless the Minister is satisfied that the applicant —
  (a) assumed in error that he was a citizen; or
  (b) did not know that he was not a citizen; or
  (c) had no reasonable opportunity or not enough time to determine his status,

the period may not be extended beyond a further two months.

(*See: Citizenship Act* Ch.12)

GENERALLY

Referred to

by Narakobi A.J. in *Tabo Sipo v Meli* (1980 Unreported) N240 at p.7.

66. — CITIZENSHIP BY DESCENT.

(1) A person who —
  (a) is born in the country on or after Independence Day; and
  (b) had one parent who was a citizen or who, if he had survived to Independence Day, would have been or would have been entitled to become, such a citizen,

is a citizen.

(2) A person —
   (a) who is born outside the country on or after Independence Day; and
   (b) who had one parent who was a citizen or who, if he had survived to Independence Day, would have been, or would have been entitled to become, such a citizen; and
   (c) whose birth is registered as prescribed by or under an Act of the Parliament made for the purposes of this subsection,

is a citizen.

67. — CITIZENSHIP BY NATURALIZATION.

(1) A person who has resided continuously in the country for at least eight years may apply to the Minister responsible for citizenship matters to be naturalized as a citizen, and the Minister may, if he is satisfied as to the matters referred to in Subsection (2), in his deliberate judgement (but subject to Division 4 (*Citizenship Advisory Committee*)), grant or refuse the application.

(2) To be eligible for naturalization, a person must —
   (a) be of good character; and
   (b) intend to reside permanently in the country; and
   (c) unless prevented by physical or mental disability, speak and understand *Pisin* or *Hiri Motu*, or a vernacular of the country, sufficiently for normal conversation purposes; and
   (d) have a respect for the customs and cultures of the country; and
   (e) be unlikely to be or become a charge on public funds; and
   (f) have a reasonable knowledge and understanding of the rights, privileges, responsibilities and duties of citizenship; and
   (g) renounce, in such manner as is prescribed by or under an Act of the Parliament, any other citizenship and make the Declaration of Loyalty.

(3) If an applicant for naturalization so requests, any child of the applicant who is under voting age at the time when the applicant is naturalized becomes a citizen by naturalization on the naturalization of the applicant.

(*See: Citizenship Act* Ch.12)

C.P.C. Report Ch.4 p.4

People born in Papua New Guinea who have no real foreign citizenship but do not become citizens automatically or by registration

32. As has been mentioned in paragraph 28 above, there are among us some people who were born in Papua New Guinea, are not Australian citizens with a right of residence in Australia, but do not have two indigenous grandparents. They are the descendants of people who came to Papua New Guinea during the colonial era, and settled here. We are unsure of the exact number of people in this category, but some Malays, some Chinese and some people with only one indigenous grandparent are included among them. They are either Australian citizens by virtue only of their birth in Papua, or Australian Protected Persons because they were born in New Guinea. They will not become Papua New Guinean citizens automatically or by registration. [p.5]

33. We do not accept the argument that Papua New Guinea should grant automatic citizenship or citizenship by registration to these people. Neither we nor our forebears had a part in bringing their foreign-born ancestors to Papua New Guinea, nor in deciding on what terms they might settle here. We consider that Papua New Guineans should know whether or not these people are truly willing to adapt themselves to the new circumstances of a post-colonial society and to make a deliberate choice to live here on that basis.

34. We believe that as the outgoing colonial power, Australia has the main responsibility for these people and that it has the obligation to ensure that they do not become stateless. We have noted that Australia has recently become a signatory to the International Convention on the Reduction of Statelessness under which contracting States which are signatories are obliged not to deprive a person of his nationality in circumstances which would mean that he would be made stateless (except in very special circumstances which are not relevant here). As all of the people in the above category are at present either Australian citizens by virtue of their having been born in Papua or are Australian Protected Persons by reason of their having been born in New Guinea, we believe the relevant provisions of the Convention would, if they were now in effect, oblige Australia to grant them full Australian citizenship rights and privileges on C-Day. Whilst it is true that the Convention will not actually come into force for a further eighteen months, we believe that, in the circumstances, Australia is morally bound to comply with the requirements of that Convention as they affect this group of people, especially as the Australian Government signed the Convention at a time when it was well aware of the possibility that some people born in Papua New Guinea might be left stateless on C-Day if Australia deprived them of their present status on that day.

35. We recommend that special provision be made to enable this group of people to apply for citizenship earlier than most other people who will not become Papua New Guinean citizens automatically or by registration. Specifically, were recommend that they be able to apply for naturalization after only three years actual residence in this country commencing on or after C-Day. During these three years, both they and we will have a reasonable opportunity to assess their place in an independent Papua New Guinea.

Foreign citizens

36. As a general rule, citizens of foreign countries who wish to become naturalized Papua New Guinean citizens should have to wait eight years after C-Day. The first eight years immediately following C-Day should provide descendants of the original inhabitants of this country with an opportunity to begin to assure their rightful place in our nation. This qualifying period should allow adequate time for foreign citizens to adapt themselves to an independent Papua New Guinea, and for Papua New Guineans to see how they fit in.

37. A further important reason for having a substantial qualifying period for foreign citizens derives from the ease with which Australians who have taken up a second citizenship may resume their Australian citizenship, even if they have previously renounced it. This provision is of great significance to Papua New Guinea because the vast majority of the foreign inhabitants of our country are Australians. They have been publicly assured by the former Minister for Immigration, Mr. Grassby, and by senior Australian officials, that they will retain certain preferential rights to permanent residence in Australia and to Australian citizenship even after they have given up that citizenship. The main effect of this provision upon Papua New Guinea is to weaken substantially our country's ability to enforce the single citizenship principle. It has made plain the need to set rather stringent conditions for the acquisition of Papua New Guinean citizenship by naturalization.

38. Of course, time spent as a resident of a country does not in itself indicate the real nature of a person's commitment. The Committee has recommended that applicants for naturalization should have to fulfil a number of other conditions (many of which are commonly included in a country's citizenship law) before they can become Papua New Guinean citizens.

39. We recognize, too, that there are foreign citizens who have ties with this country which should also be taken into account when they apply for naturalization. We have in mind people with two indigenous grandparents who have for some reason acquired a foreign citizenship; the foreign spouses of Papua New Guinean citizens; certain inhabitants of the territory formerly known as Netherlands New Guinea; and foreign residents who have lived among us continuously for more then twenty years before C-Day. These people should, we believe, be given certain concessions as to the time they must wait before they can apply for Papua New Guinean citizenship. Nonethless, all people in these groups — except for some Irianese who will qualify on C-Day — should have to wait for a time after C-Day — until they and the majority of our country's inhabitants have been able to take one another's measure in the circumstances of independence. [p.6]

Foreign citizens with two indigenous grandparents

40. There are a number of people with two indigenous grandparents who will neither become citizens automatically under the above recommendations nor be eligible to become citizens by registration on C-Day. They will have acquired a foreign citizenship not simply because they were born abroad. If they wish to become Papua New Guinean citizens, they should, like other foreign citizens, have to seek naturalization.

41. Among the people in this category will be Papua New Guineans married to foreign citizens who have obtained the citizenship of their spouses; certain people who, being partly of foreign descent, have been able to obtain full Australian citizenship rights (through being granted a Right of Residence in Australia, or being

registered or naturalized as Australian citizens); and the children of people in both categories. Many of these people made a deliberate choice to foresake their Papua New Guinean heritage for a foreign citizenship, while others have been brought up having the advantages that have gone with a foreign status under colonial rule. In the case of the people of mixed origins, the possession of a Right of Residence in Australia has carried with it very significant advantages not available to indigenous Papua New Guineans, such as the right to an expatriate salary and other conditions of service, putting them in an income bracket far above Papua New Guineans holding similar positions. The children of these foreign citizens have also been privileged by comparison with the indigenous majority.

42. These people should not, we believe, be able to acquire Papua New Guinean citizenship on C-Day. They have not been fully identified with our country. Indeed, many of them have deliberately set themselves apart from the mass of the people. Taking a realistic view, we believe full account should be taken of the attitude of our people to those who, having been born here, have had the benefits of foreign citizenship but now wish to have the advantages of Papua New Guinean citizenship. Unless our people are satisfied that such people are now genuinely committed to this country, they are unlikely to accept them, whether or not they hold citizenship of this country.

43. Nonetheless, the people in this group do retain ties here which distinguish them from complete foreigners with no relatives here. We therefore recommend that they should have to wait five years after C-Day before they can apply for naturalization as Papua New Guinean citizens. During that period, the necessary changes of attitude can be made by both groups.

44. Of course, some of the above group of foreign citizens will be people who did not themselves choose to apply for full foreign citizenship rights. And some of them may be people who have conscientiously declined to accept the advantages of foreign status in order to identify themselves with the indigenous majority. The Committee recommends that those in this group who have always identified themselves with a Papua New Guinean community should be eligible to apply for Papua New Guinean citizenship after three years residence following C-Day.

45. In order to be eligible for naturalization three years after C-Day, those foreign citizens with two indigenous grandparents should establish to the satisfaction of the Minister responsible for citizenship matters that they did not themselves seek a foreign citizenship, and that they have always identified themselves with a group of indigenous people of Papua New Guinea. They will be people whose parents sought of foreign citizenship on their behalf or who have inherited it in some other way, but who have never exercised any of the rights associated with it, nor accepted any of the privileges or other benefits which are available to those who hold that citizenship.

46. We have recommended that any of the following actions should disqualify an applicant for naturalization *under this provision*:

- acceptance of a position in public or private employment with a salary and conditions attached which were not applicable to or received by indigenous Papua New Guineans at the relevant time;
- voluntary voting in an election restricted to citizens of the country of which the applicant is a citizen; and
- obtaining social service benefits restricted to citizens of the other country.

47. In considering applications made under this provision, the minister responsible for citizenship matters should also take into account as factors militating against treating an applicant for citizenship as a person who has always identified himself with an indigenous Papua New Guinean community —

- significant property or business interests which an applicant may have in the country of which he is a citizen; [p.7]
- numerous or lengthy private visits made as an adult to the country of which he or she is a citizen (other than visits to obtain medical treatment or education which was not available in Papua New Guinea at the time);
- a lack of meaningful social relationships with those who are entitled to Papua New Guinean citizenship automatically.

It should, however, be clearly understood that a person who is disqualified by one of the above factors can still be granted citizenship after *five years* actual residence in Papua New Guinea commecing on or after C-Day.

Irianese

48. Another group of people who should not have to wait eight years after C-Day before being able to apply for naturalization comprises those indigenous people from Irian Jaya (formerly Netherlands New Guinea) who sought permanent refuge in our country before the United Nations General Assembly formally took note on 19 November 1969 of the Report of the Secretary-General on the fulfilment of his tasks under the Indonesian-Dutch Agreement of 15 August 1962. We recognize our cultural and ethnic affinity with these people, and believe that they should be able to apply for Papua New Guinean citizenship on C-Day, or eight years after they took up permanent residence in our country, whichever is the later date. We consider that they should not obtain citizenship automatically, or by registration, but that they should be granted this concession.

Foreign spouses of citizens

49. A further group of people who should not have to wait for eight years after C-Day comprises the foreign-born spouses of Papua New Guinean citizens. They should, we believe, have to wait only five years after C-Day

before they can apply to be naturalized. People who seek to be naturalized under the terms of this recommendation should have been married, and lived together with their spouses, for at least two years before they make application. This qualification is designed to ensure that the marriages of people who seek to take advantage of this concession are genuine. The Committee is determined to see that marriage is not used by foreign citizens as a device for obtaining Papua New Guinean citizenship more quickly than otherwise.

Foreign residents of more than twenty years standing

50. There are a few foreign citizens who have lived and worked among us for so long that they have come to regard Papua New Guinea as their only home. We believe that some recognition should be made of their special situtation, but not to such an extent that sentiment outweighs our responsibility to the long term interests of our people, as there are some expatriates who have lived here many years and now have dominant economic power and influence which we do not wish to entrench or legitimise. We therefore recommend that a foreign citizen, both of whose parents were foreign citizens at his or her birth, should be eligible to have the qualifying period before application can be made for naturalization reduced by one year for each twenty years that he or she has lived in Papua New Guinea before C-Day.

Conditions for naturalization

51. With the exceptions spelt out above, foreign citizens should have to wait eight years after C-Day before they can apply for naturalization as Papua New Guinean citizens. However, while we hold firmly to the view that a qualifying period of time is necessary, it is in the final analysis the heartfelt commitment to our people and the challenges which lie ahead that matter most. We firmly reject the notion that the residential requirement should, as a rule, take into account a period before C-Day. Their privileged life during the colonial period has not prepared the foreign residents in our country for life in an independent Papua New Guinea. The only people who should receive any concession in respect of time spent in Papua New Guinea before C-Day are certain Irianese and foreign residents of more than twenty years standing. They should be able to apply for naturalization a little more quickly than other foreign citizens.

52. Until very recently we, the descendants of the original inhabitants of this country have had no effective say in determining who should and who should not be able to come to our country and live among us. The Committee is also convinced that the experiences, acquaintances, and familiarity with the people and conditions of colonial times often provide little evidence of the commitment that will be required of all citizens of our independent nation. We believe that it is proper that fulfilment of the residential requirement should, as a general rule, begin on C-Day, when the citizenship law made by our people takes effect.

53. In addition to time spent in our country, we believe that applicants for naturalization [p.8] should have to satisfy other conditions too. Time spent in our midst does not in itself indicate how committed to our country an applicant really is, nor is it the only factor to be considered in deciding whether he is, generally, a suitable type of person to enter our community on a permanent basis.

54. We must be satisfied that those who seek our citizenship are genuinely concerned with the welfare and progress of our people; that they understand and respect us and are able to communicate with ordinary people; and that they are capable of contributing to our country's development. They should therefore be able to supply to the Minister responsible for citizenship matters evidence that they are not only of full age and capacity, but that —

- they are of good character;
- they are unlikely to become a charge on public funds;
- they intent to reside permanently in Papua New Guinea;
- they respect the cultures of our people;
- they specak and understand Pidgin, Hiri Motu or a local vernacular, so that they can communicate effectively with the citizens of our country;
- they have an adequate knowledge of our country's history and customs and of its citizens' rights and duties; and
- they are acceptable (as citizens) to citizens in the area where they live.

intending citizens should, in short, know the rights and obligations of citizens in relation to the national government, and they should be able to live and work in harmony with the ordinary people of Papua New Guinea.

55. We do not believe that applicants for naturalization should have to chew betel-nut, wear tapa cloth, or engage in traditional rituals. But they must, we believe, demonstrate a genuine respect for the ancient wisdom and ways of our people. Before they apply for naturalization, they should where possible or unless exempted by the Minister responsible for citizenship matters, attend courses on the rights and duties of Papua New Guinean citizens, and the history and customs of our people.

56. Potential citizens should possess skills and personal qualities that will be of benefit to our country. They should, in turn, be able to see Papua New Guinea as a country that offers them a satisfying future life. We do not believe that our country should accept as citizens people who are likely to become liabilities to us. Nor do we believe that people who seek no more than short term advantage should have the rights of citizens.

57. We naturally accept that applicants for citizenship will have normal human frailties. But we have an obligation not to admit to citizenship people who are likely to contribute little that is positive to our development. However, the Mininster responsible for citizenship matters should have power to exempt applicants with two indigenous grandparents from the requirement of full possession of the mental faculties.

58. We also recommend that, in accordance with normal international practice, applicants for naturalization should be able to apply simultaneously for naturalization of any of their children aged less than eighteen years.

GENERALLY

Referred to

by Frost C.J. in *Tei Abul v Anton Parua* [1976] PNGLR 250 at p.254 (s.67(2)(c) as illustrating that the Constitution recognizes the existence of vernacular unwritten languages which make inappropriate the common law rule that a slander must be set out in writing both in the vernacular language and in the language of the Court);

by Narakobi A.J. in *Tabo Sipo v Meli* (1980 Unreported) N240 at p.7.

68. — SPECIAL PROVISIONS RELATING TO NATURALIZATION

(1) A person who is eligible to become a citizen under Section 67(1) (*citizenship by naturalization*) and holds an executive office by virtue of being a member of an elective body shall cease to hold that office at the expiration of a period of two months after Independence Day unless within that time he makes application under that section to be naturalized and that application is granted.

C.P.C.Report Ch.4 p.11

Political Office-holders

81. We believe that political office in Papua New Guinea should, in principle, be reserved for our citizens, and that all qualified citizens should be eligible to stand for election. We should not allow citizens of foreign countries to stand for election, and to participate in the conduct of our nation's affairs. Almost no other country allows it. We should not allow it. To do so would be a denial of our sovereignty.

82. However, certain people who will not qualify for citizenship on C-Day have been freely elected to our national parliament and to membership of local government bodies by our people. They should, we believe, be able to serve out the remainder of the terms for which they were elected. They should not, however, be allowed to stand again after C-Day unless they have become Papua New Guinean citizens.

83. Further, we believe that non-citizens should not be allowed to hold executive office in, or to preside over, our National Parliament, area authorities, provincial or district [p.12] governments, or legally recognized local government bodies. The people of our country did not elect them directly to such positions. They hold them because they were elected by members of these bodies. They should, we believe, resign from the these offices at C-Day, and be replaced by citizens. They may, however, remain as ordinary members of the National Parliament, or of the other bodies specified above, until fresh elections are called.

(2) Without limiting the matters that may be taken into account in deciding on the application for naturalization, under Section 67 (*citizenship by naturalization)* the following matters shall be taken into account in deciding on an application that is made during the first eight years after Independence Day:—

(a) if the applicant is a person to whom Section 65(4) (*automatic citizenship on Independence Day*) applies, whether he acquired the right of permanent residence in Australia or became an Australian citizen otherwise than by reason of a voluntary act (other than marriage) on his part; and

(b) whether the applicant has at any time accepted pay and conditions of employment that were not in general applicable —
   (i) before Independence Day, to persons who qualify or would, if they had survived to that day, have qualified for citizenship under Section 65 (*automatic citizenship on Independence Day*); or
   (ii) after Independence Day, to citizens; and
(c) whether the major part of the investment and business interests of the applicant are and have been in the country; and
(d) whether the applicant is or has been married to a citizen or to a person who, if they had survived to Independence Day, would have been, or would have been entitled to become, a citizen, and the nature of the family ties of the applicant; and
(e) the length and nature of the residence of the applicant in the country; and
(f) any performance by the applicant of services beneficial to Papua New Guinea or its people; and
(g) any sacrifices made by the applicant in the interests of Papua New Guinea or its people; and
(h) the applicant's knowledge of *Pisin* or *Hiri Motu* or of a vernacular of the country; and
(i) whether or not the application of the applicant includes the children (if any) under voting age of the applicant; and
(j) any references given as to the good character and suitability for citizenship of the applicant; and
(k) the place of birth and the parentage of the applicant.

GENERALLY

Referred to

by Frost C.J. in *Tei Abal v Anton Parua* [1976] PNGLR at p.254 (68(2)(h) as illustrating that the Constitution recognizes the existence of vernacular unwritten languages which make inappropriate the common law rule that a slander must be set out in writing in both the vernacular language and the language of the Court).

(3) Notwithstanding anything in a Constitutional Law, a benefit, right or privilege, directly or indirectly, conferred upon "Papua New Guineans" or "natives" or "local persons" or "non-overseas persons" or "citizens" (where that term is to take effect after the making of a law relating to citizenship) by any pre-Independence law shall continue to be enjoyed only by persons who became citizens of Papua New Guinea under Section 65 (*automatic citzenship on Independence Day*) but only —
(a) for a period of ten years after Independence Day; or
(b) until an Act of the Parliament takes away that benefit, right or privilege,

whichever first occurs.

GENERALLY

Referred to

by Narakobi A.J. in *Tabo Sipo v Meli* (1980 Unreported) N240 at p.5;

by Kapi J. in *S.C.R.No 2 of 1982; Re Organic Law* [1982] PNGLR 214 at p.240 (s.68(3) provides an express exception to which s.55 of the Constitution is subject).

(4) Notwithstanding anything in a Constitutional Law, during the five years after Independence Day only persons who become citizens of Papua New Guinea under Section 65 (*automatic citizenship on Independence Day*) shall have the rights conferred by Section 53 (*protection from unjust deprivation of property*) except that during this period the rights of a person who becomes a citizen otherwise than under Section 65 (*automatic citizenship on Independence Day*) in respect of his property shall not be less than those accorded by law to non-citizens.

GENERALLY

per Kapi J. (dissenting)

It is now necessary to consider the effect of s.68(4) of the Constitution. Mr. Frame, the respondent, is not an automatic citizen but is a naturalized citizen. Section 68(4) of the Constitution must be considered as to whether it deprives Mr. Frame of the protection of the terms of s.53 of the Constitution or not. Counsel for the appellant submits that under s.68(4) of the Constitution, during the first five years after Independence, only automatic citizens may claim the protection provided for by s.53 of the Constitution. He submits that since Mr. Frame is a naturalized citizen and that his claim is made within the first five years after Independence, compensation under the Act is not subject to the provisions of s.53 of the Constitution.

Counsel for the respondent, on the other hand, submits that under s.68(4) of the Constitution, it would be competent for the Parliament to pass a law depriving non-automatic citizens of the right to compensation in respect of the land resumed. He submits that the Parliament has not passed such an Act. He further submits that the acquisition of Mr. Frame's land was made under the *Lands Acquisition Act* and that has only one meaning, and therefore s.68(4) of the Constitution has no relevance.

With respect, I do not think that the submissions made by counsel for the respondent are correct. Section 68(4) of the Constitution does not require that an Act of the Parliament should make special provision for non-automatic citizens whose land is acquired during the first five years after Independence. The sub-section quite clearly says that citizens other than automatic citizens shall not have less rights than those *accorded by law to non citizens*. The right of compensation by naturalized citizens in the first five years after Independence is the same as the rights given to non citizens by the law. As I have pointed out earlier, the rights of non citizens are provided for under the Act.

It is quite clear from these provisions of the Constitution that the protection given under s.53 of the Constitution was intended only for automatic citizens for the first five years after Independence. These provisions are consistent with the intentions of the founding fathers of our Constitution. They recognized that there was an element of control of the economy by foreigners and the impact of multi-national corporations on this country before Independence, and their desire was for Papua New Guinean automatic citizens to take control of their own economy after Independence. (Final Report of the Constitutional Planning Committee dated 13th August, 1974. See 'Impact of Multi-national Corporations on Development' pars. 78-86 at pp.2/10 to 2/11; and see 'Protection from Deprivation of Property' pars. 85-91 pp.5/1/14 to 5/1/15.) (See s.24 of the Constitution.)

It is necessary to consider the effect of s.55 of the Constitution in view of the fact that the rights that are conferred by virtue of s.68(4) seem to differentiate between classes of citizens under the Constitution; that is, the rights conferred by s.53 can only apply to automatic citizens, and not naturalized citizens, within five years after Independence. Section 55 of the Constitution provides that all citizens have the same rights, privileges, obligations and duties irrespective of race, tribe, etc. The question is whether s.55 of the Constitution overrides the provision of s.68(4). It appears that s.68(4) of the Constitution has an overriding effect over s.55 since s.68(4) reads: 'Notwithstanding anything in a Constitutional law ....' Section 55 therefore is to be read subject to the provisions of s.68(4) of the Constitution.

Having regard to all these considerations, I have come to the conclusion that naturalized citizens, for the first five years after Independence, do not have the protection in terms of s.53 of the Constitution by virtue of s.68(4) of the Constitution.

Minister for Lands v Frame [1980] PNGLR 433 at pp.466, 467; but see Greville Smith J. at pp.437-439 and Pratt J. at pp.481-484.

Note: assuming Kapi J. correctly expressed the law, that the five year period referred to above expired on the 16th September 1980.

(5) Notwithstanding anything in a Constitutional Law, but subject to Subsection (6), an Act of the Parliament made in the period of ten years after Independence Day may confer a benefit, right or privilege on persons who became citizens of Papua New Guinea under Section 65 (*automatic citizenship on Independence Day*).

GENERALLY

Comment

The effect of s.68(5) will expire immediately following the 16th September 1985.

Referred to

by Kapi J. in *S.C.R. No 2 of 1982; Re Organic Law* [1982] PNGLR 214 at p.240.

(6) An Act of the Parliament referred to in Subsection (5) —
- (a) shall not derogate the rights conferred by Sections 32 to 58 (*basic rights*) except the rights conferred by Section 55 (*equality of citizens*); and
- (b) shall be for the purpose of giving advantage or assistance to persons who become citizens of Papua New Guinea under Section 65 (*automatic citizenship on Independence Day*).

GENERALLY

Referred to

by Kapi J. in *S.C.R. No 2 of 1982; Re Organic Law* [1982] PNGLR 214 at p.240.

69. — APPLICATION FOR NATURALIZATION

(1) Subject to Subsection (2) an application for naturalization under Section 67 (*citizenship by naturalization*) must be made —
- (a) in the case of a person who has resided continuously in the country for eight years or more before Independence Day — within two months after Independence Day; and

(b) in the case of any other person — within two months after the completion by him of eight years continuous residence in the country.

(2) Where in his opinion it is just to do so, the Minister responsible for citizenship matters may in his deliberate judgement, (but subject to Division 4 (*Citizenship Advisory Committee*)) extend the periods referred to in Subsection (1) where he is satisfied that —
(a) the person was unaware of the provisions of Subsection (1); or
(b) there are special circumstances.

(*See: Citizenship Act* Ch.12).

Division 3. — Loss and Regaining of Citizenship.

70. — AUTOMATIC LOSS OF CITIZENSHIP

(1) A citizen who has reached voting age and is of full capacity who —
(a) obtains the nationality or citizenship of another country by a voluntary act (other than marriage); or
(b) exercises a right that is exclusive to nationals or citizens of another country, unless the Minister responsible for citizenship matters is satisfied that the right was exercised inadvertently; or
(c) takes an oath or makes a declaration or affirmation of allegiance to another country or to the Sovereign or Head of State of another country; or
(d) does, agrees to or adopts any act (other than marriage) by which he becomes a national or citizen of another country; or
(e) enters or serves in the armed forces of another country, except with the express approval of the Head of State, acting with, and in accordance with, the advice of the National Executive Council; or
(f) except as permitted by an Act of the Parliament, votes in a national, provincial, state or local election, or accepts elective office, of another country; or
(g) subject to Subsection (3), travels under the protection of a passport or purported passport of another country in which he is described as a citizen or national of that country.

loses his citizenship.

(2) A person who is found by a court to have obtained citizenship by a false representation, fraud or concealment of a material fact on his part loses his citizenship, unless the Minister responsible for citizenship matters is satisfied that the offence was of a minor nature and that revelation of the true fact would not have affected the grant of naturalization.

(3) Subsection (1) (g) does not apply to —

(a) a person who is absent from the country on Independence Day, who continues to travel under the protection of a passport of another country, but only until —

(i) the expiration of the then-current period of validity of the passport; or

(ii) his return to the country,

whichever first happens; or

(b) a person travelling under the protection of the passport of a parent or guardian; or

(c) a person travelling under the protection of a passport of another country with the approval of the Minister responsible for citizenship matters.

(*See*: *Citizenship Act* Ch.12).

C.P.C. Report Ch.4 p.9

Loss of Papua New Guinean Citizenship

65. The Committee believes that, as a matter of principle, citizens should not be readily deprived of their citizenship. That is one of the reasons why we do not want to make it easy for foreign citizens to be naturalized. Foreign citizens should have to demonstrate a strong commitment to our country before they can apply for naturalization. And, in admitting them to citizenship, we must recognize that our country is making a commitment to them.

66. However, in keeping with our firm opposition to dual citizenship, we recommend that any person who, while a Papua New Guinean obtains a foreign citizenship, or deliberately exercises a right which is exclusive to citizens of another country, should be deprived of Papua New Guinean citizenship. It is, of course, possible that a Papua New Guinean citizen may acquire a foreign citizenship or exercise rights exclusive to citizens of another country inadvertently. If so, then he or she should not be deprived of our country's citizenship.

67. In particular, we believe that Papua New Guinean citizens should not take (or agree to) any action other than marriage which confers a foreign citizenship upon them or entitles them to exercise rights exclusive to citizens of another country. In addition, Papua New Guinean citizens should not —

- make an oath or affirmation, or declare or acknowledge allegiance, to a foreign country (or the head of that country);
- enter or serve in the armed services of a foreign country except with the prior approval of the National Executive Council;
- vote in an election restricted to foreign citizens; or
- travel on a valid passport describing them as citizens of a country other than Papua New Guinea.

If a Papua New Guinean citizen does any of these things deliberately, then he or she should be deprived of our country's citizenship. We recommend a proviso, however, which would enable the responsible Minister to allow a person to retain his citizenship of Papua New Guinea even though he has carried a foreign passport, if to deprive him of his citizenship on this ground would be unjust. [p.10]

68. In additional, naturalized Papua New Guinean citizens should be deprived of their citizenship if they are found guilty in a court of law of —

- sedition or treason; or
- obtaining Papua New Guinean citizenship by false representations, fraud, or concealment of a material fact.

Persons found guilty of these offences will have betrayed the trust that the people of Papua New Guinea placed in them when they originally accepted them as citizens.

69. Firm as our belief is that Papua New Guineans should not be too readily deprived of their citizenship, we do not seek to prevent those citizens who wish to cut their ties with us from renouncing them. Any citizen should, we believe, be able to renounce his or her Papua New Guinean citizenship, but only in order to obtain another citizenship. We have an obligation to the international community not to allow our citizens to make themselves stateless.

70. In making our recommendations regarding loss of Papua New Guinean citizenship, we have borne in mind the possibility that the National Parliament may wish to make provision in ordinary law for citizenship to be lost in ways additional to those specified above. We believe that the Constitution should not preclude this possibility, but all laws dealing with loss of Papua New Guinean citizenship should allow for a right of appeal to the National Court by any person who believes that a decision to deprive him or her of Papua New Guinean citizenship has been wrongly or unjustly made.

71. — ACTS DONE UNDER COMPULSION OF LAW

The preceding provisions of this Division do not apply to any act done under compulsion of law of another country.

72. — RENUNCIATION OF CITIZENSHIP

(1) Subject to Subsections (2) and (3), a citizen who has reached voting age and is of full capacity may renounce his citizenship in such manner and on such conditions as are prescribed by or under an Act of the Parliament.

(*See*: *Citizenship Act* Ch.12)

(2) A person may not renounce his citizenship unless —
(a) he already holds some other nationality or citizenship; or
(b) the renunciation is for the purpose of his obtaining some other nationality or citizenship.

(3) During a time of war, citizenship may not be renounced without the prior consent of the Minister responsible for citizenship matters.

73. — REGAINING CITIZENSHIP

(1) Subject to Subsection (2), citizenship once lost can be regained —
(a) in the case of citizenship by virtue of Section 65 (*automatic citizenship on Independence Day*) or 66 (*citizenship by descent*) — only after five years' continuous residence in the country after the loss of citizenship, and in the deliberate judgement (but subject to Division 4 (*Citizenship Advisory Committee*)) of the Minister responsible for citizenship matters; and
(b) in the case of citizenship by naturalization only in accordance with the law relating to naturalization, for which purpose any period of residence in the country before the loss of citizenship shall be disregarded.

(2) Where a person —
(a) was citizen by virtue of Section 65 (*automatic citizenship on Independence Day*) or 66 (*citizenship by descent*); and
(b) married, before, on or after Independence Day, a person who was a national or citizen of another country; and
(c) became, on or during the marriage, a national or citizen of the country of which his spouse was at that time a national or citizen,

and the marriage has permanently broken up, the reference in Subsection (1) (a) to a period of five years shall be read as a reference to a period of three years commencing —
(d) if the person was, at the time when the marriage broke up, resident in the country — on the date on which it broke up; or
(e) if the person was at that time resident outside the country — on his return to reside in the country.

C.P.C. Report Ch.4 p.10

Regaining Papua New Guinean citizenship

71. Under our recommendations, it would take a deliberate action on the part of a citizen for him to lose his Papua New Guinean citizenship. We believe that this is only proper. But, by the same token, we believe that those of our country's citizens who deliberately renounce their citizenship or knowingly enjoy rights exclusive to citizens of a foreign country should be treated as the foreign citizens they chose to be if they seek to resume their Papua New Guinean citizenship. They should be required to apply for naturalization.

72. Naturalized citizens who have forsaken their Papua New Guinea citizenship and later seek to resume it, should have to reside in Papua New Guinea for a further eight years before they can apply for naturalization again. People who first acquired their Papua New Guinean citizenship either automatically or by registration should have to wait for five years after they return to Papua New Guinea after living abroad. But a person who became a citizen automatically or by registration, is married to a foreign citizen on or after C-Day, leaves the country and assumes the citizenship of the spouse, should, if the marriage breaks down, be able to regain Papua New Guinean citizenship only three years after returning here.

RECOMMENDATIONS [p.20]

Regaining Papua New Guinean citizenship

17. A person who has renounced or otherwise lost his Papua New Guinean citizenship may regain it —
    (a) in the case of a naturalized citizen, only after fulfilling the residential qualifications applicable to foreign citizens and satisfying the other conditions for naturalization of such citizens; and
    (b) subject to Recommendation 18 below, in the case of a citizen who originally obtained his Papua New Guinean citizenship automatically or by registration, and who obtained a foreign citizenship whilst residing in a foreign country, if he has completed *five years* actual residence in Papua New Guinea after resuming residence in Papua New Guinea.

18. A person who —
    (a) was originally a citizen of Papua New Guinea automatically or by registration;
    (b) on or after C-Day has been married to a foreign citizen;
    (c) has acquired the citizenship of the country of which his spouse is a citizen;
    (d) experiences a breakdown in his marriage; and
    (e) returns to Papua New Guinea after residing in a foreign country;

shall be eligible to regain his Papua New Guinean citizenship after completing three years actual residence in Papua New Guinea following his re-establishing Papua New Guinea as his real place of residence.

Note: In this recommendation, 'real place of residence' shall be taken to have the [p.21] same meaning as it has in the *Electoral Ordinance*, 1963 as amended.

74. — LOSS AND REGAINING OF CITIZENSHIP BY CERTAIN CHILDREN.

(1) Where —
    (a) a parent of a child loses his citizenship; and
    (b) the Minister is satisfied on application on behalf of the child that it is for the welfare of the child to do so,

the Minister responsible for citizenship matters may, by order, deprive the child of his citizenship.

(2) A person aggrieved by an order under Subsection (1) may appeal to the National Court.

(3) An Act of the Parliament may make special provision to facilitate the regaining of citizenship by persons who lose their citizenship by reason of the loss of citizenship by a parent.

(*See*: *Citizenship Act* Ch.12)

Division 4. — Citizenship Advisory Committee

75. — THE COMMITTEE

(1) An Act of the Parliament shall make provision for a Citizenship Advisory Committee, all of the members of which must be citizens (other than naturalized citizens).

(*See*: *Citizenship Act* Ch.12)

(2) The Committee shall consist of —
(a) four permanent members, at least two of whom are members of the Parliament other than Ministers; and
(b) one ad hoc member to represent the community in which the person to whom a matter before the Committee relates resides.

C.P.C. Report Ch.4 p.19

Composition of Committee

14. (1) The Advisory Committee on Citizenship Matters shall comprise five members, each of whom is a Papua New Guinean citizen.
(2) Two of those members shall be members of the National Parliament who shall hold office during the life of the parliament in which they are appointed.
(3) The other three members of the committee shall, subject to law, hold office for six years.

Appointment and Removal of Members of Advisory Committee

15. (1) Subject to clause (2) of this recommendation, the members of the Advisory Committee shall be appointed and removed in accordance with law by the National Executive Council after considering a submission by the Minister.
(2) Before making a submission under clause (1) above, the Minister shall consult the Permanent Parliamentary Committee concerned with citizenship matters as to —
(a) nominees for appointment to the Committee; and
(b) the removal of any member of the Committee.

76. — FUNCTIONS OF THE COMMITTEE

(1) Before taking any action under this Part in relation to a person, the Minister responsible for citizenship matters shall refer the matter to the Citizenship Advisory Committee and receive its advice.
(*Amended by Constitutional Amendment No. 5 — Citizenship*)

C.P.C. Report Ch.4 p.19

Administration of Citizenship Law — Advisory Committee on Citizenship Matters

13. The citizenship law shall be administered by the Minister who shall be advised by an Advisory Committee on Citizenship Matters —
(a) on matters concerning citizenship and naturalization generally, and on such specific matters as are referred to it by the Minister;
(b) on all applications for registration of persons as citizens;
(c) on all applications for naturalization;
(d) on all matters concerning the registration and deregistration of intending citizens; and
(e) on such other matters relating to the citizenship law as are provided for by law.

(2) If the Minister refuses to accept the advice of the committee on any matter referred to it under Subsection (1), he shall, if so requested by a person affected or by the Committee, give to the Parliament, as soon as practicable, a statement on the matter setting out the reasons for his refusal, and the Parliament may reverse his decision on such conditions as it thinks proper.

(3) The reversal by the Parliament of a decision to grant or to allow the regaining of citizenship, or to grant a certificate under Section 81 (*certificate as to citizenship*), takes effect, subject to any conditions to which it is made subject, as a deprivation of citizenship on the date of the reversal.

(4) The reversal by the Parliament of a decision to refuse to grant citizenship to a person, to deprive a person of citizenship or to refuse to grant a certificate under Section 81 (*certificate as to citizenship*) takes effect retrospectively to the date of the decision.

(5) The Committee has such powers and such other functions and duties as are conferred or imposed by or under an Act of the Parliament.

(*See*: *Citizenship Act* Ch.12)

Division 5. — General.

77. — SPECIAL PROVISIONS FOR CERTAIN PERSONS

(1) A foundling discovered at any time in the country shall, in the absence of proof to the contrary, be deemed to be the child of parents at least one of whom was, or if he had survived would have been, a citizen.

(2) Where the identity or the citizenship status of a parent of a child born in the country is unknown or doubtful, the parent shall be deemed to have been, in the absence of proof to the contrary, a person who was, or if he had survived would have been, a citizen.

(3) For the purposes of this Part, a posthumous child of a person has the same status as he would have had if he had been born immediately before the date of the death of his father.

78. — EFFECT OF ADOPTION

(1) Where the citizenship status or entitlement of a person is to be determined by reference to a parent or grandparent and the person, or a parent of the person, was adopted under a law at any time in force in the country or any other place, the status or entitlement

shall be determined by reference to the natural parents or grandparents, except that the Minister responsible for citizenship matters may, in his deliberate judgement (but subject to Division 4 (*Citizenship Advisory Committee*)), allow an adoptive parent or grandparent to be taken into account where the result would be to recognize citizenship or the entitlement to citizenship.

(2) In Subsection (1), a reference to adoption includes a reference to an adoption by custom.

79. — PLACE OF BIRTH OF CERTAIN PERSONS

For the purposes of this Part —
(a) a person born on a registered ship or aircraft shall be deemed to have been born at the place where the ship or aircraft was registered and
(b) a person born on an unregistered ship or aircraft belonging to the government of a country shall be deemed to have been born in that country.

80. — "RESIDENCE"

Subject to any Act of the Parliament, a requirement in this Part of a period of residence in a place is not satisfied by —
(a) residence in custody under sentence awaiting deportation or removal from the country; or
(b) residence as an unlawful immigrant.

81. — CERTIFICATE AS TO CITIZENSHIP

(1) A person whose status or entitlement in relation to citizenship of Papua New Guinea is, or may be, in doubt may apply to the Minister responsible for citizenship matters for a certificate under this section.

(2) If the Minister is satisfied that the applicant is, or is entitled to become, a citizen, he may, in his deliberate judgement (but subject to Division 4 (*Citizenship Advisory Committee*)), grant a certificate stating that the person is or may become a citizen by virtue of a provision specified in the certificate.

(3) Subject to Section 76 (*functions of the Committee*), a certificate under this section is (unless it is proved that it was obtained by means of a false representation, fraud or concealment of a material fact) conclusive evidence that on the material date the person concerned was, is or may become a citizen in accordance with the terms of the certificate.

PART V. — THE HEAD OF STATE

Division 1. — The Head of State

82. — QUEEN AND HEAD OF STATE

(1) Her Majesty the Queen —
  (a) having been requested by the People of Papua New Guinea, through their Constituent Assembly, to become the Queen and Head of State of Papua New Guinea; and
  (b) having graciously consented so to become,
is the Queen and Head of State of Papua New Guinea.

(2) Subject to and in accordance with this Constitution, the privileges, powers, functions, duties and responsibilities of the Head of State may be had, exercised and performed through a Governor-General appointed in accordance with Division 3 (*appointment, etc., of Governor-General*) and, except where the contrary intention appears, reference in any law to the Head of State shall be read accordingly.

C.P.C. Report Ch.7 p.1

Power belongs to the people

1. The Committee proposes that the first part of our Constitution should include an article which states:
   Power belongs to the people and it shall be exercised in accordance with this Constitution.
We believe it is important to make clear in this way that the power exercised under the Constitution is derived from the people. In the great majority of the societies that make up our nation, it was from the people rather than from kings or chiefs that power was taken by the colonial rulers. It is therefore appropriate that it be the people to whom that power should now be returned. The principle that power derives from the people provides the basis of the Constitution.

2. In Chapter 6 we outlined the provisions we proposed for the National Parliament, the body of elected representatives of the people which will exercise the power to make laws for our country. We are concerned here with the power to administer the country in accordance with those laws — that is, the executive power of Papua New Guinea.

Where should executive power lie?

3. It is important in a constitution to say where executive power lies. In accordance with the practice of most of our societies, in which decisions are made by a group, we propose that the executive power of Papua New Guinea be vested in the National Executive Council. This is the name we have chosen for the group of Ministers who, collectively, will administer the country and be responsible for this work to the National Parliament.

Arguments for and against a separate Head of State

4. In reaching this conclusion, we have given consideration to other possibilities — especially the more usual practice of vesting executive power in one person. We believe that this would be contrary to the customs of most of our people. Also, it has usually occured elsewhere for historical reasons that have little or no relevance at all to the circumstances of the present day. Thus, in some countries in earlier times, one man became the unchallenged king, usually as a result of conquest, although he often claimed that his power came from a god or gods. In more recent times, the founders of some states have created the position of president as a kind of substitute for a king. Like the king of former years, he too exercises executive power alone.

5. Many countries, however, have kept kings and queens and their representatives, such as governors-general, or else replaced them with presidents who have been given a similar role, long after they have lost effective power. With the growth of democratic systems of government, real executive power is no longer exercised by them, but by governments elected by the people. The constitutions of those countries say that the kings or queens or presidents must do what the elected governments tell them to do.

6. We believe that there is no reason why the people of Papua New Guinea should have to adopt this foreign idea. Neither kings and queens, nor governors-general or presidents, have any traditional place in our societies. This does not mean, of course, that we should not accept the British monarch, at present Queen Elizabeth II, as Head of the Commonwealth. If Papua New Guinea joins the Commonwealth we would still wish to show her our respect and affection, and to welcome her and her family with our traditional hospitality. But that is a different thing from actually vesting the executive power of Papua New Guinea in the Queen, in her representative or in a president, as Head of State.

7. The case for a separate Head of State is sometimes associated with the view that too much power should not be placed in the hands of the elected Head of Government. We have found that this view is widespread among our people; it has influenced the great majority who have expressed an opinion on the matter to reject the idea of Papua New Guinea having an executive-type president. We share this view. However, we believe that in order to avoid a concentration of power in one man, it is neither necessary nor desirable to establish a new separate Head of State to act either as a representative of, or as a substitute for, a king or queen. [p.2]

8. There is little evidence to suggest that the mere existence of a separate Head of State provides any obstacle to the emergence of a dictatorial Prime Minister. On the other hand there *is* evidence which suggests that to divide executive power between a Head of State and a Prime Minister — or even to leave a vague area of discretion to the Head of State — is to risk a serious conflict between them, resulting in a constitutional crisis which may be resolved by one or the other seizing power.

9. Two things are thus quite clear. A separate Head of State has little relevance to the cultural heritage of our people, and, in any case, the existence of such a person can be no real safeguard against too much power being exercised by the Head of Government. To guard against that possibility, we recommend that there be collective leadership in the Executive — as was suggested to us by people in various parts of the country — and that a truly effective legislature be established.

10. We have not overlooked other arguments that are sometimes put forward in favour of a separate Head of State. One of these is that a Head of State helps to symbolize national unity. We recognize that this may be true of nations which have their own king or queen, but this has often been achieved only after a long period, perhaps centuries, during which the people as a whole have come to forget the regional or foreign origins of the royal dynasty, and the battles or wars that gained it ascendency. There is no historical basis for anything of this nature in Papua New Guinea. Moreover, experience elsewhere in the Commonwealth indicates that a Governor-General acting for the Queen is unlikely to be an acceptable alternative. In few of those nations comparable to our own has such an arrangement lasted for long. Furthermore, were we to opt for a Presidential substitute, we would be creating an additional institution which, having no traditional roots, would need to gain acceptance among our diverse peoples. It is quite possible that the installing of a titular or ceremonial President would have a divisive rather than a unifying effect in Papua New Guinea.

11. It has been suggested to us that a mature and experienced person as a separate Head of State could act as an arbiter in constitutional disputes, or at least provide a source of advice to the Prime Minister in difficult times. We prefer to have constitutional matters dealt with as part of the political process — for example, in discussions or negotiations among Ministers and Parliamentary leaders, or in Parliamentary debate — or, in the last resort, by a constitutional court, rather than by a kind of father figure, whose own legitimacy may not be widely accepted.

12. Another argument put forward is that a separate Head of State could relieve the Prime Minister of some of the burdens of State ceremonial duties — such as giving speeches, laying foundation stones, opening new buildings and shows, and so on. But such duties, we believe, can and should be shared among the various Ministers and, for example, the Speaker as representative of the Parliament — a practice which would again emphasize the collective nature of our national leadership.

13. Finally, it is suggested that a separate Head of State would provide a degree of continuity in government, especially when there are political changes. We feel that the advantage of this can also be overstated: even titular Presidents are appointed for a set term, often 5 years. We have taken particular care in our recommendations to ensure an orderly transfer of power when political fortunes change.

The National Executive Council

14. We have therefore concluded that as there is no clearly demonstrable need for a Head of State, we should not create one merely because it is the usual thing to do. We believe that our proposal for vesting executive power in the National Executive Council, which comprises all Ministers, is most appropriate to our country.

GENERALLY

Referred to

by Frost C.J. in *The State v Mogo Wonom* [1975] PNGLR 311 at p.316; see also Raine J. at p.317 and Williams J. at p.320 (the Queen's functions are defined by the Constitution; the Head of State possesses no prerogative function to prosecute criminal offences).

83. — QUEEN'S SUCCESSORS

The provisions of this Constitution referring to the Queen extend to Her Majesty's heirs and successors in the sovereignty of the United Kingdom of Great Britain and Northern Ireland.

84. — PRECEDENCE

The Head of State takes precedence in rank over all other persons in Papua New Guinea, and the Governor-General takes precedence in rank immediately after the Head of State.

85. — ROYAL STYLE AND TITLES

The Style and Titles of the Head of State are as determined by Act of the Parliament, and until such an Act is made are —

Elizabeth II, Queen of Papua New Guinea and Her other Realms and Territories, Head of the Commonwealth.

Division 2. — Functions, etc., of the Head of State.

86. — FUNCTIONS, ETC.

(1) The privileges, powers, functions, duties and responsibilities of the Head of State are as prescribed by or under Constitutional Laws and Acts of the Parliament.

AS TO PREROGATIVE POWER OF HEAD OF STATE TO DISPENSE JUSTICE

per Williams J.

Section 82(1) of the Constitution provides that the Queen shall be 'Head of State'. Section 86(1) provides that the privileges, powers, functions, duties and responsibilities of the Head of State are as prescribed by or under Constitutional Laws and Acts of Parliament. A number of sections in the Constitution confer certain special powers and functions upon the Head of State. There appears to be no specific provision touching the matter now in issue.

By s.158 of the Constitution the judicial authority of the people is vested in the National Judicial System which, under s.155, consists of the Supreme Court, the National Court and such other courts as are established under s.172.

It is thus clear that the people have vested the administration of justice not in the Head of State but in the National Judicial System which consists of courts which the people themselves have created by the Constitution. This seems to me to be a clear and distinct departure from the English situation as explained by Blackstone where the people traditionally have entrusted the administration to the monarch and the courts created by him. It seems to me that a consideration of the provisions of the Constitution to which I have referred show that the position of the monarch in the system of justice in this country is completely different from the position in England and in other countries where the traditional concept is as expounded by Blackstone.

The power of judicature in this country lies in the people at large. This has been invested by the people in the courts established under the Constitution. I think it inappropriate that proceedings of a criminal nature should be brought in the name of the court, nor do I think

that proceedings should be in the name of the Public Prosecutor, whose functions are defined in s.177 of the Constitution, which, in their terms, appear inapt to meet the present situation. In my view it is appropriate that proceedings be brought by the people in their collective corporate name 'The State' (s.1).
The State v Mogo Wonom [1975] PNGLR 311 at p.320; see also Frost C.J. at p.315 and Raine J. at p.317.

(2) Except as provided by Section 96(2) (*terms and conditions of employment*), in the exercise and performance of his privileges, powers, functions, duties and responsibilities the Head of State shall act only with, and in accordance with the advice of the National Executive Council, or of some other body or authority prescribed by a Constitutional Law or an Act of the Parliament for a particular purpose as the body or authority in accordance with whose advice the Head of State is obliged, in a particular case, to act.

AS TO THE DISPLACEMENT OF THE PREROGATIVE EXERCISE OF EXECUTIVE AND JUDICAL ACTS

per Frost C.J.

Now under the Constitution the principles and rules of the common law which are adopted under Sch.2.2(1) (Adoption of Common Law) include the principles and rules relating to the Royal Prerogative, except (inter alia) to the extent that they are inconsistent with a Constitutional Law which, of course, includes the Constitution. (See Sch.2.2(1)(a) and (2); Sch.1.2). But an examination of the relevant constitutional provisions shows, in my opinion, that the powers associated with the structure of government exist only as defined therein, and thus to use the words of Quick and Garran in referring to the prerogative powers of the Governor-General in the Australian Constitution, have become 'detached from the prerogative'. *The Annotated Constitution of the Australian Commonwealth* 1901 at p.406.

The Constitution itself is a truly autochthonous Constitution established, as the preamble recites, by the will of the people, to whom 'all power belongs'. Its authority is thus original and in no way derivative from any other source. Unlike the case of Australia where the first settlers brought with them the common law, there is, to use the words of Sir Owen Dixon speaking of the American Constitution, 'no anterior law providing the source of juristic authority' for the institutions of government now established. (*The Common Law as an Ultimate Constitutional Foundation,* 31 A.L.J. 240). See also *Legislative, Executive and Judicial Powers in Australia*, Wynes (4th ed.) pp.362,364. Under the provisons of the Constitution, Her Majesty the Queen is established as the Head of State and, subject to the Constitution, the privileges, powers, functions, duties and responsibilities of the Head of State may be had, exercised and performed through a Governor-General. (s.82). But these functions, etc. of the Head of State are as prescribed under Constitutional Laws and Acts of Parliament (s.86(1)). (No prosecution function is prescribed). There is then a most significant provision that in the exercise of these functions the Head of State shall act only with, and in accordance with, the advice of the National Executive Council, or other body prescribed for the purpose. (s.86(1) and (2)). Functions thus expressly limited in their exercise can no longer be considered as part of the prerogative. (Quick and Garran (supra) at pp.404-406). The same conclusion also follows from the Structure of Government (s.99). That section provides that subject to and in accordance with the Constitution, the power, authority and jurisdiction of the People is to be exercised by the National Government (s.99(1)). It consists of three principal arms: the National Parliament — the Queen has no part —; the National Executive which consists of the Head of State acting in accordance with the advice of the National Executive Council, and the National Executive Council; and the National Judicial System, consisting of the Supreme Court, the National Court and other Courts (s.99(2), s.138 and s.139). It is significant that there is no power given to the Head of State to assent to Bills, to dissolve Parliament, or to dismiss the Prime Minister except on a motion of no confidence by the Parliament, s.142(5). There is no Commander-in-Chief of the Defence Force (s.201).

Leaving aside the legislative power, with which the Court is not concerned, whatever operation remains to be given to the express reservation of the principles and rules of the Royal Prerogative, under Sch.2.2(2), there is no provision for any prerogative executive acts. Further, the Royal Prerogative of the Monarch as the 'distributor' of justice has been displaced. (I refer to the passage from Blackstone citied by Williams J. in his judgment, which I have read). Accordingly the only conclusion open, in my opinion, is that the Head of State has no prerogative function under the Constitution to prosecute offences, whether that is considered an executive function as, in my opinion, it is, or a judicial function.
The State v Mogo Wonom [1975] PNGLR 311 at p.315; see also Raine J. at p.317, Williams J. at p.320.

'ADVICE' NOT EQUIVALENT TO 'RECOMMENDATION'

Held

'Advice' (as used in s.86(2) and (4)) has a different meaning than 'recommendation' in s.28(2) of the Constitution. A 'recommendation' need not be implemented and is not non-justiciable because of s.86(4).
The State v The Independent Tribunal, Ex parte Sasakila [1976] PNGLR 491; see Frost C.J. at p.500.

'ADVICE' NOT EQUIVALENT TO 'REPORT'

per Kapi J.

The question in this case is this: Is there any provision under the *Lands Acquisition Act* which requires or obliges the Head of State, as far as fixation of factor is concerned, to *act in accordance with* the advice of that body or authority?

Section 20 of the Act says that the Head of State may fix a factor 'after receiving a report from the Valuer-General'.

First, I do not see that the Head of State is obliged to act in accordance with this report. There is no such clear intention expressed in the section or in any other part of the Act.

Secondly, a *report* is not *advice* to the Head of State. (See judgment of Frost, C.J. in *The State v The Independent Tribunal; Ex parte Sasakila* [1976] PNGLR 491 at p.500)

A report of the Valuer-General does not come within the words of s.86(2) of the Constitution: '... or of some other body or authority prescribed by a Constitutional Law or an Act of the Parliament for a particular purpose as the body or authority in accordance with whose advice the Head of State is obliged, in a particular case, to act.'
Minister for Lands v Frame [1980] PNGLR 433 at pp.468, 469.

(3) Any instrument made by or in the name of the Head of State shall recite that it is made with, and in accordance with, the advice of the National Executive Council or of any other body or authority in accordance with whose advice the Head of State is obliged, in the particular case, to act, but failure to comply with this subsection does not affect the validity of an instrument.

(4) The question, what (if any) advice was given to the Head of State, or by whom, is non-justiciable.

NON-JUSTICIABLE

per Frost C.J.

[Referring to the purported dismissal of one Sasakila as a Minister and Member of Parliament by the Governor-General]

Stopping here, I should say that it was not questioned in these proceedings that the independent Tribunal was a body to which certiorari would lie. Insofar as it had the purported authority to dismiss, such a tribunal clearly had authority to determine questions affecting the rights of subjects; and whilst not conclusive, the applicability of the principles of natural justice as provided by the Constitution, s.28 (5), is one indication — there are others — that it also had a duty to act judicially, so that, in all the circumstances, the Tribunal is to be taken as subject to the controlling jurisdiction of the Court to issue the prerogative writ of certiorari. Apart from the constitutional significance of the dismissal of the prosecutor both as Minister and Member of Parliament, being made pursuant to an order by the Governor-General, both orders would be quashed for want of jurisdiction and error of law, and it would be open for this Court to make appropriate declaratory orders.

Accordingly it is necessary to consider the effect of the order being made by the Governor-General.

So far as the office of Minister is concerned, the relevant provisions are contained in the Constitution, s.144. That section, so far as is relevant to this case, provides for dismissal from office by the Head of State acting with, and in accordance with, the advice of the Prime Minister; or in accordance with Div.III.2. (*Leadership Code*) Subsection (4)(a) and (b). The section must be read with s.86(4) which provides that the question, what (if any) advice was given to the Head of State, or by whom, is non-justiciable. The significance of that provision is stated in the Constitution, Sch.1.7, which provides that the question may not be heard or determined by any Court or Tribunal.

Turning now to the Instrument of Dismissal by the Governor-General, the Minister can have no redress insofar as his dismissal from office as Minister is based on the invalid recommentation by the Tribunal. The reason is that the Instrument not only recites the recommendation from the appropriate Tribunal, but goes further and recites, as an additional ground, that the Governor-General has acted with, and in accordance with, the advice of the Prime Minister, and as any question concerning the nature of that advice is beyond the power of this Court the prosecutor's dismissal from his ministry must stand.

But the same defect does not apply to the prosecutor's dismissal as a Member of Parliament. The only relevant way in which the seat of Member of Parliament becomes vacant is by dismissal from office under Div. III.2.(*Leadership Code*). Constitution, s.104(2). The question is whether the Court can go behind the dismissal by the Governor-General if it is made pursuant to a recommendation which is null and void. If that recommendation amounts to advice which is non-justiciable the Member may be left without redress. Here the terms in which the Constitution is drafted are not entirely clear. The Constitution, s.28(2), provides that in the case of certain limited classes of persons to whom the Leadership Code applies, which include Members of the Parliament, the independent Tribunal shall make any recommendation to the Head of State, and then goes on to provide that the Head of State shall act in accordance with the *advice* of the independent Tribunal. The reason for the use of the term 'advice' rather than 'recommendation', it would appear, is to be found in s.86(2), which provides that in the exercise of his powers, functions etc., the Head of State shall act only with and in accordance with the advice of the National Executive Council or some other body or authority prescribed by law. Section 28(2) is in conformity with that provision. But when one turns to s.28(3), which is concerned with recommendations made by the Tribunal in the case of other classes of leaders found guilty of misconduct, the same words are used, although the recommendations are not in these cases made to the Head of State but to the appropriate appointing authority. In the latter section there would seem to be no constitutional requirement for the word 'advice' to carry any meaning other than recommendation.

I think it has to be accepted that, so far as s.28(2) and (3) are concerned the provision for the Head of State and the appropriate authority respectively, as the person and body to whom any recommendations are to be made, and the consequent obligations to take action accordingly, are to be taken as self-executing. Now there would appear to be no reason why an order for dismissal implementing an invalid recommendation should be free from attack in the ordinary way if made by an appointing authority who is not the Head of State. So a leader to whom s.28(3) applies, who is found guilty of an act of misconduct, could succeed in those circumstances in having the order for dismissal set aside. But if the word 'advice' in s.28(2) is given its constitutional meaning as provided in s.86(4), and the recommendations acted on by the Head of State are not justiciable, a leader to whom that subsection applies, if found guilty of the same act of misconduct in office, would be left with no redress if the recommendation were invalid.

To adopt an interpretation which produces such a discriminatory result would not, in my opinion, be to accord the provisions of s.28(2) their fair and liberal meaning as required under the Consitution, Sch.1.5(2).

A further pointer to the justiciability of recommendations upon which the Head of State must act under s.28(2) arises from the provision in s.28(5) that proceedings under sub-s.(1)(g), whilst not judicial proceedings, are subject to the principles of natural justice. (The precise implications of the proceedings not being judicial were not argued. The provision may be sufficient to exclude the National Court's power of review under Constitution, s.155(3)(a)). The provision bringing in the principles of natural justice would be quite ineffective unless an order for dismissal or other penalty could be impugned and set aside in the case, for example of a leader who, in his absence and without any opportunity of being heard, and thus in breach of the principles of natural justice, was found guilty of misconduct in office. The remedy could be found in the Court's inherent power to grant relief — Constitution, s.155(4).

Section 28(5) is therefore a strong indication that a recommendation is not finally conclusive against a leader but is justiciable, and that proceedings may be brought to set aside an order made either by the Head of State or other appointing authority pursuant to a recommendation alleged to be invalid.

In an endeavour to find a solution I do not consider that this Court should proceed to cut down the force of the meaning of non-justiciability. The answer, I consider, is to be found by looking at the purpose of s.86(4). That provision is certainly to be given the plenary operation of putting beyond the scrutiny of the Courts the question of what advice (if any) is given by the National Executive Council to the Head of State. But the provision seems inappropriate to the proceedings of an independent Tribunal which acts judicially, conducts its hearings in public, and makes public its decision supported by reasons.

The conclusion I have come to is that so far as the obligation of the Head of State to act on the recommendation of such a Tribunal is concerned, special and exclusive provision is made for that subject-matter in s.28, and the general provisions of s.86, except possibly sub-s.(3) which is concerned with the form of instruments, have no application. The terms of the order of dismissal which recite merely the receipt of a recommendation from the appropriate Tribunal without the use of the term 'advice' indicates that the draftsman probably took the same view. The order is thus not saved from invalidity.

The State v The Independent Tribunal, Ex parte Sasakila [1976] PNGLR 491 at pp.499-501; see also Saldanha J. at pp.504, 505 and Kearney J. at p.507, both adopting the analysis of Frost C.J.

REGULATION MADE BY HEAD OF STATE ACTING ON ADVICE: WHETHER REGULATION MAY BE CHALLENGED IN JUDICIAL PROCEEDINGS

per Pratt J.

Section 20 of the Act stipulates that the Governor-General in Council, after a report is received from the Valuer-General, may by way of regulation 'fix a factor' to be used for the purpose of arriving at a final figure, such factor being the multiplying 'factor' referred to in s. 19(1)(c)(i).

In support of this appeal, Mr. Lucas spent some time developing an argument based on s.86(4) of the Constitution, which says that the nature of the advice given to the Head of State is non-justiciable. I could not then, and I still cannot, appreciate the point of this submission. At no stage has the respondent ever concerned himself with whether or not the Governor-General received advice, or whether or not it was given to him by the Valuer-General or someone else. There was never any attack, on what took place between the Governor-General and any other persons. It is not the advice, or what was contained in that advice, or who gave that advice which forms the point of contention before this Court. What is contended is that the final figure, determined upon by the Governor-General is an incorrect figure. It is the result of the advice, the conclusion reached following consideration of whatever, if any, advice the Governor-General received which is the point in issue. In my view, the question of non-justiciability simply does not arise.

The Governor-General, of course, must act on the advice which he receives. There is no discretion vested in him as Head of State (the Constitution, s.86(2)). Having received advice, the Governor-General then gazettes the result of that advice — in this instance a figure to be used as a multiplier, by way of regulation to operate under the Act. Like any other regulation, it is of course subject to the Act and must not be ultra vires the Act. It is this figure which the Minister is obliged to use under s.22 of the *Lands Acquisition Act* for the purpose of arriving at the amount of compensation payable to the claimant. To maintain that because the Governor-General has caused a regulation to be published in the

Gazette following on advice, and because the advice received by the Governor-General is non-justiciable means that no consequent regulation can be challenged as ultra vires is a proposition of law so fundamentally misconceived as to warrant no further consideration. *Minister for Lands v Frame* [1980] PNGLR 433 at pp.476,477; see also Greville Smith J. at pp.438-440, but see Kapi J. (dissenting) at p.469 (below).

per Kapi J. (dissenting)

It therefore follows from s.86(2) of the Constitution that the Head of State *shall* act in accordance with the *advice* of *the National Executive Council.*

This is in fact, what happened in the statutory instrument (regulation) fixing the factor for this case. The regulation recites: 'Made by the Head of State, acting with and in accordance with the *advice of the National Executive Council*, after receiving a report from the Valuer-General, under the *Lands Acquisition Act* 1974.'

It follows, from the provision of s.86(2) that the Governor-General acted in accordance with the advice of the National Executive Council. Under s.86(4) and Sch.1.7 questions concerning the nature of that advice is (sic) beyond the power of this Court. In *The State v The Independent Tribunal; Ex parte Sasakila* [1976] PNGLR 491 at p.499, Frost C.J., in considering the advice of the Prime Minister, said:

> The reason is that the Instrument not only recites the recommendation from the appropriate Tribunal, but goes further and recites, as an additional ground, that the Governor-General has acted with, and in accordance with, the advice of the Prime Minister, and as any question concerning the nature of that advice is beyond the power of this Court the prosecutor's dismissal from his ministry must stand.

In this case, the Governor-General acted in accordance with the advice of the National Executive Council. This Court cannot question the advice of the National Executive Council. The fixation of the factor must stand.

It has been suggested in argument that when the court changes the factor on appeal it is not questioning the advice of the Governor-General. I find this difficult to accept in view of the clear provisions of s.86 and Sch.1.7 of the Constitution. What the Governor-General does in this case is in *accordance with advice*. When the court questions the factor it is questioning the advice in accordance with which he has acted.

Minister for Lands v Frame [1980] PNGLR 433 at p.469, but see Pratt J. at pp.476, 477(above) and Greville Smith J. at pp.438-440.

Division 3. — Appointment, etc., of Governor-General.

87. — QUALIFICATIONS FOR APPOINTMENT

(1) The Governor-General must be a citizen who —
   (a) is qualified to be a member of the Parliament (except for the reason that be occupies the office of Governor-General); and
   (b) is a mature person of good standing who enjoys the general respect of the community.

(2) The question, whether for the purposes of Subsection (1) a person is a person to whom Subsection (1) (b) applies, is non-justiciable.

(3) The Governor-General must not hold any office or position or engage in any calling other than that of, or an office or position associated with, his office as Governor-General, except with the consent of the Head of State, acting with, and in accordance with, the joint advice of the National Executive Council and the Ombudsman Commission.

GENERALLY

Referred to

by Pritchard J. in *Constitutional Reference No 1. of 1978 (s.19)* [1978] PNGLR 345 at p.374.

(4) A request for the consent of the Head of State under Subsection (3) shall not be made unless agreement on the matter in relation to which the consent is sought has been reached between the National Executive Council and the Ombudsman Commission.

GENERALLY

Referred to

by Pritchard J. in *Constitutional Reference No 1 of 1978 (s.19)* [1978] PNGLR 345 at p.374.

(5) No person is eligible for appointment as Governor-General more than once unless the Parliament, by two-thirds absolute majority vote, approves appointment for a second term, but no person is eligible for appointment for a third term.

88. — APPOINTMENT TO OFFICE.

(1) Except in the case of the first Governor-General appointed before Independence Day the Governor-General shall be appointed by the Head of State, acting with, and in accordance with, the advice of the National Executive Council given in accordance with a decision of the Parliament.

(2) A decision of the Parliament to nominate a person for appointment as Governor-General shall be made by a simple majority vote, in an exhaustive secret ballot conducted in accordance with an Organic Law.

(*See: Organic Law on the Nomination of the Governor-General Ch.1*)

(3) Subject to Subsection (5), the Speaker shall, within the period of three months before the completion of the normal term of office of the Governor-General, call a meeting of the Parliament to nominate the next Governor-General.

(4) Subject to Subsection (5), in the event of a casual vacancy in the office of Governor-General the Speaker shall, as soon as practicable, call a meeting of the Parliament to nominate the next Governor-General.

(5) If —
  (a) at a time when a meeting of the Parliament should otherwise be called under Subsection (3) or (4) a general election to the Parliament has been ordered; or
  (b) between the time when a meeting of the Parliament should otherwise be called under Subsection (3) and the date of the completion of the normal term of office of the outgoing Governor-General a general election to the Parliament is due to be held in accordance with this Constitution,

the Speaker shall not call a meeting of the Parliament in accordance with Subsection (3) or (4), as the case may be, and a nomination shall be made at the first meeting of the new Parliament as its first item of business after any formal business and the election of a Speaker.

89. — ASSUMPTION OF OFFICE.

Notwithstanding Section 90 (*Declaration of Loyalty, etc.*) for the purposes of this Constitution a person appointed as Governor-General takes office —
(a) subject to paragraph (b), at the end of his predecessor's term of office; or
(b) if he is appointed to fill a casual vacancy — on the date of his appointment.

90. — DECLARATION OF LOYALTY, ETC.

(1) Before entering upon the duties of his office, a Governor-General shall take the Oath of Allegiance and make the Declaration of Loyalty and the Declaration of Office before the Chief Justice and in the presence of the Parliament, but during a period of declared national emergency they may be taken and made in such manner as is directed by the National Executive Council.

(2) If the Governor-General has not complied with Subsection(1) before taking office —
  (a) he is suspended from office until such time as he does so; and
  (b) if he does not do so at the first reasonably available opportunity, he may be dismissed from office by the Head of State, acting with, and in accordance with, the advice of the National Executive Council given in accordance with a decision of the Parliament, and in that event is not eligible for reappointment for a period of six years.

91. — NORMAL TERM OF OFFICE

Unless he earlier dies, resigns, ceases to be qualified for office in accordance with Section 87 (*qualifications for appointment*), is dismissed under Section 90 (*Declaration of Loyalty, etc.*), or 93(1) (*dismissal from office*), or is removed from office under Section 93(2) (*dismissal from office*), the Governor-General holds office for a term of six years from the date of his assumption of office in accordance with Section 89 (*assumption of office*), plus any period that is required, in accordance with Section 88(5) (*appointment to office*), for the appointment of the next Governor-General.

92. — RESIGNATION.

(1) The Governor-General may resign from office by notice in writing to the Head of State.

(2) The resignation takes effect on its acceptance by the Head of State, acting with, and in accordance with, the advice of the National Executive Council.

93. — DISMISSAL AND REMOVAL FROM OFFICE.

(1) The Governor-General may be dismissed from office by the Head of State, acting with, and in accordance with, the advice of the National Executive Council given in accordance with either —
(a) a decision of the National Executive Council; or
(b) a decision made by an absolute majority of the Parliament.

(2) The Governor-General may be removed from office by the Head of State, acting with, and in accordance with, the advice of the National Executive Council given in accordance with a decision of the Parliament, if the Speaker advises the Parliament that two medical practitioners appointed for the purpose by the National authority responsible for the registration or licensing of medical practitioners have jointly reported to the Speaker that, in their professional opinions, the Governor-General is unfit, by reason of physical or mental incapacity, to carry out the duties of his office.

94. — SUSPENSION FROM OFFICE.

(1) The Governor-General may be suspended from office —
(a) by the National Executive Council, if he refuses or fails to act in accordance with the advice of the National Executive Council or of any other body or authority in accordance with whose advice he is obliged, in the particular case, to act, or acts, or purports to act contrary to, or without, any such advice; or
(b) in accordance with an Act of the Parliament pending an investigation for the purposes of Section 93(2) (*dismissal and removal from office*),

and pending any resultant action by the Parliament.

(2) If the Governor-General is suspended from office by the National Executive Council under Subsection (1)(a), the Prime Minister shall immediately inform the Speaker of the suspension and of the reasons for it.

(3) If the Governor-General is suspended from office under Subsection (1)(a) —
   (a) the Speaker shall, as soon as practicable, call a meeting of the Parliament at which the matter of the suspension and of the possible dismissal of the Governor-General shall be the first item of business after any formal business and, if necessary, the appointment of a Speaker; and
   (b) the suspension may be lifted at any time by decision of the Parliament; and
   (c) unless before the end of the meeting a recommendation is made in accordance with Section 93(1) (*dismissal and removal from office*) that the Governor-General be dismissed from office, the suspension ceases at the end of the meeting.

(4) If the Governor-General is suspended from office under this section, the Prime Minister shall, as soon as practicable, inform the Head of State of the suspension and of the reasons for it.

(5) A period of suspension under this section shall be taken into account in calculating for the purposes of this Division, the length of the period of service in office of the Governor-General.

95. — ACTING GOVERNOR-GENERAL.

(1) In this section, a reference to the Speaker or to the Chief Justice shall be read as a reference to the substantive holder of that office.

(2) If —
   (a) there is a vacancy in the office of Governor-General; or
   (b) the Governor-General is suspended from office; or
   (c) the Governor-General is —
      (i) on leave of absence; or
      (ii) absent from the country; or
      (iii) out of speedy and effective communication; or
      (iv) otherwise unable to perform, or is not readily available to perform, the duties of his office,

the Speaker is, subject to Subsection (3), the Acting Governor-General.

(3) If at any time to which Subsection (2) applies —
   (a) there is a vacancy in the office of Speaker; or
   (b) the Speaker is suspended from office; or
   (c) the Speaker is
      (i) on leave of absence; or
      (ii) absent from the country; or

(iii) out of speedy and effective communication; or
(iv) otherwise unable to perform, or is not readily available to perform, the duties of his office,

the Chief Justice (if he is a citizen) is the Acting Governor-General.

(4) During any period when he is the Acting Governor-General, the Speaker or the Chief Justice shall not exercise or perform any of the other powers, functions, duties and responsibilities of the office of Speaker or Chief Justice as the case may be, except that the Chief Justice may complete any proceedings actually commenced before him unless other suitable arrangements can be made.

(5) When neither the Speaker nor the Chief Justice is available (or, in the case of the Chief Justice, qualified) to be the Acting Governor-General, the powers, functions, duties and responsibilities of the Governor-General shall be exercised and performed by a Minister appointed by the Head of State on the advice of the National Executive Council for the purpose.

(6) The question, whether the occasion for the exercise or performance of a power, function, duty or responsibility by an Acting Governor-General or a Minister under this section has arisen or has ceased, is non-justiciable.

96. — TERMS AND CONDITIONS OF EMPLOYMENT.

(1) Subject to this Constitution, the terms and conditions of employment of the Governor-General are as determined by or under an Organic Law.

(*See: Organic Law on the terms and conditions of employment of the Governor-General Ch.1*).

(2) Except with the consent of the Governor-General the terms and conditions of employment of the Governor-General shall not be changed to his detriment during his term of office, and an Organic Law that so changes them shall recite the terms of the consent.

Division 4. — General

97. — CONVEYANCE OF DECISIONS.

Where any act is done, decision is made or advice is given by the Parliament or the National Executive Council under this Part, the Prime Minister shall immediately convey it to the Head of State.

98. — ACTS, ETC., OF THE HEAD OF STATE.

Unless the contrary intention appears, any act by the Head of State takes effect when it is formally advised to the Prime Minister or the National Executive Council.

PART IV — THE NATIONAL GOVERNMENT

Division 1. — General Principles

99. — STRUCTURE OF GOVERNMENT

(1) Subject to and in accordance with this Constitution, the power, authority and jurisdiction of the People shall be exercised by the National Government.

GENERALLY

Referred to

by Pritchard J. in *Constitutional Reference No 1 of 1978 (s.19)* [1978] PNGLR 345 at p.378.

(2) The National Government consists of three principal arms, namely:—
- (a) the National Parliament, which is an elective legislature with, subject to the Constitutional Laws, unlimited powers of law-making; and
- (b) the National Executive; and
- (c) the National Judicial System, consisting of a Supreme Court of Justice and a National Court of Justice, of unlimited jurisdiction, and other courts.

AS TO WHETHER THE PUBLIC SOLICITOR IS AN ARM OF THE NATIONAL GOVERNMENT

per Prentice C.J.

An 'arm of Government' would normally be an instrumentality which acts on behalf of the government. An arm acts under the control of the body of which it is part. For myself I cannot see how as a matter of fact, the Public Solicitor in carrying out his duties to advise and represent clients can be envisaged as carrying out work on behalf of or for the government.

In endeavouring to find the conceptual basis of the powers of the Public Solicitor, one refers to s.99 of the Constitution which asserts the 'power, authority and jurisdiction' of the people is to be 'exercised by the National Government'. But this is 'subject to and in accordance with the Constitution'. The Constitution and Organic Laws have created and vested powers and responsibilities in certain organisations and offices, such as Public Prosecutor, Public Solicitor, Committee of Mercy and Public Accounts Committee.

Insofar as such bodies are created independent of direction and control, they would seem to be exercising the power of the people given to them as a direct grant by the Constitution and Organic Laws and their exercise of powers could not I think be said to be an exercise of power 'by the National Government' in such a sense as would by itself constitute any of them 'an arm' of the National Government, or department or agency or instrumentality thereof within the meaning of s.219 and Sch.1.2 of the Constitution.

That the Public Solitor is not 'an arm of government', appears I consider, in the Constitutional provisions establishing the office. Section 176(1) establishes the office, that is, he is a creature of the people not of Parliament. His appointment (s.176(2)) is by the Judicial and Legal Services Commission, itself also a creature of the people (s.183) and not of the Parliament. And s.176(5) enacts that 'Subject to Section 177(2) (functions of the Public Prosecutor and the Public Solicitor), in the performance of his functions under this Constitution, the Public Solicitor is not subject to direction or control by any person or authority'.
Constitutional Reference No 1 of 1978 (s.19) [1978] PNGLR 345 at p.350; see also Wilson J. at p.361 but see Pritchard J. (dissenting) at p.384 (below).

per Pritchard J. (dissenting)

This concept of government is somewhat like a play. You have the principal actors and the supporting cast. 'Principal' means (*Concise Oxford Dictionary*) 'First in rank or importance, chief, main, leading.' The supporting cast sustains and gives strength to the principals, but each of course plays an independent role and the totality of the performers comprise the whole of the cast. If our Constitution-makers envisaged the traditional English concept of three arms of Government only, the word 'principal' need never have appeared in s.99. As I have said earlier, the Public Solicitor, Public Prosecutor and the Judicial and Legal Services Commission are created as part of the National Government under Pt. VI of the Constitution, not one of them is created under any of the three principal arms, each one is separate and each has a distinct responsibility to the people as a part of the whole of the National Government, the vast majority of their functions being directly related to the administration of justice and the judicial system.
Constitutional Reference No 1 of 1978 (s.19) [1978] PNGLR 345 at p.384; but see Prentice C.J. (above) at p.350, Wilson J. at p.361.

GENERALLY

Referred to

by Frost C.J. in *The State v Mogo Wonom* [1975] PNGLR 311 at p.316 (the Head of State is not a separate component of the National Government);

by Kearney J. in *Peter v South Pacific Brewery Ltd* [1976] PNGLR 537 at p.560 (National Parliament's unlimited powers of law making are subject to Constitutional Laws by reason of s.99(2)(a)).

(3) In principle, the respective powers and functions of the three arms shall be kept separate from each other.

COURT NOT TO ASSUME THE ROLE OF THE LEGISLATURE

per Kearney J.

In my opinion, Constitution s.10 must be applied in the light of other provisions in the Constitution, in particular s.99(3); it does not warrant an incursion by the Court upon the law-making power of Parliament, so as to create, by reading down, an Act which differs in its substance from that passed by Parliament. The Court's function remains one of construction, the ascertaining of Parliamentary intention however conjectural, and not one of legislation.
Peter v South Pacific Brewery Ltd [1976] PNGLR 537 at p.560; see also Frost C.J. at p.546.

per Miles J.

[If] the word 'application' [in s.19] were to have the wide meaning contended for, it would be difficult to see where the limits of the Supreme Court's function in being required to give advisory opinions would lie. The constitutional bodies and office holders entitled to apply under the Constitution, s.19, derive their existence from constitutional laws. The day to day carrying out of their functions involves the implementation and in a sense the 'application' of constitutional laws. However, it is in my view not consistent with the responsibility bestowed upon such bodies and office holders that they should be at liberty to require the Supreme Court to give an opinion on all matters concerning the carrying out of their functions, or in other words, the implementation of the constitutional provisions by which they are established. If this was what was intended, it would amount in effect to what has been described and condemned in the United States as 'government by judiciary' (see Crawshaw *The High Court of Australia and Advisory Opinions* (1977) 51 A.L.J. 112) which is something the Constitution of Papua New Guinea seeks in principle to avoid: the Constitution, s.99. Again it may be of some significance to note that in other countries where courts are given an advisory opinion jurisdiction, it is usually confined to questions of constitutional validity.
S.C.R. No 2 of 1981; Re s.19 of the Constitution [1981] PNGLR 518 at pp.528,529.

Referred to

by Kapi J. in *Avia Aihi v The State* [1981] PNGLR 81 at p.107 (courts not to intrude into the legislative arena.)

LEGISTURE PROHIBITED FROM USURPING THE JUDICIAL FUNCTION

per Kearney Dep.C.J.

I consider that any Act which requires a court to record a plea of guilty to an offence in circumstances in which the court is not first required to be satisfied, in its independent judgment, that the person charged wishes freely and with full understanding to admit his guilt, amounts to a usurpation by the legislative arm of government of a function reserved by the Constitution to the judicial arm of government; and is accordingly unconstitutional and a nullity, of no legal effect. I respectfully agree with the Chief Justice that the procedure set out in the provisions referred to do not amount to the summary hearing required by the proviso to the Constitution, s.37(5) and are unconstitutional for that reason. But more fundamentally, I think, they are unconstitutional because they amount to an exercise by the legislature of the judicial authority of the people in respect of criminal offences, which by the Constitution s.158(1) is vested exclusively in the National Judicial System. It is of course true that judicial authority may be conferred on other tribunals under the Constitution s.159, but that is irrelevant for present purposes, since s.159(3) prevents any such tribunal from imposing any penalty for a criminal offence.

It is clear from its structure that the Constitution contemplates a general separation of powers between the three principal arms of government — the legislature, executive and judiciary; see the Constitution s.99. As a parliamentary system with an executive responsible to Parliament, the separation of powers between the arms cannot be rigid. But the separation principle remains of basic importance in the Constitution and prohibits incursions by one arm of government upon basic functions of another. The legislation presently in question, I think, is an example of the legislature having gone too far in prescribing rules which control judicial decisions in certain cases, thus invading the realm of judicial power. It is of the essence of the judicial function that the court, when considering whether a plea of guilty should be recorded, brings to bear its own independent judgment as to whether materials put before it are probative of guilt, whether they bear that character; and also as to whether a defendant fully and freely is waiving his right to a trial, in which he cannot be convicted unless all the elements of the offence are proved against him to the required standard of proof, and is unequivocally admitting every element of the offence. The fact that the evisceration of the essential judicial function in considering whether a plea of guilty should be recorded, is achieved by the surgical knife of procedure, does not affect the character of what was done; what cannot be done directly, cannot be done indirectly. Here there are, in truth, no judicial functions for the court to perform; the legislation has wholly absorbed the judicial process.
S.C.R. No 1A of 1981; Re Motor Traffic Act [1982] PNGLR 122 at p.134; see also Kidu C.J. at p.129, Andrew J. at p.138, and Kapi J. at p.138.

(4) Subsection (2) is descriptive only and is non-justiciable.

Division 2. — The National Parliament

Subdivision A. — The Legislative Power.

100. — EXERCISE OF THE LEGISLATIVE POWER.

(1) Subject to this Constitution, the legislative power of the People is vested in the National Parliament.

C.P.C. Report Ch.6 p.1

1. In the kind of participatory democracy we envisage for Papua New Guinea, with maximum emphasis on consultation and consensus, the national legislature must clearly have a central role. We believe that while the executive must be given every opportunity to provide strong leadership in reshaping our new nation to meet the needs and aspirations of our people, it is important also that this leadership does not become autocratic so that the legislature becomes a mere rubber stamp. If government is to be truly responsive to the people, it is vital that those whom the people elect to represent them should be able to contribute actively and effectively to the government of the nation. The legislature should not be seen as a rival to the executive arm, but rather as a full and constructive partner. It can then help to ensure the overall effectiveness of government by keeping the executive accountable to the people. This is the approach that underlies our proposals.

AS TO LIMITS TO LEGISLATIVE POWER: CONSTITUTION SUPREME

per Kapi J.

The legislative power is vested in the National Parliament (s.20 of the Constitution). This power, however, is made subject to the other provisions of the Constitution. Where restrictions or limitations are placed by the Constitution, the Parliament may only legislate within these bounds; or where the Constitution provides for something, no Act of Parliament may be passed so as to be inconsistent with that provision. Where there is such inconsistency, the Act, as to the inconsistency, is invalid and ineffective. This is because the Constitution is the supreme law.
Minister for Lands v Frame [1980] PNGLR 433 at pp.470,471.

Referred to

by Frost C.J. in *Peter v South Pacific Brewery Ltd* [1976] PNGLR 537 at p.541;

by Miles J. in *S.C.R. No 4 of 1980; Re petition of M.T. Somare* [1981] PNGLR 265 at p.298.

COURTS NOT TO INTRUDE INTO LEGISLATURE'S AREA OF AUTHORITY

Referred to

by Frost C.J. in *Peter v South Pacific Brewery Ltd* [1976] PNGLR 537 at pp.546,550 (courts have no share in the exercise of legislative power);

by Prentice Dep.C.J. in *Reference No 1 of 1977* [1977] PNGLR 362 at p.377 (legislative power is vested in Parliament not the Courts; Courts should not imply terms in legislation which would substantially add to rights conferred thereby);

by Prentice Dep.C.J. in *Constitutional Reference No 1 of 1978 (s.19)* [1978] PNGLR 345 at p.367;

by Greville Smith J. (dissenting) in *Avia Aihi v The State* [1981] PNGLR 81 at p.98 (Supreme Court may not exercise inherent jurisdiction under s.155(2)(b) of the Constitution to over-ride a provision of a validly enacted statute); see also Kapi J. at p.111 (a longer note of *Avia Aihi* appears under ss.155(2) and (4) hereafter);

by Kapi J. in *Re James Allan Sannga; Peter Timereke v Duncan Ferrie and anor* (1983 Unreported) SC255 at pp.42-43; but see Kidu C.J. (Andrew J. concurring) at pp.16,17.

AS TO STANDING TO CHALLENGE CONSTITUTIONAL VALIDITY OF STATUTES

per Kapi J.

> As to what is sufficient interest, I would adopt the objective test laid down by Lord Denning in *R. v Inland Revenue Commissioners; Ex parte National Federation of Self-Employed and Small Businesses Ltd* [1980] 2 A11 ER 378. It is not possible to lay down a workable definition for all cases because each case is different. I would leave it to courts to develop the appliction of the rule in individual cases.
>
> Applying this to the present case I find that Mr. Somare would have standing. As a member of the Parliament he belongs to the governmental body which has been invested with the power of law-making by the Constitution. In relation to the issue in this case, Mr. Somare has raised, amongst other things, that the law-making body has not complied with certain provisions of the Constitution in passing the *Defence Force (Presence Abroad) Act* 1980.
>
> If anyone has interest in the matter it is the members of the legislature who make the laws. It cannot be said that he is a mere busybody meddling in other people's affairs. He, as a member of the Parliament, has standing and can bring this matter to court.
>
> *S.C.R. No 4 of 1980; Re petition of M.T. Somare* [1981] PNGLR 265 at p.295; see also Kidu C.J. at pp.273,274, Miles J. at pp.300-311, but see Kearney Dep.C.J. (dissenting) at pp.275,276, Greville Smith J. (dissenting) at pp.279-284. For more detailed analysis of this topic see under s.18(1).

GENERALLY

Referred to

by Pritchard J. in *In re Moresby North East Election Petition* [1977] PNGLR 429 at p.446 (power of Parliament to pass an ordinary Act on the same subject matter as the Constitution directs that an Organic Act be made).

(2) Subsection (1) does not prevent a law from conferring on an authority other than the Parliament legislative powers or functions (including, if the law so provides, a further power or further powers of delegation and subdelegaton).

(3) Nothing in any Constitutional Law enables or may enable the Parliament to transfer permanently, or divest itself of, legistive power.

DIVESTING OF POWER

Comment

Section 26 of the *Organic Law on Provincial Government* provides that, except in certain cases no relevant to this note, the National Parliament has no power to make an Act on a subject defined by the Organic Law as being 'primarily Provincial'. Section 26 would appear to offend s.100(3) and is, in the authors' opinion, accordingly unconstitutional and invalid.

Subdivision B — Composition of the National Parliament.

101. — MEMBERSHIP

(1) Subject to this section, the Parliament is a single-chamber legislature, consisting of —
  (a) a number of members elected from single-member open electorates; and
  (b) a number of members elected from single-member provincial electorates; and
  (c) not more than three nominated members, appointed and holding office in accordance with Section 102 (*nominated members*).

(2) An Organic Law shall make provision for the number of open and provincial electorates.

(*See: Organic Law on National Elections.*)

(3) No member may represent two or more electorates at the same time.

(4) The precise number of open electorates and of provincial electorates and their boundaries shall be determined from time to time in accordance with Section 125 (*electorates*).

(5) An alteration to the number of electorates or to the boundaries of an electorate takes effect for the purposes of the next general election and of succeeding elections.

C.P.C. Report Ch.6 p. 1

The National Parliament

2. To signify the break with the colonial past, and to emphasise the national character of the legislature, we propose that the House of Assembly be renamed the 'National Parliament'.

3. We have considered four basic questions concerning the composition of the National Parliament —
  (a) Should there continue to be only one house, or should there be an upper house as well?
  (b) Should all members be elected, or should some be nominated?
  (c) Should 'regional' electorates be retained, or should there be only 'open' electorates?
  (d) How many members should there be?

(a) One house or two

4. Although there is some attraction in the idea of a house of review, we are not convinced that a second chamber of parliament would, in practice, perform the task for which it was intended. Experience elsewhere indicates that it is by no means certain that the results would justify the expense or the much more cumbersome legislative process that a second house would entail. We have concluded that by strengthening the present legislature to make it a more effective organ of government, and by establishing also an effective system of provincial government, such case as may exist for a second house would be very substantially diminished. We therefore recommend that the National Parliament should consist of a single house.

(b) Nominated members

5. Following recommendations in the Final Report of the Second Select Committee on Constitutional Development, an amendment to the *Papua New Guinea Act* in 1971 provided that, in addition to the 100 elected members in the House of Assembly —

(a) the Administrator could choose up to four official members; and

(b) if the House decided by a two-thirds majority, a select committee could be appointed to nominate, in consultation with the Administrator, up to three further persons who would become members if approved by the vote of a simple majority of the House.

The provision for official members was removed when Papua New Guinea became self-governing on 1 December 1973. The provision for nominated members remains.

6. The case usually put forward for having nominated members is that it provides the opportunity for bringing into the parliament persons either with special qualifications or experience not available among the elected members, or from particular groups not otherwise represented. In its two years of office the present government has taken no initiative in this matter, nor has any interest in the possibility of nominating members been shown in the House. There has been, we believe, a general reluctance to see any breach of the principle that members of the legislature should be elected by the people, and a feeling that, in any case, there is no real practical need for nominated members. The Committee shares these views and, [p.2] having found public opinion divided on the issue of nominated members in the parliament, we recommend that all members be elected under a system of universal suffrage, as in practice they are at present.

(c) Regional electorates

7. In each of the three Houses of Assembly since 1964 there have [been] two kinds of members. Most members have represented open electorates for which there have been no special qualifications. In 1964, there were also 10 'special' electorates reserved for expatriate candidates. In 1968, these were abolished and replaced by 15 'regional' electorates, and this number was increased to 18, one for each administrative district, in 1972. In addition to normal qualifications, a candidate for a regional electorate has had to have the 'Intermediate Certificate', or its equivalent. This usually meant having completed a third year at high school. As mentioned in the Report of the Second Select Committee on Constitutional Development (p.4 para.27) in 1971, there was some call at that time for the removal of regional electorates. The Select Committee found this to be a minority view, and so it was in the House when a motion to abolish them, stongly supported by the present Chief Minister, was defeated.

8. Over the past three years there has been a considerable shift in opinion on this matter. From submissions made to the Committee it is clear a majority in most parts of the country now want regional electorates abolished. From discussion at our public meetings we have found that many people do not understand why there should be two kinds of member representing the same area, nor do they consider this as necessary. It is clear also that in many instances it has been very difficult for the regional member to make himself known in all parts of his electorate.

9. To these points may be added the fact that the original reason for regional electorates has been largely invalidated by the increasing number of well educated members returned from open electorates. This trend is bound to continue. We accept that the time has come for the abolition of regional electorates, and it is of note that none of the six regional members on our Committee dissented from the decision to make this recommendation.

(d) How many members

10. There are a number of factors to be considered in arriving at an appropriate number of members: cost and the efficiency of parliament, the opportunity for real participation by its members, the need to provide sufficient variety of talent. But, ultimately, the major factor in our country is adequacy of representation. In submissions to the Committee there has been widespread support for the idea of replacing regional electorates with open electorates, thereby maintaining the present total of 100 elected members. A significant minority, however, favoured more than 100 electorates. The most common reason given for an increase was that existing electorates are too large for members to travel around easily to visit the people.

11. We believe that there is a strong case for increasing the total number of open electorates to about 100, or a little more. However, this should not necessarily mean that the regional electorate should be replaced by an additional open electorate in every district. There should be some flexibility in the total number prescribed so as to provide adequately for the application of relevant criteria in the drawing of electoral boundaries by an independent commission. We refer to this commission and the drawing of boundaries later. We feel also that there should be an odd number of members. This should help to preclude a situation where a government cannot be formed because of a stalemate in an evenly divided parliament.

12. We therefore recommend that the National Parliament comprise not less than 101 nor more than 107 members, the number to be an odd number determined by the Electoral Commission in accordance with the criteria set out in the Constitution.

RECOMMENDATIONS [p.20]

National Parliament

1. (1) There shall be a National Parliament elected under a system of universal suffrage.
   (2) The National Parliament shall consist of one house.

Composition

2. The National Parliament shall comprise not less than 101 nor more than 107 elected members, the number to be an odd number determined by the Electoral Commission in accordance with the criteria laid down in Recommendation 90.

102. — NOMINATED MEMBERS

The Parliament may, from time to time, by a two-thirds absolute majority vote, appoint a person (other than a member) to be a nominated member of the Parliament.

AS TO PRACTICE

This section has never been utilized.

103. — QUALIFICATIONS FOR AND DISQUALIFICATIONS FROM MEMBERSHIP

(1) A member of the Parliament must be not less than 25 years of age.

C.P.C. Report Ch.6 p.3

Age

18. The 1970 Commission of Inquiry found that opinion in favour of making a distinction between voters and candidates was particularly strong in respect of the age qualification. Most people wanted a reduction in voting age from 21 to 18 years, and this was implemented in the 1971 legislation. There was opposition, however, to any reduction in the minimum age for candidates, and some feeling in favour of raising the age above 21 on the grounds that the majority of persons under that age lack the maturity required of a member of the House. The Commission recommended that the minimum age for candidates be left at 21, but that it should be reviewed again after the 1972 general election.

19. We have found that similar reservations on this matter continue to be widely held. After giving it full consideration we have concluded that there should be a period of five years between the voting age, which should remain at 18, and the age at which a person may be nominated as a candidate. Accordingly, we recommend that the age qualification for membership of the National Parliament be 23 years or over.

AS TO WHEN MEMBER OF PARLIAMENT MUST ACHIEVE THE AGE OF TWENTY-FIVE

per Andrew J.

I should also refer to the submission of Counsel for the Electoral Commissioner and of Counsel for the respondent. That submission, briefly stated, is that Mr. Mori was in fact a legally qualified candidate. This, it was said, flowed from s.50 of the Constitution, namely, that every citizen who is of full capacity and has reached voting age has the right and shall be given a reasonable opportunity to vote for and to be elected to, elective public office at genuine, periodic free elections and that he may hold public office. Under s.126 of the Constitution, the voting age is 18. The argument then goes that s.103 of the Constitution says only that a member of Parliament must be not less than twenty-five years of age. It does not refer to a candidate so that presumably a person over the age of eighteen could be a candidate and stand for the national elections (provided he was prepared to run the risk of completing a false nomination form by declaring that he was not under twenty-five) but that if elected he could not take his seat in Parliament.

However, I think that this argument fails at the threshold because s.50 of the Constitution is subject to the express limitations imposed by the Constitution and s.103 is just such an express limitation. The two sections can quite easily be read together. In my opinion, it is not conceivable that Parliament in adopting the Constitution could have contemplated that a man could be a candidate and stand for national electons when it was known that when he came to take his seat, he would not be qualified. It must follow from s.103 of the Constitution that if the candidate is not twenty-five when he comes to take his seat, that he has not qualified to stand in the first place.

Okuk v Nilkare (1982 Unreported) N406 at p.6.

(2) A candidate for election to the Parliament must have been born in the electorate for which he intends to nominate or have resided in the electorate for a continuous period of two years immediately preceding his nomination or for a period of five years at any time.

C.P.C. Report Ch.6 p.3

Residence

15. The Commission of Inquiry did propose a number of changes, however, and the *Electoral Ordinance* was amended in 1971 largely in accordance with its recommendations. There was some tightening of residential qualifications. Previously a person otherwise qualified could be nominated for any electorate in which he had lived for one year. It was now required that he stand for election only in an electorate in which he had his 'real place of living' or in which he had at some time lived continuously for five years. The intention of the latter qualification was to allow a person to represent the people of an area with which he had 'real home ties' even though he might have lived elsewhere for some time — by reason of his employment, for example. We believe that the grounds for this qualification will continue to have relevance for Papua New Guineans in the foreseeable future and recommend, therefore, that it be retained.

16. The alternative qualification provided that a person could be nominated as a candidate in the electorate in which he had had his 'real place of living' for a period of at least six months. This is the same as the qualifying period for electors. In other words, under the present law, a person may be nominated for the electorate in which he is entitled to be enrolled as an elector. We share the view, however, commonly held among our people, that a distinction should be made between the qualifications for electors and candidates: that, while six months' residence may be appropriate for the purpose of voting, a longer period of residence is desirable for a person to be qualified to stand for election in a particular electorate — in particular, for him to get to know the area and its people. We submit that a period of two years would be more appropriate.

17. Our recommendation for residential qualifications for election to the National Parliament is therefore two years' continuous residence in an electorate immediately prior to nomination or period of five years at some previous time.

AS TO RESIDENCE

per Frost C.J.

What does 'reside' mean?

As I have indicated, it is for the petitioner to prove that Mr. Lowa had not resided in the electorate for a continuous period of 2 years immediately preceding nomination. That was the qualification relied on by Mr. Lowa in his nomination form, and the only qualification relied on by his counsel, Mr. Andrew. The period goes back to 12th April, 1975, when Mr. Lowa was living in the house at Murray Barracks.

There is no difficulty in arriving at the meaning of 'reside'. In a tax case, it was said:

> ... the word 'reside' is a familiar English word and is defined in the *Oxford English Dictionary* as meaning 'to dwell permanently or for a considerable time, to have one's settled or usual abode, to live in or at a particular place.'

Levene v Inland Revenue Commissioners [1928] AC 217 per Viscount Cave L.C. at p.222.

That definition was applied by Lord Denning M.R. in the election case of *Fox v Stirk* [1970] 2 QB 463 at p.475, cited by Mr. Andrew.

Mr. Andrew relied also on a passage from a Queensland ease, *R. v Gillies* [1912] 6 QJPR 138 at p.140, where a similar problem arose and the candidate had to show 12 months' residence in Queensland. This is what the learned judge said:

> ... continuous residence did not mean that the applicant had to be every day of that twelve months in Queensland. It was sufficient if a man, during that twelve months had his house or fixed place of abode in Queensland, whether he was absent from time to time or not.

It is clear that during 1975 — except possibly for a period of one week to which I shall later refer — Mr. Lowa had in fact resided outside Moresby Northeast. Accordingly, the only way Mr. Andrew could put forward a case of two year's continuous residence was to rely on the doctrine, as it has been called, of 'constructive' residence, which has been developed by the courts under the electoral legislation of England. That is the legal term for the simple notion that 'a man may have more than one residence at a time. He may corporeally be residing at one place, and yet have a residence at another. He may have a place of residence to which he is free to go during the whole period.' *Durant v Carter* (1873) LR 9 CP 261 at p.266. Thus if a man spends his life at sea, he is considered resident at the house where his wife and family live ashore, even although his wife has moved and is living in a house which her husband has never seen — *The Queen v The Midland Licensing Court* [1959] SASR 229, a case also relied on by Mr. Andrew. As Lord Denning M.R. said in *Fox v Stirk* [1970] 2 QB 463, a man may have two residences, a flat in the city and a house in the country, and be resident in both.

It is to be noted however that *Fox v Stirk* was concerned with a statute in which there was no qualifying period of residence but only a qualifying date, namely one fixed day in the year. For the purposes of the present case therefore in which a continuous period of residence is required, Lord Denning's general statement is to be taken subject to the qualification laid down in the earlier English case of *Tanner v Carter* (1885) 16 QBD 231, a case where continuous residence for a prescribed period was required, that a person's claim to be a resident will be defeated if it is shown that he did not have the power to go to the house in question when he pleased throughout the period. See also *Halsbury, Laws of England*, 3rd ed., Vol. 14, p.14, where the cases are collected. The doctrine is further explained by Erle C.J. in *Powell v Guest* (1864) 18 CB (NS) 72 as follows:

> I entirely subscribe to the doctrine so clearly laid down in *Elliott on Registration*, 2nd edit. 204, where the learned author says that, 'in order to constitute residence, a party must possess at the least a sleeping apartment, but that an uninterrupted abiding at such dwelling is not requisite.' 'Absence,' he continues, 'no matter how long, if there be the liberty of returning at any time, and no abandonment of the intention to return whenever it may suit the party's pleasure or convenience so to do, will not prevent a constructive legal residence. But, if he has debarred himself of the liberty of returning to such dwelling, by letting it for a period, however short, or has abandoned his intention of returning, he cannot any longer be said to have even a legal residence there.' The learned author says he loses his character of resident 'if he has debarred himself of the liberty of returning to such dwelling,' and he gives two examples, viz. letting the house, or abandoning the intention of returning.

That passage was applied also in *Bond v Overseers of St. George, Hanover Square* (1870) LR 6 CP 312 per Brett J. at page 314.

It is plain that constructive residence implies an available residence, from which the claimant has not debarred himself from the liberty of returning.

There is no reason to suppose that the doctrine is not suitable or appropriate to the circumstances of Papua New Guinea, and accordingly it is applicable in determining the operation of the residential qualifications under the Constitution s.103.

In re Moresby North East Parliamentary Election (*No.2*) [1977] PNGLR 448 at pp.452-454.

Referred to

by Prentice Dep. C.J. in *In re Moresby North East Election Petition* [1977] PNGLR 429 at p.432; see also Pritchard J. at p.441.

(3) A person is not qualified to be, or to remain, a member of the Parliament if —

(a) he is not entitled to vote in elections to the Parliament; or

(b) he is of unsound mind within the meaning of any law relating to the protection of persons and property of persons of unsound mind; or
(c) subject to Subsections (4) to (7), he is under sentence of death or imprisonment for a period of more than nine months; or
(d) he is otherwise disqualified under this Constitution.

C.P.C Report Ch.6 p.2

Qualifications for membership

13. We consider that the qualifications for membership of the National Parliament should be in keeping with the increased responsibilities of members of the legislature in an independent Papua New Guinea; and in keeping also with the importance of the role of parliament in the system of government we recommend. We therefore propose a number of changes in the qualifications, but they are subject to certain transitional arrangements which include protection of the right of present members of the House of Assembly to retain the seats to which they have been elected until the end of their term in 1976.

Citizenship

14. Qualifications for membership of the House of Assembly were last examined in 1970 by a Commission of Inquiry into Electoral Procedures. No change was proposed in respect of the basic qualification that, in addition to being a British subject, a candidate for election to [p.3] the House should either have been born in Papua New Guinea or have lived here for at least five years. With the introduction of Papua New Guinean citizenship, this provision is no longer appropriate. We believe that, first and foremost, one should be a citizen in order to stand for election to the National Parliament. We therefore recommend that citizenship of Papua New Guinea replace the qualifications referred to above.

Literacy

20. The Second Select Committee on Constitutional Development expressed the view in its Final Report (pp.4-5, para.29) that if regional electorates were later to be abolished, 'an examination should be carried out to determine whether there should be a minimum (educational) qualification for open members e.g. to read and write'. From its experience in overseas countries it visited, the Select Committee concluded that 'this ability is very necessary if the legislature is to function efficiently and competently'.

21. It has been put to us that if we were to recommend that a literacy test be imposed for candidates for election to the National Parliament we would be cutting across one of the fundamental principles upon which we have recommended that the Constitution be based, namely that of maximizing the opportunities for participation by all of our people in the political life of the country.

22. After weighing up these arguments, and taking into account the practical difficulties of implementing, in a fair manner an appropriate literacy test, we have decided against recommending any literacy qualifications for members of the National Parliament, preferring to leave to the electors the question of the appropriate weight to be given to the degree of literacy of candidates. [p.4]

Disqualification from membership

23. Having reviewed the grounds on which a person may at present be disqualified from being elected, or from continuing, as a member of the House of Assembly, we consider that three grounds should remain unaltered — those concerning persons who are of unsound mind, who are undischarged bankrupts, or who take or agree to take any payment for services rendered in the House. We propose that three other grounds at present in force should be changed. These are the provisions relating to other paid employment, sentences arising from court convictions and absence from the House without leave.

Other paid employment

24. Under the *Papua New Guinea Act* a person is not qualified to be a member of the House of Assembly if he is a member of either the Papua New Guinea or Australian Public Services, or if he holds an office either constituted by law or specified by the High Commissioner in the Government Gazette. In our deliberations we first reached the conclusion that if public servants should be disqualified under constitutional legislation from being members of the legislature, so should others in government employment — such as teachers, employees of statutory authorities, policemen and members of the Defence Force. But this led us to question whether in principle a person should be allowed to hold any other position of paid employment whilst being a member of

Parliament. Should an employee of a business firm be treated more favourably than an employee of the government? Equally important, can a member of parliament carry out his duties adequately if he has other paid employment? Our answer to both questions was in the negative. Accordingly we recommend that to be qualified to be elected, or to continue as a member of the National Parliament a person shall not have any other paid employment.

Sentence following conviction

25. The *Papua New Guinea Act* also provides for disqualification in the case of a person who has been convicted of an offence punishable by death or imprisonment for one year or longer, and who is consequently subject to be sentenced to death or imprisonment, is under sentence of death, or undergoing imprisonment. Under this law, a person who is undergoing three months' imprisonment in respect of an offence for which the maximum sentence is one year is disqualified; but a person who is undergoing six months' imprisonment in respect of an offence for which that is the maximum sentence does not suffer this further penalty. We believe that it would be more equitable if disqualifications were related, as it is in a number of countries, to the gravity of the particular case and hence to the term of imprisonment actually imposed by the court — not to the maximum punishment for the type of offence committed.

26. Having agreed on this principle, we consider that imprisonment for a term exceeding nine months would constitute appropriate grounds for disqualification, and we recommend accordingly. In addition, however, we propose that where a member of parliament is imprisoned for a term exceeding nine months but has appealed against either his conviction or sentence he should be allowed to hold his seat pending determination of his appeal.

Absence without leave

27. The *Papua New Guinea Act* specifies, as a third ground for disqualification of a member of parliament, absence without leave from each of three consecutive meetings of the House. We recommend that this be reduced to two consecutive meetings.

Additional grounds for disqualification

28. We propose that a person may be disqualified by an Electoral Court from being elected, or from continuing, as a member of parliament if it finds that he has committed a corrupt practice in relation to his election or has breached the provisions covering electoral expenses. Recommendations on the subject of electoral expenses are outlined in the last section of this chapter. Finally, we propose also that a member may have to forfeit his seat if so ordered by the responsible tribunal as a result of a breach of the Leadership Code.

ELECTION MAY BE DISPUTED ON GROUNDS THAT CANDIDATE LACKS NECESSARY QUALIFICATIONS

Held

Sections 206 (election petition) and 228 (parliamentary references) of the *Organic Law on National Elections* are alternative procedures either of which may be utilized to bring a dispute concerning a member's eligibility before the Court.
In re Moresby North East Parliamentary Elections (No 1) [1977] PNGLR 424; see Frost C.J. at p.428.

ONCE DISQUALIFIED CANDIDATE SERVES OUT HIS PRISON SENTENCE HE MAY RE-CONTEST ELECTIONS

per Pratt J.

> I have formed the view that there is nothing in s.103 of the Constitution which would prevent the appellant from standing once again for Parliament after he had completed his [four year] term of imprisonment [for rape].
> *John Jaminan v The State* (1983 Unreported) SC262 at pp.14, 15.

GENERALLY

Referred to

by Gajewicz J. in *S.C.R No 2 of 1982; Re Opai Kunangel Amin* (1982 Unreported) SC231 at p. 35.

(4) Where a person is under sentence of death or imprisonment for a period exceeding nine months, the operation of Subsection (3)(d) is suspended until —
- (a) the end of any statutory period allowed for appeals against the conviction or sentence; or
- (b) if an appeal is lodged within the period referred to in paragraph (a), the appeal is determined.

(5) The references in Subsection (4), to appeals and to the statutory period allowed for appeals shall, where there is provision for a series of appeals, be read as references to each appeal and to the statutory period allowed for each appeal.

(6) If a free pardon is granted, a conviction is quashed or a sentence is changed to a sentence of imprisonment for nine months or less, or some other form of penalty (other than death) is substituted, the disqualification ceases, and if at the time of the pardon, quashing, change of sentence or substitution of penalty the writ for the by-election has not been issued the member is restored to his seat.

(7) In this section —
"appeal" includes any form of judicial appeal or judicial review;
"statutory period allowed for appeals" means a definite period allowed by law for appeals, whether or not it is capable of extension, but does not include an extension of such a definite period granted or that may be granted unless it is granted within that definite period.

104. — NORMAL TERM OF OFFICE.

(1) An elected member of the Parliament takes office on the day immediately following the day fixed for the return of the writ for the election in his electorate.

Referred to

by Gajewicz J. in *S.C.R No 2 of 1982; Re Opai Kunanagel Amin* (1982 Unreported) SC231 at p.43.

(2) The seat of a member of the Parliament becomes vacant —
- (a) if he is appointed as Governor-General; or
- (b) upon the expiry of the day fixed for the return of the writs for the general election after he last became a member of the Parliament; or

(c) if he resigns his seat by notice in writing to the Speaker, or in the case of the Speaker to the Clerk of the Parliament; or
(d) if he is absent, without leave of the Parliament, during the whole of three consecutive meetings of the Parliament, unless the Parliament decides to waive this rule upon satisfactory reasons being given; or
(e) if, except as authorized by or under an Organic Law or an Act of the Parliament, he directly or indirectly takes or agrees to take any payment in respect of his services in the Parliament; or
(f) if he becomes disqualified under Section 103 (*qualification for and disqualifications from membership*); or
(g) on his death; or
(h) if he is dismissed from office under Division III. 2 (*leadership code*).

UNQUALIFIED RIGHT TO RESIGN

Held

Section 104(c) confers an unqualified right upon a member of the Parliament to resign his seat by notice to the Speaker. That express constitutional right may be exercised notwithstanding that the member has been suspended from duty pending completion of an investigation under the provisions of the Leadership Code and notwithstanding that, on the authority of *In re Joseph Auna* [1980] PNGLR 500, his resignation will terminate proceedings against him under the Code. A Member's resignation automatically takes effect when the notice of resignation, in writing, is given to the Speaker.
S.C.R No 2 of 1982; Re Opai Kunangel Amin (1982 Unreported) SC231, see Kapi Dep. C.J. at pp.7, 8 (Andrew J. concurring), Bredmeyer J. at pp.12, 13, Gajewicz J. at pp.30, 38, 42; but see also Kaputin J. (dissenting) at pp.13A-22.

GENERALLY

Referred to

by Frost C.J. in *The State v The Independent Tribunal; Ex parte* Sasakila [1976] PNGLR 491 at p.500.

(3) For the purposes of Subsection (2)(d), a meeting of the Parliament commences when the Parliament first sits following a general election, prorogation of the Parliament or an adjournment of the Parliament otherwise than for a period of less than 12 days and ends when next the Parliament is prorogued or adjourned otherwise than for a period of less than 12 days.

105. — GENERAL ELECTIONS.

(1) A general election to the Parliament shall be held —
(a) within the period of three months before the fifth anniversay of the day fixed for the return of the writs for the previous general election; or

(b) if, during the last 12 months before the fifth anniversary of the day fixed for the return of the writs for the previous general election —
   (i) a vote of no confidence in the Prime Minister or the Ministry is passed in accordance with Section 145 (*motions of no confidence*); or
   (ii) the Government is defeated on the vote on a question that the Prime Minister has declared to the Parliament to be a question of confidence; or

(c) if the Parliament, by an absolute majority vote so decides.

C.P.C. Report Ch.6 p.13

Dissolution of parliament

88. Unless the National Parliament is dissolved earlier (in circumstances discussed in the next paragraph), we recommend that it be dissolved by the Speaker on a date within the last three months of its term fixed by the National Executive Council. We have recommended elsewhere that the Speaker and Ministers remain in office in a caretaker capacity during the period of a general election. The current practice by which all members continue to receive their salaries until the election should be continued.

89. We have looked closely at the question of a premature dissolution of the parliament, which is always a possibility under the Westminister system and most modifications of it. Although the practice appears sometimes to entail manipulation of the legislature, we concede that early dissolutions resulting in 'snap elections' may be useful and relevant in certain circumstances in those countries which have a well-developed party system. We are not at all convinced, however, that the practice is appropriate for Papua New Guinea. We have found public opinion to be in favour of a fixed term of four years. The expense and difficulty of holding general elections in our country provide arguments to support this view. In general, we believe also that members of the Parliament should be able to settle problems that may arise without resorting to an early dissolution which may, in any case, do nothing to help the situation.

90. We have decided to propose that an early dissolution be allowed in two kinds of circumstances. Firstly, the parliament shall be dissolved by the Speaker if, during the fourth year of its term, the National Executive Council is defeated specifically in a vote of no confidence or on an issue which the Prime Minister has declared to be one of confidence. The procedure for each of these possibilities is outlined in Chapter 7. Secondly, as a kind of [p.14] safety valve to be used in what are likely to be rather extraordinary circumstances, we propose that the Speaker dissolve parliament at any time if the parliament itself so resolves.

General elections

91. As indicated in paragraph 89, we have found wide support for retaining the present term of four years for the legislature. We consider that elections held not more than four years apart would allow the people to express their will at reasonably frequent intervals while also providing the government with a period of office sufficient to enable it to carry out a substantial programme. Concerning the precise date, we recommend that a general election be held at such time within ten weeks after every dissolution of the National Parliament as the Speaker appoints, acting in accordance with the advice of the National Executive Council.

AS TO THE LIFE OF THE FIRST PARLIAMENT

Held

A motion of no confidence pursuant to s.145 cannot validly be moved against the Government during the life of the First Parliament which under s.260(b) of the Constitution extended from Independence Day until May/June 1977, subject to the holding of a general election under s.105(1)(c).

The provisions of s.145(2) do not apply to the First Parliament because that section refers only to motions of no confidence moved in a Parliament elected at a previous general election held pursuant to the Constitution and is not therefore intended to apply to the First Parliament. *Reference No 3 of 1976* [1976] PNGLR 228; see Frost C.J. at pp.234, 236; Raine J. at p.237 and Saldanha J. at pp.238-240.

Held

If the First Parliament by an absolute majority vote pursuant to s.105(1)(c) of the Constitution decides to hold a general election, the same may be held notwithstanding that the Parliament has yet to determine the number and boundaries of electorates in accordance with s.125 of the Constitution. In such circumstances the number and boundaries of the electorates should remain the same as for the previous general election to the pre-Independence House of Assembly. *Reference No 3 of 1976* [1976] PNGLR 424; per Curiam (Frost C.J., Prentice Dep. C.J., Raine, Saldanha and Kearney JJ.) at pp.246-249.

(2) The Head of State, acting with, and in accordance with, the advice of the Electoral Commission, shall fix the first and last days of the period during which polling shall take place and the date by which the writs for a general election shall be returned.

(3) In advising the Head of State under Subsection (2), and in conducting the election, the Electoral Commission shall do its best to ensure that —
- (a) in a case to which Subsection (1)(a) applies — the date for the return of the writs is fixed as nearly as may reasonably be to the fifth anniversary of the date fixed for the return of the writs for the previous general election; and
- (b) in case to which Subsection (1)(b) or (c) applies — the date for the return of the writs is fixed as soon as may reasonably be after the date of the relevant decision of the Parliament.

106. — BY-ELECTIONS.

If the office of an elected member of the Parliament becomes vacant otherwise than by virtue of Section 104(2)(b) (*normal term of office*), an election shall be held to fill the vacancy unless the vacancy occurs —
- (a) within the period of six months before the fifth anniversary of the date fixed for the return of the writs for the previous general election; or
- (b) after the writ has been issued for an election under Section 105(1) and before the day fixed for the return of that writ, writs for a general election are issued, the first-mentioned writ shall be deemed to have been revoked.

Subdivision C. — The Speaker and the Deputy Speaker.

107. — OFFICES OF SPEAKER AND DEPUTY SPEAKER.

(1) There shall be offices of Speaker and Deputy Speaker of the National Parliament.

(2) The Speaker and the Deputy Speaker must be members of the Parliament, and shall be elected by the Parliament by secret ballot in accordance with the Standing Orders of the Parliament.

(3) The Speaker and the Deputy speaker hold office, and their offices become vacant, in accordance with the Constitutional Laws and the Standing Orders of the Parliament.

(4) No Minister may be the Speaker or Deputy Speaker, and if a Speaker or Deputy Speaker becomes a Minister he vacates his office as Speaker or Deputy Speaker, as the case may be.

C.P.C. Report Ch.6 p.4

The Speaker

29. To symbolize the central role of the National Parliament we recommend a substantial upgrading of the role of the Speaker. We propose, therefore, that he perform a number of executive functions. He should, for example, make some formal appointments and sign bills into law. We have more to say about his executive functions in Chapter 7. Here we wish to make the point that he would be acting as the principal representative of the Parliament.

30. We have considered the possibility of the Speaker being appointed from outside the parliament but have concluded that his position might be weakened if he is not, as the members are, directly elected by the people and thereby entitled to a seat as of right. We recommend, [p.5] therefore, that the Speaker continue to be elected in a secret ballot by the members from among their own number. To ensure also that he has substantive support, his election should require an absolute majority of the votes cast. Consequently, we have provided for an 'exhaustive ballot' in cases where there are more than two candidates and none has obtained such a majority in the first ballot. In keeping with the dignity and importance of his position, we recommend that, following his election, the Speaker be sworn into office by the Chief Justice.

31. To provide for continuity, the Speaker would, under our proposals, remain in office until the commencement of the first meeting of parliament following the next general election, when the first item of business is the election of the Speaker of the new parliament. If still a member, he could be re-elected or replaced. Under the *Papua New Guinea Act*, the Speaker can be removed from office at any time by the vote of a simple majority in the House of Assembly. We consider that under the new Constitution this would no longer be appropriate, and we recommend instead a modification of what is sometimes called the 'constructive vote of no confidence'. Under the procedure we propose, a motion for the removal of the Speaker must also designate a successor, and shall require the support of an absolute majority to be passed. We propose also that such a motion be signed by at least one-tenth of the total membership of the parliament and that it be subject to one week's prior notice. This procedure should ensure that any motion for the removal of the Speaker is a well-considered one. It also provides continuity if the motion is successful.

32. In addition to certain executive functions dealt with in Chapter 7, and others in respect of legislation, we recommend that the Speaker be formally vested with the responsibility for administering the affairs of the National Parliament, and with the direction and control of an independent Parliamentary Service ...

Deputy Speaker

33. We have reviewed the present arrangements in respect of the Chairman of the Committees and the Deputy Speakers. These positions are established by the Standing Orders of the House of Assembly: none is specified in the *Papua New Guinea Act*. We do not consider that the provision for Deputy Speakers works very well in practice. We recognise that it may be necessary from time to time for a member to be asked to take the chair for a brief period and we have provided for this. In normal circumstances, however, the Speaker or Deputy Speaker should preside and both should be expected to acquire a good knowledge of Standing Orders.

34. Especially in view of the extended functions and responsibilities we have proposed for the Speaker, we recommend that the position of Deputy Speaker be formally instituted and that he act as Speaker during any period when that position is vacant. He should be elected and removed in the same manner as that prescribed for the Speaker, but his election at the first meeting of parliament following a general election should take place after the appointment of the Ministers. We have also recommended arrangements to cover various circumstances in which the Speaker is absent or incapacitated.

RECOMMENDATIONS [p.21]

Speaker

6. There shall be a Speaker of the National Parliament.

7. (1) The Speaker shall be elected in a secret ballot by the members of the National Parliament from among their own number —
   (a) as the first item of business in the first meeting of the National Parliament following a general election; and
   (b) in the case of a vacancy, as provided in Recommendation 16 below.

(2) (a) To be elected Speaker, a member shall obtain an absolute majority of the formal votes cast.
   (b) The following provisions shall be made in the Standing Orders of the National Parliament for the election of the Speaker by an exhaustive ballot in cases where there are more than two candidates, and in the first ballot the leading candidate does not obtain an absolute majority of the formal votes cast:
      (i) Subject to the following sub-paragraphs, successive ballots shall be held until a candidate obtains an absolute majority of the formal votes cast.
      (ii) The number of candidates shall be reduced at each successive ballot by the exclusion of the candidate who obtained the least number of votes in the preceding ballot.
      (iii) If, in the first ballot, two or more candidates each obtain the least number of formal votes, the first ballot shall be repeated. If such a tie again results and there are only three candidates, the leading candidate shall be elected, notwithstanding the fact that he did not obtain an absolute majority of the formal votes cast. If such a tie again results, and there are more than three candidates, both candidates with the least number of formal votes shall be excluded and a second ballot conducted.
      (iv) If, in a second or subsequent ballot no candidate has an absolute majority, and two or more candidates obtain the least number of votes, the one to be excluded shall be the tied candidate who obtained the second to least number of formal votes in the proceding ballot. If in that ballot there had also been a tie, the procedure prescribed in (iii) shall be adopted.

8. Following his election by the National Parliament, the Speaker shall be sworn into office by the Chief Justice.

9. In addition to other functions prescribed in the Constitution, the Speaker shall have the responsibility for administering the affairs of the National Parliament and shall have direction and control of the Parliamentary Service.

10. In respect of the affairs of the National Parliament and of the Parliamentary Service, submissions by the Speaker to the National Executive Council shall be presented by the Prime Minister, who shall also be responsible in the parliament for any bills dealing with these matters.

11. The office of Speaker shall become vacant —
   (a) at the commencement of the first meeting of the National Parliament following the next general election after his election;
   (b) if he resigns that office in a signed letter delivered to the Clerk of the National Parliament;
   (c) if he is appointed a Minister;
   (d) if he ceases to be a member of the National Parliament for reasons other than a dissolution of the Parliament; or
   (e) if a motion for his removal from office is passed by an absolute majority of the National Parliament in accordance with Recommendation 12 below.[p.22]

12. A motion to remove the Speaker may be moved in the National Parliament only if —
   (a) the designation of his successor is included in the same motion;
   (b) the motion is signed by at least one-tenth of the total membership of the parliament; and
   (c) at least one week's prior notice of the intention to move such a motion is given.

Deputy Speaker

13. There shall be a Deputy Speaker of the National Parliament.

14. (1) The Deputy Speaker shall be elected in a secret ballot by the members of the National Parliament from among their own number —
   (a) at the next sitting of the parliament after the Prime Minister has been elected and has announced the names of the Ministers following a general election; and
   (b) at the next sitting of the parliament after a vacancy has occurred for reasons other than the commencement of the first meeting of the parliament following a general election.
(2) (a) To be elected Deputy Speaker, a member shall obtain an absolute majority of the votes cast.
   (b) Provision shall be made in the Standing Orders of the National Parliament in the manner prescribed in Recommendation 7(2)(b) above, for the election of the Deputy Speaker by an exhaustive ballot in cases where there are more than two candidates, and in the first ballot the leading candidate does not obtain an absolute majority of the votes cast.

15. The office of Deputy Speaker shall become vacant in the same circumstances as that of the Speaker under Recommendations 11 and 12 above.

108. — FUNCTIONS OF THE SPEAKER AND DEPUTY SPEAKER

(1) The Speaker is responsible, subject to and in accordance with the Constitutional Laws, the Acts of the Parliament and the Standing Orders of the Parliament, for upholding the dignity of the Parliament, maintaining order in it, regulating its proceedings and administering its affairs, and for controlling the precincts of the Parliament as defined by or under an Act of the Parliament.

(*See: Parliamentary Powers and Privileges Act Ch.24.*)

(2) In the event of a vacancy in the office of the Speaker or his absence from the country or from the Parliament, and otherwise as determined by or under a Constitutional Law, an Act of the Parliament or the Standing Orders of the Parliament, the Deputy Speaker has, subject to Section 95 (*Acting Governor-General*), all the rights, privileges, powers, functions, duties and responsibilities of the Speaker.

(3) A Constitutional Law, and Act of the Parliament or the Standing Orders of the Parliament may provide for other powers, functions, duties and responsibilities of the Speaker and the Deputy Speaker.

C.P.C. Report Ch.6 p.22

Vacancy in office of Speaker

16. At the next meeting of the National Parliament following a vacancy in the office of Speaker due to —
   (a) his ceasing to be a member of the parliament for any reason other than a dissolution of the parliament;
   (b) his resignation from that office;
   (c) his appointment as a Minister; or
   (d) his loss of office as a result of a breach of the Leadership Code

   the National Parliament shall elect a new Speaker. The Deputy Speaker shall act as Speaker in the interim period.

Absence or incapacity of Speaker

17. In respect of his functions other than that of presiding in the National Parliament, the Speaker —
   (a) *shall* empower the Deputy Speaker in a signed letter to act on his behalf when he is absent from Papua New Guinea; and
   (b) *may* empower the Deputy Speaker in a signed letter to act on his behalf —
      (i) when he is within Papua New Guinea but likely to be out of effective and prompt communication with his office;
      (ii) when he is ill or otherwise incapacitated; or
      (iii) as otherwise authorised by law.
18. Subject to Recommendation 19 below, and in respect of those functions of the Speaker other than that of presiding in the National Parliament, the Deputy Speaker *shall* act on behalf of the Speaker —
   (a) when empowered to do so by the Speaker in a signed letter;
   (b) when the First Parliamentary Committee, after considering a written report signed by two medical practitioners, has resolved that the Speaker is physically or mentally incapable of performing the duties of his office; or
   (c) in an emergency situation, when effective communication with the Speaker is impossible.

19. If, at the next meeting of the National Parliament, the Deputy Speaker is still acting on behalf of the Speaker pursuant to Recommendation 18(b) above because the Speaker has not resumed his duties, the First Parliamentary Committee shall report on the situation to the Parliament during that meeting, and shall recommend that either —
   (a) the Deputy Speaker continue to act for the Speaker, subject to confirmation by the parliament at successive meetings of the parliament; or
   (b) the Speaker be removed from office in accordance with the Constitution.

Subdivision D. — Powers, Privileges and Procedures.

109. — GENERAL POWER OF LAW-MAKING.

(1) Subject to this Constitution, the Parliament may make laws, having effect within and outside the country, for the peace, order and good government of Papua New Guinea and the welfare of the People.

PEACE ORDER AND GOOD GOVERNMENT

Comment

The words 'peace order and good government' are not words of limitation. They are words apt, at common law, to confer unlimited plenary powers of lawmaking upon a legislature. See Jennings *Constitutional Laws of the Commonwealth* Vol.1, 3rd edition, London 1962 at pp.48-52.

GENERAL

Referred to

by Kidu C.J. in *S.C.R No 4 of 1980;Re petition of M.T. Somare* [1981] PNGLR 265 at p.273 (all citizens have an interest in ensuring that legislative power is exercised subject to the Constitution. Every citizen has standing to complain to the Courts if the legislature exceeds its powers).

(2) In particular, Acts of the Parliament, not inconsistent with the Constitutional Laws, may provide for all matters that are necessary or convenient to be prescribed for carrying out and giving effect to this Constitution.

(3) No law made by the Parliament is open to challenge in any court on the ground that —
   (a) it is not for the peace, order or good government of Papua New Guinea or the welfare of the People; or
   (b) it purports to have extra-territorial effect.

(4) Each law made by the Parliament shall receive such fair, large and liberal construction and interpretation as will best ensure the attainment of the object of the law according to its true intent, meaning and spirit, and there is no presumption against extra-territoriality.

AS TO GENERAL PRINCIPLE

per Kearney J.

The process of statutory interpretation is essentially intuitive and subjective, in the absence of rules consistently applied. The Act is a Constitutional Law and thus subject to the general principles of interpretation set out in Constitution ss.10, 25(3), 63(3) and Basic Social Obligation (a), and 158(2); and to the more specific canons in Constitution ss.24, 109(4) when read with 12, and Sch.1.5. In my opinion these provisions amount to a direction to the Court that in carrying out its functions under Constitution s.18(1) the

words actually used in the Act do not have to be strictly adhered to but are to be construed with the assistance of the materials referred to in Constitution s.24, so as best to attain what Parliament intended. When Constitution ss.109(4) and 158(2) are themselves interpreted with the aid of s.24, this view is fortified: there are several references in Chapter 8 of the Report of the Constitutional Planning Committee which point against the Court taking a 'narrowly legalistic' or 'literal' approach, and thus sacrificing the 'spirit for the letter of the Constitution'. The 'dynamic character' of the Constitution is emphasized; in interpreting the laws, the judges are urged to use 'judicial ingenuity' in appropriate cases, to do justice. One consequence of this appraoch to interpretation is that the Court should not fail to give a provision the effect it considers the Parliament intended, by applying a literal or 'plain meaning' test nor should it attribute to the legislature an intention to produce a capricious or unjust result. The search throughout is for the intention of Parliament, a process which remains, formally at least, one of interpretation and not of legislation, and one in which the best guide remains the provisions of the Act itself.
The State v The Independent Tribunal; Ex parte Sasakila [1976] PNGLR 491 at pp.506,507.

'LITERAL'RULES OF INTERRETATION TO BE REJECTED

per Wilson J.

In expressing my opinion, which I now do, that the 'literal' rule of statutory interpretation is inappropriate to the circumstances of this country at this time, I have not overlooked the need for consistency or uniformity as between neighbouring jurisdictions (in this context I am referring to Papua New Guinea and Australia), and I am conscious of the special responsibility which is imposed on the Supreme Court 'to assist in the development of our indigenous jurisprudence adapted to the changing circumstances of Papua New Guinea'.

Why is the 'literal' rule of statutory interpretation inappropriate to the circumstances of this country at this time? In my judgment there is no place in a developing country where the courts, as well as the Law Reform Commission, are given special responsibilities in the process of development, for the narrow interpretation of statutes without adequate regard to the social purpose of particular legislation. Development is difficult to achieve if courts adopt too conservative an approach to the interpretation of statutes. There has been a tendency in our National Judicial System, less evident in some recent decisions of the courts but still perceptible, to over-emphasize the literal meaning of a provision at the expense of the meaning to be derived from other possible contexts; the latter including the application of the 'mischief' rule, the recognition of the general legislative purpose, as well as the obligations laid down under the Constitution such as, for example, the obligation upon the courts in interpreting the law to give 'paramount consideration to the dispensation of justice' (s.158(2) of the Constitution). The purpose of the law in the Criminal Code regarding provocation is to give to a person who has been provoked into assaulting another and thereby into committing a crime a defence in certain circumstances.

There is, therefore, no place for a literalist approach to statutory interpretation in the law of Papua New Guinea and in relation to the Criminal Code in particular; a fortiori, as here, where the application of the majority decision in *Kaporonovski v The Queen* (1973) 133 CLR. 209 in this case would justifiably bring with it the charge of narrow literalism. The letter of the law should not be allowed to prevail over the spirit of the law in a case of statutory interpretation such as this, especially where, as I see it, injustice will result if our decision is otherwise.
P.L.A.R. No 1 of 1980 [1980] PNGLR 326 at pp.335,336; see also Andrew J. at p.347; but see Greville Smith J. (dissenting) at pp.341,342.

Referred to

by Kearney Dep. C.J. in *Placer Holdings Pty Ltd v The Independent State of Papua New Guinea* [1982] PNGLR 16 at p.17 (adopting the purposive approach to the interpretation of statues and following Wilson J. in *P.L.A.R. No 1 of 1980*: above).

APPLIED

Held

A liberal interpretation of s.43 of the *Wills Probate and Administration Act* 1967 (i.e. that irregularities, informalities and statutory defects shall not invalidate a document proved to be a last will and testament) preferred over a narrower construction (that s.43 applies only to save a testamentary instrument flawed by a single such defect) because the true intent of the provision was to facilitate the legitimate aspirations of citizens to make effective testamentary disposition of their property.
Public Curator of Papua New Guinea v Public Trustee of New Zealand [1976] PNGLR 427; see Prentice Dep.C.J. at pp.427,431.

Held

Section 30 of the *Evidence Act* 1975 constitutes an exception to the hearsay rule, but should receive a fair large and liberal construction notwithstanding.
Kerr v Motor Vehicles Insurance (P.N.G.) Trust [1977] PNGLR 461; see Kearney J. at p 464.

Held

Section 62 of the *Prices Regulation Act* 1949 (requiring that traders mark and display prices on goods subject to price control, offered for sale) created a strict liability offence. The appellant (a company) contended that it had been wrongly convicted because its failure to mark prices had arisen because of an omission of its store manager and, pursuant to s.23 of the *Criminal Code*, it should not have been held criminally liable for an act or omission occurring independently of its will. Conviction upheld because, inter alia, the *Prices Regulation Act* 1949 was a law for the protection of the people and Section 109(4) of the Constitution required it to be given full effect. Section 23 of the *Criminal Code* accordingly could not be used to evade prosecution on the basis that the company's 'corporate mind' did not know of the omission.
Bromley and Manton Pty Ltd v Eremas Andrew [1978] PNGLR 498; see Pritchard J. at pp.505,506.

GENERALLY

Referred to

by Frost C.J. in *Peter v South Pacific Brewery Ltd* [1976] PNGLR 537 at p.542 (s.109(4) cannot save an unconstitutional law from being held invalid by the Court); but see also Prentice Dep.C.J. at p.558;

by Narakobi A.J. in *The State v Wapulae and ors* (1979 Unreported) N233 at p.20 (note overruled in *Acting Public Solicitor (sic) v Uname Aumane* [1980] PNGLR 510);

by Pratt J. in *Timereke v Ferrie and Johns* (1981 Unreported) N379 at p.30 (no reason to suppose an intention that automatic citizens should be precluded from making testamentary dispositions of property);

by Kapi J. in *Re James Allan Sannga; Peter Timereke v Duncan Ferrie and anor* (1983 Unreported) SC255 at p.43(Court should hesitate to develop the underlying law in areas where important policy questions ought be decided by parliament:see also annotations under Sch.2.3.).

See also under s.158(2); Sch.1.5

110. — CERTIFICATION AS TO MAKING OF LAWS.

(1) Subject to Section 137(3) (*Acts of Indemnity*) and to any Act of the Parliament made for the purposes of Subsection (3), the Speaker shall certify under the National Seal, in accordance with the Standing Orders of the Parliament, that a law has been made by

the Parliament and, subject to Subsection (2), the law comes into operation on the date of the certificate.

(2) Nothing in Subsection (1) prevents a law —
   (a) being expressed to come, or to be deemed to have come, into force on a date specified by, or fixed in accordance with, law; or
   (b) being retrospective or retroactive.

(3) An Act of the Parliament or the Standing Orders of the Parliament may make provision under which a law made by the Parliament may, at the direction of the Head of State, acting with, and in accordance with, the advice of the National Executive Council, be recommitted to the Parliament for the consideration of amendments proposed by the Head of State, acting with, and in accordance with, the advice of the National Executive Council.

C.P.C. Report Ch.6 p.9

Bill becomes law

61. We mentioned earlier, in the context of upgrading the role of the Speaker, our proposal that he perform certain executive functions, including the signing of bills into law. We do not see this as a ritualistic act in the nature of a royal or presidential assent, although it would have the same legal effect. Rather it will be a corollary, the natural outcome of the Speaker's action in certifying that a bill has been passed by the National Parliament in accordance with the Constitution and Standing Orders. We recommend that a bill become law from the date it is so certified, and that this date be no later than 28 days from the end of the meeting of parliament at which it is passed. We recommend further that any law, or parts of a law, which do not automatically come into effect when signed, or at a date specified in the bill itself, should be brought into effect by the Speaker on a date or dates fixed by the National Executive Council.

62. We recognise that there may be circumstances in which the executive will wish to have a bill recommitted before it is signed into law. It may want to ask parliament to correct an error that had been made inadvertently, or less commonly, to reconsider a bill. We think it reasonable to provide for this, but we wish to emphasise that we do not intend that the procedure should amount to any kind of veto, either directly or by means of delay. Accordingly, we recommend that a bill may be recommitted, through the appropriate Minister, no later than two weeks after it has been passed and during the same meeting of parliament; but that it may be recommitted only once, and if recommitted, must be given precedence so that it may be passed again, whether or not amended, or otherwise disposed of at the same meeting.

111. — RIGHT TO INTRODUCE BILLS, ETC.

(1) Subject to Section 210 (*executive initiative*), any member of the Parliament is entitled to introduce into the Parliament, in accordance with, and subject to any reasonable restrictions contained in, the Standing Orders of the Parliament, a petition, question, bill, resolution or motion.

(2) The petition, question, bill, resolution or motion shall be dealt with as provided by the Standing Orders of the Parliament.

(3) The Standing Orders of the Parliament may make provision for priority to be given to Government business at certain times or in certain circumstances.

C.P.C. Report Ch.6 p.8.

Introduction of Bills, motions and petitions

54. Under the system of government we propose, and especially with the increasing complexity of government, it is certain that most legislation to come before the parliament will be introduced by the government of the day. However, the particular emphasis we place on the role of parliament makes it all the more important that the Constitution should include protecion of the right of any member to introduce bills. We recommend accordingly, and propose the inclusion of similar protection for the right of members to move motions and present petitions for the consideration of parliament. Limitations on these rights in respect of financial measures are dealt with in Chapter 9.

112. — PRESIDING IN THE PARLIAMENT.

(1) Subject to Subdivision C (*the Speaker and the Deputy Speaker*) and to Subsection (2), the Standing Orders of the Parliament shall make provision in respect of the chairmanship of the Parliament and of Committees of the Whole.

(2) No Minister may preside in the Parliament or in a Committee of the Whole.

113. — QUORUM

(1) The quorum for a sitting of the Parliament is one-third of the number of seats in the Parliament at the time.

(2) The Standing Orders of the Parliament shall make provision for the action to be taken in the event of a lack of or loss of a quorum at any time.

C.P.C. Report Ch.6 p.8.

Quorum

57. We recommend that the quorum for sittings of the parliament be not less than one-third of all its members. This is, in effect, about the same as at present. We are concerned, however, to avoid the situations that have occurred from time to time when the House of Assembly has been unable to meet, or to continue to meet, because a quorum was not immediately available or had temporarily lapsed. At present, Standing Orders allow the Speaker to defer the commencement of a day's sitting for up to one hour if there is no quorum but he is satisfied there is likely to be one within that time. We recommend that this procedure be permitted if the quorum lapses at any time during a sitting.

114. — VOTING IN THE PARLIAMENT.

(1) Except as otherwise provided by a Constitutional Law or the Standing Orders of the Parliament, all questions before a meeting of the Parliament shall be decided in accordance with the majority of votes of the members present and voting.

(2) The member presiding does not have a deliberative vote except —
 (a) on a motion of no confidence in the Prime Minister, the Ministry or a Minister, in accordance with an Organic Law referred to in Section 145 (*motions of no confidence*); or

(b) on any question which requires an affirmative vote greater than a simple majority.

(3) Except as otherwise provided by a Constitutional Law or the event of an equality of votes on a question, the member presiding has a casting vote, but if he fails to use it the motion shall be deemed to be withdrawn.

(4) The Standing Orders of the Parliament shall make provision for the manner in which a vote is to be taken and recorded.

C.P.C. Report Ch.6 p.8.

Voting

58. Except where special majorities are required, all matters for decision in the parliament should be determined by a simple majority — that is, by a majority of those members present and voting. We propose that in normal circumstances such as these the Speaker, Deputy Speaker, or other member presiding should not vote unless the voting is evenly divided, in which case he should have and exercise a casting vote. This is in keeping with current law.

59. There are, however, three kinds of situation in which we believe that the Speaker, his [p.9] Deputy or another member presiding should not have a casting vote but should cast a deliberative vote as other members do. These are when a motion involves the formation or dismissal of a government — that is, a motion to elect or remove the Prime Minister, and a motion of no confidence in the National Executive Council or on a question declared by the Prime Minister to be one of confidence in the Council. The third situation is when parliament is voting on a Bill to amend the Constitution. In each of these instances, we feel that the member presiding should have the normal voting right of an elected member, and we recommend accordingly.

60. The only limitation we propose should be placed on the voting rights of members other than the Speaker or member presiding, is the common one that no member should speak or vote on any matter relating to a contract for the supply of goods or services to the government, in which he has an interest.

115. — PARLIAMENTARY PRIVILEGES, ETC.

(1) The powers (other than legislative powers), privileges and immunities of the Parliament and of its members and committees are as prescribed by or under this section and by any other provision of this Constitution.

(2) There shall be freedom of speech, debate and proceeding in the Parliament, and the exercise of those freedoms shall not be questioned in any court or in any proceedings whatever (otherwise than in proceedings in the Parliament or before a committee of the Parliament).

(3) No member of the Parliament is subject to the jurisdiction of any court in respect of the exercise of his powers or the performance of his functions, duties or responsibilities as such, but this subsection does not affect the operation of Division III.2 (*leadership code*).

(4) No member of the Parliament is liable to civil or criminal proceedings, arrest, imprisonment, fine, damages or compensation by reason of any matter or thing that he has brought by petition, question, bill, resolution, motion or otherwise, or has said before or submitted to the Parliament or a committee of the Parliament.

(5) No member of the Parliament or other person is liable to civil or criminal proceedings, arrest, imprisonment, fine, damages or compensation by reason of —
  (a) an act done under the authority of the Parliament or under an order of the Parliament or a committee of the Parliament; or
  (b) words spoken or used, or a document or writing made or produced, under an order or summons made or issued under the authority of the Parliament or a committee of the Parliament.

(6) Members of the Parliament are free from arrest for civil debt during meetings of the Parliament and during the period commencing three days before, and ending three days after, a meeting when they are travelling from their respective electorates to attend the meeting or are returning to their electorates from the meeting.

(7) No process issued by any court in the exercise of its civil jurisdiction shall be served or executed through the Speaker, an officer of the Parliament or a member of the Parliamentary Service, or within the precincts of the Parliament (as defined by or under an Act of the Parliament) while it is sitting.

(8) The powers conferred by Section 109 (*general powers of law making*) extend to the making of laws —
  (a) declaring further powers (other than legislative powers), privileges and immunities of the Parliament, and of its members and committees; and
  (b) providing for the manner in which powers, privileges and immunities provided for by or under this section may exercised or upheld.

(9) The powers and privileges conferred by or under this section do not and shall not include the power to impose or provide for the imposition of a fine, imprisonment, forfeiture of property or other penalty of a criminal nature, but this subsection does not prevent the creation of offences for the purposes of this section that are triable within the National Judicial System.

C.P.C. Report Ch.6 p.8.

Privileges and immunities

55. There is already an Ordinance dealing with privileges and immunities in respect of the House of Assembly and its members. Detailed provisions should remain in ordinary legislation, and we therefore propose that, subject to the Constitution, parliament should be authorised to determine these matters by law.

56. We believe, however, that freedom of speech, debate and proceedings in the National Parliament is of such vital importance that it should be protected in the Constitution itself, and should not be questioned in any court or place outside parliament. In addition to this general recommendation, we propose a number of specific privileges and immunities which stem directly from it: these provide protection for the Speaker or any officer of parliament in respect of the exercise of powers relating to their office; protection of members in respect of any matters they bring before parliament (or any of its Committees) by way of petition, motion, question or bill; and limited protection for members in respect of civil proceedings while parliament is meeting. We believe that these provisions are the minimum necessary to ensure that members are free to participate fully in the work of parliament, without fear or favour.

RECOMMENDATIONS [p.25]

Privileges and immunities

43. Subject to the Constitution, parliament may by law determine its privileges, immunities and powers and those of its members.

44. There shall be freedom of speech, debate and proceedings in the National Parliament, and those freedoms shall not be questioned in any court or place outside the parliament. [p.26]

45. Neither the Speaker nor an officer of the National Parliament shall be subject to the jurisdiction of a court in respect of the exercise of a power conferred on, or vested in, the Speaker or officer in his capacity as such.

46. No member of the National Parliament is liable to civil or criminal proceedings, arrest, imprisonment, fine or damages by reason of any matter or thing which he has brought by petition, question, bill, resolution, motion or otherwise, or has said, before the parliament or a committee of the parliament.

47. For the duration of any meeting of the National Parliament, members shall enjoy freedom from arrest for any civil debt.

48. No process issued by any court in the exercise of its civil jurisdiction shall be served or executed through the Speaker, the Clerk or any officer of the National Parliament or within the precincts of the parliament while it is sitting.

PROCEEDINGS NOT TO BE QUESTIONED

per Curiam (Frost C.J., Prentice Dep. C.J., Williams J.)

These proceedings concern the appointment of Mr. Michael Somare as the Prime Minister of Papua New Guinea following the general elections earlier this year. Mr. James Eki Mopio, the plaintiff, who is a member of the National Parliament, contends that the requirements of s.142(4) of the Constitution were not complied with, and on that ground seeks a declaration that the appointment of the Prime Minister was null and void and that a new election of Prime Minister should be ordered ....

After Mr. Mopio outlined his case a preliminary objection was taken by Mr. Pokwari Kale on behalf of the Speaker that what Mr. Mopio was seeking to do was to litigate before this Court the question whether a procedure prescribed for the Parliament had been complied with, and that such a question, there being no special provision in a Constitutional law to the contrary, was non-justiciable — Constitution s.134. So far as Mr. Mopio's reliance on a breach of the Standing Orders was concerned, Mr. Pokware Kale submitted that as such orders concerned the order and conduct of the Parliament's business and proceedings that matter also was non-justiciable Constitution, ss.133, 134.

Counsel relied also on the Constitution, s.115(2), which provides, so far as is relevant, that there shall be freedom of debate and proceeding in the Parliament, and the exercise of those freedoms shall not be questioned in any court or in any proceedings whatever (otherwise than in proceedings in the Parliament or before a committee of the Parliament).

Mr. Kale then referred to *Dingle v Associated Newspapers Ltd & Ors* [1960] 2 QB 405, a case in England, in which the Court applied the *Bill of Rights* 1688, s.1, art.9, to which our s.115(2) is substantially similar, and also a passage from the headnote of the earlier case of *Bradlaugh v Gossett* (1884) 12 QBD 271 which was adopted by the Court. Whilst full recognition is to be given to the autochthonous nature of the Constitution of Papua New Guinea, this passage is helpful in illustrating the meaning of s.115(2).
It is as follows:

> Reference was also made to *Bradlaugh v Gossett*, and it is sufficient to read a short portion of the headnote: 'The House of Commons is not subject to the control of Her Majesty's Courts in its administration of that part of the statute law which has relation to its internal procedure only. What is said or done within its walls cannot be inquired into in a court of law ...'
>
> There is a clear affirmation of the exclusive right of Parliament to regulate its own internal proceedings.

The Acting Principal Legal Adviser supported these submissions and referred also to the Constitution, s.115(3), which provides, so far as is relevant, 'No member of the parliament is subject to the jurisdiction of any court in respect of the exercise of his powers or the performance of his functions, duties or responsibilities as such, ...' He submitted that this section clearly conferred upon the Speaker an immunity from judicial control or supervision in the exercise of his function of conducting the election of the Prime Minister ....

These are matters which concern the conduct of the business of the Parliament and its procedure. Accordingly as the issues before the Court involve the question whether that procedure has been complied with, and also the exercise of the freedom of proceedings of Parliament and the functions and duties of the Speaker, this Court has no jurisdiction to entertain the case now before it.
James Eki Mopio v The Speaker of the National Parliament [1977] PNGLR 420 at pp.421-423.

PARLIAMENT NOT SUBJECT TO SECTION 23(2) OF THE CONSTITUTION

per Kidu C.J.

[Section 23(2)] does not confer standing. It empowers the National Court to prevent or remedy breaches of constitutional restrictions, prohibitions or duties. In this case there is no question raised of a Constitutional Law which prohibits or restricts an act or imposes a duty. It could be said that parliament is under a duty to act within the ambit of powers conferred on it by the Constitution. If it does not, can it be sent to gaol for ten years or fined K10,000 or ordered to pay compensation? To me it seems that using s.23 to punish or penalize Parliament is not what the provision was intended to do. Although the court has power to rule acts of the Parliament unconstitutional, it has no power to penalize it, nor does it have power to order it to pay compensation. (See s.115 of the Constitution.) It has no power either to stop the Parliament from making laws. The court has power only to determine whether a law made by Parliament is constitutional or unconstitutional.
S.C.R. No. 4 of 1980; Re petition of M.T. Somare [1981] PNGLR 265 at p.267.

INCONSISTENCY BETWEEN SECTION 115(5) AND CONSTITUTIONALISM

Comment

Section 115(5) is a provision which on its face runs directly counter to the sophisticated system of checks against the exercise of arbitrary power built into the Constitution. Read literally it gives absolute protection to any person carrying out any order of the Parliament.

It is conceivable that this result was intended by the framers of the Constitution although the records are silent upon this point. If so it would entrench in the Constitution the same absolute immunity from judicial scrutiny that the English courts were forced to concede to the Parliament in the *Case of the Sherriff of Middlesex* (1840) 11 Ad & E 273. This result would, however, sigificantly undermine the guarantees of human rights purportedly conferred by Division 3 of the Constitution as no Court could challenge or check the excesses of the Parliament by punishing those acting under its direction albeit unconstitutionally.

One way of avoiding this consequence would be to read this provision as if the word 'lawful' were impliedly inserted before the words 'authority' and 'order' in Subsection 5(a). Such a reading would, however, reduce the effect of the provision to nought as it is inconceivable that anyone could be punished for obeying the lawful direction or order of the Parliament. Despite this objection it may well be that such a reading is to be preferred, given the potential for abuse otherwise revealed.

GENERALLY

Referred to

by Miles J. in *S.C.R. No 4 of 1980; Re petition of M.T. Somare* [1981] PNGLR 265 at p.299.

116. — DISALLOWANCE OF SUBORDINATE LAWS.

(1) All subordinate legislative enactments made under an Act of the Parliament —
  (a) shall be tabled in the Parliament as soon as practicable, and in any event within seven sitting days of the Parliament, after being made; and

(b) are subject to disallowance in whole or in part by decision of the Parliament,

in accordance with Section Sch. 1.18 (*disallowance, etc.*) and the Standing Orders of the Parliament.

(2) Subject to Section Sch. 1.18 (*disallowance, etc.*) an Act of the Parliament may make further provision as to the disallowance of a subordinate legislative enactment or part of a subordinate legislative enactment under this section, and as to the effect of such a disallowance on or in respect of rights and liabilities under or affected by the disallowed enactment or part.

(3) Failure to comply with Subsection (1) does not invalidate a subordinate legislative enactment.

C.P.C. Report Ch.6 p.7

Power of disallowance

48. Many regulations, rules, by-laws and orders are made by the government under the authority of enactments of the legislature. Under existing procedures, these are tabled in the House and automatically referred to the Subordinate Legislation Committee for consideration and report. As the original legislative body, the House of Assembly has the power to disallow subordinate legislation. We recommend that this power be provided for in the Constitution.

49. We have, however, reviewed the present system of committees and our proposals include the abolition of the Subordinate Legislation Committee. We think it is too much to expect a single committee to scrutinise effectively subordinate legislation covering all possible subjects ....

RECOMMENDATIONS [p.25]

Powers of disallowance

37. All regulations, rules, by-laws and orders made under an enactment of the National Parliament shall be tabled in the parliament within seven days of their making if parliament is meeting, or if it is not meeting, within seven days of the commencement of the next meeting of the parliament, and shall be referred to the appropriate permanent parliamentary committees for consideration and report.

38. (1) The National Parliament shall have power to disallow any regulations, rules, by-laws or orders made under an enactment of the parliament, not later than the last sitting day of the meeting following that at which those regulations, rules, by-laws or orders were tabled.

(2) Where a motion of disallowance is moved in the National Parliament within the period specified in clause (1), that motion shall also be debated and voted upon within that period — *provided that* notice of the motion is given at least one sitting day before the motion is moved.

117. — TREATIES, ETC.

(1) In this section, unless the contrary intention appears —

"treaty" means an agreement between States that —

(a) is governed by international law; and

(b) creates a relationship binding at international law on Papua New Guinea,

whether embodied in a single instrument or in two or more related instruments and whatever may be its designation, but does not include a visiting forces agreement entered into in accordance with Section 206 (*visiting forces*);

"treaty document" means —

(a) the text of a treaty that it is proposed to accept or to ratify; or
(b) a statement of the effect of such a treaty; or
(c) a copy of the document by which it is intended that Papua New Guinea will express its consent to be bound by such a treaty.

(2) Subject to Subsection (3), the consent of Papua New Guinea to be bound as a party to a treaty may be given only —
(a) by the Head of State, acting with, and in accordance with, the advice of the National Executive Council; or
(b) by a Minister authorized either generally or specifically for the purpose by the Head of State, acting with, and in accordance with, the advice of the National Executive Council; or
(c) otherwise in accordance with international law, usage and practice,
and in accordance with this section.

(3) Subject to Subsection (5), the consent of Papua New Guinea to be bound as a party to a treaty shall not be given —
(a) unless a treaty document relating to the treaty has been presented to the Parliament for at least 10 sitting days; or
(b) if within 10 sitting days of the Parliament after the day on which the treaty document was presented to the Parliament the Parliament, by an absolute majority vote, disapproves the giving of the consent.

(4) The fact that the Parliament has disapproved the giving of the consent of Papua New Guinea to be bound as a party to a treaty does not prevent the re-presentation to the Parliament of a treaty document relating to the treaty, and in that event Subsection (3) once again applies.

(5) Subsection (3) does not apply if —
(a) the Parliament has, by an absolute majority vote, waived the requirements of that subsection; or
(b) both the Speaker (acting on behalf of the Parliament) and the Prime Minister are satisfied that the giving of the consent of Papua New Guinea to be bound as a party to the treaty is too urgent a matter to allow of compliance with that subsection, or that compliance would not be in the national interest.

(6) A certificate of the Speaker as to any matter arising under this section is, before all courts and all persons acting judicially, conclusive evidence of the facts certified to.

(7) Notwithstanding the consent of Papua New Guinea to be bound as a party to a treaty, no treaty forms part of the municipal law of Papua New Guinea unless, and then only to the extent that, it is given the status of municipal law by or under a Constitutional Law or an Act of the Parliament.

(8) Legislative approval or ratification of a treaty does not, without more, give it the status of municipal law for the purposes of Subsection (7).

C.P.C. Report Ch.6 p.7

50. We believe that it is desirable also that the National Parliament should have some say as to whether or not our country should enter into proposed treaties or other international agreements, conventions or acts which give rise to rights or obligations on the part of Papua New Guinea at international law. We recommend that in normal circumstances all such treaties, agreements, etc. be tabled in the parliament and referred to the appropriate permanent committee for consideration and report; and that no such commitment be accepted by the government until it has been before parliament for eight (extendable to twelve) sitting days. We recommend also, however, tha t this requirement be waived if, in any particular case, the Prime Minister and the Speaker (acting on behalf of parliament) jointly certify that the matter is too urgent for the normal procedure to be complied with.

RECOMMENDATIONS [p.25]

39. (1) Subject to clause (2) below, unless the parliament otherwise in any particular case resolves, no treaty, convention, agreement, or other act which gives rise to rights or obligations on the part of Papua New Guinea at international law shall be entered into by the National Executive Council until it has been tabled in the National Parliament for not less than eight sitting days — *provided that* parliament may resolve to extend this period to twelve sitting days.

(2) The requirement in clause (1) above shall not apply in any particular case where the Speaker (acting on behalf of the parliament) and the Prime Minister jointly certify that the matter is too urgent for compliance with that requirement.

(3) Where the parliament, during the period referred to in clause (1) resolves that a treaty, convention, agreement, or other act be not entered into, the National Executive Council shall not enter into that treaty etc.

AS TO PRE-INDEPENDENCE INTERNATIONAL ARRANGEMENTS

Held

International 'arrangements' not amounting to treaties made before Independence do not survive the attaining of Independence under Sch. 2.6(2) of the Constitution as a pre-Independence 'law'.
Costello v The Controller of Civil Aviation (No 1) [1977] PNGLR 229; see Prentice J. at p.236.

AS TO THE DIFFERENCE BETWEEN FORMAL AND INFORMAL INTERNATIONAL AGREEMENTS

per Kapi J.

At international law, whether an agreement is treated as formal (treaty) or informal such as notes verbal and oral, depends on the gravity of the problems and its political implications (see D.P. O'Connell *International Law* Vol. 1, 2nd ed., London 1970) vol. 1, p.195).

Our Constitution under s.117 deals with formal treaties as understood at international law. I would expect that our Government will use these provisions to commit Papua New Guinea in international agreements in matters which are of great importance. I would consider that the use of our defence force on foreign soil for purposes of maintaining law and order is of the greatest importance. International commitment or obligation of this nature ought to be entered in into by way of treaty under s.117. This is clearly envisaged by s.117 only with the exception of agreement entered under s.206 of the Constitution (see s.117(1) of the Constitution).
S.C.R. No 4 of 1980 (No 2); Re petition of M.T. Somare [1982] PNGLR 65 at p.79.

AS TO RELATIONSHIP BETWEEN TREATIES AND INTERNATIONAL OBLIGATIONS REFERRED TO IN SECTION 202 OF THE CONSTITUTION

per Miles J.

Counsel for the petitioner submitted that an international obligation arose under s.202 only if there was an agreement recognisable in international law between Papua New Guinea as a sovereign nation and some other sovereign nation. He conceded that such agreement need not be formalised as a treaty (as to which see the Constitution s.117) and I would agree that an international obligation within s.202 does not have to arise from a treaty. The recommendation of the Constitutional Planning Committee referred to 'international or treaty' obligations (p.13/9 par. 16) and the dropping of the word 'treaty' from the final draft was in my view no more than a recognition that treaty obligations are one type of a wider range of international obligations. In this respect it may be of relevance to record that in the official *Memorandum on the Legality of United States Participation in the Defence of Vietnam* (1966) 54 Department of State Bulletin 474 . . . , the United States justified its action in Vietnam in terms of 'commitments', 'undertakings', 'international obligations' and 'assurances', although the use of the term 'international obligation' was reserved for the situation which had arisen under treaty.
S.C.R. No 4 of 1980 (No 2); Re petition of M.T. Somare [1982] PNGLR 65 at p.84.

Subdivision E. — The Committee System.

118. — PERMANENT PARLIAMENTARY COMMITTEES.

(1) In order to ensure full and active participation by backbenchers in the work of the Parliament and of government, there shall be the following Permanent Parliamentary Committees which, in principle, should cover all major fields of the activities of the National Government:—
- (a) a Public Accounts Committee, established in accordance with Subdivision VIII. 1.C (*the Public Accounts Committee*); and
- (b) such other committees as are determined by the Parliament from time to time.

(2) The Parliament shall, subject to this Constitution, make provision by Organic Law, by Act of the Parliament, Standing Order or otherwise, for the establishment, membership, jurisdiction, functions, powers and procedures of the Permanent Parliamentary Committees, and in particular for empowering such a Committee to call for persons, papers and records.

(3) No Minister may be a member of a Permanent Parliamentary Committee.

(4) In principle, membership of the Permanent Parliamentary Committees should be spread as widely as practicable among the backbenchers.

C.P.C. Report Ch.6 p.9

Permanent Parliamentary Committees

66. Our most significant proposals for the legislature — those dealing with a new system of permanent

parliamentary committeess — stem directly from our concern to ensure that the National Parliament will be a truly effective body. On the basis of our own experience, we are dissatistied with the way the House of Assembly works. Our proposal that there should be a thorough review of Standing Orders is one result of this dissatisfaction. We feel strongly that parliamentary procedures should be changed so that they are more appropriate to our needs. But the essence of the problem lies in the role parliament is to play. As mentioned in the [p.10] introductory chapter of this Report, we are by no means alone in expressing concern that parliament should be permitted to have a more constructive role than is usually provided for it, particularly in a Westminster-type system of government and its variations. We are convinced that a strong system of committees is the most effective way of giving parliament that constructive role.

67. The committees we propose would provide much greater opportunities than exist at present for members on either side of the House who do not become Ministers to contribute usefully to the government of the country. Under the existing system there is often neither the time nor the means to carry out adequately the basic parliamentary functions. With their increasing volume and complexity, legislation and reports cannot be satisfactorily considered during normal sessions of the legislature, nor can there be adequate probing and checking of government activity. Both functions would be greatly facilitated by the use of committees which can act while parliament is in recess. These committees could also work constructively by carrying out inquiries into various matters of national importance either referred to them by parliament or nominated on their own initiative.

68. We propose that the present standing committees known collectively as 'subject committees' be abolished. The sole function of these committees is to 'consider and inform' themselves on any bill, motion or paper referred to them by the House. They have no deliberative powers and are not permitted to pass any motion relating to matters brought before them. The fact that they have become moribund is readily understandable. We recommend that they be replaced by Permanent Parliamentary Committees, intially three in number, each with responsibility for a group of subjects, and called, respectively, the First, Second and Third Parliamentary Committees. Provision is included for additional committees to be established if experience indicates that more are warranted. We prefer the term 'permanent' to the more vague word 'standing', but the intention is the same: the permanent committees would be appointed for the full term of each parliament. There should also be three other Permanent Committees to which we shall refer separately — the General Committee and the Private Business Committee, later in this Chapter, and the Public Accounts Committee, in Chapter 9, 'Financial Control'.

Composition of permanent committees

69. Under our proposals, most permanent parliamentary committees would consist of 10 to 12 members (not being Ministers or the Speaker), who should be broadly representative of opinion in the parliament. With parliament divided between Government and Opposition this would mean a government majority (e.g. of a ratio 6:4, 6:5 or 7:5); but we recommend also that the chairman and deputy chairman of each committee, elected by the committee itself from among its own number, would in these circumstances, be Government and Opposition members respectively. The membership of each committee would be subject to approval by resolution of the parliament. To perform their functions effectively, the committees should have adequate finance, facilities and suitably qualified staff.

Subject areas

70. We recommend that these Permanent Parliamentary Committees have specific responsibilities in subject areas as follows:—

First Parliamentary Committee:

constitutional matters; foreign relations, trade and investment; defence; police; public employment.

Second Parliamentary Committee:

finance; industry; natural resources.

Third Parliamentary Committee:

social welfare (including health and education); justice.

A general Parliamentary Committee (discussed below), in which the chairmen and deputy chairmen of the other permanent committees meet under the chairmanship of the Speaker would draw up the details of how specific matters should be allocated to the committees within the framework laid down, and make recommendations for these to be incorporated in Standing Orders. It would be the responsibility of the General Parliamentary Committee to resolve any 'demarcation' disputes that might arise, and to review the overall allocation from time to time with a view to recommending any changes to parliament. In addition, however, to provide greater flexibility and to take into account the likelihood that some matters would overlap the areas of responsibility of more than one committee, we propose that the committees be allowed to meet jointly to consider any matter, or to set up joint sub-committees for that purpose. [p.11] ...

72. In addition, so that parliamentarians can participate more readily in government, we propose that the present artificial barriers between Ministers and other members, and between legislators and bureaucrats, be reduced by providing for co-operation between them in the preparation of legislation. We intend this proposal to apply more particularly to legislation arising from substantive statements, papers or reports made or tabled in parliament or from resolutions of parliament. It is not intended to affect the right of a government to seek the implementation of its basic policies through its own legislation.

73. Another important area of committee activity would be that relating to reports and papers presented to parliament. Too often in the past the House of Assembly has been unable to give proper consideration to reports dealing with even the most important of subjects. A recent example was the Report of the Committee of Inquiry into Land Matters, which was hardly debated at all. We therefore recommend that the permanent parliamentary committees consider and make recommendations on any reports or papers referred to them by parliament.

74. We propose also that the First, Second and Third Permanent Parliamentary Committees, (and others like them) be given the power to carry out inquiries of their own into matters of national importance — either referred to them by parliament or nominated on their own initiative — and to report their findings and recommendations to parliament. They may, in this context, perhaps also prepare relevant draft legislation. Recent developments in a number on countries, some with conservative parliamentary traditions, have shown that inquiries by parliamentary committees can produce very constructive and illuminating contributions to government, and can do much also to stimulate greater interest and participation by the public in the consideration of national affairs.

75. Finally, we recommend that the First, Second and Third Permanent Parliamentary Committees act, in their own spheres of responsibility, as consultative bodies in the appointment of persons to a number of statutory positions provided for in the Constitution or by law. While preserving the right of the executive to appoint those officers who have the major responsibility for tendering it advice and carrying out its policies, our recommendations open up the selection process in a number of constitutional and statutory offices where it is imperative that the holders should enjoy widespread confidence in the community. In some cases, we propose that selection be by specially constituted bodies in which the executive has representation but not control. In others, we recommend that the National Executive Council have power of appointment but that it may not be exercised until after the Council has consulted the appropriate parliamentary committee.

76. Positions to which it is proposed that this latter procedure apply include those of members of the Public Services Commission and other similar bodies, the Chairman of the National Broadcasting Commission, officers who are also Electoral Boundaries Commissioners and the most senior officers of the Police and Defence Forces. We see this form of consultation as a realistic and useful compromise between straight out appointment by the executive on the one hand, and approval by the legislature on the other. It is intended to help bring about some consensus on these appointments, and thereby to avoid their becoming the subject of contentious political debate.

Powers

77. In order that the Permanent Parliamentary Committees may effectively perform their functions, we recommend that, with certain exceptions (mentioned below), they have powers similar to those of the present Public Accounts Committee, Public Works Committee, and Economic Development Committee — such as the power to enforce the attendance of witnesses and examine them under oath, affirmation or otherwise, and to compel the production of documents, including decisions of the National Executive Council. Witnesses appearing before the committees would have reasonable protection from self-incrimination or civil action in respect of their evidence.

78. Under our proposals, however, privilege would extend to Council decisions if their release would seriously prejudice national security or proposed fiscal or revenue measures. We [p.12] propose also that Ministers be exempt from subpoena by any committee. Our recommendations provide instead for procedures designed to promote maximum co-operation between the committees and Ministers. Thus Ministers would be notified in advance of the agenda of committee meetings and when matters relevant to their portfolios are under discussion, they would be entitled to attend those meetings, to address them and, except for voting, to participate fully in their proceedings.

General Committee

79. In addition to the three permanent committees with specific responsibilities for subject areas, we recommend that, with the exception of Private Members Business (discussed below), all matters concerning the internal operation of the National Parliament be dealt with by a single permanent committee of senior members. This committee, to be known as the General Parliamentary Committee, would consist of the Speaker, the Chairmen and Deputy Chairmen of the other permanent committees, and, if he is not otherwise included, the Deputy Speaker. In addition to the functions already described in paragraphs 36-37 (concerning senior positions in the Parliamentary Service) and paragraph 70 (concerning the allocation of subject areas among the other permanent committees), the General Parliamentary Committee would assume the functions of the House, Library, Broadcasting of Parliamentary Proceedings, and Standing Orders committees, which it would replace. Two of these committees have not so far been appointed by the present House.

80. Of the remaining committees currently provided for, the functions of the Budget and Economic Development Committees could be taken over by the permanent committees described in paragraph 70, and possibly those of the Public Works Committee also. A similar recommendation is made in paragraph 49 concerning the present Subordinate Legislation Committee. The Privileges Committee would remain, to be appointed as required. Finally, there is the Private Business Committee for which we propose some modifications in procedure.

Private Business Committee

81. We recommend that Standing Orders continue to provide that on one sitting day per week or, if the sittings of parliament are rearranged as a result of the review of Standing Orders, during an equivalent proportion of parliament's sitting time, precedence be given to the consideration of Private Business. The order in which items are considered should continue to be determined by the Private Business Committee, consisting of the Speaker, Deputy Speaker and five other members (not being Ministers), who are broadly representative of opinion in the parliament. We recommend that in determining the order of business, the Committee give preference to private members' bills over motions. We recommend also that the Committee be empowered to consult any member about a bill or motion he has submitted and that, subject to the approval of the member concerned, such a bill or motion might be withdrawn by leave of the Committee rather than by leave of parliament as a whole. Such a procedure, we believe, would increase the efficiency with which the legislature is able to deal with Private Business.

Summary

82. We have gone into some detail to explain our proposals for a new system of parliamentary committees because of the importance we attached to them and hence our wish that they be understood. We would emphasise that they are intended to contribute to the more effective working of a truly democratic parliamentary system. Although it would be part of their job to review government activity, and it is important that they do so, they should not be regarded as a challenge to the executive. We see the committees rather as fulfilling a role complementary to that of the executive; and the success of their work will depend a great deal on active co-operation between committee members and their staff, on the one hand, and Ministers and their departmental officers, on the other.

119. — CHAIRMEN AND DEPUTY CHAIRMEN.

(1) There shall be a Chairman and a Deputy Chairman of each Permanent Parliamentary Committee.

(2) In principle, either the chairman or the Deputy Chairman of each Permanent Parliamentary Committee should be a member of the Parliament who is recognized by the Parliament as being generally committed to support the Government in the Parliament, and the other should be a member of the principal party or group, or coalition of parties or groups, that is recognized by the Parliament as being not so committed.

(3) Subject to any Act of the Parliament and to the Standing Orders of the parliament, in the event of the absence or non-availability to act of the Chairman (sic), the Deputy Chairman has all the rights, privileges, powers, functions, duties and responsibilities of the Chairman.

120. — ROLES OF CHAIRMEN AND DEPUTY CHAIRMEN OF PERMANENT PARLIAMENTARY COMMITTEES.

(1) The Chairman and Deputy Chairman of each Permanent Parliamentary Committee shall be granted full access to each Minister having responsibilities relevant to the jurisdiction and functions of his Committee and, by arrangement with the Minister, to the head of the Minister's department, and are entitled to be briefed and consulted on major policy issues.

(2) In relation to any information given to or obtained by them under Subsection (1), the Chairman and the Deputy Chairman are under the same obligation, whether by law or by convention, as to con-

fidentiality as is the Minister but this principle does not prevent the Chairman or Deputy Chairman from briefing the members of his Permanent Parliamentary Committee on major policy issues.

(3) In relation to any information given to him under Subsection (2), a member of a Permanent Parliamentary Committee is under the same obligation, whether by law or convention, as to confidentiality as is the Minister.

121. — SESSIONAL COMMITTEES, SELECT COMMITTEES, ETC.

Nothing in this Subdivision prevents the Parliament from establishing Sessional or Select Committees or other committees for any purpose, or prevents the Parliament from sitting as a Committee of the Whole.

C.P.C. Report Ch.6 p.12

Select Committees

83. We recommend that, as at present, the National Parliament have the power to establish Select Committees at any time to inquire into, and report upon, any particular matters.

122. — ARRANGEMENT OF PARLIAMENTARY BUSINESS IN RELATION TO COMMITTEES.

The business of the parliament shall be so arranged as to allow reasonable time for committees of the Parliament to perform their functions adequately, and the Standing Orders of the Parliament shall make provision to ensure that such time is allowed either within or outside the sitting hours of the Parliament.

C.P.C. Report Ch.6 p.11

71. The Permanent Parliamentary Committees, under our proposals, would play a vital part in the legislative process. We recommend that, unless the requirement is waived by a resolution supported by an absolute majority, each bill presented to parliament be referred to the appropriate committee for consideration and report. We believe that as a result it is more likely that legislation would be considered on its merits than at present. However, the proposal does allow the government to by-pass the committees in appropriate cases in the same way as it can at present expedite the second reading of a bill by moving the suspension of Standing Orders. Both procedures require an absolute majority. There is also a safeguard against any committee unduly holding up passage of a bill. Unless parliament grants to a committee an extension of time, debate may proceed on a bill after eight sitting days.

123. — MEMBERSHIP OF PARLIAMENTARY COMMITTEES.

Each committee of the Parliament shall consist only of members of the Parliament, but nothing in this section prevents the establishment, by statute or otherwise, of commissions or committees of any other kind.

Subdivision F. — Calling, etc., of the Parliament.

124. — CALLING, ETC.

(1) The Parliament shall be called to meet not more than 21 days after the day fixed for the return of the writs for a general election, and shall meet not less frequently than three times in each period of 12 months, and, in principle, for not less than nine weeks in each such period.

(2) An Organic Law shall make provision for the calling of meetings of the Parliament.

(*See: Organic Law on the First Meetings of the National Parliament* (expired 31.12.75); *Organic Law on the calling of Meetings of the Parliament Ch.1.*)

(3) Subject to Subsections (1) and (2), an Act of the Parliament or the Standing Orders of the Parliament may make provision in respect of the sittings of the Parliament.

C.P.C. Report Ch.6 p.31

Summoning the National Parliament

78. The Chief Justice shall, after consultation with the Speaker and the Prime Minister, summon the National Parliament no earlier than fourteen days nor later than twenty-one days after a general election.

79. The Speaker shall appoint such other time of meeting of the National Parliament as the National Executive Council fixes according to law, and shall give such prior notice of meetings as is provided by law.

Meetings

80. In any period of twelve months, there shall be at least three meetings of the National Parliament, and the meetings held shall have a total duration of at least nine weeks.

Subdivision G. — Electorates and Elections.

125. — ELECTORATES.

(1) The number of open electorates and of provincial electorates and their boundaries shall be determined by the Parliament in accordance with recommendations from a Boundaries Commission from time to time, at intervals determined by or under an Organic Law, being intervals of not more than 10 years.

(2) In recommending open electorates and open electorate boundaries, the Boundaries Commission shall, taking into account any considerations laid down by an Organic Law, endeavour to ensure that all open electorates contain approximately the same population, within limits prescribed by an Organic Law.

(3) The Parliament may accept or reject, but may not amend, any recommendation of the Boundaries Commission under Subsection (1).

(4) The Boundaries Commission is not subject to direction or control by any person or authority.

(5) An Organic Law shall make further provision for and in respect of the appointment, constitution and procedures of the Boundaries Commission, and for safeguarding its independence, and in relation to the procedures for formulating and considering its recommendations.

(6) An Organic Law relating to provinces or to provincial government may confer or impose on the Boundaries Commission powers, functions, duties or responsibilities in relation to the boundaries of provinces and of provincial electorates.

(*See: Organic Law on National Elections Ch.1.*)

C.P.C. Report Ch.6 p.14

Electoral Commission

92. We have given careful consideration to the question of who should be in charge of carrying out elections, including the registration of voters. At present it is the responsibility of the Chief Electoral Officer, who is appointed under normal public service procedures and is a member of the Department of the Interior. As such, although he must act in accordance with the *Electoral Ordinance*, he is nevertheless, like any other public servant, subject to the policy instructions of his Head of Department and, ultimately, of his Minister.

93. This is the situation in many countries, but in others it is considered more appropriate that the officer responsible for conducting elections should not be open to direct political control. Consequently, he is vested with a measure of independence. We support the adoption of this approach in Papua New Guinea. It would place the officer concerned in a more clearly impartial position and, especially in the context of a developing party system, would provide some assurance to our people that elections are conducted fairly. We therefore recommend that an Electoral Commission be established and that, in respect of its functions prescribed in the Constitution or by law, it should not be subject to the direction or control of any other person or body.

94. We propose that for the purpose of conducting national and provincial elections, the Electoral Commission consist of a single commissioner. We consider also that it would be appropriate for the Electoral Commission to be formally appointed by the Speaker of the National Parliament acting on the advice of a special selection committee. We recommend this procedure and that the committee comprise the Prime Minister or another Minister representing him (chairman), the Chairman and Deputy Chairman of the First Parliamentary Committee which is responsible for constitutional matters, a provincial Premier elected by all the Premiers, and the Chairman of the Public Services Commission. The conditions of service of the Electoral Commissioner, along with those of other constitutional office-holders, are included in Chapter 14.

Boundaries Commissioners

95. Another matter fundamental to the conduct of elections is that of electoral boundaries. Who should draw them, how often, and on the basis of what criteria? Under the present *Electoral Ordinance* electoral boundaries have been twice redrawn by a special committee of five persons appointed by the then Administrator. The committee included the Chief Electoral Officer, the Surveyor-General and the Commissioner for Local Government, although the Ordinance allows other persons with similar qualifications to act in their place. We consider that the drawing of national and provincial electoral boundaries should be another function of the Electoral Commission. For this purpose, however, the Commission should be augmented by four Boundaries Commissioners, including both professional officers and laymen, with one or two additional Commissioners when provincial electoral boundaries are being considered. As Boundaries Commissioners, we recommend the Surveyor-General and Government Statistician (each of whom might be represented by a deputy from time to time); two persons nominated by the National Parliament, who may not be members of parliament or of any

provincial assembly, nor public servants or provincial government employees; and, in the drawing of provincial boundaries, a person nominated by the assembly of the province concerned, subject to the same disqualifications as the nominees of the National Parliament. With parliament divided between Government and Opposition, we envisage that the two parliamentary nominees would be initially proposed by Government and Opposition members respectivly.

Redrawing electoral boundaries

96. At present the *Electoral Ordinance* provides that boundaries should be redrawn whenever the composition of the House of Assembly changes or whenever directed by the Administrator — now [p.15] High Commissioner. Because of the number of seats in the House was increased at each election (sic), boundaries have so far been redrawn twice, with effect from 1968 and 1972. With the introduction of the Constitution it is unlikely that there will be subsequent changes in the composition of the legislature for some time. The main factors that are likely to justify the future redrawing of electoral boundaries are increases and shifts of population. We therefore recommend that boundaries be redrawn after each official five-yearly census or, in any event, at not more than six-yearly intervals.

97. The procedure we propose for the approval of new electoral boundaries by the legislature does not vary greatly from that followed in the past. Following publication of provisional boundaries, a three-month period for objections and its consideration of those objections, the Electoral Commission should present its final recommendations to parliament. The Parliament should have the right to approve or reject the recommendations as a whole, but not to amend them. If the recommendations are approved, the new boundaries should be gazetted to come into effect at the next national and provincial elections. If they are rejected, the Commission should present its recommendations again, with such amendments as it sees fit, within a period of three months. Should parliament reject them a second time, the next general and provincial elections should be held in accordance with the existing boundaries.

98. We have considered carefully the criteria upon which electoral boundaries should be based. Most of the submissions we have received express the view that all electorates should have *about* the same number of people in them, but that other factors should also be taken into account. We agree with this view. At present the *Electoral Ordinance* includes the distribution of population as only one of six criteria to be taken into account and does not accord it any priority. This has contributed to the present anomalies whereby the estimated population of electorates at the 1972 elections varied from 17,900 to 44,400. We propose the adoption of population quota for electorates, from which actual numbers may vary by up to 20 per cent in order that other factors can also be considered.
(*Note*: The 'quota' would be the number arrived at by dividing the total population of the country by the minimum number seats in the parliament. To take a clear example, with a total population of 2,500,000 and a total of 100 seats, the quota would be 25,000 per electorate. If the maximum variation allowed were 20 per cent (that is, 5,000 where the quota is 25,000), electorates could vary in population from 20,000 to 30,000.)

99. We recommend that the degree of variation from the quota be determined on the basis of the following criteria: density of population; physical features and communications; existing electoral boundaries and those of provinces, local government council and administrative areas; and community and diversity of interests. This last criterion, however, should not be interpreted too narrowly in terms of tribal or linguistic affiliations. Although not constituting a majority of the views expressed to us, support for this factor was substantial. It was also the basis for objections to some of the provisional boundaries drawn by the Electoral Boundaries Distribution Committee in 1971. When objections were based on the grounds *only* of tribal or linguistic affiliations, they were rejected by the Committee. We agree with this approach. To act otherwise would lead, in the end, to the need for hundreds of electorates.

GENERALLY

Referred to

per Curiam (Frost C.J., Prentice Dep.C.J., Raine, Saldanha and Kearney JJ.) in *Reference No 3 of 1976* [1976] PNGLR 242 at pp.245-249 (if the first Parliament by an absolute majority vote decides to hold a general election pursuant to s.105(1)(c) of the Constitution, such election may be held notwithstanding that Parliament has not yet determined the number of open and provincial electorates and their boundaries under s.125);

by Pritchard J. in *In re Moresby North East Election Petition* [1977] PNGLR 429 at p.446;

by Kidu C.J. in *S.C.R. No 2 of 1981; Re s.19 of the Constitution* [1981] PNGLR 518 at pp.519,520 (under s.19 of the Constitution the court has power to give an opinion on any question relating to the interpretation or application of a Constitutional Law; however, a question arising as to the accuracy of electoral maps adopted by the Parliament is not such a question); see also Kapi J. at pp.421-424 and Miles J. at pp.525-530.

126. — ELECTIONS

(1) Elections to the Parliament shall be conducted, in accordance with an Organic Law, by an Electoral Commission.

(2) General elections shall be held in accordance with Sections 105 (*general elections*) and 106 (*by-elections*), as required.

(3) The members of the Parliament (other than the nominated members) shall be elected under a system of universal, adult, citizen suffrage in accordance with Section 50 (*right to vote and stand for public office*) and the other Constitutional Laws, and the voting age is 18 years.

(4) A citizen's right to vote in an election to the Parliament is as provided by Section 50 (*right to vote and stand for public office*).

(5) No non-citizen may vote in an election for the Parliament.

(6) The Electoral Commission is not subject to direction or control by any person or authority.

(7) An Organic Law shall make provision for and in respect of —
 (a) the appointment, constitution and procedures of the Electoral Commission, and for safeguarding its independence; and
 (b) the electoral system; and
 (c) safeguarding the integrity of elections; and
 (d) appeals to the National Court in electoral matters.

(8) An Organic Law relating to provinces or provincial government may confer or impose on the Electoral Commission powers, functions, duties or responsibilities in relation to provincial elections. (*Added by Constitutional Amendment No 2. — Provincial Government Elections*)

(*See: Organic Law on National Elections* Ch.1.)

C.P.C. Report Ch.6 p.15

Qualification for electors

100. We recommend that only citizens of Papua New Guinea be eligible to vote in elections for the National Parliament. Otherwise, however, we consider that the present qualifications for electors should be retained: 18 years of age or over, the residence in an electorate for a period of at least six months. Citizens who have shifted residence and have not lived for six months in their new electorate would be entitled to vote in the electorate in which they last lived for six months.

System of voting

101. Most colonial territories inherit the voting system found in the countries that have ruled them. There are many different methods of voting, but the preferential system is rare outside Australia. It has been transferred to Papua New Guinea with the exception that here it is not compulsory to give a preference to every candidate. The use of preferences is optional.

102. In his Report on the 1972 general election (p.18), the Chief Electoral Officer said that the optional preferential system 'is becoming more and more complicated and time consuming'. He added that the 'system must be completely revised with a view to making it simple and less complicated so that it is easily understood by both polling officials and voters'. After indicating that most members in 1972 were elected virtually by 'first-past-the-post' voting, the Chief Electoral Officer concluded:

> It is time Papua New Guinea looked realistically and critically at its [p.16] voting system and made its own decision as to what is suitable for its future electoral needs.

In accordance with our general approach, we fully agree with this view.

103. In looking at alternative voting systems, we reject any form of proportional representation. Although often regarded as the 'fairest' system, proportional representation is also very complicated and it is usually found in countries where there are well developed political parties. On both these grounds, proportional representation would be unsuitable for Papua New Guinea.

104. The single most common voting system is 'first-past-the-post' which is favoured by the Chief Electoral Officer. This system is used by Britain, the U.S.A., New Zealand and most of their former colonial territories in Africa, Asia and the Pacific that have became independent. Under this system, the people vote for only one candidate and the candidate with the most votes is declared elected.

105. Those who oppose 'first-past-the-post' voting argue that, where there are more than two candidates, it is possible for one of them to win without obtaining an absolute majority (that is, more than half) of the votes; and, where there are many candidates, he can win with a fairly small proportion of the votes. Although it is true that this can happen in 'first-past-the-post' voting, it is also true of the preferential system in which the use of preference is optional, as it is in Papua New Guinea.

106. In 1970, a Commission of Inquiry into Electoral Procedures in Papua New Guinea said that the people did see the value of the preferential system even if they did not understand how it worked. In particular, the Commission stated that people were worried that under 'first-past-the-post' voting, the candidate from the biggest clan or language group would always win though that group might form only a small minority in the electorate as a whole. The Commission concluded that most people wanted to keep the preferential system, and predicted that there would be an increase in the number of people who used their preferences at elections.

107. Two points need to be made about this. Firstly, the evidence of elections in this country is not conclusive one way or the other in regard to the prospects of a candidate from the biggest group. Because so many people do *not* use their preferences, such a candidate can, and often does, win under the present system. But it is also true that a candidate from a smaller group has often been in the lead after the first count (that is, the equivalent of 'first-past-the-post') because bigger groups have split their votes between two or more candidates.

108. Secondly, it is by no means clear that an increasing number of people are using their preferences. It was found in the 1972 election that in only 13 electorates was the candidate who led on the first count defeated after preferences had been distributed. In none of these did the winning candidate receive an absolute majority of votes. In fact, in all the electorates in which the winner *did* receive an absolute majority, he had also led on the first count, and in relatively few of these (7) was it necessary to distribute preferences at all. By contrast, where preferences were distributed through numerous counts, winning candidates often received less than a third of the total valid votes cast.

109. On the basis of their own experience, and with the help of a fair summary of the arguments in favour of the two systems of voting, a clear majority of those who have made submissions have asked for a change to 'first-past-the-post'. The Committee agrees. In addition to the fact that the optional preferential system has not produced the advantages often claimed for it, 'first-past-the-post' voting will mean that the people may vote only for the person they really want (something many are doing now). The system is easier to understand, easier to run, and the results become known much more quickly. For all these reasons, we recommend a change to the 'first-past-the-post' system.

Absentee voting

110. In his Report on the 1972 general election)(p.11), the Chief Electoral Officer commented that 'absentee voting is continuing to give 'headaches' to the electoral officials, because of its complexity and questionable worth'. He added that about three-quarters of all absentee votes at the last two elections had to be rejected because of the difficulty of identifying the voters as belonging to the electorate concerned. Absentee votes have never made any difference to the result of an election in Papua New Guinea. 'The whole operation', he concluded, 'is a waste of money and time'.

111. We agree with this view. We accept also the argument put forward by the Chief [p.17] Electoral Officer that a person who is away from his electorate for less than six months (the limit now imposed by law for absentee voting) and anxious to vote in his home electorate should be able to continue to do so by applying for a postal vote. We propose, however, that there should be a strict time limit so that all postal votes must be received by the Returning Officer concerned by the end of the polling period. This may necessitate closing applications for postal votes at, say, one week prior to the start of polling.

(*Note*: To cast an *absentee vote*, an elector may go to a polling booth in any electorate, and request and mark a ballot paper for his home electorate. When the ballot boxes are opened, the absentee ballot paper is sent to the Returning Officer in the home electorate.
To cast a *postal vote*, an elector may apply for a ballot paper either to his nearest electoral office or by post to the Returning Officer in his home electorate. If he is found to satisfy the requirements, the ballot paper is issued to him. This must be done no later than the day before polling starts. He then marks it and posts it back to the Returning Officer.
Under existing rules, the official result can be delayed for up to two weeks after polling has closed waiting for absentee and postal votes to arrive.)

112. After conferring with senior members of the Chief Electoral Office, we believe that in simplifying the system of voting — by adopting 'first-past-the-post' and restricting voting by absentees to the use of postal ballots — the whole electoral machinery will run more smoothly. In addition, this should mean that the polling period can be reduced, and also the period following an election before the final results are known. These last advantages will have the very important effect of reducing the time it will take to confirm an existing government in office or to establish the need for a new one to be formed. We believe that minimizing one period of political uncertainty at election times is to be welcomed.

General electoral provisions

113. We are most concerned at the decline in the proportion of eligible electors who are voting in general elections. According to official figures, only 60 per cent of persons eligible to vote actually did so in the 1972 elections, compared with 64 per cent in 1968 and 72 per cent in 1964. We recognise that in significant measure this is a political problem, but we believe that everything possible should be done to ensure that the electoral machinery is geared to maximum participation. The Constitution should require that the electoral law contain provisions designed to ensure that, so far as is practicable, any person entitled to vote at an election of members of the National Parliament should have a reasonable opportunity of doing so. We recommend accordingly. In addition as an ultimate safeguard, we propose that any election at which fewer than 30 per cent of persons eligible to vote did so, be declared invalid and a fresh election ordered.

Candidates' deposits

114. We have given careful consideration to the question of what deposit should be paid by candidates in respect of their nominations for election to the National Parliament. We agree that a reasonable deposit should be paid to help ensure that the act of nominating is regarded with appropriate seriousness. However, we believe that the deposit should not be set at a figure so high that it is likely to exclude a great many people merely because they cannot afford the sum involved. There is a very real danger that this would be the effect of implementing the recent resolution of the House of Assembly which proposes a deposit of $200. We recommend that the deposit for candidates should remain at $100.

AS TO SAFEGUARDING THE INTEGRITY OF ELECTIONS

Held

The principle that the integrity of elections should be safeguarded (s.126(7)(c)) requires that candidates must strictly comply with prescribed electoral qualifications. Failure to satisfy the residency test must result in ineligibility to be nominated as a candidate or to be a Member of Parliament for that electorate.
In re Moresby North East Parliamentary Elections (No 2) [1977] PNGLR 448, see Frost C.J. at p.456.

Held

There is nothing in the Constitution to empower the Electoral Commissioner to abridge any time prescribed by the *Organic Law on National Elections* for the issue of writs etc.
In the Matter of the Organic Law on National Elections and In the matter of Iambakey Okuk (1983 Unreported) S248; see per Curiam at p.3.

SYSTEM OF ELECTION MUST COMPLY WITH SECTION 50 OF THE CONSTITUTION

Held

An amendment to the *Organic Law on National Elections* which required a candidate for election to Parliament to lodge a K1000 deposit on nomination was invalid as effectively prohibiting the exercise of the right under s.50(1) of a citizen to offer himself for election. Such a right may be regulated or restricted (see Constitution s.50(2)) but cannot lawfully be extinguished.) *S.C.R. No 2 of 1982; Re Organic Law* [1982] PNGLR 214.

SECTION 126(7) DIRECTORY, NOT MANDATORY

per Pritchard J.

If s.126(7) were mandatory as opposed to directory, and the Organic Law had in fact been passed after Independence, the matter may be different. That it is not mandatory is in my view clear. For a start, there is no time fixed or indicated within which Organic Laws should be enacted. As an example those required under s.129 and s.130 to deal with the integrity of political parties and candidates have never been enacted. It was because of apprehension as to when the Parliament of the newly independent Papua New Guinea might enact the Organic Laws authorized by the Constitution, that led the Constituent Assembly itself to create those Organic Laws it felt were required at Independence by the system of Provisional Organic Laws. The Deputy Chief Justice has referred to the rush involved in such exercise in his draft judgment.

In *Liverpool Borough Bank v Turner* (1861) 30 LJ Ch. 379 at p.380 Lord Campbell said 'No universal rule can be laid down as to whether mandatory enactments shall be considered directory only or obligatory with an implied nullification for disobedience. It is the duty of the courts of justice to try to get at the real intention of the legislature by carefully attending to the whole scope of the statute to be construed'. In *Pearse v Morrice* (1834) 2 A & E 84 at p.96, Taunton J. said that he understood 'the distinction to be, that a clause is directory where the provisions contain mere matter of direction and nothing more, but not so where they are followed by such words as 'that anything done contrary to the provisions shall be null and void to all intents'.'

Looking then at s.126(7) first. It gives no clear guideline at all as to what extent an Organic Law should provide for appeals to the National Court in electoral matters. It certainly does not provide that an Organic Law 'alone', 'solely' or 'exclusively' should so provide. Nor does it provide that any provision in any other law contrary to its requirement should be invalid. The whole concept of Organic Laws is that, when they are passed as such, they become very difficult to amend (s.17 of the Constitution) and secondly, when they are passed as such, any ordinary Act inconsistent with them must be construed subject to them (s.10 Constitution) and they, of course, must prevail. In other words when Parliament is satisfied to enact as an Organic Law in the strict sense provisions, similar to those in Pt. XVIII, then the new Organic Law will attain the full status of an Organic Law and prevail over the present Pt. XVIII which, at that point of time would, in all probability, be repealed in any event. ....

I therefore believe that if an Act of the Parliament creates an Organic Law, giving the status of an Ordinary Act only to matters which are required in a directory rather than in a mandatory manner to be the subject of an Organic Law, such provisions have full legal effect, until Parliament in its considered judgment decides it is appropriate to enact an Organic Law which is suitable to be cloaked with the invulnerability of an Organic Law provided by the Constitution.

In re Moresby North East Election Petition [1977] PNGLR 429 at pp.445-447; see also Prentice Dep.C.J. at pp.435,436, Williams J. at p.439.

NATIONAL COURT DOES NOT SIT AS A COURT OF DISPUTED RETURNS TO DETERMINE ELECTION PETITIONS

per Kidu C.J.

The Constitution makes no differentiation between the term 'National Court' in s.126 and any other provision therein when the same term is used... If the Parliament or found-

ing fathers of our Constitution had intended that [a] special tribunal be set up to hear electoral petitions they would have made specific provision either in the Constitution or in the *Organic Law on National Elections*.
In the Matter of the Organic Law on National Elections; Malipu Balakau v Paul Torato and anor (1983 Unreported) SC256 at p.10; see also Kapi Dep. C.J. at p.13, Andrew J. at pp.23,24.

ELECTION PETITION UNDER ORGANIC LAW MUST STRICTLY COMPLY WITH ALL CONDITIONS PRECEDENT

per Curiam (Kidu C.J., Kapi Dep.C.J., Andrew J.)

In a petition dated 16th July 1982 and filed in the Registry of the National Court pursuant to s.208 of the *Organic Law on National Elections* the petitioner has disputed the validity of the election of the first-named respondent as member for the electorate of Gumine Open. That result had been declared on 28th June 1982.

There is no dispute that the petition does not contain the occupations of the attesting witnesses as required by s.208(D) of the Organic Law.

In *Mapun Papol v Antony Temo* [1981] PNGLR 178, the National Court had cause to consider whether compliance with an equivalent section to s.208 (i.e. s.184 of the *Provincial Government (Electoral Provisions) Regulations* 1977) was mandatory or not. In that case the petition did not contain the signatures of attesting witnesses. The court there found that the equivalent to s.210 meant that unless the requirements of the equivalent of ss.208 and 209 were complied with, there could be no proceedings in the National Court as a matter of law. The requisites in ss.208 and 209 are conditions precedent to instituting proceedings by way of petition to the National Court. In our view it is clear that all the requirements in ss.208 and 209 must be complied with. Section 208 is in mandatory terms and being the *Organic Law on National Elections* it is a Constitutional Law. Section 210 simply precludes any proceeding unless ss.208 and 209 are complied with.

It may be said that the requirement that a witness's occupation must be stated is not important or that it is not suitable to the circumstances of the country. But the method of disputing an election given by ss.206 and 208 of the Organic Law is a right given by statute. The Organic Law gives no power to dispense with any of the requirements. This is a statutory creature and if any such power is given it must be found in the provisions of the applicable legislation (see *Mapun Papol v Antony Temo*(supra)).

Furthermore, it seems to us that the statute has clearly expressed its intention that a petition must strictly comply with s.208. It is not difficult to see why. An election petition is not an ordinary cause (In *Re Norwich Election Petition; Birbeck v Bullard* (1886) 2 TLR 273) and it is a very serious thing. It is basic and fundamental that elections are decided by the voters who have a free and fair opportunity of electing the candidate that the majority prefer. This is a sacred right and the legislature has accordingly laid down very strict provisions before there can be any challenge to the expression of the will of the majority.

In our opinion it is beyond argument that if a petition does not comply with all of the requirements of s.208 of the *Organic Law on National Elections* then there can be no proceedings on the petition because of s.210.
S.C.R. No 4 of 1982; Re Delba Biri v Bill Ginbogl Ninkama [1982] PNGLR 342 at pp.344,345.

Referred to

per Curiam (Kidu C.J., Kapi Dep.C.J., Andrew J.) in *S.C.R. No 5 of 1982; Hugo Berghauser and ors v Joseph Aoae* [1982] PNGLR 379 at pp.381-383 (strict compliance required: no provision for joint petitions disputing the validity of an election or return);

by Kidu C.J. and Pratt J. in *In the Matter of the Organic Law on National Elections and In the Matter of Kuberi Epi and ors* (1982 Unreported) SC247 at p.4 (strict compliance with the requirements of the Organic Law does not necessitate the strict interpretation of such sections. The matter of interpretation is governed by Sch.1.5);

per Curiam (Kidu C.J., Kapi Dep.C.J., Kaputin J.) in *In the Matter of the Organic Law on National Elections and In the Matter of Iambakey Okuk* (1983 Unreported) SC248 at p.3 (there is nothing in the Constitution which would enable the Electoral Commission to abridge the time permitted by the Organic Law for the issue of writs etc.).

GENERALLY

Referred to

by Pritchard J. (dissenting) in *Constitutional Reference No 1 of 1978 (s.19)* [1978] PNGLR 345 at p.381 (Electoral Commission is a 'governmental body' within the meaning of Sch.1.2 of the Constitution);

by Andrew J. in *Okuk v Nilkare* (1982 Unreported) N406 at p.6 (no nomination may be valid if the person nominating is under age 25);

by Andrew J. in *In the Matter of the Organic Law on National Elections; Malipo Balakau v Paul Torato and anor* (1983 Unreported) SC256 at p.24.

Subdivision H. — Protection of Elections from Outside or Hidden Influence.

127. — PURPOSE OF SUBDIVISION H.

The purpose of this Subdivision is to protect elections and to prevent candidates from being, or appearing to be or to have been, improperly or unduly influenced by outside (especially foreign) or hidden influences, and an Organic Law may make provision, in addition to the provisions expressly referred to in this Subdivision, for achieving that purpose.

128. — "REGISTERED POLITICAL PARTY".

In this Subdivision, "registered political party" means a political party or organization registered under an Organic Law made for the purpose of Section 129(1)(a) (*integrity of political parties*).

129. — INTEGRITY OF POLITICAL PARTIES.

(1) An Organic Law shall make provision —
- (a) requiring any political party or organization having political aims and desiring to nominate a candidate for election to the Parliament, or to publicly support such a candidate as representing its views, to register with the Electoral Commission such reasonable particulars as are prescribed by Organic Law; and
- (b) requiring any such party or organisation to disclose to the Ombudsman Commission or some other authority prescribed by the law in such manner, at such times and with such details as are prescribed in or under the law —

(i) its assets and income, and their sources; and
(ii) its expenditure on or connected with an election or the support of a candidate; and

(c) prohibiting non-citizens from membership of, and from contributing to the funds of, any such party or organization; and
(d) defining the corporations and organizations that are to be regarded as non-citizens for the purpose of a provision made for the purposes of paragraph (c); and
(e) limiting the amount or contributions that such a party or organization may receive from any source or sources; and
(f) requiring persons who have made, or may have made, contributions to any such party or organization to give to the Ombudsman Commission or some other authority, details of any such contribution.

(2) Where another authority is prescribed by the law under Subsection (1)(b), that authority —
(a) shall be composed of a person or persons who are declared under paragraph (i) of the definition of "constitutional office-holder" in Section 221 (*definitions*) to be a constitutional office-holder; and
(b) is not subject to direction or control by any person or authority.

(3) An Organic Law made for the purposes of Subsection (1) may provide that the value of any assistance given otherwise than in cash shall be taken into account as expenditure or contributions for any purpose of that subsection or of that law.

C.P.C. Report Ch.6 p.17

Restrictions on financing parties and candidates

115. Over recent years in many countries there have been increasingly determined efforts to find ways of preventing the corruption of political parties and election candidates. The problem is an exceedingly difficult one to solve and it is unlikely that any country has found the complete answer in the various kinds of legislation that have been adopted. We believe, however, that this should not discourage Papua New Guinea from making its own efforts to prevent corruption of this nature; and we believe that the time to act is now, when we are about to become an independent state and before corruption has the chance to take root.

116. The problem, as we see it, is twofold: firstly, to prevent parties and candidates from receiving financial and other material assistance on such a scale that there is a grave danger of their becoming the tools, whether consciously or not, of their benefactors, and in particular to prevent foreign interests from distorting our electoral process in this manner; secondly, to prevent a situation where most of our people are virtually excluded from national political office because they are unable to raise sufficient funds to compete effectively against their weathier countrymen. Our recommendations are [p.18] intended to meet these problems.

117. We propose that candidates in national elections should not declare, or allow to be declared, their affiliation with a political party or political association unless that party or association is registered. The function of registering political parties and associations should be performed by the Registrar-General, who should have independence in this matter. We provide for appeals to the courts against any decision to refuse or cancel registration. All organisations registered as political parties or associations must declare, once a year, their assets and liabilities, sources of income and amount received from each source, but this information should not include individual membership fees or the names of those who pay them. The financial information would be tabled annually in Parliament.

118. We propose further that no political party or association be allowed to accept benefits totalling more than the amount prescribed by law from any one source in one year. We recommend that the amount prescribed initially in legislation should be $1,000. We propose, however, that there should be a prohibition on political parties or associations receiving any contribution of funds or other benefit from a non-citizen or from any company, firm or other body which is effectively controlled by non-citizens.

119. We realise that this prohibition will adversely affect the functioning of the existing parties. So that national political parties will be able to function effectively without relying on donations and other benefits given to them by foreigners (corporations or individuals), we recommend that the Government should immediately explore ways of fairly distributing finance among them from a central fund made up of moneys derived from a specific tax or levy (e.g. on all companies paying company tax) and donations from foreigners. The finance distributed would be sufficient to enable political parties to pay for the running expenses of a national office, including the salaries and travelling expenses of an adequate staff, and also to assist the parties in conducting national election campaigns. There are a number of countries where schemes of this nature have been introduced. We believe that a suitable one could be established here so that political parties can contribute constructively to the political life of the country.

RECOMMENDATIONS. [p.33]

Political parties — restrictions on finance

100. A candidate for election to the National Parliament may not declare or allow to be declared his affiliation with a political party or political association unless that party or association is registered.

101. (1) There shall be a Registrar-General, who shall be a public officer, and whose functions shall include the registration of political parties and associations.
(2) In respect of that function he shall not be subject to the direction or control of any other person or authority.
(3) Registration of a political party or association shall not be refused or cancelled except on reasonable grounds and in accordance with law.
(4) An appeal shall lie to the National Court of Justice against refusal or cancellation of registration of a political party or association.

102. Organisations registered as political parties or political associations shall be required to declare, annually, their assets and liabilities, their sources of income, and the amount received from each source —
provided that this information shall not include individual membership fees and the names of those who, bona fide, pay them.

103. Financial information declared by political parties and political associations shall be submitted annually to the Speaker for tabling in the National Parliament.

104. (1) No registered political party may accept benefits totalling more than the amount prescribed by law from any one source in one year.
(2) The amount to be prescribed initially by law shall be $1,000.

105. A contribution to the funds of, or the conferring of a benefit upon, a registered political party or political association by a non-citizen, or by any company, firm or other body which is effectively controlled by non-citizens shall be prohibited. ('Contribution' includes money to establish a political party or association.)

106. In view of the need to ensure that national political parties have sufficient funds to continue to function effectively without relying on donations and other benefits given to them by foreigners (corporations and individuals), the government should immediately explore ways of fairly distributing finance among such parties from a central fund made up of moneys derived from — [p.34]
(a) a specific tax or taxes (or levy), for example on all companies which pay income tax; and
(b) donations from foreigners.

107. The finance distributed should be sufficient to enable all registered national political parties to pay for the running expenses of a national office, including the salaries and travelling expenses of an adequate staff, and also to assist these parties in conducting national election campaigns.

NO LAW YET ENACTED

Referred to

by Pritchard J. in *In re Moresby North East Election Petition* [1977] PNGLR 429 at p.445;

by Pritchard J. in *Constitutional Reference No 1 of 1978 (s.19)* [1978] PNGLR 345 at p.374.

130. — INTEGRITY OF CANDIDATES.

(1) An Organic Law shall make provision —
(a) requiring a candidate or former candidate for election to the Parliament to disclose to the Ombudsman Commission or some other authority prescribed by the law, in such manner, at such times and with such details as are prescribed by or under the law —
(i) any assistance (financial or other) received by him in respect of his candidature, and its source; and
(ii) the amount or value of his electoral expenses; and
(b) prohibiting a candidate or former candidate for election to the Parliament from accepting from a non-citizen assistance (financial or other) in respect of his candidature; and
(c) defining the corporations and organizations that are to be regarded as non-citizens for the purposes of a provision made for the purposes of paragraph (b); and
(d) regulating or restricting the amount or kind of such assistance that may be received from any source other than a registered political party; and
(e) prohibiting a candidate for election to the Parliament from holding himself out as representing any party or organization other than a registered political party that has publicly adopted him as its candidate.

(2) Where another authority is prescribed by the law under Subsection (1)(b), that authority —
(a) shall be composed of a person or persons who are declared under paragraph (i) of the definition of "constitutional office-holder" in Section 221 (*definitions*) to be a constitutional office-holder; and
(b) is not subject to direction or control by any person or authority.

(3) An Organic Law made for the purposes of Subsection (1) may make provision for further defining what are to be regarded as assistance and electoral expenses for any purpose of that subsection or of that law, and in particular may provide that —
(a) the value of hospitality (including meals, accommodation and transport) of a kind and to a degree recognized by custom in the country shall not be taken into account as assistance; and
(b) the personal expenses of a candidate shall not be taken into account as electoral expenses.

(4) In this section —
"electoral expenses", in relation to a candidate, means expenses incurred (whether before, during or after an election to the Parliament, including expenses incurred before the issue of the writ for election) by him or on his behalf on account of or in respect of the election;
"personal expenses", in relation to a candidate, means any reasonable costs incurred by him personally for travel and for living away from his home for the purposes of the election.

C.P.C. Report Ch.6 p.18

Election expenses of candidates

120. We propose that every person who is elected to the National Parliament should, within three months of the declaration of his election, submit to the Ombudsman Commission a statement showing the total expenditure associated with his election campaign, including the source of each item of expenditure and the total sum or value of benefits from each source. (We define the term 'expenditure' in our detailed recommendations).

121. Our proposals require that the total campaign expenditure permitted, expressly or tacitly, by any candidate for election to Parliament should not exceed the maximum amount prescribed by law. We recommend that the initial maximum should be fixed at $1,500, which appears to us as being sufficient to cover the cost of any reasonable campaign in a Papua New Guinea open electorate. There should be a similar provision relating to the maximum permissible from any source other than a political party. We recommend an initial maximum of $500. In keeping with our proposals for a similar prohibition in respect of political parties, we recommend also that no candidate for election to Parliament be permitted to accept, either directly or indirectly, any benefit in relation to his candidature from any non-citizen, or from any company, firm or other body which is effectively controlled by non-citizens.

122. We propose that a breach of the provisions limiting election expenses and receipt of benefits in relation to candidature for election to Parliament constitute an offence. The penalty should, according to law, be a fine or, in the case of a serious offence, imprisonment or loss of office as a member of Parliament.

123. It is our intention that these restrictions on the financing of political parties and election candidates should be incorporated in a Schedule to the Constitution, and that they should be able to be amended by a bill supported by an absolute majority of members of Parliament. (The actual financial limits would be prescribed in ordinary legislation.) We have in mind that the need for changes to these provisions may soon become apparent in the light of experience here and in other countries where similar restrictions have only recently been imposed.

RECOMMENDATIONS. [p.34]

Limitation on election expenses

108. No candidate for election to the National Parliament may accept, agree to accept or, at the time of his nomination, have accepted any benefit in relation, either directly or indirectly, to his candidature from a non-citizen, or from any company or firm or other body which is effectively controlled by non-citizens.

109. Every person who is elected to the National Parliament shall, within three months of the declaration of his election, submit to the Ombudsman Commission a statement showing the total expenditure associated with his election campaign.
Note: 'Expenditure' in this Recommendation includes the value of all gifts and services provided without charge in respect of personal expenses and reasonable living and travelling costs incurred before, during and after the election by that person or, with his permission, express or implied, on his behalf.

110. The statement shall specify the source of each item of expenditure and the total sum or value of benefits received from each source.

111. (1) The total campaign expenditure by, or permitted (expressly or tacitly) by a candidate for election to the National Parliament shall not exceed the maximum amount prescribed by law for such expenditure.
(2) The amount to be prescribed initially by law shall be $1,500.

112. (1) No candidate for election to the National Parliament may accept from any one source benefits in relation, either directly or indirectly, to his candidature, totalling more than the amount prescribed by law, other than from a registered political party.
(2) The amount to be prescribed initially by law shall be $500.

113. (1) A breach of the provisions limiting election expenses and receipt of benefits in relation to candidature for the National Parliament shall constitute an offence.
(2) The penalty for an offence under clause (1) above shall, according to law, be a fine or, in the case of serious offence, imprisonment or loss of office as a member of the Parliament.

NO LAW YET ENACTED

Referred to

by Pritchard J. in *In re Moresby North East Election Petition* [1977] PNGLR 429 at p.445;

by Pritchard J. in *Constitutional Reference No 1 of 1978 (s.19)* [1978] PNGLR 345 at p.374.

Subdivision I. — General.

131. — THE PARLIAMENTARY SALARIES TRIBUNAL.

(1) A Parliamentary Salaries Tribunal is hereby established.

(2) The Tribunal shall consist of —
(a) a judicial officer, appointed by the Judicial and Legal Services Commission, who shall be the Chairman; and
(b) a person with wide practical experience in wage fixation, appointed by the Public Services Commission; and
(c) a member of the Public Services Commission, appointed by that Commission.

(3) The Tribunal is solely responsible for fixing from time to time, at intervals determined by it —
(a) the salaries, allowances and benefits, financial and otherwise (other than pensions or retirement benefits which shall be fixed by a Parliamentary Committee), for all or any members of the Parliament; and
(b) the salaries, allowances and benefits, financial and otherwise (other than pensions or retirement benefits), for all or any members of Provincial Assemblies (including any Speakers appointed from outside the Assemblies). (*Added by Constitutional Amendment No. 6. — Parliamentary Salaries Tribunal (Amendment of Section 131)*).

(4) An Act of the Parliament shall make provision for the powers and procedures of the Tribunal, and generally in respect of it.

(*See: Parliamentary Salaries Tribunal Act* Ch.25;
Parliamentary Salaries (Constitutional Change Act) Act 1981;
Parliamentary Members Retirement Benefits Act 1981.)

C.P.C. Report Ch.6 p.6

Parliamentary Salaries Tribunal

40. The salaries and allowances of members of parliament are frequently the cause of controversy. Those in Papua New Guinea are no exception. The authority to fix the salaries and allowances of our Ministers and members of the House of Assembly has been vested in the Australian Minister for External Territories, now the minister responsible for Papua New Guinea matters. It was he who authorised last year's increase in the salaries of Ministers who were not members of the Executive Council, but he did so on the advice of the Papua New Guinea Government. This became the subject of acrimonious debate in the House. It is largely to avoid this kind of situation that some countries establish independent tribunals to determine the remuneration of all parliamentarians, including Ministers. We believe this to be a desirable precedent for Papua New Guinea to follow.

41. We recommend that a Parliamentary Salaries Tribunal be established comprising three persons: a judge or magistrate (as chairman), a person experienced in salary or wage fixation, and a member of the Public Services Commission. The members of the Tribunal should be appointed by the National Executive Council, following consultation with the General Parliamentary Committee, for terms of six years.

42. The Tribunal should be vested with the authority to determine the salaries, allowances, pensions and other benefits of all members of the National Parliament, including the Prime Minister, Deputy Prime Minister and other Ministers, and parliamentary office-holders such as the Speaker and Deputy Speaker, the Leader and Deputy Leader of the Opposition and the party Whips. The Tribunal should also have the powers of a

Commission of Inquiry. We recommend that determinations be made at intervals of four years, but that a particular interval might be reduced to a minimum of two years if the parliament decided that an earlier review was warranted.

43. We believe that the legislation providing for the Tribunal should include those matters which the Tribunal should take into account in making its determinations. We propose that these should be: the National Goals and Directive Principles in the Constitution; the general state of the economy; changes in the cost of living; the general level of salaries and wages in the community; and the relative responsibilities of Ministers, parliamentary office-holders and other members of parliament, subject to the need to avoid undue disparity between the levels of remuneration of these groups.

132. — THE PARLIAMENTARY SERVICE

(1) An Act of the Parliament shall make provision for and in respect of a Parliamentary Service, separate from the other State Services.

(*See: Parliamentary Service Act* Ch.26)

(2) Within the Service, there shall be an office of Clerk of the National Parliament who shall, subject to Subsection (3), be the head of the Service.

(3) The Service shall be subject to the direction and control of the Speaker and shall perform its functions impartially.

C.P.C. Report Ch.6 p.5

Parliamentary Service

35. If the National Parliament is to work effectively it will need to be served by a staff which is competent, sufficient in number, and responsible to the legislature alone. At present parliamentary staff are members of the Department of the House of Assembly, which is established with a limited degree of autonomy in the Public Service legislation. The staff should continue to be under the direction and control of the Speaker, but we propose that its independence of the executive be formalised by establishing a Parliamentary Service under separate legislation.

36. The Service should be headed by the Clerk of the National Parliament, who should be appointed by the Speaker after he has consulted the National Executive Council (the new term we recommend for the present Executive Council), the General Parliamentary Committee (the permanent committee with special responsibilities concerning the operation of parliament), and the Public Service Commission. We recommend here an upgrading of the Clerk's position but his general conditions of service are included with those of other constitutional office-holders in Chapter 14.

37. Other officers of the Parliamentary Service should be appointed by the Speaker on the advice of the Clerk, and in the case of senior positions, after consultation with the General Parliamentary Committee. Although the Parliamentary Service would remain independent of the public services, arrangements should be such as to allow transfers and promotions between them, with protection of service rights. We propose that the Speaker have control over conditions of service and establishment matters in the Parliamentary Service, but subject to consultation with the Prime Minister or the Minister assisting him in respect of the public services, and in the case of establishment matters involving senior positions with the General Parliamentary Committee. [p.6]

38. We recommend that within the Parliamentary Service there should be —
(a) a Parliamentary Research and Information Service, and
(b) an Office of the Parliamentary Counsel,

whose functions should be to provide research and legal services (including parliamentary drafting services) for the Speaker, Committees of the parliament, non-ministerial members, and for Ministers in respect of matters relating to their own electorates. We envisage, however, that the main emphasis in the work of the research and legal staff is likely to be on assisting the permanent parliamentary committees which will have a major role under our proposals. This should also ensure that specialist staff have greater continuity of work than at present.

39. Our proposals include initial maximum establishments which provide for up to eight research officers and two parliamentay counsel to be appointed at a level which should attract able and well qualified staff. There should also be four executive officers to serve the permanent parliamentary committees. Overall, this represents only a slight increase in the present establishment for such staff in the Department of the House of Assembly as a number of the present positions are not filled. But it does involve a general upgrading of senior positions to take account of the greater responsibility which will be placed on these officers as a result of our proposals for the legislature.

GENERALLY

Referred to

by Pritchard J. (dissenting) in *Constitutional Reference No 1 of 1978 (s. 19)* [1978] PNGLR 345 at p.381 (Clerk of the Parliament as a Constitutional office holder).

133. — STANDING ORDERS.

The Parliament may make Standing Orders and other rules and orders in respect of the order and conduct of its business and proceedings and the business and proceedings of its Committees, and of such other matters as by law are required or permitted to be prescribed or provided for by the Standing Orders of the Parliament.

C.P.C. Report Ch.6 p.27

RECOMMENDATIONS

Other procedures

61. Subject to the Constitution, the National Parliament may regulate its own procedure and for this purpose shall make Standing Orders.

62. A thorough review of all Standing Orders of the House of Assembly should be made so that they are made appropriate to the needs of the National Parliament of Papua New Guinea.

GENERALLY

Referred to

per Curiam (Frost C.J., Prentice Dep.C.J. Williams J.) in *James Eki Mopio v The Speaker of the National Parliament* [1977] PNGLR 420 at p.421;

by Miles J. in *S.C.R. No 4 of 1980; Re petition of M.T. Somare* [1981] PNGLR 265 at p.299.

134. — PROCEEDINGS NON-JUSTICIABLE.

Except as is specifically provided by a Constitutional Law, the question, whether the procedures prescribed for the Parliament or its committees have been complied with, is non-justiciable, and a certificate by the Speaker under Section 110 (*certification as to making of laws*) is conclusive as to the matters required to be set out in it.

C.P.C. Report Ch.6 p.12

Disputes

84. We propose that any disputes about membership of the parliament — such as whether a person has been properly elected or whether a vacancy has occurred — should be determined by a judge of the National Court constituted as the Electoral Court, and that appeals should lie to the Supreme Court (that is, the new appellate court proposed in Chapter 8). In general, however, other disputes arising from the procedures of parliament should not be subject to the jurisdiction of any court. Thus, for example, the election of the Speaker should be conclusively determined by the certificate of the Chief Justice, and the election of other office-holders, including the Prime Minister, by the certificate of the Speaker. The Speaker's certificate should be conclusive also in respect of disputes as to whether a bill has been [p.13] validly passed or a motion of disallowance carried. We consider that disciplinary procedures should not be reviewable in any court. We recommend, however, that questions concerning the extent and nature of parliamentary privilege should be dealt with by the National Court, with appeals lying to the Supreme Court.

RECOMMENDATIONS [p.27]

Disputes

60. (1) Questions concerning the extent and nature of parliamentary privilege shall be subject to the jurisdiction of the National Court with appeals lying to the Supreme Court.
(2) With the exception of cases covered by clause (1) above and questions concerning membership of the parliament covered in Recommendation 20, disputes arising from the procedures of parliament shall not be subject to the jurisdiction of any court.
(3) The election of the Speaker shall be conclusively determined by the certificate of the Chief Justice and the election of other office-holders, including the Prime Minister, by the certificate of the Speaker.
(4) Question as to whether a bill has been validly passed or a motion of disallowance carried shall be conclusively determined by the certificate of the Speaker.
(5) Disciplinary procedures of the National Parliament shall not be reviewed by any Court.

PROCEDURES FOR ELECTION OF THE PRIME MINISTER ARE NON-JUSTICIABLE

per Curiam (Frost C.J., Prentice Dep. C.J., Williams J.)

These proceedings concern the appointment of Mr. Michael Somare as the Prime Minister of Papua New Guinea following the general elections earlier this year. Mr. James Eki Mopio, the plaintiff, who is a member of the National Parliament, contends that the requirements of s.142(4) of the Constitution were not complied with, and on that ground seeks a declaration that the appointment of the Prime Minister was null and void and that a new election of Prime Minister should be ordered . . .

After Mr. Mopio outlined his case a preliminary objection was taken by Mr. Pokwari Kale on behalf of the Speaker that what Mr. Mopio was seeking to do was to litigate before this Court the question whether a procedure prescribed for the Parliament had been complied with, and that such a question, there being no special provision in a Constitutional law to the contrary, was non-justiciable — Constitution, s.134. So far as Mr. Mopio's reliance on a breach of the Standing Orders was concerned, Mr. Pokwari Kale submitted that as such orders concerned the order and conduct of the Parliament's business and proceedings that matter also was non-justiciable. Constitution, ss.133, 134.

Counsel relied also on the Constitution, s.115(2), which provides, so far as is relevant, that there shall be freedom of debate and proceeding in the Parliament, and the exercise of those freedoms shall not be questioned in any court or in any proceedings whatever (otherwise than in proceedings in the Parliament or before a committee of the Parliament).

Mr. Kale then referred to *Dingle v Associated Newspapers Ltd & Ors* [1960] 2 QB 405, a case in England, in which the Court applied the *Bill of Rights* 1688, s.1, art.9, to which our s.115(2) is substantially similar, and also a passage from the headnote of the earlier case of *Bradlaugh v Gossett* (1884) 12 QBD 271 which was adopted by the Court. Whilst full recognition is to be given to the autochthonous nature of the Constitution of Papua New Guinea, this passage is helpful in illustrating the meaning of s.115(2).
It is as follows:

> Reference was also made to *Bradlaugh v Gossett*, and it is sufficient to read a short portion of the headnote: 'The House of Commons is not subject to the control of Her Majesty's Courts in its administration of that part of the statute law which has relation to its internal procedure only. What is said or done within its walls cannot be inquired into in a court of law . . .' There is a clear affirmation of the exclusive right of Parliament to regulate its own internal proceedings.

The Acting Principal Legal Adviser supported these submissions and referred also to the Constitution, s.115(3), which provides, so far as is relevent, 'No member of the Parliament is subject to the jurisdiction of any court in respect of the exercise of his powers or the performance of his functions, duties or responsibilities as such, . . .' He submitted that this section clearly conferred upon the Speaker an immunity from judicial control or supervision in the exercise of his function of conducting the election of the Prime Minister . . .

These are matters which concern the conduct of the business of the Parliament and its procedure. Accordingly as the issues before the Court involve the question whether that procedure has been complied with, and also the exercise of the freedom of proceedings of Parliament and the functions and duties of the Speaker, this Court has no jurisdiction to entertain the case now before it.

James Eki Mopio v The Speaker of the National Parliament [1977] PNGLR 420 at pp. 421-423.

Referred to

by Miles J. in *S.C.R. No 4 of 1980; Re petition of M.T. Somare* [1981] PNGLR 265 at p.299.

135. — QUESTIONS AS TO MEMBERSHIP, ETC.

The National Court has jurisdiction to determine any question as to —

(a) the qualifications of a person to be or to remain a member of the Parliament; or

(b) the validity of an election to the Parliament.

(*See: Organic Law on National Elections* Ch.1.)

C.P.C. Report Ch.6 p.12

Disputes

84. We propose that any disputes about membership of the parliament — such as whether a person has been properly elected or whether a vacancy has occurred — should be determined by a judge of the National Court constituted as the Electoral Court, and that appeals should lie to the Supreme Court (that is, the new appellate court proposed in Chapter 8).

NATIONAL COURT MAY REFER POINTS OF CONSTITUTIONAL INTERPRETATION TO THE SUPREME COURT AND THE SUPREME COURT MAY ENTERTAIN IN EXCEPTIONAL CASES (AS AN APPEAL) INTERLOCUTORY APPLICATIONS FROM THE NATIONAL COURT

per Prentice Dep.C.J.

The respondent to an election petition has, by application to the Supreme Court, caused the hearing of the petition against his election to be stopped. The Chief Justice sitting as the National Court had given a ruling that the petitioner was entitled to rely in a petition under s.112, *National Elections Act*, on a question of lack of qualification in the respondent. Following the cessation of the hearing, leave to appeal has been sought against this ruling on the basis that it was an 'interlocutory judgment' (s.14 *Supreme Court Act*). In addition a writ of prohibition against the continuance of the hearing of the petition has been sought.

For myself, in an ordinary case, I would be reluctant to rule that the Supreme Court should so interfere with a hearing before the National Court. I consider that as a general rule the Supreme Court should not interfere with a National Court hearing until it had reached a conclusion — unless, in an exceptional case, the National Court itself referred a case for decision before finality. That finality should normally be obtained in the National Court before appeal were sought therefrom, is called for, in my opinion, by the geography and circumstances of this country, and the organization of its superior courts. Mr McAlary has presented an argument that s.155(2) of the Constitution, which vests an inherent power in the Supreme Court to review all the judicial acts of the National Court, renders invalid s.14 of the *Supreme Court Act* which requires leave to appeal from an interlocutory judgment. In my opinion the argument is unacceptable. Such a result would render every decision of the National Court (even, for example, on questions of reception of evidence) susceptible to appeal, and presumably before finality of decision. The potentially catastrophic effect upon the work of National and Supreme Courts of such an interpretation is immediately apparent. In my view, s.14 of the *Supreme Court Act* does not infringe upon the powers conferred by the Constitution, but merely regulates their exercise — indeed in an eminently reasonable particular . . .

In the hearing before the National Court it appears to have been assumed by the counsel involved that s.18 of the Constitution did not debar the National Court from interpreting Constitutional laws in an election petition, because the section itself expresses its provisions to be 'subject to the Constitution', and s.135 of the Constitution vested the National Court with 'jurisdiction to determine *any question* as to the qualifications of a person to be or to remain a member of the Parliament or the validity of an election to the Parliament' (emphasis mine); which would, it was apparently agreed, include any ancillary interpretation of a Constitutional Law. Nevertheless, it might well have transpired that during, or at the end of, the hearing, counsel might have sought that such an interpretation point be referred, or the Chief Justice might have wished to refer such a point — in compliance with the Supreme Court's 'inherent power to review all judicial acts of the National Court' (s. 155(2)(b) of the Constitution) — this despite s.220 of the *Organic Law on National Elections*, which enacts that 'a decision of the National Court is final and conclusive and without appeal, and shall not be questioned in any way'. An Organic Law must of course be read subject to the Constitution (s.10(a) of the Constitution).

For the reason that such a reference might have been and could be made, and because the Chief Justice who is engaged in the National Court hearing, is known to be retiring in a few weeks, I would agree that this hearing should continue as a matter of convenience, justice and necessity, as an appeal.

In re Moresby North East Election Petition [1977] PNGLR 429 at pp.430–432; see also Williams J. at p.440 and Pritchard J. at pp.442, 445.

AS TO JURISDICTION OF THE NATIONAL COURT

per Kapi J.

Under s.18(1) of the Constitution the Supreme Court has original jurisdiction to the exclusion of other courts as to any question relating to the interpretation or application of the Constitution. However, his jurisdiction is subject to the Constitution. Where the Constitution specifically empowers any other court other than the Supreme Court to decide a question regarding the interpretation and application of the Constitution then that court shall consider the question. Such examples can be found in s.57 and s.135 of the Constitution, where the National Court is empowered to deal with these matters.

S.C.R. No 4 of 1980; Re petition of M.T. Somare [1981] PNGLR 265 at pp.296, 297; see also Miles J. at p.313.

136. — VALIDATION OF ACTS OF THE PARLIAMENT.

Where a person who has purported to sit or vote as a member of the Parliament at a meeting of the Parliament or of a committee of the Parliament —

(a) was not duly qualified to be elected or appointed, or to continue, as a member of the Parliament; or

(b) had vacated his office as a member of the Parliament,

all things done or purporting to have been done by the Parliament or by the committee, as case may be, shall be deemed to have been as validly done as if that person had, when so sitting or voting, been duly qualified to be elected or appointed or to continue as a member of the Parliament, or had not vacated his office, as the case may be.

Division 3. — Special Instances of the Legislative Power.

137. — ACTS OF INDEMNITY.

(1) If —
(a) a provision of a Constitutional Law has been contravened or not complied with; and
(b) the Parliament is satisfied that —
(i) the contravention or non-compliance was made in good faith and in exceptional circumstances for the purpose, or with the intention, of upholding this Constitution or protecting Papua New Guinea, or of dealing with an emergency for which no provision or no adequate provision appeared to exist; and
(ii) no blameworthiness attaches to some person or some persons concerned in the contravention or non-compliance,

the Parliament may make a special law (to be known as an "Act of Indemnity") in relation to that person or those persons.

(2) An Act of Indemnity shall —
(a) specify the contravention or non-compliance; and
(b) certify as to the Parliament's satisfaction concerning the matters specified in Subsection (1)(b)(i) and (ii); and
(c) identify or provide for the identification of the person or persons to whom it relates; and
(d) provide for the making of full compensation to any person suffering injury as a result of the contravention or non-compliance; and
(e) be made in accordance with the procedures laid down by this Constitution for the making of Organic Laws; and
(f) be passed by an absolute majority vote of the Parliament.

(3) Before the Speaker certifies under Section 110 (*certification as to making of laws*) as to the Act, he shall refer the question, whether the Act complies with this section, for the opinion of the Supreme Court in accordance with Section 19 (*special references to the Supreme Court*), and until the Court advises that the Act does so comply he shall not so certify it.

(4) An Act of Indemnity —
(a) relieves, and shall be expressed to relieve, the person or persons concerned from all liability for, and from all legal consequences of, the contravention or non-compliance; and
(b) if a person concerned has been convicted of an offence in respect of or arising out of the contravention or non-compliance, takes effect as a free pardon,

but in respect only of acts done before the Parliament was formally advised of the intention to propose the Act.

(5) An Act of Indemnity does not take effect as a Constitutional Law.

(6) An Act of Indemnity shall not be amended or extended in any way, and its repeal does not affect the operation of Subsection (4).

Referred to

by Pritchard J. in *Constitutional Reference No 1 of 1978 (s.19)* [1978] PNGLR 345 at p.367.

Division 4. — The National Executive.

Subdivision A. — The National Executive and the Executive Power.

138. — VESTING OF THE EXECUTIVE POWER.

Subject to this Constitution, the executive power of the People is vested in the Head of State, to be exercised in accordance with Division V.2 (*functions, etc., of the Head of State*).

C.P.C. Report: see extracts under s.82 (Queen and Head of State).

EXCLUDES PREROGATIVE EXERCISE OF EXECUTIVE ACTS

Held

The Head of State may act only with and in accordance with the advice of the National Executive Council or other body prescribed for that purpose (s.86(1) and (2)). There is no provision for any prerogative exercise of executive power.
The State v Mogo Wonom [1975] PNGLR 311; see Frost C.J. at p.316; see also Raine J. at p.317, Williams J. at pp.319, 320.

139. — THE NATIONAL EXECUTIVE.

The National Executive consists of —

(a) the Head of State acting in accordance with Division V.2 (*functions, etc., of the Head of State*); and

C.P.C. Report: See extracts under s.82 (Queen and Head of State).

(b) the National Executive Council.

C.P.C. Report Ch.7 p.2

The National Executive Council

14. We have therefore concluded that as there is no clearly demonstrable need for a Head of State, we should not create one merely because it is the usual thing to do. We believe that our proposal for vesting executive power in the National Executive Council, which comprises all Ministers, is most appropriate to our country.

140. — CONFERRING OF POWERS, ETC., OUTSIDE THE NATIONAL EXECUTIVE.

Except where the contrary intention appears, nothing in this Constitution prevents an Organic Law or a statute from conferring or imposing powers, functions, duties or responsibilities on a person or authority outside the National Executive.

C.P.C. Report Ch.7 p.2

15. There are a few very specific executive functions which we propose should be vested in persons or bodies other than the National Executive Council, and which shall be performed strictly in accordance with the Constitution. In the case of the Speaker (mentioned below) these functions do not allow him to exercise any personal discretion.

16. Our recommendations envisage that the Head of Government, whom we propose should have the title of Prime Minister, will be the leader of the group of Ministers — the first among equals. As outlined below, separate provisions are therefore recommended in regard to his appointment and powers.

RECOMMENDATIONS [p.7]

Executive power of Papua New Guinea

3. Except as otherwise provided in the Constitution, the executive power of Papua New Guinea shall be vested in the National Executive Council and shall be exercised either by that Council directly or through members of that Council or officers subordinate to it . . . [p.8]

5. Subject to the Constitution, nothing shall prevent the National Parliament from conferring executive functions on persons or authorities other than the National Executive Council.

Subdivision B. — The Ministry.

141. — NATURE OF THE MINISTRY: COLLECTIVE RESPONSIBILITY.

The Ministry is a Parliamentary Executive, and therefore —

(a) no person who is not a member of the Parliament is eligible to be appointed to be a Minister, and, except as is expressly provided in this Constitution to the contrary, a Minister who ceases to be a member of the Parliament ceases to hold office as a Minister; and

(b) it is collectively answerable to the People, through the Parliament, for the proper carrying out of the executive government of Papua New Guinea and for all things done by or under the authority of the National Executive; and

(c) it is liable to be dismissed from office, either collectively or individually, in accordance with this Sub-division.

C.P.C. Report Ch.7 p.2

17. In order to ensure that decisions are in fact made collectively, we have proposed basic rules of procedure for meetings of the National Executive Council. In normal circumstances, executive decisions should be made only after due consideration and by at least a minimum number of Ministers. We have therefore recommended that a submission to the National [p. 3] Executive Council should be circulated to all Ministers at least two weeks before any decision on it is made. Decisions of the Council must also be made by not less than one-third of the Ministers. This should reinforce the concept of collective responsibility. The same principle leads us to recommend that full minutes of proceedings be kept and distributed to Ministers. They must have a clear record of the decisions for which they are collectively responsible. Our recommendations include procedures which may be adopted whenever urgent action by the Council is required . . .

Ministers to be chosen from within Parliament

23. We propose that the Prime Minister and other Ministers should all be chosen from among members of the National Parliament. We have considered the possibility of allowing some Ministers to be nominated from outside the Parliament in order for example, to obtain the services of persons with particular professional skills. However, as indicated in Chapter 6, we have concluded that the elective principle should not be contravened and we have found little public support for including a provision of this nature. Meanwhile, arrangements can conveniently be made to have specialist advisers available as required when Parliament is sitting.

24. We believe, however, that the present system by which Ministers are nominated by a special committee of the House, and the Ministers in turn choose the Chief Minister from their own number, has outlived its purpose and that the disadvantages of such a cumbersome procedure have become increasingly apparent. We have therefore sought an elective procedure which will directly involve the Parliament and yet cope with a possibly fluid political situation.

RECOMMENDATIONS [p.12]

28. A motion for the removal of a Minister (other than the Prime Minister) may be moved in the National Parliament only on the grounds of inability to perform the functions of his office, whether arising from infirmity of body or mind, or misbehaviour, and if —

(a) the motion is signed by at least one-tenth of the total membership of the Parliament;
(b) the motion is supported by a majority of the First Parliamentary Committee in a report to the Parliament; and
(c) at least one week's prior notice of the intention to move such a motion is given.

AS TO COLLECTIVE RESPONSIBILITY AND THE BUREAUCRACY

per Kidu C.J.

No legislation confers on the Minister for Police the power to direct and control the Secretary for Police. The *Public Service Act* contains no such provision or provisions.

Although the Minister for Police is not specifically empowered to direct and control either the force or the Commissioner, or the Secretary for Police, he has political responsibility for them. He has therefore the duty to ensure that the force and the Commissioner have funds to carry out the functions. He is also responsible for speaking on their behalf when they are under criticism. The Minister, therefore has the *right* to be informed of all aspects of police operations. He has the right to request the head of the police force to provide information relating to the force.

A Minister is part of a Ministry which is given the responsibility by the Constitution to govern Papua New Guinea ....

How can Ministers be responsible for the executive government of this country if their departmental heads, Police Commissioners, etc. refuse to brief and inform them?

The executive government is a conglomerate of Ministers, public officers, statutory bodies, the police force, defence force, etc. The only body in the country that can hold this mass of men, etc. together is the National Executive Council. This is particularly reflected in the Constitutional provisions already mentioned in ss.141, 148 and 149.

Each Minister is responsible to the National Executive Council for the functions etc. of his portfolio. In turn the National Executive Council is responsible to the people. It is this responsibility that carries with it the right of the Minister to be advised and informed of the activities, performances, problems of those who are under his political responsibility.

It is the responsibility of civil servants to advise their Ministers. Granted neither the Constitution nor the *Police Act* nor the *Public Service Act* specifically so provides.

However, the governmental structure set out in the constitutional laws and statutes would not function if civil servants were not obliged to advise their Ministers.

S.C.R. No 1 of 1982; Re Bouraga [1982] PNGLR 178 at pp.186,187; see also Pratt J. at pp.202-208 (note however, in the case of departmental heads, that the only mechanism for enforcing this duty is the threat of dismissal under Sch.1.10(4).)

GENERALLY

Referred to

by Frost C.J. in *Reference No 2 of 1976* [1976] PNGLR 228 at p.232 (dissatisfaction with government policy may be expressed by motion of censure falling short of motion of no confidence); see also Saldanha J. at p.240.

142. — THE PRIME MINISTER.

(1) An office of Prime Minister is hereby established.

(2) The Prime Minister shall be appointed at the first meeting of the Parliament after a general election and otherwise from time to time as the occasion for the appointment of a Prime Minister arises, by the Head of State, acting in accordance with a decision of the Parliament.

(3) If the Parliament is in session when a Prime Minister is to be appointed, the question of the appointment shall be the first matter for consideration, after any formal business and any nomination of a Governor-General or appointment of a Speaker, on the next sitting day.

(4) If the Parliament is not in session when a Prime Minister is to be appointed, the Speaker shall immediately call a meeting of the Parliament, and the question of the appointment shall be the first matter for consideration, after any formal business and any nomination of a Governor-General or appointment of a Speaker, on the next sitting day.

(5) The Prime Minister —
(a) shall be dismissed from office by the Head of State if the Parliament passes, in accordance with Section 145 (*motions of no confidence*), a motion of no confidence in him or the Ministry, except where the motion is moved within the last 12 months before the fifth anniversary of the date fixed for the return of writs at the previous general election; and
(b) may be dismissed from office in accordance with Division III.2 (*leadership code*): and
(c) may be removed from office by the Head of State, acting in accordance with a decision of the Parliament, if the Speaker advises the Parliament that two medical practitioners appointed by the National Authority responsible for the registration or licensing of medical practitioners have jointly reported in accordance with an Act of the Parliament that, in their professional opinions, the Prime Minister is unfit, by reason of physical or mental incapacity, to carry out the duties of his office.

(6) The Prime Minister may be suspended from office —
(a) by the tribunal appointed under an Organic Law made for the purposes of Section 28 (*further provisions*), pending an investigation into a question of misconduct in office within the meaning of Division III.2 (*leadership code*), and any resultant action; or

(See: Organic Law on the Duties and Responsibilities of Leadership Ch.1.)

(b) in accordance with an Act of the Parliament, pending an investigation for the purposes of Subsection (5)(c), and any resultant action by the Parliament.

(*See*: *Prime Minister Act* Ch.27)

C.P.C. Report Ch.7 p.3

Appointment of the Prime Minister

25. We recommend that the Parliament itself should elect the Prime Minister by means of an ordinary resolution when Parliament meets after a general election. If a vacancy occurs at other times the election of a new Prime Minister by the same procedure would take place at the next sitting if Parliament is in session, or, if it is not, at a meeting to be convened within fourteen days of the vacancy. [p.4]

26. It is unlikely, but nevertheless possible, that no motion designating a member as Prime Minister will gain majority support when the Parliament first takes up the question. To cover this possibility, we propose that adjournments of up to three sitting days at a time be allowed for further political negotiations.

27. This system should work satisfactorily in a variety of circumstances — whether there be a number of parties, none at all, or only one party. If any party or coalition of parties has an effective majority, it will have no difficulty in seeing that its leader is elected. If no such party or coalition has a majority, the Parliament might elect the leader of the largest group, and it would then be up to him to form either a minority government or to try to create a majority through choosing a particular combination of Ministers. Our proposal allows for a maximum of flexibility.

28. Once he is elected, we recommend that the Prime Minister be formally appointed and sworn in by the Speaker. This is one of the executive functions of the Speaker to which we have referred. In making the appointment, the Speaker would be acting on behalf of the people's representatives in Parliament.

RECOMMENDATIONS [p.10]

Tenure of office of Prime Minister

19. The Speaker shall revoke the appointment of the Prime Minister —
   (a) if he ceases to be a member of the National Parliament for any reason other than that there has been a dissolution of the Parliament;
   (b) if he delivers to the Speaker a signed letter of resignation from that office;
   (c) if another person is elected Prime Minister at the first meeting of the National Parliament following a general election;
   (d) if a motion of no confidence in the National Executive Council in which a new Prime Minister is designated is passed by an absolute majority of the National Parliament under recommendation 20 below;
   (e) if a motion for the removal of the Prime Minister from office, in which a new Prime Minister is designated is passed by —
      (i) a simple majority of the National Parliament under recommendation 16(2)(c) above, or
      (ii) an absolute majority of the National Parliament under recommendation 25(2) below.
   (f) if his removal from office is ordered by the tribunal provided for in Part E of Chapter 8 as a result of a breach of the Leadership Code.

Vacancy in office of Prime Minister

21. (1) Subject to recommendation 22 below, if a vacancy occurs in the office of Prime Minister due to —
      (a) his ceasing to be a member of the National Parliament for any reason other than that there has been a dissolution of the Parliament;
      (b) his resignation from that office; or
      (c) his removal from office as a result of a breach of the Leadership Code;
   there shall be an election of a new Prime Minister by ordinary resolution of the [p.11] Parliament as provided for in clause (2) below.

   (2) (a) if a vacancy under clause (1) occurs during the period of a meeting of the National Parliament, the first item of business at the next sitting of the Parliament after the vacancy occurs shall be the election of a new Prime Minister — *provided that* the election may be deferred for up to three sitting days at a time if the Parliament so resolves;

(b) if a vacancy under clause (1) occurs at a time when the National Parliament is not meeting, if the Parliament is not due to meet within fourteen days of the vacancy occurring the Speaker shall convene a meeting of the Parliament not earlier than seven days nor later than fourteen days after the vacancy occurs, and the first item of business at the first sitting of the Parliament at that meeting shall be the election of a new Prime Minister, *provided that* the election may be deferred for up to three sitting days at a time if the Parliament so resolves; and

(c) if a vacancy under clause (1) occurs when the National Parliament is dissolved, the election of a new Prime Minister shall take place at the first meeting of the Parliament following the general election in accordance with recommendation 14 above.

(3) If a vacancy occurs under clause (1) above, the Deputy Prime Minister shall act as Prime Minister until a new Prime Minister is elected under clause (2) above, or, if there is a vacancy also in the office of Deputy Prime Minister, the Senior Minister shall so act.

AS TO FIRST PARLIAMENT

Held

Section 142(5)(a) applies only to a Prime Minister in office during a Parliament elected for a five year term and is not intended to apply to the first Parliament established under s.269.
Reference No 2 of 1976 [1976] PNGLR 228; see Frost C.J. at pp.232-236; see also Raine J. at p.237, Saldanha J. at pp.238-240.

AS TO JUSTICIABILITY

Held

The courts have no jurisdiction to entertain an application which seeks a declaration that the appointment of the Prime Minister is invalid on the ground that s.142(4) of the Constitution has not been complied with. Questions concerning the conduct of the Parliament and its procedures are non-justiciable (see also under s.134).
James Eki Mopio v The Speaker of the National Parliament [1977] PNGLR 240 per Curiam (Frost C.J., Prentice Dep. C.J., Williams J.) at pp.421,423.

GENERALLY

Referred to

by Kapi Dep.C.J. in *S.C.R. No 2 of 1982; Re Opai Kunangel Amin* (1982 Unreported) SC231 at p.8; see also Kaputin J. at pp.22,23.

143. — ACTING PRIME MINISTER.

(1) Subject to Subsection (2), an Act of the Parliament shall make provision for and in respect of the appointment of a Minister to be Acting Prime Minister to exercise and perform the powers, functions, duties and responsibilities of the Prime Minister when —
- (a) there is a vacancy in the office of Prime Minister; or
- (b) the Prime Minister is suspended from office; or
- (c) the Prime Minister is —
  - (i) absent from the country; or
  - (ii) out of speedy and effective communication; or
  - (iii) otherwise unable or not readily available to perform the duties of his office.

(*See*: *Prime Minister Act* Ch.27.)

(2) Where a Prime Minister is dismissed under Section 142(5)(a) (*the Prime Minister*) the person nominated under Section 145(2)(a) (*motions of no confidence*) —
   (a) becomes the Acting Prime Minister until he is appointed a Prime Minister in accordance with Section 142(2) (*the Prime Minister*); and
   (b) may exercise and perform all the powers, functions, duties and responsibilities of a Prime Minister.

(3) The question whether the occasion for the appointment of an Acting Prime Minister or for the exercise or performance of a power, function, duty or responsibility by an Acting Prime Minister, under this section has arisen or has ceased, is non-justiciable.

C.P.C. Report Ch.7 p.5

Continuity of government

35. We have taken particular care to provide for procedures to ensure that the country has a national government at all times. Thus, during the period when Parliament is dissolved and there is a general election, the National Executive Council stays in office until either the present Prime Minister or a successor is appointed following his election by the new Parliament. Whoever becomes Prime Minister would then have the right to construct a new Ministry. He may or may not choose any of the former Ministers. These procedures are similar to those found in most parliamentary systems.

36. We have provided separately, in paragraphs 38 and 39 below, for the procedures to be followed should there be a vacancy in the office of Prime Minister arising, for example from the death or resignation of the incumbent. However, it would be possible for all Ministers to resign so that, in effect, there is a resignation by the National Executive Council as a whole. A government might decide to do this if the Parliament rejected its Budget or other major legislation, but it need not necessarily do so. We have made specific provision for Parliament to replace a government that appears to have lost majority support, but we expect that Parliament itself will evolve its own convention in respect of the circumstances in which a government ought to resign. If the Ministry as a whole does resign, we propose that the resignations take effect from the time of the appointment of a new Prime Minister following his election by Parliament.

37. The election of a new Prime Minister in these circumstances would take place at the next sitting of Parliament, although we have provided for the possibility of adjournments in paragraph 26. If Parliament is not meeting at the time, it must be convened by the Speaker within fourteen days. Until the appointment of a new Prime Minister, the outgoing government would remain in office in a 'caretaker' capacity — that is, it would not embark on any major policy initiative during that period. In this latter respect, the arrangement would be like that existing during the period of a general election, when a government would be expected to exercise similar restraint.

Acting Prime Minister

38. We recommend that when the Prime Minister advises the Speaker on the appointment of Ministers, he designates the Deputy Prime Minister and, to act as a subsequent deputy if required, the Senior Minister, and that they be appointed accordingly. If a vacancy arises in the office of Prime Minister — for example, from death or resignation — the Deputy Prime Minister automatically acts in his place until a successor is appointed following an election by Parliament. Should, however, there be a vacancy at that time in the office of Deputy Prime Minister also, then the Senior Minister shall act.

39. As in paragraph 37, the election of a new Prime Minister would take place at the next sitting of Parliament after the vacancy occurs, with the possibility of adjournments provided for in paragraph 26. If Parliament is not meeting at the time, it must be convened by the Speaker within fourteen days. However, should the vacancy occur when the Parliament is [p.6] dissolved, the Acting Prime Minister would stay in office until a new Prime Minister is appointed after the general election.

40. Arrangements have also been set out for the delegation of responsibilities to the Deputy Prime Minister (or Senior Minister) in the absence or incapacity of the Prime Minister, including the procedure to be followed should the Prime Minister be incapacitated to the extent that he is unable himself to effect such a delegation.

GENERALLY

Referred to

by Frost C.J. in *Reference No 2 of 1976* [1976] PNGLR 228 at p.234 (as to relationship of s.143(2) with s.145: Parliament has a real choice, the members knowing who would become Prime Minister if a motion of no-confidence is successful).

144. — OTHER MINISTERS.

(1) There shall be such number of Ministers (other than the Prime Minister), not being less than six or more than one quarter of the number of members of the Parliament from time to time, as is determined by or under an Organic Law.

(*See: Organic Law on the Number of Ministers* Ch.1.)

C.P.C. Report Ch.7 p.3

Size of the Ministry

21. In setting the minimum and maximum number of Ministers we have taken into account several factors in addition to the general one of efficiency. We propose a minimum of 15 ministers. This would allow a smaller ministry than at present, should circumstances warrant it, while at the same time allowing a reasonably representative spread. We propose a maximum equal to one-quarter of the total membership of the Parliament, effectively 25-27, so as to preclude the possibility of the executive becoming so large as to dominate the legislature.

22. However, we have also been conscious of the need to discourage any unnecessary increase in the number of ministers beyond the present 20. We take this view both because of the expense involved and because the introduction of provincial government might be expected to reduce the workload on some ministers in the future. We therefore propose that any increase in the number beyond 20 should require the approval of the Parliament by resolution passed by an absolute majority.

(2) The Ministers, other than the Prime Minister, shall be appointed by the Head of State, acting with, and in accordance with, the advice of the Prime Minister.

C.P.C. Report Ch.7 p.4

Appointment of other Ministers

29. We propose that the Prime Minister be empowered to choose the other Ministers from within the Parliament, and to allocate portfolios among them. Similarly, he would have the power to remove a Minister and to reshuffle portfolios. The actual appointment of Ministers and the revocation of their appointments would be by the Speaker, acting on the advice of the Prime Minister. (He must follow this advice; he has no discretion in this and similar matters).

30. These proposals should help to ensure that a Ministry which is formed is reasonably cohesive and works as a team. The *formal* powers they provide for the Prime Minister are common in parliamentary systems. However, the extent to which the Prime Minister, in *actual practice*, has a free hand in choosing or changing the Ministry would depend on prevailing political circumstances.

31. These circumstances could vary considerably but, where there is a party system in operation, they would include:

(a) whether the Prime Minister's party has the numbers to form a government alone or needs the support of other parties in a coalition;

(b) whether the party or parties which form the government have adopted formal rules which either permit the Prime Minister alone to choose the Ministers or require them to be elected by all the parliamentary representatives of the party or parties concerned (sometimes where the latter rule applies the Prime Minister alone is given the right to allocate portfolios); and
(c) whether the Prime Minister has achieved such personal dominance in his party, or perhaps in the Parliament as a whole, that his own decisions in this matter are accepted without question. The degree of personal dominance achieved by a Prime Minister would, of course, be a vital factor whether or not there is a party system.

By their nature these factors arise from the political process and can not be provided for by the Constitution.

Delays in forming a Ministry

32. We recognise that, in certain political circumstances, a newly elected Prime Minister might require additional time to negotiate the formation of a Ministry. We have provided for this situation. Thus, if the Prime Minister is unable, immediately following his appointment, to nominate at least the minimum number of Ministers required for the National Executive Council (that is, 15), we recommend that the Speaker, acting on the advice of the Prime Minister, adjourn the Parliament for up to three sitting days. When Parliament resumes, the Prime Minister would either nominate his Ministers or, if negotiations have proved difficult or are not concluded, he might seek a further adjournment. It would rest with Parliament as to whether the Prime Minister's request is agreed to, but if it is not, members would have the right to move for his replacement. This should provide a deterrent against undue delays in the formation of the Ministry, and also a check on the powers of the Prime Minister during these periods when he may act alone in place of the National Executive Council.

(3) A Minister other than the Prime Minister may be suspended from office in accordance with an Organic Law made for the purposes of Section 28(2) (*further provisions*).

(4) A Minister other than the Prime Minister —
  (a) shall be dismissed from office by the Head of State if the Parliament passes, in accordance with Section 145 (*motions of no confidence*), a motion of no confidence in him; and
  (b) may be dismissed from office —
    (i) by the Head of State, acting with, and in accordance with, the advice of the Prime Minister; or
    (ii) in accordance with Division III.2 (*leadership code*).

(*See*: *Organic Law on the Duties and Responsibilities of Leadership* Ch.1.)

C.P.C. Report Ch.7 p.5

Removal of Ministers

33. We have found that it is a widely held opinion among our people that Parliament should have the power to require the removal of an individual Minister. We agree with this view, but to avoid undermining the principle of collective responsibility — that is, that the Ministers accept joint responsibility for matters of policy — we recommend that an individual Minister may be removed on two grounds only:
(1) inability to perform his duties, 'arising from infirmity of body or mind': and
(2) 'misbehaviour', which should be interpreted as meaning gross personal misbehaviour regarded as unfitting to his office.

34. Certain safeguards are included in this proposal. No motion for the removal of a Minister may be moved unless —
- it is signed by a least one-tenth of the members of Parliament;
- it is supported by a majority of the First Parliamentary Committee in a report to the Parliament; and
- one week's notice of the motion is given.

In addition, to be successful, the motion must be passed by an absolute majority — that is, by over half of the total membership of the Parliament. (See also C.P.C Report Ch.7 p.4 under s.144(2))

REASONS FOR PRIME MINISTER'S ADVICE FOR DISMISSAL OF MINISTER MAY NOT BE EXAMINED

per Saldanha J.

> The Governor-General's order of dismissal reads —
> I . . . acting with, and in accordance with, the advice of the Prime Minister and having received a recommendation from the appropriate tribunal, hereby dismiss Moses Sasakila from the offices of member of the Parliament and Minister.

It will be noticed that the Governor-General dismissed Mr. Sasakila both as member of Parliament and as Minister. There were two bases for the dismissal; firstly the advice of the Prime Minister, and, secondly the recommendation of the Tribunal. . . .

The Tribunal could neither dismiss nor recommend dismissal of Mr. Sasakila as Minister. To the extent that the Governor-General purported to dismiss Mr. Sasakila as Minister on the recommendation of the Tribunal the dismissal was null and void. But in dismissing Mr. Sasakila as Minister the Governor-General also acted on the advice of the Prime Minister. Now, 'the question, what (if any) advice was given to the Head of State or by whom, is non-justiciable:' s.86(4) of the Constitution. The question of Mr. Sasakila's dismissal as Minister following the advice of the Prime Minister cannot be heard or determined by this Court: Sch.1.7 of the Constitution.

The net result is that Mr. Sasakila's dismissal as member of Parliament is null and void but his dismissal as Minister insofar as it is based on advice from the Prime Minister is valid. If the Prime Minister wants Mr. Sasakila back in office as Minister there is nothing to prevent him from advising the Governor-General to re-appoint him.

The State v The Independent Tribunal; Ex parte Sasakila [1976] PNGLR 491 at p.504; see Frost C.J. at p.491, Kearney J. at p.507.

Referred to

by Kapi J. in *Minister for Lands v Frame* [1980] PNGLR 433 at p.468.

GENERALLY

Referred to

by Frost C.J. in *Reference No 2 of 1976* [1976] PNGLR 228 at p.232 (Prime Minister may dismiss Ministers during the term of the First Parliament).

145. — MOTIONS OF NO CONFIDENCE.

(1) For the purposes of Sections 142 (*the Prime Minister*) and 144 (*other Ministers*), a motion of no-confidence is a motion —
- (a) that is expressed to be a motion of no confidence in the Prime Minister, the Ministry or a Minister, as the case my be; and
- (b) of which not less than one week's notice, signed by a number of members of the Parliament being not less than one-tenth of the total number of seats in the Parliament, has been given in accordance with the Standing Orders of the Parliament.

(2) A motion of no confidence in the Prime Minister or the Ministry —
- (a) moved during the first four years of the life of Parliament shall not be allowed unless it nominates the next Prime Minister; and
- (b) moved within 12 months before the fifth anniversary of the date fixed for the return of the writs at the previous general election shall not be allowed if it nominates the next Prime Minister.

(3) A motion of no confidence in the Prime Minister or the Ministry moved in accordance with Subsection (2)(a) may not be amended in respect of the name of the person nominated as the next Prime Minister except by substituting the name of some other person.

(4) A motion of no confidence in the Prime Minister or in the Ministry may not be moved during the period of six months commencing on the date of the appointment of the Prime Minister.

C.P.C. Report Ch.7 p.6

Changing the government

41. One of the major principles in our recommendations for the National Executive Council is that it should be responsible to the National Parliament. Basically this means that Ministers are individually and collectively answerable to members of the Parliament for their executive actions and policies, including the work of their Departments. Ultimately, however, it means that Parliament must be able to change the government.

42. For the first three years of the Parliament's term we propose an adaptation of what has been called the 'constructive vote of no confidence'. Under this procedure, a vote of no confidence in the National Executive Council may be moved if it has been signed by one-tenth of the members and at least one week's notice has been given. To be successful, it must be passed by an absolute majority of the Parliament.

43. In addition we propose two further conditions. First, in order to ensure some stability in government, such a motion may not be moved unless the Prime Minister has been in office for at least six months. In practice this is likely to mean that if the Parliament is dissatisfied with the government, it may try to change it at the second meeting after the one at which it comes into office. The government should therefore have at least one meeting of Parliament in between in order to show something of its legislative programme.

44. The second condition provides the basis for the description 'constructive vote of no confidence'. Such a motion may be moved only if it concludes (sic) the name of the proposed successor to the Prime Minister. If the motion is successful, it thereby incorporates the election of a new Prime Minister. Accordingly, the Speaker revokes the appointment of the defeated Prime Minister and appoints his named successor, who is then free to choose his own ministry.

45. There are four main advantages in this procedure. Firstly, it reduces the element of uncertainty that might follow the fall of a government; one Prime Minister automatically gives way to another. Secondly, it ensures that the Speaker does not exercise any discretion as to who should be appointed to succeed the outgoing Prime Minister. Thirdly, the Parliament has a real choice; members know who will become Prime Minister if the motion is successful. Fourthly, it should ensure that a motion of no confidence is moved in all seriousness. It would still be open to the Parliament to register its strong opposition to, or dissatisfaction with, a particular government policy or action by adopting a motion that falls short of one of no confidence — such as a motion of censure.

AS TO OPERATION OF SECTION 145

per Frost C.J.

It will be seen that so far s.145 is concerned para.(1) is concerned with formal matters, and the provisions relevant to the question before the Court are confined to para.(2), and possibly para.(4). The notion behind s.145(2)(a) is 'the constructive vote of no confidence' as it was referred to by the Constitutional Planning Committee (see Final Report (supra), at Ch.7, p.6, paras.41-45). Under the Constitution, for the first four years of the life of the Parliament a motion of no confidence may only be moved if it nominates the next Prime Minister. If the motion is successful, it thus also constitutes a decision of the Parliament entitling the person nominated to be appointed the next Prime Minister under s.142(2). This explains the term 'constructive'. In the meantime that person becomes the Acting Prime Minister until he is appointed Prime Minister (s.143(2)(a)). The main advantages which the Constitutional Planning Committee saw in this procedure are that it reduces the element of uncertainty that might follow the fall of a government, the Parliament has a real choice, the members knowing who would become Prime Minister if the motion was successful, and it should ensure that such a motion is moved in all seriousness (op. cit., para.45). It is

appropriate that such a motion moved in the fifth and final year of the life of the Parliament, as provided in sub-s.145(2)(b), should not nominate the next Prime Minister because under s.105(1)(b) if the motion is passed, the consequence is different for a general election is to be held.
Reference No 2 of 1976 [1976] PNGLR 228 at p.234; see also Raine J. at pp.236,237 (the works 'may not be moved' in s.145(5) mean 'shall not be moved'), Saldanha J. at pp.238-240.

AS TO FIRST PARLIAMENT

Held

Section 145(2) applies only to a Ministry in office during a Parliament elected for a five year term and is not intended to apply to the First Parliament established under s.269.
Reference No 2 of 1976 [1976] PNGLR 228 per Frost J. at pp.232-236; see also Raine J. at p.237, Saldanha J. at pp.238-240.

146. — RESIGNATION.

(1) The Prime Minister may resign from office by notice in writing to the Head of State.

(2) A Minister other than the Prime Minister may resign from office by notice in writing to the Prime Minister.

UNQUALIFIED RIGHT TO RESIGN

Comment

In *S.C.R. No 2 of 1982; In re Opai Kunangel Amin* (1982 Unreported) SC231, the Supreme Court held (Kapi Dep. C.J., Andrew, Bredmeyer and Gajewicz JJ.; Kaputin J. dissenting) that s.104(c) confers an unqualified right upon a member of the Parliament to resign his seat by notice to the Speaker. The Court held that express right may be exercised notwithstanding that the member has been suspended from duty pending completion of an investigation into his conduct under the provisions of the Leadership Code and notwithstanding that, on the authority of *In re Joseph Auna* [1980] PNGLR 500, his resignation will terminate proceedings against him under the Code. The Court held that a Member's resignation took effect automatically when the notice of resignation in writing was given to the Speaker. Although the same argument would appear to apply to a resignation by a Minister (except as provided for by s.147(2)(b)) it would not seem to be appropriate in the case of the Prime Minister who, pursuant to s.147(2), is obliged to remain in office after resignation until the appointment of his successor.

The better view would appear to be that a suspended Prime Minister remains subject to the Leadership Code, notwithstanding a proffered resignation, until Parliament acts to appoint his successor.

147. — NORMAL TERM OF OFFICE

(1) Unless he earlier —
(a) dies; or
(b) subject to Subsection (2), resigns; or
(c) subject to Subsection (3), ceases to be qualified to be a Minister; or
(d) is dismissed or removed from office,
a Minister (including the Prime Minister) holds office until the next appointment of a Prime Minister.

(2) Notwithstanding Subsection (1)(b) —
  (a) a Prime Minister who resigns; and
  (b) a Ministry that resigns collectively,
shall continue in office until the appointment of the next Prime Minister.

(3) Notwithstanding Subsection (1)(c), a Minister who —
  (a) ceases, by reason of a general election, to be a member of the Parliament; but
  (b) remains otherwise qualified to be a member of the Parliament,
shall continue in office until the next appointment of a Prime Minister.

GENERALLY

Referred to

by Frost C.J. in *Reference No 2 of 1976* [1976] PNGLR 228 at p.235;

by Gajewicz J. in *S.C.R. No 2 of 1982; In Re Opai Kunangel Amin* (1982 Unreported) SC231 at p.31.

148. — FUNCTIONS, ETC., OF MINISTERS.

(1) Ministers (including the Prime Minister) have such titles, portfolios and responsibilities as are determined from time to time by the Prime Minister.

(2) Except as provided by a Constitutional Law or an Act of the Parliament, all departments, sections, branches and functions of government must be the political responsibility of a Minister, and the Prime Minister is politically responsible for any of them that are not specifically allocated under this section.

(3) Subsection (2) does not confer on a Minister any power of direction or control.

C.P.C. Report Ch.7 p.4

Appointment of other Ministers

29. We propose that the Prime Minister be empowered to choose the other Ministers from within the Parliament, and to allocate portfolios among them. Similarly, he would have the power to remove a Minister and to reshuffle portfolios. The actual appointment of Ministers and the revocation of their appointments would be by the Speaker, acting on the advice of the Prime Minister. (He must follow this advice; he has no discretion in this and similar matters). . . . . [p.6]

46. We propose thast a general system of government departments be maintained. Accordingly, we have provided for each department to be under the direction and control of a Minister and, subject to that direction and control, under supervision of a Head of Department. The method of appointment, tenure and certain other conditions of service of Heads of Departments are included separately in Chapter 12, 'The Public Services'.

AS TO 'POLITICAL RESPONSIBILITY'

per Kapi J.

What is the *political responsibility* of the Minister? The term is not defined. In my opinion the political responsibility of Minister involves —

(a) all matters concerning a department, section, branch or function of government which require the deliberations or decision of the National Executive Council as a matter of responsibility of the National Executive Council as the executive government of Papua New Guinea. (See s.149(3) of the Constitution). It would be the political responsibility of a Minister of the particular department, etc. to submit, advise, inform, report or brief the National Executive Council to enable the National Executive Council to make decisions as the executive government of Papua New Guinea regarding the particular branch of government.
This would include such matters as budget priorities and allocations.

(b) inform, report or answer questions in the Parliament or the public through news media regarding any matter concerning the function of the government as a member of the Cabinet which is responsible for the executive arm of the Government.

This responsibility is more in the nature of doing the groundwork for the National Executive Council for purposes of executive decisions under s.149(3) of the Constitution and simply informing the public through Parliament or news media of the workings of the executive arm of the government on the particular branch or department of government. That is as far as the political responsibility of a Minister can go.
S.C.R. No 1 of 1982; Re Bouraga [1982] PNGLR 178 at p.196.

NO POWER OF DIRECTION AND CONTROL CONFERRED BY CONSTITUTION BUT NO PROHIBITION UPON ITS GRANT

per Kidu C.J.

This Constitutional Law, in my view, does four things.

(a) it vests in the Prime Minister of Papua New Guinea the power to determine what ministerial title a particular Minister is to have; and
(b) what a Minister's responsibilities must be; and
(c) of what departments, sections, branches and functions of government a Minister has political responsibility; and
(d) that s.148(2) 'does not confer on a Minister any power of direction or control.'

It does not say that a Minister has no power of direction or control *whatsoever* over a department, section, branch and function of government of which he/she has political responsibility. It is my view that s.148 merely says that the fact that it (i.e. s.148) vests in a Minister the political responsibility over a department, section, branch, etc in itself confers no powers of direction or control over these bodies. I cannot also see that s.148 prohibits Parliament from making laws vesting in Ministers power of direction and control over matters for which they have political responsibility.
S.C.R No 1 of 1982; Re Bouraga [1982] PNGLR 178 at pp.184, 185 see also Kapi Dep. C.J. at p.197, Pratt J. at p.206.

Comment

Although the judges, with the exception of Kidu C.J. (at p.189); in *S.C.R. No 1 of 1982; Re Bouraga* [1982] PNGLR 178, referred only to the possibility of the Parliament conferring powers of direction and control there would appear to be nothing to prevent the National Executive Council by-passing this step and conferring such powers directly on a Minister by a delegation under s.149(4) of the Constitution.

Held

Although Heads of Department have a responsibility to keep their Minister informed, a Minister has no authority to issue an order that he be briefed as to a particular matter.
S.C.R. No 1 of 1982; Re Bouraga [1982] PNGLR 178 per Kidu C.J. at pp.182—188, Kapi J. at pp.196,197, Pratt J. at pp.199-207.

Subdivision C. — The National Executive Council.

149. — THE NATIONAL EXECUTIVE COUNCIL.

(1) A National Executive Council is hereby established.

(2) The Council shall consist of all the Ministers (including the Prime Minister when he is present as Chairman).

(3) The functions of the Council are —
(a) to be responsible, in accordance with this Constitution, for the executive government of Papua New Guinea; and
(b) such other functions as are allocated to it by this Constitution or any other law.

(4) Except where the contrary intention appears, nothing in this Constitution prevents the powers, functions, duties or responsibilities of the Council from being exercised, as determined by it, through a Minister.

(5) Subject to any Organic Law or Act of the Parliament, the procedures of the Council are as determined by it.

C.P.C. Report: see extracts under s.139 and s.140.

AS TO DELEGATION OF POWER

Held

The National Executive Council may delegate to a Minister those powers of direction and control not conferred under s.148 of the Constitution.
S.C.R. No 1 of 1982; Re Bouraga [1982] PNGLR 178 per Kidu C.J. at p.189.

150. — THE SECRETARY TO THE NATIONAL EXECUTIVE COUNCIL.

(1) An office of Secretary to the National Executive Council is hereby established.

(2) Subject to any Act of the Parliament, the functions and responsibilities of the Secretary of the Council shall be as determined by the Council.

C.P.C. Report Ch.7 p.3

18. We propose also the establishment of a Secretariat with specific responsibilities to be carried out under the direction of the Prime Minister. Not least among its functions should be that of following up the decisions of the Council so as to ensure they are implemented without undue delay and that, where appropriate, there is the necessary degree of co-ordination. If there are second thoughts about some decisions, they should be brought up again for review, not merely set aside by an individual Minister or Department.

Subdivision D. — The Power of Mercy.

151. — GRANT OF PARDON, ETC.

(1) Subject to this Subdivision, the Head of State, acting with, and in accordance with, the advice of the National Executive Council, may grant to a person convicted of an offence or held in penal detention under a law of Papua New Guinea —
(a) a pardon, either free or conditional; or
(b) a remission or commutation of sentence; or
(c) a respite of the execution of sentence; or
(d) a less severe form of punishment for that imposed by any sentence,

and may remit or refund, in whole or in part, any fine, penalty or forfeiture paid or payable to a governmental body.

(2) Where an offence has been committed, the Head of State, acting with, and in accordance with, the advice of the National Executive Council, may grant a pardon, either free or conditional, to an accomplice who gives evidence that leads to the conviction of a principal offender.

(3) Except in a case referred to in Subsection (2) or as otherwise permitted by or under an Act of the Parliament, the exercise of the power conferred by Subsection (1) shall not be held out, offered or promised in advance of conviction.

(4) Nothing in this section prevents the establishment by law of systems of probation, parole or release on licence, or any similar systems.

(*See*: *Probation Act* 1979.)

C.P.C. Report Ch.8 p.12

122. We recognize that it is important for the Executive to have the power to commute sentences of death, to grant pardons, and to reduce sentences. This power is, of course, a normal one for any Executive. It enables the Government to rectify injustices which [p.13] only become apparent after the time for an appeal against a conviction or sentence has passed. For example: —

> There might be a case where a young man takes the blame for an offence committed by an older man in his clan. The true situation might become apparent some years after the young man has been convicted, and sentenced to a long term of imprisonment.
> In these circumstances, the executive needs to have power to grant a pardon to the young man on the grounds that his conviction and secntence were wrong.

123. We are, however, concerned to try to ensure that the power of mercy is exercised only in an appropriate case and in a just manner. We propose that an advisory committee on the executive power of mercy be established to investigate and make recommendations in cases where the Executive is giving consideration to exercising this power.....

132. It will be noted that in accordance with our general policy of breaking away from common law terms which are not well understood by our people, we have refrained from using the traditional British term 'prerogative' in the context of the power of mercy; we prefer to use the word 'power'.

GENERALLY

Referred to

by Wilson J. in *The State v Mathias Peter Joseph Evertz* (1979 Unreported) N193 at p.8 (interests of those adversely affected by failure to commence an appeal within the allowed time thought adequately protected under s.151).

152. — ADVISORY COMMITTEE ON THE POWER OF MERCY.

(1) An Organic Law shall make provision for and in respect of an Advisory Committee on the Power of Mercy, and for and in respect of its appointment, constitution, powers and procedures.

(*See: Organic Law on the Advisory Committee on the Power of Mercy* Ch.1.)

(2) Before giving any advice to the Head of State under Section 151(1) (*grant of pardon, etc.*), the National Executive Council shall consider a report from the Advisory Committee.

C.P.C. Report Ch.8 p.13

124. The Committee should consist of five citizens, including at least one woman, appointed by the Minister responsible for justice after consulting with appropriate bodies or groups. These might include, for example, the Melanesian Council of Churches.

125. The membership of the Committee should be —
(a) a doctor who has had experience in psychiatry;
(b) a lawyer;
(c) a member of parliament;
(d) a minister of religion; and
(e) a person who has had experience in community work....

127. We believe that the Minister responsibile for justice should consult the Committee before giving any advice to the National Executive Council in a case where consideration is or may be given to commuting a death sentence, granting a pardon, reducing a sentence of imprisonment, or paying back a fine.

128. The Committee proposes also that, whenever the advisory Committee is consulted, its Chairman be entitled to ask for all relevant information to be made available concerning the court hearing and other aspects of the case. The Minister should be obliged to make this information available. Included in it should be a report on the case by the trial judge or presiding magistrate (as the case may be).

129. The Advisory Committee should consider any case referred to it by the Minister and make a report to him within a reasonable time.

130. Neither the Minister nor the National Executive Council should be obliged to accept the recommendations contained in the report of the Advisory Committee. However, we believe that if it has all the relevant facts placed before it, together with a recommendation from an independent body such as the Advisory Committee, it is likely that the Council will make sound decisions in exercising its power of mercy.

131. We have recommended that the requirement of consultation with the Advisory Committee may be waived in certain circumstances. It is proposed that if the Public Prosecutor certifies that it is in the interests of justice to do so, the Executive may, without the necessity to consult the Committee, decide to grant a pardon or a reduction of sentence to an accomplice who gives evidence aginst a principal offender who is subsequently convicted.

Referred to

by Wilson J. in *The State v Mathias Peter Joseph Evertz* (1979 Unreported) N193 at p.8

Subdivision E. — General.

153. — VALIDITY OF EXECUTIVE ACTS.

(1) Subsections (2), (3) and (4) are subject to any Constitutional law or Act of the Parliament.

(2) The question whether the procedures prescribed for the National Executive Council have been or are being complied with, is non-justiciable.

(3) The question, whether any, and if so what report has been given to the National Executive Council by the Advisory Committee on the Power of Mercy, is non-justiciable.

(4) No act of a Minister is open to challenge on the ground that he was not empowered to perform the act, if some other Minister, or any Minister, was so empowered.

(5) This section does not limit the jurisdiction or powers of the Ombudsman Commission, or of an authority or tribunal established under Division III.2 (*leadership code*).

Division 5. — The Administration of Justice.

Subdivision A. — General Structure and Principles of the National Justice Administration.

154. — THE NATIONAL JUSTICE ADMINISTRATION.

The National Justice Administration consists of —
(a) the National Judicial System; and
(b) the Minister responsible for the National Justice Administration; and
(c) the Law Officers of Papua New Guinea.

C.P.C. Report Ch.8 p.1

1. In Papua New Guinea there have always been traditional peaceful means of resolving disputes and doing what is right in conflict situations, according to traditional notions of justice. With the establishment of modern institutions in our country, the courts of justice, as developed elsewhere, are gradually becoming generally acceptable institutions in our society. The advent of the Constitution and Independence provides the opportunity for these courts, appropriately modified to suit our needs, to become a vital part of the foundations on which our people seek freedom, fulfilment and total development, both personal and national.

2. The courts constitute the third pillar of the government of a country. They have a different function from those of the executive and the legislature, namely that of peacefully determining conflicts that arise between individuals; between different levels of government (in some countries); and between individuals and government; in accordance with law and justice. They may also have an important advisory function, through which they can assist in the avoidance of potential disputes. In countries which have a written Constitution the highest courts often have the important task of deciding matters relating to the interpretation and enforcement of the Constitution. In this unique role courts should be key instruments through which peaceful development in a society can take place.

3. It is a fundamental principle of any free country that the men and women who sit to hear and determine disputes that come before them as members of the judiciary should not be improperly influenced to make decisions for or against any particular person or group. The Committee has made a number of recommendations in this Chapter, and elsewhere in this report, designed to ensure that people of Papua New Guinea are governed by law, not according to the whims of powerful individuals or groups. That aim, in fact, underlies the very idea of having a constitution at all.

4. We believe that the cardinal principle that the courts should be independent of the legislature and the executive must be firmly established under our Constitution. Those who legislate and those who exercise executive power should not also be responsible for dispensing justice in our new nation. The people who have that responsibility, namely judges and magistrates, should be sufficiently secure in their positions so that they are able to make their decisions without fear of personal repercussions.

5. The courts do not, however, exist in a vacuum. Like other institutions of the government of a country they are caught up in political realities, and often their decisions have important political consequences.

6. In carrying out their judicial role, judges and magistrates must take full account of the goals of the society in which they live; they must be attuned to the wishes of that society and to that extent must be politically conscious (although not party politically conscious). In Chapter 2, 'National Goals and Directive Principles', we have spelt out what we believe to be the goals of Papua New Guinea and we have recommended that our judges uphold the Constitution and interpret the laws made under it in the spirit of those goals and principles.

7. At the same time, the judiciary has a duty to protect the rights of the individual and minority groups: its job is not simply to reflect the will of the Government of the day. The judges will be particularly concerned with this role in deciding cases which arise under the proposed provisions concerning human rights in Chapter 5.

8. These two principles may well be contradictory in a given situation and the courts are therefore faced with the need to make a satisfactory compromise between them.

9. Let us take the example of a situation in which the existing law is either not clear, or alternatively, there appears to be no law which covers the case. In these circumstances, we believe the judge or magistrate who is hearing the case should use judicial ingenuity to do justice as between the parties, taking full account of the national goals and principles of policy as well as the rights of the individual.

10. We do not underestimate the difficulties with which judges and magistrates are faced. They must on the one hand avoid appearing to encroach upon the role of the legislature or to act as a brake on the executive government's legitimate efforts in trying to promote development: yet on the other hand they must endeavour to ensure that an injustice is not done in a particular case, and that the rights of individuals or minority groups are not unreasonably overridden. [p.2]

11. These problems are in the nature of the judicial role, but they are particularly acute in an emerging state such as Papua New Guinea. We believe that our recommendations on the judiciary will enhance the independent status which courts in Papua New Guinea now have, and that our judges and magistrates will be equal to the task which faces them. The method of appointment of judges and magistrates which we propose, is designed to promote the involvement of all three arms of government — the executive, legislature and judiciary-in this important process. We believe that this mechanism will encourage members of all three arms to feel part of the nation's overall system of government. We consider that there is good reason to believe, therefore, that Papua New Guinean men and women of integrity and ability will welcome appointment to judicial office, thereby assisting in safeguarding the rights, liberties and freedoms which belong to the people as we move ahead in all aspects of our development.

12. The emergence of Papua New Guinea as a sovereign state should, we recommend, be marked by cutting the legal ties between our judicial system and that of Australia. We propose that a new Supreme Court be the final court of appeal for Papua New Guinea. This recommendation has very strong support from our people, who see it as an important benefit of independence to have final judicial decisions made within the country. This step should enable the body of law which is developing in Papua New Guinea to reflect, to a much greater degree than at present, our own values and circumstances. That evolutionary process will occur most rapidly if the principle that past decisions of the highest courts bind courts at a lower level in the judicial hierarchy (and arguably the highest courts themselves), is applied with maximum flexibility.

13. We are concerned that justice should be done throughout the country, and that our people, wherever they may be, should have ready access to the courts and to legal assistance. The system of administration of justice cannot function effectively if it is only people of wealth or status who are able to afford legal representation in the courts, or who are able to travel to places where lawyers are located. We have therefore recommended the establishment of the office of Public Solicitor as an independent constitutional office. We would hope that steps will soon be taken to establish branches of his office in additional centres besides Port Moresby and Rabaul.

14. To ensure that prosecutions for criminal offences are not subject to improper political interference, we have recommended the establishment of the office of Public Prosecutor. The person who is appointed to this position will also be an independent constitutional office-holder.

15. We recognize that it is important for the Public Prosecutor to take due account of public policy in exercising his discretion to prosecute or to discontinue prosecutions. However, the final decisions on prosecutions should be made by him in the exercise of his independent judgement.

16. As a means of ensuring that the executive power of mercy is not used in an arbitrary way, we have recommended the establishment of an Advisory Committee on the Power of Mercy whose function it should be to give advice to the Executive on most matters in respect of which that power may be used.

17. We have provided also for the highest court in the country, the Supreme Court, to have exclusive jurisdiction to resolve most disputes concerning provisions of the Constitution, and to give advisory opinions on many constitutional questions.

18. As we believe that justice should be administered in accordance with the ideas of our people, we have decided to emphasize this by recommending that justice be administered in the name of the people.

Referred to

by Prentice C.J. in *Constitutional Reference No 1 of 1978 (s.19)* [1978] PNGLR 345 at p.349 (Law Officers form part of National Justice Administration but not part of National Judicial System); see also Wilson J. at p.361 and Pritchard J. (dissenting) at pp.367,368;

by Pratt J. in *S.C.R. No 2 of 1981; Re s.19(1)(f) of the Criminal Code* [1982] PNGLR 150 at p.176.

155. — THE NATIONAL JUDICIAL SYSTEM.

(1) The National Judicial System consists of —
- (a) the Supreme Court; and
- (b) the National Court; and
- (c) such other courts as are established under Section 172 *(establishment of other courts)*.

C.P.C. Report Ch.8 p.2

19. Ordinary citizens tend to come into direct contact with the courts only in times of trouble; when they are accused of having done something wrong themselves or when a wrong has been done to them. As we have said above, it is a function of the courts to apply general laws and principles of justice in particular cases. As part of our first recommendation we propose that this function be performed by the Judiciary.

20. Members of our Judiciary should have integrity, appropriate professional qualifications and experience. They should be in a position to withstand outside pressures in exercising their judgement, yet be responsive to the needs and wishes of our society. They should pledge themselves in public to uphold our country's Constitution in accordance with the national goals and directive principles of policy. [p.3]

Structure of the judiciary

21. The foundation of our legal system is and will remain the good sense and social organization of our people. The system of village courts which the House of Assembly has approved should provide a suitable means of developing our traditional judicial institutions and of significantly influencing the evolution of the imposed court system and the common law which it applies.

22. At the apex of our court system should be a new Supreme Court comprising three judges, and a National Court of Justice, in which a single judge will sit. These courts will replace the present Full Court of the Supreme Court and the Supreme Court respectively.

23. We recommend that Parliament should be able to provide for additional lower courts as necessary to handle disputes which would not be appropriately dealt with in either the highest courts or in the village courts. The present District Courts and Local Courts come into this category.

Generally

Referred to

by Raine J. in *The State v Mogo Wonom* [1975] PNGLR 311 at p.318 (no part of the power to dispense justice is vested in Her Majesty as Head of State; the people have vested all judicial power in the National Judicial System); see also Williams J. at p.320;

by Wilson J. in *Constitutional Reference No 1 of 1978 (s.9)* [1978] PNGLR 345 at p.361 (Public Solicitor not part of National Judicial System and accordingly is neither a part of one of the principal arms of the National Government under s.99 nor a lesser arm of the National Government); see also Prentice C.J. at p.349, but see Pritchard J. (dissenting) at pp.367,368;

by Kidu C.J. in *Avia Aihi v The State* [1981] PNGLR 81 at p.87; see also Greville Smith J. at p.94.

(2) The Supreme Court —
(a) is the final court of appeal; and

(*See: Supreme Court Act* Ch. 37.)

C.P.C. Report Ch.8 p 2

The Supreme Court

24. The highest court in the country should be the Supreme Court, which should be the final appeal court for all cases heard under Papua New Guinean law. We believe that the provision of a right to appeal against judgements of our courts to foreign courts would undermine our sovereignty as a nation, and would perpetuate the incorporation in our legal system of values alien to our own. Submissions we have received have firmly opposed the continuance of appeals to a foreign court such as the High Court of Australia.

25. In its general jurisdiction the Supreme Court should hear cases that have been dealt with first in the National Court or a lower court other than a village court. In carrying out this function it would hear appeals against judgements given by these courts in both criminal and civil cases.

26. We propose also, that the Supreme Court should have a key role in resolving constitutional disputes, our recommendations in this regard being included in Part E of this Chapter 'Resolution of Constitutional Questions'.

27. The Supreme Court should consist of three judges of the National Court, presided over by the Chief Justice or his Deputy or the most senior judge sitting as a member of the Court for a particular case. Clearly, any judge who has heard a case in the National Court should not be eligible to sit on the Supreme Court to hear an appeal against an earlier verdict of his own.

28. Taking account of the likelihood that in the long term, when there is much appellate work to be done by the Supreme Court, Parliament may properly wish to appoint some of our most able National Court Judges as full-time Supreme Court Judges, we have made an appropriate recommendation to allow for this situation.

SECTION 155(2)(a) DOES NOT CONFER JURISDICTION

per Kidu C.J.

I hold the view that there is no doubt the intention of s.155(2)(a) was merely to ensure that everyone understood that there would be no appeals from the Supreme Court of Papua New Guinea to any Courts outside. It does not by itself give any extra jurisdictions to the Supreme Court. The jurisdiction of the Supreme Court is given by other provisions.
In the Matter of the Organic Law on National Elections: Malipu Balakau v Paul Torato and anor (1983 Unreported) SC256 at p.12.

(b) has an inherent power to review all judicial acts of the National Court; and

AS TO SUPREME COURT PRE-EMPTING JUDGMENT OF THE NATIONAL COURT

per Prentice Dep.C.J.

The respondent to an election petition has, by application to the Supreme Court, caused the hearing of the petition against his election to be stopped. The Chief Justice sitting as the National Court had given a ruling that the petitioner was entitled to rely (sic) in a petition under s.112, *National Elections Act,* on a question of lack of qualification in the respondent. Following the cessation of the hearing, leave to appeal has been sought against this ruling on the basis that it was an 'interlocutory judgment' (s.14 *Supreme Court Act*). In addition a writ of prohibition against the continuance of the hearing of the petition has been sought.

For myself, in an ordinary case, I would be reluctant to rule that the Supreme Court should so interfere with a hearing before the National Court. I consider that as a general rule the Supreme Court should not interfere with a National Court hearing until it had reached a conclusion — unless, in an exceptional case, the National Court itself referred a case for decision before finality. That finality should normally be obtained in the National Court before appeal were sought therefrom, is called for, in my opinion, by the geography and circumstances of this country, and the organization of its superior courts. Mr. McAlary has presented an argument that s.155(2) of the Constitution, which vests an inherent power in the Supreme Court to review all the judicial acts of the National Court, renders invalid s.14 of the *Supreme Court Act* which requires leave to appeal from an interlocutory judgment. In my opinion the argument is unacceptable. Such a result would render every decision of the National Court (even, for example, on questions of reception of evidence) susceptible to appeal, and presumably before finality of decision. The potentially catastrophic effect upon the work of the National and Supreme Courts of such an interpretation is immediately apparent. In my view, s.14 of the *Supreme Court Act* does not infringe upon the powers conferred by the Constitution, but merely regulates their exercise — indeed in an eminently reasonable particular. It does not appear to me that a ruling during the course of the hearing of a case (though sometimes for convenience called such) is an 'interlocutory judgment' within the meaning of s.14 of the *Supreme Court Act*. Such an 'interlocutory judgment', in my opinion, is one which gives a decision upon a particular motion or summons before the Court. The distinction between the two types of decision, an interlocutory judgment on the one hand and a ruling on the other, may be illustrated by the fact that a ruling might be vacated or altered during the course of a hearing. I am satisfied that an effective 'review' of the National Court's proceedings, within the meaning of s.155 of the Constitution, can be obtained on appeal...

In the hearing before the National Court it appears to have been assumed by the counsel involved that s.18 of the Constitution did not debar the National Court from interpreting Constitutional Laws in an election petition, because the section itself expresses its provisions to be 'subject to the Constitution', and s.135 of the Constitution vested the National Court with 'jurisdiction to determine *any question* as to the qualifications of a person to be or to remain a member of the Parliament or the validity of an election to the Parliament' (emphasis mine); which would, it was apparently agreed, include any ancillary interpretation of a Constitutional Law. Nevertheless, it might well have transpired that during, or at the end of, the hearing, counsel might have sought that such an interpretation point be referred, or the Chief Justice might have wished to refer such a point — in compliance with the Supreme Court's 'inherent power to review all judicial acts of the National Court' (s.155(2)(b) of the Constitution) — this despite s.220 of the *Organic Law on National Elections,* which enacts that 'a decision of the National Court is final and conclusive and without appeal, and shall not be questioned in any way'. An Organic Law must of course be read subject to the Constitution (s.10(a) of the Constitution).

For the reason that such a reference might have been and could be made, and because the Chief Justice who is engaged in the National Court hearing, is known to be retiring in a few weeks, I would agree that this hearing should continue as a matter of convenience, justice and necessity, as an appeal.

In re Moresby North East Election Petition [1977] PNGLR 429 at pp.430-432; see also Williams J. at p.439, Pritchard J. at pp.442,443.

A PRIVATIVE CLAUSE CANNOT EXCLUDE THE SUPREME COURT'S INHERENT POWER TO REVIEW THE JUDICIAL ACTS OF THE NATIONAL COURT

Held

Although s.220 of the *Organic Law on National Elections* provides that 'a decision of the National Court is final and conclusive and without appeal, and shall not be questioned in any way', the Organic Law must be read subject to the inherent power of the Supreme Court to review all judicial acts of the National Court entrenched by s.155(2)(b) of the Constitution.
In re Moresby North East Election Petition [1977] PNGLR 429; see Prentice Dep.C.J. at p.432, Pritchard J. at p.442.

Held

Section 220 of the *Organic Law on National Elections* (see above) is valid insofar as it prohibits all appeals because there is no constitutional right to appeal in matters other than criminal proceedings. Section 220 however cannot cut down or exclude the Supreme Court's inherent discretionary power under s.155(2)(b) to review all judicial acts of the National Court. A dissatisfied petitioner although he has no right of appeal may still seek to invoke this inherent power of review.
In the Matter of the Organic Law on National Elections; Malipu Balakau v Paul Torato and anor (1983 Unreported); SC256; see Kidu C.J. at pp.2-8, Kapi Dep.C.J. (dissenting) at pp.15-21, Andrew J. at pp.25,26)

AS TO THE NATURE OF THE PROCESS OF REVIEW

Comment

There has been little detailed examination given to the nature of the process of review. In *Avia Aihi v The State* [1981] PNGLR 81, Kearney Dep.C.J. and Kapi J. each regarded the process of review as analogous to the process of appeal (see Kearney Dep.C.J. at p.92, Kapi J. at p.108). However in *State v District Land Court; Ex parte Caspar Nuli* [1981] PNGLR 192, Bredmeyer J. made clear his opinion that appeal and review were not, in legal theory, identical concepts (at p.193). A similar conclusion was expressed by Andrew J. in *In the Matter of the Organic Law on National Elections; Malipu Balakau v Paul Torato and anor* (1983 Unreported) SC256 when (at p.25) he said:

> I am unable to agree with the finding in [*Avia Aihi's*] case which was obiter that a review within the meaning of s.155(2)(b) has no distinction from an appeal .... It is in my view a separate and additional power, an inherent one, to any statutory right to appeal. The circumstances in which it may be invoked are established in *Avia Aihi's* case. Being of such a unique nature I simply cannot see how it can be equated with any statutory right of appeal.

Assuming Bredmeyer and Andrew JJ. are correct, it still remains for the Court to clarify the practical distinction, if any, that exists between proceedings by way of appeal and review.

THE SUPREME COURT'S INHERENT POWER TO REVIEW THE JUDICIAL ACTS OF THE NATIONAL COURT MAY BE EXERCISED AFTER TIME LIMITED FOR APPEAL HAS EXPIRED.

Comment

The case of *Avia Aihi v The State* [1981] PNGLR 81 arose out of the following facts: on the 17th March 1979 Avia Aihi was sentenced to life imprisonment after her conviction for murder.

Section 21 of the *Supreme Court Act* 1975 gave her the right to appeal against her sentence with the leave of the court. Section 27 of the *Supreme Court Act* 1975 however provided as follows:

> (1) Subject to Sub-section (2), where a person convicted decides to appeal or to obtain leave to appeal to the Supreme Court, he shall give notice of appeal, or notice of application for leave to appeal, as the case may be, in the manner prescribed by the Rules of Court within 40 days after the date of conviction.
>
> (2) The time within which notice of appeal, or notice of an application for leave to appeal, may be given may be extended at any time by the Supreme Court on application made within 40 days after the date of conviction.

Avia Aihi did not comply with s.27 — that is, no notice of application for leave to appeal or extension of time was applied for within forty days after her conviction.

However, on the 8th May 1980, more than twelve months after her conviction and sentence, the Public Solicitor filed on her behalf a notice seeking leave to appeal.

Counsel for the applicant submitted that s.27 of the *Supreme Court Act* did not operate to bar his client from appealing against her sentence because the right of appeal against conviction and sentence was a guaranteed right under s.37(15) of the Constitution and the Supreme Court should protect this right as required by s.57 of the Constitution. In the alternative it was argued that the Supreme Court had power under s.155(4) of the Constitution to make an order to enforce this right. Counsel also submitted that the Supreme Court had a discretion under s.155(2)(b) to allow the applicant to have her conviction reviewed.

The court (Kidu C.J., Kearney Dep.C.J., Greville Smith, Andrew, Kapi JJ.) unanimously rejected the arguments based upon s.37(15) and s.155(4) but held, Greville Smith and Kapi JJ. dissenting, that s.155(2)(b) invested the Supreme Court with an unfettered discretionary jurisdiction to hear an application to review despite the applicant having lost the right to appeal or to apply for leave to appeal. The court held that this discretionary jurisdiction should only be exercised in exceptional circumstances; the onus being upon the applicant to persuade the court to exercise such discretion. Each of the judges expressed himself at length upon the subject (Kidu C.J. at pp.87,88; Kearney Dep.C.J. at pp.92,93; Greville Smith J. (dissenting) at pp.94-99; Andrew J. at pp.99-102; Kapi J. (dissenting) at pp.108-112). Set out below are extracts of the leading majority and dissenting judgments. Note also Kidu C.J.'s remarks (at p.87) that the Supreme Court may not cut down the powers invested in it by Constitution and should be bold in stating the fact of its power.

per Kearney Dep.C.J. at pp.92,93.

> This court, as part of the Nationa l Judicial System, is invested with the judicial authority of the people: the Constitution, s.158(1). That is the exclusive and ultimate source of its authority.
>
> The word 'inherent' in the Constitution, s.155(2)(b), I think, indicates that it is direct from that unlimited well that the court's authority under that provision is derived; it is not a reference to a power possessed by the court simply because it is a court.
>
> The word 'inherent' also connotes that within the limits of the subject-matter of the Constitution, s.155(2)(b) — 'judicial acts of the National Court' — the power of review of this Court is plenary. In the absence of express constitutional provision, that power and its exercise cannot be restricted by any Act of Parliament; there is no express constitutional provision — see per Andrew J. in *Constitutional Reference No 1 of 1979* [1979] PNGLR 329 at p.401. So, for example, a privative clause would be of no effect — see the illustration by Pritchard J. in ***In re Moresby North East Election Petition; Patterson Lowa v Goasa Damena*** [1977] PNGLR 429 at p.442. Contrast the Constitution, ss.155(3)(a) and 155(3)(e), as regards the National Court.
>
> Whether the power is to be exercised in a particular case must always remain wholly a matter for this Court, in its discretion. I consider that it is a truly discretionary jurisdiction, of much the same type as that of the Privy Council in exercising what the common law recognizes as its inherent prerogative to grant special leave to appeal, though an applicant has no right by statute to appeal.
>
> I consider that this Court's discretionary and reserve power under the Constitution, s.155(2)(b), is additional to the power and jurisdiction vested in the court under the Constitution, s.155(2)(c); this appears clearly from the language used. The latter is dependent in part on the exercise of legislative power by Parliament; the former is not. The latter is subject to limits imposed by Acts; the former is not.
>
> It is to be expected that the final court of appeal in the National Judicial System would be expressly vested by the Constitution with a discretionary jurisdiction of the type in the Constitution, s.155(2)(b), so as to ensure the dispensation of justice; it is a common feature of many judicial systems. The policy of the Constitution in this respect is made strikingly clear in s.155(5) as regards the National Court.
>
> No distinction is to be drawn in my opinion, as regards the Constitution, s.155(2)(b), between the concepts of 'jurisdiction' and 'power'. In normal language usage, 'jurisdiction' connotes the authority of a court to exercise judicial power in a specific case; while 'judicial power' is the totality of the powers of a court, when it embarks upon the hearing of a case within its jurisdiction. The Constitution, s.155(2)(b), however, vests in the court an unrestricted authority to review certain judicial acts; and that, in effect, is a grant of jurisdiction. A grammatical support for this view is the reference to 'other jurisdiction'

in the Constitution, s.155(2)(c). Further, it appears that the 'inherent power' in the Constitution, s.155(4) is characterized as a 'jurisdiction' in the Constitution s.155(3)(d), although the 'power' there referred to in fact accords more closely with the strict sense of the word. The Constitution, s.155(2)(b) and s.155(2)(c), are clearly two distinct and separate heads of jurisdiction.

I would accordingly uphold Mr. Wilson's second submission. I consider that the applicant, a person affected by a judicial act of the National Court, lacking now any right to have that act reviewed, may yet ask this Court to exercise its inherent and discretionary power to review, under the Constitution, s.155(2)(b); and the court may hear the appeal.

Whether or not this Court would exercise that power and grant leave to appeal, depends on the circumstances of the particular case. It is wholly discretionary, but I think that in general leave would be granted only in exceptional circumstances where some substantial injustice is manifest, or the case is of special gravity.

per Kapi J. (dissenting) at pp.109-112

Can the applicant find any assistance under s.155(2)(b)? This provision deals with the power to review any act of the National Court. This power to review is no different from the power of review given to the Supreme Court by the *Supreme Court Act*. In my view there is no magic in the words '*an inherent power to review* all judicial acts of the National Court.' The *inherent power to review* all judicial acts of the National Court simply means that power which is essential to the existence and function of the court from the very fact that it is the final court of appeal. It needs no constitutional provision to say it. It is inherent in the court by the very nature of its existence as the final court of appeal. However the framers of the Constitution chose to put this in the Constitution, s.155(2)(b). In the context of review by way of prerogative writ, this Court has inherent power at common law to supervise the proceedings of the inferior courts. This power is now inherent in the Constitution (s.155(2)(b) — in relation to acts of the National Court and s.155(4) in relation to other bodies). However, the procedure to obtain such a writ and grounds for granting such writ still remain the subject of Rules of Court and the common law as may be adopted or rejected under Sch.2.2 of the Constitution. The *only difference now is that no Act of the Parliament can take this power away*. Any Act of the Parliament which seeks to take this power away will be declared invalid. Section 27(2) of the *Supreme Court Act* does not affect the power of review under s.155(2)(b) of the Constitution. The power of the court to review a sentence imposed by the National Court still remains. [It is] only that this particular applicant has lost the right to invoke that power. What then is the extent of this power? As I have already pointed out this power is to review all acts of the National Court. However, the power of review can only be exercised if it is invoked by a person who has the right to appeal. Who can invoke such power? In my view s.155(2)(b) cannot be of any assistance in determining who is entitled to invoke that power. It does no more than simply invest a power to review in the Supreme Court but does not give it the power to determine who may appeal and other incidental matters regarding the appeal procedure. In my view it certainly does not give it the power to determine who may have a right to extend time. These are matters which are determined by the Parliament in the *Supreme Court Act*.

In considering the preliminary issue, s.155(2)(b) cannot be of any assistance. It should be noted that s.155(2)(b) is only concerned with *reviewing acts of the National Court*. The *preliminary issue* raised in this case *is not an act of the National Court* but an operation of s.27 of the *Supreme Court Act*. The appeal against sentence which is the act of the National Court has not yet come before this Court. I see no difficulty in the Supreme Court reviewing the sentence in this case under s.155(2)(b) provided the applicant has a right of appeal and can bring the notice of application for leave to appeal against sentence. I find that there is nothing in the *Supreme Court Act* or the Constitution which gives the applicant the right to apply for an extension of time .....

However, it is significant to note that such an order for an extension of time *can only be made upon application made by a person who is entitled to apply* for such extension. Under s.27(2) of the *Supreme Court Act* a convicted person can only apply within the forty day period. At the most it can be said that the Supreme Court would have power to extend time under s.155(2)(b) of the Constitution. The difficulty in the applicant's case is that she has lost this right to invoke the power of the extension of time. Similarly, under s.27(1) while the Supreme Court still has the inherent power to review the sentence in this case, the applicant has lost the right of appeal at the expiration of the forty day limit. The power to review and the power to extend time has nothing to do with the right of a person to invoke these powers. Consequently I find that the applicant has no right, or no standing, to make this application.

I appreciate that the provisions of the *Supreme Court Act* on limitation of time in which to appeal by convicted persons is too short. This is particularly so in view of the fact that most people who are convicted are uneducated and are ignorant of this limitation. However it is not competent of this Court to question the justice or injustice of a statute. The court can only investigate whether the Parliament in passing a statute has done so within the powers given under the Constitution. See *Carltona Ltd v Commissioners of Works and Others* [1943] 2 All ER 560, at p.564.

It has not been suggested that s.27 of the *Supreme Court Act* is contrary to a provision of the Constitution. I find that s.27 of the Act is valid. It is not inconsistent with s.155(2)(b) of the Constitution. They deal with different issues.

Such injustice in a statute can only be remedied by the Parliament by an amendment to the Act.

To find that s.27 of the *Supreme Court Act* is validly enacted by the Parliament on the one hand and then on the other hand find that the Supreme Court has inherent jurisdiction to override the provision under s.155(2)(b) to give the applicant a right to apply is, in my view, contrary to the doctrine of separation of powers. With respect, I find it difficult to resolve that this Court can override a provision of a validly enacted statute. Legislative power is vested in the National Parliament (s.100 of the Constitution). Only the Parliament can amend a statute.

This Court has peculiar power of formulating a new rule of law under Sch.2.3 of the Constitution. The court can only do this if there is no applicable rule of law. In the instant case the provisions of the *Supreme Court Act* are directly on point.

The substance of my decision then is this. The Supreme Court has an inherent power of review under s.155(2)(b) of the Constitution to review all acts of the National Court. This power cannot be taken away by an Act of the Parliament.

Section 27 of the *Supreme Court Act* has not been found to be inconsistent with s.155(2)(b). This is because s.27 deals with the *right of persons of appeal* rather than the power of review by the Supreme Court. The right of a person to appeal is given by the statutes. In the instant case the right of a person to appeal is restricted to within forty days by s.27 of the *Supreme Court Act.* The restriction of the right of appeal under the *Supreme Court Act* is not inconsistent with the right of appeal guaranteed by s.37(15) of the Constitution. The applicant is left with s.27 of the *Supreme Court Act.* Section 27 of the *Supreme Court Act* can only be amended by the Parliament and not by this Court.

THE SUPREME COURTS' INHERENT POWER TO REVIEW THE JUDICIAL ACTS OF THE NATIONAL COURT MAY BE EXERCISED EVEN AFTER THE DISMISSAL OF AN APPEAL FROM THAT COURT

per Bredmeyer J.

I have considered whether the court should hear an appeal from an appellant ... who has escaped custody or, ... who has not answered bail ... If an appellant escapes custody or jumps bail ... the court may in its discretion adjourn the case or dismiss the appeal. If the appeal is dismissed and the applicant should later surrender into custody, he may apply in England for an extension to appeal out of time. In Papua New Guinea s.29 of the *Supreme Court Act* does not allow for such an extension of time unless the application is itself made within the 40 day time limit; he may however apply for a review of the decision under s.155(2)(b) of the Constitution as interpreted by the Court in *Avia Aihi v The State (No 2)* [1982] PNGLR 44.

Keko Aparo and ors v The State (1983 Unreported) SC249 at p.12.

Held

The Supreme Court may, pursuant to s.155(2)(b), alter the terms of a warrant of commitment issued by a National Court judge to make it conform to law notwithstanding that the person affected has not raised the issue and has abandoned his appeal.

Saki v The State [1980] PNGLR 33; see Kearney A.C.J., see also Greville Smith and Pratt JJ. at p.35.

AS TO PRINCIPLES UPON WHICH INHERENT JURISDICTION IS TO BE EXERCISED

per Kidu C.J. and Andrew J.

It must be emphasized from the outset that the power vested in this court by s.155(2)(b) will not be exercised as a matter of course. The reason is quite obvious. Where statutory appeal provisions are not complied with there must be shown convincing reasons why this court should exercise its constitutional power ... [The applicant] filed an application for leave to appeal fourteen months after her conviction .... For her to be allowed to have her sentence (of life imprisonment) reviewed by this court pursuant to s.155(2)(b) she must satisfactorily explain why she did not comply with s.27 of the Act [as to time limits for the institution of appeals] and also show that her case merits a hearing by this court.
Avia Aihi v The State (No 2) [1982] PNGLR 44 at pp.45,46, see also Kapi J. at p.61 (principles to be applied are: 1. leave will not be granted as a matter of course; 2. there must be substantial reasons given for the delay; 3. there must be some legal merit on the grounds of appeal; and 4. whether leave is granted or not is in the discretion of the Court).

AS TO PROCEDURE

per Kearney Dep.C.J.

The question before us is whether the applicant should be granted leave to appeal. This has been argued as an issue largely distinct from the merits of an appeal. The case has not simply been split into two parts, but three, as this hearing follows an earlier hearing and ruling directed solely to the preliminary question as to whether the Court had jurisdiction to entertain the application see ... *Avia Aihi v The State* [1981] PNGLR 81. So we have had separate hearings on jurisdiction and the grant of leave; and there will be a separate hearing on the merits of the appeal. In retrospect, I think it was unfortunate that the Court permitted the presentation of argument in this trifoliate manner; no good purpose has been served; the ultimate resolution of the vital question has been unduly prolonged; and the Court is now in the invidious position of tacitly ruling on the probability of success of an appeal the merits of which, as presently constituted, it is yet to hear ...

I should add one comment. Although this hearing has been accepted as being directed solely to the question of whether leave to appeal should be granted, strictly a prior question requires to be answered. It is whether the Court should exercise its jurisdiction under the Constitution, s.155(2)(b) and hear the applicant on the question of leave. Only if that is answered in the affirmative does the question of whether leave should be granted, arise.
Avia Aihi v The State (No 2) [1982] PNGLR 44 at pp.57.

Referred to
by Kapi J. (dissenting) in *In the Matter of the Organic Law on National Elections; Malipu Balakau v Paul Torato and anor* (1983 Unreported) SC256 at pp.17,18.

GENERALLY

per Kaputin J.

In Papua New Guinea the Supreme Court has a constitutional duty to form its independant opinion as to what are the proper inferences from evidentiary facts.
John Pok v The State (1983 Unreported) SC254 at pp.11,12.

Referred to

by Kapi J. in *Acting Public Solicitor [sic] v Uname Aumane* [1980] PNGLR 510 at p.530;

by Greville Smith J. in *S.C.R. No 2 of 1981; Re s.19(1)(f) of the Criminal Code* [1982] PNGLR 150 at pp.166,167;

by Kidu C.J. and Andrew J. in *In the Matter of the Organic Law on National Elections; Jabara v Okuk* (1983 Unreported) SC246 at p.12;

per Curiam (Kidu C.J. Kapi Dep.C.J., Andrew J.) in *Burns Philp (New Guinea Ltd) v Maxine George* (1983 Unreported) SC244 at p.2.

(c) has such other jurisdiction and powers as are conferred on it by this Constitution or any other law.

(*See: Supreme Court Act* Ch.37.)

(3) The National Court —
(a) has an inherent power to review any exercise of judicial authority; and
(b) has such other jurisdiction and powers as are conferred on it by this Constitution or any law,

(*See: National Court Act* Ch.38.)

except where —
(c) jurisdiction is conferred upon the Supreme Court to the exclusion of the National Court; or
(d) the Supreme Court assumes jurisdiction under Subsection (4); or
(e) the power of review is removed or restricted by a Constitutional Law or an Act of the Parliament.

C.P.C. Report Ch.8 p.3

The National Court of Justice

29. There should be a National Court of Justice consisting of the Chief Justice, the Deputy Chief Justice and other judges, with broad power to dispense justice throughout the country, and also in cases which involve a law of this country but arise outside Papua New Guinea. We have provided for the National Court's jurisdiction to be altered by ordinary law (provided that law specifically refers to the jurisdiction of the court), as we believe it is important not to unduly limit the power of parliament to make changes in the jurisdiction of the highest courts, as well as of subordinate courts. We also wish to maximise the scope for a Law Reform Commission to recommend significant changes in the present judicial system if it thinks they are necessary.

AS TO WHAT CONSTITUTES AN EXERCISE OF JUDICIAL AUTHORITY

per Prentice C.J.

It will be noted that the National Court's 'power of review' is related to exercises of 'judicial authority'. The latter term is not defined in the Constitution, though 'judicial officer' is stated to mean 'a Judge or Magistrate of a court within the National Judicial System (other than a magistrate or member of a village court) in his capacity as such.' The exercise of power by administrative bodies is not normally regarded as an 'exercise of judicial authority,' though sometimes such bodies are required by their creating statutes to 'act judicially'. I see no reason to justify the construction of the phrase 'power of review' in s.155(3)(e) and s.155(5) differently from that it is expressed to have in s.155(3)(a) — namely a power to review any exercise of judicial authority, which should in my opinion exclude exercise of power by administrative (non-judicial) bodies. In so far therefore as s.61AA of the *Migration Act* 1963 excludes an appeal to any court by way of 'review'. (sic) It does not in my opinion trespass upon a grant of power by the Constitution itself as to review of exercises of 'judicial authority.'

Premdas v The Independent State of Papua New Guinea [1979] PNGLR 329 at p.337; see also Saldanha J. at p.360 and Andrew J. at p.401.

REVIEW MAY BE EXERCISED OVER NON-JUDICIAL TRIBUNALS UNDER JURISDICTION CONFERRED BY SECTION 155(3)(b) AND SECTION 59 OF THE CONSTITUTION

per Kapi J.

It has been suggested by the appellants that the Minister for Transport and Civil Aviation is not a judicial authority and therefore the National Court has no inherent power to review the exercise of his authority under s.155(3)(a) of the Constitution. This provision was considered in *Premdas v The Independent State of Papua New Guinea* [1979] PNGLR 329. However this submission is not destructive as the National Court has jurisdiction and powers conferred on it by s.155(3)(b) of the Constitution. It appears from the majority judgments in the *Premdas* case (supra) that the National Court has such other powers conferred under this provision by the common law of England. The question is what are the powers given by the common law of England?

In this case we are concerned with the principles of natural justice. These principles are set out under s.59 of the Constitution which reads:

(1) Subject to this Constitution and to any statute, the principles of natural justice are the rules of the underlying law known by that name developed for control of judicial and administrative proceedings.

(2) The minimum requirement of natural justice is the duty to act fairly and, in principle, to be seen to act fairly.

These principles are the common law principles of natural justice as adopted under Sch.2.2 of the Constitution or as developed under Sch.2.3 and s.60 of the Constitution. *Iambakey Okuk v Fallscheer* [1980] PNGLR 274 at p.279; but see also Prentice C.J. in *Premdas v The Independent State of Papua New Guinea* [1979] PNGLR 329 at pp.337,338; see also Saldanha J. at p.361 and Andrew J. at p.401. Note, for detailed annotations as to natural justice see under ss.59-62.

PROHIBITION OF APPEAL DOES NOT AFFECT APPLICATION FOR REVIEW BY WAY OF PREROGATIVE WRIT

per Bredmeyer J.

Caspar Nuli has applied under 0.81 r.1 of the *Rules of the National Court* for an order to show cause why a writ of certiorari should not issue to quash a decision given by the District Land Court at Kimbe on 13th April, 1981.

The decision of the District Land Court was given under s.60 of the *Land Disputes Settlement Act* 1975 on an appeal from a decision of the Local Land Court. By s.61 the effect of a decision of a District Land Court 'is final and not subject to appeal in any way'. That section prevents any appeal to the National Court of Justice but it is not effective to prevent an application for review by means of a prerogative writ. Under s.155(3) of the Constitution the National Court has 'an inherent power to review any exercise of judicial authority' and under s.155(4) the National Court has 'an inherent power to make, in such circumstances as seem .... proper, orders in the nature of prerogative writs and such other orders as are necessary to do justice in the circumstances of a particular case'. Appeal and review are two different things. Appeal is prevented by s.61 but review is open by those sections of the Constitution. Even if s.155 of the Constitution did not exist, at common law certiorari lies even where a statute declares the decision of an inferior court to be 'final' for that only prevents an appeal, and an application for an order for certiorari is not an appeal: *R. v Medical Appeal Tribunal, ex parte Gilmore* [1957] 1 QB 574.
The State v District Land Court [1981] PNGLR 192 at p.193.

Referred to

by Frost C.J. in *The State v The Independent Tribunal; Ex Parte Sasakila* [1976] PNGLR 491 at p.501.

AS TO PURPORTED REMOVAL BY PARLIAMENT OF THE NATIONAL COURT'S POWER OF REVIEW

per Narakobi A.J.

The Constitution s.155(3)(a) makes it clear that the National Court has an inherent power to review any exercise of judicial power or authority and such other jurisdiction and powers as are conferred on it by this Constitution or any law. That power may be removed or restricted by a Constitutional Law or an Act of the Parliament (s.155(3)(e)).

It is argued that s.9 of the *National Land Registration Act* (sic) excluded the National Court's jurisdiction. That, in my view is not correct.

Subsection (5) of s.155 of the Constitution makes it abundantly clear that whatever the restrictions an Act of the Parliament might seek to place on the jurisdiction of the National Court pursuant to s.155(3)(e), it the National Court nevertheless has an inherent power of review where, in its opinion, there are over-riding considerations of public policy in the special circumstances of a particular case. In other words, the Act simply cannot cut out the jurisdiction of the National Court to review any exercise of judicial authority.
Reve Mase v The Independent State of PNG (1980 Unreported) N260 at p.3.

Referred to

by Kearney Dep.C.J. in *Avia Aihi v The State* [1981] PNGLR 81 at pp.92,93; see also Kidu C.J. at p.88, Greville Smith J. at p.94.

NATIONAL COURT MAY EXERCISE A LIMITED POWER OF REVIEW OVER ITS OWN JUDICIAL ACTS

Held

Section 155(3) authorizes the National Court to review its own decisions during the period between the termination of a case and the close of the circuit. Accordingly the court will review a sentence imposed upon a convict if it were shown that it had sentenced upon a mistaken understanding of certain relevant facts.
The State v Kaupa Ungi [1980] PNGLR 199; see Narakobi A.J. at p.203.

NATIONAL COURT MAY MAKE ORDERS IN THE NATURE OF PREROGATIVE WRITS NOTWITHSTANDING THE PROVISIONS OF THE RULES OF COURT

per Bredmeyer J.

Order 81 r.2 reads:

> Orders to show cause shall be to show cause before the Full Court, unless the matter appears to be one of urgency, in which case the Court or Judge may make the Order returnable before a single Judge in Court or Chambers.

I consider O.81 r.2 ultra vires s.155(3)(a) and s.155(4) of the Constitution. Those subsections give the National Court the power to review any exercise of judicial authority and to make orders in the nature of prerogative writs and that clearly implies a power to make orders nisi and orders absolute.
The State v District Land Court [1981] PNGLR 192 at p.197 (Note, however, that the new National Court Rules adopted in July 1983 have been significantly revised. They now contain no provision equivalent to O.81 r.2).

GENERALLY

Referred to

by Narakobi A.J. in *Enga Kilu v John Moroby* (1980 Unreported) N246 at p.6 (National Court reviewing sentence imposed by Magistrate);

by Quinlivan A.J. in *The State v Jacob Toroken (Coroner)* (1981 Unreported) N281 at p.16;

by Narakobi A.J. in *Wapele v Constable Sepa* (1981 Unreported) N292 at p.3;

by Kearney Dep.C.J. in *The State v Giddings* [1981] PNGLR 423 at p.434 (National Court reviewing exercise of discretion by District Land Court);

by Quinlivan A.J. in *Marben v Gesa* (1981 Unreported) N314(M) at pp.8-12.

(4) Both the Supreme Court and the National Court have an inherent power to make, in such circumstances as seem to them proper, orders in the nature of prerogative writs and such other orders as are necessary to do justice in the circumstances of a particular case.

C.P.C. Report Ch.8 p.3

Powers of Supreme Court and National Court

30. We have recommended that these courts have the powers of superior courts of record, that is, the powers which the present Full Court of the Supreme Court and Supreme Court now have.

AN OVERVIEW

Comment

The history of judicial application of s.155(4) has been one of restraint. With three exceptions: *State v Luku Wapulae and ors* (1980 Unreported) N233, the judgment at first instance in *S.C.R. No 2 of 1981; Re s.19(1)(f) of the Criminal Code* [1982] PNGLR 150 and *Dent v Thomas Kavali* [1981] PNGLR 488 (the first-mentioned two of which were subsequently reversed by unanimous holdings of the Supreme Court), the judges have refrained from construing s.155(4) as a mandate to 'over-ride' the ordinary law.

Notwithstanding this history of restraint it has been surprisingly difficult to state concisely the effect of s.155(4). This is because although the Supreme Court has reached unanimous decisions in several cases in which the interpretation of s.155(4) has been in issue, individual judges have expressed divergent reasons for their conclusions. Broadly, these divergent holdings can be grouped into two categories.

The narrow view, neatly expressed by Kapi J. in *S.C.R. No 2 of 1981; Re s.19(1)(f) of the Criminal Code* [1982] PNGLR 150 at pp.169-171 is that the words 'such orders as are necessary to do justice' must be construed ejustem generis with the words that precede them. Thus, in Kapi J.'s view, s.155(4) confers upon the National and Supreme Courts only the power to make orders having the character of the prerogative writs and then only in so far as is necessary to do justice *according to law*. This narrow view has commanded occasional support (see for example Greville Smith J. in the same case at p.167) but appears unlikely to gain majority approval.

The preponderance of judicial opinion instead appears to favour the slightly wider formulation originally expressed by Kearney Dep.C.J. in *Avia Aihi v The State* [1981] PNGLR 81 at pp.90-92 and later developed by him in *S.C.R. No 2 of 1981; Re s.19(1)(f) of the Criminal Code* [1982] PNGLR 150 at p.157,158. In these judgments Kearney Dep.C.J. asserted that there was no reason for the Courts to limit the words 'such other orders' by the application of the ejustem generis rule. Implicitly Kearney Dep.C.J. rejected Kapi J.'s view that the expression 'justice' meant only justice 'according to law'.

However, Kearney Dep.C.J. also rejected any suggestion that s.155(4) was intended to confer an unlimited jurisdiction on the National and Supreme Courts such as would enable those Courts to grant judicial remedies whenever they were moved to do so by the justice of the claimants' case. Instead he held that s.155(4) was intended to have no effect at all upon the 'primary rights' of the parties before the Court. In Kearney Dep.C.J.'s view the question of whether a claimant possesses a legal right is one to be decided by the ordinary law entirely independently of s.155(4). Section 155(4) only applies once that question has been answered and it empowers the court to tailor its remedies (limited only by the Court's own discretion) such that those primary rights may be adequately protected.

In *SCR No 2 of 1981: Re s.19(1)(f) of the Criminal Code* [1982] PNGLR 150, Kearney

Dep.C.J.'s views were adopted by Kidu C.J. at p.155 and, with some reservations, by Pratt J. at pp.173-176 so as to form the majority opinion of the Court.

In *Placer Holdings Pty Ltd and Land Act* [1982] PNGLR 326, Kapi Dep.C.J., who had earlier advocated a narrower construction of the section, found himself constrained to follow that majority.

For completeness it should be noted that a third and yet wider view of s.155(4) was briefly advocated by Bredmeyer J. In *Dent v Thomas Kavali* [1981] PNGLR 488 and in *Public Employees Association of Papua New Guinea v Public Service Commission* (1983 Unreported) SC253, Bredmeyer J. appeared to be laying the ground for rejecting the proposition that s.155(4) can only be used to protect pre-existent legal rights. However in *Aundak Kupil v The State* (1983 Unreported) N435 his Honor reviewed the cases in which the section had been discussed and concluded:

> Those cases have decided that the latter words [of s.155(4)] are disjunctive from the former, that is the latter orders do not have to be in the nature of prerogative writs. The section is a grant of power or of jurisdiction. It does not affect the primary rights of parties which are determined by the substantive law. It is no warrant for the court allowing a new cause of action for example. The section encompasses remedies, adjectival and procedural orders. It enables the Court to tailor its remedies to the circumstances of an individual case to ensure that the primary rights of a party are protected.

In our opinion the above extract from Bredmeyer J.'s judgment states accurately the now settled law.

AS TO THE LEGAL SOURCE OF JURISDICTION TO MAKE ORDERS IN THE NATURE OF PREROGATIVE ORDERS AND DECLARATORY ORDERS.

per Bredmeyer J.

> Although O.4 r.11 [of the Rules of the National Court] appears to confer a power on the court to grant declaratory orders and judgments, albeit expressed in a negative way, in view of the Constitution, s.184, and the other statutory provisions cited, it should be interpreted as relating only to matters of practice and procedure. Although the Rules are 'continued in force' by s.14 of the *National Court Act* I consider that they remain rules of court, and as such are subordinate to any statute. Any statute passed which conflicted with a rule of court would override it, see the Constitution, s.184(4). In my view, O.4 r.11 is a rule, not a statutory provision, and must be read down as relating to matters of practice and procedure.
>
> I consider the National Court's jurisdiction or power to grant a declaratory order comes from the Constitution, s.155(4), in particular the latter words of that section. Section 155(4) reads:
>
> > Both the Supreme Court and the National Court have an inherent power to make, in such circumstances as seem to them proper, orders in the nature of prerogative writs and such other orders as are necessary to do justice in the circumstances of a particular case.
>
> Likewise I consider that the power of the pre-Independence Supreme Court of Papua New Guinea to grant a declaratory order did not come from O.4 r.11 but rather from the statutory provisions conferring on that court the powers of the Court of Chancery in England. I propose merely to allude to the statutes which produced that result. Section 6 of the *Supreme Court Act* 1949 conferred on the Supreme Court of the Territory of Papua and New Guinea the same jurisdiction in relation to the Territory of Papua as that exercised by the Supreme Court of the pre-war Territory of Papua, and, in relation to the Territory of New Guinea, the same jurisdiction as that exercised by the Supreme Court of the pre-war Territory of New Guinea. The Supreme Court of pre-war Papua had the jurisdiction of the Supreme Court of Queensland (s.10 of the *Courts and Laws Adopting Ordinance* of 1888, and s.6 of the *Papua Act,* 1905). Likewise the Supreme Court of pre-war New Guinea also had the jurisdiction of the Supreme Court of Queensland (s.11 of the *Judiciary Ordinance* 1921 (N.G.)). The Supreme Court of Queensland in turn had the equitable jurisdiction of the Lord High Chancellor in England (s.22 of the *Supreme Court Act,* 1867 of Queensland). And the Court of Chancery before 1883 could make binding declarations of right whereas the common law courts could not. In 1883 a rule was made, similar to the Papua New Guinea rule, which introduced a very big change in the law of declaratory judgments; it enabled the court to make a binding declaration of right whether or not any consequential relief was or could be claimed, see historical note in *Supreme Court Practice* 1967, vol.1, par.15/16/1.

It follows from my analysis that in seeking a declaratory order the plaintiff is seeking to invoke s.155(4) of the Constitution which is the supreme law of Papua New Guinea and superior to any statute (ss.10 and 1 1 of the Constitution).
Dent v Thomas Kavali [1981] PNGLR 488 at pp.490,491.

Referred to

by Bredmeyer J. in *Public Employees Association of Papua New Guinea v Public Service Commission* (1983 Unreported) SC253 at p.12.

ENABLES THE THICKETS OF TECHNICALITY APPLYING AT COMMON LAW TO THE PREROGATIVE WRITS TO BE SWEPT ASIDE

per Kearney J.

In these proceedings Mr Boston seeks a certiorari. It is clear that this Court has power to review by certiorari the Tribunal's decision and recommendation, to ensure that it kept within its powers and observed the law in that which it did. Constitution ss.60, 155(4) and Sch.2.4. enlarge the scope of certiorari beyond that which it has in the common law of England, and enable the thickets of technicality and inconsistency to be cut away, with the beneficial result that the law concerning judicial control is not here bedevilled by complex restrictive procedures and practices.
The State v The Independent Tribunal; Ex Parte Sasakila [1976] PNGLR 491 at p.505.

Referred to

by Kearney J. in *Billy Keri v George Kogia and ors* (1978 Unreported) N153 at p.2 (court may treat an appeal as an application for certiorari).

INCLUDES JURISDICTION TO GRANT INTERLOCUTORY INJUNCTIONS

per Frost C.J.

It is plain that s.155(4) cannot be taken so far as to enable a court to make a final decision upon the circumstances of a particular case without regard to the principles of law or equity applicable for its determination.

However, I do not consider that the power to make 'such other orders as are necessary to do justice in the circumstances of a particular case' can be confined to matters of procedure only. Giving the words their fair and liberal meaning as required by the Constitution, Sch.1.5(2), the provision, in my opinion, extends to jurisdiction also, and enables a court to make an order in the nature of an interlocutory injunction, if the requirements of the section are met, even although no jurisdiction to make the order exists under the principles of common law or equity. The express reference 'to the circumstances of a particular case', in my opinion, leave no room for a more restrictive construction to be adopted.

Where a case for interlocutory relief falls within the well established principles of equity, there is no need for the claimant to have recourse to s.155(4). It is sufficient for the purposes of this case to hold that full regard must be given to the balance of considerations affecting each party in reaching a conclusion whether or not a particular order is necessary under the section to do justice in the circumstances of a particular case. On the facts, in my opinion it has been shown by the plaintiff that the Court's power should be exercised in its favour.
Mauga Logging Company Pty Ltd v South Pacific Oil Palm Development Pty Ltd (No 1) [1977] PNGLR 80 at p.85.

AS TO LIMITS UPON JURISDICTION

per Prentice J.

It was sought by the Government to contend that s.155(4) did not amount to a *grant* of jurisdiction or power.

If the Constitution be regarded as making a distinction clearly between jurisdiction and power, s.155(4) must at least be regarded as a grant of power. There appears no other source by which the power specified therein could have been granted by the people to the court so as to enable that section to be read as merely declaratory. But I do not apprehend the section to have given the Supreme Court jurisdiction to review by writs in the nature of prerogative writs, matters other than those normally coming within the purview of courts, (such as status, property, contract and so on), or involving the enforcement of the Constitution and the rights it guarantees. One does not envisage that thereby alone this Court becomes potentially seized of enquiries into how, and how fairly, executive decisions were arrived at, or those say of private committees such as political parties, football clubs, parents and friends associations, and so on. 'The administrative process is not, and cannot be, a succession of justiciable controversies .... The prospect of judicial relief cannot be held out to every person whose interests may be adversely affected by administrative action.' (S.A. de Smith, *Judicial Review of Administrative Action* (2nd ed., 1968), p.3). I would answer question 4, 'No; s.61AA of the *Migration Act* 1963 is not unconstitutional; but it cannot prevent the jurisdiction of the National and Supreme Courts being invoked in support of alleged Constitutional Rights and against alleged breaches of the Constitution.' *Premdas v The Independent State of Papua New Guinea* [1979] PNGLR 329 at pp.337,338; see also Saldanha J. at pp.360,361,368, Wilson J. at p.389, Andrew J. at p.401.

AUTHORISES THE NATIONAL COURT TO AWARD PERIODIC PAYMENTS INSTEAD OF LUMP SUM DAMAGES

per Bredmeyer J.

The power to make the periodic orders I propose comes I think from s.155(4) of the Constitution which reads:

> (4) Both the Supreme Court and the National Court have an inherent power to make, in such circumstances as seem to them proper, orders in the nature of prerogative writs and such other orders as are necessary to do justice in the circumstances of a particular case.

and in particular from the latter words of that subsection 'such other orders as are necessary to do justice in the circumstances of a particular case'. The ambit of that power has been discussed in a number of cases: *Mauga Logging Co. Pty Ltd v South Pacific Oil Palm Development Pty Ltd* [1977] PNGLR 80, *Premdas v The Independent State of Papua New Guinea* [1979] PNGLR 329, *Avia Aihi v The State* [1981] PNGLR 81, *New Guinea Cocoa (Export) Co. Pty Ltd v Basis Vedbaek* [1980] PNGLR 205, and *Dent v Kavali* [1981] PNGLR 488. Those cases have decided that the latter words are disjunctive from the former, that is that the latter orders do not have to be in the nature of prerogative writs. The section is a grant of power or of jurisdiction. It does not affect the primary rights of parties which are determined by the substantive law. It is no warrant for the courts allowing a new cause of action for example. The section encompasses remedies, adjectival and procedural orders. It enables the courts to tailor its remedies to the circumstances of an individual case to ensure that the primary rights of a party are protected. The section has been used to justify a *Mareva* injunction and a declaration of right. I consider it could be used to justify the arrest of a ship on the issue of a writ, an *Anton Piller* Order, and the issue of a writ and the entry of judgment in a foreign currency (now widely allowed in England as a common law development following *Milianges v George Frank (Textiles) Ltd* [1976] A.C. 443).

The periodic orders I propose in this case fall within the ambit of s.155(4). I have not allowed a new cause of action. The cause of action and the measure of damages for future economic loss and future medical expenses are within the existing common law. The existing common law requires the future loss and expenses to be estimated as weekly sums to be computed into a lump sum by the use of interest tables based on my estimate of the working life expectancy for economic loss, and the life expectancy for future medical expenses. It then requires me to make some reduction on the assumption that the possible adverse vicissitudes of life are likely to outweigh the possible adverse favourable vicissitudes. My periodic orders are simply an alteration in the form in which the money I estimate for the plaintiffs' future economic loss and medical expenses are given to them. It is an alteration in the remedy and I believe that orders for periodic payments which cease on death are a more precise and exact way of arriving at the same result, namely compensation for the plaintiffs' future economic loss and medical needs. I consider that the orders are necessary to do justice to the parties in the circumstances of this particular case. A lump sum payment based on a three-year life span would be unjust to the plaintiffs if they should live longer than three years and to the defendant if they should die before then.

The Supreme Court and National Court should not hesitate to use s.155(4) to make new law on occasions and on other occasions to declare parts of the English common law and equity inapplicable and inappropriate to the circumstances of Papua New Guinea under Constitution Sch.2.2.

Aundak Kupil v The Independent State of Papua New Guinea (1983 Unreported) N435 at pp.54-56.

AS TO WHETHER SECTION 155(4) PERMITS THE NATIONAL OR SUPREME COURTS TO OVER-RIDE TIME LIMITS IMPOSED BY STATUTE FOR THE DOING OF AN ACT.

per Kearney Dep.C.J.

I agree with the views of Prentice C.J. and Andrew J. in *Premdas v The Independent State of Papua New Guinea* ([1979] PNGLR 329 at pp.337,401) that the Constitution, s.155(4), involves at least a grant of power to the courts. I consider that the sub-section gives unfettered discretionary power both to this Court and the National Court so to tailor their remedial process to the circumstances of the individual case as to ensure that the primary rights of parties before them are protected. And so, for example, the development of remedial process such as the *Mareva* injunction need not be as tortuous here as in England. But the Constitution, s.155(4) cannot affect the primary rights of parties; these are determined by law. In the circumstances of this case, the applicant now has lost the right to have her sentence reviewed. That extinction of her primary right comes about by operation of law; that is, by her failure to comply with s.27 of the Act. The Constitution, s.155(4), cannot be used to re-create a primary right, once extinguished.

Avia Aihi v The State [1981] PNGLR 81 at p.91; see also Kidu C.J. at pp.84,85, Kapi J. at p.107.

per Kapi Dep.C.J.

This is a Notice of Motion by the applicant seeking declarations:

(a) that the applicant be allowed to nominate as a candidate in Kundiawa for the forthcoming elections; and

(b) that he be declared as nominated pursuant to s.92 of the *Organic Law on National Elections* ....

I should set out the facts for the purposes of deciding this point of law. It appears from the applicant's version of events that on the morning of of the last day of nomination, he paid a nomination fee of K100 at the Bureau of Management Services Office as directed by Electoral Commission officials and was on his way to nominate at the Electoral Office when he was arrested by the police on a warrant of arrest in connection with a traffic offence. According to him, he pleaded with the policement to allow him to nominate before being taken away to the court hearing. However, he was informed that he should attend the court hearing and that he would have enough time to nominate afterwards. However, by the time he returned to nominate, the hour of nomination had lapsed. He alleges that the police have acted wrongfully in not allowing him to nominate in these circumstances and therefore his right to stand for elective office under s.50(1)(d) of the Constitution was infringed. For the purposes of deciding the preliminary point before me, I will assume that the police have infringed the right of the applicant to stand for public office. The question of law is —

> Do I have power to direct that the nomination period which closed on 15th of April 1982 be extended and the Electoral Commissioner accept the nomination of the applicant during any extension which I may order? ....

It is not disputed that in the instant case, nominations were opened on the 18th of March 1982 and closed on the 15th of April 1982. During this period all citizens had the right to nominate according to the the Organic Law. If this right was denied by any person or authority during that period the Court would enforce that right during the nomination period under s.57 of the Constitution. However, it would appear that such an application was not made during the nomination period in the instant case.

When the nomination period closed on the 15th of April 1982, no citizen had the right to nominate for public office. That is the effect of the Organic Law. Citizens have no right to exercise this right after the period expires. Having lost the right to nominate at at the

expiration of time, a citizen cannot use the provisions of s.155(4) of the Constitution to restore the right. See *Avia Aihi v The State* [1981] PNGLR 81. See also *S.C.R. No 2 of 1981; Re s.19* [1981] PNGLR 518. [Comment: but what of the powers under s.57?].
In re Organic Law on National Elections [1982] PNGLR 289 at pp.289-291.

per Bredmeyer J.

It follows from my analysis that in seeking a declaratory order the plaintiff is seeking to invoke s.155(4) of the Constitution which is the supreme law of Papua New Guinea and superior to any statute (ss.10 and 11 of the Constitution).

I consider the National Court thus has constitutional power to grant a declaratory order (and under the earlier part of s.155(4) a certiorari order) in disregard of the time limit on appeal imposed by s.121(2) of the *Land Act*. That is consistent with the decision of five judges of the Supreme Court in *Avia Aihi v The State* [1981] PNGLR 81. There the Supreme Court held that it had power to entertain a criminal appeal under s.155(2) of the Constitution despite the appellant's failure to comply with the 40-day time limit on appeal imposed by s.27 of the *Supreme Court Act* 1975. Any statutory provision inconsistent with a constitutional provision is invalid to the extent of the inconsistency (Constitution, s.11).

For these reasons I consider the plaintiff is not barred by s.121(2) of the *Land Act* from seeking a declaratory order. Whether or not he succeeds in getting a declaration lies in the discretion of the court. There is abundant authority that a declaration is a discretionary remedy.
Dent v Thomas Kavali [1981] PNGLR 488 at p.491.

Referred to

by Kapi J. in *Mapun Papol v Antony Temo* [1981] PNGLR 178 at p.181 (*Avia Aihi* followed);

per Curiam (Kidu C.J., Kapi Dep.C.J., Andrew J.) in *S.C.R. No 4 of 1982; Re Delba Biri v Bill Ginbogl Ninkama* [1982] PNGLR 342 at p.348 (*Avia Aihi* followed);

by Kapi Dep.C.J. in *Placer Holdings Pty Ltd and Land Act* [1982] PNGLR 326 at p.329 (*Avia Aihi* followed).

DOES NOT PERMIT THE NATIONAL COURT TO SENTENCE OR OTHERWISE MAKE A DISPOSITION OF AN OFFENDER OTHERWISE THAN AS PROVIDED BY THE CRIMINAL CODE

per Kearney Dep.C.J.

... I adhere to the view of s.155(4) I expressed in *Avia Aihi v The State* [1981] PNGLR 81, a case which turned on s.155(2)(b). I consider that s.155(4) is directed solely to the power of the Court to issue preventive or remedial judicial process for the purpose of protecting or enforcing a party's primary rights. It is concerned with a party's secondary rights. For this categorization of rights see e.g. Jowitt, 2nd ed, Volume 2, pp.1581-2. The process must be within judicial power e.g. an injunction. See the *Mikasa (NSW) Pty Ltd v Festival Stores* (1972) 127 CLR 617 at p.631.

I might add that I agree with Pratt J. that there is no reason why the term 'other orders' referred to in s.155(4), should be construed ejusdem generis with 'orders in the nature of prerogative writs'. That was also I think the view of Frost C.J. in *Mauga Logging* [1977] PNGLR 80 at p.85. The linking phrase is ' ... such ... as ... '; this is to be read as a phrase and given its ordinary meaning which does not connote any referral back to a category of orders already described. Provided the 'other orders', of an adjectival character and within judicial power to make, are properly characterized as 'necessary to do justice in the circumstances of (the) particular case', the Court is competent to make them. I would reserve for further consideration the question of the power of the Court under s.155(4) in a case where a law limits the permissible adjectival process; but in principle no law can detract from the Court's stated inherent power to issue such orders. It is, however, unnecessary to decide whether the order made here is adjectival.

As to the criminal law, it is considered of the essence of the legislative function of Parliament in a democracy to provide both for the type of behaviour which is to be subject to criminal sanction, and the punishment which conviction is to attract. It is of the essence of judicial power, as regards the criminal law, to decide whether an accused has contravened the law; and, if so, to assess the proper disposition *within* whatever range and type of disposition Parliament permits. The *Criminal Code Act* 1974 is an adopted Act of the Parliament, under the Constitution, Sch. 2.6. It provides exhaustively for the punishment of Code offences; see s.2 of the Act, and ss.18,19 and many provisions of the Code ....

In this case the trial judge has effected a disposition of the case in a way not permitted by the law. I consider that he has, with respect, strayed beyond the field of judicial competence into a field reserved to the Parliament. The principle of separation of powers permeates the Constitution .... the Constitution, s.155(1) must be read in the light of the separation of powers; and cannot authorize the making of an order other than one within the judicial power. I respectfully agree with Greville Smith J. that 'justice' means 'justice according to law'.

I have considerable sympathy with the difficulty in which the trial judge found himself. He thought it surprising that the accused had been charged. I was similarly surprised in *The State v Meli Heti* [1977] PNGLR 173, but I think that the most that can be done, in the absence of some provision such as the Queensland Criminal Code s.657A, is to apply the Criminal Code s.19(1)(f). Unfortunately, that leaves the accused with the stain of a conviction, for what was, on the facts, an offence of a trivial nature,

S.C.R. No 2 of 1981; Re s.19(1)(f) of the Criminal Code [1982] PNGLR 150 at pp.158,159; see also Kidu C.J. at pp.154,155, Greville Smith J. at pp.163-168, Kapi J. at pp.171-173, Pratt J. at pp.172-176.

Referred to

by Narakobi A.J. in *The State v Luku Wapulae and ors* (1980 Unreported) N233 at p.18 (as authority for making an order for compensation in a criminal matter. Note this decision was reversed in *Acting Public Solicitor [sic] v Uname Aumane* [1980] PNGLR 510 but without reference to s.155(4);

GENERALLY

Referred to

by Saldanha J. in *The State v The Independent Tribunal; Ex Parte Sasakila* [1976] PNGLR 591 at p.505;

by Prentice Dep.C.J. (dissenting) in *Paul Aika and ors v Caspar Uremany* [1976] PNGLR 46 at pp.53,54 (both the National Court and the Supreme Court have jurisdiction to hear bail applications at first instance and a person refused bail by the National Court may apply as of right to the Supreme Court);

by Pritchard J. in *Kuijk v Kuijk* [1977] PNGLR 253 at pp.255,256 (substantial compliance with prescribed forms is sufficient: omissions may be corrected by the Court acting pursuant to s.155(4));

per Curiam (Frost C.J., Prentice Dep.C.J., Williams, Kearney and Pritchard JJ.) in *Reference No 1 of 1977* [1977] PNGLR 362 at p.363;

by Pritchard J. in *Re Condon and National Airline Commission of Papua New Guinea* [1978] PNGLR 1 at p.14;

per Curiam (Andrew, Pratt, Miles JJ.) in *The State v Viula Onea* [1980] PNGLR 186 at p.187 (application for writ of habeus corpus is always treated as an urgent matter which takes precedence over all other matters. Section 155(4) considered as affecting procedural matters under Supreme Court Rules);

by Narakobi A.J. in *The State v Yaulipa Bulaim and ors* (1980 Unreported) N234 at p.6 (as authorizing the National Court to refuse to accept an accused's plea of guilty when in the Court's opinion it is not safe to accept that plea);

by Narakobi A.J. in *Enga Kilu v John Moroby* (1980 Unreported) N246 at p.6:

by Bredmeyer J. in *New Guinea Cocoa (Export) Co. P/L v Ba[illegible]is Vedbaek* [1981] PNGLR 205 at p.214 (as authorizing the making of an order for the arrest of a vessel);

by Narakobi A.J. in *State v Kaupa Ungi* [1980] PNGLR 199 at p.203 (see note of decision under s.155(3));

by Narakobi A.J. in *State v Yale Gesie and ors* (1980 Unreported) N254 at p.17;

by Narakobi A.J. in *Reva Mase v The Independent State of Papua New Guinea* (1980 Unreported) N260 at pp.6,7;

by Miles J. in *State v Police Appeal Tribunal; Ex parte Lawrence Allen Sausau* (1980 Unreported) N220 at p.1;

by Kapi Dep.C.J. in *Acting Public Solicitor [sic] v Uname Aumane and ors* [1980] PNGLR 510 at p.530;

by Kearney A.C.J. in *Saki v The State* [1980] PNGLR 33 at p.35 (see note of decision under s.155(2));

by Andrew J. in *Sudi Yaku v Commissioner of Police; Ex parte The State* [1980] PNGLR 27 at pp.28,29;

by Kearney Dep.C.J. in *The State v Giddings* [1981] PNGLR 423 at p.434 (District Land Court is subject of writ of certiorari);

by Quinlivan A.J. in *The State v Jacob Toroken, (Coroner);* (1981 Unreported) N281 at p.16 (as to grant of writ of prohibition);

per Curiam (Andrew, Miles, Bredmeyer JJ.) in *Port Moresby City Council v The Sheriff of Papua New Guinea* [1981] PNGLR 477 at pp.478,479 (as conferring jurisdiction to issue writ of mandamus and as to grounds therefor);

by Miles J. in *Vian Guatal v The Independent State of Papua New Guinea* [1981] PNGLR 230 at p.234 (pursuant to s.155(4) a court may refuse to be a party to what amounts to an abuse of process);

by Bredmeyer J. in *State v District Land Court* [1981] PNGLR 192 at pp.193,197 (see note of decision under s.155(3));

by Kapi Dep.C.J. in *Hetura Paz Development Co. Pty Ltd v Niugini Nius Pty Ltd and ors* [1982] PNGLR 250 at p.252 (as to jurisdiction to grant injunctive relief);

by Pratt J. in *Simon Karl v The Public Prosecutor* (1982 Unreported) N388(L) at p.2;

by Kapi Dep.C.J. in *Employers Federation of Papua New Guinea v Papua New Guinea Waterside Workers and Seamans Union and ors* (1982 Unreported) N393 at p.8 (as to jurisdiction to grant injunctive relief);

by Greville Smith J. in *Placer Holdings Pty Ltd v The Independent State of Papua New Guinea* [1982] PNGLR 16 at p.19 (matter remitted for trial judge to exercise his discretion according to law);

by Kidu C.J. and Andrew J. in *In the Matter of the Organic Law on National Elections; Jabara v Okuk* (1983 Unreported) SC246 at p.4; see also Kapi Dep.C.J. at pp.12,13.

(5) In a case referred to in Subsection (3)(e), the National Court has nevertheless an inherent power of review where, in its opinion, there are over-riding considerations of public policy in the special circumstances of a particular case.

ORIGIN OF SECTION 155(5): CANNOT BE EXCLUDED BY PRIVATIVE CLAUSE

per Narakobi A.J.

The Constitution s.155(3)(a) makes it clear that the National Court has an inherent power to review any exercise of judicial power or authority and such other jurisdiction and powers as are conferred on it by this Constitution or any law. That power may be removed or restricted by a Constitution Law or an Act of the Parliament (s.155(3)(e)).

It is argued that s.9 of the *National Land Registration Act* (sic) excluded the National Court's jurisdiction. That, in my view is not correct.

Subsection(5) of s.155 of the Constitution makes it abundantly clear that whatever the restrictions an Act of Parliament might seek to place on the jurisdiction of the National Court pursuant to s.155(3)(e), it the National Court nevertheless has an inherent power of review where, in its opinion, there are over-riding considerations of public policy in the special circumstances of a particular case. In other words, the Act simply cannot cut out the jurisdiction of the National Court to review any exercise of judicial authority.

It may be that this power is an unnecessary judicial surveillance of executive or even parliamentary activity. However, I think it is a vital, if not the most crucial safeguard in a Constitutional democracy. If by legislative enactments, interested and aggrieved persons could be excluded from ever approaching the courts for conflict resolution we would quickly reach a situation whereby the excluded aggrieved parties will resort to violence and severe political agitation to seek redress. Rule of Law would, by legislative action give way to rule of the mob.

I recall, in the making of the Constitution days those largely involved in government service, arguing strongly that Subsection(5) should not exist. It was my strong personal protest that led to the inclusion of Subsection(5). I foresaw then an over-anxious executive, having every command of the Legislature, enacting laws, taking away or restricting human liberties, under written law and leaving the aggrieved with no recourse to a court of law, and justice and conscience.

Our Constitution is a fragile and flexible document. Various sections can be changed with different degrees of parliamentary approval. All sections can be changed by the Parliament. The people have no direct say, except through the elected representatives in the change of any provisions of their Constitution. A strong Executive with popular Parliamentary support may easily change or even subvert the will and the judicial power of the people, expressed through the Constitution, to be vested in the National Judicial System (s.158).

It is all the more important that the courts be not excluded ultimately from providing a forum in which competing interests of parties, including the State may be contested under prior acknowledged rules, designed to extract truth and under disinterested referees.

The judicial authority of the people is rightly vested in the National Judicial System (s.158). Other law may confer judicial authority in other tribunals (s.159(1) of the Constitution) outside the National Judicial System. But that cannot take away the National Court's inherent power under s.155(4) to make whatever orders appropriate to do justice, and its inherent power of review under s.155(5) of the Constitution.

Furthermore s.166 of the Constitution makes it very clear that the National Court is a court of unlimited jurisdictiion. It is also a superior court of record (s.163(2)).

Reva Mase v The Independent State of Papua New Guinea (1980 Unreported) N260 at pp.3,4.

AS GIVING ACCESS TO THE COURT IN THE LAST RESORT IF PROCEDURES UNDER THE PROVINCIAL GOVERNMENTS (MEDIATION AND ARBITRATION PROCEDURES) ACT 1981 FAIL.

Held

The *Provincial Government (Mediation and Arbitration Procedures) Act* 1981 which provides for the compulsory non-judicial settlement of disputes between Provincial Governments and the National Government by means of conciliation and arbitration does not alter a government party's right to bring its complaint before an impartial body for settlement. And, if all such procedures should ultimately fail, then that party would have recourse to the National Court under s.155(5). The Act accordingly is not invalid.

Milne Bay Provincial Government v Roy Evara and anor [1981] PNGLR 63; see Andrew J. at p.66.

GENERALLY

Referred to

by Kearney J. in *Cory v Blyth (No 4)* [1976] PNGLR 525 at p.531;

by Prentice C.J. in *Premdas v The Independent State of Papua New Guinea* [1979] PNGLR 329 at p.337 (see note of judgment under s.155(3));

by Narakobi A.J. in *Koniare Wapele v Constable Sepa* (1981 Unreported) N292 at p.3;

by Kearney Dep.C.J. in *Avia Aihi v The State* [1981] PNGLR 81 at p.93 (ultimate power of court to control the dispensation of justice referred to).

(6) Subject to any right of appeal or power of review of a decision, it is the duty of all persons (including the Law Officers of Papua New Guinea and other public officers in their respective official capacities), and of all bodies and institutions, to comply with and, so far as is within their respective lawful powers, to put into effect all decisions of the National Judicial System.

156. — THE LAW OFFICERS.

(1) The Law Officers of Papua New Guinea are —
- (a) the principal legal adviser to the National Executive; and
- (b) the Public Prosecutor; and
- (c) the Public Solicitor.

C.P.C. Report .... See extracts under Section 177.

AS TO CONSTITUTIONAL STATUS OF THE PUBLIC SOLICITOR

Held

The Public Solicitor is neither part of the National Judicial System nor is he a 'State Service' whose conduct the Ombudsman Commission has jurisdiction to investigate pursuant to s.219(1)(a)(i) of the Constitution. Further, the Public Solicitor does not come within the description 'other Governmental body' whose conduct the Commission has jurisdiction to investigate under s.219(1)(a)(ii).

The Public Solicitor is intended to be independent in the exercise of his professional duties. He is a Law Officer of Papua New Guinea and a Constitutional Office Holder. He is, however, as a lawyer, subject to the inherent power of the National and Supreme Courts to supervise his professional conduct.
Constitutional Reference No 1 of 1978 (s.19) [1978] PNGLR 345; see Prentice C.J. at pp.348-351, Wilson J. at pp.359-365, Pritchard J. (dissenting) at pp.383-389.

GENERALLY

Referred to

by Pritchard J. in *Ex parte Smedley* [1978] PNGLR 156 at p.159 (court should respect the constitutional office of the Public Prosecutor to the extent that where criminal charges are pending against a non-citizen, and the Public Prosecutor objects to that person leaving Papua New Guinea, an application for permission to leave should be refused);

by Wilson in *Mathias Evertz v The State* [1979] PNGLR 174 at p.178.

(2) An Act of the Parliament shall make provision for and in respect of the office referred to in Subsection (1)(a).

(*See: Principal Legal Adviser Act* Ch.54.)

157. — INDEPENDENCE OF THE NATIONAL JUDICIAL SYSTEM.

Except to the extent that this Constitution specifically provides otherwise, neither the Minister responsible for the National Justice Administration nor any other person or authority (other than the Parliament through legislation) outside the National Judicial System has any power to give directions to any court, or to a member of any court, within that System in respect of the exercise of judicial powers or functions.

C.P.C Report Ch.8 p.1

2. The courts constitute the third pillar of the government of a country. They have a different function from those of the executive and the legislature, namely that of peacefully determining conflicts that arise between individuals; between different levels of government (in some countries); and between individuals and government; in accordance with law and justice. They may also have an important advisory function, through which they can assist in the avoidance of potential disputes. In countries which have a written Constitution the highest courts often have the important task of deciding matters relating to the interpretation and enforcement of the Constitution. In this unique role courts should be key instruments through which peaceful development in a society can take place.

3. It is a fundamental principle of any free country that the men and women who sit to hear and determine disputes that come before them as members of the judiciary should not be improperly influenced to make decisions for or against any particular person or group. The Committee has made a number of recommendations in this Chapter, and elsewhere in this report, designed to ensure that people of Papua New Guinea are governed by law, not according to the whims of powerful individuals or groups. That aim, in fact, underlies the very idea of having a constitution at all.

4. We believe that the cardinal principle that the courts should be independent of the legislature and the executive must be firmly established under our Constitution. Those who legislate and those who exercise executive power should not also be responsible for dispensing justice in our new nation. The people who have that responsibility, namely judges and magistrates, should be sufficiently secure in their positions so that they are able to make their decisions without fear of personal repercussions.

5. The courts do not, however, exist in a vacuum. Like other institutions of the government of a country they are caught up in political realities, and often their decisions have important political consequences.

6. In carrying out their judicial role, judges and magistrates must take full account of the goals of the society in which they live; they must be attuned to the wishes of that society and to that extent must be politically conscious (although not party politically conscious). In Chapter 2, 'National Goals and Directive Principles', we have spelt out what we believe to be the goals of Papua New Guinea and we have recommended that our judges uphold the Constitution and interpret the laws made under it in the spirit of those goals and principles.

7. At the same time, the judiciary has a duty to protect the rights of the individual and minority groups: its job is not simply to reflect the will of the Government of the day. The judges will be particularly concerned with this role in deciding cases which arise under the proposed provisions concerning human rights in Chapter 5.

8. These two principles may well be contradictory in a given situation and the courts are therefore faced with the need to make a satisfactory compromise between them.

9. Let us take the example of a situation in which the existing law is either not clear, or alternatively, there appears to be no law which covers the case. In these circumstances, we believe the judge or magistrate who is hearing the case should use judicial ingenuity to do justice as between the parties, taking full account of the national goals and principles of policy as well as the rights of the individual.

10. We do not underestimate the difficulties with which judges and magistrates are faced. They must on the one hand avoid appearing to encroach upon the role of the legislature or to act as a brake on the executive government's legitimate efforts in trying to promote development; yet on the other hand they must endeavour to ensure that an injustice is not done in a particular case, and that the rights of individuals or minority groups are not unreasonably overridden. [p.2]

11. These problems are in the nature of the judicial role, but they are particularly acute in an emerging state such as Papua New Guinea. We believe that our recommendations on the judiciary will enhance the independent status which courts in Papua New Guinea now have, and that our judges and magistrates will be equal to the task which faces them. The method of appointment of judges and magistrates which we propose, is designed to promote the involvement of all three arms of government — the executive, legislature and judiciary — in this important process. We believe that this mechanism will encourage members of all three arms to feel part of the nation's overall system of government. We consider that there is good reason to believe, therefore, that Papua New Guinean men and women of integrity and ability will welcome appointment to judicial office, thereby assisting in safeguarding the rights, liberties and freedoms which belong to the people as we move ahead in all aspects of our development.

THE INDEPENDENCE OF THE JUDICIARY

per Wilson J.

The independence of the judiciary is guaranteed by the Constitution of the Independent State of Papua New Guinea itself. The Constitution provides the protective safeguards of judicial independence.

The independence of the judiciary is further recognised in the Criminal Code and, in particular, in those sections which make it an offence for any person to conspire to (s.131), or attempt to (s.139) obstruct, prevent, pervert or defeat the course of justice.

The independence of the judiciary is the key to freedom under the law. For evidence that this is so, one needs to look no further than the national goals and directive principles that are stated to underlie the Constitution and, in particular, the first aim, viz. integral human development. This part of the preamble to the Constitution provides:

> We declare our first goal to be for every person to be dynamically involved in the process of freeing himself or herself from every form of domination or oppression so that each man or woman will have the opportunity to develop as a whole person in relationship with others.

One of the basic rights guaranteed under the Constitution is the right to the full protection of the law which is ensured by a subsidiary right to have the existence or extent of a civil right or obligation determined, in a case going to court, 'by an independent and impartial court' (s.37(1)). In s.99(3) of the Constitution the notion of the separation of powers is recognised. Section 99(3) provides:

> (3) In principle, the respective powers and functions of the three arms (of government) shall be kept separate from each other.

Section 157 of the Constitution imposes a duty on the Minister for Justice as the Minister responsible for the national justice administration and on all other persons or authorities (other than the Parliament through legislation) not to give directions to any court, or to a member of any court, within the national judicial system in respect of the exercise of judicial powers or functions. The independence of the national judicial system, of which the judiciary forms a part, is further recognised in s.176(3)(a) and (5), s.183(4) and s.223. The Judicial Declaration that each member of the judiciary is required, by s.249 of the Constitution, to make before entering upon the duties of, or exercising any of the powers of, his office is inconsistent with there being any erosion of the concept of the independence of the judiciary. The Judicial Declaration is in the following terms:

> JUDICIAL DECLARATION
>
> I, , do promise and declare that I will well and truly serve the Independent State of Papua New Guinea and its People in the office of that I will in all things uphold the Constitution and the laws of the Independent State of Papua New Guinea, and I will do right to all manner of people in accordance therewith, without fear or favour, affection or ill-will.

By virtue of the making of such a declaration independence becomes a vital part of a judge's judicial integrity.

Perhaps the most important aspect of judicial independence is independence from the interference, control and direction of the Executive, i.e. the Government. It is the Government that has the greatest de facto power in the State. Its ability to interfere is probably greater than that of any other individual or group.

Most crucial in a sovereign, independent and democratic nation is the watchful presence of independent and fearless judges able and willing to do justice between citizen and State according to the law and vigilant to ensure that the State and its officers do not exceed their legal powers.

In *Sirros v Moore* [1975] QB 118 at pp.146-147 the words of Fox J. in *Taaffe v Downes* (1813) 3 Moo. PC 36 at pp.51-52 were approved in the Court of Appeal in England:

> It is necessary to the free and impartial administration of justice, that the persons administering it should be uninfluenced by fear and unbiased by hope ... A judge must — a judge ought to be uninfluenced by any personal consideration whatsoever operating upon his mind, when he is hearing a discussion concerning the rights of contending parties; otherwise, instead of hearing them abstractedly, a considerable portion of his attention must be devoted to himself. There is something so monstrous in the contrary doctrine, that it would poison the very source of justice, and introduce a system of servility, utterly inconsistent with the constitutional independence of the judges ... and ... utterly inconsistent with the preservation of the rights and liberties of the subject.

The essence of independence is that the judge, in the discharge of his functions, reaches his decisions because of his analysis, legal knowledge and understanding, his training, his system of values as has been discovered by him in the jurisdiction where he is serving, and no-one else's, lead him to particular conclusions. That independence is demonstrated in the judge's refusal to submit to any external pressures to reach conclusions different from those which, in his evaluation of the law and interpretation of the material before him, appear to be the right ones. It is also demonstrated when in an appropriate case the protective sanctions are applied. It is not being suggested that the judge should insulate himself from his community. He must be sensitive to social trends, be prepared to listen to informed criticism of his decisions, particularly on the interpretation of the law, and above all to adopt a critical approach towards his own functions and responsibilities in times of social change.

Judicial independence at its heart derives from the judge's own determination to be free to make up his own mind in the end. The purpose of such independence in Papua New Guinea is to entrust to suitably equipped individuals in whom general confidence lies the resolution of conflicts according to standards embodied in the Constitution and the rules of law. Such confidence derives from the assurance that those individuals are not responsible to any of the parties interested in the outcome of the decision.

Re Rooney (No 2) [1979] PNGLR 448 at pp.492-494.

AS TO WHAT CONSTITUTES A 'DIRECTION'

Held

A letter (set out fully at p.453 of the judgment) written by the Honourable Mrs Nahau Rooney, Minister for Justice, to the Chief Justice containing material highly critical of an (interlocutory) decision of the National Court and criticizing the Court for jeopardizing its independence and neutrality by intervening in a matter 'which is obviously the sole prerogative of the Government' was not a 'direction' within the meaning of s.157 although it came very close to it. What can constitute such a direction considered.

Re Rooney (No 2) [1979] PNGLR 448; see Wilson J. at p.502.

GENERALLY

Referred to

by Pritchard J. in *Constitutional Reference No 1 of 1978 (s.19)* [1978] PNGLR 345 at p.382.

Subdivision B. — The Judicial Power.

158. — EXERCISE OF THE JUDICIAL POWER.

(1) Subject to this Constitution, the judicial authority of the People is vested in the National Judicial System.

AS TO CONSTITUTIONAL RELATIONSHIP BETWEEN THE JUDICIARY AND THE HEAD OF STATE

per Williams J.

Section 82(1) of the Constitution provides that the Queen shall be 'Head of State'. Section 86(1) provides that the privileges, powers, functions, duties and responsibilities of the Head of State are as prescribed by or under Constitutional Laws and Acts of Parliament. A number of sections in the Constitution confer certain special powers and functions upon the Head of State. There appears to be no specific provision touching the matter now in issue.

By s.158 of the Constitution the judicial authority of the people is vested in the National Judicial System which, under s.155, consists of the Supreme Court, the National Court and such other courts as are established under s.172. It is thus clear that the people have vested the administration of justice not in the Head of State but in the National Judicial System which consists of courts which the people themselves have created by the Constitution. This seems to me to be a clear and distinct departure from the English situation as explained by Blackstone where the people traditionally have entrusted the administration to the monarch and the courts created by him. It seems to me that a consideration of the provisions of the Constitution to which I have referred show that the position of the monarch in the system of justice in this country is completely different from the position in England and in other countries where the traditional concept is as expounded by Blackstone.

The power of judicature in this country lies in the people at large. This has been invested by the people in the courts established under the Constitution. I think it inappropriate that proceedings of a criminal nature should be brought in the name of the court, nor do I think that proceedings should be in the name of the Public Prosecutor, whose functions are defined in s.177 of the Constitution, which, in their terms, appear inapt to meet the present situation. In my view it is appropriate that proceedings be brought by the people in their collective corporate name 'The State' (s.1).
The State v Mogo Wonom [1975] PNGLR 311 at p.320; see also Frost C.J. at p.316 and Raine J. at pp.317,318.

AS TO THE ABSORPTION OF THE PREROGATIVE POWER OF 'PARENS PATRIAE' BY THE NATIONAL JUDICIAL SYSTEM

per Frost C.J.

Motion for approval of compromise of an action. The action is brought under the *Law Reform (Miscellaneous Provisions) Act* 1962, Pt. IV, for the benefit of the widow and three infant children of a deceased husband and father whose death it is claimed was caused by the negligence of the defendant.

When the motion first came before me I indicated that I was satisfied that the compromise was beneficial to the infants and should be approved. However, I adjourned the hearing to consider the basis of the Court's jurisdiction having regard to the provisions of the new Constitution.

In *Bradford v Bradford* [1975] PNGLR 305 which was also an application for approval of a compromise it was accepted that that part of the Royal Prerogative whereby the Queen is parens patriae, under which prior to Independence the judicial power to approve compromises was held to exist, continues in force. See also *Katundi and Katundi (Infants) v Hay* [1940] St RQJ 39. Judgment in the former case, however, was given upon the same day as in the case of *The State v John Mogo Wonom* [1975] PNGLR 311.

> In my opinion it follows from the judgments in *The State v John Mogo Wonom* that it is no longer the law that that part of the prerogative is delegated by Her Majesty to the Judges. It has been displaced by reason of the constitutional provision that, subject to the Constitution, the judicial power of the people is vested in the National Judicial System (Constitution s.158(1)). But there can be no doubt that the judicial power of the people is as plenary as the Royal Prerogative which attached to the Queen as the dispenser of justice or as parens patriae, and is amply sufficient to support the well-established rules for the protection of infants.
> *Monomb Yamba v Geru* [1975] PNGLR 322 at p.323.

Referred to

by Narakobi A.J. in *Re The Adoption of Children Act 1968* (1980 Unreported) N221 at p.3;

by Miles J. in *Acting Public Prosecutor v Clement Maki and anor* (1981 Unreported) SC205 at p.28.

AS TO SEPARATION OF POWERS

Held

A law requiring a court to convict an accused without even an (ex parte) hearing should he fail to appear in answer to a summons is an invasion by the legislature of the judicial power of the people vested, in respect of criminal offences, exclusively in the National Judicial System by s.159(3).
S.C.R. No 1A of 1981; Re Motor Traffic Act [1982] PNGLR 122, see Kidu C.J. at p.129, Kearney Dep.C.J. at pp.134-136 (see extracts of this judgment under s.99(3)), Andrew J. at p.138 and Kapi J. at p.138.

Referred to

by Greville Smith J. (dissenting) in *Avia Aihi v The State* [1981] PNGLR 81 at p.98 (Section 158(1) does not confer power on the judiciary to usurp the function of the legislature: see note of above decision under s.155(2)).

AS TO STANDING

per Kapi J.

> Furthermore, Mr Somare, as a citizen, has standing. A citizen has standing where a question of non-compliance with the Constitution by the Parliament is involved.
>
> This stems from the fact that the legislative power belongs to the people (citizens). This power is vested in the Parliament by the Constitution. The power given to the Parliament is to be exercised in accordance with the Constitution (s.100). If the Parliament has not complied with the Constitution and the members of the Parliament are not willing to bring the matter before the court then, in my view, a citizen can. A citizen, under our Constitution, has not only an interest for the due observance of the law but, more than this has the legislative power. I do not think that standing ought to be restricted to members of the Parliament or leaders of political parties in the Parliament. They are politicians and may have political reasons for not wanting to come to court. Our Constitution would be at stake if nobody had standing in those circumstances.
>
> It might be said that such a view might open the floodgates and the courts might be swamped with too many cases. I observe that in other countries this policy consideration often restricts the scope of locus standi. With respect, this is no question of policy. Under our Constitution the legislative power belongs to the people. The question is, would the ordinary citizens have any standing in court if the legislative power is not exercised in accordance with the Constitution? A citizen would have standing for the reasons I have already given. I do not think it is proper for this Court to deny a citizen right to locus standi by a policy consideration. After all, the judicial power belongs to the people (s.158 of the Constitution). It is the people's court and let them come by the hundreds if they have the right to come.

S.C.R. No 4 of 1980; Re petition of M.T. Somare [1981] PNGLR 265 at p.296; see also Kidu C.J. at p.273 but note the more limited view of Miles J. at p.312; Kearney Dep.C.J. (at pp.275,276) and Greville Smith J. (at pp.283,284) dissenting; for detailed analysis of this issue see under s.18(1).

GENERALLY

Referred to

by Narakobi A.J. in *Reva Mase v The Independent State of New Papua New Guinea* (1980 Unreported) N260 at p.4;

by Narakobi A.J. in *The State v Luku Wapulae and ors* (1980 Unreported) N233 at p.18.

(2) In interpreting the law the courts shall give paramount consideration to the dispensation of justice.

'LITERAL' RULES OF INTERPRETATION TO BE REJECTED

per Wilson J.

Before I complete my references to the provisions of the Constitution it is appropriate to mention s.158(2) which provides: 'In interpreting the law the courts shall give paramount consideration to the dispensation of justice.'

In expressing my opinion, which I now do, that the 'literal' rule of statutory interpretation is inappropriate to the circumstances of this country at this time, I have not overlooked the need for consistency or uniformity as between neighbouring jurisdictions (in this context I am referring to Papua New Guinea and Australia), and I am conscious of the special responsibility which is imposed on the Supreme Court 'to assist in the development of our indigenous jurisprudence adapted to the changing circumstances of Papua New Guinea'.

Why is the 'literal' rule of statutory interpretation inappropriate to the circumstances of this country at this time? In my judgment there is no place in a developing country where the courts, as well as the Law Reform Commission, are given special responsibilities in the process of development, for the narrow interpretation of statutes without adequate regard to the social purpose of particular legislation. Development is difficult to achieve if courts adopt too conservative an approach to the interpretation of statutes. There has been a tendency in our National Judicial System, less evident in some recent decisions of the courts but still perceptible, to over-emphasize the literal meaning of a provision at the expense of the meaning to be derived from other possible contexts; the latter including the application of the 'mischief' rule, the recognition of the general legislative purpose, as well as the obligations laid down under the Constitution such as, for example, the obligation upon the courts in interpreting the law to give 'paramount consideration to the dispensation of justice' (s.158(2) of the Constitution). The purpose of the law in the Criminal Code regarding provocation is to give to a person who has been provoked into assaulting another and thereby into committing a crime a defence in certain circumstances.

There is, therefore, no place for a literalist approach to statutory interpretation in the law of Papua New Guinea and in relation to the Criminal Code in particular; a fortiori, as here, where the application of the majority decision in *Kaporonovski v The Queen* (1973) 133 CLR 209 in this case would justifiably bring with it the charge of narrow literalism. The letter of the law should not be allowed to prevail over the spirit of the law in a case of statutory interpretation such as this, especially where, as I see it, injustice will result if our decision is otherwise.

P.L.A.R No 1 of 1980 [1980] PNGLR 326 at pp.335,336; see also Andrew J. at p.347 but see Greville Smith J. (dissenting) at pp.341,342.

Referred to

by Kearney J. in *The State v The Independent Tribunal; Ex Parte Sasakila* [1976] PNGLR 491 at pp.506,507;

by Kearney Dep.C.J. in *Placer Holdings Pty Ltd v The Independent State of Papua New Guinea* [1982] PNGLR 16 at p.17 (adopting the purposive approach to the interpretation of statutes and following Wilson J. in *P.L.A.R. No 1 of 1980* [1980] PNGLR 326).

AS A SOURCE OF JURISDICTION TO DISPENSE JUSTICE

Comment

Goldring in *The Constitution of Papua New Guinea* (1978) stated at p.124:

> The reference in the Constitution in the opening words of s.10 must, it is submitted, include a reference to s.158(2); thus what appears to be the establishment of a system of positive law incorporates also a direction to the judicial system to apply .... not only the rules of positive law but also the undefined indefinite and abstract concept of justice which is left to the courts to identify and apply.

The courts, however, have shown little inclination to trouble themselves with the philosophical difficulties suggested by Goldring (see pp.124-127). In *S.C.R. No 4 of 1980; Re petition of M.T. Somare* [1981] PNGLR 265 Miles J. (at p.297) noted that the Constitution recognised in s.158(2) that justice and law were not necessarily co-extensive and in *The State v Luku Wapulae and ors* (1980 Unreported) N233 Narakobi A.J. described the National Court as a 'court of justice, not of legality' (at p.18). And, without expressly stating reasons, the Courts have, on a number of occasions, referred to s.158(2) as a *source* of jurisdiction or judicial power.

For example, in *The State v Woila (No 2)* [1978] PNGLR 113, Kearney J. relied upon s.158(2) to support his conclusion that an accused could sit next to his counsel and need not remain in the dock (see at p.117) and in *The State v Yaulipa Bulaim and ors* (1980) Unreported) N234, Narakobi A.J. relied upon s.158(2) to support his conclusion (see at p.6) that the Court had an inherent power to refuse to accept a plea of guilty in appropriate circumstances. In *Mauga Logging Co Pty Ltd v Okura Trading Co Ltd* [1978] PNGLR 259 Kearney J. relied upon s.158(2) as conferring upon the Court an inherent power to stay an action brought in breach of an arbitration clause (at p.260). A further recent example is provided by *Busina Tabe v The State* (1983 Unreported) SC260 in which McDermott J. (Gajewicz J. concurring) held that when 'by no means senior' prosecution and defence counsel each omitted to place an important piece of potentially exculpatory evidence before the trial judge, the Supreme Court could exercise its power under s.158(2) to allow for the reception of 'fresh evidence', quash the conviction and order a new trial. (See at pp.10-13)

On yet other occasions s.158(2) has been relied upon as a reason for rejecting a rule of common law thought not to work justice in the context of Papua New Guinea. For example, in *S.C.R. No 4 of 1980; Re petition of M.T. Somare* [1981] PNGLR 265, Kapi J. relied upon, inter alia, s.158(2) as justifying rejecting the common law principles applying to the question of locus standi (at p.292) and, in *The State v Birch* [1978] PNGLR 79, Greville Smith J. held that s.158(2) was relevant to the determination of whether a principle of common law was appropriate to the circumstances of Papua New Guinea (at p.87).

These cases, however, must be contrasted with two lines of authority which restrict the application of s.158(2). In several cases the Courts have warned that 'justice' does not mean justice for a particular applicant but rather justice for all (see for example *State v Wemp Mapa* (1979 Unreported) SC151 per Andrew J. at p.3 and *James Neap v Independent State of Papua New Guinea* (1983 Unreported) SC228 per Pratt J. at p.3).

More significant is the line of authority holding that 'justice' means 'justice according to law'. Acceptance of this view necessarily implies that s.158(2) may neither be availed of as a source of judicial power nor as a justification for not applying the positive law. Early holdings to this effect can be found in *The Government of Papua New Guinea and Davies v Barker* [1977] PNGLR 386 (per Frost C.J. at p.392 and Prentice Dep.C.J. at p.398); *Smedley v The State [No 2]* [1980] PNGLR 379 (per Wilson J. at pp.388,389) and *Avia Aihi v The State* [1981] PNGLR 81 (per Greville Smith J. at p.97).

This restrictive view appears now to be established as the orthodox approach following the joint decision of the court in *S.C.R. No 4 of 1982; Re Delba Biri v Bill Ginbogl Ninkamal* [1982] PNGLR 342. In that case the Court (Kidu C.J., Kapi Dep.C.J. and Andrew J.) held at pp.348,349:

> It was submitted that failure to include an attesting witness's occupation [in an Electoral Petition] was a minor matter and that it would be unjust that a petition should fail for this reason and that accordingly there is or should be power to grant an amendment to cure the defect. But in our opinion the requirements of s.208 reflect the special nature of electoral petitions. These requirements are, as we have said, strict and mandatory and we think they serve, inter alia, or attempt to limit the frivolous petition and to ensure as far as is possible that the petition is genuine.

> It is also our view that s.158(2) of the Constitution must mean the dispensation of justice *according to law*. It cannot mean the dispensation of justice in accordance with some notion of what is thought to be fair and reasonable to the exclusion of the stated intention of Parliament. In our opinion, the section means justice according to law and the law here is that as set out in a Constitutional Law.

This case appears to have settled the law and overruled the reasoning of the cases which have referred to s.158(2) as a source of jurisdiction, but the decisions of McDermott and Gajewicz JJ. in *Busina Tabe* (see above) may keep the debate open.

GENERALLY

Referred to

by Kapi J. in *Acting Public Solicitor [sic] v Uname Aumane and ors* [1980] PNGLR 510 at p.535 (relevant to interpreting Rule 33 of the *Supreme Court Rules* 1977);

by Kearney Dep.C.J. in *S.C.R. No 1A of 1981; Re the Motor Traffic Act* [1982] PNGLR 122 at p.136; note s.158(2) is incorrectly referred to as s.158(a) in the Report.

159. — TRIBUNALS, ETC., OUTSIDE THE NATIONAL JUDICIAL SYSTEM.

(1) Subject to Subsection (3), nothing in this Constitution prevents an Organic Law or a statute from conferring judicial authority on a person or body outside the National Judicial System, or the establishment by or in accordance with law, or by consent of the parties, of arbitral or conciliatory tribunals, whether ad hoc or other, outside the National Judicial System.

(2) Nothing in, or done in accordance with, Subsection (1) affects the operation of Section 155(4) or (5) (*the National Judicial System*).

(3) No person or body outside the National Judicial System has, or may be given, power to impose a sentence of death or imprisonment, or to impose any other penalty as for a criminal offence, but nothing in this subsection prevents —

(a) the imposition, in accordance with law, of disciplinary detention or any other disciplinary punishment (other than death) by a disciplinary authority of a disciplined force on persons subject to the disciplinary law of the force; or

(b) the imposition, in accordance with law, of disciplinary punishments (other than death or detention) on members of other State or provincial services; or

(c) the imposition of reasonable penalties (other than death or detention) bý an association on its members for breaches of its rules.

VESTS JURISDICTION TO TRY CRIMINAL OFFENCES EXCLUSIVELY IN THE NATIONAL JUDICIARY SYSTEM

per Kearney Dep.C.J.

> ... But more fundamentally, I think, [the impugned statutory provisions] are unconstitutional because they amount to an exercise by the legislature of the judicial authority of

the people in respect of criminal offences, which by the Constitution s.158(1) is vested exclusively in the National Judicial System. It is of course true that judicial authority may be conferred on other tribunals under the Constitution s.159, but that is irrelevant for present purposes, since s.159(3) prevents any any such tribunal from imposing any penalty for a criminal offence.
S.C.R. No 1A of 1981; Re Motor Traffic Act [1982] PNGLR 122 at p.134; see also Kidu C.J. at p.129.

AS TO WHAT CONSTITUTES IMPRISONMENT

per Curiam (Kapi Dep.C.J., Kaputin and McDermott JJ.)

... Section 159 (3) of the Constitution deals with imposition of imprisonment or other penalties. It does not deal with other forms of deprivation of liberty as are enumerated in s.42 of the Constition. We find that detention for the purposes of deportation under s.14 of the *Migration Act* is not an imposition of penalty or imprisonment and is specifically provided for by s.42(1)(g) of the Constitution. We therefore find that s.159 of the Constitution has no application to the present case.
Perryman v The Minister for Foreign Affairs and Trade [1982] PNGLR 339 at p.340.

Referred to

per Curiam (Prentice C.J., Saldanha and Andrew JJ.) in *Constitutional Reference No 2 of 1978; Re Corrective Institutions Act 1957* [1978] PNGLR 404 at pp.405,409 (quaere whether corrective institution offences are to be included in the phrase 'criminal offences').

CREATES AN EXPRESS EXCEPTION FOR DISCIPLINARY PROCEEDINGS

per Bredmeyer J.

Section 159(3) says that the only courts that can punish for a criminal offence are the offical Courts of the National Judicial System — but excluding certain disciplinary punishment which can be imposed under certain laws ... I do not consider that the disciplinary offences of the *Public Service Act* are criminal offences but, even if they are, they are expressly saved by s.159(3) of the Constitution.
Public Employees Association of Papua New Guinea v Public Service Commission (1983 Unreported) SC253 at p.12.

GENERALLY

Referred to

by Narakobi A.J. in *Reva Mase v The Independent State of Papua New Guinea* (1980 Unreported) N260 at p.4;

by Bredmeyer J. in *Amaiu v Commissioner of Corrective Institutions and The State* (1983 Unreported) N417 at p.50 (suggesting that in order to allow Corrective Institutions staff the power to punish detainees for corrective institutions offences an amendment would be needed to s.159).

(4) In Subsection 3(a), "disciplined force" has the same meaning as in Section 207 (*definition of "disciplined force"*).

Subdivision C. — The Supreme Court of Justice.

160. — ESTABLISHMENT OF THE SUPREME COURT.

(1) A Supreme Court of Justice is hereby established.

(2) The Supreme Court is a superior court of record and accordingly, subject to any Act of the Parliament, has the power to punish the offence against itself commonly known as contempt of court.

C.P.C. Report Ch.8 p.19

Powers of the Supreme Court and the National Court

8. The Supreme Court and the National Court shall be superior courts of record and, except as otherwise provided by the Constitution or by law, shall have all the powers of such a court.

AS TO CONTEMPT BY MEMBER OF NATIONAL EXECUTIVE COUNCIL

per Wilson J.

I am clearly satisfied that the power to punish for contempt of court is expressly reserved to the Supreme Court by s.160(2) which provides:

> The Supreme Court is a superior court of record and accordingly, subject to any Act of the Parliament, has the power to punish the offence against itself commonly known as contempt of court.

(See also s.37(2) of the Constitution.) Not only does s.23 [of the Constitution] not amount to a code covering the field and excluding the application of the law of contempt but also it expressly reserves other sanctions contained in 'a Constitutional Law or any Act of the Parliament' including the sanctions under the Leadership Code. As the Constitution itself is a constitutional law (see Sch.1.2 to the Constitution) and as s.160(2) appears in the Constitution, it is clear that it was the intention of the framers of the Constitution that contempt of the Supreme Court would be separately punishable by the Supreme Court.

All persons guilty of contempt of the Supreme Court are liable to be punished for that offence against the court. Members of the National Executive Council and acting in their capacities as such are not immune. If such an important immunity was to be given, one would have expected to see an express provision to that effect in the Constitution itself. The Minister for Justice is not immune from prosecution for contempt of court, in the same way as the Minister does not have immunities that are conferred upon the Crown by the adopted common law. The Minister is not answerable only to the people through the Parliament.

Re Rooney (No 2) [1979] PNGLR 448 at pp.502,503.

161. — COMPOSITION OF THE SUPREME COURT.

(1) The Supreme Court shall consist of the Chief Justice, the Deputy Chief Justice and the other Judges of the National Court (excluding the acting Judges).

(2) Subject to Section 162(2) (*jurisdiction of the Supreme Court*) and for the purposes of any hearing, the Supreme Court shall consist of at least three Judges.

(3) In a hearing that consists of at least three Judges, the Chief Justice, the Deputy Chief Justice or the most senior Judge available shall preside over the court.

C.P.C. Report Ch.8 p.3

27. The Supreme Court should consist of three judges of the National Court, presided over by the Chief Justice or his Deputy or the most senior judge sitting as a member of the Court for a particular case. Clearly, any judge who has heard a case in the in the National Court should not be eligible to sit on the Supreme Court to hear an appeal against an earlier verdict of his own.

28. Taking account of the likelihood that in the long term, when there is much appellate work to be done by the Supreme Court, Parliament may properly wish to appoint some of our most able National Court judges as full-time Supreme Court Judges, we have made an appropriate recommendation to allow for this situation.

RECOMMENDATIONS [p.18]

The Supreme Court

4. (1) There shall be a Supreme Court which shall be the final court of appeal for Papua New Guinea constituted, subject to the Constitution, in accordance with law.
(2) When the Supreme Court is determining any matter other than a pre-trial matter it shall comprise not fewer than three judges sitting together, presided over by the Chief Justice, or if he is not a member of that Supreme Court, the Deputy Chief Justice, or if neither the Chief Justice nor the Deputy Chief Justice is a member of that court, the most senior of the judges of that Supreme Court.
(3) Subject to clause (4) below, the Supreme Court shall be constituted by judges of the National Court.
(4) Parliament may by law provide for the appointment by the Judicial and Legal Service Commission of National Court Judges as full-time judges of the Supreme Court.
(5) A judge who hears a case in the National Court shall not be eligible to be a member of the Supreme Court which hears and determines an appeal from any decision in that case.

162. — JURISDICTION OF THE SUPREME COURT.

(1) The jurisdiction of the Supreme Court is as set out in —
(a) Subdivision II.2.C (*constitutional interpretation*); and
(b) Subdivision III.3.D (*enforcement*); and
(c) Section 155 (*the National Judicial System*),
and otherwise as provided by this Constitution or any other law.

C.P.C. Report Ch.8 p.3

The Supreme Court

24. The highest court in the country should be the Supreme Court, which should be the final appeal court for all cases heard under Papua New Guinean law. We believe that the provision of a right to appeal against judgements of our courts to foreign courts would undermine our sovereignty as a nation, and would perpetuate the incorporation in our legal system of values alien to our own. Submissions we have received have firmly opposed the continuance of appeals to a foreign court such as the High Court of Australia.

25. In its general jurisdiction the Supreme Court should hear cases that have been dealt with first in the National Court or a lower court other than a village court. In carrying out this function it would hear appeals against judgements given by these courts in both criminal and civil cases.

26. We propose also, that the Supreme Court should have a key role in resolving constitutional disputes, our recommendations in this regard being included in Part E of this Chapter — 'Resolution of Constitutional Questions'. [See under s.18].

GENERALLY

Referred to

by Saldanha J. in *Premdas v The Independent State of Papua New Guinea* [1979] PNGLR 329 at p.360; see also Andrew J. at p.400;

by Kidu C.J. in *Avia Aihi v The State* [1981] PNGLR 81 at pp.87, 88 (as showing that s.155(2)(b) of the Constitution confers a grant of power and jurisdiction on the Supreme Court);

see also Andrew J. at pp.99, 102.

by Kapi Dep.C.J. (dissenting) in *In the Matter of the Organic Law on National Elections; Malipu Balakau v Paul Torato and anor* (1983 Unreported) SC256 at p.21 (*Supreme Court Act* is intended to implement the jurisdiction of the Supreme Court).

(2) In such cases as are provided for by or under an Act of the Parliament or the Rules of Court of the Supreme Court, the jurisdiction of the Supreme Court may be exercised by a single Judge of that Court, or by a number of Judges sitting together.

(3) The jurisdiction of the Supreme Court may be exercised by a Judge or Judges of that Court notwithstanding that it is being exercised at the same time by another such Judge or Judges.

(4) The jurisdiction of the Supreme Court may be exercised either in court or in chambers, as provided by or under an Act of the Parliament or the Rules of Court of the Supreme Court.

Subdivision D. — The National Court of Justice.

163. — ESTABLISHMENT OF THE NATIONAL COURT.

(1) A National Court of Justice is hereby established.

(2) The National Court is a superior court of record and accordingly, subject to any Act of the Parliament, has the power to punish the offence against itself commonly known as contempt of court.

C.P.C. Report Ch.8 p.3

The National Court of Justice

29. There should be a National Court of Justice consisting of the Chief Justice, the Deputy Chief Justice and other judges, with broad power to dispense justice throughout the country, and also in cases which involve a law of this country but arise outside Papua New Guinea. We have provided for the National Court's jurisdiction to be altered by ordinary law (provided that law specifically refers to the jurisdiction of the court), as we believe it is important not to unduly limit the power of Parliament to make changes in the jurisdiction of the highest courts, as well as of subordinate courts. We also wish to maximise the scope for a Law Reform Commission to recommend significant changes in the present judicial system if it thinks they are necessary.

GENERALLY

Referred to

by Prentice Dep.C.J. in *In re Moresby North East Election Petition* [1977] PNGLR 429 at p.431 (discussed, without deciding, whether a prerogative writ should issue from the Supreme Court to the National Court, itself a superior court of record);

by Narakobi A.J. in *The State v Luku Wapulae and ors* (1980 Unreported) N233 at p.18 (note reversed in *Acting Public Solicitor [sic] v Uname Aumane* [1980] PNGLR 510;

by Narakobi A.J. in *The State v Kaupa Ungi* [1980] PNGLR 199 at p.203;

by Narakobi A.J. In *Reva Mase v The Independent State of Papua New Guinea* (1980 Unreported) N260 at p.4.

164. — COMPOSITION OF THE NATIONAL COURT.

The National Court shall consist of —

(a) the Chief Justice, and
(b) the Deputy Chief Justice; and
(c) subject to Section 165(2) (*Acting Judges*) not less than four or more than six other Judges, or such greater number as is determined by or under an Act of the Parliament.

C.P.C. Report Ch.8 p.18

RECOMMENDATIONS

National Court of Justice

6. There shall be a National Court of Justice (referred to below as 'the National Court'). The Judges of the National Court shall be —
   (a) the Chief Justice;
   (b) the Deputy Chief Justice; and
   (c) not fewer than three other judges of the National Court, whose number, subject to the Constitution, may be determined by law.

165. — ACTING JUDGES.

(1) A person who is qualified under Section 168 (*qualifications*) for appointment may be appointed to be an acting Judge of the National Court —
   (a) to fill temporarily a vacancy; or
   (b) in the case of the absence from duty for any reason of a Judge of that Court; or
   (c) to meet a temporary unexpected workload or other exigency of the business of the Court.

(2) An appointment under Subsection (1)(c) may be made without reference to the numerical limit imposed by Section 164 (*composition of the National Court*).

C.P.C. Report Ch.8 p.23

33. If the office of any judge is vacant, or if any judge is for any reason unable to perform the functions of his office, or if the state of business in the National Court or the Supreme Court makes it necessary, the Judicial and Legal Service Commission may appoint a person qualified for appointment as a judge to be temporarily a judge of the National Court and of the Supreme Court, *provided that* an appointment under this provision may not continue for a period exceeding twelve months.

34. A person who is over the retiring age for judges may nevertheless be appointed an acting judge, unless he is over the age of sixty-five years.

35. Subject to the proviso to Recommendation 33 above, any person appointed under this provision to be temporarily a judge shall hold office for the period of his appointment, or if no such period is specified, until his appointment is revoked by the Judicial and Legal Service Commission, *provided that* the Judicial and Legal Service Commission may permit a person whose appointment to act as a judge has expired, or been revoked, to continue to act as a judge for such period as may be necessary to enable him to deliver judgement or to do any other thing in relation to proceedings that were commenced before him prior to the expiry or revocation of his appointment.

166. — JURISDICTION OF THE NATIONAL COURT.

(1) Subject to this Constitution, the National Court is a court of unlimited jurisdiction.

(2) In particular, the National Court has the jurisdication set out in —
(a) Section 22 (*enforcement of the Constitution*); and
(b) Subdivision III.3.D (*enforcement*); and
(c) Section 155 (*the National Judicial System*),
and otherwise as provided by this Constitution or any other law.

(3) Subject to any Act of the Parliament and to the Rules of Court of the National Court, the jurisdiction of the National Court may be exercised by a single Judge of that Court, or by a number of Judges sitting together.

(4) The jurisdiction of the National Court may be exercised by a Judge or Judges of that Court notwithstanding that it is being exercised at the same time by another Judge or other Judges.

(5) The jurisdiction of the National Court may be exercised either in court or in chambers, as provided by or under an Act of the Parliament or the Rules of Court of the National Court.

C.P.C. Report Ch.8 p.18

RECOMMENDATIONS

Jurisdiction of the National Court

7. Subject to the Constitution, and to any law which specifically refers to its jurisdiction the National Court shall have all the jurisdiction which may be necessary for the [p.19] administration of justice, and may exercise such further powers and determine such other matters as may be provided for by law.
Note: It is intended that this jurisdiction will include extraterritorial jurisdiction.

AS TO JURISDICTION CONFERRED

per Miles J.

Having regard to the unlimited jurisdiction of the National Court (Constitution, s.166) this Court has jurisdiction to determine the current disputes between the parties. The claim for necessaries is a claim in contract or possibly quasi-contract. The counterclaim is for wrongful arrest or detention of property, trespass to a vessel and trespass to chattels. All these causes of action are justiciable at common law and therefore in the National Court, regardless of whether the jurisdiction of the court includes the jurisdiction, practices and procedures of admiralty courts as they exist or existed in other countries....

There must however be some limit to the jurisdiction of this Court. Section 166 itself provides that it is subject to the Constitution. Without wishing to lay down a definitive interpretation of s.166, I think s.166 has to be read subject to Sch. 2.6 of the Constitution, in othe r words, within the laws applicable to Papua New Guinea by virtue of the Constitution itself. The Court's jurisdiction is not restricted as to subject matter or as to remedy. *Milan Capek v The Yacht 'Freja' (No 2)* [1980] PNGLR 161 at pp.164, 168, 169.

Held

It follows from the fact that the National Court is a court of unlimited jurisdiction that the Court may exercise the power of parens patriae directly; it is no longer the law that that power is part of the prerogative delegated by Her Majesty to the Judges.
Monomb Yamba v Geru [1975] PNGLR 322; per Frost C.J. at p.324.

Referred to

by Prentice C.J. in *Premdas v The Independent State of Papua New Guinea* [1979] PNGLR 329 at pp.336, 337 (as specifically vesting in the National Court power to enforce the Constitution); see also Saldanha J. at pp.359, 360 and Andrew J. at p.400;

by Kapi J. in *Milan Capek v The Yacht 'Freja'* [1980] PNGLR 57 at p.61 (Section 166(1) may be construed as conferring Admiralty jurisdiction on the National Court);

by Bredmeyer J. in *New Guinea Cocoa (Export) Co Pty Ltd v Basis Vedbaek* [1980] PNGLR 205 at p.214 (Section 166 as, inter-alia, conferring power on the National Court to order the arrest of a ship).

GENERALLY

Referred to

by Prentice Dep. C.J. in *Paul Aika and ors v Caspar Uremany* [1976] PNGLR 46 at p.53 (National Court may sit comprised of more than one judge);

by Narakobi A.J. in *Reva Mase v The State* (1980 Unreported) N260 at p.4.

167. — ASSISTANT JUDGES.

Subject to this Section, an Act of the Parliament may make provision for and in respect of the appointment of Assistant Judges of the National Court, and for and in respect of their qualifications, privileges, powers, functions, duties and responsibilities, and of their terms and conditions of employment.

C.P.C. Report Ch.8 p.4

Assistant Judges

34. Because Papua New Guinean lawyers were not trained until very recently, we will continue to rely on foreign judges for some years to come. Whilst this situation might be acceptable in a pre-independence period, it will obviously not be consistent with the principle of our national sovereignty after Independence.

35. We already have a number of qualified Papua New Guinean lawyers with basic training in all the major branches of the law and who also possess a good sense of justice.

36. Some of these lawyers should, we believe, be appointed as assistant judges after three years of experience in the practice of the law. These appointees should be seen partly as trainee judges under their more experienced foreign brother judges, but more significantly, these appointments should represent a deliberate policy to have our own people control the courts of our country soon after Independence.

37. We recognize the value of long experience in the practice of law. At the same time we are very much aware that the majority of people who go before the courts are the indigenous people. It is only right that our own lawyers should begin to adjudicate among our people in the highest courts if the judicial process of settling disputes is to gain legitimacy.

38. Our own people would be the best judges where the cultures and customs of Papua New Guineans are concerned. Much of the present English common law has evolved over many centuries. Our common law must begin to evolve and our own judges are the best people to promote its development. These reasons have led us to recommend that the assistant judges play a more important role than might otherwise be the case. The assistant judges should participate fully in the court process, subject of course to the overriding decision of the judge with whom the assistant judge is sitting in the event of a difference of opinion on a question of law. As to questions of fact, we believe careful consideration should be given by the legislature to maximizing the effectiveness of assistant judges' participation, particularly in criminal cases. The assistant judges should sit with different judges in different court cases to gain wide experience and to benefit from the experience of all the judges. The assistant judges should be eligible for full appointments on proven ability.

GENERALLY

Comment

Section 167 has not been availed of since Independence.

Subdivision E. — Apppointment, etc., of Judges.

168. — QUALIFICATIONS.

The qualifications for appointment as a Judge are as determined by or under an Act of the Parliament.

(*See: National Court Act* Ch.38.)

C.P.C. Report Ch.8 p.3

Qualifications of Judges

31. As we said earlier Judges should, we believe, be persons of integrity who are professionally qualified as lawyers, and have adequate legal experience. We consider that the qualifications of judges should be set by law rather than in the Constitution itself, so that they can be changed by parliament as circumstances alter. For example, when more of our own people have had a number of years experience as lawyers, the requirements concerning legal experience might be made more rigorous. [p.4]

32. We recommend that non-citizen judges should be lawyers who have had at least five years experience in the practice of law either in Papua New Guinea or in another country with a similar legal system. Judges from countries with legal systems similar to that in Papua New Guinea should also be eligible for recruitment as judges, as should citizens who hold a law degree and have had at least five years experience as a Resident Magistrate.

33. Some citizens may graduate from one of our country's universities, but not practise law initially. They, too, should be eligible to become judges — six years after graduating, provided that they have been practising law for at least three years after they have obtained full admission to practise as lawyers. These proposed qualifications for judges give greater scope for appointing Papua New Guineans to the bench of the Supreme Court and the National Court than do the present provisions of the *Papua New Guinea Act*. Non-citizens would be eligible for appointment as judges on the same basis as at present.

169. — APPOINTMENT, ETC., OF THE CHIEF JUSTICE.

(1) An office of Chief Justice of Papua New Guinea is hereby established.

(2) The Chief Justice shall be appointed by the Head of State, acting with, and in accordance with, the advice of the National Executive Council given after consultation with the Minister responsible for the National Justice Administration.

(3) In addition to his other powers, functions, duties and responsibilities, the Chief Justice, after consultation with the other Judges, is responsible for the organization of the affairs and the administration of the business of the Supreme Court and the National Court (other than, except to the extent allowed by or under an Act of the Parliament, matters relating to the National Public Service).

(4) Where —
(a) there is a vacancy in the office of Chief Justice; or
(b) the Chief Justice is absent from the country or is absent from duty; or
(c) the Chief Justice is unable or unavailable to act; or
(d) the Chief Justice so directs,
the powers, functions, duties and responsibilities (other than as acting Governor-General) of the Chief Justice may be exercised and performed by the next most senior Judge who is available.

(5) The question, whether the occasion for the exercise or performance of the powers, functions, duties and responsibilities of the Chief Justice by another Judge under this section has arisen or has ceased, is non-justiciable.

C.P.C. Report Ch.8 p.4

Chief Justice

39. The Chief Justice will be the head of the judiciary. On certain important occasions, such as the calling together of a new National Parliament and the swearing-in of the Speaker, the Chief Justice will play a significant ceremonial role under our recommendations in Chapter 6, 'The Legislature'. He should also be responsible, in consultation with the other judges, for the day-to-day administration of the business of the Supreme Court and of the National Court.

40. The Chief Justice should be a man of undoubted integrity and professional standing. Because his decisions and actions are likely to have such a great influence upon public attitudes towards the legal system and the judiciary, and upon the way in which laws are applied, it is of great importance that he be accepted by all major political groups as being clearly impartial. He should nevertheless, be responsive to the circumstances of Papua New Guinean society.

41. We recommend that the Prime Minister should initially consult the Minister responsible for justice on a proposed appointment of a Chief Justice. The Prime Minister should then consult the National Executive Council and the Permanent Parliamentary Committee responsible for justice, jointly, before making the appointment. Under this procedure the opportunity is given initially to the Minister responsible for justice, and later to the Permanent Parliamentary Committee jointly with members of the National Executive Council, to express [p.5] views as to the merits of proposed (or possible) appointees. This procedure should, we believe, ensure that the appointment of a person as Chief Justice will have broad political support.

170. — APPOINTMENT OF OTHER JUDGES.

(1) An office of Deputy Chief Justice of Papua New Guinea is hereby established.

(2) The Deputy Chief Justice and the other Judges of the National Court (other than the Chief Justice) and acting Judges shall be appointed by the Judicial and Legal Services Commission.

(*See:* Section 183 Constitution)

(3) No appointment of an acting Judge shall continue for a period of more than 12 months, but one extension for a period of not more than 12 months may be granted by the Judicial and Legal Services Commission.

(4) The question, whether the occasion for the appointment of an acting Judge has arisen or has ceased, is non-justiciable.

C.P.C. Report Ch.8 p.5

42. The selection of the Deputy Chief Justice, other judges and magistrates also requires a careful assessment of the professional ability and individual character of potential appointees. Particularly in a developing country such as Papua New Guinea, judges should normally be not unsympathetic to the executive and legislative branches of government, and as we have indicated above, always have a real appreciation of the circumstances of the country in which they work, if their judgements are to be just.

43. We have therefore recommended that judges (including the Deputy Chief Justice) should be selected by a body composed of people who are likely to take into account all of these factors. We do not believe that judges should be chosen simply by the Government of the day in consultation with the judiciary though of course the act of appointing a judge is, in fact, an executive one, and in most countries, including Australia and Britain, the appointment of judges of the higher courts is made by the executive alone. As well as the views of the executive and the judiciary, opinions expressed from the standpoint of people with a variety of backgrounds, experience and values should, we believe, be brought to bear on the choice of those who are to become judges.

171. — SENIORITY OF JUDGES.

(1) Subject to Subsection (2), the Chief Justice is the most senior Judge, the Deputy Chief Justice is the second senior Judge and the other Judges (other than acting Judges) have seniority according to the dates of their respective appointments, unless otherwise stated in an instrument of appointment.

(2) Unless otherwise stated in an instrument of appointment, acting Judges —
  (a) rank in seniority after the other Judges; and
  (b) have seniority as between themselves according to the dates of their respective appointments or last appointments, as the case requires.

Subdivision F. — Inferior Courts, the Magisterial Service, etc.

172. — ESTABLISHMENT OF OTHER COURTS.

(1) Subject to this Constitution, Acts of the Parliament may establish, or provide for the establishment of, courts within the National Judicial System in addition to the Supreme Court and the National Court, and may define, or provide for the definition of, their respective powers, functions and jurisdictions and their relationship with other components of the National Judicial System.

(*See: District Courts Act* 1963; Reserved Ch.40, *Local Courts Act* 1963; Reserved Ch.41)

(2) Courts established under Subsection (1) may include courts intended to deal with matters primarily by reference to custom or in accordance with customary procedures, or both.

(*See: Village Courts Act* Ch.44, *Organic Law on Provincial Government* Ch.1).

AS TO WHAT CONSTITUTES A COURT

Held

Visiting justices hearing charges arising out of corrective institution offences under the *Corrective Institutions Act* constitute a court within the meaning of s.172.
Constitutional Reference No 2 of 1978; Re Corrective Institutions Act 1957 [1978] PNGLR 404.

Referred to

by Pratt J. in *S.C.R. No 1 of 1981; Re Intergroup Fighting Act 1977* [1981] PNGLR 151 at p.168.

GENERALLY

Referred to

by Williams J. in *The State v Mogo Wonom* [1975] PNGLR 311 at p.320;

by Prentice C.J. in *Constitutional Reference No 1 of 1978 (s.19)* [1975] PNGLR 345 at p.345; see also Pritchard J. at p.382.

(3) Full-time members of courts established under Subsection (1) (other than courts referred to in Subsection (2)) shall be appointed by the Judicial and Legal Services Commission, and may be removed from office in accordance with an Act of the Parliament, but only for incapacity or misbehaviour, (including, if applicable, misconduct in office).

(4) Acts of the Parliament may make provision for or in respect of the appointment and removal from office of members of courts referred to in Subsection (2).

173. — ESTABLISHMENT OF THE MAGISTERIAL SERVICE.

(1) A service to be known as the Magisterial Service is hereby established.

(2) The Magisterial Service consists of —
  (a) the Chief Magistrate; and
  (b) subject to Section 174 (*magistrates, etc., outside the Magisterial Service*), all other members of courts established under Section 172 (*establishment of other courts*); and

(c) such other persons employed in connexion with the National Judicial System as are prescribed by or under Acts of the Parliament.

(3) The Chief Magistrate is responsible to the Judicial and Legal Services Commission for the efficient functioning and operation of the Magisterial Service.

(4) Subject to the Constitutional Laws, an Act of the Parliament shall make provision for and in respect of the Magisterial Service.

(*See: Magisterial Service Act* Ch.43.)

C.P.C. Report Ch.8 p.6

The Magisterial Service

57. We have recommended that a Magisterial Service consisting of the Chief Magistrate and other full-time magistrates be established, and that responsibility for ensuring the independence and effective functioning of the Service be vested in the Judicial and Legal Service Commission. This should ensure that full-time magistrates, (who now carry out a substantial proportion of the judicial work in Papua New Guinea), have their independence safeguarded and also are given adequate opportunities for promotion within a career service.

GENERALLY

Referred to

by Pritchard J. in *Constitutional Reference No 1 of 1978 (s.19)* [1978] PNGLR 345 at p.382 (the considerable administrative responsibility of the Chief Magistrate discussed).

174. — MAGISTRATES, ETC., OUTSIDE THE MAGISTERIAL SERVICE.

(1) Unless and except to the extent that an Act of the Parliament makes provision to the contrary, members of village courts are not, as such, members of the magisterial Service.

(2) An Act of the Parliament may provide for part-time members of courts established under Section 172 (*establishment of other courts*), who need not be members of the Magisterial Service.

175. — THE CHIEF MAGISTRATE.

(1) An office of Chief Magistrate is hereby established.

(2) The Chief Magistrate shall be appointed by the Judicial and Legal Services Commission.

(3) Unless and except to the extent that an Act of the Parliament makes provision to the contrary, the Chief Magistrate is *ex officio* a member of all courts (other than village courts) established under

Section 172 (*establishment of other courts*), and, if provision is made for grades of powers, functions or jurisdiction within any such courts, has all the powers, functions and jurisdiction of the highest grades.

(4) In the performance of his functions under Section 173(3) (*establishment of the Magisterial Service*), the Chief Magistrate shall carry out any directions or instructions of the Judicial and Legal Services Commission.

C.P.C. Report Ch.8 p.6

The Chief Magistrate

58. We recommend the establishment of the office of Chief Magistrate. To be qualified for [p.7] appointment to this office a person must have the same qualifications as those for a judge.

59. We propose that the Chief Magistrate be an additional member of the Judicial and Legal Service Commission for the purposes of appointing other full-time Magistrates and determining general policy directives in relation to the Magisterial Service.

60. The Chief Magistrate should also be the person who has day-to-day responsibility for the efficient functioning of the Magisterial Service, carrying out any direction by the Commission in relation to the Service.

61. His term of office and protection against arbitrary suspension or removal from office should be the same as for a judge.

GENERALLY

Referred to

by Pritchard J. in *Constitutional Reference No 1 of 1978 (s.19)* [1978] PNGLR 345 at p.382 (the judicial and administrative responsibilities of the Chief Magistrate discussed).

Subdivision G. — The Public Prosecutor and the Public Solicitor.

176. — ESTABLISHMENT OF OFFICES.

(1) Offices of Public Prosecutor and Public Solicitor are hereby established.

C.P.C. Report: See under s.177(1) and s.177(2)

AS TO THE NATURE OF THE OFFICE OF PUBLIC SOLICITOR

Held

The Public Solicitor is neither part of the National Judicial System nor is he one of the State Services whose conduct the Ombudsman has jurisdiction to investigate under s.219(1)(a)(i) of the Constitution. Further, the Public Solicitor does not come within the description 'other governmental body' for the purposes of s.218(1)(a)(iii). He is not an 'arm of the government'. Section 176(1) establishes that he is a creature of the people, not the Parliament (see at p.350). The Public Solicitor is intended to be independent in the exercise of his professional duties. He is, however,

subject to the inherent power of the National Court to supervise his professional conduct as a lawyer.
Constitutional Reference No 1 of 1978 (s.19) [1978] PNGLR 345; see Prentice C.J. at pp.350-354 and Wilson J. at pp.360-362; but see also Pritchard J. (dissenting) at pp.367-371 and 382-384.

AS TO THE NATURE OF THE OFFICE OF PUBLIC PROSECUTOR

per Pratt J.

> ... Section 176 of the Constitution, which sets up the office of Public Prosecutor and, inter alia, established that in the performance of his functions, he will not be subject to direction or control by any person or authority. There are very obvious reasons why this should be so. In their wisdom the framers of the Constitution considered it undesirable, at least at the present stage of development in Papua New Guinea, for the prosecuting authority to be subject to the various pressures which fall on the shoulders of an Attorney-General in other jurisdictions ..... It is clear that a tremendous reliance has been placed on the individual integrity and sense of fair play of the person occupying the office of Public Prosecutor. Because he is not subject however to the usual checks and balances which would normally apply to an Attorney-General under the common law .... one must look very closely at the legislation which governs the powers and responsibilities of the Public Prosecutor. Indeed, he has almost complete freedom from the normal restraints and checks which would apply to any Attorney-General in the performance of his high office.
> *Smedley v The State* [1980] PNGLR 379 at p.403.

GENERALLY

Referred to

by Kapi J. in *Acting Public Solicitor (sic) v Uname Aumane and ors* [1980] PNGLR 510 at p.531 (see note under s.177(2)).

(2) The Public Prosecutor and the Public Solicitor shall be appointed by the Judicial and Legal Services Commission.

GENERALLY

Referred to

by Prentice C.J. in *Constitutional Reference No 1 of 1978 (s.19)* [1978] PNGLR 345 at p.350; see also Pritchard J. at p.367.

(3) Subject to this Constitution —
- (a) in the performance of his functions under this Constitution the Public Prosecutor is not subject to direction or control by any person or authority; but
- (b) nothing in paragraph (a) prevents the Head of State, acting with, and in accordance with, the advice of the National Executive Council, giving a direction to the Public Prosecutor on any matter that might prejudice the security, defence or international relations of Papua New Guinea (including Papua New Guinea's relations with the Government of any other country or with any international organization).

GENERALLY

Referred to

by Frost C.J. in *The State v Mogo Wonom* [1975] PNGLR 311 at p.317 (Subsection 3 is not relevant to the 'ultimate authority' of the people to prosecute offences);

by Wilson J. in *Re Rooney (No 2)* [1979] PNGLR 448 at p.493 (referred to as part of the independence of the National Judicial System).

(4) The Prime Minister shall table in the National Parliament any direction to the Public Prosecutor at the next sitting of the Parliament after the direction is given unless, after consultation with the Leader of the Opposition, he considers that tabling of the direction is likely to prejudice the security, defence or international relations of Papua New Guinea.

(5) Subject to Section 177(2) (*functions of the Public Prosecutor and the Public Solicitor*), in the performance of his functions under this Constitution the Public Solicitor is not subject to direction or control by any person or authority.

GENERALLY

Referred to

by Prentice C.J. in *Constitutional Reference No 1 of 1978 (s.19)* [1978] PNGLR 345 at p.350; see also Wilson J. at p.357;

by Wilson J. in *Re Rooney (No 2)* [1979] PNGLR 448 at p.493 (referred to as part of the independence of the National Judicial System).

177. — FUNCTIONS OF THE PUBLIC PROSECUTOR AND THE PUBLIC SOLICITOR.

(1) The functions of the Public Prosecutor are —
- (a) in accordance with an Act of the Parliament and the Rules of Court of the Supreme Court and the National Court, to control the exercise and performance of the prosecution function (including appeals and the refusal to initiate and the discontinuance of prosecutions) before the Supreme Court and the National Court, and before other Courts as provided by or under Acts of the Parliament; and
- (b) to bring or to decline to bring proceedings under Division III.2 (*leadership code*) for misconduct in office.

(*See: Public Prosecutor (Office and Functions) Act* Ch.338)

C.P.C. Report Ch.8 p.10

92. It is not generally appreciated that, if a person is suspected of committing a criminal offence, it does not follow automatically that he should be prosecuted. The person who is responsible for making the decision as to whether or not to prosecute, usually a police officer, must use discretion in deciding whether or not to bring criminal proceedings against the suspect.

93. In the ordinary case, the person responsible for launching a prosecution considers the evidence against the person suspected of committing an offence, and decides whether that evidence is sufficient to justify having the person tried in court for the offence. If it is, a prosecution is normally commenced.

94. However, in some cases, wider considerations may be involved. It is not always in the public interest to go through the whole process of the criminal law if, at the end of the proceedings, perhaps because of mitigating circumstances, or because of what the defendant has already suffered, only a nominal punishment is likely to be imposed.

95. In other cases, the offence which has been committed may be a breach of an old law which most people no longer regard as relevant. In this situation also, the person responsible for deciding whether or not to prosecute may reasonably decide that, in the circumstances, it would not be in the public interest to bring proceedings.

96. In common with leaders in many other old and new Commonwealth states and elsewhere, we believe that the person who has final responsibility for commencing, and discontinuing prosecutions in the superior courts has a duty, in deciding whether or not to authorise a prosecution, to ascertain all the relevant facts, including the effect which a particular prosecution, successful or unsuccessful as the case may be, would have upon public morale and order. He should also take into account any other considerations of public policy. For the person responsible for the performance of this important onerous task to be free from improper political pressure, and to be able to act in such a manner that he is seen to be acting justly, we believe he should have independent status which is guaranteed by the Constitution.

97. Accordingly, we have recommended the establishment of a constitutional office known as the 'Public Prosecutor'. The holder of this office should be specifically made independent by providing that he is not subject to direction or control by any other person or body in exercising constitutional powers and functions.

98. We do not envisage, however, that the Public Prosecutor would completely ignore the views of the Executive in regard to cases which have serious political implications — for example, in the case of an act which might constitute treason. In these situations, we would expect that the Public Prosecutor would consult the Minister responsible for justice, or the Prime Minister, as to the political effects of a decision either to prosecute or not to prosecute. The Public Prosecutor could then take into account the views of the Executive on the public policy aspect of the case when making his own decision as to whether or not to prosecute (or to discontinue a prosecution). [p.11]

Powers

101. We propose that the Public Prosecutor have power to commence, continue or discontinue any prosecution in any court, but we have enabled Parliament to pass a law that limits the right of the Public Prosecutor to deal with a case which is within the jurisdiction of either a village court or of Defence Force judges. We have recommended that two further specific powers be conferred on the Public Prosecutor, namely —

- the power to take proceedings against any 'leader' for breach of a provision in the proposed Leadership Code, (which is set out in Chapter 3, 'The Leadership Code'); and
- the power to advise the Commissioner of Police on any criminal matter, either on request or on his own initiative.

AS TO THE FUNCTIONS OF THE PUBLIC PROSECUTOR

per Kapi J.

> ... The primary function of the Public Prosecutor is to control the exercise and performance of the prosecution including appeals and refusal to initiate or discontinue prosecutions before the National and Supreme Courts. Under s.177(1) of the Constitution the Public Prosecutor's functions are:
>
> (a) In accordance with an Act of the Parliament and the Rules of Court of the Supreme Court and the National Court ....
>
> Pursuant to this constitutional provision the *Public Prosecutor (Office and Functions) Act* 1977 was enacted and sets out the functions of the Public Prosecutor in more detail. It is significant to note that under Section 177 of the Constitution, the performance of the prosecution function is not only in accordance with an Act of the Parliament but also in accordance with the Rules of the Supreme Court and the National Court ....
>
> *Acting Public Solicitor (sic) v Uname Aumane* [1980] PNGLR 510 at p.531.

AS TO THE INSTITUTION OF PRIVATE CRIMINAL PROSECUTIONS

Held

The power conferred upon the Public Prosecutor to control the exercise and performance of the prosecution function does not impinge upon the common law right conceded to everyone, and applying as part of the law of Papua New Guinea by virtue of Sch. 2.2, of testing the legality of any conduct of which he disapproves by a criminal prosecution.
Re Rooney (No 2) [1979] PNGLR 448; see particularly Greville Smith J. at p.517.

PROSECUTIONS TO BE IN NAME OF THE STATE

Held

Prosecutions should neither be in the name of the Crown (it having no constitutional role in their conduct) nor in the name of the Public Prosecutor. Prosecutions should be brought in the corporate name of the people.
The State v Mogo Wonom [1975] PNGLR 311; see Williams J. at p.320.

GENERALLY

Referred to

by Pritchard J. in *Ex parte Smedley* [1978] PNGLR 156 at pp.159,160 (a court should respect the office of Public Prosecutor to the extent that where criminal charges are pending against a non-citizen and the Public Prosecutor objects to that person leaving the country, any application for permission to leave should be refused);

by Pritchard J. in *Constitutional Reference No 1 of 1978 (s.19)* [1978] PNGLR 345 at p.367.

(2) The functions of the Public Solicitor are to provide legal aid, advice and assistance for persons in need of help by him, and in particular —
- (a) to provide legal assistance to a person in need of help by him who has been charged with an offence punishable by imprisonment for more than two years; and
- (b) notwithstanding the provisions of Section 176(5) (*establishment of offices*) he shall provide legal aid, advice and assistance to any person when directed to do so by the Supreme Court or the National Court; and
- (c) in his discretion in any matter, whether of a criminal or civil nature provided that such assistance shall be —
  - (i) limited to advice and preparation of documents in any proceedings in respect of which an Act of the Parliament prohibits legal representation of any party to the proceedings; and
  - (ii) granted in accordance with an order of priorities relative to the resources of the Public Solicitor laid down by an Act of the Parliament.

C.P.C. Report Ch.8 p.11

103. In countries such as England and Australia, there is a long tradition of an independent private legal profession, the members of which are supposed to protect the rights of the individual. However, individuals or corporations seeking legal advice or representation in courts of law are expected to pay quite high fees to these

private practitioners. While this tradition might be sufficient to meet the needs of those who are able to pay for these services, it has on the whole proved quite unsatisfactory for those who are unable to pay for such service.

104. In those coutries the 'poor person's' needs are supposed to be met mainly by lawyers who volunteer to represent the 'poor' for little or no fee. This practice has a number of severe limitations. Experienced private lawyers usually have little time to assist these people. Because of the small fees payable, the tendency has generally been for relatively young and inexperienced lawyers to take the poor person's case, doing so mostly for experience. Furthermore, the range of matters in respect of which legal aid has been made available, has generally been very limited.

105. The Australian Government has recently recognised these difficulties and has now established a national, government-paid, professionally independent Legal Aid Service.

106. In Papua New Guinea an effective legal aid service has been provided over the last fourteen years by the Office of the Public Solicitor, which has given representation to Papua New Guineans (and some expatriates) who could not afford to pay private lawyers to represent them in courts or to give them advice about their rights. This Office has been developed especially to meet the needs of the indigenous people, the great majority of whom cannot afford to pay legal fees, particularly in criminal cases.

107. The Public Solicitor's Office has had a considerable degree of independence over the years, despite the fact that it has been a branch of the Law Department. However, because of its lack of statutory independence, the Office has on one occasion at least, been made subject to direction by the Secretary for Law.

108. We do not consider that private practitioners will be able to provide legal services on the scale and of the nature required by our people in the future, nor do we think they can be expected to do so. We are convinced that the Office of the Public Solicitor is the best institution to provide legal assistance to the great majority of our people.

109. No-one should be denied legal assistance by reason of his financial circumstances or the fact that he or she is unable to establish contact with persons of authority or influence. Law Courts we believe should be available to all persons, not just to persons who have money.

110. We have found public opinion throughout the country to be in favour of making the Public Solicitor's Office constitutionally independent of the executive government. We ourselves believe that this independence is essential in order to provide legal services to the majority of our people and to protect the rights of individuals and small groups. [p.12]

The Grant of Legal Aid

114. We recommend that the Public Solicitor be specifically empowered to grant legal assistance to an individual or a group on the basis of 'need'. We have defined 'need' in broad terms that are similar to the definition of 'impecuniosity' which the Public Solicitor has been applying for a number of years.

115. We have also proposed that the Public Solicitor be empowered to charge an appropriate sum towards the cost of providing legal aid in cases where a person cannot afford to go to a private practitioner but could make a contribution towards that cost.

116. We appreciate, of course, that the extent to which legal service can be provided by the Public Solicitor's Office to those entitled to such assistance will depend on the availability of lawyers and their supporting staff, and reasonable facilities being provided for them. We have therefore recommended that the Public Solicitor should be provided with adequate qualified and supporting staff and facilities.

Powers and Functions

117. We have recommended that the Public Solicitor *shall* provide legal aid to any person who is in 'need' and is to be tried in the National Court of Justice on a criminal charge. The Public Solicitor has had this responsibility in respect of trials in the present Supreme Court since his Office was first established.

118. We also propose that the Public Solicitor should have a discretion to provide legal representation in cases where a person is charged with a serious offence, but the trial is taking place in a subordinate court. We recommend that the term 'serious offence' should include any offence which may at present be tried in the Supreme Court.

119. Other recommended discretionary powers of the Public Solicitor include the power to commence and provide legal representation in appeals against convictions or sentences in lower courts and other powers and functions concerning civil and criminal matters according to law.

AS TO A DIRECTION BY THE COURT TO PROVIDE LEGAL AID

per Wilson J.

... Although s.177(2)(b) vests in both the Supreme Court and the National Court a wide discretion regarding the giving of directions to the Public Solicitor, such a discretion must be exercised '...judicially according to rules of reason and justice, not arbitrarily or capriciously or according to private opinion'. (*House v The King* (1936) 55 CLR 499 per Starke J. at p.503) ...

In exercising my discretion I have taken into account the following facts and circumstances:

1. Legal advice ... was given by the Public Solicitor to the applicant.
2. The Constitution does not guarantee any right in a convicted person to legal assistance on an appeal against conviction
3. There is no rule of law or rule of practice to the effect that convicted persons should be entitled to receive legal assistance for the purposes of having their appeals against convictions prepared and argued for them.
4. The Court should be slow to intervene in the area of provision of legal aid, advice and assistance, which is the primary function of the Public Solicitor, and should therefore be slow to interfere with the Public Solicitor's discretion.
5. The Public Solicitor has limited resources with which to discharge his functions and is entitled to determine an order of priorities for the expenditure of such resources......
6. There is an absence of substantial reasons or special circumstances which, in the interests of justice, would require the Court to direct that legal assistance be given.

For these reasons the application will be refused.

Mathias Evertz v The State [1979] PNGLR 174 at pp.179,180.

Referred to

by Pratt J. in *Simon Karl v The Public Prosecutor* (1981 Unreported) N388(L) at pp.1-4 (principles in *Mathias Evertz v The State* (above) explained and affirmed).

GENERALLY

Referred to

by Prentice C.J. in *Constitutional Reference No 1 of 1978 (s.19)* [1978] PNGLR 345 at pp.350-352; see also Wilson J. at p.363 and Pritchard J. at pp. 371, 386.

(3) A person aggrieved by a refusal of the Public Solicitor to provide legal aid may apply to the Supreme Court or the National Court for a direction under Subsection (2)(b).

C.P.C. Report Ch.8 p.12

Right of Application to National Courts where legal aid refused

120. In order to ensure that legal aid is not unreasonably refused by the Public Solicitor, we have recommended that a person should have a right to apply to the National Court for a certificate that he should be granted legal aid. Where the National Court is satisfied that legal aid has been wrongly refused the Court may direct the Public Solicitor to immediately grant legal aid to the person concerned. If such a certificate is issued, the Public Solicitor would be reguired to grant legal assistance to that person in accordance with the certificate, (either with or without conditions as to the payment of a contribution towards the cost of providing that assistance.

AS TO WHAT CONSTITUTES A REFUSAL TO PROVIDE LEGAL AID

Held

Where the Public Solicitor provides assistance in the form of far-ranging investigation, research and legal advice but then declines to proceed with an appeal an applicant cannot complain that he is aggrieved by a refusal to provide legal aid. Instead recourse must be had to s.177(2)(b).
Mathias Evertz v The State [1979] PNGLR 174; see Wilson J. at pp. 178-180.

AS TO PRINCIPLES TO BE APPLIED BY THE COURT

Held

The principles expressed by Wilson J. in *Mathias Evertz v The State* [1979] PNGLR 174 (see under s.177(2)) apply to applications under s.177(3).
Simon Karl v The Public Prosecutor (1981 Unreported) N388(L); see Pratt J at pp.1-4.

GENERALLY

Referred to

by Pritchard J. (dissenting) in *Constitutional Reference No 1 of 1978 (s.19)* [1978] PNGLR 345 at pp.385, 386 (not a reason to preclude the Ombudsman Commission investigating the administrative acts of the Public Solicitor).

(4) For the purposes of this section the need of a person is to be interpreted in relation to each particular case and, without limiting the generality of this expression, account shall be taken of the means of the person to meet the probable cost.

(5) An Act of Parliament may make provision for the Public Solicitor to make a reasonable charge for services provided by him to persons in need of his help whom he considers are able to make a contribution towards the cost of these services.

(*see: Public Solicitor (Charges) Act* Ch. 337.)

GENERALLY

Referred to

by Pritchard J. (dissenting) in *Constitutional Reference No 1 of 1978 (s.19)* [1978] PNGLR 345 at p.371.

(6) An Act of the Parliament may confer, or may provide for the conferring of, additional functions, not inconsistent with the performance of the functions conferred by Subsections (1) and (2), on the Public Prosecutor or the Public Solicitor.

GENERALLY

Referred to

by Pritchard J. (dissenting) in *Constitutional Reference No. 1 of 1978 (s.19)* [1978] PNGLR 345 at p.371.

Subdivision H. — Removal from Office of Senior Judicial and Legal Office-holders.

178. — GROUNDS OF REMOVAL.

A Judge, the Public Prosecutor, the Public Solicitor or the Chief Magistrate may, during his term of office, be removed from office only —

(a) for inability (whether arising from physical or mental infirmity or otherwise) to perform the functions and duties of his office; or

(b) for misbehaviour; or

(c) in accordance with Division III.2 (*leadership code*), for misconduct in office.

C.P.C. Report Ch.8 p.11

Suspension and Removal

102. We have recommended that similar provision should be made for the suspension and removal from office of the Public Prosecutor as is made in respect of judges. .... [p.13]

121. Similar provisions to those applicable to the Public Prosecutor should apply to the Public Solicitor. ... [p.21]

24. The Chief Magistrate shall have the same term of office and protection from arbitrary suspension or removal as a judge.
Note: Provision should be made by law in respect of the qualifications, term of office, salary and other conditions of service, discipline, retirement age, removal etc., of full-time magistrates. Such provision should give these magistrates security of tenure similar to that recommended in respect of judges.

GENERALLY.

Referred to

by Wilson J. in *Constitutional Reference No. 1 of 1978 (s.19)* [1978] PNGLR 345 at p.360; see also Pritchard J. (dissenting) at p.368;

by Pratt J. in *Smedley v The State* [1980] PNGLR 379 at p.403.

179. — REMOVAL FROM OFFICE OF CHIEF JUSTICE.

(1) If the National Executive Council is satisfied that the question of the removal from office of the Chief Justice should be investigated, the Head of State, acting with, and in accordance with, the advice of the National Executive Council, may —

(a) appoint a tribunal under Section 181 (*constiution, etc., of tribunals*); and

(b) refer the matter, together with a statement of the reasons for its opinion, to the tribunal for investigation and report to it.

(2) If the tribunal reports that there are good grounds for removing the Chief Justice from office, the Head of State, acting with, and in accordance with, the advice of the National Executive Council, may, by notice in writing to the Chief Justice, remove him from office.

(3) The Prime Minister shall send a copy of the notice, together with a copy of the report of the tribunal, to the Speaker for presentation to the Parliament, and shall also forward copies to the Judicial and Legal Services Commission.

C.P.C. Report Ch.8 p.23

Removal of the Chief Justice

39. If the Prime Minister is satisfied that the question of removing the Chief Justice ought to be investigated —

(a) he shall, after first consulting the Minister responsible [p.24] for justice and subsequently consulting, two bodies jointly, namely, the National Executive Council and the Permanent Parliamentary Committee responsible for justice, appoint a tribunal to which he shall refer the matter. The tribunal shall consist of three judges, chosen from among judges of the National Court of Papua New Guinea, and judges of a court of a unlimited jurisdiction in a country which has a legal system which the Judicial and Legal Service Commission considers similar to that of Papua New Guinea, one of whom shall be appointed chairman by the Commission; and

(b) that tribunal shall enquire into the matter and report its findings to the Prime Minister, (a copy of those findings being forwarded simultaneously to the Commission), who shall act in accordance with the recommendations of the tribunal.

180. — REMOVAL FROM OFFICE OF OTHER JUDGES, ETC.

(1) If the Judicial and Legal Services Commission is satisfied that the question of the removal from office of a Judge (other than the Chief Justice), the Public Prosecutor, the Public Solicitor or the Chief Magistrate should be investigated, it may —

(a) appoint a tribunal under Section 181 (*constitution, etc., of tribunals*); and

(b) refer the matter, together with a statement of the reasons for its opinion, to the tribunal for investigation and report to it.

(2) If the tribunal reports that there are good grounds for removing the Judge, Public Prosecutor, Public Solicitor or Chief Magistrate from office, the Judicial and Legal Services Commission, may, by notice in writing to the Judge, Public Prosecutor, Public Solicitor or Chief Magistrate, as the case may be, remove him from office.

(3) The Commission shall send a copy of the notice, together with a copy of the report of the tribunal, to the Speaker for presentation to the Parliament.

C.P.C. Report Ch.8 p.8

Removal of judges from office

75. The grounds upon which constitutional office-holders should be disqualified from holding office, and the way in which they should be removed are dealt with in general terms in Part A of Chapter 14.

76. We believe that judges should be removed from office before their term of office is completed only in the most serious of circumstances. Their fixed term, and assured conditions of employment after their term has expired, are a vital guarantee of their judicial independence.

77. As is the case with other constitutional office-holders there are, however, certain circumstances in which a particular judge should not be allowed to continue in office. These include situations in which a judge is guilty of misbehaviour (including gross negligence and breach of the Leadership Code), or is physically or mentally incapable of performing his duties. In such circumstances, the Judicial and Legal Service Commission should be able to suspend from office a judge other than the Chief Justice, pending an investigation by a tribunal of three judges chosen by the Commission. We have been concerned to ensure that this tribunal of three judges not only *is* impartial but *is seen* to be impartial. We have therefore recommended that judges from a court of unlimited jurisdiction in a country which has a legal system similar to that of Papua New Guinea and former judges of the present Supreme Court, as well as judges (and former judges) of the National Court, should be eligible for appointment to the tribunal.

78. The Judicial and Legal Service Commission should then either allow a judge to remain in office, or remove him, as the tribunal recommends. The Commission should also be able, in its discretion, to revoke suspensions, but in any event a suspension should automatically cease if the tribunal recommends that the judge concerned ought not to be removed.

181. — CONSTITUTION, ETC., OF TRIBUNALS.

(1) A tribunal for the purposes of Section 179 (*removal from office of Chief Justice*) or 180 (*removal from office of other Judges, etc.*) shall consist of a Chairman and two other members, each of whom must be —
  (a) a Judge or former Judge of the Supreme Court or of the National Court; or
  (b) a former Judge or acting Judge of the pre-Independence Supreme Court; or
  (c) a Judge or former Judge of a court of unlimited jurisdiction of a country with a legal system similar to that of Papua New Guinea, or of a court to which an appeal from such a court lies.

(2) The tribunal shall make due inquiry into any matter referred to it without regard to legal formalities or the rules of evidence, and shall inform itself in such manner as it thinks proper, subject to compliance with the principles of natural justice.

C.P.C. Report; see under s.180.

182. — SUSPENSION.

(1) Where a question has been referred to a tribunal under this Subdivision —
  (a) the Head of State, acting with, and in accordance with, the advice of the National Executive Council, in the case of the Chief Justice; or
  (b) the Judicial and Legal Services Commission, in any other case,

may suspend the person concerned from office pending the report of the tribunal, and may remove the suspension at any time.

(2) Unless otherwise determined by the Head of State, acting with, and in accordance with, the advice of the National Executive Council, or by the Judicial and Legal Services Commission, as the case may be, the suspension shall be on full pay.

(3) Where at the time of the suspension, a suspended Judge or Chief Magistrate was dealing with any judicial proceedings, he may continue and complete those proceedings, unless the Judicial and Legal Services Commission in the case of the Chief Justice, or the Chief Justice in any other case, otherwise orders.

C.P.C. Report Ch.8 p.24

Suspension of Judges

40. Where the question of removing a judge on the grounds of misbehaviour or inability to perform the functions of his office has been referred to the appropriate tribunal —

(a) in the case of a judge other than the Chief Justice, the Judicial and Legal Service Commission may suspend that judge from performing the functions of his office. Any such suspension may at any time be revoked by the Commission, and shall in any case cease to have effect if the tribunal recommends to the Commission that the judge should not be removed; or

(b) in the case of the Chief Justice, the Prime Minister may, after first consulting, jointly, the National Executive Council and the First Parliamentary Committee, suspend the Chief Justice from performing the functions of his office. Any such suspension may at anytime be revoked by the Prime Minister, after consulting the Ministerial bodies referred to above, and shall in any case cease to have effect if the tribunal recommends to the Prime Minister that the Chief Justice should not be removed.

GENERALLY

Referred to

by Pritchard J. (dissenting) in *Constitutional Reference No 1 of 1978 (s.19)* [1978] PNGLR 345 at p.368.

Subdivision 1. — The Judicial and Legal Services Commission.

183. — ESTABLISHMENT OF THE COMMISSION.

(1) A Judicial and Legal Services Commission is hereby established.

(2) Subject to Subsection (3), the Commission consists of —

(a) the Minister responsible for the National Justice Administration, or a person nominated by him, who is the Chairman; and
(b) the Chief Justice; and
(c) the Deputy Chief Justice; and
(d) the Chief Ombudsman; and
(e) a member of the Parliament appointed by the Parliament.

(3) When the Commission is considering a matter relating to the appointment or removal from office of a member of the Magisterial Service, or any other matter relating to the Magisterial Service prescribed for the purposes of this subsection by or under

an Act of the Parliament, the Chief Magistrate is (except in a matter involving himself) an additional member of the Commission.

(4) The Commission is not subject to direction or control by any person or authority.

(5) An Organic Law may make further provision in respect of the constitution, powers, functions, duties and responsibilities of the Commission, and for guaranteeing its independence.

(*See: Organic Law on the Judicial and Legal Services Commission* Ch.1)

C.P.C. Report Ch.8 p.5

44. The power to choose judges should, we believe, be vested in a body chaired by the Minister responsible for justice, which should be named the 'Judicial and Legal Service Commission'. Certain other powers and functions should also be vested in the Commission under the Constitution and by law. It should comprise the following five people —

- the Minister responsible for Justice, who would be Chairman;
- the Chief Justice;
- a lawyer of the National Court, nominated by the Minister responsible for justice;
- the Chief Ombudsman (who would be the head of the Ombudsman Commission which, in Chapter 11, we propose should be established); and
- a lawyer nominated by the Permanent Parliamentary Committee responsible for justice.

45. This combination of people should ensure that persons chosen as judges are thought to be just by people whose concern is the proper administration of justice, the representation of public opinion, and the protection of the rights of citizens both as individuals and groups; that they are well regarded as lawyers by the judiciary and by their professional colleagues; and that they are sympathetic to the cultures and values of Papua New Guinean society.

46. We would expect that, before attending a meeting of the Commission at which a person is to be chosen as a judge, the Minister responsible for justice would informally consult the Prime Minister and possibly some of his National Executive Council colleagues also, to ascertain their views as to the suitability of potential appointees. Thus the Government's views, which we believe to be important in this context, should be adequately represented in the Commission.

47. Our recommendations as to the composition of the proposed Judicial and Legal Service Commission constitute a middle course between the various systems of appointing judges by politicians alone (as in most countries of the world) on the one hand, and formally exlcuding politicians from the appointment process by placing it in the hands of members of the judiciary and the Chairman of the Public Service Commission, (as in a few states of the Commonwealth) on the other.

48. Our proposed Commission is somewhat similar to the authority in Israel which is responsible for appointing judges. It too is chaired by the Minister for Justice, but is a larger body, comprising nine members of whom two are members of the government, two are parliamentarians, three are judges, and the other two are practising lawyers. [p.6]

49. We have noted that of the Judicial Service Commissions established in certain other new Commonwealth states, some of which have two or even three judges (or former judges) as members, there has been a significant trend, since they were established at Independence, either for their powers of appointment to be substantially reduced so that they now appoint magistrates only, not judges, or for their independent status to be eroded. This fact has reinforced our view that politicians representing both the executive and the legislature should have a direct say in the appointment of judges, particularly when the judges who are appointed will be deciding major constitutional issues. If politicians do not have this influence we consider it less likely that they will accept judicial decisions which they regard as politically unpopular or as increasing the limitations on their own powers.

50. A further serious disadvantage of excluding politicians from the process of appointing judges is that it is likely to increase the danger (which is almost always present in emerging states), of a serious break-down in communication between the judiciary and the other arms of government. Such a situation might result in the very independence of the judges, which the people very much want to see established, being threatened.

51. In Britain where the independence of the judiciary is well established, there is a strong link between all three arms of government — the legislature, the executive and the judiciary — through the Lord Chancellor, who is a member of the legislature (the House of Lords) a member of cabinet, and the head of the judiciary. We do not propose a system which goes so far in establishing this link but we believe the British precedent is a useful one to be taken into account.

GENERALLY

Referred to

by Pritchard J. (dissenting) in *Constitutional Reference No 1 of 1978 (s.19)* [1978] PNGLR 345 at p.368;

by Wilson J. in *Re Rooney (No 2)* [1979] PNGLR 448 at p.492 (as an element in the independence of the national judicial system).

Subdivision J. — Miscellaneous.

184. — RULES OF COURT.

(1) The Judges of the Supreme Court or of the National Court may make rules of court, not inconsistent with a Constitutional Law or an Act of the Parliament, with respect to the practice and procedure in and in relation to the Supreme Court or the National Court, as the case may be.

(2) Without limiting the generality of Subsection (1), the rules may make provision for and in respect of —
- (a) the practice and procedures in the offices of the Supreme Court and the National Court; and
- (b) the service and execution of process and judgements of the Supreme Court and the National Court; and
- (c) the service and execution within the country of process and judgements of foreign courts; and
- (d) the issue by the Supreme Court or the National Court of letters of request for the service in a foreign country of process of the Supreme Court or the National Court, as the case may be, or for the examination of witnesses in a foreign country; and
- (e) the costs of and relating to proceedings in the Supreme Court or the National Court; and
- (f) the methods of pleading; and
- (g) the attendance of witnesses and the taking of evidence; and
- (h) the means by which particular facts may be proved, and the manner in which evidence of particular facts may be given, in any proceedings or in any application in connexion with, or at any stage of, any proceedings.

(3) The Rules of Court may require or permit legal argument to be submitted in writing.

(4) If an Act of the Parliament comes into force that is inconsistent with a rule of court, the rule ceases to have effect to the extent of the inconsistency.

(5) All rules of court shall be forwarded by the Chief Justice to the Speaker, for presentation to the Parliament, as soon as practicable after being made, and may be disallowed by the Parliament.

C.P.C. Report Ch.8 p.9

82. We have recommended that, subject to the Constitution and any law, the judges of the National Court (or a majority of them) may make Rules of Court regarding the procedure of the National Court and the Supreme Court. Notice of the making of these rules should be published in the Government Gazette, and a copy of them forwarded by the Chief Justice to the Speaker of the National Parliament and to the Minister responsible for justice within fourteen days of publication.

83. We propose that the Speaker shall, when he receives Rules of Court, promptly table them in Parliament. Parliament may disallow them (or part of them) not later than the final day of the meeting following that at which the Rules are tabled.

AS TO WHICH MATTERS MAY BE GOVERNED BY RULES OF COURT

per Kapi J.

Matters of practice and procedure may be defined to include the form and manner of conducting all litigation before the courts. This includes everything that leads up to the commencement of litigation in court to final judgment and to its enforcement and appeal. If any form of litigation is to commence at all and to come to some final judgment and enforcement, the meaning of 'practice and procedure' would necessarily include time limits in which acts may be done in the process.
Acting Public Solicitor [sic] v Uname Aumane [1980] PNGLR 510 at p.532.

per Bredmeyer J.

... By s.184(2)(e) ... the rules may make provision for the costs of and relating to proceedings in the National Court. The rules of the National Court thus ... are limited to the costs of proceedings *in the National Court* ... I consider then that National Court when hearing an appeal from the [Taxation] Review Tribunal can award costs for work done before that court ... but not the legal costs incurred by a party before the Review Tribunal as that is not a proceeding in the National Court nor within the scope of the practice and procedure of the National Court.
Theiss Bros (Pacific) Pty Ltd v Chief Collector of Taxes [1982] PNGLR 385 at p.393; see also Kidu C.J. at pp.387,388.

GENERALLY

Referred to

by Kidu C.J. in *Acting Public Solicitor [sic] v Uname Aumane* [1980] PNGLR 510 at pp.512, 513 (Rules of court may not be inconsistent with an Act of Parliament); see also Kearney Dep. C.J. at p.516, Greville Smith J. at pp.519, 521, Andrew J. at p.526 and Kapi J. at pp.532, 533.

185. — LACK OF PROCEDURAL PROVISION.

If in the circumstances of a particular case before a court no provision, or no adequate provision, is made in respect of a matter of practice or procedure, the court shall give ad hoc directions to remedy the lack or inadequacy.

AS TO EXPRESS RULES OF PRACTICE AND PROCEDURE

Held

Section 185 has no application where the law expressly sets out procedures to bring a matter before the Court. In such circumstances there is no lack of practice or procedure. Section 185 may not be used to amend the law.
S.C.R. No 5 of 1982: Hugo Berghauser and ors v Joseph Aoae [1982] PNGLR 379 at pp.382,383.

AS TO UNCERTAINTY AND INADEQUACY OF PROCEDURES

per Williams J.

> The statutory provisions relating to appeals from the [Liquor Licensing] Commission are unclear and unsatisfactory, particularly in relation to the material to be furnished to this Court on appeal. It seems rare indeed for an appeal to be brought from a decision of the Commission ...
>
> I think that in the circumstances the proper course to have been followed was for directions to be sought in relation to the conduct of the matter ... I propose to deal with the matter on the basis of an application for directions. Having regard to the uncertainty and possible inadequacy of the procedures laid down I think it is open for me to give ad hoc directions pursuant to s.185 of the Constitution of Papua New Guinea.
> *Evangelical Lutheran Church of New Guinea v Peninsula Hotels Pty Ltd* [1977] PNGLR 147 at pp.150, 151.

AS TO LACK OF PROCEDURE

Held

In a case in which the Constitution requires that a person convicted of an offence is entitled to have his conviction and sentence reviewed by a higher court but no provision for such an appeal exists it is the duty of the Court to make both specific provision for the particular case before it and general provision for future cases under the power conferred by s.185 of the Constitution.

Accordingly, in the case of convictions under ss.26 and 27 of the *Corrective Institutions Act* when no provision for an appeal existed, it was ordered, pending legislation to correct the omission, that appeals would lie to the National Court and that such appeals should be brought in accordance with the provisions of the *Local Courts Act*.
Constitutional Reference No 2 of 1978; Re Corrective Institutions Act 1957 [1978] PNGLR 404.

GENERALLY

Referred to

by Kapi J. in *Minister for Lands v Frame* [1980] PNGLR 433 at p.472;

by Miles J. in *S.C.R. No 2 of 1981; Re s.19 of the Constitution* [1981] PNGLR 518 at p.530.

186. — JURIES AND ASSESSORS.

Nothing in this Division prevents the establishment, by or under an Act of the Parliament, of a system of juries or assessors.

(*See: National Court Assessors (T.N.G.) Act* Ch.42)

187. — REPORTS BY JUDGES.

(1) The Judges shall, at least once in each period of 12 months, at such times as are fixed by or under an Act of the Parliament or, subject to any such Act, by the Head of State, acting with, and in accordance with, the advice of the National Executive Council, give to the Head of State, for presentation to the Parliament, a report on the work of the National Judicial System, with such recommendations as to improvement as they think proper.

(2) Nothing in Subsection (1) prevents the Judges from making, on their own initiative or at the request of the Parliament or of the National Executive, other reports on any aspect of the work of the National Judicial System.

C.P.C. Report Ch.8 p.21

Reports

25. (1) At least once a year, a report on the functioning and administration of the judiciary shall be forwarded by the Chief Justice after consultation with the other judges to the Speaker, who shall table the report in the National Parliament not later than during the first meeting of the Parliament after he has received the report. A copy of the report shall simultaneously be forwarded to the Minister responsible for justice. [p.22]

(2) Each report shall include -
(a) a carefully considered opinion as to the extent to which the various courts are meeting the needs of the people;
(b) an overall view of any legal and administrative difficulties that may have been encountered by the judiciary, and recommendations on ways in which such difficulties might be overcome or minimized;
(c) in particular, an analysis by the Chief Magistrate of the functioning of the Magisterial Service and of courts of summary jurisdiction; and
(d) such other matters as the Chief Justice after consultation with the other judges and the Chief Magistrate considers should be brought to the attention of parliament in the interests of justice and its effective administration.

Referred to

by Greville Smith J. in *S.C.R. No 2 of 1981; Re s. 19(1) (f) of the Criminal Code* [1982] PNGLR 150 at p.165 (as a reason why the court should be inclined to caution in developing the underlying law).

PART VIA. — PROVINCIAL GOVERNMENT AND LOCAL LEVEL GOVERNMENT.

(Added by Constitutional Amendment No. 1 — Provincial Government)

187A. — PROVINCIAL GOVERNMENT SYSTEM

There shall be a system of Provincial Government for Papua New Guinea in accordance with this Part.

C.P.C. Report Ch.10 p.1

1. There is widespread discontent with the present distribution of power in our country, and a deep yearning among our people for a greater say in the conduct of their affairs. If the Committee's recommendation in Chapter 7, 'The Executive', that the Constitution should explicitly vest power in the people, is to be more than legal rhetoric, then opportunities must be provided for our people to participate meaningfully in those aspects of government that directly concern them. The recommendations we make in this chapter are designed to provide such opportunities.

2. When Europeans first settled in Papua New Guinea, they did not find a political vacuum on the shores and plains, or in the mountains and valleys, of our islands. Our ancestors lived and worked in communities — villages, hamlets, clans and tribes — with their own forms of social organisation, appropriate to their needs. However, colonial rule has had an important impact upon the character and life styles of our people. It placed new requirements upon them. It ignored, or opposed, or sought to alter, our traditional forms of social organisation without proper consultation with our people. It deprived us of self-government, and even of self-respect. The proud independence of our local communities was replaced by dependence — upon the all-powerful representative of the colonial government, the *kiap*.

3. Colonial rule has brought peace between once-warring communities, roads and other forms of material progress. But the price of these changes has been the establishment of a system of government that has not made adequate provision for local initiative.

4. Nonetheless, our people have demonstrated an outstanding capacity to endure and to tolerate the oppressive and paternalistic policies of successive colonial rulers. The aspirations that underlie the discontent and yearning referred to in the opening sentence of this chapter provide a sure sign that their will has not been broken. But, the system of government that is Australia's legacy to us provides no real outlet for these aspirations.

5. In our *Second Interim Report*, we described the present system of government of Papua New Guinea as 'highly centralized' and 'bureaucratic'. Our report continued:

> All significant decisions affecting the lives of people in every part of the country are made in Konedobu. Such a system cannot motivate our people to become self-expressive through constructive and self-reliant involvement. On the contrary it can only stifle initiative as it has done in the past.

6. Since these remarks were made, we have received a report from two distinguished experts who were made available to the Committee by the Commonwealth Secretariat to act as specialist consultants on a number of matters of relevance to this chapter. Their report provided ample confirmation of our views. As Professors W. Tordoff and R.L. Watts themselves put it:

> . . . in our experience of political systems in Asia, Africa and the Caribbean, we have not come across an administrative system so highly centralized and dominated by its bureaucracy.

7. The many hundreds of oral and written submissions we have received on 'Central — Regional — Local Government Relations' indicate that people in all parts of the country are dissatisfied with this state of affairs. Our people feel powerless and frustrated. Decisions that can and should be made locally are made in Konedobu. The structure of government bequeathed to us by our colonial rulers has placed power in the hands of public servants rather than the people whom this bureaucracy should serve . . . .

The importance of district-level government

9. The Committee has devoted a great deal of time, and much earnest thought, to its consideration of item (b) in its terms of reference, 'Central — Regional — Local Government Relations and District Administration'. We have asked ourselves fundamental questions about the proper distribution of power in our society, and carefully weighed the alternative answers. We have been assisted in our deliberations by specialist consultants from overseas, and by advice and special studies prepared for us locally. We have paid close attention to the [p.2] submissions we have received. We believe that the recommendations contained in this chapter embody the views of the overwhelming majority of our people; that they provide the necessary safeguards for those minority groups who would otherwise be fearful for their own future; and that they are workable.

10. In our *First Interim Report*, we recorded the tentative conclusion that a clear majority view seemed to be emerging from the oral and written submissions we had received that government should be restructured and brought under political control at the district level.

11. In our *Second Interim Report*, we quoted both the Deputy Chief Minister, Dr. John Guise, Member for Alotau, and the late Leader of the Opposition, Mr. Matthias ToLiman, Member for Gazelle, as early and forceful advocates of a system of elected district-level government. We also pointed out that the present Leader of the Opposition, Mr. Tei Abal, Member for Wabag has been a consistent supporter of this concept, and that it is in harmony with the themes underlying the government's Eight Aims, particularly decentralisation.

12. Approximately 200 discussion groups in all parts of the country responded to a paper which we prepared on this subject. Three-quarters of them felt that the present system of government at district level should be changed. And the same proportion favoured the establishment of a system of elected assemblies to govern at the district level. Overwhelming support for both of these views was expressed at public meetings which we attended throughout the country.

13. Last September, we reported that the people of Bougainville wanted arrangements to be made for the establishment of a form of district-level government, pending publication and implementation of our recommendations. Since then, support for the idea of district-level government has grown. Demands have already been made in half of the districts of Papua New Guinea for the establishment of district-level government without delay.

14. Our recommendation that a system of district-level government should be established in the Constitution is designed to achieve several ends at once: decentralization; greater participation in decision-making by local leaders; and greater co-ordination of developmental activities undertaken by government officers in the districts.

15. We have already explained how important we think it is that government should be brought closer to the people. Decentralization of government services will make them more accessible to the people they should serve. Decentralization of decision-making will make government more responsive to local wishes and needs.

16. Government activity in the districts will also become more effective if it is brought under local political control. In becoming involved in policy and decision-making at the district level, our leaders will become more closely aware of the limitations and difficulties encountered by government in the development of their areas. Public servants who work in accordance with the wishes of local leaders will become more effective because they will also be able to work in the name of these leaders. Their activities are therefore more likely to enjoy the full support and co-operation of the local people. And, a strong district-level government will provide a framework, and a stimulus, for the co-ordination of government activity in each district.

17. The Committee has received a number of submissions, and an amount of critical comment on its recommendations, which seem to turn counter to what has been said above. The most serious of these counter-proposals have come from people who advocate some form of regional government for Papua New Guinea.

18. The advocates of regional government often seek the same ends as ourselves. They share many of our misgivings at the *status quo*, but they are, we believe, mistaken in the solutions they propose.

19. Most of the submissions which we have received in support of the establishment of a system of regional government have come from individuals. Few of them have appeared at our meetings. And, they seem to have enjoyed no discernible support among members of the discussion-groups that were organized for us by the Government Liaison Branch. A few of the advocates of regional government have favoured the establishment of a federal system of government in Papua New Guinea. The overwhelming majority of our people favour the maintenance of a unitary state.

20. Advocates of regional government also differ among themselves as to the number of regions there should be, and where their boundaries should be drawn. Most of them seem to favour a total of four or five regions based on the regional administrative divisions of [p.3] certain government departments. Generally, they favour Papua, the Highlands, the New Guinea Islands, and coastal districts of New Guinea mainland, although they disagree as to the likely affiliation of the Southern Highlands in particular. Some proponents of regional government have sought to take account of Bougainvillean feeling by suggesting that Bougainville should be regarded as a separate region. It is clear that Bougainvilleans certainly do not wish to form part of a region embracing all of the five existing districts in the New Guinea Islands.

21. The Committee believes that a system of regional government is not unlikely to repeat those very shortcomings in the present system of government which the advocates of regional government tend to decry. The so-called regions of Papua New Guinea tend to embrace people as diverse as those found in the country at large. There are great obstacles to communication within the regions. To the ordinary villager, regional headquarters are likely to seem almost as remote as Konedobu. We are convinced that government must be brought much closer to the people.

22. One of the most powerful arguments against establishing regional governments concerns the impetus they would be likely to give to regionalism — to the exacerbation of tensions between different regions, particularly the Highlands and Papua. The Committee does not believe that the attachments and the identities of people who are beginning to think of themselves in regional terms should necessarily be discouraged. But, we do believe that it would be unwise to institutionalize these attachments. To endanger the present fragile form of unity in our country by providing inducements to local leaders to think in regional terms would be to abdicate the mandate we have from the overwhelming majority of our people to secure the foundations of a united Papua New Guinea.

23. No detailed arguments have been brought to our attention to support the concept of regional government. But, the submissions we have received seem to assume that there is a certain ethnic homogeneity to each region.

24. We are basically doubtful of any theory that fails to take full account of the diversity of our country at the local level. We distrust any attempt to employ a limited unity to divide us. The experience of a number of recently independent state, including Nigeria, should serve as a warning of the dangers attendant upon the establishment of a small number of large, politically powerful regions, in which ethnic sentiments serve as a basis for regional unity and deep national division.

25. Finally, we feel concerned lest the establishment of regional governments should divert the energies of potential national leaders into regional politics. Our country needs the services of all capable men and women. We cannot afford a situation to develop in which leaders' energies are devoted to activities that do not contribute to nation-building. A system of district-level governments should enable our people to avoid most of these pitfalls.

26. Earlier in this chapter, we drew attention to some of the positive advantages we feel are likely to result from the establishment of district-level governments. All of them require that power be vested in a representative body. An advisory body would lack the power to respond effectively to local desires. It would also lack the ability to ensure that developmental activity in each district would be properly co-ordinated. An elective assembly with substantial powers, including financial powers of its own, is essential if meaningful decisions are to be made at the district level, and if action is to follow those decisions.

27. Effective government at both the national and district levels requires that there be strong links with the villages. The government and development of our country depend upon the village people. We attach the very greatest importance to government at the village level. But, we do not believe that the Constitution can or should do more than facilitate the participation of village people in government, and encourage the national and district-level governments to respect our country's diverse local communities.

28. We are conscious of the important role that can be played by associations spontaneously formed by the people outside the framework of local government established by the central government. We anticipate that such bodies will be formed in parts of the country that presently lack them, and that support for them will grow. They are vital expressions of that self-esteem, self-reliance and desire for participation in development that we are determined to foster. We are, however, unable to foresee a situation in which these bodies might act as the main link between the national government and village people throughout the country. We believe that such bodies should seek representation on district-level assemblies as the leaders of a number have declared they will. But, much as we believe in self-reliance, we recognize that the people of many districts require some assistance in devising structures through which they might effectively participate in their own development and government. Hence, our proposal that a system of a district-level governments be established without undue delay. [p.4]

29. The people of an increasing number of districts are becoming ever more conscious of the interests and problems that they share. The district is more than a simple administrative unit. It is, in fact, an important political unit with much of the administrative infrastructure necessary for further political development. It is also a known quantity: it poses no new problems of identity.

30. Thus, the system of district-level governments we recommend should be capable of accommodating present demands for the granting of significant autonomy to particular parts of the country. It should, indeed, harness them to those importants tasks of nation-building that lie before us all.

31. We recognize that the system of district-level government that we favour cannot be established overnight. But, there is a basis of existence from which the development of such a system can proceed, through stages we have recommended in the transitional provisions of this chapter. A start can and should be made at once. District-level governments can be set up without major dislocation to the present administrative system. Apart from a certain number of changes in the law, the most urgent requirements for this task are dedication to the goals we have specified — dedication shared by public servants and politicians alike.

A flexible system of provincial government established in Constitution

32. The diversity of our country is one of its greatest strengths. We are fortunate that Papua New Guinea does not have large ethnic groups competing for power at the national level, and that our cultural heritage is nonetheless so rich and varied.

33. We must ensure that our Constitution recognizes the value of our diverse national heritage, and fosters its development. We must not allow a dull uniformity to be imposed upon our people in the name of unity. But, we must also ensure that our country's Constitution preserves and expresses those values and aspirations which we all share.

34. The system of district-level governments we propose opens up new opportunities for our people to become involved in determining how their affairs should be conducted. In recommending that certain parts of it should be entrenched in the Constitution, we seek to provide reassurance for minority-groups fearful for their future.

35. We believe that the system of district-level governments recommended in this Chapter recognizes the diversity of our country, while fostering co-operation. It provides certain guarantees, entrenched in the Constitution, for those who may be anxious at majority rule. It gives expression to certain values which Papua New Guineans share. It is flexible in that it provides for local variation, and is capable of accommodating change. Above all, it creates opportunities for those who would use them.

36. We believe that the system of district-level governments we propose must meet present needs and provide for future aspirations. We have recommended that a number of statements of principle be included in the Constitution to make it quite clear that it should do so. And, to signify the break we believe must be made from the old Colonial system of district administration, we recommend that the present districts be renamed 'provinces', and that their governments should be known as 'provincial governments'.

187B. — GRANT OF PROVINCIAL GOVERNMENT

An Organic Law shall provide for, or make provision in respect of, the granting to a province of provincial government after consultation, as prescribed by an Organic Law, with the province.

(*See: Organic Law on Provincial Government* Ch.1)

TRANSITIONAL PROVISION

Comment

Constitutional Amendment No.1 Provincial Government, s.5 provided:

5. — TRANSITIONAL PROVISION FOR FORMER PROVINCIAL GOVERNMENT BODIES.

(1) An Organic Law may make provision in respect of the relations between former provincial government bodies and the system of provincial government provided for by the preceding provisions of this Law, and in particular may provide that some or all of such bodies may or shall be regarded as provincial governments for some or all of the provisions of the Constitution as amended by this Law.

(2) An Organic Law may make provision for or in respect of the continued operation of the *Provincial Government (Preparatory Arrangements) Act* 1974, as in force from time to time, and its relationship with the system of provincial government.

(3) In this section, 'former provincial government body' means a provincial government body as defined in Section Sch. 1.2(1) of the Constitution as in force immediately before the making of this Law.

Section 5 was not expressed to form part of the Constitution, but is, presumably, to be regarded as a Constitutional Law.

(*See: Organic Law on Provincial Government* Ch.1)

187C. — CONSTITUTION, FUNCTIONS, ETC., OF PROVINCIAL GOVERNMENTS.

(1) Subject to this Part, an Organic Law shall make provision in respect of the constitution, powers and functions of a provincial government.

(*See: Organic Law on Provincial Government* Ch.1)

(2) For each provincial government, there shall be established —

(a) an elective, or mainly elective, provincial legislature with such powers as are conferred by law; and

C.P.C. Report Ch.10 p.5

43. We have demonstrated above how important it is that government should not only be decentralized but that it should be brought under political control at the provincial level. We believe that it is vital that a body comprising directly elected representatives of the people should be established to exercise that control in each province. It should be called the 'Provincial Assembly'.

44. The Provincial Assembly should be the legislative and policy-making body for each provincial government. It should also have ultimate control over the performance of each provincial government's administrative responsibilities.

45. The Committee believes that the members of each Provincial Assembly should, in principle, be directly elected by the people. They should be answerable to the people at periodic elections.

46. At present, local government councils are represented on Area Authorities. The people of the various districts are only indirectly represented. The councillors who sit on Area Authorities were chosen to represent their wards at council level. They were not chosen by the people to represent them at district level.

47. A person who is an acceptable representative at one level of government may be quite unacceptable at another. Holders of political offices at each level of government should be separately elected. It is only as a purely interim measure that we recommend that the Provincial Assembly of a Stage One provincial government may be indirectly elected, like an Area Authority, until the first provincial elections after the Constitution comes into force are held.

48. The Constitution should, we believe, make general provision for the establishment of a directly elected Provincial Assembly in each province. The detailed arrangements should be spelt out in ordinary legislation.

49. The Constitution should provide a framework for provincial government. It should not be burdened with unnecessary detail. In proposing that the remaining recommendations in this section should be brought into effect through ordinary legislation, we hope that this framework will also remain flexible. The principles underlying our recommendations should be entrenched in the Constitution. But the National Parliament should have the power to vary the ways in which they are put into effect according to circumstance.

50. The number of representatives on each Provincial Assembly should be large enough to enable all major local groups to be adequately represented. It should not be so large that the assembly cannot function efficiently and with a minimum of formality.

51. The size we propose for each Provincial Assembly is one representative for every 10,000 people in the province, except that no Provincial Assembly should comprise fewer than 15 members. But, it must be possible, we believe, for the exact number of representatives in each assembly to vary somewhat from the standard so that provincial boundaries can be drawn to take account of local groupings (in accordance with the rules recommended in Chapter 6, 'The Legislature'). The Committee recommends that the Electoral Commission provided for in Chapter 6 should be given the power to increase or decrease the number of electorates for each Provincial Assembly by a maximum of two. [p.6]

Co-opted members

52. We have already stated our belief that holders of political office at different levels of government should be separately elected. We therefore see no reason to give members of the National Parliament the *right* to sit on Provincial Assemblies, nor to compel Provincial Assemblies to co-opt them. Members of the National Parliament are paid to act as full-time representatives of their people at the national level. Their energies ought not to be diverted into provincial politics, nor should Provincial Assemblies be required to give them a voice in a representative body to which they were not elected.

53. But, we do believe that communication and co-operation between political leaders at the national and provincial levels should be encouraged. We therefore recommend that each Provincial Assembly should be given the power to co-opt members of the National Parliament to sit and take part in debates in the assembly. However, members of the National Parliament should not be allowed to vote in Provincial Assemblies. They have no mandate from the people to do so.

54. Lest the members of a Provincial Assembly should seek to give greater voice to only one or a few of the members of the National Parliament from their province, we recommend that each Provincial Assembly should be allowed to choose only between co-opting all or none of the members of the National Pariiament from the province.

55. Otherwise, there is no reason to allow for people to be co-opted to Provincial Assemblies. Our leaders are quite capable of making wise decisions by themselves. They can consult whatever outside interests and experts they like. But, as the elected representatives of the people, they must accept responsibility for their own decisions. Members of Provincial Assemblies should therefore be able to discuss matters freely among themselves, unhindered by the interventions of outsiders. To provide for the co-option of other persons to membership of Provincial Assemblies would undermine the principle of representative government, which is their very basis.

(b) a provincial executive; and

C.P.C. Report Ch.10 p.7

63. Each Provincial Assembly will need a small executive body, which we recommend should be called the 'Provincial Council'. Subject to the overriding authority of the Provincial Assembly, the Provincial Council should be responsible for supervising the development and implementation of the provincial government's policies and programmes. It should control the activities of the provincial government's staff, and oversee their work between meetings of the Provincial Assembly.

64. The Committee has given careful consideration to the optimal size of the Provincial Council, and especially to the desirability of limiting its membership. We believe that it should be kept reasonably small in size. We recommend that it should, at most, comprise no more than one-third of the membership of the Provincial Assembly.

65. In recommending that a limit be placed on the maximum size of each Provincial Council, the Committee intends to facilitate decision-making by the political executive of each province. The limit should also help to keep expense to a moderate level, for members of Provincial Councils will need to be properly recompensed for what will be relatively onerous duties. Our proposed limit on the size of each Provincial Council should ensure that the provincial executive cannot dominate the assembly numerically.

(c) an office of head of the provincial executive.

C.P.C. Report Ch.10 p.7

66. There should be a person at the head of each provincial government who presides over all of its activities and acts as its representative in dealings with the national government and other provincial governments. We do not believe that a public servant can properly play such a role. The head of the provincial government must, we believe, be a political figure, chosen by the members of the Provincial Assembly from among their own number or elected directly by the people of the province.

67. We believe that the election of a political head of each provincial government is an integral feature of the whole system of provincial government recommended in this Chapter. The functions to be performed by the head of each provincial government will be essentially political. The office itself will symbolize the new order of decentralized political control we favour.

68. The head of the provincial government should be called the 'Premier' — the first person of the province. The Premier should be a member of both the Provincial Council and the Provincial Assembly.

69. The office of Premier should be provided for in the Constitution, as the Premiers will, we envisage, have a major role to play at the national level, particularly in resolving disputes between governments. But the manner in which each Premier is to be chosen and can be removed from office should be spelt out in the documents that establish each provincial government.

70. The Premier should, as a rule, be chosen by the members of Provincial Assembly from among their own number. That method of selection has received the greatest support in the submissions we have received. But, in one district in particular, strong support was expressed for the view that the Premier should be directly elected by the people of the province. We therefore recommend that provision should be made in the documents establishing a provincial government for direct election of the Premier if two-thirds of the members of the first directly elected Provincial Assembly in that province vote in favour of such a system. We leave it to individual Provincial Assemblies to determine for themselves how their Premiers should be removed from office.

(3) An Organic law shall provide for the minimum number of members for the provincial legislature and the maximum number of members that may be appointed as nominated members of the legislature.

(4) An Organic Law shall make provision for and in respect of —
  (a) grants, conditional or unconditional or both, by the National Government to provincial governments; and
  (b) the imposition and collection of taxation by provincial governments,

and may make other financial provision for provincial governments, to an extent reasonably adequate for the performance of their functions.

C.P.C. Report Ch.10 p.12

Finance

111. Unless they have adequate funds at their disposal, provincial governments will be ineffective. Without final control over certain sources of revenue, they will be powerless.

112. Both the national government and provincial governments should have the financial resources to carry out their respective responsibilities. The allocation of revenue to both levels of government should be appropriate to the distribution of powers and functions. We believe that the Constitution should vest final control over certain revenue-raising powers in provincial governments. Without that control provincial governments may be unable to undertake programmes of their own.

113. An overwhelming majority of the submissions made to us on 'Central-Regional-Local Government Relations' expressed support for the view that provincial governments should be able to raise money by collecting taxes and licence fees from the people in their provinces. The Committee is of the same opinion, and has consulted a number of experts as to how it might best be put into effect. We believe that our recommendations on the allocation of revenue between the national government and provincial governments provide a workable framework for the system of provincial government recommended in this Chapter.

114. Certain major taxes should remain under the control of the national government if our country's economy is to be efficiently managed and its vital interests are to be properly secured. They comprise both direct and indirect taxes. They are taxes which are most appropriately levied on a nation-wide basis, and taxes which may be collected most effectively by the national government. We recommend that the power to raise the following taxes should be vested by the Constitution in the national government:

- import and export duties;
- excise duties;
- taxes on corporate profits;
- taxes on personal income; and
- royalties on minerals, timber, fish, oil, natural gas, and private hydro-electric projects.

The power to raise all of these taxes should be exercised only in accordance with law, as we have recommended in Chapter 9, 'Financial Control'.

115. In addition to the major sources of revenue listed above, the national government should be responsible for the negotiation of foreign aid, foreign loans and medium – as well as long-term domestic loans. Papua New Guinea's economic relations with the outside world, and government indebtedness at all levels, should, in principle, remain under the ultimate control of the National Parliament.

116. The most important potential sources of government revenue in Papua New Guinea will therefore be under the control of the national government. Provincial governments will have to rely upon the national government for financial assistance if they are to carry out their responsibilities properly. This assistance may take a number of forms:

- conditional grants;
- unconditional grants;
- the unconditional allocation of shares of revenues raised by specified taxes; and
- the unconditional allocation of shares of a pool of revenues raised by the national government.

The national government may also secure loans on behalf of provincial governments.

117. The Committee believes that grants made by the national government to provincial governments should, in principle, have as few conditions attached to them as necessary. And, the conditions attached to grants should never be unreasonable.

Sources of revenue under the control of provincial governments

118. The Committee has already emphasized how important it is that provincial governments [p.13] should have revenue-raising powers of their own. The national government should provide provincial governments with adequate financial assistance for them to perform their lawful functions in a manner consistent with the National Goals and Directive Principles recommended in Chapter 2, but they should not be unduly dependent upon it. We recommend that authority to raise specified forms of taxation and to levy fees for certain kinds of licences should be vested in provincial governments by the Constitution.

119. The Committee has thought very carefully about the revenue-raising powers which might be placed under the final control of provincial governments. We believe that our recommendations provide a framework within which the spirit of self-reliance might be fostered in the provinces without contributing to the preservation or growth of inequalities between them. The implementation of our recommendations should also induce provincial governments to act in a financially responsible manner: under the proposed arrangements, they will make decisions concerning not only the expenditure of national governments funds — both grants and loans — but the use of their own revenue-raising powers.

120. We recommend that the Constitution should give provincial governments the authority to impose and to collect the following taxes:

- produce sales taxes and cesses; (sic).
- sales taxes on beverages, petrol and diesel fuel;
- entertainment taxes and
- land taxes.

121. All of these taxes can be readily and cheaply collected by provincial governments. A decision to impose any of them — and a decision to impose a land tax or a tax upon the sale of agricultural produce in particular — would raise issues of considerable political sensitivity. We believe that such issues can best be resolved through close consultation between the body responsible for the imposition of these taxes and the people directly affected. All of these taxes should be levied in such a way that local economic and agricultural conditions can be taken into account. For these reasons, we recommend that final control over these sources of potential revenue should be vested in provincial governments.

122. In recommending that the power to levy particular taxes should be vested in either the national or provincial governments, the Committee does not mean to imply that any or all of these taxes should necessarily be imposed. Our recommendations are intended to provide a framework within which individual governments may exercise their legal powers according to the needs, wishes, and financial resources of their people. In our opinion, it would be inadvisable for a provincial government to impose a tax upon land. Land taxes are unacceptable to our people. But, insofar as government at any level should have the power to levy a land tax, we believe that it should be provincial government.

123. In addition to the power to raise revenue through levying the taxes listed above, provincial governments should have the power to issue, and to levy fees for:

- mobile trading licences;
- liquor licences;
- motor vehicle and drivers' licences and registrations; and
- entertainment licences.

124. Provincial governments should have to difficulty in administering these licensing powers. The fees raised should provide a small, but useful, income for provincial governments. The power to issue these licences should enable provincial governments to regulate a number of important activities in their areas. Armed with these licensing powers, provincial governments will be able to see that their people are adequately served by mobile traders, hotels, transport facilities, and theatres, for example, and that local entrepreneurs and joint ventures are provided with opportunities to participate equitably in the economic life and development of the provinces.

125. The Committee also recommends that fines and fees levied in provincial courts (the present 'District Courts') should accrue to provincial governments. Court fees and fines should be imposed with due regard to local circumstances. The revenue they yield should be used so as to benefit the province in which each court sits.

126. The Committee has sought to secure the financial position of provincial governments by recommending that the power to raise the taxes and to levy the fees listed above should be [p.14] vested in provincial governments by the Constitution. But, we are only too well aware of the ways in which the central governments of other countries have used their powers of taxation so as to restrict effective access by lower levels of government to sources of revenue that are legally theirs. We are concerned lest a similar situation be allowed to develop in Papua New Guinea. We therefore recommend that the Constitution should state quite directly that the revenue-raising powers of the national government should not be employed so as to limit the effective use by provincial governments of theirs.

127. Co-operation between governments is also important if their various taxes and fees are to be equitably and efficiently levied. The national government may need help from provincial governments to ensure that its taxes are properly administered at the local level. Provincial governments may need help from the national government, or from one another, in collecting taxes and fees that they have imposed. We recommend that the Constitution should say quite explicitly that the national government and provincial governments should co-operate in the collection of lawfully levied taxes... [p.15]

135. Provincial governments will not be able to finance all of their activities from the revenue sources which we have recommended should be placed under their control. We have not sought to make them financially self-sufficient. Provincial governments will have to rely upon the national government for financial assistance.

136. The Committee believes that the national government should make grants rather than loans to provincial governments. It should attach as few conditions to its grants as necessary. The national government should not seek to dominate, nor to manipulate, provincial governments. It should make grants to provincial governments to enable them to develop and carry out plans of their own.

137. The recurrent expenditures of provincial governments should generally be met, we believe, from funds made available in the form of unconditional grants from the national government. These grants should be allocated according to the following criteria:

- need;
- derivation;
- compensation;
- equalization;
- national welfare;
- conservation, restoration and improvement of the human and physical environment; and
- stabilization of services.

138. Each provincial government should receive enough money to meet essential expenditures incurred in the performance of its lawful functions. Money for this purpose should be allocated to each province according to need. The needs of each province should be determined by the size of the population its government serves, and the relative costs involved in providing that population with essential services. These costs tend to vary with the geographical size of each province. It costs more per head to provide certain services to people in the Western District, for example, than to people in more densely settled areas. We therefore recommend that money granted to provincial governments on the basis of the needs criterion should be distributed according to the population and area of each province.

139. Provincial governments should receive grants from the national government, on the same basis as that specified in the preceding paragraph, to be used for minor capital projects. These are projects valued at no more than $50,000 each, which provincial governments should be able to undertake on their own authority.

140. Some parts of our country contribute more to government revenue than other parts. Proper regard should be paid to this fact when grants are made to the provinces. We recommend that money should be granted to provincial governments in accordance with the principle of derivation, that is, money should be returned to the various provinces in the same proportion as they have contributed to the national government's revenues. This principle should be invoked so as to take particular account of the royalties levied on natural resource projects, and of each province's contribution to revenue raised through the export of agricultural produce.

141. The national government's policies and activities may affect various parts of our country in different ways. Some provinces may have to bear a disproportionate share of the costs and burdens of national development. We believe that money should be allocated among the provinces to provide compensation for the differential impact of national government policies. Provinces which suffer certain disadvantages in contributing to the overall development of Papua New Guinea should receive compensation.

142. The Committee believes that all of our people should have equal access to government services. They should be able to share equally in the fruits of development. We believe that money should be redistributed among the provinces in order to assist provincial governments to make services as readily available to people in the less developed parts of the country as they are to the rest.

(5) An Organic Law shall make provision for the devolution and delegation to each provincial government of substantial powers of decision-making and substantial administrative powers in respect of matters of direct concern to the province.

(6) An Organic Law shall make provision in respect of the legislative powers of provincial governments.

(*See: Organic Law on Provincial Government* Ch.1; *Provincial Government (Transfer of Activities) Act* 1983)

C.P.C. Report Ch.10 p.8

78. The many hundreds of submissions we have received from all parts of the country have provided ample confirmation of the view expressed in our *First* and *Second Interim Reports* that there is a strong and widespread demand in Papua New Guinea that political power be decentralized. This has been made clear in the responses of discussion groups to a number of questions we asked them in order to ascertain where they felt primary responsibility for a range of governmental functions should lie. Their submissions indicate that they see an important role for provincial governments in relation to education, health, agriculture, public works, and other governmental activities. The thousands of people who addressed us at public meetings spoke to similar effect.

79. The Committee's deliberations on the distribution of powers and functions between the national government and provincial governments have been among the most difficult and time-consuming of all. But, the recommendations we make on this distribution are what give this entire Chapter meaning.

80. We cannot claim to have completed our work on this subject. We know what powers and functions our people want brought under the control of provincial government; and our own objectives are clear. But, even after our own lengthy and careful deliberations, and participation in a number of detailed discussions with government officers, we must nevertheless confess that the list of powers and functions which we believe should be vested in each level of government requires some refinement. That refinement will require considerable technical expertise.

81. However, the recommended distribution of powers and functions, which we have appended to this Chapter, should not be left to legal or other technical experts to refine on their own. The distribution of powers and functions between various levels of government is a matter [p.9] in which technical considerations often have a profound effect upon substance. That is why we have recommended that a special body comprising four members of this Committee should be appointed to work with expert consultants in preparing the legislation which gives effect to the recommendations in this Chapter. We must not allow the very substance of our recommendations to be dissolved in technical questions at the end of our work.

82. We have agreed very strongly for the decentralization of power to the provincial level. We must also do what we can to ensure that relations between provincial governments and local government bodies in their areas do not replicate those that have pertained between the national government and the districts under the colonial system we have inherited. Decentralization should not stop at the district or provincial level. The communities in which most of our people live, and the organizations through which they conduct their affairs, have an important role to play in our country's development.

83. If the system of provincial government we favour is to represent a real break from the recent past, then provincial governments will have to demonstrate genuine respect for the wishes and practices of the communities in their areas, as well as those of bodies exercising governmental functions at the local level.

84. We refer deliberately to 'bodies exercising governmental functions at the local level' rather than local government councils. Frustration with the existing system, and a desire for self-expression, has led a number of groups of people in various parts of the country to organize themselves independently of the official local government system. Many of them deserve the same respect and protection as local government councils. We recommend that provision should be made for their official recognition.

85. But, while we do not wish to undermine the autonomy and operations of effectively functioning local government bodies, we believe that responsibility for government at the local level should, in principle, be vested in the next highest level of government, that is, in provincial governments. The national government should not deal directly with local government bodies, except with the consent of the relevant provincial governments. Provincial government should assume responsibility for the organization and conduct of local government in their areas. The Constitution should protect the existing rights and powers actually exercised by local government bodies before the Constitution comes into force, but each Provincial Assembly should otherwise be ultimately responsible for government at the local level. In a small province, this may mean that existing local government bodies may combine with the provincial government.

86. Very few of our people have advocated the continuance of the present Area Authority system. They prefer to be governed by directly elected representatives at the district level. Many complaints have also been made, including some by members of Area Authorities, at the powerlessness of the present Area Authorities. That is why the distribution of powers and functions is of such great concern to us. The fate of the new system of decentralized political control recommended in this Chapter depends upon the powers and functions that are placed under the control of provincial governments. They must be substantial if our people are to have faith in the new system.

87. We have appended to this Chapter a proposed division of powers and functions between the national and provincial governments. It comprises three lists.

88. The 'A' list comprises those powers and functions over which the national government should, we believe, always retain final control. Responsibility for the conduct of our country's foregin relations and defence should be vested exclusively in the national government if the integrity of Papua New Guinea is to be safeguarded. The efficient and equitable development of the country requires that the national government retain the final power to make national policies concerning natural resources, health, education and public works, for example, although provision should still be made for provincial governments to participate meaningfully in policy-making on all of these subjects.

89. Responsibility for the National Executive Council and the National Parliament belongs, by definition, to the national government. Certain other institutions, for example, the National Cultural Centre and the National Library should also be national responsibilities, as their names would imply, but provincial governments should be encouraged to play a part in the establishment and operation of local branches. Certain aspects of financial policy, postal and telecommunications services, and the keeping of some records, are also properly national responsibilities. But, the complete 'A' list must be examined with care if the full ramifications of the proposed distribution of powers and functions are to be appreciated.

90. The need to safeguard the integrity of Papua New Guinea, to develop the country efficiently in the interests of its citizens, and to ensure that its international [p.10] responsibilities are fulfilled, have all played a part in determining which powers and functions of government we have recommended for inclusion in the 'A' list. So have the views of our people, and a proper sense of which services the national government ought itself to provide for the people of all provinces.

91. We believe that the national government should strive to the utmost to see that its responsibilities even in relation to powers and functions that appear in the 'A' list are exercised in close consultation with provincial and local authorities. The police, for example, should work in close accord with provincial governments, and the senior police officer in each province should be encouraged to consult regularly, and to co-ordinate his officers' activities, with the provincial government.

92. The 'C' list comprises those powers and functions which should be vested in provincial governments by the Constitution. This list represents the bare minimum of those powers and functions which we believe should be placed under the control of provincial governments if there is to be a real change from past practice. It is intended to provide a guarantee to all provincial governments that they will always have certain powers at their disposal, unless the Constitution is amended. The 'C' list is a gesture towards the future rather than the realization of our ultimate intentions.

93. The powers and functions in the 'C' list tend to concern matters that are mainly of provincial or local concern. Many of the powers and functions specified are the local aspects of national policies. They are the basis upon which the system of provincial government recommended in this Chapter should be founded, and from which it should grow.

94. The real key to the future of provincial government is the 'B' list. It comprises those powers and functions which may be transferred to provincial governments, either in part or in whole, by agreement between the governments concerned. The powers and functions on the 'B' list represent the grey area between the minimum guarantees provided by the 'C' list and the fulfilment of our hope for a decentralized system of government with as much power as possible devolved upon provincial authorities.

95. It is impossible to prepare a complete list of governmental powers and functions. As society changes, so do the activities in which governments become involved. We do not regard the lists of powers and functions appended to this Chapter as definitive. The 'A' list provides a minimum framework for development within a unitary state. The 'C' list guarantees a minimal autonomy to provincial governments. The 'B' list is as accurate an approximation of the outstanding powers and functions of government in Papua New Guinea as we have been able to secure. It should properly comprise all of the powers and functions of government other than those in the 'A' and 'C' lists. It is, in intention, a residual list, and we recommend that final responsibility for all of the powers and functions listed in it, and for all otherwise unspecified powers and functions of government, should be vested in the national government. That responsibility should be delegated to, or devolved upon, provincial governments to the maximum practicable extent.

(7) A question of the adequacy of provision made under Subsection (3), (4), (5) or (6) is non-justiciable.

(*See: Organic Law on Provincial Government* Ch.1.)

187D. — INCONSISTENCY AND JUSTICIABILITY OF PROVINCIAL LAWS

(1) Subject to any Constitutional Law, the application by its own force of an Act of the Parliament is not affected by a provincial law.

(2) Nothing in this Part authorizes the making of a provincial law, or authorizes any other action, that is inconsistent with —
(a) this Constitution (and in particular with Division 3 (*Basic Rights*)); or
(b) an Organic Law,
and all questions as to such consistency are justiciable.

(3) In order to avoid fruitless controversy and litigation, an Organic Law may provide that a question as to the effect of Subsection (1) is non-justiciable either absolutely or to the extent or in the cases prescribed by the Organic Law, except in proceedings between the National Government and a provincial government, or between governments.

(*See: Organic Law on Provincial Government* Ch.1)

187E. — SUSPENSION OF PROVINCIAL GOVERNMENTS.

(1) Where —
(a) there is wide-spread corruption in the administration of the province; or
(b) there has been gross mis-management of the financial affairs of the province; or
(c) there has been a break-down in the administration of the province; or
(d) there has been deliberate and persistent frustration of, or failure to comply with, lawful directions of the National Government; or
(e) the provincial government has deliberately and persistently disobeyed applicable laws, including the National Constitution, an Organic Law, the Provincial Constitution or any national legislation applicable to the province,
the National Executive Council may provisionally suspend the Provincial Government concerned, subject to confirmation by a simple majority vote of the Parliament.

(2) An Organic Law may make provision for and in respect of the procedures to be followed in the exercise of the powers under Subsection (1); and

(3) An Organic Law may make provision for further defining any matter referred to in Sub-Section (1)(a), (b), (c), (d) or (e).

(Subsections (1), (2) and (3) amended by Constitutional Amendment No. 7 — Suspension and Re-establishment of Provincial Governments)

(See: Organic Law on Provincial Government Amendment No 2 (Suspension and Re-establishment) Law)

(4) The National Executive Council may suspend a provincial government that cannot carry out its functions effectively because of a war or of a national emergency declared under Part X affecting the province or the whole of the country.

(5) While a provincial government is suspended, its powers and functions are vested in and shall be exercised by or on behalf of the National Executive Council, in accordance with an Organic Law.

(6) Where a provincial government is suspended —
(a) in the case of a suspension under Subsection (4), the Minister responsible for provincial affairs shall, as soon as practicable and in any event not later than the first meeting of the Parliament after the suspension, table in the Parliament a report on the suspension, the reasons for it and the circumstances of it; and
(b) at each meeting of the Parliament during the suspension the Minister responsible for provincial affairs shall report to the Parliament on the measures taken to re-establish the provincial government.

C.P.C. Report Ch.10 p.23

198. Throughout our deliberations on 'central — regional — local — government relations', the Committee has sought to secure the autonomy of provincial government without undermining the role of the national government as guardian of the overall national interest. This objective has not been easy to obtain and we are aware that situations might arise in which it may become impossible. We believe that the Constitution should make specific provision for such situations. It should define when and how provincial governments might be suspended by the national government.

199. The Committee believes that provincial governments should be suspended only in the most serious of circumstances, and even then as a last resort. The suspension of a provincial government would represent at least a temporary breakdown in the system of government recommended in this Chapter. Care should be taken to see that it also provides an opportunity for a fresh start to be made in any province in which the provincial government has been suspended.

200. The Committee recommends that the National Executive Council should have the power to suspend a provincial government when —

- there is widespread corruption among elected officials or government employees;
- gross financial mismanagement has occurred;
- there has been a breakdown of administration in a province;
- there has been deliberate and prolonged frustration of lawfully made national government directives;
- the provincial government has persistently exceeded its lawful powers;
- a State of Emergency has been declared in accordance with the Constitution; or
- a majority of the members of a Provincial Assembly voted that the government which they control should be suspended.

201. The national government should take over all of the responsibilities of a suspended provincial government with the aim of restoring it as soon as possible. The Minister responsible for provincial government affairs should make a full report to the National Parliament at its next meeting on the circumstances which prompted the suspension of a provincial government. Fresh elections should be called within six months of the suspension of a provincial government, and should be held within the following three months.

202. The National Parliament should have the power to extend the period for which a provincial government is suspended by six months at a time, provided that an absolute majority of members support a motion to that effect. If the period of suspension is extended, the Minister responsible for provincial government affairs should make a full report to each successive meeting of the National Parliament on the state of affairs in the province until such time as he is able to report that the provincial government concerned has been re-established.

203. The Committee believes that provincial governments should be suspended in only the most [p.24] serious of circumstances. But, the national government should exercise its power before the orderly development and constitutional government of the country as a whole are imperilled.

204. The national government should do all that it can to prevent circumstances requiring the suspension of a government from arising. Every effort should be made to restore a province in which the government has been suspended to normal as soon as possible.

187F. — RE-ESTABLISHMENT OF PROVINCIAL GOVERNMENT.

(1) Subject to Subsections (2) and (3), if a provincial government is suspended arrangements shall be made to re-establish it and to hold fresh elections and make fresh appointments (if necessary) to the provincial legislature within nine months from the effective date of the provisional suspension under Section 187E(1) (*suspension of a provincial government*) or of the definitive suspension under Section 187E(4).

(*Subsection (1) amended by Constitutional Amendment No.7 — Suspension and Re-establishment of Provincial Governments*)

(2) Subject to Subsections (3) and (4), where —

(a) a provincial government is suspended under Section 187E(4) (*suspension of provincial governments*) as a result of a declaration of a national emergency under Section 228 (*declaration of national emergency*); and

(b) the declaration is extended under Section 239(3) (*parliamentary control*),

the period of nine months referred to in Subsection (1) runs from the end of the meeting (or if there are more such extensions than one the last meeting) of the Parliament at which the declaration is so extended.

(3) A period of nine months referred to in the preceding provisions of this section may be extended by periods, each not exceeding six months, by the Parliament by an absolute majority vote.

(4) Subject to Subsection (3), where a provincial government is suspended under Section 187E(4) (*suspension of provincial governments*) the period of suspension, unless earlier terminated, ends at the end of nine months after the end of the war or national emergency concerned.

C.P.C. Report Ch.10 p.42

63. (4) Subject to the Constitution, the Minister responsible for provincial government affairs shall announce (by notice in the Government Gazette) the date on which new elections to the Provincial Assembly (including the office of Premier) shall be held, not later than six months after the provincial government was suspended, and those elections shall be held not later than nine months after the provincial government was suspended.

(5) The period of time for which a provincial government is suspended may be successively extended for up to six months at a time if the individually [p.43] recorded votes of an absolute majority of the members of the National Parliament support a motion to that effect.

(6) If the period of time for which a provisional government has been suspended is extended in accordance with Clause (5) above, the Minister responsible for provincial government affairs shall report to each successive meeting of the National Parliament on the state of affairs in the province until such time as the date of new provincial elections has been announced in accordance with Clause (4) above.

187G. — GRADATIONS OF PROVINCIAL GOVERNMENTS.

Nothing in any law is inconsistent with this Part so far as it provides for the full status, powers or functions of provincial government to be acquired by a provincial government in stages, or provides for a gradation of provincial governments.

C.P.C. Report Ch.10 p.4

Establishment in stages

37. We have already emphasized how important it is that the framework of the system of provincial government we propose should be established in the Constitution. We have also indicated that we believe that the system we favour cannot be set up at a single stroke. We therefore recommend that provision be made for provincial governments to be established in stages, and that the procedures through which they are first set up and then developed should be specified in the Constitution.

38. We envisage that provincial governments may be developed in three stages. But most of our recommendations are concerned with the third and last stage. It alone meets the real needs for our people.

39. We believe that Stage Three provincial governments should be established in all provinces as soon as possible. But, while arrangements are being made for the universal implementation of Stage Three, Stage One and Stage Two provincial governments should be set up — even before the Constitution comes into force.

40. In recommending that provision be made for provincial government to be established in stages, the Committee is in no way implying that the various stages should be seen as long term alternatives to one another. The submissions we have received show quite clearly [p.5] that our people envisage no alternative to what we have described as Stage Three provincial governments. We do not recommend that there should be any long term alternative to Stage Three. And, we warn against those who might seek to undermine our proposals by arguing — falsely — that the three stages we provide for can be seen as alternative answers to our people's needs.

41. Our recommendation that provision be made for the phased establishment of provincial governments must not be used as a blind for delay. It does not signify a willingness to wait, but an urgent commitment that a start be made at once to recognise our country's system of government in accordance with our people's wishes.

42. We recognize that the implementation of our proposals may encounter administrative problems. That is why we have provided for a phased approach, which builds, where appropriate, upon existing Area Authorities. But, to ensure that the system of provincial governments we propose is established with a due sense of urgency, we recommend that the initiative for change should be constitutionally vested in provincial leaders. And, to make plain our intention that Stage Three provincial governments should be established throughout the country as soon as possible, we recommend that those provisions in the Constitution which deal with Stage One and Stage Two provincial governments should be transitional provisions.

187H. — INTER-GOVERNMENTAL RELATIONS.

(1) An Organic Law shall make provision for and in respect of a National Fiscal Commission, to advise, and to make recommendations to, the National Executive Council and the Parliament on the allocation of unconditional grants by the National Government to provincial governments, and as between provincial governments, and as to other fiscal matters relating to provincial government.

(*See: Organic Law on Provincial Government* Ch.1)

C.P.C. Report Ch.10 p.17

150. It is inevitable that provincial governments will have to rely upon the national government for financial assistance. Unconditional grants for recurrent expenditures and minor capital projects will be the lifeblood of the system of provincial government recommended in this Chapter. We therefore recommend that the Constitution should set out the criteria according to which such grants should be made. We also recommend that the courts should have no jurisdiction over disputes concerning their application. They should be non-justiciable.

151. In Chapter 9, 'Financial Control', we recommended that, except as otherwise provided in the Constitution, ultimate authority over both the raising and expenditure of all public monies should be vested in the National Parliament. We also recommended that the National Parliament should not be able to exercise this authority unless a measure has first been recommended by the National Executive Council. We do not believe that the allocation of grants to provincial governments should be exempted from either rule. We are, however, also of the opinion that the national government's control over the allocation of unconditional grants to provincial governments should be tempered. Provision should be made for views other than those of national politicians to be considered when proposed allocations are discussed by the National Executive Council and the National Parliament.

152. The Committee has looked carefully at the possibility that grants might be allocated by negotiation between the national government and provincial governments. We think that the views of provincial governments should be taken into account when proposed allocations are prepared for consideration by the National Parliament. But, experience in other countries leads us to believe that such a system would not be appropriate to Papua New Guinea, in that negotiations on such a vital issue as government finance tend to generate tensions, rivalries, and controversies between governments. Our recommendations are designed to facilitate co-operation between governments.

153. After careful consideration of the available options, the Committee has come to the conclusion that the Constitution should provide for the establishment of a body which should be known as the 'National Fiscal Commission'. The National Fiscal Commission should make recommendations every four years on the allocation of unconditional grants by the national government to provincial governments during the next four years. Its recommendations should be tabled in the National Parliament.

154. The National Fiscal Commission should comprise three members who should be appointed (or reappointed) for terms of four years by the National Executive Council following consultation with the Permanent Parliamentary Committee concerned with provincial government affairs. Two of the Commission's members should be persons with professional qualifications and experience in accountancy, economics, or law. A third member should be professionally qualified in one of the social sciences. These recommendations are designed to ensure that the members of the National Fiscal Commission are neither too strongly oriented towards the executive arm of the national government, nor antipathetic towards its objectives; and that they will take social as well as economic considerations into account in framing their recommendations. The National Fiscal Commission should be exempted from the provision in Chapter 14, 'General', that the majority of the members of all collective bodies established in the Constitution should be citizens. The people chosen to become members of this Commission should be the best available from anywhere in the world. Other countries have found it useful to appoint neutral outsiders to similar bodies.

155. The Committee believes that the National Fiscal Commission's reports to the National Parliament are likely to play an important role in moderating inter-governmental conflicts over finance. They should provide a considered view of the demands made by individual provincial governments, and a counter to excessive centralism in the National Executive Council. They should enable the National Parliament to consider proposed allocations of unconditional grants to provincial governments on their merits. And, they will allow both the national government and provincial governments to plan ahead.

(2) An Organic Law shall make provisions for and in respect of a council consisting of —
- (a) the Prime Minister, or a Minister nominated by him; and
- (b) each head of a provincial executive, or a member of the provincial executive nominated by him; and
- (c) representatives, appointed in accordance with the Organic Law, or provinces that do not have provincial government (including provinces whose provincial governments are suspended); and
- (d) the Minister responsible for provincial affairs; and
- (e) the Minister responsible for financial matters.

(3) The Chairman of the Council referred to in Subsection (2) shall be —
- (a) the Prime Minister; or
- (b) in the absence or unavailability to act of the Prime Minister — the Minister responsible for provincial affairs; or
- (c) in the absence or unavailability to act of both the Prime Minister and the Minister responsible for provincial affairs — a member of the Council appointed by the Prime Minister for the purpose.

(4) The Council referred to in Subsection (2) shall meet at least once in every period of 12 months to discuss, amongst other matters of mutual concern, fiscal and administrative arrangements between governments.

C.P.C. Report Ch.10 p.21

182. Throughout this Chapter, the Committee has placed considerable stress upon the need for the national government and provincial governments to consult and co-operate with one another. We have sought, in our recommendations to provide a framework for governmental inter-dependence; one which secures the autonomy of provincial governments without undermining the unity of our nation. The same themes and objectives have guided our attempts to devise means through which the policies of the national government and provincial governments can be co-ordinated by their political leaders.

183. We have already suggested that one of the main tasks of each Provincial Premier should be to represent the government of his province in its dealings with the national government and other provincial governments. We intend that he should do so in more than a formal sense. We recommend that each Provincial Premier should have the right to attend meetings of the National Executive Council at which important matters directly affecting his province are discussed. The minister responsible for provincial government affairs — who should be generally responsible for facilitating communications between governments — should advise a premier in advance when such matters are to be discussed by the National Executive Council.

184. The Committee believes that there is a need for a forum in which the Prime Minister and the Provincial Premiers (or their respective representatives) can meet periodically to discuss matters of common concern. We recommend that the Constitution should make explicit provision for such a body and that it should meet at least once a year. We recommend that it be called the 'Premiers' Council'.

185. The Committee envisages that discussions in the Premiers' Council will be both wide ranging and informal. We anticipate that the Council will develop into a major forum for review by the leaders of the participating governments of the entire system of provincial government recommended in this Chapter. It will provide opportunities for the exchange of ideas between governments, and in particular for bringing the needs, hopes and grievances of provincial governments to the attention of national politicians. We recommend that the Premiers' Council should have the power to make direct reports (including recommendations for alteration of the provincial government system) to the National Executive Council and the National Parliament. It should also play a role in the resolution of inter-governmental disputes.

186. The Prime Minister should have the power to call meetings of the Premiers' Council, provided that at least three weeks notice (or such other notice as may be required by law) is given. He should be required to do so within a month of receiving a written request for a meeting bearing the signatures of at least three provincial premiers.

(5) A major function of the Council established under Subsection (2) shall be avoid legal proceedings between governments by providing a forum for the non-judicial settlements of inter-governmental disputes.

(6) An Organic Law made for the purposes of Subsection (2) may vest in the Council established under that subsection mediatory or arbitral powers or functions in relation to inter-governmental disputes.

(*See: Organic Law on Provincial Government* Ch.1; *Provincial Government (Mediation and Arbitration Act* 1981)

C.P.C. Report Ch.10 p.22

194. Despite the emphasis that we have placed upon the need for co-operation and consultation between governments, and the ways in which we have sought to facilitate joint policy making and action, the Committee recognizes that inter-governmental disputes will almost inevitably arise. Provincial governments may disagree or decline to co-operate with one another, or with the national government.

195. If a matter over which two or more governments differ cannot be resolved by negotiation, then it should be referred for mediation by an independent body comprising one or more persons who are acceptable to the parties of the dispute. If the disputants cannot agree upon the composition of such a body, or if the mediating body fails to find a solution, then they should be free to refer the dispute to the Premiers' Council. The Premiers' Council should determine whether to try to resolve the dispute itself, or to appoint a body to mediate on its behalf. We have already recommended that the Prime Minister should have the power to call meetings of the Premiers' Council. We have also proposed that he be required to do so upon receipt of a written request signed by at least three provincial premiers. We believe that these recommendations should ensure that the Premiers' Council will meet within a reasonable time to discuss serious disputes. In the case of a dispute which involves only two provinces, the Prime Minister or another premier would have to be convinced that the dispute was important enough to warrant a special meeting of the Premiers' Council. Provincial governments should be encouraged to resolve their own differences. [p.23].

196. The Committee believes that disputes between governments can best be resolved by political means. We believe that court action tends to produce unnecessarily rigid and legalistic solution to what are often essentially political disputes. Unlike the parties to inter-governmental disputes, the courts are not directly answerable to the people. It is for these reasons that we have recommended that some of the most important constitutional provisions concerning the operation of the provincial government system should not be justiciable. It is also why we believe that the national government and provincial governments should have recourse to the courts only after the procedures outlined above have been employed and only if the dispute concerns a matter of law. The Supreme Court should hear inter-governmental disputes that concern matters of law.

197. The foregoing recommendations should not apply in respect of disputes other than inter-governmental disputes. Individuals or groups who seek to take action or to protect themselves against the National Government or a provincial government should take direct action through the courts, the Ombudsman Commission, their elected representatives, or such other means as are provided, as may be appropriate in each case. The courts should guard against governments that might seek to circumvent the recommended procedures for resolving inter-governmental disputes by acting through individual persons or groups.

AS TO JUSTICIABILITY OF INTER-GOVERNMENTAL DISPUTES

Comment

Pursuant to Constitution s.187H(5) and (6) the Parliament enacted the *Organic Law on Provincial Government*. Section 84 thereof provides:

The Premier's Council shall meet at least once in each year to discuss . . . any other matters concerning inter-provincial and inter-governmental problems, with a view, in particular, to avoiding legal proceedings between governments by providing a forum for the non-judicial settlement of inter-governmental disputes.

In *Milne Bay Provincial Government v Roy Evara and anor* [1981] PNGLR 631, Andrew J. held (at p.66):

> The Constitution and the Organic Laws are the supreme laws of Papua New Guinea (Constitution s.11). By Sch.1.7 of the Constitution where a constitutional law declares a question non-justiciable, the question may not be heard or determined by any court or tribunal. In my view the purport and intent of the Constitution and the *Organic Law on Provincial Government* is to declare [an inter-government] dispute such as has arisen here, to be non-justiciable.

However, in a passage seemingly directly inconsistent with the above (also at p.66) Andrew J. further held that if conciliation and arbitration under the *Provincial Governments (Mediation and Arbitration Procedures) Act* 1981 should ultimately fail, a party to such a dispute would have recourse to the National Court under the provisions of s.155(5) of the Constitution.

It is submitted that Andrew J. in concluding that the Constitution requires all intergovernmental disputes to be heard by mediation and arbitration distorts the language of both s.187H of the Constitution and s.84 of the *Organic Law on Provincial Government.* There is nothing in either provision, it is submitted, which expressly or by implication adopts the C.P.C.'s recommendation set out in paragraph 196 above. This view, however, does not conclude the issue as to whether inter-governmental disputes are or are not justiciable. If Andrew J. is wrong as suggested, that question would turn on the validity of the *Provincial Government (Mediation and Arbitration Procedures) Act* 1981 which expressly purports to exclude the jurisdiction of the Courts in all such disputes. It is submitted that that law is valid pursuant to s.159(1) of the Constitution. However, such an exclusion could not operate to exclude the National Court's 'review jurisdiction' under s.155(3) and s.155(5) [see annotations under those sections]. Note also that the terms of s.4 of the *Provincial Government (Mediation and Arbitration Procedures) Act* were amended in 1983 to allow the National Court to hear a dispute where it concerns a matter of law or where the dispute has not been resolved to the satisfaction of a party after the exhaustion of the procedures set out under the Act.

(7) Other provision may be made by statute or administrative act for consultation between the National Government (including any Permanent Parliamentary Committee with special responsibility for provincial affairs) and all or any provincial governments, and between provincial governments.

187I. — LOCAL AND VILLAGE GOVERNMENTS

(1) Until a provincial law of a province makes provision for government at the local level, the *Local Government Act* 1963, as in force from time to time, continues to apply in respect of such government in the province.

(2) An Organic Law may make provision for the respective powers of the National Government and of provincial governments concerning local level government.

(3) Upon the establishment of provincial government for a province, any Local Government Area Authority having jurisdiction over all or part of the area of the province is abolished in relation to the area of the province.

(4) Notwithstanding anything in any other law, a Local Government Council or a Local Government Special Purposes Authority in a

province that has provincial government may be suspended or abolished only with the consent of the National Executive or the Parliament, and of the provincial executive or the provincial legislature.

(5) For the purposes of this section, the Gazelle Peninsula Trust established by the *Gazelle Peninsula Affairs (Temporary Provisions) Act* 1973, as in force from time to time, shall be deemed to be a Local Government Council.

(*See: Organic Law on Provincial Government* Ch.1; *Local Government Act* Ch.57; *Local Government Service Act* Ch.58)

C.P.C. Report Ch.10 p.24

210. The Committee has already recommended that the Constitution should vest responsibility for government at the local level in provincial governments. But, the rights and powers of existing local government bodies should receive some protection. We recommend that the Constitution should provide that local government bodies should retain control over those powers and functions which they had actually exercised power (sic) at the establishment of provincial government. They should also be allowed to continue to draw revenue from those sources from which they had actually derived it, except that the national government should cease to make direct grants of money to local government bodies. The national government should make grants to provincial governments in accordance with our recommendations. Provincial governments should provide such financial assistance that may be appropriate to local government bodies. [p.25]

211. The Committee is very conscious of the wide gap that has hitherto existed between the powers and functions vested in law in local government councils, and those that they were actually able to exercise. That is why we have recommended that local government bodies should retain control over only those powers and functions which really were theirs. All other powers and functions of government at the local level should be placed under the control of provincial governments.

212. The Committee believes that provision should be made for local government bodies to transfer their powers, functions and sources of revenue to provincial governments by negotiation. Provincial governments should have the power to take over any or all of the powers and functions of local government bodies on their own authority, provided that two-thirds of the members of the Provincial Assembly in the province concerned agree to a motion to that effect. A three-quarters majority should be required for a Provincial Assembly to abolish a pre-existing local government body.

213. The preceding recommendations are designed to smooth the introduction of a new tier of representative government between the national government and local government bodies. They are intended to provide protection for existing local government bodies, and to facilitate their integration into the provincial government system. We believe that the national government has certain obligations towards existing local government bodies. We have tried to ensure that they will be met. But, in principle, we believe that local governments should be organized to meet local needs. That is why we recommend that responsibility for government at the local level should henceforth be vested in provincial governments.

214. Provincial governments should provide for the establishment, re-establishment and organization of local government in their areas. They should determine the powers, functions, staff and financial resources that should be placed under the control of local government bodies.

215. The Committee believes that local government has a most important role to play in the overall government and development of our country. Provincial governments should be encouraged to respect and decentralise power upon local government bodies. We recommend that control over local government should itself be decentralized. That is why our Report does not deal with detail with the organization, powers and conduct of government at the local level.

187J. — REPORTS ON PROVINCIAL AND LOCAL LEVEL GOVERNMENTS.

The Minister responsible for provincial affairs shall, at least once in each period of 12 months, at such times as are fixed —

(a) by or under an Act of the Parliament; or

(b) subject to any such Act, by the Head of State acting with, and in accordance with, the advice of the National Executive Council,

present to the Head of State, for presentation to the Parliament, a report on the working of the systems of provincial government and government at the local level.

(*See: Organic Law on Provincial Government* Ch.1; *Local Government Act* Ch.57)

PART VII. — THE STATE SERVICES

Division 1. — Introductory

188. — ESTABLISHMENT OF THE STATE SERVICES.

(1) The following State Service are hereby established:-
- (a) the National Public Service; and
- (b) the Police Force; and
- (c) the Papua New Guinea Defence Force; and
- (d) the Parliamentary Service.

(2) Acts of the Parliament may make provision for or in respect of other State Services.

GENERALLY

Referred to

by Prentice C.J. in *Constitutional Reference No 1 of 1978 (s. 19)* [1978] PNGLR 345 at p.348; see also Wilson J. at pp.355, 360 and Pritchard J. (dissenting at p.381);

by Kapi J. in *S.C.R. No 1 of 1982; Re Bouraga* [1982] PNGLR 78 at p.191.

189. — CIVILIAN CONTROL.

All of the State Services other than the Defence Force shall be civilian services, and all of the State Services shall be subject at all times to ultimate civilian control.

C.P.C. Report: See under s.196(1) and s.201(2)

Division 2. — The Public Services Commission

190. — ESTABLISHMENT OF THE COMMISSION.

(1) A Public Services Commission is hereby established.

(2) The Commission shall consist of not less than four members, who shall be appointed by the Head of State, acting with, and in accordance with, the advice of the National Executive Council given after consultation with any appropriate Permanent Parliamentary Committee.

(3) All of the members of the Commission must be citizens.

(4) Subject to this Constitution, an Organic Law shall make provision for and in respect of the appointment and the terms and conditions of employment of the members of the Commission, and for and in respect of its constitution, powers and procedures.

(*See: Organic Law on the Public Services Commission* Ch.1)

C.P.C. Report Ch.12 p.1

1. In the government of any country, a vital role is performed by the various public services — that is, those people who work for government departments, statutory authorities and, where they exist, provincial or state governments. It is on these people that governments rely for much of their professional and technical advice, and it is they who are responsible for implementing government policies. Their role is particularly important in new nations where governments are usually more actively and directly involved in the development process. It follows that the arrangements made for the overall control and supervision of the public services are fundamental to the success of any government in carrying out its improvement programme and in the provision of services for the people.

2. In considering this question, we have been guided by three basic principles:
(1) the need to ensure that any government of the day has a permanent body of officers who will serve it loyally and impartially, and who have been appointed to their positions on the basis of merit;
(2) the need for the government to have control over the management of the public services so as to ensure that they do the job they are required to do with maximum efficiency and economy; and
(3) as an important aspect of both (1) and (2) — the need for co-ordination of the various government departments and statutory authorities in respect of both personnel matters and government policies on conditions of service and establishments.

3. In order that the first two principles may be fully implemented, we propose that two separate bodies be established:
- a Public Services Commission, responsible for personnel matters, and
- a Department responsible for management matters in the public services. [p.2].....

Public Services Commission

8. In order to have career officers who will provide the government of the day with loyal and impartial service, we believe that the Public Services Commission, as the body to determine matters which vitally affect those officers as individuals, should be independent. We have also found that opinion in all parts of the country strongly supports an independent body of this kind so that, for example, merit should be the major criterion for decisions on appointments and promotions, rather than personal friendships and ethnic or political affiliations.

Composition and appointment

9. We propose that the Public Services Commission should comprise four members who, together, would be broadly representative of the various areas of the country. They should be appointed by the National Executive Council, but only after the posts have been advertised and the First Parliamentary Committee has been consulted on the candidates available for appointment. As in the case of other positions, the requirement for consultation is intended to help bring about some consensus on important appointments and to avoid their becoming the subject of contentious political debate. To help ensure that the Commission enjoys widespread confidence and does not become dominated by one man, we recommend also that the position of chairman be rotated annually among its members.

10. The tenure of members of the Commission should be the same as that of other constitutional office-holders, that is six years, but with an initial term of three years during a ten-year period from the date when the Constitution comes into force. Members would be eligible for reappointment comes into force. Members would be eligible for reappointment for six-year terms but, if not reappointed, they would be entitled to a position at a salary and on conditions not less favourable than those which they enjoyed at the time their term of office expired.

191. — FUNCTIONS OF THE COMMISSION.

(1) Subject to this Constitution, the Public Services Commission shall be responsible, in accordance with an Act of the Parliament, for —
(a) the efficient management and control of the National Public Service; and
(b) all personnel matters connected with the National Public Service; and
(c) such other matters in relation to the other State Services, the provincial services and the services of other governmental bodies as are prescribed by Constitutional Laws or Acts of the Parliament. (*Amended by Constitutional Amendment No. 3. — Provincial Government (Consequential Amendments), s.5*).

(*See: Public Service Act* Ch.67)

(2) It is a special function of the Commission to keep under continuous review the State Services (other than the Defence Force), the provincial services and the services of other governmental bodies, and to advise, either on its own initiative or on request, the National Executive and any authority responsible for any of those services on organizational matters and the co-ordination of effort, and in particular on conditions of employment, with a special view to avoiding wasteful duplication of effort and competition. (*Amended by Constitutional Amendment No. 3. — Provincial Government (Consequential Amendments), s.5*).

(3) Nothing in Subsection (2) gives the Commission any power of direction or control.

C.P.C. Report Ch.12 p.1

5. By ***management matters***, we mean matters about ***groups*** of public servants, or about the public service ***as a whole***. Thus, the Department responsible for management matters would have the responsibility for such things as —

- size and organisation of government departments, including classification of positions (that is 'establishments');
- efficiency and economy of departments;
- conditions of service — that is, salary scales, rules about leave and allowances, etc;
- recruitment, training and localisation of staff. .... [p.3]

16. For many years to come Papua New Guinea is likely to be short of skilled manpower. In view of this, we recommend reducing the barriers between those employed in government departments and most statutory authorities so that for the purposes of appointments, promotions, transfers, dismissals and disciplinary control, all these officers would constitute a single national service under the Public Services Commission. We

recommend further that this 'umbrella' arrangement should include those public servants working for provincial governments. While both statutory authorities and provincial governments would retain their separate autonomy in matters of policy, the arrangement is intended to allow greater flexibility in the allocation of staff from an overall national viewpoint.

AS TO JURISDICTION OF THE NATIONAL PUBLIC SERVICES COMMISSION OVER THE COMMISSIONER OF POLICE

Held

In the absence of any statutory provision pursuant to s.191(1) (c) the Public Services Commission has no responsibility for the management of State Services other than the National Public Service. The Public Services Commission accordingly has no power or authority to lay disciplinary charges against the Commissioner of Police.
S.C.R. No 1 of 1982; Re Bouraga [1982] PNGLR 178, (see in particular Kidu CJ at p.183, Kapi J. at pp.194,195, Pratt J. at pp.200,201).

AS TO JURISDICTION OVER 0FFICERS APPOINTED UNDER SECTION 193 OF THE CONSTITUTION

Held

The responsibility of the Public Services Commission for personnel matters connected with the National Public Service (which, by s.194, includes decisions in relation to appointment, promotion, demotion, suspension, discipline, removal etc.) does not apply (Kidu C.J.) or at least does not apply in respect of discipline and dismissal (Kapi and Pratt JJ.) to those officers appointed pursuant to s.193. Such officers appointed under the Constitution may only be removed or disciplined in the manner prescribed by Sch.1.10(4). Any Act or provision inconsistent with Sch. 1.10 (4) (ie providing for discipline and dismissal by the Commission) is, to the extent of the inconsistency, invalid.
S.C.R. No 1 of 1982; Re Bouraga [1982] PNGLR 178 (see in particular Kidu C.J. at p.184, Kapi J. at pp. 194,195, Pratt J. at pp.209-212).

192. — INDEPENDENCE OF THE COMMISSION.

The Public Services Commission is responsible to the National Executive Council, but, subject to Section 193 (*appointments to certain offices*), in personnel matters —

(a) it shall comply with any general directions as to policy from the Head of State, acting with, and in accordance with, the advice of the National Executive Council; and
(b) it is otherwise not subject to direction or control by any person or authority.

C.P.C. Report Ch.12 p.2

11. We propose that there should be two main limitations on the independence of the Commission. First, it should be subject to general policy directives of the National Executive Council, but any directives of this kind must be tabled in the National Parliament. An example of a general policy directive would be an instruction to ensure that the senior positions in any department are not dominated by officers who come from one particular area of the country.

Senior appointments in public services

12. We support the widely accepted principle that the government must have confidence in those who have the major responsibility for tendering it advice and carrying out its policies.

13. Secondly, therefore, although the Commission would be consulted on the respective merits of the candidates, it should be the National Executive Council that selects persons to be appointed Heads of Departments and also those to be appointed to a number of other senior posts which involve special statutory responsibilities. For some of these appointments the appropriate Parliamentary Committee should be consulted also. We propose, in addition, that all these positions be advertised so that people both within and outside the public services may apply.

GENERALLY

Referred to

by Pritchard J. (dissenting) in *Constitutional Reference No 1 of 1978 (s.19)* [1978] PNGLR 345 at p.382 (Commission subject to investigation by Ombudsman).

193. — APPOINTMENTS TO CERTAIN OFFICES.

(1) This section applies to and in respect of the following offices and positions:-

(a) all offices in the National Public Service the occupants of which are directly responsible to the National Executive Council or to a Minister; and

(b) the offices of the members of the Boundaries Commission; and

(c) the office the occupant of which is responsible for the administration of the Government broadcasting service, or, if that responsibility rests with a board or commission, the chairman or president of the board or commission; and

(d) the offices of the persons (including members of boards or commissions) responsible for the administration of any of the State Services; and

(e) the office of Commissioner of Police; and

(f) the office of Commander of the Defence Force; and

(g) the office of Secretary to the National Executive Council; and

(h) such other offices and positions as are prescribed by an Act of the Parliament for the purpose,

other than the offices of the members of the Public Services Commission.

(2) All appointments (whether temporary or substantive) to offices to which Subsection (1)(b), (c), (e) and (h) apply shall be made by the Head of State, acting with, and in accordance with, the advice of the National Executive Council given after consultation with the Public Services Commission and any appropriate Permanent Parliamentary Committee, and a report concerning each of them shall be given to the Parliament by the responsible Minister as soon as possible after it has been made.

(3) All appointments (whether temporary or substantive) to which Subsection (1)(a), (d), (f) and (g) apply and such other offices and positions as are prescribed by an Act of the Parliament for the purpose of this subsection, shall be made by the Head of State, acting with, and in accordance with, the advice of the National Executive Council given after consultation with the Public Services Commission.

(4) An Act of the Parliament may make provision for and in respect of a temporary appointment to an office to which this section applies until such time as it is practicable to make an appropriate substantive appointment in accordance with Subsection (2).

(*See: Public Service Act* Ch.67)

C.P.C. Report Ch.12 p.2

12. We support the widely accepted principle that the government must have confidence in those who have the major responsibility for tendering it advice and carrying out its policies.

13. Secondly, therefore, although the Commission would be consulted on the respective merits of the candidates, it should be the National Executive Council that selects persons to be appointed Heads of Departments and also those to be appointed to a number of other senior posts which involve special statutory responsibilities. For some of these appointments the appropriate Parliamentary Committee should be consulted also. We propose, in addition, that all these positions be advertised so that people both within and outside the public services may apply.

AS TO TEMPORARY APPOINTMENTS

Held

A person appointed pursuant to s.193(3) to fill a vacancy in the office of Secretary, Department of Works and Supply, for a period of six months is a Head of Department within the meaning of s.26(1) of the Constitution (Leadership Code).
Constitutional Reference No.1 of 1978 (s.18) [1878] PNGLR 460.

AS TO DISCIPLINE AND DISMISSAL OF SECTION 193 APPOINTEES

Held

Officers appointed under s.193 may be removed or disciplined only in the manner prescribed by Sch. 1.10(4) which must be read as one with s.193. Such officers are not subject to the Public Services Commission's general power to discipline public servants conferred by s.191 of the Constitution.
S.C.R. No 1 of 1982; Re Bouraga [1982] PNGLR 178 (See Kidu C.J. at p.184, Kapi J. at pp.194,195, Pratt J. at pp.209-212).

AS TO RESIGNATION OF A SECTION 193 APPOINTEE

per Board of Enquiry

We are not persuaded that because the appointment of the Secretary for Police is made by the Head of State acting with, and in accordance with, the advice of the National Executive Council after consultation with the Public Service Commission that resignation must follow the same course. In our view the essential requirement is reasonable notice to the employing authority, namely the Public Service Commission.
In the matter of a Board of Inquiry appointed under the provisions of Section 83(2) of the Public Service (Interim Arrangements) Act 1973 (1982 Unreported) N367 at p.6 (quaere whether this decision is implicitly overruled by *S.C.R. No 1 of 1982; Re Bouraga*, see above).

194. — "PERSONNEL MATTERS".

In this Division, "personnel matters" means decisions and other service matters concerning an individual whether in relation to his appointment, promotion, demotion, transfer, suspension disciplining or cessation or termination of employment (except cessation or termination at the end of his normal period of employment as determined in accordance with law), or otherwise.

GENERALLY

Referred to

by Pritchard J. (dissenting) in *Constitutional Reference No 1 of 1978 (s.19)* [1978] PNGLR 345 at p.382:

by Kidu C.J. in *S.C.R. No 1 of 1982; Re Bouraga* [1982] PNGLR 178, at p.184, see also Pratt J. at pp.209-211.

Division 3. — The State Services Generally

195. — ORGANIZATION, ETC., OF THE STATE SERVICES.

Subject to this Part, Acts of the Parliament may make provision for or in respect of the State Services, and in particular for and in respect of —

(a) the structures and organizations of the State Services; and
(b) the employment of persons in the State Services; and
(c) the terms and conditions of appointment to, and of employment in, the State Services.

GENERALLY

Referred to

by Prentice C.J. in *Constitutional Reference No 1 of 1978 (s.19)* [1978] PNGLR 345 at p.348;

by Pratt J. in *S.C.R. No 1 of 1982; Re Bouraga* [1982] PNGLR 178 at p.200.

Division 4. — Special Provisions in Relation to the Police Force.

196. — CONTROL OF THE POLICE FORCE.

(1) The Police Force is subject to the control of the National Executive Council through a Minister.

(2) The Minister has no power of command within the Police Force, except to the extent provided for by a Constitutional Law or an Act of the Parliament.

C.P.C. Report Ch.13 p.1

1. Every society has some means to maintain its laws, to preserve peace among its people, and, when needed, to defend them from outside attack. As societies become larger and more complex it is usually necessary to establish

special groups of people to exercise these functions. Because a strict degree of discipline and, in some circumstances, the use of force is required, these groups are sometimes called the 'disciplined forces'. The two most important are the Police Force and the Defence Force.

Civilian control

2. At the outset we wish to emphasise our belief in the general principle that where the people of a country wish to maintain a democratic parliamentary system, it is vital that the disciplined forces should at all times be subject to the control of the elected government through a civilian Minister. Both the Police and Defence Forces are responsible to the government in the same way as, for example, the public services and the teaching service. Senior members of these Forces may be required to advise the government, through their respective Ministers, on matters relating to law enforcement and defence but, like public servants, their function is not to make policy themselves, but to implement policy decided upon by the government.

3. Following the principles we have outlined, we propose that there be a Papua New Guinea Police Force which, except in matters relating to prosecutions, shall at all times be subject to the direction and control of the National Executive Council acting through a civilian Minister. The exception is in keeping with our recommendation concerning the independence of the Public Prosecutor in Chapter 8 on the Administration of Justice.

AS TO DIRECTIONS BY A MINISTER

Held

In the absence of any delegation by the N.E.C. of its power of control to the Minister for Police, the Minister for Police has neither power of direction or control over the Commissioner of Police nor powers under s.196 to issue orders to the Commissioner. The Minister however, in order to discharge his political responsibility may request information as to the functioning of the force from the Commissioner. The Commissioner, whilst not legally obliged to, ought to provide answers to the Minister.
S.C.R. No 1 of 1982; Re Bouraga [1982] PNGLR 178 (see Kidu C.J. at pp.185-189, Kapi J. at pp.201-208.

AS TO DELEGATION TO THE MINISTER

per Kidu C.J.

Subsection (1) puts it beyond doubt that the Police Force is subject to ultimate control of the Government of the day. The Minister himself, although vested with the political responsibility of the Force and the Commissioner hold no power to direct or control. However, I see no difficulty in the National Executive Council delegating its power or control to the Minister. This may be effected under s. 149(4) of the Constitution.
S.C.R. No 1 of 1982; Re Bouraga [1982] PNGLR 178 at p.189.

197. — FUNCTIONS OF THE POLICE FORCE.

(1) The primary functions of the Police Force are, in accordance with the Constitutional Laws and Acts of the Parliament —
  (a) to preserve peace and good order in the country; and
  (b) to maintain and, as necessary, enforce the law in an impartial and objective manner.

C.P.C. Report Ch.13 p.1

7. We recommend that the functions of the Police Force be defined as preserving the peace and maintaining the laws of Papua New Guinea in accordance with the Constitution.

POLICE FORCE GENERALLY SUBJECT TO CONTROL OF NATIONAL EXECUTIVE COUNCIL

Held

The functions set out in s.197(1) are subject to the control of the National Executive Council. That means the Police Force must carry out those functions within the terms of s.197(1) and where there is a direction given by the N.E.C. pursuant to s.196, that direction must be followed. Subsection (2) however, precludes the N.E.C. giving directions in relation to particular prosecutions and restricts it to giving directions of general policy.
S.C.R. No 1 of 1982; Re Bouraga [1982] PNGLR 176; see Kidu C.J. at p.189, Kapi J. at p.198.

GENERALLY

Referred to

by Pratt J. (Kapi Dep.C.J. and Bredmeyer J. concurring) in *The State v The Principal Magistrate District Court, Port Moresby; Ex parte the Public Prosecutor* (1983 Unreported) SC243 at p.8 (functions of police force include bringing malefactors before justice by way of an information).

(2) Insofar as it is a function of the Police Force to lay, prosecute or withdraw charges in respect of offences, the members of the Police Force are not subject to direction or control by any person outside the Force.

AS TO RELATIONSHIP WITH PUBLIC PROSECUTOR

Held

The constitutional function of members of the police force to prosecute charges in respect of offences is not subject to the control of any person including the Public Prosecutor. The Constitution establishes that as a matter of principal the police will not be controlled in this role except when Parliament decrees. Any such decree would need to be in the clearest terms. Section 197(2) is not, however, contravened by s.4(ga) of the *Public Prosecutor (Office and Functions) Act* 1977 which vests in the Public Prosecutor, in respect of offences listed in Sch. 1A of the Criminal Code, the discretion to elect that in such a case, proceedings shall be way of a summary trial. Such a provision does not offend s.197(2) because the police still retain independent power to lay charges and prosecute insofar as it remains their function to do so. All the Act does is to remove from the police the function of prosecuting offences under Sch. 1A of the Criminal Code when the Public Prosecutor exercises the right of election conferred upon him by the *Public Prosecutor (Office and Functions) Act* 1977.
The State v The Principal Magistrate District Court Port Moresby; Ex parte the Public Prosecutor (1983 Unreported) SC243; see Pratt J. (Kapi Dep.C.J. and Bredmeyer J. concurring) at pp.6-9.

198. — COMMISSIONER OF POLICE

There shall be, within the Police Force, an office of Commissioner of Police, who shall be responsible for the superintendence, efficient organization and control of the Force in accordance with an Act of the Parliament.

(*See: Police Force Act* Ch.65.)

C.P.C. Report Ch.13 p.1

4. We recommend that there be a Commissioner of Police who, subject to the direction and control of the Minister, should have superintendence of the Force. Under the present legislation, the Commissioner, Deputy Commissioner and Assistant Commissioners are, in effect, chosen and appointed by the Executive Council. We recommend that the successor to that body called the National Executive Council under our proposals — also have this power, but that the appointments be made only after the Minister has consulted the Public Services Commission and the First Parliamentary Committee.

5. As in the case of constitutional office-holders, the requirements for consultation with a Parliamentary Committee is intended to help bring about some consensus on the appointment of the senior officers of the Police Force, and thereby to avoid their becoming the subject of contentious political debate. It is obviously important that those at the top of the Police Force should enjoy widespread confidence in the community.

AS TO CONSTITUTIONALITY OF CREATION OF DEPARTMENT OF POLICE

per Kapi J.

Section 198 of the Constitution is clear that the superintendence and efficient organization of the police force is the responsibility of the Commissioner. This is an exclusive responsibility. The only requirement is that the responsibility must be carried out in accordance with the Act.

By creation of a Department under the *Public Service (Interim Arrangements) Act*, this took away some of the responsibilities of the Commissioner . . . and gave them to a different organization set up under a different legislation.

To the extent that the creation of the Department of the Police is set up to take-over some functions of the Commissioner it is inconsistent with s.198 and therefore unconstitutional. In law there can be no Department of Police and Secretary of Police. Every function that the Commissioner performs including those designated to be performed by the Secretary of Police all fall within the functions of the Commissioner of Police.

S.C.R. No 1 of 1982; Re Bouraga [1982] PNGLR 178 at pp.192,193; see also Kidu C.J. at p.184 but see Pratt J. at p.200, leaving the question open.

Referred to

by Board of Inquiry in *In the matter of a Board of Inquiry appointed under the provisions of Section 83(2) of the Public Services (Interim Arrangements) Act 1973* (1983 Unreported) N367 at p.2.

199. — OTHER FORCES

There shall be only one Police Force in Papua New Guinea, but this section does not prevent —

(a) the creation of reserve or special forces, or other similar forces (by whatever name known); or

(b) the creation of special bodies, or the authorization of persons other than members of the Police Force, for the administration or enforcement of particular laws; or

(c) the conferring of police powers on persons who are not members of the Police Force.

by or under an Act of the Parliament.

AS TO ENFORCEMENT

Comment

It is arguable that the private establishment of a force of similar nature to the police force is a constitutional 'crime' and may be punished pursuant to s.23. The question, however, is not likely to arise as the establishment of such a force is expressly made subject to criminal sanctions under s.50A of the Criminal Code; see for example *Koniel Alar and Hosea Biu v The State* [1979] PNGLR 300 at p.304.

Division 5. — Special Provisions in Relation to the Defence Force.

200. — RAISING UNAUTHORIZED FORCES.

(1) It is strictly forbidden to establish, organize, equip, train or take part in or associate with a military or para-military force, or to organize or take part in military or para-military training, except such as is provided for by this Constitution, or to plan, prepare for or assist in the raising or training of such a force or in such training.

(2) Subsection (1) does not prevent —
   (a) the establishment of a reserve, auxiliary or special force (by whatever name known) as part of the the Defence Force; or
   (b) the establishment of civilian components of the Defence Force, or the establishment or recognition of non-combatant units or organizations within, attached to or associated with the Defence Force,

   in accordance with an Act of the Parliament.

(3) An act of the Parliament may provide that Subsection (1) does not apply to the armed forces of any other country specified in or under the Act, or to the civilian components of, or to the non-combatant units or organizations whether, attached to or associated with such forces.

C.P.C. Report Ch.13 p.4

29. Our first recommendation is that the Constitution should include a provision that states that no person or body may raise any armed military or para-military force except as provided in the Constitution itself. In other words, other armed forces should be specifically prohibited.

AS TO ENFORCEMENT

Comment

The establishment of other armed forces may be punished either directly under s.23 of the Constitution or pursuant to ss. 51, 52 and 53 of the Criminal Code.

GENERALLY

Referred to

by Prentice C.J. in *Koniel Alar and Hosea Biu v The State* [1979] PNGLR 300 at p.304.

201. — CONTROL OF THE DEFENCE FORCE

(1) There shall be no office of Commander-in-Chief of the Defence Force, whether honorary or otherwise.

(2) The Defence Force is subject to the superintendence and control of the National Executive Council, through the Minister responsible for the Defence Force.

(3) No serving member of the Defence Force may be the Minister responsible for the Defence Force.

(4) The Minister responsible for the Defence Force shall not use any military rank or title, and, except to the extent provided for by Constitutional Law or an Act of the Parliament, has no power of command within the Defence Force.

C.P.C. Report Ch.13 p.4.

30. We recommend that the Defence Force be subject at all times to the direction and control of the National Executive Council acting through a civilian Minister responsible for Defence. There are two exceptions to this, both involving the Prime Minister. Firstly, the Council shall, in specified cases, act through the Commander-in-Chief. We propose that this formal title be accorded to the Prime Minister in recognition of his position as the Head of Government and as a symbol of civilian control. As Commander-in-Chief he makes a number of senior appointments, and has such other functions as are provided for by law. But in each case he shall act in accordance with the advice of the National Executive Council. Secondly, we recommend that any call-out of the Defence Force be proclaimed by the Prime Minister in his capacity as Head of Government, but again acting in accordance with the advice of the National Executive Council.

Referred to

by Frost C.J. in *The State v Mogo Wonom* [1975] PNGLR 311 at p.316;

by Kapi J. in *S.C.R. No 4 of 1980 (No 2); Re petition of M.T. Somare* [1982] PNGLR 65 at p.79;

by Kapi J. in *S.C.R. No 1 of 1982; Re Bouraga* [1982] PNGLR 178 at p.191.

(5) There shall be —
- (a) within the Defence Force, an office of Commander of the Defence Force, who shall be the principal military adviser to the Minister responsible for the Defence Force on matters relating to the Defence Force; and
- (b) within the National Public Service, an officer of the Service, who shall be the principal civilian adviser to the Minister on matters relating to the Defence Force,

and each of whom shall have such other powers, functions, duties and responsibilities as are prescribed by or under an Act of the Parliament.

C.P.C. Report Ch.13 p.4

Higher command organization and Defence Department

31. After studying various options available for higher defence organization we supported the proposal, since announced in the Minister's statement, that there be a dual but integrated structure by which the Minister would be advised by senior civilian and military officers of equal status. Accordingly, we recommend that there be a Commander of the Defence Force, who shall be the principal military adviser to the Minister; and a Secretary for Defence, who shall be his principal civilian adviser. We agree with the view that in order to ensure civilian control, the Minister must have access to civilian as well as military advice. But, in any case, there are many considerations, both civil and military, to be taken into account in formulating defence policy and these should be brought together. We therefore propose that, subject to the direction and control of the Minister, the Secretary and the Commander jointly supervise a Department of Defence in which civilian and military personnel are integrated, working side by side.

202. — FUNCTIONS OF THE DEFENCE FORCE

The functions of the Defence Force are —

- (a) to defend Papua New Guinea and its territory; and
- (b) to assist in the fulfilment by Papua New Guinea of its international obligations; and
- (c) to provide assistance to civilian authorities —
  - (i) in a civil disaster; or
  - (ii) in the restoration of public order and security on being called out in accordance with Section 204 (*call-out in aid to the civil power*); or
  - (iii) in accordance with an Act of the Parliament during a period of declared national emergency under Part X. (*emergency powers*); and
- (d) to perform, as directed, functions and services of a civil nature so as to participate to the maximum in the task of national development and improvement,

either within the country or outside it, in accordance with this Constitution and Acts of the Parliament.

(*See*: *Defence Act* Ch.74.)

C.P.C. Report Ch.13 p.1

8. In our deliberations on the Defence Force we have been concerned with both its functions and the manner in which it is controlled in relation to the maintaining of democratic, constitutional government in our country. We discuss here some considerations which underlie our proposals. [p.2]

9. We stated earlier that the Defence Force is responsible to the elected government in the same way as the public services and the teaching service. Soldiers, like public servants and teachers, have particular jobs to do in the interests of the country.

10. There are, however, two important differences. Firstly, members of the Defence Force spend much more of their time training for functions which they may never actually have to carry out. No other people who work for the government are in a position comparable with that of an army in the normal circumstances of peace-time, and in the apparent absence of any threat from outside the country in the foreseeable future.

11. Secondly, the Defence Force is trained to use force in a situation where more peaceful methods, if they have been tried, have failed. Soldiers are taught to obey the orders of their superior officers, to fight and if necessary, to kill — not to discuss, to persuade or to negotiate.

12. Experience in many countries shows that armies are therefore not always very patient with the slower and more difficult methods that have to be used by elected governments. Ministers cannot just give orders without taking into account the views of the people who elected them or of those of the members of Parliament to whom they are more immediately responsible.

13. In recent years a number of countries in different parts of the world have experienced military coups; that is the armed forces have used violence, or the threat of violence, to overthrow the government and to take power themselves. Sometimes this has happened because the political leaders were corrupt or dictatorial, or a country had very serious financial difficulties. But at other times it has been because the military leaders were themselves ambitious for power, or did not agree with the government's policies, or were encouraged to take over by another country that did not like those policies.

14. In some cases the military leaders were more honest or efficient than the politicians they displaced; in others they were just as corrupt or no more successful in solving a country's problems. But, in any case, it is usually true that people have very little freedom when the army takes power, and military men, once they have seized power, don't like giving it up. In a number of countries the armed forces have ruled for many years and have suppressed any organized opposition to their rule.

15. It is relevant to note that in many countries it has been possible for a relatively small army to overthrow the government. Neither careful training nor the teaching of respect for civilian authority has necessarily had much effect. Nor have personal friendships among the political and military leaders of a country prevented coups — especially as they have often been planned by officers below the level of top command.

16. We are not pessimistic about the future of the Defence Force in an independent Papua New Guinea, nor do we wish to appear to be so. But we think it would be folly to ignore entirely experience elsewhere. It has been estimated that there were 85 successful or attempted military coups throughout the world between 1951 and 1963; and from 1963 to 1969 the number in Africa alone was nearly 40. In view of this record we believe we would have failed in our duty had we neglected to give very serious consideration to the role of the Defence Force.

17. The major justification for the existence of armies is to provide protection from external enemies. It is, we believe, a matter for the most serious consideration that this country will have an army of more than three and a half thousand men in a situation where, for the foreseeable future, there appears to be no likelihood of external attack. Indeed, at the time of the preliminary drafting of this Report, we were not aware of any statement from either the Papua New Guinea or the Australian Government that would indicate any official view that the Defence Force was a necessary, or adequate, shield against an external aggressor.

18. In April, however, an important statement on defence policy was made in the House of Assembly by the Minister for Defence, Foreign Relations and Trade. In this statement, the Minister said that the Government has no reason to expect any major external attack in the foreseeable future but, if such attacks did occur, it 'would count on the fact that our more powerful neighbours could not avoid being concerned in the interests of their own security'.

19. The Minister indicated that the external defence role of our own Force is primarily that of a deterrent against 'small-scale infringements of our sovereignty', possibly of an intimidatory nature, 'which we should be able to cope with ourselves'. His statement added that the government did not see any such problems in the foreseeable future but attributed this situation 'in significant measure' to the presence of the Defence Force. Along with other matters, this is a view for the House of Assembly to weigh carefully in forming its own judgement. [p.3]

20. Prior to the Minister's statement there had been some official indications, informal and none very explicit, that the Defence Force should have a role also in the maintaining of internal security. The Minister has now confirmed that the Defence Force might be 'summoned to help' in 'more extreme situations beyond the ability of the Police' to handle.

21. The implications of using the military for dealing with civil disorder have not yet been the subject of serious debate by our country's own elected representatives in the House of Assembly. We had concluded that with the approach of independence it was time this matter was given full consideration. The Minister's statement now provides additional reason for this.

22. For our own part, on grounds we explain later, we have very serious reservations about the possibility of a future Papua New Guinea Government using the army against its own people in any but the most extreme cases of civil disorder, and then subject also to specific conditions. The Minister's statement appears to move away from earlier indications that a more comprehensive approach to military involvement in maintaining public order was being contemplated, but we believe that further clarification is required, and that the issue involved should be thoroughly discussed.

23. There are some other aspects of the Papua New Guinea Defence Force that have caused us concern. The Force has always been an integral part of the Australian armed forces, and it will remain so until the moment of independence. This had had two important effects.

24. Firstly, whatever may have been taught to the soldier in their 'civics' lessons, until quite recently there has been no real link with the Papua New Guinea Government or the country's own political leaders. For practical purposes, it has been to the Australian army and its representatives in Papua New Guinea, rather than to any political institutions of our own, that the Defence Force has been orientated.

25. Secondly, this has been reinforced by the fact that its barracks and other installations, plant and equipment have all been provided at a standard that has little relevance to the circumstances of Papua New Guinea. This standard will be most difficult to maintain unless the Australian Government is willing to provide, and our own government willing to accept, continuing military aid at the massive levels of the past. And if this were to occur, it would be contrary to our proposal that the national goals of the country should include the need to ensure that its sovereignty is not reduced by external political, economic or military dependence. The alternative would be for the $20-$30 million per year to be paid entirely or mostly from our own budget. We feel sure that, if given the choice, most of our people would prefer such sums to be spent on implementing the government's Eight Point Improvement Plan.

26. Closely related to, and arising from, the points discussed, is the elitist nature of the Defence Force. While we appreciate the importance of morale in any armed force, there is danger if this is maintained at the cost of a genuine feeling of identity with the majority of our people; and if there is therefore a lack of sympathy with policies that give much higher priority to increases social and economic development than to military expenditure.

27. We have noted from the Minister's statement that there have been a number of developments intended to alleviate some of these problems, starting with the creation of the Minister's own portfolio and of a Defence Division within the Chief Minister's Department. The Minister has emphasised the need for the Defence Force to share its expensive supporting facilities and services with other agencies of government as far as practicable; and he has spelt this out with particular reference to engineering and sea and air transportation. This would appear to be a rational and common-sense policy but, nonetheless, a cautionary note might perhaps be expressed. There could be some grounds for unease if our country were to receive capital aid tagged for the Defence Force, but the consequential maintaining of expanded facilities were then justified on grounds that they were used for civil purposes. It could be argued that it would be better in such circumstances for increased resources to be allocated direct to the appropriate civil departments.

28. More generally, however, we welcome the Minister's emphasis on changing arrangements and systems which, though appropriate while the Defence Force was an Australian force, are quite inappropriate for Papua New Guinea — changes that are necessary to provide 'the kind of Force we want'. Despite the underlying reservations on certain matters about which we, as a Committee charged with recommending a Constitution, are naturally concerned, we recognize the need for the protection of our country's interests from external threat — whether, for example, by military incursion or encroachment on our fishing grounds. Although the military may, in certain circumstances, provide assistance in civil matters, and we have provided for this, our recommendations are based on the assumption that if Papua New Guinea is to have a competent and professional Defence Force, it should be firmly orientated towards external defence and, of course, be subject to the control of our constitutionally elected government at all times. ... [p.4]

Functions of the Defence Force

32. We believe that it is desirable that the functions of the Defence Force should be clearly set out and that they be exercised in accordance with the Constitution. We propose that the Defence Force should have four basic functions —
(1) the defence of Papua New Guinea;
(2) the fulfilment of international or treaty obligations of Papua New Guinea;
(3) the provision of assistance to the civil authorities of Papua New Guinea in the circumstances of a state of Emergency proclaimed in accordance with the Constitution; and
(4) the performance of services of a civil nature in Papua New Guinea or elsewhere as directed from time to time.

33. We recognize, as the Minister has pointed out, that some activities of the Defence Force involve more than one of these broad functions. Thus, for example, maritime surveillance, by patrol boats is an integral part of the general defence function, but it may also extend to the civil function of policing our fishing grounds and, if necessary, arresting foreign vessels considered to be breaking the law.

34. The provision of assistance to the civil authorities during a state of emergency covers those circumstances outlined in the section on emergency powers in Chapter 5. They include the occurrence of natural disasters, such as earthquakes, eruptions, hurricanes and floods, and of such action by persons as it likely to cause deprivation of supplies essential to life. At those times the Defence Force could be called upon to help provide relief. Also included is the occurance of such action by persons as is likely to endanger the public safety. If a State of Emergency is proclaimed in this kind of stitution the Defence Force could be required to help restore peace and order. We discuss this more fully in a later section. (see under s.204)

35. The fourth function — the performance of services of a civil nature — is intended to cover various forms of civic action, search and rescue activities, and special transportation assignments, in which the technical facilities of the Defence Force, in particular, can be put to civil use. We believe that it is important, however, that it always be made clear to the people of any area concerned that it is the government that directs such work to be done. We [p.5] include also the safeguard that these services are not to be performed in circumstances in which a state of emergency could lawfully be proclaimed unless such a proclamation is already in force. Finally, this function is not restricted to Papua New Guinea. We envisage that the occasion might arise when the government wants the Defence Force to assist a neighbouring country — for example, in search and rescue work, or with a special transportation problem.

AS TO WHETHER SECTION 202 EXHAUSTIVELY SPECIFIES THE FUNCTIONS OF THE DEFENCE FORCE

Held

Parliament cannot assign to the Defence Force a function outside its constitutional functions, which are exhaustively specified in s.202. Section 205 does not enlarge those functions. That section merely sets out mandatory procedures which are to be followed if the Defence Force is to engage in certain activities in the course of carrying out its s.202 functions.
S.C.R. No 4 of 1980 (No 2); Re petition of M.T.Somare [1982] PNGLR 65; see Kearney Dep.C.J. at p.69, Greville Smith J. at pp.71,72, Kapi J. at p.75, Miles J. at p.81.

AS TO WHAT CONSTITUTES AN INTERNATIONAL OBLIGATION

Comment

In 1980 the then Chief Minister for the Condominium of the New Hebrides (later Prime Minister of Vanuatu) requested the government of Papua New Guinea to provide the government of New Hebrides/Vanuatu with troops to perform post independence peacekeeping functions in that country. The question of whether the committal of troops in those circumstances was constitutional was brought before the Supreme Court and considered in *S.C.R. No 4 of 1980 (No 2); Re petition of M.T. Somare* [1982] PNGLR 65. Whilst the decision in that case was decided on technical grounds not relevant to this note, all the judges remarked upon the meaning to be given to the expression 'international obligation' in s.202(b). A clear majority of the Court (Kidu C.J., Greville Smith, Kapi and Miles JJ.) rejected the view that the Court was bound to accept the executive's opinion as to whether an international obligation was in existence. As Miles J. remarked, 'The executive should not be in a position to create an international obligation merely by saying that one exists' (at p.88).

As to what constitutes an international obligation, see Greville Smith J. at p.73, Kapi J. at pp.75-80 and Miles J. at pp.85-88 (adopted by Kidu C.J. at p.67). From these judgments it is clear that an interna tional obligation cannot be constituted by a mere request from another nation for military assistance followed by Papua New Guinea's agreement to provide that aid (but see Kearney Dep.C.J. at p.69). It must be an international obligation, the nature of which is recognised by international law.

AS TO ONUS OF PROOF

per Kearney Dep.C.J.

> .... It is a fundamental principle that he who contends that an Act is unconstitutional, must prove it. In this case, it came to this, that the Petitioner had to prove that no relevant 'international obligations' existed to warrant the Vanuatu peace-keeping operation under the Constitution s.202(b). It is of course usually difficult to prove a negative, but the attempt must be made ... the intervener cannot suffer from the petitioner's failure to do what the law requires him to do.
> *S.C.R. No 4 of 1980 (No 2); Re petition of M.T. Somare* [1982] PNGLR 65 at pp.69,70; see also Greville Smith J. at pp.72-75, Miles J. at p.90, but see Kidu C.J. at p.68 and Kapi J. at pp.77,78.

203. — APPLICATION OF GENERAL LAW

Since it is necessary that the Defence Force and the members of the Defence Force have no special position under the law except to such extent as is required by the nature of the Force as a disciplined force and its peculiar functions, duties and responsibilities, it is hereby declared that, except as is specifically provided by a Constitutional Law or an Act of the Parliament, the Defence Force and the members of the Defence Force are subject to all laws in the same way as other bodies and persons.

AS TO CIVIL LIABILITY WHILST ON DUTY

Held

There is no rule of law applicable in Papua New Guinea under which a member of the Defence Forces is precluded from recovering damages from a fellow member or the State for injuries caused by the fellow member's negligence in the course of non-warlike duties.
Vian Guatal v The Independent State of Papua New Guinea [1981] PNGLR 230; see Miles J. at p.239.

GENERALLY

Referred to

by Andrews J. in *Benas Openefa v Willie Wagera* (1980 Unreported) N242 at p.3.

204. — CALL-OUT IN AID TO THE CIVIL POWER

(1) The Defence Force or a part of the Defence Force may be called out to perform functions under Section 202(c)(ii) (*functions of the Defence Force*) only by the Head of the State, acting with, and in accordance with, the advice of the National Executive Council.

(2) When called out in accordance with Subsection (1), the Defence Force or a part of the Defence Force —
   (a) does not have, and shall not be given, any power or protection that would not be possessed by the Police Force or the members of the Police Force in similar circumstances; and
   (b) shall support the Police Force for so long and so far as is necessary to enable the Police Force to restore public order and security; and
   (c) in so doing shall act only on, and to the extent specified in, a request by the appropriate civilian authority in accordance with an Act of the Parliament; and
   (d) shall cease to act in support of the Police Force when directed to do so by the Head of State, acting with, and in accordance with, the advice of the National Executive Council.

C.P.C. Report Ch.13 p.5

42. We have given very serious consideration to the manner in which civil disorder should be dealt with, and to the circumstances in which the Defence Force might be permitted to become involved. People have the right to go about their daily lives free from threat by others, and the government has the duty to protect that right by maintaining peace and order. We think it is important, however, to distinguish carefully between various situations which might arise.

43. The great majority of disturbances should be dealt with by the police. Urban rioting and inter-tribal fighting will almost always come within this category. But there could be disturbances that are of such intensity or which are so wide-spread that the police are unable to cope and the authority of the government is seriously challenged. We believe that it is only in these circumstances, which would warrant the proclamation of a State of Emergency, that the Defence Force should be used to restore peace and order. And it is only in regard to this kind of situation that the term 'internal security situation' is really appropriate.

44. It follows from this that we support the government's expressed view that the Defence Force should be used only 'as a last resort'. In all we have said earlier it is implicit that the Defence Force should not have a political role — that is, it should not be involved in the [p.6] internal politics of the country. It must be realized that if the Force is called upon to restore peace and order, it is carrying out a political role — and it is made clear to all that the government is dependent upon use of the army to maintain its authority.

45. There are other reasons for deep concern about the use of the Defence Force in any but the most grave internal situations. Any realistic assessment of the requirements of maintaining peace and order must take into account situations where the police might need to use tear gas and batons. There will probably be occasions also when police might need to be armed with loaded rifles — as, in certain circumstances, when guarding political leaders or vital installations. But a policeman is trained to exercise personal discretion in carrying out his duties, and to do so as a member of the general community. An important aspect of this training is an emphasis on the use of minimum force.

46. The situation is very different with soldiers, who are trained as a force to repel outside aggressors. They are trained to kill and the rifle is an integral part of their equipment. They are also trained to obey others without question. Even with modifications in their training programme, it would be placing a very heavy burden upon soldiers to expect them to have a strong sense of individual responsibility for their actions in a situation of civil disorder.

47. We believe there is a great difference between police being equipped with rifles to guard people or installations in special circumstances, and soldiers using guns to restore order when there is, for example, urban rioting or inter-tribal fighting. We feel sure that the people of this country would react with bitterness and horror at the use of 'military methods' in such situations, and that irreparable damage could be done to the standing of any government which allowed this to happen except in extreme circumstances. The use of the Defence Force in this way could also have a most serious effect on its morale.

48. We emphasise most strongly, therefore, that the Police Force alone should be used for maintaining peace and order in all situations except those which have deteriorated to such an extent that the government considers it necessary to proclaim a State of Emergency in accordance with the Constitution. Only then, and subject to specific safeguards, should units of the Defence Force be used.

49. We believe that this is a reasonable interpretation of the 'last resort' concept in a country which wishes to adhere to the principles of constitutional democracy. We recognize that this proposal goes against any wider interpretation which would permit the Defence Force to be used in a secondary, back-up role in support of the police in a variety of situations. According to that interpretation, there could be what has been called a 'graduated response': in some circumstances the Defence Force personnel would be used to provide logistic support and supplies for the police; in others, they would assist the police in such activities as cordoning off and searching areas, manning road blocks and policing curfews; in still others, they would be directly involved, for example, in the controlling and dispersal of crowds, especially if police resources became exhausted but police, rather than military, methods were still appropriate.

50. These levels of involvement could all occur prior to the actual deployment of Defence Force units. In a deteriorating situation, what might begin as provision of logistic support or some other, relatively minor form of assistance, could end in full and direct army involvement. The use of the army at an early stage could in fact be seen as a provocative act and seriously aggravate a situation it was intended to remedy.

51. We recognize the practical advantage of allowing the Defence Force to provide logistic support for the police when required — this would cover transport, quartering, supplies, communications and so on — but we consider that this should be done by members of the Force acting in a non-combatant capacity. We recommend accordingly.

52. More generally, however, we believe that the answer to the possibility of a deteriorating public order situation is not to involve the Defence Force in an active role — with all the risks that this would entail — but to increase the resources of the police so that with logistic support, if necessary, they are able to cope with all situations except those where police methods are no longer adequate, and there is no alternative but to call in the military. We think such occasions would be rare and of a kind that would justify the proclamation of a State of Emergency. Under the Constitution, the National Parliament would then be summoned and the use of Defence Force units would be the subject of parliamentary scrutiny and debate.

53. To give greater assurance that the Police Force will be able to carry out its responsibilities, we recommend that the Force be increased in numbers, and that, so far as practicable, it be adequately equipped for the communications, transport and other logistic requirements of its extended role. We note from the Defence Minister's statement that the [p.7] government has begun an expansion programme for the Police Force which might reduce the likelihood that help would be needed from the Defence Force.

54. We appreciate that, to be truly effective, such a programme would require considerable financial and other resources, but it is possible that this problem might be met, at least in part, by a re-allocation of existing resources. Indeed, especially in the light of our conclusion that use of the army for handling civil disorder should be restricted to the rare occasion of a State of Emergency, we believe there is a strong case for an inquiry into the relative allocation of resources between the Police and Defence Forces. We return to this later.

55. To sum up, we believe that these proposals are based on a realistic and sober assessment of the situation in Papua New Guinea, and of experience elsewhere. We repeat our belief that there is great danger in providing for the early involvement of the military (other than in a non-combatant, logistic supporting role) in cases of civil disorder. This is the job of the police. If it is thought that the Police Force as at present established and equipped may prove inadequate for the task, then, so far as is practicable, it should be given both the numbers and

equipment that are necessary. We believe that the military should be used for military purposes; that to use it as an auxiliary police force except in extreme circumstances is to put our Constitution and all that in stands for at great risk.

205. — ACTIVE SERVICE

(1) Except for the purposes of defence against attack, the Defence Force or a part of the Defence Force —
  (a) may be ordered on active service only by the Head of State, acting with, and in accordance with, the advice of the National Executive Council; and
  (b) may be sent out of the country only by the authority of and on conditions imposed by the Head of State, acting with, and in accordance with, the advice of the National Executive Council.

(2) The Defence Force or a part of the Defence Force may not be ordered on, or committed to —
  (a) active service; or
  (b) an international peace-keeping or relief operation,
outside the country without the prior approval of the Parliament.

(3) If practicable before, and in any event as soon as practicable after, action is taken under Subsection (1) or the Defence Force becomes engaged in war or warlike operations or in defence against attack, the Parliament shall be advised of the action taken, or likely to be taken, and of the reasons for it, and shall be given an opportunity to debate the matter.

(4) Subsection (1)(b) does not prevent —
  (a) the Defence Force or a part of the Defence Force being sent out of the country for normal administrative or training purposes; or
  (b) any action that is required or permitted by an Act of the Parliament for the purposes of enforcing a law

C.P.C. Report Ch.13 p.5

36. We have been aware of the need to formulate a constitutional position concerning the authority to send units of the Defence Force into action overseas. It is clear that should Papua New Guinea itself be under attack, or in imminent danger of attack, the government must be completely free to dispatch units outside the country if such action is regarded as necessary or expedient for the more effective defence of Papua New Guinea.

37. We believe also that our government should be able to respond promptly to a request for our participation in an international peace-keeping force such as those organized by the United Nations. As a safeguard, however, we propose that for any such service to continue beyond a period of 28 days, it should require the approval of the National Parliament.

38. In other circumstances, we have reservations about commiting units of the Defence Force to active service outside Papua New Guinea — expecially in view of the possibilities such action has for escalation of the conflict, and for division of opinion at home. We recommend, therefore, that with the exceptions referred to above, such commitments be made only after the approval of the National Parliament has been obtained. We do not think that Papua New Guinean forces should be sent to fight in wars in other countries unless the Parliament has first had the opportunity to debate and decide the matter.

Liaison with the National Parliament

39. In Chapter 6 on the Legislature, we emphasized that although strong leadership is required of the Executive, the role of the National Parliament should, nonetheless, be one of full and constructive partnership. Thus, while the responsibility for maintain ing the country's security — both external and internal — lies with the Executive, there is no matter in which it is more important to our democratic system of government that a spirit of consulation and consensus should prevail.

40. If the Defence Force becomes engaged in any war, declared or otherwise, or in any warlike operations, it may not always be practicable for the National Parliament to meet in the normal way. We believe, however, that in the event of an outbreak of hostilities, it should be summoned as soon as practicable so that the Prime Minister may report on the situation; and we recommend the inclusion of such a provision. Should any part of the Defence Force be used to restore peace and order in a state of emergency, Parliament would be summoned in accordance with the relevant constitutional provisions recommended elsewhere.

41. It is unlikely, however, that there would be an outbreak of hostilities without any warning; a situation would normally have deteriorated over a period of time. Similarly, there would be prior indications of any situation within the country in which it eventually became necessary to use the Defence Force to restore peace and order. We propose that, in such circumstances, and so far as it is practicable, The National Executive Council should keep the First Parliamentary Committee (as the Committee concerned with defence matters) informed of developments.

DOES NOT EXTEND THE PERMISSIBLE FUNCTIONS OF THE DEFENCE FORCE

Held

Section 205 does not enlarge the functions assigned to the Defence Force by s.202. Section 205 merely sets out mandatory procedures which must be followed if the Defence Force is to engage in the activities specified in s.205 in the course of carrying out its s.202 functions.
S.C.R. No 4 of 1980 (No 2); Re petition of M.T. Somare [1982] PNGLR 65; see Kearney Dep.C.J. at p.69, Greville Smith J. at pp.71,72, Kapi J. at p.75, Miles J. at p.81.

Referred to
by Kapi J. in *S.C.R. No 4 of 1980; Re petition of M.T. Somare* [1981] PNGLR 265 at pp.284,286; see also Miles J. at pp.310, 311.

206. — VISITING FORCES

(1) An Act of the Parliament may make provision for or in respect of —
- (a) the presence in the country, by arrangement with the National Executive, of forces of another country; and
- (b) the presence in another country of the Defence Force or a part of the Defence Force,

and in particular for or in respect of —
- (c) the concession to courts or tribunals, and to service authorities, of the other country of jurisdiction over members of its forces (other than citizens of Papua New Guinea) in relation to some or all civil and criminal matters; or
- (d) the assertion of the exclusive jurisdiction of courts and tribunals of Papua New Guinea, and of Defence Force authorities, over members of the Defence Force in another country.

(*See: Defence (Visiting Forces) Act* Ch 77; *Defence (Presence Abroad) Act* 1980.)

(2) Except in relation to its own members or to civilian components of, or civilians accompanying, the force, a visiting force of another country shall not be used in the country in any role in which the Defence Force may not be used, and accordingly any law that restricts the role, powers or functions of the Defence Force or of members of the Defence Force applies equally to visiting forces and members of visiting forces.

(3) A law made for the purposes of Subsection (1) may apply, in whole or in part, to civilian components of, or civilians accompanying, the Defence Force or a part of the Defence Force, or to civilian components of, or civilians accompanying a visiting force.

GENERALLY

Referred to

by Kapi J. in *S.C.R. No 4 of 1980; Re petition of M.T. Somare* [1981] PNGLR 265 at p.284;

by Miles J. in *S.C.R. No 4 of 1982 (No 2); Re petition of M.T. Somare* [1982] PNGLR 65 at p.90 (*Defence Force (Presence Abroad) Act* 1980 not unconstitutional).

Division 6 — Special Provisions relating to Disciplined Forces.

207. — DEFINITION OF "DISCIPLINED FORCE"

(1) The following are, for the purposes of this Division, disciplined forces:—
- (a) the Police Force; and
- (b) the Defence Force; and
- (c) any other force or service that —
  - (i) is established by or under a statute; and
  - (ii) is declared by an Organic Law to be a disciplined force for the purpose of this Division.

(2) For the purposes of any Organic Law made for the purposes of this Division, a person acting, as required or authorized by law, under the direction of a member of a disciplined force, for the purpose of assisting in the performance of the functions or duties of the member or of the force, shall be deemed to be a member of that force.

208. — PROTECTION OF MEMBERS OF DISCIPLINED FORCES

(1) Because of the special nature of disciplined forces and of their operations, it is a primary duty of their members to obey lawful orders, and accordingly an Organic Law shall make special provision for relieving a member of such a force from responsibility for the consequences of —

(a) carrying out a lawful order; or
(b) carrying out an order which he honestly, and on reasonable grounds believed to be a lawful order, in which case the onus of establishing his belief and the reasonable grounds on which it was based, shall be upon him.

(2) Without derogating any other right to compensation from an authority responsible for the disciplined force concerned, an Organic Law made for the purposes of Subsection (1) shall make provision for any liability to make compensation that would otherwise lie on a member of a disciplined force to lie on the authority responsible for the force.

(*See: Organic Law on the Relief of Members of Disciplined Forces from the Responsibility for the Consequences of Carrying out a Lawful Order* Ch.1.)

AS TO CIVIL LIABILITY FOR NEGLIGENCE

Held

There is no rule of law applicable in Papua New Guinea under which one member of the Defence Force is precluded from recovering damages from a fellow member or the State for injuries caused by the fellow member's negligence in the course of non-warlike duties. Section 208(2) effectively preserves the right of any person to take action against the State to recover compensation for injury caused by the conduct of a member of a disciplined force acting pursuant to a lawful order.
Vian Guatal v The Independent State of Papua New Guinea [1981] PNGLR 320; see Miles J. at pp.237-239.

GENERALLY

Referred to

by Andrew J. in *Benas Openefa v Willie Wagera* (1980 Unreported) N242 at p.7 (the importance of soldier's obedience to lawful orders is recognized by s.208).

PART VIII — SUPERVISION AND CONTROL

Division 1 — Public Finances.

Subdivision A — The Parliament and Finance

209. — PARLIAMENTARY RESPONSIBILITY

(1) Nothwithstanding anything in this Constitution, the raising and expenditure of finance by the National Government, including the imposition of taxation and the raising of loans, is subject to authorization and control by the Parliament, and shall be regulated by an Act of the Parliament.

C.P.C. Report Ch.9 p.1

1. The principle that parliament should have ultimate control over the raising and expenditure of government funds follows logically from the Committee's recommendation Chapter 7, 'The Executive', that the members of the National Executive Council should be collectively responsible to the National Parliament. 'Parliamentary Control of the Purse' provides the legislature with one of its most important checks upon the actions and intentions of the executive. Parliamentary control over public monies secures for the elected representatives of the people final say over the economic aspects of the government's development plans.

Ultimate Parliamentary Authority

2. The Committee recognises that the National Parliament cannot exercise detailed control over each individual revenue-raising measure or every item of government expenditure. The executive arm of the government requires some flexibility in its negotiations with potential lenders or aid givers. It must be capable of responding quickly and effectively to changes in the international economy or in economic conditions in Papua New Guinea, so as to safeguard the country's interests. The executive must be able to seize opportunities, and to meet situations of difficulty or urgency as they arise.

3. Parliament may do no more than set the broad limits within which loans may be negotiated, taxes imposed, aid received, and government funds spent. It may establish procedures to ensure the honesty of those who handle government funds, and to hold them accountable for their actions. The National Parliament should, we believe, scrutinise very carefully any proposal to delegate the power to levy or alter revenue-raising measures, to authorise loans, or to spend public monies, to another body. It should also be wary of permanent appropriations by statute. The principle of ultimate parliamentary control over public monies is, we believe, vital. However, we do not believe that it would be wise to limit the National Parliament constitutionally in respect of these matters. Parliament cannot exercise detailed control over every aspect of the management of public funds. In a system of responsible government, the parliament entrusts certain responsibilities to the executive, while the executive, in turn, must display respect for the parliament. Our recommedations are designed to ensure that *ultimate* authority over all aspects of public finance shall be vested in National Parliament.

Revenue Raising

4. Papua New Guinea obtains public monies from three main sources:
— domestic taxation
— domestic and foreign loans
— foreign aid

In Chapter 2, 'National Goals and Directive Principles', we have attempted to link the procedures set out in this Chapter for the raising and expenditure of government funds with the ends for which we believe these procedures should be employed. We have also tried to specify there the objectives for which public monies should, we believe, be used. But in this Chapter we are not directly concerned with the uses to which public monies might be put, but with the procedures through which they are raised, allocated, and spent.

5. All taxes, rates, duties, (including excises), levies or impositions imposed by the government should be set according to law. This recommendation does not prevent the parliament from empowering the executive to set the precise levels of certain taxes by regulation. It therefore allows for some flexibility in the setting of particular taxes by the government (within limits and according to procedures set by National Parliament), without weakening parliament's ultimate control over the raising of taxes.

6. Similarly, the Committee recognises that the National Parliament cannot approve the precise details of every government loan. The executive must be able to seek money where it is available on reasonable terms. But the National Parliament must be able to keep at least general control over the country's indebtedness. It must be able to prevent the raising of unnecessary loans, to determine the framework within which loans are negotiated, and to guard against Papua New Guinea becoming unduly dependent upon particular lenders.

AS TO WHAT CONSTITUTES A TAX

Held

Schedule 1.2 defines taxation as including rates charges and fees and imposts of any kind. Accordingly, an 'economic fee' of K400 per pupil imposed by the Board of Governors of the Port Moresby Multi-Racial High School on all students following a certain curriculum was a 'tax' within the meaning of s.209(1) of the Constitution. The operation of s.209(1) is not precluded by reason of the fact that a benefit such as tuition at school is provided in respect of the fee.
Mairi v Alkan Tololo and ors (No 2) [1976] PNGLR 125; see particularly Prentice Dep.C.J. and Williams J. at p.139.

Referred to

by Prentice Dep.C.J. in *James Saleng Mileng v Alkan Tololo* [1976] PNGLR 447 at p.457.

AS TO PRINCIPLES OF INTERPRETATION TO BE APPLIED TO TAXING PROVISIONS

per Prentice Dep. C.J., Williams J.

This provision in s. 209 (1) of the Constitution is similar in kind to that first introduced in England by the *Bill of Rights* in 1689, 1Wm. & M. sess.2, c.2. In accordance with the Constitution it is necessary to give this constitutional section 'its fair and liberal meaning', and to construe it so that it will take effect and not become attenuated. We consider that it must be construed so that it will maintain parliamentary responsibility for revenue raising and 'ultimate parliamentary control over public moneys', as contemplated by the recommendations of the Constitutional Planning Committee (Final Draft, Chapter 9, at 2, 3 and 5). But to do so, we think it is incumbent upon the court to follow a well-trodden road of interpretation. This path suggests that for the imposition of a charge upon the subject to be legal, a clear and unambiguous intention must be shown in a Statute. Insofar as the *Education Act* is sought to be relied on as giving powers to raise revenue, what has been said about taxing acts seems appropriate; 'In a taxing Act one has to look at what is clearly said. There is no room for intendment. There is no equity about a tax. There is no presumption as to a tax. Nothing is to be read in, nothing is to be implied, one can only look fairly at the language used.' And again, 'If the case is not brought within the words of the statute, interpreted according to their natural meaning; and if there is a case which is not covered by the statute so interpreted, that can only be cured by legislation and not by any attempt to construe it benevolently in favour of the (State)'. (See the cases collected in *Craies on Statute Law*, 6th ed., 113 to 114). To render imposition of tax for the raising of revenue constitutional, the statutory grant of power must be clear and unambiguous and the circumstances bringing it into operation sufficiently clear. That the operation of s.209 (1) of the Constitution ought not to be precluded by reason of the fact that a benefit such as tuition at school is provided in respect of the fee, or that a fee is paid voluntarily, is illustrated by *Attorney-General v Wilts United Dairies, Limited* (1921) 37 TLR 884 and 38 TLR 781.
Mairi v Alkan Tololo and ors (No 2) [1976] PNGLR 125 at pp.138, 139; see also Frost C.J. at p.130.

Referred to

by Frost C.J. in *James Saleng Mileng v Alkan Tololo* [1976] PNGLR 447 at pp.451, 452 (comprehensive analysis of the reasons supporting the need for clear and unambiguous statutory authorization for a tax); see also Prentice Dep.C.J. at p.457, Williams J. at p.462.

GENERALLY

Referred to

by Pritchard J. (dissenting) in *Constitutional Reference No 1 of 1978 (s.19)* [1978] PNGLR 345 at p.371.

(2) For each fiscal year, there shall be a National Budget comprising estimates of finance proposed to be raised, and estimates of proposed expenditure, by the National Government in respect of the fiscal year, and appropriations for the service of that year, and such other supplementary Budgets and appropriations as are necessary.

C.P.C. Report Ch.9 p.2

12. The presentation of the annual budget and statement of account to the legislature provides a most important opportunity for the audited results of one year's government activity to be related to estimates for the following year, and for both of these to be examined against the government's long range economic plans. It provides a most useful occasion for parliament to review progress being made towards the attainment of national objectives. The Committee therefore recommends that the present system whereby the Minister responsible for finance submits an annual budget to the parliament be continued, and that parliament be given the opp ortunity to review the raising and expenditure of government funds during the previous year. The Permanent Parliamentary Committee responsible for financial matters should be given adequate opportunity to examine the budget in depth before it is finally approved.

13. At present, the government publishes quarterly statements of government revenue and expenditure. This practice is useful for those engaged in economic and financial management. The Committee recommends that it be continued, but it does not propose that it be required in the Constitution.

14. At present, the annual budget is presented to the Parliament almost two months after the commencement of the financial year with which it deals, and funds often do not become available until the third or, sometimes, the fourth month. If a budget is to be a true plan for future expenditure, it should ideally be presented to the National Parliament before or at the beginning of the financial year. The Committee therefore recommends that the timing of the presentation of the budget to the National Parliament, or the dates on which money becomes available from Australia, should be changed so that the budget can be debated before some of the money contained in it has already been spent.

(3) Before any Budget or appropriation is prepared for submission to the Parliament, the National Executive Council shall consult with any appropriate Permanent Parliamentary Committee, but this subsection does not confer any right or impose any duty of consultation after the initial stages of the preparation of the Budget or appropriation.

C.P.C. Report Ch.9 p.2

15. As indicated above, the Committee recognises the importance of executive initiative in the presentation of financial proposals to the National Parliament. But, the executive must be open to proposals and reactions from back-bench representatives of parliament in relation to both the raising and expenditure of government funds. We therefore recommend that the National Executive Council should consult with the appropriate Permanent Parliamentary Committee before the annual budget is prepared, so that it may take account of a broad range of opinion on budgetary matters. Such consultation would enable a representative group of [p.3] back-bench members of parliament to make their views on budgetary policy known to the government. It would provide an opportunity for the exchange of information and ideas. Short-run programmes might be considered in the light of long range plans. Changes can be more readily fitted into the overall framework of the budget at this stage than after the budget has been presented.

210. — EXECUTIVE INITIATIVE

(1) The Parliament shall not provide for the imposition of taxation, the raising of loans or the expenditure of public moneys of Papua New Guinea except on the recommendation of the Head of State, acting with, and in accordance with, the advice of the National Executive Council.

(2) The Parliament may reduce, but shall not increase or re-allocate, the amount or incidence of, or change the purpose of, any proposed taxation, loan or expenditure.

C.P.C. Report Ch.9 p.2

10. The Committee recognises that the day-to-day management of the national economy must be in the hands

of the National Executive Council. The National Executive Council must be able to raise and spend government funds according to law. Ministers should be able to bring their financial requirements before parliament. Parliament must be able to scrutinise these proposals carefully and in depth. But the detailed management of the economy should remain the responsibility of the executive. The government should be able to introduce the programmes upon which it was elected.

11. If the principle that parliament should have ultimate control over the raising and expenditure of public monies is to have meaning, then the National Parliament needs to have the power to examine the budget as a whole, and to reject it in whole or in part. Parliament should, we believe, have the power to cut particular items of expenditure or particular taxes proposed by the executive. Members must be able to move and to pass motions and amendments in protest against particular provisions of the government's budgetary proposals. But the ultimate task of management, of raising, allocating, re-allocating and then spending government funds, remains an executive responsibility.

211. — ACCOUNTING, ETC., FOR PUBLIC MONEYS.

(1) All moneys of or under the control of the National Government shall be dealt with and properly accounted for in accordance with law.

(2) No moneys of or under the control of the National Government shall be expended except as provided by this Constitution or by or under an Act of the Parliament.

C.P.C. Report Ch.9 p.2

7. The provision that all government funds must be paid into a Consolidated Fund, and that expenditure from it must be made according to law, ensures that the National Parliament has ultimate control over all revenue raised, including foreign aid. The establishment of a Consolidated Fund provides a useful device for keeping regular account of the country's overall financial situation.

8. There may be occasions on which the government wishes to set aside certain funds for special purposes, and to keep them apart from the Consolidated Fund established in the Constitution. The Committee's recommendation does not prevent this, but it requires that this may be done only with the approval of the National Parliament, which may require that regular reports be made to it on transactions involving such funds.

212. — REVENUE AND EXPENDITURE WITHOUT PRIOR APPROVAL.

(1) If at the beginning of a fiscal year the Parliament has not made provision for public expenditure for that year, the National Executive may, in accordance with an Act of the Parliament, expend out of the Consolidated Revenue Fund, without authorization other than this section, amounts not exceeding in total one-third of the budgetted expenditure by the National Government during the immediately preceding fiscal year.

(2) The authority conferred by Subsection (1) lapses when the Parliament has made provision for the public expenditure for the fiscal year in question, and any amounts expended by virtue of that subsection are a charge against the expenditure so provided for and shall be properly brought to account accordingly.

C.P.C. Report Ch.9 p.3

Revenue and Expenditure without prior approval

16. As a rule, public monies should neither be raised nor spent without prior parliamentary approval. There may, however, be occasions when it is simply impossible for the National Parliament to approve estimates of revenue and expenditure before the beginning of a particular financial year. It may be, for example that the National Parliament cannot be brought together before the close of a financial year, because an election is in progress, or because of an unforeseen emergency, or for some other reason; or that a meeting of parliament lapses for want of a quorum before the estimates for the first few months of the next financial year can be approved; or that a new government is formed so close to the end of a financial year that it does not have time to prepare its own estimates before the commencement of the next financial year.

17. The Committee believes that the entire work of government should not come to a halt in such circumstances. But it also recommends that a firm limit be set to what the executive can do without parliament's prior approval.

18. We therefore recommend that an amount not exceeding in total one-third of the estimated expenditures for the preceding year should be available to the Minister responsible for finance to draw upon to maintain the normal services of government until parliament can be brought together. The expenditures he authorises should be held against the expenditures that the National Parliament later approves for that year.

19. The inclusion in the Constitution of a provison in line with this recommendation should not be taken to mean that the committee favours a continuation of the current practice, whereby the government asks the parliament to grant it Supply to enable its work to continue during the following financial year until the budget approved by the parliament comes into effect. Indeed, we strongly believe that the government should seek prior parliamentary approval of all revenue raising and expenditure. This provision is intended to deal with circumstances in which the National Executive Council is for some reason unable to obtain such approval.

Subdivision B. — The Auditor-General.

213. — ESTABLISHMENT OF THE OFFICE OF AUDITOR-GENERAL.

(1) An office of Auditor-General is hereby established.

(2) The Auditor-General shall be appointed by the Head of State, acting with, and in accordance with, the advice of the National Executive Council given after receiving reports from the Public Services Commission and the Public Accounts Committee.

(3) In the performance of his functions under this Constitution, the Auditor-General is not subject to the control or direction of any person or authority.

C.P.C. Report Ch.9 p.3

24. Sound and honest financial administration is basic to the development of our country, and to the effectiveness and reputation of its government. Public monies must be raised and spent as the law provides. It is the task of the Auditor-General to investigate whether public monies are properly handled, and to report his findings to the National Parliament at least once a year.

25. The office of Auditor-General should, we believe, be established in the Constitution. [p.4] It must be independent of outside political control.

26. The Auditor-General should be as independent as possible of all involvements beyond his official duties. He must be able to pursue his lawful investigations without inhibition, and report the results of his inspections and audits directly to the National Parliament.

214. — FUNCTIONS OF THE AUDITOR-GENERAL.

(1) The primary functions of the Auditor-General are to inspect and audit, and to report at least once in every fiscal year (as provided

by an Act of the Parliament) to the Parliament on the public accounts of Papua New Guinea, and on the control of and on transactions with or concerning the public moneys and property of Papua New Guinea, and such other functions as are prescribed by or under a Constitutional Law.

(*See: Public Finances (Control and Audit) Act* Ch.36.)

(2) Unless other provision is made by law in respect of the inspection and audit of them, Subsection (1) extends to the accounts, finances and property of —
(a) all arms, departments, agencies and instrumentalities of the National Government; and
(b) all bodies set up by an Act of the Parliament, or by executive or administrative act of the National Executive, for governmental or official purposes.

(*See: Public Bodies (Financial Administration) Act* Ch.6)

(3) Notwithstanding that other provision for inspection or audit is made as provided for by Subsection (2), the Auditor-General may, if he thinks it proper to do so, inspect and audit, and report to the Parliament on, any accounts, finances or property of an institution referred to in that subsection, insofar as they relate to, or consist of or are derived from, public moneys or property of Papua New Guinea.

(4) An Act of the Parliament may expand, and may provide in more detail for, the functions of the Auditor-General under Subsections (1), (2) and (3), and may confer on the Auditor-General additional functions and duties not inconsistent with the performance of the functions and duties conferred and imposed by those subsections.

(*See: Public Finances (Control and Audit) Act* Ch.36.)

C.P.C. Report Ch.9 p.4

27. The Auditor-General's main function is to check that the raising and expenditure of government funds takes place in the manner approved by the parliament, and that all transactions involving such funds have been properly accounted for. He should be able to report to the National Parliament when he finds examples of waste and extravagance in the use of public monies. His jurisdiction should extend to all bodies that make use of government funds, including government departments, provincial governments, and all other statutory bodies.

28. It is important that the Auditor-General be supplied with adequate facilities and suitably trained staff to perform his duties effectively. Any suggestion that his functions might be performed by auditors in private practice in Papua New Guinea acting as his agents should, we believe, be rejected. We have recommended above that the position of Auditor-General should be independent of outside direction and control. In Chapter 14, 'General', and Chapter 3, 'Leadership Code', we have made detailed recommendations designed to secure this independence. It would, therefore, run counter to all that we have said on this subject if a person in private practice in Papua New Guinea were to act as an agent of the Auditor-General. An auditor in private employ or in business on his own account in Papua New Guinea would not be subject to the restrictions which we have

recommended (in Chapters 3 and 14) should be placed upon the Auditor-General. Further, the size of the profession in Papua New Guinea makes it all-too-likely that a n auditor acting as an agent of the Auditor-General would become privy to information which might place him in a difficult position in relation to the interests of his private clients. The Auditor-General must, therefore, be given adequate staff of his own, and that staff as well as the office of Auditor-General should be filled as soon as possible by citizens with appropriate qualifications. Meanwhile, shortages of suitable staff in Papua New Guinea should be met by recruitment, and if necessary, secondment, from overseas.

Subdivision C. — The Public Accounts Committee.

215. — ESTABLISHMENT OF THE COMMITTEE.

There shall be a Public Accounts Committee, which is a Permanent Parliamentary Committee for the purposes of Subdivision VI.2.E (*the Committee system*).

C.P.C. Report Ch.9 p.4

29. In addition to the Auditor-General, there should, we believe, be a group of parliamentarians outside the ministry charged with the specific responsibility of scrutinizing the administration of government funds. They should receive the reports of the Auditor-General, and ex amine them in detail. They should be empowered to initiate their own independent enquiries into the administration and expenditure of public monies.

216. — FUNCTIONS OF THE COMMITTEE.

(1) The primary function of the Public Accounts Committee is, in accordance with an Act of the Parliament, to examine and report to the Parliament on the public accounts of Papua New Guinea and on the control of and on transactions with or concerning, the public moneys and property of Papua New Guinea.

(*See: Public Finances (Control and Audit) Act* Ch.36.)

(2) Subsection (1) extends to any accounts, finances and property that are subject to inspection and audit by the Auditor-General under Section 214(2) (*functions of the Auditor-General*), and to reports by the Auditor-General under that subsection or Section 214(3) (*functions of the Auditor-General*).

(3) An Act of the Parliament may expand, and may provide in more detail for, the functions of the Committee under Subsections (1) and (2), and may confer on the Committee additional functions and duties not inconsistent with the performance of the functions and duties conferred and imposed by those subsections.

C.P.C. Report Ch.9 p.4

30. The Committee therefore recommends that a permanent Parliamentary Committee with the specific responsibility of reporting to the parliament on the administration of government funds should be established in accordance with the recommendations in Chapter 6, 'The Legislature'. This Committee should be able to examine all government accounts as it sees fit, to call for witnesses and documents, and to recommend changes in the administration of public monies (sic).

31. The Committee is firmly of the opinion that this committee must be provided with staff suitably trained to assist it in its work. Ideally, it would have people trained in accountancy or economics at its disposal, able to carry out detailed investigations on the committee's behalf. The work of the Auditor-General should also be readily available to the committee. We have already recommended that this committee should be expressly charged with the responsibility of examining the Auditor-General's reports. It should have the power to summon the Auditor-General to give evidence before it, and to call for his papers. However, it is most important, we believe, that the Auditor-General and the Permanent Parliamentary Committee concerned with the scrutiny of p ublic accounts should work together more closely and rather less formally than the preceding recommendations might imply. Their work is very closely related. Co-operation between them is essential, and would, we believe, be mutually reinforcing. We therefore recommend that the Auditor-General should assist the committee in its investigations by being available to brief it as required, and that all of his working papers should be at the committee's disposal.

32. The Permanent Parliamentary Committee whose establishment we have recommended above should have the responsibility of ensuring that the executive is accountable in detail to the legislature for its administration of government funds. It is therefore important that it should be representative of opinion in the National Parliament, and that it should not be open to domination by members of the National Executive Council. We therefore recommend that Ministers should not have the *right* in the case of this committee to attend meetings and to take part in discussions as they choose. This committee must be free to determine for itself who (including Ministers) may, and who may not, take part in its proceedings. We urge members of the National Parliament to choose a man of independent mind as its chairman.

GENERALLY

Referred to

by Pritichard J. (dissenting) in *Constitutional Reference No 1 of 1978 (s.19)* [1978] PNGLR 345 at p.371.

Division 2. — The Ombudsman Commission.

217. — THE OMBUDSMAN COMMISSION.

(1) There shall be an Ombudsman Commission, consisting of a Chief Ombudsman and two Ombudsmen.

C.P.C. Report Ch.11 p.1

1. The 'Ombudsman Commission' is one of the new institutions which our people, in their submissions to us, have clearly decided is necessary to meet their changing needs as Papua New Guinea moves to independence. We fully support their views, and have accordingly recommended the establishment of this important body, which we describe below. In our traditional societies, there were many customs and beliefs which imposed restrictions on land use, on human relations and on personal obligations. These traditional controls are no longer adequate to cope with the increasingly interdependent nature of our societies and the widespread activities of government.

2. The government of our country today must have a substantial police force to maintain internal stability. Our defence force guards against external attack. The government must also provide roads, education and health services and make it possible for our people to find meaningful employment; the parliament has to make laws to govern the wise use of our resources. When conflicts arise, our courts are equipped to settle disputes amicably.

3. The modern control system has become very complex, and many men and women who are trained to administer those controls, cannot be adequately supervised. The decisions of these men and women in the public service and in semi-government institutions affect a great number of people. Sometimes, even the most diligent public servant makes errors. Because of the size of the public service, careful superintendence of all government officials is difficult. Some public servants take advantage of this, and their negligence, or wilful abuse of administrative power, can result in hardship or injustice being caused to many.

The role of the Ombudsman

4. In a number of industrialised countries, the office of the Ombudsman has been established to fill the gaps in the scope of the court system, and to strengthen the integrity of the public service. The 'Ombudsman' is an independent government official who receives complaints about government agencies mainly from people who feel they have been unfairly or unreasonably dealt with by officials. This work involves the Ombudsman in

investigating these complaints (and sometimes initiating investigations himself) and, if he finds evidence of, for example, administrative injustice or unreasonable delay in taking action, he makes recommendations to remedy the situation.

5. The court system is for various reasons restricted in being able to provide a remedy in many situations even when it is clear that an obvious wrong has been done to someone. Courts for instance, are reluctant to inquire into the fairness or otherwise of an administrative decision, on the basis that administrative decisions and actions are of the essence of the exercise of executive power, and only if it is clear either that a particular executive act or decision was beyond the scope of a specific executive power, or there has been an obvious mistake in law, or the rules of natural justice have been ignored, do the courts see intervention on their part as being justified.

6. Some countries have evolved intricate systems of administrative tribunals to deal with grievances of one sort or another arising from acts or decisions of public servants. These tribunals work under flexible rules of procedure. Whilst not closing the door to similar tribunals being developed in Papua New Guinea in the future, we confine our recommendations in this field for the time being to proposing the establishment of an ombudsman.

7. A few years ago many people doubted that the institution of the Ombudsman would be suitable to the developing nations. It was argued that the members of the public service in countries such as ours were too inexperienced and prone to excessive use of power, and that the executive was too strong to allow an ombudsman to function properly. Yet many new States have established an ombudsman in recent years, and some of these have been very successful in helping to make administration more responsive to the public, and promoting the idea that a member of the public is entitled to redress if he has been unfairly or unreasonably dealt with by a government officer.

8. There is, however, a tendency in some developing countries to see the role of the Ombudsman as a substitute for or an alternative to the courts. We believe that our Ombudsman Commission should have more the supervisory and investigatory role in relation to those vested with the administrative power to make decisions, rather than for the Commission to be seen as a substitute for the courts.

9. This does not mean that we see the Ombudsman as in any way less significant. In fact, [p.2] we recognize that sometimes access to courts is diffcult, for psychological or other reasons, and that the courts are not always able to provide redress sufficiently promptly or in the most effective way. In such situations, the ombudsman could be the more appropriate channel for the redress of grievances.

10. In recommending the establishment of the Ombudsman Commission we have given consideration to the kinds of arguments which were raised some years ago, when the possibility of introducing the institution of the ombudsman was first raised in Papua New Guinea. The view that an ombudsman would reduce the scope of members of parliament to serve the interests of their constituents by obtaining redress for their complaints, has been rejected in many countries since then, and we, too find it unconvincing.

11. Members of the House of Assembly are not themselves in a position to investigate complaints of administrative injustice or malpractice — they are obliged to rely upon senior public servants to do this. These people may themselves be involved in the matter complained of, and if so, are unlikely to make a satisfactory investigation of it. Even if a senior officer is not personally involved, a departmental inquiry is unlikely to be as searching as one made by an independent body such as an ombudsman. An ombudsman has the staff, the expertise, the authority and the independence to make a thorough investigation, and is in a position to persuade the department or authority concerned to take corrective action if this is necessary. In our view, the person complaining is therefore far more likely to obtain redress through an ombudsman than through a member of parliament.

12. If an ombudsman were established, the member of parliament could, of course, refer complaints to him, and probably gain more credit in the eyes of his constituents than he does at present, since there would be a better chance of injustices being redressed.

13. The second main argument against the establishment of an ombudsman in Papua New Guinea is that it is unnecessary in view of the fact that we have a Public Solicitor's Office which can handle most of the kinds of complaints with which an ombudsman might otherwise be concerned.

14. We reject this argument also, on the basis that there is a clear distinction between the respective roles of the two institutions — the ombudsman in his general jurisdiction being concerned mainly with matters concerning the bureaucracy which are best dealt with by administrative means or do not involve a cause of action which could be tried in court. Furthermore, the Public Solicitor does not have the necessary power of investigation to carry out the functions of an ombudsman. He is bound by the ordinary rules of evidence and procedure while the procedures of an ombudsman are not so limited, and are more flexible.

15. We did, in fact, consider the possibility of combining the functions of the Public Solicitor with those of the proposed Ombudsman Commission, but ultimately decided against such a recommendation on the grounds that the differences between the respective roles and procedures of these two institutions were such as to make it undesirable to merge them. We foresaw an extremely difficult situation arising when the Ombudsman Commission decided that disciplinary or criminal proceedings should be taken against a particular leader, and

referred the matter to Public Prosecutor. The leader might then wish to obtain legal aid in respect of his defence against any charges laid against him by the Public Prosecutor. If the Ombudsman Commission and the Public Solicitor's Office were part of the same organization, neither the leader nor the community would feel justice could be done in such cases.

16. There are, of course, considerable advantages in having some degree of administrative co-ordination between these two institutions. We have therefore proposed that in the provinces, the same person should act as agent for both bodies. This matter is dealt with in detail later in this chapter.

GENERALLY

Referred to

by Wilson J. in *Constitutional Reference No 1 of 1978 (s.19)* [1978] PNGLR 345 at p.355; see also Pritchard J. (dissenting) at p.371.

(2) The members of the Commission shall be appointed by the Head of State, acting with, and in accordance with, the advice of an Ombudsman Appointments Committee consisting of —
(a) the Prime Minister, who shall be Chairman; and
(b) the Chief Justice; and
(c) the Leader of the Opposition; and
(d) the Chairman of the appropriate Permanent Parliamentary Committee, or, if the Chairman is not a member of the Parliament who is recognized by the Parliament as being generally committed to support the Government in the Parliament, the Deputy Chairman of that Committee; and
(e) the Chairman of the Public Services Commission.

C.P.C. Report Ch.11 p.3

23. While it is clearly of great importance that the Commission have the confidence of the people, it is also important that it should enjoy the confidence of the Government. Bearing this in mind, we recommend that the members of the Commission should be appointed by a special committee chaired by the Prime Minister, its other members being —

- the Chief Justice;
- the Chairman of the First Parliamentary Committee;
- the Deputy Chairman of the First Parliamentary Committee;
- a Provincial Premier or Chairman chosen by all the Provincial Premiers and Chairmen annually; and
- the Chairman of the Public Services Commission.

This composition would mean that the most senior members of all three arms of government at the national level, as well as a Premier on behalf of the provincial governments and the Chairman of the Public Service Commission would be involved in the selection of the Ombudsmen. This, we consider, should mean that those appointed as Ombudsmen would have broad political, judicial and public service support — an essential prerequisite if this new institution is to be effective. Once appointed, the Chief Ombudsman and the other Ombudsman would be quite independent of any political or other authority or group.

GENERALLY

Referred to

by Pritchard J. (dissenting) in *Constitutional Reference No 1 of 1978 (s.19)* [1978] PNGLR 345 at p.371.

(3) The salary and other conditions of employment of the Chief Ombudsman shall not be less than or inferior to the salary and other conditions of employment of a Judge other than the Chief

Justice and the Deputy Chief Justice without taking into account any conditions of employment personal to that Judge.

(4) The salary and other conditions of employment of the Ombudsmen shall be not less than or inferior to the salary and other conditions of employment of the Public Prosecutor, without taking into account any conditions of employment personal to any particular Public Prosecutor.

C.P.C. Report Ch.11 p.4

33. In order to able to attract people with the ability which we consider is vital to the success of the Commission, and also to provide the appropriate recompense for the responsibilities which he will be shouldering, we recommend that the Chief Ombudsman be paid a salary and allowances which are at least equivalent to those of a judge, whilst the other Ombudsmen should be paid only slightly less — equivalent to the salary and allowances payable to the Public Prosecutor and the Public Solicitor. This recommendation is in line with the practice in most other countries where the institution of the ombudsman has been established.

GENERALLY

Referred to

by Pritchard J. (dissenting) in *Constitutional Reference No 1 of 1978 (s.19)* [1978] PNGLR 345 at p.372.

(5) In the performance of its functions under Section 219 (*functions of the Commission*) the Commission is not subject to direction or control by any person or authority.

(6) The proceedings of the Commission are not subject to review in any way, except by the Supreme Court or the National Court on the ground that it has exceeded its jurisdiction.

C.P.C. Report Ch.11 p.10

Immunities of the Commission

75. We propose that the protection from legal proceedings which is normally given to Ombudsmen elsewhere be given to the Ombudsman Commission. This protection would ensure that legal action could not be taken against the Commission in respect of its actions or opinions, or of any steps taken by those acting on its behalf, unless it could be shown that the Commission or any of those persons had acted in bad faith. Our recommendation extends to the Commission the immunity from harassment by legal action which is enjoyed by, for example judges and magistrates. It does not, however, prevent criminal proceedings being brought against an ombudsman or an officer of the Commission if it is alleged an offence has been committed by him.

•

RECOMMENDATIONS [p.16]

Immunities of the Commission

25. (1) No proceeding, opinion or expression of the Commission shall be reviewable in any court.

(2) No proceeding, either criminal or civil, shall lie against the Commission or any member of the Commission or any police officer employed to serve or execute any summons or order of the Commission, for anything done or said or omitted by the Commission or by any member or officer of the Commission or any such police officer in discharging the responsibilities or orders of the Commission under the Constitution or any law unless it is shown that the Commission or any of the above persons acted in bad faith.

GENERALLY

Referred to

by Pritchard J. (dissenting) in *Constitutional Reference No 1 of 1978 (s.19)* [1978] PNGLR 345 at p.372.

(7) An Organic Law shall make further provision in respect of the appointment, powers, procedures and immunity of the Commission.

(*See*: *Organic Law on the Ombudsman Commission* Ch.1.)

C.P.C. Report Ch.11 p.3

24. The qualifications which we believe the Chief Ombudsman should have are primarily personal, not formal. We consider that it is essential that the person who is chosen as Chief Ombudsman should have complete integrity, independence of mind, and high standing (but not necessarily status) in the community. He should also be a person of resolution, who can cope with frustrations and overcome administrative inertia. We have accordingly made our recommendations in these terms.

25. Other characteristics which would also be invaluable in a Chief Ombudsman would be tact, initiative, thoroughness, an ability to persuade, and some background in public administration.

26. A number of ombudsmen in other countries have a legal background but we do not see this as an essential qualification in respect of the Chief Ombudsman of Papua New Guinea, as we have recommended that there be a full time legal adviser (counsel) to the Commission. In any event, [p.4] the qualifications for one of the other Ombudsmen include legal qualifications and experience as an option.

27. We do, however, believe it is of great importance that he be a citizen of this country, who has a good appreciation of Melanesian thinking and actions, and who can speak and negotiate with politicians and senior public servants with the authority that only a Papua New Guinean holding this office would have.

Qualifications of the other Ombudsmen

28. Although, as we have explained, we consider that the Chief Ombudsman should be chosen on the basis of his personal qualities rather than because he has particular professional qualifications, we believe it is important, if the Ombudsman Commission is to be fully effective, for one of the other Ombudsmen to have qualifications and experience in accountancy, and for the other to have an administrative or legal background. We have recommended accordingly. This recommendation ensures that the Commission includes people who have knowledge and experience in at least two of the several fields of activity with which the Commission will be concerned.

29. The Ombudsman with the accountancy background will be particularly concerned with the Leadership Code enforcement side of the Commission's activitities, though obviously there will be many matters arising out of the Commission's other responsibilities with which the 'Accountant Ombudsman' will be concerned.

30. The personal qualities of these two Ombudsmen will also be important. Like the Chief Ombudsman, unless they enjoy the respect and trust of the politicians, public servants and other people with whom they are in contact in course of their work, their task is likely to prove difficult.

31. In view of the present shortage of Papua New Guineans with the required background, we do not exclude the possibility that in the immediate future one of these two Ombudsmen might be a foreign citizen.

GENERALLY

Referred to

by Pritchard J. (dissenting) in *Constitutional Reference No 1 of 1978 (s.19)* [1978] PNGLR 345 at p.372.

(8) In this section "conduct" includes —
- (a) any action or inaction relating to a matter of administration; and
- (b) any alleged action or inaction relating to a matter of administration.

REDUNDANT PROVISION

Comment

There is no reference to 'conduct' in s.217.

218. — PURPOSES OF THE COMMISSION.

The purposes of the establishment of the Ombudsman Commission are —
- (a) to ensure that all governmental bodies are responsive to the needs and aspirations of the People; and
- (b) to help in the improvement of the work of governmental bodies and the elimination of unfairness and discrimination by them; and
- (c) to help in the elimination of unfair or otherwise defective legislation and practices affecting or administered by governmental bodies; and
- (d) to supervise the enforcement of Division III.2 (*leadership code*).

C.P.C. Report Ch.11 p.2

17. Papua New Guinea's ombudsman should be available to assist ordinary people throughout the country who feel aggrieved by actions or omissions of the bureaucracy or of any institution of government. We consider that our ombudsman should also have the important responsibility of supervising and enforcing the Leadership Code, to ensure that our leaders do not compromise national, provincial or local interests for personal and selfish ends. Our ombudsman should have the necessary powers to investigate charges of corruption or other types of abuse of public office, and to ensure that appropriate action is taken against those who break the provisions of the Code.

18. We realize that it may be argued by some in government that the existence of such an institution could be unnecessarily restrictive of the initiative and th e independent discretion of the government and its officers. The government may sometimes be embarrassed by disclosures or recommendations made by the ombudsman. These we believe, are not sufficient reasons for not [p.3] having an ombudsman. Such arguments have been put forward in other countries shortly before the establishment of an ombudsman, yet in virtually all cases the work carried out by the ombudsman has proved, on balance, to be clearly beneficial to the effective functioning of governmental institutions and to citizens generally.

19. Another function we consider the Commission is well suited to carrying out is that of enforcing legislation prohibiting discriminatory practices. To date no legal action has been brought in any court for an offence against the *Discriminatory Practices Ordinance*, yet it is common knowledge that discrimination against Papua New Guineans on racial grounds is still common.

20. We have given careful consideration to the question of whether a single person or a number of people should hold this office. We believe, as do our people, that because of the diverse nature of our society and the collective way in which it is our custom to settle disputes, three persons should be members of what we call the Ombudsman Commission. One of these should be the Chairman. He is to be called the Chief Ombudsman.

21. It seems that our people support the concept of ministerial responsibility, and our recommendations in Chapter 7, 'The Executive', reflect this. We therefore recommend that the Ombudsman Commission should not question the merits of a Minister's policy decision unless maladministration was involved either in the advice given to the Minister before the decision was made or in the implementation of the decision. We have also made it clear that the Commission is not permitted to question the decision of a court on its merits.

AS TO RELATIONSHIP OF SECTION 218 WITH SECTION 219

Held

Section 219 is to be construed in association with (Prentice C.J. at p.374) and read together with (Pritchard J. at p.387) s.218.
Constitutional Reference No 1 of 1978 (s.19) [1978] PNGLR 345; see also Wilson J. at p.355, Pritchard J. at p.372.

219. — FUNCTIONS OF THE COMMISSION

(1) Subject to this section and to any Organic Law made for the purposes of Subsection (7), the functions of the Ombudsman Commission are —

(a) to investigate, on its own initiative or on complaint by a person affected, any conduct on the part of —

(i) any State Service or provincial service, or a member of any such service; or

(ii) any other governmental body, or an officer or employee of a governmental body; or

(iii) any local government body, or an officer or employee of any such body; or

(iv) any other body set up by statute —

(A) that is wholly or mainly supported out of public moneys of Papua New Guinea; or

(B) all of, or the majority of, the members of the controlling authority of which are appointed by the National Executive,

or an officer or employee of any such body; and

(v) any member of the personal staff of the Governor-General, a Minister or the Leader or Deputy Leader of the Opposition; or

(vi) any other body or person prescribed for the purpose by an Act of the Parliament,

specified by or under an Organic Law in the exercise of a power or function vested in it or him by law in cases where the conduct is or may be wrong, taking into account, amongst other things, the National Goals and Directive Principles, the Basic Rights and the Basic Social Obligations; and (*Amended by Constitutional Amendment No. 3. — Provincial Government (Consequential Amendments), s.6)*

(b) to investigate any defects in any law or administrative practice appearing from any such investigation; and

(c) to investigate, either on its own initiative or on complaint by a person affected, any case of an alleged or suspected discriminatory practice within the meaning of a law prohibiting such practices; and

(d) any functions conferred on it under Division III.2 (*leadership code*); and

(e) any other functions conferred upon it by or under an Organic Law.

(*See*: *Organic Law on the Ombudsman Commission.* Ch.1)

C.P.C. Report Ch.11 p.5

37. We recommend that the Commission should have a general jurisdiction similar to that possessed by Ombudsmen in other countries, but that in addition it should have two specific areas of responsibility — one concerned with the supervision and enforcement of the Leadership Code which, in Chapter 3, we have recommended be incorporated as a schedule to the Constitution, and the other the enforcement of legislation prohibiting discriminatory practices.

General jurisdiction

38. The Commission's general jurisdiction should, we believe, be very broad, covering the full range of administrative activities of government departments and authorities. Experience in other countries has shown that attempts to define an ombudsman's jurisdiction in a detailed way have been unproductive as they have led to numerous disputes over its exact limits. We believe it is far better to define the scope of the Commission's general functions broadly, give the Commission scope for rejecting complaints or declining to investigate a particular matter on the basis of certain specific provisions in the Constitution or in ordinary legislation, and also to state in the Constitution certain matters in respect of which the Commission is to have no power to investigate. Our recommendations have been made accordingly.

39. The proposed general jurisdiction of the Commission enables it to enquire into the conduct of persons such as those in a government department, a disciplined force, (the Defence Force, the Police Force, etc.) statutory authority, local government council, the staff of a Minister, constitutional office-holders, members of government committees, and in the Parliamentary Service.

40. We recommend that the Commission be able to investigate, either after receiving a complaint, or on its own initiative, acts or omissions by officials which appear to it to be instances of maladministration or unfairness. The Commission also should be able to look into any apparent defects or unfairness in laws made by parliament or in the way in which such laws are being applied by those responsible for administering them. Our purpose here is to ensure that the Commission is able to recommend that action be taken to remedy a situation where injustice is being caused, even though this is not due to an administrative action or omission, but to an unsatisfactory provision in an Act of Parliament or a regulation or rule made under it.

Supervision of Leadership Code and discriminatory practices legislation

41. Turning to the two specific areas of jurisdiction which we propose that the Commission should have, we recommend that it have power to enquire into —

- possible breaches of the Leadership Code by any leader; and
- possible breaches of any law prohibiting discriminatory practices.

42. In Chapter 3, 'The Leadership Code', we have indicated our view as to the importance of the role of the Commission in seeing to it that the Leadership Code is observed by leaders. We do not underestimate the difficulty or the heavy responsibility which this task will entail; indeed it is partly for this reason that we have recommended that the Commission be a three person body rather than a body consisting of a single person only, as in most countries which have an ombudsman. We feel that a group of three persons will be in a better position to cope with the pressure of work and the discussions with Ministers and senior government officers in regard to matters which at times are likely to be of a very delicate nature.

43. In respect of its jurisdiction in relation to breaches of discriminatory practices legislation, it is our belief that the ineffectiveness of the *Discriminatory Practices Ordinance* is due in large part to the fact that there is no supervising body such as the Race Relations Board in the United Kingdom with responsibility for investigating complaints of racial discrimination and taking steps to have discriminatory actions dealt with administratively. Experience in other countries clearly shows the need for a watchdog body of this kind to oversee the enforcement of such legislation.

AS TO 'CONDUCT'; see under s.219(8).

AS TO JURISDICTION TO INVESTIGATE ACTIONS OF THE PUBLIC SOLICITOR

Held

The Public Solicitor is neither a State Service (whose conduct the Ombudsman Commission has jurisdiction to investigate pursuant to s.219(1)(a)(i)) nor does that office come within the description 'other governmental body' pursuant to s.219(1)(a)(ii). The whole tenor of s.219 is

directed towards administrative rather than professional legal activities.
Constitutional Reference No 1 of 1978 (s.19) [1978] PNGLR 345; see Prentice C.J. at pp.348-351, Wilson J. at pp.359-365, Pritchard J. (dissenting) at pp.383-389: see also note under s.219(8).

GENERALLY

Referred to

by Prentice C.J. in *Premdas v The Independent State of Papua New Guinea* [1979] PNGLR 329 at p.346 (declining to answer whether the actions of the Minister for Foreign Affairs and Trade and of a Committee of Review in ordering the deportation of an alien were within the investigatory powers of the Ombudsman Commission); see also Raine Dep.C.J. at p.351, Saldanha J. at p.368, Wilson J. (dissenting) at p.390 and Andrew J. at p.402.

(2) Subject to Subsections (3), (4) and (5), and without otherwise limiting the generality of the expression, for the purpose of Subsection (1) (a) conduct is wrong if it is —

(a) contrary to law; or
(b) unreasonable, unjust, oppressive or improperly discriminatory, whether or not it is in accordance with law or practice; or
(c) based wholly or partly on improper motives, irrelevant grounds or irrelevant considerations; or
(d) based wholly or partly on a mistake of law or of fact; or
(e) conduct for which reasons should be given but were not,

whether or not the act was supposed to be done in the exercise of deliberate judgement within the meaning of Section 62 (*decisions in "deliberate judgement"*).

Referred to

by Prentice C.J. in *Constitutional Reference No 1 of 1978 (s.19)* [1978] PNGLR 345 at p.347; see also Pritchard J. (dissenting) at pp.373, 389 ('conduct' verges into the field of law).

(3) The Commission shall not inquire into the justifiability of a policy of the National Government or a Minister, or a provincial government or a member of a provincial executive, except insofar as the policy may be contrary to law or to the National Goals and Directive Principles, the Basic Rights or the Basic Social Obligations, or of any Act of the Parliament. (*Amended by Constitutional Amendment No.3 — Provisional Government (Consequential Amendments) s.6)*

(4) The Commission shall not inquire into the exercise of a rule-making power by a local government body.

(5) The Commission shall not inquire into a decision by a court, except insofar as the decision may show an apparent defect in law or administrative practice to which Subsection (1)(b) would apply.

C.P.C. Report Ch.11 p.5

44. The specific limitations on the jurisdiction of the Commission which we recommend are designed to ensure that the Commission does not enquire into the correctness of actual decisions [p.6] made by courts in exercising their judicial functions, or into policies made by Ministers (either collectively through the National Executive Council, or individually) which have influenced particular decisions. Our recommendations do, however, enable the Commission to enquire into improper influence which may have been brought to bear in relation to a judicial decision, or to the formulation of a ministerial policy.

GENERALLY

Referred to

by Prentice C.J. in *Constitutional Reference No 1 of 1978 (s.19)* [1978] PNGLR 345 at p.347; see also Pritchard J. (dissenting) at pp.373, 378.

(6) Except as provided by or under Division III.2 (*leadership code*), the Commission's powers of enforcement are limited to publicity for its proceedings, reports and recommendations, to the making of reports and recommendations to the Parliament and other appropriate authorities as provided by an Organic Law, and to the giving of advice.

C.P.C. Report Ch.11 p.7

54. After considering a complaint or any matter which it has been investigating on its own initiative, we believe the Commission should, if it thinks a government department or authority, or any person ought to —

- consider a matter further;
- take a specific action;
- modify or cancel any administrative act;
- alter a regulation or rule;
- explain more fully the administrative act concerned,

advise the Minister responsible for the department or authority concerned of its recommendations. The Commission should have power to request a responsible Minister or head of authority to inform it of action taken after receiving a recommendation of the Commission, within a time limit specified by the Commission.

55. We further propose that if the Commission finds that unfair or otherwise objectionable provisions are contained in legislation, the Commission should bring this to the notice of the National Parliament or the provincial assembly or recognised local body exercising governmental functions, whichever of these is the appropriate body.

56. Our proposal in this regard exemplifies a basic distinction between the role of an ombudsman and that of a court, namely, the action which each body takes after reaching a conclusion about a matter before it. Whereas a court makes an order which binds the parties to the case, the ombudsman makes recommendations for action to be taken, but cannot himself compel a person or authority to follow his recommendation.

57. This is one of the reasons why we consider it to be so important that members of the Ombudsman Commission should have support from politicians at the national and provincial level, from the Public Services Commission, and from the judiciary. If the Chief Ombudsman and the other Ombudsmen have this vital support, the recommendations of the Commission are likely to be acted upon in the great majority of cases. Experience overseas seems to show the considerable [p.8] weight which recommendations of Ombudsmen who have the respect and trust of those in government and of the general public, can carry.

58. We recommend that if, after having considered a complaint and obtained such evidence and information as it thinks necessary, the Commission forms the opinion that a government department, an authority, or any person should consider a matter further; take some specific action; modify or cancel any administrative act; alter a regulation or ruling; explain an administrative action more fully to a person affected by it; or take any other step, the Commission should advise the Minister responsible for the department or authority concerned of its recommendations.

59. Normally the Commission would not make a recommendation unless it has found an error or improper action by the department or authority concerned, but we envisage that it would be free to suggest improvements in method, procedure or policy even when the existing practice may be legally correct. In this way the Commission may help one department or authority to learn about and take advantage of the procedures of another.

60. The Commission is likely to recommend quite often that action be taken by the department or authority concerned to correct an error or unfair decision. If the department or authority has power to do so we would expect that in most cases the necessary corrective action would be carried out.

61. However, to try to ensure that the Commission's recommendations are considered and acted upon promptly, we propose that it be empowered to request the responsible Minister or head of an authority to advise it within a certain time of the action it has taken in relation to the Commission's recommendations. In cases where no action is taken within the specified time, and no good reasons for this inactivity are given, the Commission might well make an unfavourable report on the matter in the manner indicated below under the heading — 'Publication of recommendations'.

62. As mentioned above, we have made specific provision for cases where injustice is being caused because (or partly because) the relevant legislation is unsatisfactory. In these cases, we propose that the Commission should make known its views in a report to the National Parliament or the appropriate provincial assembly, area authority or legally recognized local body exercising powers and functions of government.

63. By making this recommendation we do not suggest that the Commission need be a general social reformer, but we believe it does have an obligation to draw attention to Acts and regulations that have unreasonably harsh effects.

Publication of recommendations

64. Bringing its views into the open is the Commission's only way of gaining the support of the public in respect of a particular matter it has investigated. We believe that the Commission should be able to publish a recommendation even when a department, authority or person has accepted it. For example, publicity may be necessary to call the attention of other administrators or of Ministers to the need for better procedures in a particular field. Also publicity helps to remind people generally that the Ombudsman Commission is functioning in their interests.

65. However, we believe publicity should come at the end, not at the beginning of discussions which the Commission has with the department, authority or person concerned. Persuasion should be the main method of gaining a favourable response from those whose activities the Commission is investigating. However, where it finds a clear breach of the Leadership Code, or of discriminatory practices legislation, it should normally refer the matter to the Public Prosecutor with a recommendation for appropriate proceedings to be taken by him.

66. In most cases, it would be only when persuasion fails that the Commission would publish its findings and rely upon public opinion having an influence in relation to a particular issue.

67. We propose that the publication of recommendations be made by the Commission to one or other of —
- the Prime Minister;
- the National Executive Council;
- the Speaker of the National Parliament for tabling in parliament;
- the Minister responsible for the Public Services; [p.9]
- the Judicial and Legal Service Commission;
- the Chief Justice or the Chief Magistrate;
- the Chairman of the Public Services Commission;
- a Provincial Premier or Chairman;
- any other person or body that the Commission considers may be concerned and should receive a copy of the recommendations.

To guard against one-sidedness in its published recommendations, we propose that the Commission be required, when publishing an opinion which is 'unfavourable' to an authority or official to include the substance of any explanation of an error or malpractice or the rejection of any recommendation of the Commission which the authority or official has made.

68. We envisage that before announcing a conclusion or recommendation which criticizes a department, authority or any person, the Commission will advise that body or person of its intention and provide it (or him) with a copy of the text of the conclusion or recommendation. This should ensure that the Commission's conclusions are not affected by any factual errors, as these could be pointed out at that stage.

GENERALLY

Referred to

by Prentice C.J. in *Constitutional Reference No 1 of 1978 (s.19)* [1978] PNGLR 345 at p.347; see also Pritchard J. (dissenting) at p.373.

(7) An Organic Law shall make provision in respect of the powers and procedures of the Commission, and in particular —
   (a) shall, subject to paragraph (b), make provision for the Commission to have access to all available relevant information; and
   (b) may impose reasonable restrictions on the availability of information; and
   (c) shall make provision to ensure the secrecy or confidentiality of secret or confidential information made available to the Commission or to a member of the Commission or of its staff; and
   (d) may limit or restrict to a reasonable extent and in a reasonable manner the jurisdiction of the Commission in relation to any matters or class of matters, and in particular in relation to national security; and
   (e) shall make provision for and in respect of publicity for the proceedings, reports and recommendations of the Commission.

(*See: Organic Law on the Ombudsman Commission* Ch.1.)

C.P.C. Report Ch.11 p.6

45. We believe it important that the Commission should have maximum flexibility in deciding the ways in which complaints are received and acted upon, the extent to which the Commission will investigate particular matters, and how often and to whom it distributes its recommendations. Informality should be a keynote of the Commission's procedures if it is to gain the support of our people. We envisage that many complaints to the Commission will be made verbally and that there will be no charge for lodging a complaint with the Commission.

46. To ensure that no adverse recommendation or report about a person whose conduct is investigated by the Commission is made unless that person is given the opportunity to put forward his version of the relevant circumstances, we have recommended that the Commission be required to give that person a hearing before making a report or recommendation of that nature. This provision would apply in respect of all aspects of the Commission's jurisdiction. It does not mean, however, that a person has a right to a hearing before the Commission simply because it has begun to make enquiries into his work or other activities. Such a requirement would unduly hamper the Committee's (sic) work and would not be justified in our view, since many inquiries will not lead to any criticism of particular persons.

47. We have specifically recommended that government departments and all other authorities whose activities are subject to investigation by the Commission should give it their co-operation and assistance in respect of information the Commission considers is necessary for it to carry out its responsibilities. This co-operation will clearly be essential if the Commission is to be able to function efficiently.

48. Other powers which we recommend the Commission should have are —

- powers in relation to the supervision and enforcement of the Leadership Code, apart from those set out in Chapter 3;
- subject to one limitation, the power to issue subpoenas (summonses to witnesses) to compel people to appear before the Commission to give evidence or produce documents;
- the power to enforce any subpoena issued by the Commission;
- subject to one limitation, the power to enter, inspect and call for any document in any house or building occupied or controlled by any department, authority or person in respect of which (or whom) the Commission has jurisdiction. (We have provided for specified buildings to be 'off limits' for members or officers of the Commission, if there is an agreement to this effect between the Prime Minister and the Chief Ombudsman, on the basis that serious prejudice would be likely to be caused to national security or Papua New Guinea's relations with other countries if a member or officer of the Commission were to enter the particular building).

49. These broad powers of compulsory process are invariably given to Ombudsmen elsewhere in order that they may obtain needed information. In fact, experience has shown that the power to issue subpoenas is rarely used, as information is normally given freely. This may not, however, always be the case when the proposed Commission is investigating, for instance, a possible breach of the Leadership Code. Though it is likely that the Commission will be mainly concerned with investigating individual complaints, we have recommended that it be empowered to look into general problems which become apparent in the course of its work.

Rights and duties of witnesses

50. We recommend that witnesses who appear before the Commission should have the same rights, duties and immunities as do witnesses who appear before the National Court. [p.7]

Investigation of complaints

51. In order that the Commission may have the kind of discretion which is normally given to Ombudsmen to decline to investigate complaints which they do not believe justify the time and expense which would be involved, we have recommended that the Commission may make such a decision in any one of a number of specified circumstances. These include, for instance, that —

- the grievance is outside the Commission's jurisdiction;
- the complaint is trivial or not made in good faith;
- the person complaining has another remedy which he could reasonably seek;
- the complaint has been delayed for too long to justify investigating it;
- other complaints are more worthy of attention.

52. We would emphasize that the Commission has a discretion to decline to investigate complaints which fall under one of the heads listed in our recommendations, but that it is not obliged to do so in such cases. Thus, even though a complainant might be able to obtain a remedy through court action, the Commission could decide to deal with the matter on the basis that it would be likely to obtain a more satisfactory solution to the problem by administrative means. Even if the Commission declines to investigate a particular complaint, we propose that it should have power to enquire generally into the matter complained of, and related problems.

53. After completing its consideration of a matter, the Commission should, we believe, suitably inform the complainant, and also any government department, authority, or other person or body concerned. This does not mean that we envisage the Commission always giving reasons for declining to investigate a complaint — the Commission should be able to decide a suitable response in certain cases, e.g. where the complainant has psychological problems rather than problems involving governmental authorities. However, normally we would expect the Commission to give full reasons for any action it takes (or decides not to take).

GENERALLY

Referred to

by Pritchard J. (dissenting) in *Constitutional Reference No 1 of 1978* (*s.19*) [1978] PNGLR 345 at p.373.

(8) In this section "conduct" includes —
(a) any action or inaction relating to a matter of administration; and
(b) any alleged action or inaction relating to a matter of administration.

PROVIDES AN EXHAUSTIVE DEFINITION OF CONDUCT

per Wilson J.

It is in this context that I consider it necessary to interpret what the words underlined by me in s. 219(8) of the Constitution mean, which provides:
(8) In this section, '*conduct*' includes —
(a) *any action or inaction relating to a matter of administration;* and
(b) *any alleged action or inaction relating to a matter of administration.*
In my opinion the list of matters set out in sub-sub-ss. (a) and (b) of sub-s.(8), albeit a short one and in the context of this ombudsman legislation, was intended to be exhaustive notwithstanding the use of the word 'includes'. A similar conclusion was reached by a majority of the High Court of Australia in *Y.Z. Finance Co. Pty Ltd v Cummings* (1964) 109 CLR 395 which re-affirmed the principles laid down by Lord Watson speaking for the Privy Council in *Dilworth v Commissioner of Stamps* [1899] AC 99 and in particular at p.105:

> The word 'include' is very generally used in interpretation clauses in order to enlarge the meaning of the words or phrases occurring in the body of the statute; and when it is so used these words or phrases must be construed as comprehending, not only such things as they signify according to their natural import, but also those things which the interpretation clause declares that they shall include. But the word 'include' is susceptible of another construction, which may become imperative, if the context of the Act is sufficient to show that it was not merely employed for the purpose of adding to the natural significance of the words or expressions defined. It may be equivalent to 'mean and include', and in that case it may afford an exhaustive explanation of the meaning which, for the purposes of the Act must invariably be attached to those words or expressions.

The context of Div. 2 of Pt. VII is 'sufficient to show that "includes" was not merely employed for the purpose of adding to the natural significance of the words or expressions defined'. In reaching such a conclusion it is necessary to consider the whole Constitution and, in particular, Div. 2 of Pt. VIII. This ombudsman legislation is clearly designed to protect the public against maladministration as well as discriminatory practices and abuses of leaders.

The powers of the Ombudsman Commission, save and except with regard to discriminatory practices and under Div. III.2 (leadership code), are limited to the investigation of administrative conduct. 'Conduct' in s.219 of the Constitution means any ac tion (or alleged action) or inaction (or alleged inaction) relating to a matter of administration. It is government officials or public servants or members of the State Services who perform most of the administrative functions at which ombudsman legislation of this type is primarily directed. If one looks at the mischief aimed at by the ombudsman legislation in Papua New Guinea, the object was to protect the public from maladministration by government officials and hardly to protect the public (which already has recourse to other remedies) from professional misconduct or the mal-performance of legal aid services. In *Judicial Review of Administrative Action* (3rd ed.) by S.A. de Smith, the learned author discusses the role of the ombudsman and (at p.7) says it is:

> to investigate and report on complaints of injustice caused by maladministration on the part of the central government and its officials in respect of matters where recourse to the courts or tribunals is normally unavailable.

There is a further reference at p.47:

> His function is to investigate complaints by individuals or bodies corporate . . . who claim to have 'sustained injustice in consequence of maladministration' by central government bodies, or persons or bodies acting on their behalf, performing (or failing to perform) administrative (as distinct from judicial or legislative) functions.

Benjafield and Whitmore, *Principles of Australian Administrative Law* (4th ed.) state (at p.157) as follows:

> The office of Ombudsman is of Scandinavian origin and basically the holder of the modern office is expected to be the community's 'watchdog' over the activities of the administration.

It is also to be noted that in some jurisdictions the ombudsman is described as the 'Commissioner for Administrative Investigation to be called The Ombudsman' (see, for example, the Victorian legislation).

I therefore conclude that the powers of investigation of the Ombudsman Commission are limited to the investigation of conduct relating to a matter of administration.

Constitutional Reference No 1 of 1978 (s.19) [1978] PNGLR 345 at pp.362, 363; see also Prentice C.J. at p.349, Pritchard J. (dissenting, but agreeing as to the above) at p.384.

220. — REPORTS BY COMMISSION.

(1) The Ombudsman Commission shall, at least once in each period of 12 months, at such time as is fixed by or under an Act of the Parliament or, subject to any such Act, by the Head of State, acting with, and in accordance with, the advice of the National Executive Council, give to the Head of State, for presentation to the Parliament, a report on the functions and workings of the Commission, with such recommendations as to improvement as the Commission thinks proper.

(*See: Organic Law on the Ombudsman Commission* Ch.1.)

(2) Nothing in Subsection (1) prevents the Commission from making, on its own initiative or at the request of the Parliament or of the National Executive, other reports on any aspect of the functions and workings of the Commission.

C.P.C. Report Ch.11 p.9

69. As in the case of other constitutional office-holders (see Chapter 14 'General'), we recommend that the Commission submit to the Speaker for presentation to the National Parliament at least annual reports on its activities. These need not include the names of those who are immediately concerned if to do so would cause unjustified hardship. If named authorities or persons are mentioned and criticised in a report, we recommend that the substance of their replies to the criticism must be included in the report.

GENERALLY

Referred to

by Wilson J. in *Constitutional Reference No 1 of 1978 (s.19)* [1978] PNGLR 345 at p.357; see also Pritchard J. (dissenting) at pp.371, 374.

PART IX. — CONSTITUTIONAL OFFICE-HOLDERS AND CONSTITUTIONAL INSTITUTIONS.

221. —DEFINITIONS.

In this Part —
"constitutional institution" means any office or institution established or provided for by this Constitution, other than an office of Head of State or of a Minister, or the National Executive Council;
"constitutional office-holder" means —
(a) a Judge; or
(b) the Public Prosecutor or the Public Solicitor; or
(c) the Chief Magistrate; or
(d) a member of the Ombudsman Commission; or
(e) a member of the Electoral Commission; or
(f) the Clerk of the Parliament; or
(g) a member of the Public Services Commission; or
(h) the Auditor-General; or
(i) the holder of any other office declared by an Organic Law or an Act of the Parliament to be a constitutional office for the purposes of this Part.

C.P.C. Report Ch.14 p.1

4. The Committee has recommended earlier in this Report the establishment of a number of offices which we believe should be free from outside direction and control. They comprise:

- the Chief Justice and other judges of the National Court of Justice
- the Chief Ombudsman and the other Ombudsmen
- the Public Prosecutor
- the Public Solicitor
- the Electoral Commissioner
- the Clerk of the National Parliament
- the members of the Public Services Commission

- the Auditor-General
- the Chief Magistrate

It may be that the National Parliament will wish to treat some other holders of high office in the same manner as these office-holders — whom we call 'constitutional office-holders' — and we have provided accordingly.

5. The persons appointed to all of these offices must be of undoubted integrity if they are to fulfil the trust that we believe should be placed in them. They, in turn should be protected from external pressures, although not in such a way that they become remote from the society in which they work. A balance must be struck between the need for them to be able to perform their duties fearlessly and without hindrance, and the need to ensure that they carry out their work honestly and with due regard for the people of Papua New Guinea.

GENERALLY

Referred to

by Pritchard J. in *Ex parte Smedley* [1978] PNGLR 156 at p.159;

by Prentice C.J. in *Constitutional Reference No 1 of 1978 (s.19)* [1978] PNGLR 345 at pp.348, 352; see also Wilson J. at p.360, Prentice J. (dissenting) at pp.370, 380, 381;

by Wilson J. in *Mathias Evertz v The State* [1979] PNGLR 174 at p.178.

222. — OTHER PROVISIONS RELATING TO CONSTITUTIONAL OFFICE-HOLDERS AND CONSTITUTIONAL INSTITUTIONS.

This Part shall be read subject to any other provisions of this Constitution relating to particular constitutional office-holders or particular constitutional institutions.

223. — GENERAL PROVISION FOR CONSTITUTIONAL OFFICE-HOLDERS.

(1) Subject to this Constitution, Organic Laws shall make provision for and in respect of the qualifications, appointment and terms and conditions of employment of constitutional office-holders.

(*See*: *Organic Law on Certain Constitutional Office-holders* Ch.1; *Organic Law on the Terms and Conditions of Employment of Judges* Ch.1.)

(2) In particular, Organic Laws shall make provision guaranteeing the rights and independence of constitutional office-holders by, amongst other things —

(a) specifying the grounds on which, and the procedures by which, they may be dismissed or removed from office, but only by, or in accordance with the recommendation of, an independent and impartial tribunal; and

(b) providing that at the end of their periods of office they are entitled, unless they have been dismissed from office, to suitable further employment by a governmental body, or to adequate and suitable pensions or other retirement benefits, or both, subject to such reasonable requirements and conditions (if any) as are laid down by an Organic Law.

(*See*: *Organic Law on the Guarantee of the Rights and Independence of Constitutional Office-holders.* Ch.1)

C.P.C. Report Ch.14 p.1

7. No person should be allowed to hold high public office indefinitely. All persons who exercise power on behalf of the people should, we believe, have their work periodically evaluated by the body that originally chose them.

8. We need to place considerable trust in the persons appointed to the constitutional [p.2] offices listed above. The Committee has, therefore, given very careful consideration to the manner in which they should be appointed, and their qualifications for office. We appreciate that it would not be proper to hold them accountable for particular decisions and actions. But, we do believe that it should be possible, at specified intervals, to consider their continued suitability for office in a rapidly changing society.

9. We propose that constitutional office-holders (other than judges) should be appointed for terms of six years. At the expiration of each term, holders of such offices should be eligible for reappointment in the same manner as they were first appointed.

10. However, in order to facilitate localisation, we believe that no person who is not a citizen should be appointed to a constitutional office for a term greater than three years. And, for the first ten years after the Constitution comes into force, while our country is still short of Papua New Guineans with appropriate training and experience, we recommend that citizens be appointed for an initial term of three years, after which they may be reappointed for terms of six years.

11. We have outlined above our belief that no person should hold a constitutional office indefinitely. But, we are also concerned to ensure that constitutional office-holders are able to perform their functions independently of outside pressures.

12. We propose that all constitutional office-holders who are citizens of Papua New Guinea should have their future guaranteed. Those office-holders who are recruited from a position in public employment for an initial term of three years, and who are not then reappointed, should be offered another position in the public employment at a salary and on conditions similar to those they enjoyed prior to their recruitment. A constitutional office-holder who is not re-appointed at the expiration of a six year term should be guaranteed a position in public employment with a salary and conditions which are not inferior to those attached to his constitutional office. In this way, we believe that the constitutional offices can be filled by people sensitive to the changing needs of our country, yet free from personal and professional pressure.

GENERALLY

Referred to

by Prentice C.J. in *Constitutional Reference No 1 of 1978 (s.19)* [1978] PNGLR 345 at p.352; see also Wilson J. at p.360.

(3) A constitutional office-holder may not be suspended, dismissed or removed from office during his term of office except in accordance with a Constitutional Law.

C.P.C. Report Ch.14 p 4.

31. In recommending that the holders of the constitutional offices listed above should be independent in the performance of their functions, we have recognised that they should not be easily dismissed. We have therefore specified the circumstances in which a constitutional office-holder can be removed from office, and how allegations against him are to be dealt with.

32. Chronic infirmity of mind or body should be grounds for dismissal. However, that infirmity needs to be carefully evaluated, as to allegations of misconduct, breach of the Leadership Code and gross negligence (which are likely to compromise the integrity and effectiveness of an office). We therefore recommend that a special tribunal of three judges should be appointed to investigate and report on allegations which the body that first appointed a constitutional office-holder feels are serious enough to warrant such an investigation. The appointing body should be able to suspend a constitutional office-holder from his office while an investigation is in progress. The recommendations of that tribunal as to whether or not a particular constitutional office-holder should be removed from office should be carried out by the appointing body.

(4) The total emoluments of a constitutional office-holder shall not be reduced while he is in office, except —
 (a) as part of a general reduction applicable equally or proportionately to all constitutional office-holders or, if he is a member of a State Service, to members of that service; or
 (b) as a result of taxation that does not discriminate against him as a constitutional office-holder, or against constitutional office-holders generally.

C.P.C. Report Ch.14 p.3.

23. We have recommended that the constitutional office-holders listed above should be independent of outside direction and control. To ensure their independence, they should not be directly beholden to, or dependent upon, either the executive or the legislature for their salary and conditions.

24. It is, we believe, desirable that the salary and conditions of all people in public employment in Papua New Guinea, including constitutional office-holders, should be set by the government. Those benefits should be appropriate to the circumstances of Papua New Guinea, and in accordance with the National Goals and Directive Principles. In times of trouble, the government should have the power to reduce all salaries and conditions according to law. Or there may be times when the National Parliament believes that salaries and conditions generally should be held down or even reduced as a matter of principle. But the salary, conditions and other benefits attached to each constitutional office should be reduced during a particular incumbent's tenure of office only if the reduction he suffers is common to all constitutional office-holders.

25. In principle, we believe that constitutional office-holders should be free, both personally and professionally, from political pressure. We therefore recommend that the salary, allowances and other benefits attached to their offices be paid directly from a consolidated fund. In that way, the professional activities of constitutional office-holders are less-likely to be influenced by pressures brought to bear upon their personal lives.

(5) The office of a constitutional office-holder may not be abolished while there is a substantive holder of the office but this subsection does not apply to the abolition of any additional constitutional office created by an Act of the Parliament.

(6) Nothing in this section prevents the making by or under an Organic Law or an Act of the Parliament of reasonable provision for the appointment of a person to act temporarily in the office of a constitutional office-holder.

C.P.C. Report Ch.14 p.4

33. There may be times when it is difficult to appoint someone promptly to fill a vacant constitutional office, or when a constitutional office-holder is for some reason — including illness or suspension from office — unable to perform his duties. At such times, the body that has the power to make appointments to a particular office should be able to make acting appointments of appropriately qualified people, for up to one year at a time — until a normal appointment can be made, or until the holder of the office concerned is able to take up his duties again. The appointing body should also have the power to revoke an acting appointment to a constitutional office at any time.

224. — SPECIAL PROVISION FOR CONSTITUTIONAL INSTITUTIONS.

(1) Subject to this Constitution, Organic Laws and Acts of the Parliament shall provide, or shall make provision for, the powers and procedures of constitutional institutions, and generally for facilitating the performance of their functions, duties and responsibilities.

(2) Subject to this Constitution, if no provision is made under Subsection (1) a constitutional institution —
- (a) may provide, to the extent of the deficiency, for its own procedures; and
- (b) has all reasonable powers that are necessary or convenient for the exercise and performance of its powers, functions, duties and responsibilities.

225. — PROVISION OF FACILITIES, ETC.

Without limiting the generality of any other provision of this Constitution, it is the duty of the National Government and of all other governmental bodies, and of all public office-holders and institutions, to ensure, as far as is within their respective legal powers, that all arrangements are made, staff and facilities provided and steps taken to enable and facilitate, as far as may reasonably be, the proper and convenient performance of the functions of all constitutional institutions and of the offices of all constitutional office-holders.

(*See*: *Organic Law on the Guarantee of the Rights and Independence of Constitutional Office-holders* Ch.1)

GENERALLY

Referred to

by Pritchard J. (dissenting) in *Constitutional Reference No 1 of 1978 (s.19)* [1978] PNGLR 345 at p.370 (an officer of the public service whilst acting on behalf of a constitutional office-holder is not subject to direction or control in the exercise of those functions by any person other than that constitutional office-holder).

PART X. — EMERGENCY POWERS.

Division 1. — Introductory.

226. — DEFINITIONS.

In this Part, unless the contrary intention appears — "declaration of a national emergency" means a declaration under Section 228 (*declaration of national emergency*);

"emergency" includes, without limiting the generality of the expression —
- (a) imminent danger of war between Papua New Guinea and another country, or of warlike operations threatening national security; and
- (b) an earthquake, volcanic eruption, storm, tempest, flood, fire or outbreak of pestilence or infectious disease, or any other natural calamity whether similar to any such occurrence or not, on such an extensive scale as to be likely to endanger the

public safety or to deprive the community or any substantial proportion of the community of supplies or services essential to life; and

(c) action taken, or immediately threatened, by any person that is of such a nature, and on so extensive a scale, as to be likely to endanger the public safety or to deprive the community or any substantial portion of the community of supplies or services essential to life;

C.P.C. Report Ch.5 Part 2 p.6

1. (1) In this Chapter 'State of Emergency' means any period during which —
   (a) Papua New Guinea is at war; or
   (b) there is in force a gazetted proclamation by the National Executive Council declaring that a State of Emergency exists.

(2) A proclamation made by the National Executive Council shall not be effective unless it contains a declaration that the National Executive Council is satisfied —
   (a) that an emergency has arisen as a result of the imminent danger of war between Papua New Guinea and another state or of warlike operations threatening national security;
   (b) that an emergency has arisen as a result of an earthquake, volcanic eruption, hurricane, flood, fire, outbreak of pestilence or infectious disease, or other calamity whether similar to these occurrences or not; or
   (c) that action has been taken, or is immediately threatened by any person, of such a nature, and on so extensive a scale as to be likely to endanger the public safety or to deprive the community or any substantial portion of the community of supplies or services essential to life.

(3) A proclamation of a State of Emergency shall be made in respect of Papua New Guinea as a whole if it is based on paragraph (a) of clause (2) above, but may be made in respect of Papua New Guinea as a whole or any part of Papua New Guinea if the proclamation is based on the circumstances set out in paragraph (b) or (c) above.

"Emergency Act" means an Act of the Parliament made for the purposes of this Part and in accordance with Section 230 (*Emergency Acts*);

"Emergency Committee" means an Emergency Committee appointed under Section 240 (*Emergency Committees*), and includes a Temporary Emergency Committee appointed and in office under Section 241 (*Temporary Emergency Committees*);

"emergency law" means —

(a) an Emergency Act, or

(b) an Emergency Regulation;

"emergency order" means an order made under an emergency law, as provided for by Section 232 (*emergency orders*);

"Emergency Regulation" means a law that is made in accordance with Section 231 (*Emergency Regulations*);

"internment" means detention that is authorized by or under a law the validity of which depends solely on this Part, but does not include the detention of a member of the armed forces of another country as a prisoner of war;

"period of declared national emergency" means any period during which —

(a) Papua New Guinea is at war with another country by virtue of a declaration under Section 227 (*declaration of war*); or

(b) a declaration of a national emergency is in force under Section 228 (*declaration of national emergency*).

Division 2. — Periods of Declared National Emergency.

227. — DECLARATION OF WAR.

The Head of State, acting with, and in accordance with, the advice of the National Executive Council, may publicly declare that Papua New Guinea is at war with another country.

228. — DECLARATION OF NATIONAL EMERGENCY.

(1) If the National Executive Council is of the opinion that an emergency exists or is about to come into being such that it is necessary that the powers conferred by the succeeding provisions of this Part be available, the Head of State, acting with, and in accordance with, the advice of the National Executive Council, may publicly declare the existence of a national emergency in relation to the whole or part of the country.

(2) Unless it is impracticable to do so, a declaration under Subsection (1) shall be made in relation to a part of the country only after prior consultation with the Emergency Committee.

C.P.C. Report Ch.5 Part 2 p.1

1. In every country there are times of great national crisis or emergency due to war, very serious civil disturbances such as organized attacks on many government officers, or natural disaster, such as a famine, an earthquake or a fire. The first and third of these situations are all too familiar to many of us, who remember the Pacific War and natural disasters such as the Mount Lamington eruption in 1951 and the Highlands' famine in 1972.

2. Fortunately, in recent years, there has been no state of civil disorder which has been so serious as to require a declaration of a State of Emergency.

3. We recognize that in preparing the Constitution we must face the reality that very difficult civil disorder situations may possibly arise in the long term future, and that proper provision should be made in the Constitution to enable the Government to cope with them.

4. We have given very careful thought to the question of what powers should be exercised by the executive government in public emergency situations, as we fully appreciate the need to ensure that, on the one hand, the executive is able to cope with crisis situations promptly and effectively, whilst on the other hand, the rights of individuals should not be disregarded. Too often, in other countries, the wide powers which governments are able to exercise in public emergency situations are used arbitrarily, without regard to the fundamental rights and freedoms of the people. Sometimes too, governments use such powers to undermine opposition parties and their leaders without justification.

Underlying Principles

5. In the proposals which follow, we have adopted a number of important principles, namely that —
   1. The introduction and continuation of emergency powers should be subject to effective and regular parliamentary control.
   2. Emergency powers legislation should be treated in the context of the human rights provisions of the Constitution.
   3. The emergency powers authorized by law should involve limiting the normal legal protection of the rights and freedoms of citizens only to the extent that is strictly necessary to deal with the particular circumstances of a given emergency.
   4. Such powers should not, except in extraordinary circumstances which are recognized as such by the great majority of members of parliament voting in favour of a suspension of the relevant protective provisions of the Constitution concerning personal liberty, and protection of law, include the power to detain a person without trial.

5. A heavy onus rests on the Government of the day to clearly establish that the conditions in fact exist which make necessary the authorisation, continuation or use of any particular power.
6. Effective safeguards against abuse and over use of emergency powers should be provided in respect both of the introduction of each individual power and of its exercise.
7. Any legislative limitation of the ordinary right of the individual to protection of his personal liberty should be balanced by the provision of special procedures to ensure that persons are not deprived of their liberty without sufficient cause, that they are not held for an unreasonably long period without being tried, and that compensation is given to those who are improperly detained.
8. As far as possible, emergency powers and procedures in relation to detention without trial should be seen to be distinguished from ordinary powers and procedures. In particular it is generally preferable that members of the judiciary be not asked to undertake tasks the performance of which may well jeopardise public confidence in the impartiality and fairness of the ordinary institutions of justice.[p.2]
9. Emergency legislation should apply only to emergency situations, and statutory instruments made under that legislation should apply only to a particular State of Emergency, and cease to have effect when that State of Emergency ends.
10. Actions taken under emergency legislation should be subject to scrutiny not only in relation to the statutory powers under which they may be authorised, but in respect of the actual situation in the context of which they are taken.

229. — TERMINATION OF PERIODS OF DECLARED NATIONAL EMERGENCY.

A declaration of war or of a national emergency may be revoked at any time —

(a) by the Head of State, acting with, and in accordance with, the advice of the National Executive Council; or

(b) by decision of the Parliament.

C.P.C. Report Ch.5 Part 2 p.2

11. We have also made provision for a proclamation of a State of Emergency to be revoked at any time either by the National Executive Council or by a resolution passed by a simple majority in parliament.

Division 3. — Emergency Measures.

230. — EMERGENCY ACTS.

(1) Before or during a period of declared national emergency, the Parliament may make Acts of the Parliament (to be known as "Emergency Acts") to make provision for dealing with the emergency, and with matters arising out of it.

(2) An Emergency Act shall be expressed to be an Emergency Act.

(3) Except to the extent necessary to bring it into effective operation at the time when it otherwise comes into operation, an Emergency Act made before the commencement of a period of declared national emergency shall not come into operation until the commencement of the period.

231. — EMERGENCY REGULATIONS.

(1) Subject to this Part, at any time before the end of the period of 24 hours after the Parliament first meets after commencement of a

period of declared national emergency the Head of State, acting with, and in accordance with, the advice of the National Executive Council, may make laws (to be known as "Emergency Regulations") to make provision for dealing with the emergency concerned, and with matters arising out of it if, and to the extent that, the nature of the emergency or its requirements necessitate the making of the provision before the Parliament can reasonably consider the matter.

(2) An Emergency Regulation shall be immediately forwarded to —
 (a) the Speaker for presentation to the Parliament; and
 (b) an Emergency Committee in accordance with Section 242(1)(a) (*functions, etc., of Emergency Committees*) or where no Emergency Committee has been established, to the Temporary Emergency Committee established under Section 241 (*Temporary Emergency Committees*).

(3) Unless earlier extended by decision of the Parliament an Emergency Regulation expires at the end of the period of 28 days after the making of the declaration of the emergency, or at the end of the period of 14 days after the Parliament first meets after the commencement of the period of declared national emergency, whichever first happens.

232. — EMERGENCY ORDERS.

(1) An emergency law may make provision for the giving of orders, not inconsistent with the emergency law, by persons authorized to do so by or under the law.

(2) No emergency law shall purport to confer powers to make orders that could not be made in the form of an emergency law.

(3) An order shall, if practicable, be in writing and be notified to the appropriate authority appointed by law.

(4) As far as practicable, details of, or copies of, all orders given in accordance with this section shall immediately be forwarded to —
 (a) the Speaker for presentation to the Parliament; and
 (b) the Emergency Committee in accordance with Section 242(1)(a) (*functions, etc., of Emergency Committees*) or where no Emergency Committee has been established, to the Temporary Emergency Committee established under Section 241 (*Temporary Emergency Committees*).

233. — CONTENT, OPERATIONS, ETC., OF EMERGENCY LAWS.

(1) Subject to this Part, an emergency law may make provision for the peace, order and good government of the country to the extent reasonably required for achieving its purpose.

(2) Notwithstanding the provisions of Sections 12 and 13 but subject to Subsections (3) and (4), an emergency law may alter, wholly or partly, and absolutely or subject to conditions, any provision of Division III.3 (*basic rights*), any Organic Law made for the purposes of any such provision or any other law (other than a Constitutional Law) to the extent reasonably necessary to deal with the emergency concerned, and with matters arising out of it, but only so far as is reasonably justifiable in a democratic society having a proper regard for the rights and dignity of mankind.

(3) An emergency law —
- (a) may not alter —
  - (i) Section 35 (*right to life*); or
  - (ii) Section 36 (*freedom from inhuman treatment*); or
  - (iii) Section 45 (*freedom of conscience, thought and religion*); or
  - (iv) Section 50 (*right to vote and stand for public office*); or
  - (v) Section 55 (*equality of citizens*); or
  - (vi) Section 56 (*other rights and privileges of citizens*); and
- (b) may provide for interment only in accordance with Division 5 (*internment*); and
- (c) may alter Section 37 (*protection of the law*) or Section 42 (*liberty of the person*) only to the extent allowed by paragraph (b).

(4) In addition, an Emergency Regulation may not alter —
- (a) Section 46 (*freedom of expression*); or
- (b) Section 47 (*freedom of assembly and association*); or
- (c) Section 49 (*right to privacy*); or
- (d) Section 51 (*right to freedom of information*),

and may not provide for a sentence of imprisonment for a period exceeding nine months.

(5) In the case of an inconsistency between a valid emergency law and any other law, the law made later prevails.

C.P.C. Report Ch.5 Part 2 p.2

12. We recognize the need for the executive to be able, in times of emergency, to firmly control manpower, supplies and services to ensure that the abilities of both skilled and unskilled people are utilized in the most effective way, and that vehicles, aircraft, ships, essential services and basic supplies are used to the best advantage. Thus, the executive could direct particular individuals to carry out certain tasks considered essential, could ration products such as petroleum, food and clothing, and use trucks and aircraft to transport supplies quickly to wherever they were needed.

Right to a fair trial

13. We have given very careful consideration to the question of whether, in an emergency situation, the executive should be empowered to imprison people whom it believes are involved in activities which it regards as a threat to the security of the country. These activities might be of a terrorist nature or might be those of a collaborator with enemy forces.

14. We are aware that in many countries the government has the power of preventive detention, which it does not hesitate to use, but we do not accept that such a power is essential to the Government of this country in any emergency situation which we can foresee. Unlike the pre-independence situation in a number of other countries which, until recently, were subject to colonial rule, Papua New Guinea does not have any legislation which permits preventive detention. Difficult civil disorder situations in various parts of the country have been handled in the past without resorting to preventive detention, and we do not consider that provision for such legislation is justified. We believe that the right to a fair trial is fundamental in a democratic society and that preventive detention cannot be justified except if our country is at war, or is in the grip of an extreme form of internal crisis due to widespread terrorist or guerilla activity or civil war. We have therefore made no recommendation empowering the Government to exercise powers of preventive detention. [p.3]

Safeguards against abuse of possible power of preventive detention

15. The Committee does, however recognize that at some time in the future a situation of civil strife may arise which is so grave that a very substantial number of Members of Parliament will be prepared to accept, during the crisis period, a suspension of the provisions of the Constitution which ensure that a person is not held in custody without a fair trial. This would enable legislation to be passed providing for detention without trial of, for instance, alleged tourist (sic) [terrorist] leaders.... [p.7]

Control of manpower

3. Nothing in the Committee's recommendation in Part 1 of this Chapter (Human Rights and Obligations) concerning protection from forced labour shall invalidate any law insofar as the law authorises the taking, during a State of Emergency, of measures that are reasonably required in the interests of peace and order and the welfare of Papua New Guinea to deal with a situation that exists during that State of Emergency.

Control of products and services

4. Nothing in the Committee's recommendations in Part 1 of this Chapter shall invalidate a law which, during a State of Emergency, empowers the responsible Minister, with the approval of the National Executive Council to make such orders concerning the production, importation, storage, supply, use, distribution and sale of any product or service declared by that Minister to be an 'emergency item', or the requisition of such vessels, aircraft or vehicles as are reasonably required to deal with a situation that exists during that State of Emergency.

Suspension of human rights provisions concerning personal liberty and protection of law

5. (1) Any provision in Recommendation 2 or Recommendation 6 in Part 1 of this chapter may be suspended in accordance with this recommendation during a State of Emergency to enable the passing of a law which authorises the taking, during that State of Emergency, of measures that are reasonably required for the purpose of dealing with a situation that exists during that State of Emergency.

234. — RELEASE FROM CUSTODY ON EXPIRY, ETC., OF EMERGENCY REGULATIONS.

Subject to any Act of the Parliament made for the purpose of dealing with the effect of the expiry or revocation of a particular Emergency Regulation, any person held in custody under or for the purposes of an emergency Regulation shall be released from custody on its expiry or repeal, unless he is also held in custody under some other law.

AS TO MEANING OF EXPRESSION 'UNDER OR FOR THE PURPOSES OF'

Comment

As detention without trial (internment) is not authorized under Emergency Regulations (see s.233(3)(b) and s.244), it is necessary to determine what s.234 refers to. On its face it appears to require the immediate release from custody of all persons held pending trial or imprisoned for an offence prescribed by an Emergency Regulation whenever such Regulation expires. This may lead to the peculiar result that although an Emergency Regulation can provide penalties for offences of up to nine months imprisonment (see s.233(4)), no person, no matter how grave his breach, may be held in prison for the full term of his sentence if the Emergency Regulations under which he has been convicted expire or are repealed.

235. — CUSTODY OF MEMBERS OF PARLIAMENT UNDER EMERGENCY REGULATIONS OR IN INTERNMENT.

If a member of the Parliament is held in custody under an Emergency Regulation, or is an internee, he shall, at all times when the Parliament is in session or when a committee (of which he is a member) of the Parliament is meeting, be released, on such conditions (if any) as are prescribed by an Act of the Parliament, into the custody of the Parliament in order to allow him to attend to his parliamentary duties, unless he is also held in custody under some other law.

(*See*: *Emergency (Custody of Members of Parliament) Act* Ch.33B)

236. — REVOCATION, ETC., OF EMERGENCY LAWS, ETC.

(1) An Emergency Act may be altered —
- (a) by an Act of the Parliament; or
- (b) in an urgent case, where to do so would not be contrary to the positive intention expressed by a resolution of the Parliament dealing with the particular emergency, by an Emergency Regulation.

(2) An Emergency Regulation may be altered at any time —
- (a) by the Head of State, acting with, and in accordance with, the advice of the National Executive Council; or
- (b) by an Emergency Act; or
- (c) by decision of the Parliament.

(3) An emergency order may be disallowed at any time by decision of the Parliament.

AS TO EFFECTIVENESS OF SECTION 236(1)(b)

Comment

Because s.231 prohibits the making of Emergency Regulations after the end of twenty-four hours after the Parliament first meets after the declaration of national emergency, s.236(1)(b) will not permit urgent alterations after that period. This almost eliminates the usefulness of the provision.

237. — AUTOMATIC TERMINATION OF EMERGENCY LAWS, ETC.

(1) Subject to Section 238 (*extension of Emergency Acts*) an emergency law, unless it has expired under Section 231(3) (*Emergency Regulations*) or unless earlier repealed shall be deemed to be

repealed immediately after the end of the day on which the period of declared national emergency ends.

(2) Where an Emergency Regulation which has amended or repealed any law in force immediately before the regulation took effect, is deemed to be repealed under Sub-section (1), the repeal of that regulation shall revive the previous law from the date of that repeal as if the repealed regulation had not been made.

238. — EXTENSION OF EMERGENCY ACTS.

(1) Subject to Subsection (2), to the extent that its extension is necessary to deal with the results or aftermath of the period of declared national emergency and is reasonably justifiable in a democratic society that has a proper regard for the rights and dignity of mankind, the operation of an Emergency Act may be extended from time to time, after the end of the period of declared national emergency, by decision of the Parliament by an absolute majority vote, for a period or periods each not exceeding two months.

(2) After the end of the period of declared national emergency, internment may be continued only in accordance with Section 244(6) (*laws providing for internment*).

Division 4. — Parliamentary Supervision and Control.

239. — PARLIAMENTARY CONTROL.

(1) Unless the Parliament is in session at the commencement of a period of declared national emergency, it shall be called to meet as soon as practicable, and in any event not more than 15 days, after the commencement of the period and thereafter during the period at intervals each not exceeding two months.

(2) At each meeting of the Parliament during a period of declared national emergency the Prime Minister shall present to the Parliament a statement setting out —
(a) the reasons for the declaration of war or of the national emergency, or for the continuance of the period; and
(b) the reasons for any new Emergency Regulations; and
(c) a report on the operation of the emergency laws.

(3) Unless earlier revoked, a declaration of a national emergency expires at the end of the period of 21 days after its making, but may be extended from time to time by decision of the Parliament by an absolute majority vote, for a period or periods each not exceeding two months.

C.P.C. Report Ch.5 Part 2 p.2

6. We believe that it is essential that Parliament have a central role in ensuring that the country, or part of the country, is under a State of Emergency only where the circumstances are so serious as to justify this. We recommend that to enable parliament to carry out this role effectively, the National Executive Council should be required, when it makes a declaration of a State of Emergency, to clearly state its reasons for so doing. It should explain to the National Parliament and the nation the circumstances which have led to the decision to declare a State of Emergency. This statement should be sufficiently specific to enable the parliament to debate it meaningfully.

7. A proclamation of a declared State of Emergency should take effect when it is published in the Government Gazette, but it should remain in force for only a very short period unless parliament approves an extension of the State of Emergency.

8. We have recommended that if parliament is sitting at the time of the proclamation, or is about to meet, the State of Emergency should automatically cease after eight days unless parliament, by a resolution carried by an absolute majority of the members, approves an extension for a period of not more than two months.

9. If parliament is not sitting or scheduled to sit within seven days of the proclamation, the declaration of Emergency should last for fifteen days instead of eight, but parliament should be called together as soon as practicable, (in any case not more than fourteen days after the proclamation has been made), in order that members may debate the declaration of Emergency, and decide whether or not there is sufficient justification for its being extended.

10. We have made provision for parliament to grant further extensions of a State of Emergency for two months at a time.

AS TO THE EFFECTIVENESS OF PARLIAMENTARY CONTROL

Comment

Although Parliament's active support would be required for the Executive to have recourse to the more significant emergency powers, including those of internment, it is arguable that a determined executive could continue to govern by Emergency Regulations for a period without the support of Parliament. This possibility is suggested by the absence of any provision preventing the executive from repeatedly redeclaring a state of national emergency and remaking Emergency Regulations as they expire or are revoked by resolutions of the Parliament. Only an executive temporarily immune from dismissal by a no confidence motion (see Section 145(4)) could, however, pursue such a confrontationist course with any likelihood of political survival.

It is to be noted that the above comment assumes that the courts of Papua New Guinea would follow the common-law rules which permit (in the absence of legislation to the contrary) the remaking of disallowed regulations: *Victorian Stevedoring and General Contracting Co. and Meakes v Dignan* (1931) 46 CLR 73 at pp.129, 130 per Evatt J. Those common law rules might, however, be held not to be applicable to the circumstances of Papua New Guinea (see Sch.2.2). If the courts did reject them they presumably would be free to apply principles developed under Sch.2.3 more consistent with the principle of the supremacy of Parliament.

Note also that statutory intervention has achieved just such a result in the case of those regulations which may be disallowed under s.116 of the Constitution. Such regulations may not be remade within six (6) months of the date of their disallowance: see s.91 of the *Interpretation Act* Ch.2.

240. — EMERGENCY COMMITTEES.

(1) An Act of the Parliament shall provide for and in respect of the appointment of committees of the Parliament (to be known as "Emergency Committees") in respect of a period or periods of declared national emergency.

(*See: Emergency Committees Act* Ch.33A.)

(2) No Minister may be a member of a Committee.

(3) A Committee shall be available to meet at all times during the period in respect of which it was appointed.

(4) Subject to the availability of members to meet in accordance with Subsection (3), a Committee should, in principle, be broadly representative of the various parts of the country and of parties and groups in the Parliament.

241. — TEMPORARY EMERGENCY COMMITTEES.

(1) An Act of the Parliament or the Standing Orders of the Parliament shall make provision for and in respect of the appointment of a Temporary Emergency Committee to hold office if a period of declared national emergency commences at a time when the Parliament is not in session and an Emergency Committee has not been established in accordance with Section 240 (*Emergency Committees*) in respect of the period.

(See: Emergency Committes Act Ch.33A.)

(2) A Temporary Emergency Committee ceases to hold office (except for the purpose of making a report in accordance with Section 242(2) (*functions, etc., of Emergency Committees*) as to events occurring during its term of office) —
- (a) at the time of the establishment of an Emergency Committee in accordance with Section 240 (*Emergency Committees*) in respect of the period of declared national emergency; or
- (b) at the end of the first meeting of the Parliament after its establishment,

whichever first occurs.

242. — FUNCTIONS, ETC., OF EMERGENCY COMMITTEES.

(1) The Prime Minister shall ensure that —
- (a) copies of all emergency laws and, so far as is practicable, of all emergency orders, are forwarded immediately to the Emergency Committee; and
- (b) subject to any Emergency Act, the Committee is fully provided with information concerning, and is fully consulted concerning, developments in the situation and in particular concerning proposed emergency laws and the operation of existing emergency laws.

(2) At each meeting of the Parliament during a period of declared national emergency the Emergency Committee shall present to the Parliament a statement as to —
- (a) whether or not the period of declared national emergency should continue; and

(b) the justification for and the operation of the emergency laws; and

(c) whether or not any emergency law should be altered,

and such other related matters as it thinks fit.

(3) As soon as practicable after receipt by him of a request to do so from the Emergency Committee and in any event not more than 15 days afterwards, the Speaker shall call a meeting of the Parliament to consider —

(a) any statements by the Committee under Subsection (2) and by the Prime Minister under Section 239(2) (*Parliamentary control*); and

(b) whether or not the period of declared national emergency should be allowed to continue; and

(c) whether or not an emergency law should be altered,

and such other matters as the Parliament thinks fit.

243. — PRIORITY OF EMERGENCY BUSINESS IN PARLIAMENT.

During a period of declared national emergency, and while any emergency law is in force, the first priority shall, subject to any express provision of this Constitution to the contrary, be given to any question, notice, motion or other Parliamentary process relating to the emergency or to an emergency law.

Division 5. — Internment.

244. — LAWS PROVIDING FOR INTERNMENT.

(1) The internment of persons may be permitted only by an Act of the Parliament.

(2) An Act referred to in Subsection (1) —

(a) must be made by an absolute majority vote; and

(b) takes effect on a date fixed by an absolute majority vote made after the commencement of a period of declared national emergency and, after at least four days' notice of the relevant motion has been given; and

(c) subject to Subsection (6), authorizes internment only during a period of declared national emergency.

(3) Subject to Subsection (4), at least four days' notice of the intention to introduce to the Parliament a proposed law to permit internment must be given, and the proposed law must be circulated, in accordance with the Standing Orders of the Parliament, to all members of the Parliament at least four days before the proposed law is made.

(4) During a time of war, the periods of four days prescribed in Subsection (3) are reduced to 24 hours.

(5) In his certificate given under Section 110 (*certification as to making of laws*) the Speaker must certify that the requirements of Subsection (2)(a) and (b) and of Subsection (3) or (4), as the case may be, have been complied with.

(6) Internment may continue after the end of the period of declared national emergency only to the extent that is reasonably required for the orderly and peaceful repatriation, resettlement or re-establishment of internees.

C.P.C. Report Ch.5 Part 2 p.3

15. The Committee does, however recognize that at some time in the future a situation of civil strife may arise which is so grave that a very substantial number of members of Parliament will be prepared to accept, during the crisis period, a suspension of the provisions of the Constitution which ensure that a person is not held in custody without fair trial. This would enable legislation to be passed providing for detention without trial of, for instance, alleged tourist (sic) [terrorist] leaders.

16. Our recommendations provide for this contingency. Whilst we propose that the passing of a law providing for preventive detention at any time other than during a State of Emergency be prohibited, we have allowed for the provisions of the Constitution protecting the right to a fair trial to be suspended by a resolution of the National Parliament passed by a special majority. That majority should, we believe be a substantial one, namely two thirds of the members of the National Parliament.

17. We appreciate that in situations of this kind it can be very important that appropriate action be taken promptly. On the other hand, where a matter which is so basic as is the right not to be held in custody except upon conviction in court after a fair trial (or in accordance with a court order made in respect of a person who is awaiting trial) is at stake we believe Members of Parliament should be allowed sufficient time to read the proposed legislation carefully, and give thought to its implications.

18. Our proposal is that in time of war, a motion for the suspension of the provisions of the Constitution concerning the fundamental right of personal liberty, or the right to the protection of the law, should be voted upon only after twenty four hours have passed following the moving of the motion. In a situation where a State of Emergency exists other than because the country is at war, there should be a longer period of time allowed members before they are obliged to vote on the motion. This period should, we believe, be seven days.

19. We further recommend that the bill providing for preventive detention must be circulated to members either before the motion for the suspension of the relevant constitutional provisions is moved, or at the same time. We consider that it should not be possible for the bill to be passed until after the motion for the suspension of the relevant provisions of the Constitution has been passed.

20. We recommend that in the event that the Constitution is suspended in this way, Parliament should be able to end the suspension by passing a resolution to that effect by a simple majority. In any event, we propose that the suspension would end automatically when the State of Emergency ceases .... [p.5]

31. To avoid any doubt as to the intention that immediately after a State of Emergency ends all persons who have been detained during the Emergency must be released, we have recommended that a specific provision to this effect be included in the Constitution.

245. — INTERNMENT.

(1) The following provisions apply to and in relation to an internee:-

(a) an internee and his next-of-kin or other close relative in the country shall, as soon as practicable and in any case not more than seven days after the commencement of his internment, be furnished with a statement in writing in a language that he understands specifying in detail the grounds upon which he is interned; and

(b) subject to Section 244(6) (*laws providing for internment*), an internee (other than an alien enemy) shall be released from detention at the end of the period of two months after his internment unless an independent and impartial tribunal established under paragraph (e) has reviewed his case and found that sufficient cause has been shown for his internment; and

(c) subject to Section 244(6) (*laws providing for internment*) an internee (other than an alien enemy) shall be released from detention at the end of the period of six months after his internment; and

(d) an internee (other than an alien enemy) is entitled to have his case reviewed by an independent and impartial tribunal established under paragraph (e) as soon as practicable after he has been interned, and in any case not more than one month after the commencement of his internment, and afterwards at intervals not exceeding two months; and

C.P.C. Report Ch.5 Part 2 p.3

24. We have recommended that subject to two exceptions, no person should be kept in preventive detention for longer than two months unless a review tribunal has reported to the responsible Minister, before the end of that period, that in its opinion sufficient cause has been shown for the detention. The exceptions relate to a situation in which Papua New Guinea is at war with another country. In these circumstances a person who is a national of a country with which Papua New Guinea is at war would not have the right to have his case considered by a review tribunal, whilst any other person detained would not have an automatic review of his case — he would have to request a review.

25. We have recommended a number of other safeguards concerning detained persons other than [p.4] those who are foreign enemies in time of war, namely that —

- within twenty-four hours of his being detained, a person shall be given a statement in writing, in a language he understands, which sets out in detail the grounds on which he has been detained. Furthermore, his next of kin must be given a copy of the statement within fourteen days of his being detained;
- not more than ten days after a person has been detained, notification of the detention shall be published in the Gazette and particulars must be given there of the provision of law under which the detention is authorized;
- not more than one month after the commencement of his detention, and subsequently at intervals of not more than three months, the case of a detained person (other than a person who has been detained in time of war) must be reviewed by a review tribunal;
- at the expiration of a period of six months, a person in detention (other than a person who has been detained in time of war) must be either released or charged with a specific offence for which he can be brought to trial;
- reasonable facilities are to be made available to the detained person (including the opportunity to apply for legal aid), to enable him to consult a lawyer of his own choice, and the legal representative he chooses should be permitted to make representations on his behalf to a review tribunal;
- when his case is reviewed by the tribunal, the detained person shall be entitled to appear in person or by his legal representative; and
- while in detention, the person must be treated at least as favourably as a remand prisoner awaiting trial, since he would not have been convicted of any crime.

(e) an Organic Law shall provide for the establishment of the independent and impartial tribunal referred to in this section and that the Chairman of the tribunal shall be a person qualified to be a Judge of the National Court; and

(*See: Organic Law on the Internment Tribunal* Ch.1.)

(f) the Organic Law referred to in paragraph (e) shall provide that as far as practicable where the case of an internee is being reviewed on a second or subsequent occasion, a majority of the members (including the Chairman) of any tribunal referred to in that paragraph which conducts that review shall be different from the members of any such tribunal which previously reviewed the case of that detainee; and

C.P.C. Report Ch.5 Part 2 p.3

23. The first of these provisions requires the establishment of an independent, impartial review tribunal comprising a chairman (who should be an experienced lawyer qualified for appointment as a judge) and two other members, all of whom would be appointed by the Judicial and Legal Service Commission, within three days of the commencement of any law permitting preventive detention.

(g) subject to Subsection (5), where a tribunal established under paragraph (e) finds that a citizen has been interned wrongly or without sufficient reason —
  (i) the Head of State, acting with, and in accordance with, the advice of the National Executive Council shall order that he be released; and
  (ii) he is entitled to compensation, in accordance with law, for the internment and any consequences of it; and

(h) subject to Subsection (5), where a tribunal established in accordance with paragraph (e) finds that there are no longer sufficient grounds for the internment of a citizen, the Minister responsible for national security shall order that he be released immediately; and

(i) a person released from internment in accordance with paragraphs (c), (g) or (h) shall not again be interned substantially on the same facts unless a change in circumstances relating to the grounds of the original internment gives these facts a new significance; and

C.P.C. Report Ch.5 Part 2 p.4

26. We recommend that review tribunals should have power to make binding recommendations to the responsible Minister as to whether they consider sufficient reasons have been shown by the executive for detaining particular persons. Although such tribunals would *not* be courts of law hearing only legally admissible evidence in respect of charges of specific criminal offences, we believe it is extremely important that the executive be bound to accept and act upon their recommendations except in time of war. Otherwise, the tribunals would be likely to be ineffective.

27. We believe that a review tribunal should also have power to make binding recommendations and fair compensation should be paid to people who have been detained without justification. As well as providing redress for the unfortunate person who has been unjustifiably detained, this provision might also have some effect as a deterrent to the executive carrying out arbitrary arrests of innocent people under preventive detention powers.

(j) internees shall be kept separated, as far as practicable, from other persons in custody, and shall receive treatment not less favourable than that afforded to persons in custody awaiting trial for offences; and

(k) the names and places of residence of internees shall be published in the National Gazette and in any newspaper which has a national circulation, within 14 days of the internment, and at monthly intervals afterwards; and

(l) the Minister responsible for national security shall present to the Parliament at each meeting of the Parliament during the period of declared national emergency, but in any event, at intervals not exceeding six months, reports concerning all internees, their treatment, the review of their cases and action taken in regard to them.

C.P.C. Report Ch.5 Part 2 p.4

29. In order that parliament and people generally may be kept informed, at regular intervals, as to exactly how many people are detained at a given time, and who the detainees are, we recommend that in every month in which parliament sits during a State of Emergency the responsible Minister should make a report to parliament in which these important facts are set out. Such reports should also indicate the number of cases in which a review tribunal has made recommendations, and the action taken in respect of each case in which a recommendation has been made for a person to be released. Thus Members of Parliament would have the opportunity of supervising the administration of the preventive detention legislation — a truly vital role.

30. As parliament is unlikely to be meeting continuously during a State of Emergency, we have also recommended that the responsible Minister publish in the Government Gazette each month the information concerning detained persons which he is required to table in parliament.

(2) An internee shall be given adequate facilities to prepare and make representations to the review tribunal referred to in Subsection (1)(e) either personally or through a lawyer, and in particular shall be allowed full access to a lawyer (and if necessary to legal aid) and the services of a competent interpeter if required.

(3) An internee shall —

(a) be permitted to appear in person before the review tribunal; and

(b) be permitted to be represented by a lawyer and a friend before the review tribunal.

(4) The tribunal shall forward copies of its findings and recommendations to the internee and to his next-of-kin or other close relative in the country when they are furnished to the Minister responsible for national security.

C.P.C. Report Ch.5 Part 2 p.4

28. It is further proposed that the part of a tribunal's report which sets out its view as to whether or not the Government has shown sufficient reason for detaining a person, and the recommendations it has made based on that view, should be promptly made available to the detained person, and to his next of kin. This would enable action to be taken in the National Court, on behalf of the detained person, if the recommendations of the tribunal were not acted upon promptly.

(5) Where in his opinion it is necessary to do so in the interests of national security or public order, the Head of State, acting with, and in accordance with, the advice of the National Executive

Council may refuse to make an order in accordance with Subsection (1)(g) or (h) for the release of an internee, but in that event, except in time of war —

(a) he shall promptly present to the Parliament a report stating that he has refused to release the internee and setting out the reasons for his refusal; and

(b) the Parliament may order that the internee be released.

(6) Where an order is made in accordance with Subsection (5) —

(a) the internee shall be released in accordance with the order; and

(b) Subsection (1)(i) applies as though the order were an order under Subsection (1)(g) or (h), as appropriate.

(7) An Organic Law, an Act of the Parliament or an emergency law may make further provision, not inconsistent with this section, in respect of the treatment, security and discipline of internees.

(8) The provisions of the Geneva Convention Relative to the Protection of Civilian Persons in Time of War of August 14 1949, and any other international convention relating to interned persons, shall be complied with in relation to persons protected by them, and in addition such of those provisions that are of general application and can appropriately be applied to interned citizens shall be complied with in relation to such internees.

Division 6. — Miscellaneous.

246. — EXTENSION OF TENURE OF PARLIAMENT AND GOVERNOR-GENERAL.

During a period of declared national emergency the Parliament may, by an absolute majority vote, extend its term of office, or the term of office of the Governor-General, or both, for a term not exceeding the length of the period and such time afterwards as is necessary to allow a general election to be arranged and held, or for a Governor-General to be appointed, as the case requires.

PART XI. — MISCELLANEOUS.

247. — LEGAL CAPACITY OF THE INDEPENDENT STATE OF PAPUA NEW GUINEA.

(1) Papua New Guinea has power to acquire, hold and dispose of property of any kind, and to make contracts, in accordance with an Act of the Parliament.

(*See: Lands Acquisition (Development Purposes) Act* Ch.192; *Government Contracts Act* Ch.34.)

(2) Papua New Guinea may sue and be sued, in accordance with an Act of the Parliament.

(*See: Claims by and against the State Act* Ch.30.)

AS TO WHETHER SECTION 247 CONFERS A SUBSTANTIVE RIGHT TO SUE THE STATE

Comment

Subsection (2) confers a right to sue the State 'in accordance with an Act of the Parliament'. An interesting question is whether the words 'in accordance with an Act of the Parliament' are words of limitation (i.e. so that a right to sue will not exist save as conferred by an Act) or of procedure only (so that a substantive right to sue can be said to be directly conferred by the Constitution and so that an Act may only regulate the manner of its exercise). It is submitted that the view that the sub-section confers a substantive right is to be preferred not only because it is consistent with fundamental constitutional objectives (the citizen to be ruled by a state governed by law), but also because a literal reading of Subsection (2) suggests that a right was intended to be conferred. An analogous problem was considered by the High Court of Australia in *Downey v Prior* (1960) 103 CLR 353. In that case s.219 of the *Local Government Act* 1919 (N.S.W.) provided: 'Any elector may at the council's office inspect the books of account .... as prescribed'. No method of inspection was subsequently prescribed. The court held that the prescription of a method was not essential to complete the right of inspection granted by the section. In the absence of prescription the right could be exercised in any appropriate manner. A similar approach to the construction of s.247(2) would, it is submitted, be appropriate for Papua New Guinea, particularly given that the National and Supreme Courts have powers to make ad-hoc rules of procedure as necessary under s.185 of the Constitution and given that s.11(2) of the Constitution requires, where possible, that the provisions of the Constitution be read as self-executing.

248. — VESTING OF RIGHTS AND LIABILITIES OF FORMER GOVERNMENT.

All property that was, immediately before Independence Day, vested in the body corporate at that time known as "the Government of Papua New Guinea" is, on that day, vested in Papua New Guinea, and all rights and liabilities (actual or contingent) of that body immediately before that day are, on that day, rights and liabilities of Papua New Guinea.

249. — DECLARATIONS BY CERTAIN OFFICE-HOLDERS.

Subject to any Organic Law, every person who is subject to Division III.2 (*leadership code*) before entering upon the duties of or exercising any of the powers of his office, shall make —

(a) unless he has made it on a previous occasion or is exempt from making it under —
   (i) Section 251(1) (*taking of certain oaths, etc., by non-citizens*); or
   (ii) Section 272 (*oaths, affirmation, etc.*),

   the Declaration of Loyalty; and

(b) in the case of —
  (i) a judicial officer — the Judicial Declaration; or
  (ii) an office-holder other than a judicial officer — the Declaration of Office.

C.P.C. Report Ch.14 p.2

13. It is important, we believe, that all constitutional office-holders should be publicly committed to uphold the Constitution, including the values embodied in the National Goals and and Directive Principles in Chapter 2, and the Leadership Code in Chapter 3. They should, we recommend, take an oath or make an affirmation (according to individual conscience) in the form set out in Schedule 3 of this Report before they take up the duties of their offices. It should be impressed upon them that these pledges are no mere formalities: they have been carefully composed by and for those with a genuine personal commitment to the objectives they specify.

GENERALLY

Referred to

by Wilson J. in *Re Rooney (No 2)* [1979] PNGLR 448 at pp.493, 494.

250. — MAKING OF DECLARATION OF LOYALTY, ETC.

(1) Subject to any provision of a Constitutional Law making special provision for the purpose, the Oath of Allegiance, the Declaration of Loyalty, the Judicial Declaration or the Declaration of Office (or any other oath, affirmation or declaration that is required or permitted to be taken or made by or for the purposes of a Constitutional Law) may be taken or made before any person appointed for the purpose by or under an Act of the Parliament, or in the absence of any such Act, before a person appointed for the purpose by the Head of State, acting with, and in accordance with the advice of the National Executive Council.

(2) Notwithstanding the provision of Subsection (1), an oath, affirmation or declaration referred to in that subsection is binding and effectual no matter before whom it is taken or made.

251. — TAKING CERTAIN OATHS, ETC., BY NON-CITIZENS.

(1) If —
  (a) it is desirable that a non-citizen be appointed to an office under a statute; and
  (b) it is a requirement that in order to be qualified for appointment, or to enter upon the duties or exercise the powers of the office, a person must take the Oath of Allegiance or make the Declaration of Loyalty, or take or make some oath, affirmation or declaration; and
  (c) the National Executive Council is satisfied that, by reason of the law of some other country, to take the oath of allegiance or make the Declaration of Loyalty, or take or make the other oath, affirmation or declaration, in the prescribed manner or

form would or might adversely affect the nationality or citizenship status of the person concerned,

the Head of State, acting with, and in accordance with, the advice of the National Executive Council, may, by order, substitute some oath, affirmation or declaration or, if thought necessary, exempt the person from the requirement.

(2) Notwithstanding Subsection (1), the non-citizen is subject to all laws as if he had made the Declaration of Loyalty, or had taken or made the other oath, affirmation or declaration, as the case may be.

(3) Nothing in Subsection (1) applies to or in respect of the Judicial Declaration.

252. — THE NATIONAL GAZETTE.

There shall be an official journal of the National Government, which shall be known as the National Gazette or by such other name as is given by or under an Act of the Parliament.

253. — SLAVERY, ETC.

Slavery, and the slave trade in all their forms, and all similar institutions and practices, are strictly prohibited.

AS TO INTERNATIONAL CONVENTIONS

Comment

It is anomalous that s.253 appears under 'Part XI Miscellaneous' of the Constitution rather than under those sections of the Constitution which are concerned with human rights. For analogous human rights provisions of international law, see:
European Convention on Human Rights, Article 4(1);
Universal Declaration of Rights, Article 4.

254. — FILLING OF OFFICES, ETC.

In principle —

(a) no constitutional office shall be left unfilled on a substantive basis for longer than is necessary for it to be filled by an appropriate appointee; and

(b) no person shall hold more than one public office at the same time except where one such office is so much associated with, or related to, another, or where the holding of one such office is so relevant to the holding of another, as to make it desirable that the offices be held jointly; and

(c) public offices of similar importance or standing, and in particular offices in any statutory board or committee, should be filled by persons from the various areas of the country.

255. — CONSULTATION.

In principle, where a law provides for consultation between persons or bodies, or persons and bodies, the consultation must be meaningful and allow for a genuine interchange and consideration of views.

AS TO WHAT CONSTITUTES CONSULTATION

Comment

Section 255 has not been referred to in any reported decision of a post-Independence court. The question of what constitutes consultation was, however, considered by the pre-Independence Full Court of the Supreme Court in *Paikara v Nau* [1971-72] PNGLR 345. That case turned on the interpretation of s.18 of the *Local Government Act* 1963 which granted power to the Administration to take certain action 'after consultation with the council or councils concerned'. The Court (Minogue C.J., Clarkson and Kelly JJ.) in a joint decision held (at p.368):

> We agree that the administration is obliged to consult with the Council — the Ordinance says so. But it does not lay down any procedure to be followed nor does it require any accord to be reached. The nature and extent of the communication necessary to constitute a consultation could depend on the nature and complexity of the proposal, where and when it originates, say previous communications or even a refusal of the Council.

The above passage would appear to correctly state the law applicable to s.255. However, it needs to be stressed that under s.255 consultation must be *both* meaningful and allow for genuine interchange and consideration of views. Thus, whilst the degree of communication necessary to constitute a consultation will vary from case to case (and to that extent be essentially a political rather than a legal consideration), it is clear that there must be a *minimum* content to constitute a consultation. Thus, it is submitted that the mere notification of an intended action to the other party without more would not amount to consultation within the meaning of s.255.

256. — REPORTS BY PUBLIC OFFICE-HOLDERS, ETC.

Subject to this Constitution, an Act of the Parliament may make provision for and in respect of annual and other reports by a constitutional office-holder or any other public office-holder, or by a constitutional institution or any other statutory body.

257. — PROOF OF ACTS OF THE CONSTITUENT ASSEMBLY.

(1) All courts, Judges and persons acting judicially shall take judicial notice of all acts and proceedings of the Constituent Assembly.

GENERALLY

Referred to

by Quinlivan A.J. in *Marben v Gesa* (1981 Unreported) N314(M) at p.4.

(2) An act of, or the proceedings of, the Constituent Assembly may be proved for any purposes by the production of —

(a) a certificate under the hand, or purporting to be under the hand, of the Speaker of the pre-Independence House of Assembly; or

(b) a document under the hand, or purporting to be under the hand, of the Clerk or other proper officer of the pre-Independence House of Assembly and purporting to be the minutes or other official record of the proceedings of the Constituent Assembly.

AS TO AVAILABILITY OF RECORDS OF PROCEEDINGS

Comment

To date, the proceedings of the Constituent Assembly have not been published. Unpublished records exist in some library collections, see for example papers held by the Department of Justice Library.

258. — CONSTITUTIONAL REGULATIONS.

(1) The Head of State, acting with, and in accordance with, the advice of the National Executive Council, may make regulations, not inconsistent with a Constitutional Law or an Act of the Parliament, prescribing all matters that by a Constitutional Law are required or permitted to be prescribed or provided for by Constitutional Regulation.

(*See: Electoral Regulation* 1977.)

(2) All Constitutional Regulations shall be tabled in the Parliament as soon as practicable after being made, and may be disallowed by the Parliament at any time.

AS TO LAW APPLICABLE TO CONSTITUTIONAL REGULATIONS

Comment

There are no rules expressly governing the legal effect of failure to table the commencement of, or the repeal of, a Constitutional Regulation.

Constitutional Regulations are not Constitutional Laws (see Sch.1.2 definition of Constitutional Law) for the purposes of Sch.1.17, nor are they governed by the provisions of s.116 of the Constitution or s.63 of the *Interpretation Act* Ch.2. This lacunae means that rules ordinarily applying to delegated legislation in Papua New Guinea do not apply to Constitutional Regulations. To fill this gap common law principles apply (Sch.2.2) unless held inappropriate to the circumstances of Papua New Guinea. For an outline of the common law rules see *Institute of Patent Agents v Lockwood* [1894] AC 347 (failure to table renders delegated legislation inoperative) and *Kay v Goodwin* (1860) 6 Bing 582 (repeal/disallowance obliterates legislation as completely as if it had never been passed).

GENERALLY

Referred to

by Kapi J. in *SCR No 2 of 1981; Re Opai Kunangel Amin* (1982 Unreported) SC231 at p.4.

259. — INDEPENDENT TRIBUNALS.

Unless otherwise provided for by a Constitutional Law, in any case where a Constitutional Law requires the appointment of an independent tribunal, the members of that tribunal shall be appointed from a list of names approved by the Judicial and Legal Services Commission.

PART XII. — CONSTITUTIONAL REVIEW.

260. — GENERAL CONSTITUTIONAL COMMISSION.

(1) An Act of the Parliament shall make provision for and in respect of the establishment, at or after the end of the period of three years commencing on Independence Day, of a General Constitutional Commission.

(*See: Constitutional Commission Act* Ch.21A.)

(2) The members of the Commission shall —
- (a) be appointed by the Head of State, acting with, and in accordance with, the advice of the National Executive Council given after consultation with any appropriate parliamentary committee; and
- (b) be broadly representative of the different areas of the country; and
- (c) give balanced representation of the major parties and groups in Parliament.

(3) Each member of the General Constitutional Commission must be —
- (a) a member of the Parliament; or
- (b) a member of a provincial government or local government body; or
- (c) a member of a State Service; or
- (d) some other citizen with relevant expertize.

(4) The General Constitutional Commission shall inquire into the working of this Constitution and the Organic Laws.

(5) As soon as is reasonably practicable after its appointment, the General Constitutional Commission shall forward a report of its findings to the Speaker for presentation to the Parliament, together with its recommendations (if any) as to amendment of this Constitution, and new or amended Organic Laws or other laws or administrative procedures.

(*See: Final Report of the General Constitutional Commission* 1983)

261. — INTERIM CONSTITUTIONAL COMMISSION.

(1) An Act of Parliament shall provide that until the Constitutional Commission is established there shall be an Interim Constitutional Commission the membership of which is in accordance with Section 260(2) and (3) (*General Constitutional Commission*).

(*See: Constitutional Commission (Interim Provisions) Act* Ch.21 (repealed)).

(2) The Interim Constitutional Commission shall consider proposed alteration of this Constitution or of any Organic Law, and report to Parliament before there is an opportunity for debate of the proposed legislation.

262. — SUBORDINATE COMMISSIONS AND COMMITTEES.

(1) Acts of the Parliament may make provision for and in respect of —
(a) a Commission on Provincial Government, the primary function of which shall be to investigate the workings of the system of provincial government; and
(b) other commissions and committees to investigate such other aspects of the working of this Constitution as the Parliament thinks desirable. (*Replaced by Constitutional Amendment No. 1 — Provincial Government, s.3*)

(2) The commissions and committees established in accordance with Subsection (1)(b) shall report to the General Constitutional Commission on the subject matters of their respective investigations, with such recommendations (if any) as they think desirable, in time to allow the General Constitutional Commission to report to the Parliament in accordance with Section 260 (*General Constitutional Commission*).

(3) The General Constitutional Commission shall ensure that any reports of commissions or committees established in accordance with Subsection (1)(b) are forwarded to the Speaker for presentation to the Parliament before or at the same time as its report is so forwarded.

263. — FURTHER DEFINITION, ETC.

Acts of the Parliament may make provision for further defining the terms of reference of the General Constitutional Commission and any other commissions or committees established in accordance with Section 262 (*subordinate commissions and committees*).

PART XIII. — IMMEDIATE AND TRANSITIONAL PROVISIONS.

Division 1. — General.

264. — EFFECT OF PART XIII.

The provisions of this Part, and of any Provisional Organic Law or Organic Law made for the purposes of Section 267 (*transitional laws*), have effect notwithstanding anything in the preceding provisions of this Constitution.

GENERALLY

Referred to

by Frost C.J. in *Reference No 2 of 1976* [1976] PNGLR 228 at p.234 (overriding effect to be given by s.264 to s.269(4) does not in itself prevent the application of other relevant provisions of the Constitution to the First Parliament).

265. — DISSOLUTION OF THE CONSTITUENT ASSEMBLY.

The Constituent Assembly, having performed its duty to frame and adopt, on behalf of the People, a Constitution, and its other duties, is dissolved.

266. — PROVISIONAL LAWS.

(1) If before Independence Day the Constituent Assembly has made an instrument expressed to be a Provisional Organic Law, the instrument takes effect, on Independence Day, as if it were an Organic Law made and coming into effect on that day.

(2) If before Independence Day the Constituent Assembly has made an instrument expressed to be a Provisional Act of the Parliament made for the purpose of bringing any provision of this Constitution into effective operation on Independence Day, the instrument takes effect, on Independence Day, as if it were an Act of the Parliament made and coming into effect on that day.

AS TO FORMAL REQUIREMENTS OF ORGANIC LAWS

per Williams J.

The argument for the appellant proceeds that by reason of s.126(7) of the Constitution only an Organic Law can make provision for and in respect of appeals to the National Court in Electoral matters and that, because of the statement contained in s.1(1) of the instrument made by the Constituent Assembly that Part XVIII is intended to take effect as an Act of the Parliament, Part XVIII is not an Organic Law which complies with the requirements of s.126(7) of the Constitution which, it is said, is a mandatory provision. In consequence the respondent could derive no assistance from the provisions of Pt. XVIII to confer on him the status of a petitioner. Whilst the National Court had jurisdiction to determine any question as to the qualifications of a person to be or to remain a member of the Parliament (s.135 of the Constitution) the respondent had no standing to invoke that jurisdiction.

The concept underlying an Organic Law as distinct from an ordinary Act of Parliament is that a proposed law to alter an Organic Law must, in accordance with s.14 of the Constitution, be supported on a division by a prescribed majority of votes expressed on at least two occasions after opportunity for debate on the merits whereas the amendment of an ordinary Act requires merely a majority of votes of the members present voting (s.144 of the Constitution).

To my mind the question reduces itself to one of ascertaining the intention of the framers of the Constitution in enacting s.126(7). That section is very general in its terms stating that an Organic Law shall make provision 'for and in respect of' the several matters referred to in the section. The framers of the Constitution contemplated, in adopting s.12(3), that an Organic Law may contain provisions that would be subject to the stringent provisions of s.14 of the Constitution relating to amendment and also provisions which would not.

Section 126(7) which makes provision with respect to a member relating to elections including appeals to the National Court in electoral matters itself contains no indication as to where the line should be drawn, that is to say which matters should be subject to the provisions of s.14 and which should not.

It seems to me that this is the reverse of the usual kind of case where Constitutional provisions are made and subsequently an Act is passed which is called into question as being outside the authority of the Constitution. In this case, however, the Constituent Assembly made the instrument and adopted the Constitution itself on the same day. Included in the Constitution was s.266 the clear purpose of which was, to, my mind, to adopt and give the force of law to Provisional Organic Laws and Provisional Acts made by the Constituent Assembly prior to Independence Day.

The instrument in question in this case was one which, on its face, was expressed to be a Provisional Organic Law for the purpose of implementing ss.125 and 126 of the Constitution and thus is of the kind of instrument referred to in s.266(1). I think that it must be attributed to the framers of the Constitution (the same body as that which produced the instrument) that they were aware of the form and content of it and that, by adopting s.266 of the Constitution, gave to it force and effect on Independence Day as an Organic Law for the purposes of s.126(7) of the Constitution. In so doing I think that they gave a clear indication that it fulfilled their intention underlying the making of ss.126(7) and 12 of the Constitution. In other words, I am unable to see how it can be said that an instrument is outside the authority conferred by the Constitution when the Constitution itself makes provision to give the instrument force and effect. I would, accordingly, hold that the petitioner was entitled to invoke the jurisdiction of the National Court.
In re Moresby North East Election Petition [1977] PNGLR 429 at pp.439,440; see also Prentice Dep.C.J. at pp.435,436, Pritchard J. at pp.444,445.

GENERALLY

Referred to

by Frost C.J. in *The State v The Independent Tribunal; Ex parte Sasakila* [1976] PNGLR 491 at p.495;

by Kidu C.J. in *SCR No 2 of 1982; Re Organic Law* [1982] PNGLR 214 at p.218;

by Kapi Dep.C.J. (dissenting) in *In the matter of the Organic Law on National Elections: Malipu Balakau v Paul Torato and anor* (1983 Unreported) SC256 at p.21.

267. — TRANSITIONAL LAWS.

(1) A Provisional Organic Law or an Organic Law may make whatever provision seems necessary or desirable for a smooth transition from pre-Independence arrangements to arrangements under this Constitution and, in particular, but without limiting the generality of the foregoing, for securing —

(a) the immediate filling of offices, and the immediately effective operation of institutions under this Constitution where there were corresponding pre-Independence offices or institutions; and

(b) the continued effect of acts done or commenced before Independence Day under pre-Independence laws.

(2) A Provisional Organic Law or an Organic Law made for the purposes of Subsection (1) may declare what were the pre-Independence offices and institutions that correspond with offices and institutions under this Constitution.

(*See*: *Organic Law on Certain Constitutional Office-holders* Ch.1; *Organic Law on immediate and transitional constitutional provisions* Ch.1; *Organic Law on the Public Services Commission* Ch.1.)

268. — FIRST GOVERNOR-GENERAL.

If before Independence Day —

(a) the Constituent Assembly has nominated by a simple majority vote, in an exhaustive secret ballot a person to be the first Governor-General; and

(b) Her Majesty, Elizabeth II, having consented to become Queen and Head of State of Papua New Guinea has signified her approval to that person becoming the Governor-General,

that person becomes the first Governor-General on Independence Day.

269. — FIRST PARLIAMENT, ELECTORATES, ETC.

(1) Notwithstanding anything in this Constitution, but subject to Subsection (6) the open and regional electorates for the pre-Independence House of Assembly established immediately before Independence Day are the first open and provincial (as the case may be) electorates for the Parliament.

(2) Notwithstanding anything in this Constitution but subject to any Organic Law on national electoral matters —

(a) each member of the pre-Independence House of Assembly in office immediately before Independence Day (including a member who although he is or may be disqualified under Section 37(4)(a) of the *Papua New Guinea Act* 1949-1975 of

Australia has been confirmed in his membership by resolution of the House of Assembly) is the first member of the Parliament for his electorate and shall continue to hold office unless or until —

(i) his seat becomes vacant by virtue of Section 104(2)(a), (b),(c),(d),(e),(g) or (h) (*normal term of office*); or

(ii) he becomes a person who has been convicted of and is under sentence of imprisonment, or is subject to be sentenced (other than a person who has been released on recognizance to appear and receive judgement when called upon), for an offence punishable by imprisonment for one year or longer, as in Section 50(1)(a) (*right to vote and stand for public office*); or

(iii) he becomes disqualified under Section 103(3)(b) or (d) (*qualifications for and disqualifications from membership*); and

(b) the pre-Independence Speaker and Chairman of Committees in office immediately before Independence Day are the first Speaker and Deputy Speaker, respectively, of the Parliament; and

(c) the electoral rolls in effect immediately before Independence Day are the first electoral rolls for the first open and provincial electorates (as the case may be).

(3) The Boundaries Commission shall recommend to the Parliament the number of open electorates and their boundaries for determination by the Parliament under Section 125(1) (*electorates*) as soon as possible after Independence Day.

(4) Unless a general election to the Parliament is held earlier under Section 105 (*general elections*) the term of the first Parliament is —

(a) the balance of the term of the pre-Independence House of Assembly remaining unexpended immediately after Independence Day; and

(b) the period up to the first general election held after Independence Day and the first general elections shall be held, as directed by the Head of State, acting with, and in accordance with, the advice of the Electoral Commission, in the months May and June 1977.

(5) If the Parliament has not made a determination under Section 125(1) (*electorates*) in time for the first general elections held after Independence Day —

(a) the number and boundaries of the open electorates shall remain the same as for the previous general elections; and

(b) the number of provincial electorates shall be as determined by an Organic Law; and

(c) the boundaries of the provincial electorates shall be as determined by the Head of State, acting with, and in accordance with, the advice of the Boundaries Commission, but so that the boundaries of the provincial electorates —

(i) enclose all the territory of open electorates within each province; and

(ii) so near as may be, coincide with the boundaries of the provinces as defined in the Organic Law on Provincial Boundaries and the boundaries of the National Capital District as defined in the Organic Law on the Boundaries of the National Capital District.

(6) If a provincial electorate consists of two or more provinces, an Organic Law shall make adequate provision for —

(a) the declaration of each province as a provincial electorate; and

(b) each electorate to be represented by a provincial member,

as soon as practicable after Independence Day.

AS TO ELECTIONS FOR THE FIRST PARLIAMENT

Held

A motion of no confidence under s.145 of the Constitution may not effectively be moved against the government during the life of the first Parliament (from Independence Day to May or June 1977: see s.269(4)(b)) which life may only be shortened by a general election under s.105(1)(c). The provisions of s.145(2)(b) do not apply to the First Parliament. *Reference No 2 of 1976* [1976] PNGLR 228; see Frost C.J. at pp.231-234, Raine J. at p.237, Saldanha J. at pp.239,240.

Held

A general election may be held if the Parliament, by an absolute majority vote, so decides under s.105(1)(c) of the Constitution, notwithstanding that the Parliament has not determined the number of open and provincial electorates and their boundaries in accordance with s.125 of the Constitution. In such a case the number and boundaries of the electorates should remain the same as for the previous general elections for the pre-Independence House of Assembly.
Reference No 3 of 1976 [1976] PNGLR 242; see per Curiam (Frost C.J., Prentice Dep.C.J., Raine, Saldanha and Kearney JJ.) at pp.248,249.

GENERALLY

Referred to

by Frost C.J. in *In re Moresby North East Parliamentary Election (No 2)* [1977] PNGLR 448 at p.451.

270. — FIRST MINISTRY.

(1) The pre-Independence Chief Minister in office immediately before Independence Day is the first Prime Minister.

(2) The other Ministers of the pre-Independence House of Assembly in office immediately before Independence Day are the other first Ministers.

GENERALLY

Referred to

by Frost C.J. in *Reference No 2 of 1976* [1976] PNGLR 228 at p.232 (Constitution s.144(4)(a) providing for the dismissal of ministers other than the Prime Minister applies to any minister in office during the first Parliament).

271. — FIRST JUDGES.

Notwithstanding anything in this Constitution —

(a) the pre-Independence Chief Justice in office immediately before Independence Day is the first Chief Justice of Papua New Guinea; and

(b) the Senior Puisne Judge in office immediately before Independence Day is the First Deputy Chief Justice of Papua New Guinea; and

(c) each Judge in office immediately before Independence Day is a Judge of the National Court; and

(d) each acting Judge in office immediately before Independence Day is Acting Judge of the National Court,

on the same terms and conditions that were applicable to him before Independence Day but in no case shall his term of office exceed three years from the date of his present appointment.

GENERALLY

Referred to

by Prentice Dep.C.J. in *Reference No 1 of 1977* [1977] PNGLR 362 at p.373 (task of interpreting the striking document that forms the Constitution of Papua New Guinea comes to be performed somewhat invidiously by a Supreme Court comprised still of expatriate judges).

272. — OATHS, AFFIRMATION ETC.

(1) Notwithstanding anything in this Constitution, but subject to Section 250 (*making of Declaration of Loyalty etc.*) and Section 251 (*taking certain oaths, etc., by non-citizens*) —

(a) the first Governor-General shall take the Oath of Allegiance and make the Declaration of Loyalty and the Declaration of Office; and

(b) the first Prime Minister and other Ministers, and the first Speaker and Deputy Speaker, shall make the Declaration of Loyalty and the Declaration of Office; and

(c) the first Chief Justice and other Judges shall make the Judicial Declaration,

in public on Independence Day, at such place, and in such manner and form, as are directed by the Prime Minister.

(2) If it is not practicable for a person referred to in Subsection (1)(a),(b) or (c) to comply with the requirements of Subsection (1), he shall take and make the necessary oath or Declarations, or both,

as the case requires, at such time and place, and in such manner and form, as are directed by the Head of State, acting with, and in accordance with, the advice of the Prime Minister.

(3) Any provision of this Constitution preventing a person referred to in Subsection (1)(a),(b) or (c) from entering upon the duties of his office until he has taken the oath of allegiance or made the Declaration of Loyalty, the Declaration of Office or the Judicial Declaration (as the case requires) is suspended pending compliance with the preceding provisions of this section.

273. — TREATIES APPLYING BEFORE INDEPENDENCE.

The provisions of Section 177 (*treaties, etc.,*) do not prevent the Head of State, acting with, and in accordance with, the advice of the National Executive Council, from making a declaration that an international commitment that, immediately before Independence Day, applied to the territory at that time known as Papua New Guinea or a component part of that territory may, by agreement, be treated as if it were binding on Papua New Guinea for a period not exceeding five years after that day.

GENERALLY

Referred to

by Kapi J. in *S.C.R. No 4 of 1980 (No 2); Re Petition of M.T.Somare* [1982] PNGLR 65 at p.77.

274. — COMPOSITION OF CERTAIN CONSTITUTIONAL INSTITUTIONS.

Except where expressly provided otherwise in a Constitutional Law, until 16 September 1985, where a constitutional institution other than the Supreme Court or the National Court is composed of more than one person, the majority of those persons must be citizens, but failure to comply with this section does not invalidate any act of the institution.

C.P.C. Report Ch.14 p.5

38. It is, we believe, essential that the institutions established in our home grown Constitution should be, and be seen to be, under the control of citizens of this country. We therefore recommend that, with the exception of only two constitutional bodies, at least the majority of the members of all collective bodies established in the Constitution should be citizens.

39. All members of the National Parliament must be citizens if sovereignty is really to be ours. We also believe that for the first ten years after the Constitution comes into force all of the members of the Public Services Commission should be indigenous citizens. We appreciate, however, that our country is likely to be short of certain skilled and experienced personnel for a number of years to come. During these years we shall need the assistance of foreign citizens who have the necessary skills. But, localization of decision-making is vital if the country is really to be run as our people wish, and localization of personnel must therefore remain an urgent objective.

40. We therefore recommend that the majority of members of collective bodies established in the Constitution should, from the inception of these bodies, be citizens. We exempt only the courts and the Fiscal Commission recommended in Chapter 10, 'Provincial Government'. Our country is short of trained Papua New Guinean lawyers generally, and particularly of lawyers qualified to sit on the National Court of Justice. It may also be short of people who are qualified to serve as members of the Fiscal Commission. But, even in these two cases, rapid localization remains our objective.

41. This recommendation should be regarded as a transitional provision. We do not believe that the holders of high public office in ten years time should be other than citizens. By then, this recommendation should be an anachronism. However, we have not made it impossible for non-citizens to be appointed to high constitutional office even then.

275. — CHAIRMANSHIP OF TRIBUNAL TO REVIEW INTERNMENTS.

Until 16 September 1985, in addition to persons who are qualified to be appointed as Judges of the National Court, a person who holds office as a magistrate of the highest grade or classification is eligible for appointment as Chairman of a tribunal appointed in accordance with Section 245(1)(e) (*internment*).

SCHEDULES.

SCHEDULE 1.

Rules for Shortening and Interpretation of the Constitutional Laws.

PART 1. — INTRODUCTORY.

Sch. 1.1. — APPLICATION OF SCHEDULE 1.

(1) The rules contained in this Schedule apply, unless the contrary intention appears, in the interpretation of the Constitution and of the Organic Laws.

(2) Unless adopted by law for the purpose, they do not apply to any other law.

UNLESS THE CONTRARY INTENTION APPEARS

per Curiam (Kidu C.J., Kapi Dep.C.J., Andrew J.)

Section 2(2) of the *Organic Law (on National Elections)* provides that notwithstanding any other law, where a time limit is imposed under this law for the taking of an action, then unless the contrary intention appears, that time is mandatory. When this is read in conjunction with s.208(e) of the Organic Law, it is clear that the limit of two months following the declaration of the result of the election, in which to file the petition, is a rigid limit of time .... Although it was not raised in argument we refer to Sch.1.16 of the Constitution:

Sch.1.16 EFFECTS OF TIME LIMITS.
(1) When in a constitutional law a time limit is imposed for the doing of an act .... and in a particular case it is not practicable to comply with that limitation, the period shall be deemed to be extended by whatever period is necessary to make compliance practicable.
...
However, this schedule is subject to Sch.1.1 .... We have already found that the Organic Law expresses a rigid limit of time and this is clearly a contrary intention to Sch.1.16 and therefore makes Sch.1.16 inapplicable.
S.C.R. No 4 of 1982; Re Delba Biri v Bill Ginbogl Ninkama [1982] PNGLR 342 at pp.346,349.

Referred to

by Wilson J. in *Constitutional Reference No 1 of 1978 (s.19)* [1978] PNGLR 345 at p.358;

by Pratt J. in *S.C.R. No 1 of 1982; Re Bouraga* [1982] PNGLR 178 at pp.209,211 (there is no contrary intention to be found in s.191 of the Constitution to displace the operation of Sch.1.10(4) and where Sch.1.10(4) is inconsistent with an Act of Parliament, Sch.1.10(4) being a Constitutional Law, shall prevail); see also Kidu C.J. at p.182;

per Curiam (Kidu C.J., Kapi Dep.C.J. and Andrew J.) in *S.C.R. No 5 of 1982; Hugo Berghauser and ors v Joseph Aoae* [1982] PNGLR 379 at pp.381,382 (Section 208 of the *Organic Law on National Elections* specifies that an election petition shall be signed and filed by a single petitioner and makes no provision for joint petitions; accordingly as the contrary intention appears, Sch.1.8(b) (which provides that words in the singular include the plural) held to have no application).

PART 2. — GENERAL.

Sch. 1.2. — MEANING OF CERTAIN EXPRESSIONS.

(1) In this Constitution or an Organic Law —
"absolute majority vote", in relation to proceedings in the Parliament, means —
(a) if qualified by reference to a certain fraction or percentage, affirmative votes equal to not less than that fraction or percentage of the total number of seats in the Parliament; or
(b) if not so qualified, affirmative votes equal to more than one half of the total number of those seats;
"act" includes omission or failure to act;
"Act of the Parliament" means a law (other than a Constitutional Law) made by the Parliament, and includes a subordinate legislative enactment made under any such law;
"alter", in relation to any provision of this Constitution or any other law, includes repeal (with or without re-enactment or the making of other provision), amend, modify, suspend (or remove a suspension) or add to the words or effect of the provision;
"committee", in relation to the Parliament, includes a subcommittee of a committee of the Parliament;
"Constitutional Law" means this Constitution, a law altering this Constitution or an Organic Law;

GENERALLY

Referred to

by Frost C.J. in *The State v Mogo Wonom* [1975] PNGLR 311 at p.315;

by Prentice Dep.C.J. in *In re Moresby North East Election Petition* [1977] PNGLR 429 at p.435;

by Pritchard J. (dissenting) in *Constitutional Reference No 1 of 1978 (s.19)* [1978] PNGLR 345 at p.368:

by Wilson J. in *Re Rooney (No 2)* [1979] PNGLR 448 at p.503;

by Miles J. in *S.C.R. No 2 of 1981; Re s.19* [1981] PNGLR 518 at p.527 (a mere Parliamentary resolution is not a Constitutional Law);

by Kearney Dep.C.J. in *S.C.R. No 2 of 1982; Re Organic Law* [1982] PNGLR 214 at p.223;

by Kaputin J. in *S.C.R. No 2 of 1982; Re Opai Kunangel Amin* (1982 Unreported) SC231 at p.17.

"the country" means the area of Papua New Guinea;
"custom" means the customs and usages of indigenous inhabitants of the country existing in relation to the matter in question at the time when and the place in relation to which the matter arises, regardless of whether or not the custom or usage has existed from time immemorial;

AS TO WHAT CONSTITUTES CUSTOM

per Kapi Dep.C.J.

> It is clear from the definition of custom that it develops from time to time. The significance of this is that while custom may have developed in the past and in relation to what may be regarded as 'traditional property', custom is likely to develop in relation to what may be regarded as 'modern property'. . . . The crucial question to ask, is whether any custom has developed in relation to a particular type of property. . . . To illustrate the point it would be wrong to conclude that shares in a company are modern property, therefore custom can have no regulation over it. The proper approach would be to ask whether a custom in a particular community has developed as far as distribution of company shares are concerned, upon death.
> *Re James Allan Sannga: Peter Timereke v Duncan Ferrie and anor* (1983 Unreported) SC255 at p.23; see also at p.43.

Referred to

by Kapi J. in *Acting Public Solicitor (sic) v Uname Aumane* [1980] PNGLR 510 at p.541;

by Kapi J. in *S.C.R. No 4 of 1980; Re petition of M.T. Somare* [1981] PNGLR 265 at pp.287,288 (see extract under Sch 2.1(1)).

"the day fixed for the return of the writs for a general election" means —

(a) in the case of a general election where there is no extension of the time for the return of any writ or the time for the return of all writs is extended — the day by which the writs are to be returned; and

(b) in any other case — the day by which the majority of the writs are to be returned;

"the Declaration of Office" means a declaration in the form in Schedule 3;

"the Deputy Leader of the Opposition" means the member of the Parliament (if any) recognized by the Parliament as being the second principal speaker on behalf of those members of the Parliament who are not generally committed to support the Government in the Parliament;

"deliberate judgment", in relation to an act, has the meaning and effect attributed to it by Section 62 (*decisions in "deliberate judgment"*);

"Emergency Regulation" means a law that is made in accordance with Section 231 (*Emergency Regulations*);

"fiscal year", in relation to any activity of the National Government, means the period of 12 months commencing on 1 July or on such other date as is fixed by an Act of the Parliament for the purpose;

(*See: Fiscal Year (Change) Act* Ch.350)

"of full capacity", in relation to a person means that he is not of unsound mind within the meaning of any law relating to the custody or protection of the persons or property of persons of unsound mind;

"government body" means —

(a) the National Government, or
(b) a provincial government, or
(c) an arm, department, agency or instrumentality of the National Government or a provincial government; or
(d) a body set up by statute or administrative act for governmental or official purposes; (*Amended by Constitutional Amendment No. 1 — Provincial Government, s.4*)

GENERALLY

Referred to

by Prentice C.J., in *Constitutional Reference No 1 of 1978 (s.19)* [1978] PNGLR 345 at p.350 ('government body' does not include those bodies which are independent of the executive's direction and control and which obtain their power from a direct Constitution grant. Accordingly the expression does not include the Public Solicitor); see also Wilson J. at pp.358, 360, 361 and Pritchard J. (dissenting) at pp.381-383.

"Judge" means a Judge of the Supreme Court or a Judge of the National Court;

"Judge of the National Court" means the Chief Justice, the Deputy Chief Justice or a Judge, and includes an acting Judge;

"Judge of the Supreme Court" means a Judge of the National Court, other than an acting Judge;
"the Judicial Declaration" means a declaration in the form in Schedule 4;
"judicial officer" means a Judge or Magistrate of a court within the National Judicial system (other than a magistrate or member of a village court) in his capacity as such;
"law" includes the underlying law;

ACCORDING TO LAW

Comment

As to the meaning of the expression 'according to law' see the cases referred to under s.37(4)(a).

GENERALLY

Referred to

by Prentice Dep.C.J. in *Constitutional Reference No 1 of 1977 (Sch 2.3)* [1978] PNGLR 295 at p.297;

by Kidu C.J. in *Avia Aihi v The State* [1981] PNGLR 81 at p.85;

by Kearney Dep.C.J. in *S.C.R. No 1A of 1981; Re Motor Traffic Act* [1982] PNGLR 122 at p.136.

"lawyer" means a person who has been admitted to practice as a lawyer under an Act of the Parliament;

(*See: Lawyers Act* Ch.91.)

"the Leader of the Opposition" means the member of the Parliament (if any) recognized by the Parliament as being the principal speaker on behalf of those members of the Parliament who are not generally committed to support the Government in the Parliament;
"local government body" includes a local government council and a local government authority established under the pre-Independence law known as the *Local Government Act* 1963 or any other law;
"medical practitioner" means a person who has been admitted to practice as a medical practitioner under an Act of the Parliament;

(*See: Medical Services Act* Ch.92.)

"the Minister" in relation to any Constitutional Law, provision, matter or thing, means the Minister for the time being administering that Constitutional Law or provision, or the Minister for time being administering the Constitutional Law or provision that governs that matter or thing, as the case may be;

"misconduct in office" means misconduct in office as described in Section 27 (*responsibilities of office*) or as prescribed by an Organic Law made for the purposes of Section 28 (*further provisions*);

"the National Gazette" includes any Special National Gazette or National Gazette Extraordinary, and any supplement to a National Gazette;

"Papua New Guinea" means the Independent State of Papua New Guinea;

"personal staff", in relation to the Governor-General, a Minister, the Leader of the Opposition or the Deputy Leader of the Opposition, means the staff supplied to him by or under an Act of the Parliament at the public expense, not being members of the National Public Service in their capacities as such;

(*See: Ministerial Personal Staff Act* Ch.22.)

"pre-Independence law" has the same meaning as in Section Sch.2.6 (*adoption of pre-Independence laws*);

"the pre-Independence Supreme Court" means the pre-Independence court known as the Supreme Court of Papua New Guinea, the Supreme Court of the Territory of Papua and New Guinea or the Supreme Court of the Territory of Papua — New Guinea;

"principles of natural justice" means the principles referred to in Division III.4 (*principles of natural justice*), and where those principles have been altered in accordance with Section 60 (*development of principles*), or by an Act of the Parliament, includes those principles as so altered;

"provincial law" means a law made or adopted by a provincial legislature, and includes a subordinate legislative enactment made under any such law; (*Added by Constitutional Amendment No. 1 — Provincial Government, s.4*)

"public accounts of Papua New Guinea" includes all accounts, books and records of, or in the custody, possession or control of, the National Executive or of a public officer, relating to public property or public moneys of Papua New Guinea;

"public moneys of Papua New Guinea" includes moneys held in trust by the National Executive or a public officer in his capacity as such, whether or not they are so held for particular persons;

"public office-holder" means —

(a) a member of any of the State services or of a provincial service; or (*Amended by Constitutional Amendment No. 1 — Provincial Government, s.4*)
(b) any other constitutional office-holder; or
(c) the holder of any office or position established by statute for administrative or governmental purposes; or
(d) the holder of any other office or position declared by a statute to be a public office;

GENERALLY

Referred to

by Prentice C.J. in *Constitutional Reference No 1 of 1978 (s.19)* [1978] PNGLR 345 at p.348 (as appearing to make a clear distinction between constitutional office holders and members of the National Public Service).

"the public trustee" means the officer (by whatever title known) charged with the duty of administering deceased intestate estates;

"seat", in relation to the Parliament, includes —
(a) the position of an elected member, whether or not the position is for the time being filled; and
(b) where there is for the time being a nominated member appointed in accordance with Section 102 (*nominated members*) — the position of that nominated member;

"statute" means an Act of the Parliament, an Emergency Regulation or a provincial law, and includes a subordinate legislative enactment made under any such law; (*Replaced by Constitutional Amendment No 1 — Provincial Government, s.4*)

"subordinate legislative enactment" means a regulation or any other instrument (whether of a legislative nature or not) made under a statute;

"taxation" includes rates, charges and fees and imposts of any kind;

GENERALLY

Referred to

by Frost C.J. in *Mairi v Alkan Tololo and ors* [1976] PNGLR 125 at p.130; see also Prentice Dep.C.J. and Williams J. at p.138.

"time of war" means a period during which a declaration under Section 227 (*declaration of war*) is in force;

"the underlying law" means —
(a) the underlying law provided for by an Act of the Parliament under Section 20(1) (*underlying law and pre-Independence statutes*); and

(b) until such time as there is an Act of the Parliament, the underlying law prescribed in Schedule 2 (*adoption, etc., of certain laws*);

GENERALLY

Referred to

by Bredmeyer A.J. in *Brown v Motor Vehicles Insur. (PNG) Trust* [1980] PNGLR 409 at p.415, Fn;

by Bredmeyer J. in *Aundak Kapil v The Independent State of Papua New Guinea* (1983 Unreported) N435 at pp.4, 12.

"village court" means a court referred to in Section 172(2) (*establishment of other courts*).

(2) Unless the contrary intention appears, where an expression is defined for any purpose in this Schedule, or otherwise in a Constitutional Law, then for that purpose all grammatical variations and cognate and related expressions are to be understood in the same sense.

(3) Unless the contrary intention appears, a reference in a Constitutional Law to an institution, office or other thing shall be read as a reference to the appropriate institution, office or thing established or provided for by this Constitution, or referred to in the Preamble to this Constitution.

GENERALLY

Referred to

by Frost C.J. in *Reference No 2 of 1976* [1976] PNGLR 228 at p.233 (the expression 'previous general election' in s.105(1)(a) and (b) of the Constitution must refer to an election conducted under the Constitution and cannot mean the previous general election of the House of Assembly before Independence).

Sch. 1.3. — FORM OF THE CONSTITUTIONAL LAWS.

(1) The Preamble to this Constitution (being the provisions that end immediately before the heading to Part I) forms part of this Constitution, but expresses general principles and therefore must be read subject to any other provision of this Constitution, though it may be used as an aid to interpretation in cases of doubt.

GENERALLY

Referred to

by Prentice Dep.C.J. (dissenting) in *Peter v South Pacific Brewery Ltd* [1976] PNGLR 537 at p.538;

by Frost C.J. in *Reference No 1 of 1977* [1977] PNGLR 362 at p.363 (the Basic Rights provisions of the Preamble referred to to illustrate that rights may be subject to limitations effected to protect the legitimate public interest);

by Prentice C.J. in *Premdas v The Independent State of Papua New Guinea* [1979] PNGLR 329 at p.340; see also Saldanha J. at p.370.

Comment

For further references to the application of the Preamble see under the Introductory paragraph of the National Goals and Directive Principles and under s.25(3) and (4) infra.

(2) The heading or head-notes to the various sections of a Constitutional Law do not form part of the Law, but other headings and notes do form part of the Law.

GENERALLY

Referred to

by Frost C.J. in *Peter v South Pacific Brewery Ltd* [1976] PNGLR 537 at p.546;

by Frost C.J. in *Reference No 1 of 1977* [1977] PNGLR 362 at p.356;

by Prentice C.J. in *Constitutional Reference No 1 of 1978 (s.19)* [1978] PNGLR 345 at p.349; see also Wilson J. at pp.359, 360 and Pritchard J. (dissenting) at p.368;

by Greville Smith J. in *S.C.R. No 2 of 1981; Re s.19(1)(f) of the Criminal Code* [1982] PNGLR 150 at p.167.

(3) Each provision of a Constitutional Law takes effect as a Constitutional Law.

GENERALLY

Referred to

by Kearney Dep.C.J. in *S.C.R. No 2 of 1982; Re Organic Law* [1982] PNGLR 214 at p.223;

by Kaputin J. (dissenting) in *S.C.R. No 2 of 1982; Re Opai Kunangel Amin* (1982 Unreported) SC231 at p.17.

(4) Where a reference in a provision of a Constitutional Law to another provision of that Law, or to a provision of another Constitutional Law, is followed by words in brackets describing, or purporting to describe, the effect of the provision so referred to, the description or purported description does not, unless the contrary is expressed, affect the meaning or effect of the provision so referred to.

Sch. 1.4. — CONSTITUTIONAL LAWS SPEAK FROM TIME TO TIME.

A Constitutional Law speaks from time to time.

SPEAKING FROM TIME TO TIME

Comment

This means that words in Constitutional Laws are to be interpreted in accordance with their current meanings and applied so as to include things not known or invented at the time of their coming into operation if such things on a fair and liberal construction of the law fall within its ambit.

For a full exposition of the effect of this rule see D.C. Pearce, *Statutory Interpretation in Australia* (2nd edition) 1981 at pp.33-36.

Sch. 1.5. — FAIR MEANING TO BE GIVEN TO LANGUAGE USED.

(1) Each Constitutional Law is intended to be read as a whole.

GENERALLY

Referred to

by Kearney J. in *The State v The Independent Tribunal, Ex Parte Sasakila* [1976] PNGLR 491 at p.506;

by Prentice Dep.C.J. in *In re Moresby North East Election Petition* [1977] PNGLR 492 at p.434;

by Frost C.J. in *In re Moresby North West Parliamentary Election* [1977] PNGLR 338 at p.345 (applied as assisting the construction of s.141(1)(a) of the *Organic Law on National Elections*);

by Prentice Dep.C.J. in *Reference No 1 of 1977* [1977] PNGLR 362 at p.373;

by Wilson J. in *Constitutional Reference No 1 of 1978 (s.19)* [1978] PNGLR 345 at pp.359,361 (applied to assist in the construction of the expression 'National Government');

by Wilson J. In *Premdas v The Independent State of Papua New Guinea* [1979] PNGLR 329 at p.375;

by Kidu C.J. in *Avia Aihi v The State* [1981] PNGLR 81 at p.85 (applied to assist in ascertaining the meaning of the word 'law' in s.35(15) of the Constitution);

by Kaputin J. (dissenting) in *S.C.R. No 2 of 1982; Re Opai Kunangel Amin* (1982 Unreported) SC231 at p.18;

by Kidu C.J. and Pratt J. in *In the matter of the Organic Law on National Elections; Kuberi Epi v Tony Farapo and anor* (1983 Unreported) SC247 at p.4;

by Bredmeyer J. in *Public Employees Association of Papua New Guinea v Public Services Commission* (1983 Unreported) SC253 at p.9 (Subsection 37(3) and s.159(3) of the Constitution should be read together as a whole).

(2) All provisions of, and all words, expressions and propositions in, a Constitutional Law shall be given their fair and liberal meaning.

FAIR AND LIBERAL MEANING

Comment

The requirement to give all words, expressions and propositions contained in a Constitutional Law their 'fair and liberal meaning' has been referred to frequently by the judiciary. However, with the exception of Kearney J. (as he then was) in *The State v The Independent Tribunal, Ex Parte Sasakila* [1976] PNGLR 491 (see below) there has been little extended analysis of the nature of this duty. Indeed if the views of Kidu C.J. and Pratt J. as expressed in their recent decision *In the matter of the Organic Law on National Elections; Kuberi Epi v Tony Farapo and anor* (1983 Unreported) SC247 (see below) gain general acceptance the principles expressed in Sch.1.5 will cease to be of any significance.

Considerably more judicial attention has been given to the principles of statutory (non-constitutional) interpretation. Extracts from and references to these cases may be found particularly under s.109(4) and s.158(2). The authors submit that the rejection of the literal approach to statutory interpretation (see Wilson J. in *P.L.A.R. No 1 of 1980* [1980] PNGLR 326 at pp.335, 336) (extract appears under s.158(2)), evidenced by these cases is also mandated, in respect of Constitutional Laws, by Sch.1.5(2) . Note s.158(2) applies to all laws, whether or not Constitutional in nature.

per Kearney J.

The process of statutory interpretation is essentially intuitive and subjective, in the absence of rules consistently applied. The Act is a Constitutional Law and thus subject to the general principles of interpretation set out in Constitution ss.10, 25(3), 63(3) and Basic Social Obligation (a), and 158(2); and to the more specific canons in Constitution ss.24, 109(4) when read with 12, and Sch.1.5. In my opinion these provisions amount to a direction to the Court that in carrying out its functions under Constitution s.18(1) the words actually used in the Act do not have to be strictly adhered to but are to be construed with the assistance of the materials referred to in Constitution s.24, so as best to attain what Parliament intended. When Constitution ss.109(4) and 158(2) are themselves interpreted with the aid of s.24, this view is fortified: there are several references in Chapter 8 of the Report of the Constitutional Planning Committee which point against the Court taking a 'narrowly legalistic' or 'literal' approach, and thus sacrificing the 'spirit for the letter of the Constitution'. The 'dynamic character' of the Constitution is emphasized; in interpreting the laws, the judges are urged to use 'judicial ingenuity' in appropriate cases, to do justice. One consequence of this approach to interpretation is that the Court should not fail to give a provision the effect it considers the Parliament intended, by applying a literal or 'plain meaning' test nor should it attribute to the legislature an intention to produce a capricious or unjust result. The search throughout is for the intention of Parliament, a process which remains, formally at least, one of interpretation and not of legislation, and one in which the best guide remains the provisions of the Act itself.
The State v The Independent Tribunal; Ex Parte Sasakila [1976] PNGLR 491 at pp.506, 507; see also Frost C.J. at p.501.

per Prentice Dep. C.J.

One reminds oneself that the Constitutional neither relies upon nor springs from any source but the will of the people of Papua New Guinea and that every effort should be made to avoid the intrusion into its interpretation of extraneous ideas or vestigial paternalism from the preceding colonial period. The Constitution itself provides many clear fingerposts to assist its interpreters. Among these are its requirements that:

(a) all its provisions are to be given their fair and liberal meaning (Sch.1.5(1), (2));
(b) all laws are to be interpreted so as to give effect to, or not derogate from, the National Goals and Directive Principles — where possible (s.25);
(c) all persons are entitled to certain defined basic rights and freedoms and the full protection of the Law (National Goals and Directive Principles 'Basic Rights (a)'; s.37);
(d) the debates on the Constitution and the reports of the Constitutional Planning Committee may be used in aid where relevant;
(e) in interpreting the law the Courts shall give paramount consideration to the dispensation of justice (s.158(2) — a provision to be considered in association with those relating to development of an underlying law (s.20: Sch.2.3, 2.4, 2.5) and to the principles of natural justice (s.59(1)).

Reference No 1 of 1977 [1977] PNGLR 362 at pp.373, 374.

per Kidu C.J. and Pratt J.

As was said during argument however, we do not for one moment consider this duty [to read each constitutional law as a whole and to give such law their fair and liberal meaning] carries with it an encouragement to abandon the normal principles of interpretation as set out in that part of our underlying law known as the common law. For indeed those principles are valuable aids to construction when attempting to obtain clarity from what admittedly in the eyes of at least one party is ambiguous.
In the matter of the Organic Law on National Elections; Kuberi Epi v Tony Farapo and ors (1983 Unreported) SC247 at p.4.

GENERALLY

Referred to

by Prentice Dep.C.J. and Williams J. in *Mairi v Alkan Tololo and ors (No 2)* [1976] PNGLR 125 at p.136;

by Frost C.J. in *Reference No 2 of 1976* [1976] PNGLR 228 at p.235;

by Raine J. in *Cory v Blyth (No 1)* [1976] PNGLR 274 at p.278;

per Curiam (Frost C.J., Prentice Dep.C.J., Raine, Saldanha and Kearney JJ.) in *Reference No 3 of 1976* [1976] PNGLR 242 at p.278;

by Frost C.J. in *Peter v South Pacific Brewery Ltd* [1976] PNGLR 537 at p.542; see also Prentice Dep.C.J. (dissenting) at p.557;

by Frost C.J. in *Mauga Logging Company Pty Ltd v South Pacific Oil Palm Development Pty Ltd (No 1)* [1977] PNGLR 80 at p.85 (restrictive construction of s.155(4) of the Constitution rejected as, inter alia, inconsistent with Sch.1.5(2));

by Wilson J. in *Constitutional Reference No 1 of 1978 (s.19)* [1978] PNGLR 345 at p.361; see also Pritchard J. (dissenting) at p.389;

by Prentice C.J. in *Premdas v The Independent State of Papua New Guinea* [1979] PNGLR 329 at p.344 (Section 41 of the Constitution to be given a 'general application'); see also Wilson J. (dissenting) at pp.374, 375;

by Kidu C.J. in *Avia Aihi v The State* [1981] PNGLR 81 at p.88 (restrictive interpretation of s.155(2)(a) of the Constitution rejected); see also Greville Smith J. (dissenting) at p.97;

by Miles J. in *S.C.R. No 1 of 1981; Re Inter-Group Fighting Act 1977* [1981] PNGLR 151 at pp.169-172 (Sch.1.5(2) is not inconsistent with the principle of the underlying law that an ambiguous provision ought to be construed in favour of the liberty of the subject);

by Kidu C.J. in *S.C.R. No 2 of 1981; Re s.19 of the Constitution* [1981] PNGLR 518 at p.520;

by Kidu C.J. in *In the Matter of An Application for Bail: Keating v The Independent State of Papua New Guinea* (1983 Unreported) SC257 at p.5 (as relevant to the interpretation of the word 'justice' in s.42(6)of the Constitution).

Sch.1.6. — STATEMENTS OF GENERAL PRINCIPLE.

Where a provision of a Constitutional Law is expressed to state a proposition "in principle", then —

(a) an act (including a legislative, executive or judicial act) that is inconsistent with the proposition is not, by reason of that inconsistency alone, invalid or ineffectual; but

(b) if the act is reasonably capable of being understood or given effect to in such a way as not to be inconsistent with the proposition it shall be so given effect to.

Sch.1.7. — "NON-JUSTICIABLE".

Where a Constitutional Law declares a question to be non-justiciable, the question may not be heard or determined by any court or tribunal, but nothing in this section limits the jurisdiction of the Ombudsman Commission or of any other tribunal established for the purposes of Division III.2 (*leadership code*).

GENERALLY

Comment

For detailed references to the effect of Sch.1.7 in relation to s.86(4) see under that Section.

Referred to

by Frost C.J. in *The State v The Independent Tribunal; Ex Parte Sasakila* [1976] PNGLR 491 at p.499; see also Saldanha J. at p.504;

by Kapi J. in *Minister for Lands v Frame* [1980] PNGLR 433 at p.504;

by Andrew J. *in Milne Bay Provincial Government v Roy Evara and anor* [1981] PNGLR 63 at p.66 (the purport and intent of the Constitution and the *Organic Law on Provincial Government* is to declare intergovernmental disputes to be non-justiciable).

Sch.1.8. — GENDER AND NUMBER.

In a Constitutional Law —

(a) words importing the masculine gender include females; and

(b) words in the singular include the plural and words in the plural include the singular.

GENERALLY

Referred to

per Curiam (Kidu C.J., Kapi Dep.C.J. and Andrew J.) in *S.C.R. No 5 of 1982; Hugo Berghauser and ors v Joseph Aoae* [1982] PNGLR 379 at pp.381,382 (Schedule 1.8(b) not applied because of contrary intention apparent on the face of the provision being interpreted);

by Bredmeyer J. in *S.C.R. No 2 of 1982; Re Opai Kunangel Amin* (1982 Unreported) SC231 at p.12.

Sch.1.9. — PROVISION WHERE NO TIME PRESCRIBED.

Where no time is prescribed or allowed within which an act is required or permitted by a Constitutional Law to be done, the act shall or may be done, as the case may be, with all convenient speed and as often as the occasion arises.

GENERALLY

Referred to

by Prentice C.J. in *Constitutional Reference No 1 of 1978 (s.19)* [1978] PNGLR 345 at p.351.

Sch.1.10. — EXERCISE AND PERFORMANCE OF POWERS AND DUTIES.

(1) Where a Constitutional Law confers a power or imposes a duty, the power may be exercised, or the duty shall be performed, as the case may be, from time to time as occasion requires.

(2) Where a Constitutional Law confers a power or imposes a duty on the holder of an office as such, the power may be exercised, or the duty shall be performed, as the case may be, by the holder (whether substantive or other) for the time being of the office.

(3) Where a Constitutional Law confers a power to make any instrument or decision (other than a decision of a court), the power includes power exercisable in the same manner and subject to the same conditions (if any) to alter the instrument or decision.

(4) Subject to Subsection (5), where a Constitutional Law confers a power to make an appointment, the power includes power to remove or suspend a person so appointed, and to appoint another person temporarily in the place of a person so removed or suspended or, where the appointee is for any reason unable or unavailable to perform his duties, to appoint another person temporarily in his place.

AS TO OFFICERS APPOINTED UNDER SECTION 193 OF THE CONSTITUTION.

Held

Officers appointed pursuant to s.193 may be removed or disciplined only in the manner prescribed by Sch.1.10(4) which must be read as one with s.193. Such officers are not subject to the Public Service Commission's general power to discipline public servants granted by s.191 of the Constitution.
S.C.R. No 1 of 1982; Re Bouraga [1982] PNGLR 178, see Kidu C.J. at p.184, Kapi J. at pp.194-195, Pratt J. at pp.209-212.

(5) The power provided for by Subsection (4) is exercisable only subject to any conditions to which the exercise of the original power of appointment was subject.

GENERALLY

Referred to

by Kidu C.J. in *S.C.R. No 1 of 1982; Re Bouraga* [1982] PNGLR 178 at p.182.

Sch.1.11. — DETERMINATION OF APPROPRIATE AUTHORITY.

Where a Constitutional Law refers to "the appropriate Permanent Parliamentary Committee", the Parliament shall determine which Permanent Parliamentary Committee is the appropriate committee for the purpose and where the Parliament fails to do so the Speaker may so determine.

Sch. 1.12. — POWER OF MAJORITY OF MORE THAN TWO PERSONS, AND QUORUMS.

(1) Where a Constitutional Law requires or permits an act or thing to be done by more than two persons, a majority of them may do it.

(2) Subsection (1) does not affect any requirement of a quorum, and, subject to Subsection (3), where no quorum is prescribed for a body the quorum is the full membership of the body.

(3) A power conferred by a Constitutional Law, otherwise than on the body in question, to determine the procedures of a body includes power to determine a quorum.

(4) The exception contained in Subsection (3) does not apply to the National Executive Council.

Sch.1.13. — ATTAINMENT OF AGE.

For any purpose of a Constitutional Law, a person attains a certain age at the first moment of the relevant anniversary of his birth.

Sch.1.14. — REFERENCES TO SERIES.

(1) Where in a Constitutional Law a reference is made to a series by reference to two numbers, one at the beginning and one at the end of the series, each of those numbers forms part of the series.

(2) The reference in Subsection (1) to numbers include, where the elements of a series are identified by letters or in some other manner, references to letters or that other means of identification.

Sch.1.15. — RESIDENCE.

(1) Where in a Constitutional Law there is a requirement for any purpose of permanent residence or of continuous residence in a place (including the area of Papua New Guinea), an Organic Law may provide that —
   (a) periods of temporary absence from that place shall be counted as periods of residence in that place; or
   (b) periods of temporary absence from that place shall not be counted as periods of residence in that place but otherwise do not affect the continuity of residence.

(2) In Subsection (1), "temporary absence" means, subject to Subsection (3), absence for temporary purposes with the intention of returning.

(3) An Organic Law may further provide for the definition of classes of absence that constitute or do not constitute temporary absence for the purposes of any provision of a Constitutional Law.

(*See: Organic Law on Residence* Ch.1.)

Sch.1.16. — EFFECT OF TIME LIMITS.

(1) Where in a Constitutional Law a time limit is imposed for the doing of an act (whether the provision is mandatory, directory or permissive, and whether it is positive or negative), and in a particular case it is not practicable to comply with that limitation, the period shall be deemed to be extended by whatever period is necessary to make compliance practicable.

DOES NOT APPLY TO LEGISLATION OTHER THAN CONSTITUTIONAL LAWS.

Referred to

by Kapi J. (dissenting) in *Avia Aihi v The State* [1981] PNGLR 81 at p.105 (not applicable to the provisions of the *Supreme Court Act* governing criminal appeals);

by Kapi J. in *Mapun Papol v Antony Temo* [1981] PNGLR 178 at p.181 (not applicable to the *Provincial Government (Electoral Provisions) Regulations* 1977).

(2) The operation of Subsection (1) is not excluded by a provision that unqualifiedly specifies a time limit or a maximum time limit.

GENERALLY

Referred to

per Curiam (Kidu C.J., Kapi Dep. C.J., Andrew J.) in *S.C.R. No 4 of 1982; Re Delba Biri v Bill Ginbogl Ninkama* [1982] PNGLR 342 at p.349; (the operation of Subsection (1) may be displaced by a clear contrary intention as provided for by Sch.1.1).

Sch.1.17. — REPEAL, ETC.

(1) The repeal of a Constitutional Law or a part of a Constitutional Law does not —

(a) revive anything (including a statute or any part of the underlying law) that was not in force or existing immediately before the repeal took effect; or

(b) affect the previous operation of the repealed provisions or anything duly done or suffered under them; or

(c) affect any right, privilege, obligation or liability acquired, accrued or incurred under the repealed provisions; or

(d) affect any penalty, forfeiture or punishment incurred in respect of an offence committed against the repealed provisions; or

(e) affect any investigation, legal proceeding or remedy in respect of any such right, privilege, obligation, liability, penalty, forfeiture or punishment,

and any such investigation, legal proceeding or remedy may be instituted, continued or enforced, and the penalty, forfeiture or punishment may be imposed, as if the repealed provisions had continued in force.

(2) In particular, the repeal of a Constitutional Law or a part of a Constitutional Law does not —

(a) affect any liability under Division III.2 (*leadership code*); or

(b) prevent the Ombudsman Commission or any other tribunal established for the purpose of that Division from investigating any act,

to which the repealed provisions were relevant.

(3) Where a Constitutional Law or a part of a Constitutional Law is repealed and re-enacted (with or without modification), references in any other law to any of the repealed provisions shall, unless the contrary intention appears, be read as a reference to the amended or replacing provision.

(4) In this section, "repeal" includes revocation, suspension and expiry.

Sch.1.18. — DISALLOWANCE, ETC.

(1) Where a Constitutional Law provides that a law may be disallowed, the disallowance takes effect in the same way as a repeal of a provision of a Constitutional Law takes effect except that, if the disallowed law altered any other law, the disallowance revives the other law as in force before the alteration.

(2) For the purpose of Subsection (1), a refusal or failure by the Parliament to confirm, approve or extend a law that requires such confirmation, approval or extension has the same effect as a disallowance.

Sch.1.19. — INDEPENDENCE.

Where a Constitutional Law provides that a person or institution is not subject to control or direction, or otherwise refers to the independence of a person or institution, that provision does not affect —

(a) control or direction by a court; or
(b) the regulation, by or under a Constitutional Law or an Act of the Parliament, of the exercise or performance of the powers, functions, duties or responsibilities of the person or institution; or
(c) the exercise of jurisdiction under Division III.2 (*leadership code*), Subdivision VIII.1.B (*the Auditor-General*), or Subdivision VIII.1.C (*the Public Accounts Committee*),

and does not constitute an appropriation of, or authority to expend, funds.

Sch.1.20. — REGULATION OF ACTS, ETC.

A provision of a Constitutional Law that provides for the regulation of an act or thing does not extend to prohibition, whether in law or in affect.

AS TO REGULATION, RESTRICTION AND PROHIBITION

per Kearney Dep.C.J.

> ... In the ordinary use of language 'regulate' does not include 'prohibit' ... And ... Sch.1.20 makes it clear that a law passed under the Constitution s.50(2) cannot, under the guise of regulating, in law or in effect prohibit the exercise of the s.50(1) rights. But I think that regulating the exercise of a right will very frequently involve the imposition of some degree of restriction on its exercise ... The difference between regulating and restricting is one of degree, not of kind, and I think the distinction is this: that power to restrict ... can extend to prohibition, while the power to regulate ... cannot.
> *S.C.R. No 2 of 1982; Re Organic Law* [1982] PNGLR 214 at p.225; see also Kapi J. at pp.234,240.

Referred to

by Frost C.J. in *Reference No 2 of 1976 [1976]* PNGLR 228 at p.235.

PART 3. — SPECIAL PROVISIONS RELATING TO THE OFFICE OF HEAD OF STATE.

Sch.1.21. — "THE HEAD OF STATE"; "THE GOVERNOR-GENERAL".

For the avoidance of doubt, it is hereby declared that —

(a) in this Constitution —
  - (i) a reference to "the Head of State" is a reference to the Queen and Head of State of Papua New Guinea for the time being and includes a reference to the person or persons exercising sovereignty over the United Kingdom of Great Britain and Northern Ireland in the event of the youth or incapacity of the person in that sovereignty; and
  - (ii) a reference to "the Governor-General" does not include a reference to the Queen or the person exercising sovereignty over the United Kingdom of Great Britain and Northern Ireland; and
  - (iii) a reference to "the Head of State" is a reference to the Queen or a person exercising sovereignty over the United Kingdom of Great Britain and Northern Ireland or, where such a person does not act personally, to the Governor-General as the representative of the Queen or that person; and

(b) the question, whether in performing a function or carrying out a duty as Head of State the Governor-General is acting in accordance with the will or opinion of the person exercising sovereignty over the United Kingdom of Great Britain and Northern Ireland, is non-justiciable and is not subject to the jurisdiction of the Ombudsman Commission or any other person or authority.

GENERALLY

Referred to

by Kapi J. (dissenting) in *Minister for Lands v Frame* [1980] PNGLR 433 at p.470.

Sec. 18. SCHEDULE 2.

Adoption, etc., of Certain laws.

Sch.2.1. — RECOGNITION, ETC., OF CUSTOM.

(1) Subject to Subsections (2) and (3), custom is adopted, and shall be applied and enforced, as part of the underlying law.

AS TO THE HIERARCHY OF THE UNDERLYING LAW AND AS TO JUDICIAL METHODOLOGY

per Kapi J.

The laws of Papua New Guinea are set out under s.9 of the Constitution, one of which is the underlying law. (Section 9(f) of the Constitution). The underlying law of Papua New Guinea is made up of three sources which are set out under Sch.2 of the Constitution. Sch.2.1, custom; Sch.2.2, common law and Sch.2.3, formulation of new law (development of the underlying law). The order in which these laws are listed under Sch.2 is not without significance. In a case where the underlying law of Papua New Guinea is in question or is an issue, the enquiry should always begin with the examination of custom which is applicable under Sch.2.1 of the Constitution. Custom which is adopted in accordance with Sch.2.1 of the Constitution is superior to common law because common law is only applicable to the extent that it is not inconsistent with custom as adopted under Sch.2.1 of the Constitution. (Sch.2.2(1)(c) of the Constitution). The extent to which common law is applicable cannot be determined without determining what the custom says.

Formulation of new law under Sch.2.3 of the Constitution does not arise until it is established that custom under Sch.2.1 and common law under Sch.2.2 are inapplicable. Schedules 2.1, 2.2 and 2.3 of the Constitution set out the manner in which such laws may be adopted, applied and enforced as part of the underlying law. Schedule 2.4 of the Constitution is a general provision applicable to all three sources of the law adopted under Schedules 2.1, 2.2 and 2.3 of the Constitution. Schedule 2.4 of the Constitution is concerned with the development of these laws from time to time in a manner appropriate to the circumstances of the country.
S.C.R. No. 4 of 1980: Re petition of M.T. Somare [1981] PNGLR 265 at pp.285,286.

per Miles J.

It may be appropriate to break off here in order to deal with what counsel for the petitioner in his submission-in-chief called 'judicial methodology', especially as it relates to custom and to development of the underlying law. It was submitted that when a court is considering the underlying law applicable to a case before it, it should first consider whether custom as adopted applied and enforced in Sch.2.1 provides an appropriate rule of law. It was submitted that only if custom did not provide an appropriate rule of law should the court then move on to consider what rule of common law, if any, was applicable as part of the underlying law.

This approach as I understand it, is similar to that recommended by the Law Reform Commission in its report *The role of customary law in the legal system* and the draft legislation contained therein. However I do not think it is incumbent upon a court observing the transitional provisions of the Constitution, s.20(2), and Sch.2.1, Sch.2.2 and Sch.2.3 to proceed in the manner and the order suggested. In my view a court in Papua New Guinea does not discharge its duty under Sch.2 of the Constitution without considering all the matters adverted to in Schedules 2.1 and 2.2, and if necessary Sch.2.3. But this means little more than that a court in this country may not apply the common law without due regard to whether it is inconsistent with a constitutional law or a statute, or custom, or inappropriate to the circumstances of the country. The order in which these various factors are taken into consideration cannot be of any consequence. The suggested requirement that a court must positively decide that custom is inapplicable before it can proceed to consider the common law carries with it the obligation to commence the case with a comprehensive inquiry into all possibly relevant custom. This would place a burden upon judges and lawyers which in the light of their present training and experience would be difficult to discharge, to say the least.

S.C.R. No 4 of 1980; Re petition of M.T. Somare [1981] PNGLR 265 at pp.303,304.

Comment

There is no authoritative decision yet resolving whether Kapi J.'s or Miles J.'s approach to judicial methodology is correct but pragmatic considerations might seem to favour the acceptance of the less rigid approach of Miles J.; in this regard see the comment of Kidu C.J. in *The State v Paul Pokolo* (1983 Unreported) N404 at pp.6-9 (see under).

AS TO WHAT CONSTITUTES CUSTOM: AND AS TO AREA OF RECOGNITION OF THE CUSTOM REQUIRED

per Kapi. J.

... Custom is defined under the Constitution: (Sch.1.2) .....

A similar definition is also provided for by the *Native Customs (Recognition) Act* 1963 (as amended). The first difficulty that arises is that the indigenous inhabitants of this country have different customs applying in various matters. Where parties come from the same custom area there is no difficulty as the custom would apply to both. However there is a difficulty when the parties before the court are from different custom areas or where the subject matter before the court is a National matter or a National issue. The question then arises as to what is the custom applicable. I am aware of only one case dealing with this situation. The case is *Hevago-Koto v Sui-Sibi* [1965-66] PNGLR 59. This was a decision of the late Chief Justice, Sir Alan Mann. The issue in that case arose out of different legislation but the question was whether there was a customary marriage. The case before his Honour involved two parties from different areas with different customs relating to marriage. In dealing with these differences his Honour said, at p.61:

> It was argued that the child should be regarded as the product of a union recognized as a native customary marriage. The difficulty arises here out of the use of the words 'customary' and 'marriage'. The parties belong to completely unrelated native groups. The applicant is from the southern highlands, the respondent is related to people from the western and eastern parts of Papua. She can apparently please herself to a large extent to which group she may choose to attach herself, but leading an urbanized life, she does not appear to have made any decisive choice. Whatever the position may be, there appears to be no community of native people recognizing any notion of customary marriage whose customs could extend to both parties in this case. Customary rules might apply by the usual process of tolerance if the family settled down as a unit within any of the groups concerned, but the differences between the parties are so great that it appears to be certain that this will never happen.

In my view before a custom is adopted and enforced as part of the underlying law under Sch.2.1 of the Constitution it must be established that there is a community of indigenous inhabitants of this country which recognize a certain customary rule. In a case which involves a dispute between two individuals regarding their private rights, it must be established that a custom which the court proposes to adopt as law is recognized and extends to both parties. In a case which involves an issue which has a general application to the whole country such as whether the Leader of the Opposition has locus standi, as in this case, it must be established that there is a custom which is common to all societies throughout the country. Custom as is referred to under Sch.2.1 of the Constitution is not created by the court but is discovered as a matter of fact and adopted as law.

S.C.R. No 4 of 1980; Re petition of M.T. Somare [1981] PNGLR 265 at pp.287, 288; see also Kidu C.J. at p.272 and Miles J. at p.304.

Referred to

by Prentice C.J. in *Constitutional Reference No 1 of 1977 (Sch.2.3)* [1978] PNGLR 295 at p.297;

by Kapi Dep.C.J. in *Re James Allan Sannga: Peter Timereke v Duncan Ferrie and anor* (1983 Unreported) SC255 at p.23 (see extract under Sch.1.2 'custom').

AS TO REASONS WHY CUSTOM HAS NOT BEEN FULLY RECOGNIZED BY THE COURTS

per Kidu C.J.

I am aware of criticisms by some legal practitioners that the Courts are failing to take custom into account and also failing to develop the underlying law as required by the Constitution. I do not wish to be defensive; rather I will make some remarks which might explain to academics and practitioners the reasons why Courts have not taken any active part in the recognition of customs and also in the development of the underlying law.

There are basically two reasons why custom is not recognized by the Courts and the underlying law not been developed.

(1) In almost every case that has come before the National Court (and also the Supreme Court) lawyers have not made any attempts either to produce evidence or material necessary for the Judges both in the National Court and the Supreme Court to use to recognize custom or to develop the underlying law.
Judges have not the time and resources to undertake their own researches in most cases and it is unfair for lawyers to expect too much from judges who are already over worked and under rewarded.

(2) The Parliament of this country has failed to perform its duties as given to it by the Constitution (see s.20).

The State v Paul Pokolo (1983 Unreported) N404 at pp.7, 8.

CUSTOM NOT TO AFFECT THE CONSTRUCTION OF WRITTEN LAWS

per Miles J.

It would therefore seem that [Schedule 2.1] constitutional considerations require s.219 [of the *Criminal Code*] (being part of a statute) to be read and construed without regard to custom or at least regardless of any custom that may be inconsistent with it.
The State v Leo Nimo [1980] PNGLR 129 at p.137.

Referred to

by Prentice C.J. in *Sanguma Wauta v The State* [1978] PNGLR 326 at p.333 (see extract under Sch.2.1(2)).

RECOGNITION OF CUSTOM IS NOT ALWAYS INCONSISTENT WITH THE COMMON LAW: COMMON LAW AWARDS OF DAMAGES TO BE REDUCED IF CUSTOMARY COMPENSATION ALSO RECEIVED

per Bredmeyer J.

To recognise and enforce customary compensation to the exclusion of common law damages 'would result in an injustice' to the Plaintiff and would not be in the public interest under s.3(1)(a) of the *Customs Recognition Act* .... I consider it is [in] the public interest to allow common law damages less customary compensation and against the public interest to allow both to the plaintiff.
Aundak Kapil v The Independent State of Papua New Guinea (1983 Unreported) N435 at pp.14, 16.

AS TO JURISDICTION TO HEAR A CLAIM BASED UPON CUSTOM IN DISTRICT COURTS

per Bredmeyer J.

> ... Mr. Lightfoot's first argument was that the District Court had no jurisdiction to hear a bride price claim under s.29(1) of the *District Courts Act* 1963 which reads as follows:
> 29 *Civil jurisdiction*
> (1) Subject to this Act, in addition to any jurisdiction conferred by any other law in force in the Territory or a part of the Territory a court has jurisdiction *in all personal actions at law or equity* where the amount of the claim ... does not exceed ... (emphasis mine).
> Mr. Lightfoot argued that the phrase 'personal actions at law' means actions arising out of contract or tort at common law. ...
> I consider that the phrase 'at law' in s.29 means more than at common law. It clearly includes statute law. For example a number of statutes create a cause of action but do not expressly confer jurisdiction on the District Court to hear those actions — yet those actions have in the past been heard, and I think properly so, in the District Court.....
> I consider that phrase 'at law' means allowed by the law of the land and encompasses common law, statutory law and also customary law. The Constitution has given a more important role to customary law than it hitherto enjoyed. Prior to Independence there were a number of statutory provisions dealing with customary law, the chief of which was the *Native Customs (Recognition) Act* 1963. That Act remains in force, but under the hierarchy of laws carefully established by the Constitution custom now occupies premier place in the underlying law. By Sch.2 of the Constitution custom is applied first to a problem and, only if it is inapplicable, due to one of the circumstances specified in Sch.2.1, is the court to turn to the English common law and equity. I think it consistent with the important place given to custom by the Constitution that I should interpret the phrase 'at law' in s.29 to include personal actions for the recovery of a debt, or chattel or for damages arising out of customary torts and contracts. The claim for K800 for enticement or bride price was a personal action in that sense based on a customary tort which is not inconsistent with the Constitution, or any statute, or repugnant to the general principles of humanity. I consider that the magistrates had jurisdiction to hear the claim.
> *Henry Aisi v Malaita Hoala* [1981] PNGLR 199 at pp. 201-203.

Referred to

by Bredmeyer J. in *Gabriel Buku v Margaret Rikian* (1982 Unreported) N335(M) (following *Henry Aisi v Malaita Hoala* (above));

by Kearney Dep.C.J. in *Camilus Billy v Jubilee* (1981 Unreported) N360(M) (following *Henry Aisi v Malaita Hoala* (above)).

GENERALLY

Referred to

by Prentice C.J. in *Reference No 1 of 1977* [1977] PNGLR 295 at pp.297, 298; see also Raine Dep.C.J. at p.299, Saldanha J. at p.300 (a prerequisite condition for the Court's exercise of its power under Sch.2.3 to 'develop the law' is that the Court must be satisfied that there is no rule of custom governing the matter pursuant to Sch.2.1);

by Narakobi A.J. in *State v Wapulae and Ors* (1980 Unreported) N233 at pp.16-20 (judges may order a convicted person to pay customary pig compensation despite absence of any enabling provision in the Criminal Code: note overruled in *Acting Public Solicitor [sic] v Uname Aumane* [1980] PNGLR 510);

by Kapi J. in *Acting Public Solicitor [sic] v Uname Aumane* [1980] PNGLR 510 at p.541 (Section 7(e) of the *Native Customs (Recognition) Act* 1963 which provides that custom shall be taken into account in determining the penalty (if any) to be imposed on a guilty party means that a judge may increase or decrease the sentence depending on whether custom mitigates or aggravates the offence but does not permit the imposition of punishments other than those prescribed by the written criminal law);

by Narakobi A.J. in *The State v Yale Gesie* (1980 Unreported) N254 at p.17 (the fact that custom would regard the killing of a reputed sorcerer as 'not unreasonable' taken into account in sentencing for wilful murder);

by Kearney Dep.C.J. in *The State v Andrew Tovue* [1981] PNGLR 8 at p.11;

by Greville Smith J. in *S.C.R. No 4 of 1980; Re Petition of M.T. Somare* [1981] PNGLR 265 at p.278;

by Kapi J. in *S.C.R. No 1A of 1981; Re Motor Traffic Act* [1982] PNGLR 122 at p.138;

by Greville Smith J. in *S.C.R. No 2 of 1981; Re s.19(1)(f) of the Criminal Code* [1982] PNGLR 150 at pp.164,165;

by Kidu C.J. (Andrew J. concurring) in *Re James Allan Sannga: Peter Timereke v Duncan Ferrie and anor* (1983 Unreported) SC255 at pp.16, 17 (because the *Infants Act* does not apply to 'native' and 'part native' children, guardianship of such children is exclusively the province of customary law): but see also Kapi J. (dissenting) at pp.42,43 (the matter requires the court to declare the underlying law and the court should decline to do so as it involves policy considerations more properly dealt with by the legislature).

(2) Subsection (1) does not apply in respect of any custom that is, and to the extent that it is, inconsistent with a Constitutional Law or a statute, or repugnant to the general principles of humanity.

REPUGNANT TO THE GENERAL PRINCIPLES OF HUMANITY

per Wilson J.

> . . . However strong the evidence of custom might have been (and it must be noted that it was not strong here), such a custom, in so far as it condoned acts of canniblism, could not be adopted and applied in this Court, because unquestionably it is repugnant to the general principles of humanity and, as this judgment so finds, it is unlawful. It is unnecessary to attempt to define or to attempt to specify what those general principles of humanity are. To answer the question of whether certain conduct is repugnant to the general principles and humanity all that one needs to do is to see if one can reconcile the concept that it is permissible for a person to cut up, for eating purposes, the dead body of a man with the notions contained in the Constitution. Undoubtedly there can be no reconciling of the two.
>
> In the Preamble to the Consitution the '*worthy* customs' of the people 'which have come down to us from generation to generation' are acknowledged. The word 'worthy', which I have emphasized, was quite obviously used in order to draw a distinction between worthy customs on the one hand and unworthy customs on the other. The latter are, by implication, rejected. Also in the Preamble the people assert that, 'respect for the dignity of the individual' is a basic principle of society, and the need to guard the 'national identity, integrity and self-respect' is recognised. Cannibalism, if a custom, must necessarily be unworthy and demeaning to the dignity of the individual; such a practice is hardly conducive to self-respect.
>
> Without indulging in a detailed analysis of the precise words used in the Constitution, the practice of cannibalism would certainly seem to be contrary to the spirit and intent of that part of the Constitution which acknowledges that, all persons, as individuals, are entitled to certain fundamental human rights and freedoms.
>
> *State v Aubafo Feama and ors* [1978] PNGLR 301 at pp.310, 311.

Referred to

by Bredmeyer J. in *Aundak Kapil v The Independent State of Papua New Guinea* (1983 Unreported) N435 at pp.10,11 (the custom of sanctioning the non-payment of customary compensation by the killing or threatened killing of a member of the debtor clan, is repugnant to the general principles of humanity).

NOT TO BE APPLIED IF INCONSISTENT WITH A CONSTITUTIONAL LAW OR A STATUTE

per Prentice C.J.

Custom is to be adopted, applied and enforced as part of the underlying law (Sch. 2.1) but *not* where it is inconsistent with .... a Statute (Sch 2.2). A custom that could be shown to regard sexual intercourse between customary adopting father and adopted daughter, as equivalent to 'incest' as defined [by the *Criminal Code*] would be inconsistent with the provisions of s.266 and could not be allowed to vary it by imposing criminal liability under the code when none otherwise lay.
Sanguma Wauta v The State [1978] PNGLR 326 at p.333; see also Raine Dep.C.J. at pp.334, 335, Wilson J. at pp.335, 336.

Held

Even if it could be shown that by custom 'big men' have rights to speak in any forum, the custom would not confer special rights of standing before judicial bodies upon those 'big men' because such special rights would be contrary to Constitution s.55(1) which provides that all citizens are to have the same rights, privileges, obligations and duties.
S.C.R. No 4 of 1980; Re petition of M.T. Somare [1981] PNGLR 265; see Kidu C.J. at p.271.

Referred to

by Kidu C.J. in *The State v Paul Pokolo* (1983 Unreported) N404 at pp.8, 9;

by Kidu C.J. (Andrew J. concurring) in *Re James Allen Sannga; Peter Timereke v Duncan Ferrie and anor* (1983 Unreported) SC255 at p.17 (where a statute has quite clearly provided for a subject no custom or common law is applicable): see also Kapi J. at pp.25, 26;

by Bredmeyer J. in *Aundak Kapil v The Independent State of Papua New Guinea* (1983 Unreported) N435 at pp.11,16 (custom of sanctioning the non-payment of customary compensation with killing or the threat of killing is not adopted as it is inconsistent with, inter-alia, ss.35 and 37(1) of the Constitution).

(3) An Act of the Parliament may —
- (a) provide for the proof and pleading of custom for any purpose; and
- (b) regulate the manner in which, or the purposes for which, custom may be recognized, applied or enforced; and
- (c) provide for the resolution of conflicts of custom.

(*See: Customs Recognition Act* Ch.19)

AS TO PROOF OF CUSTOM

per Kapi J.

Under Sch.2.1(3) of the Constitution an Act of Parliament may:
- (a) provide for the proof and pleading of custom for any purpose; and
- (b) regulate the manner in which, or the purposes for which, custom may be recognized applied or enforced and
- (c) provide for the resolution of conflicts of custom.

Since the adoption of the Constitution, the Parliament has yet to pass such an Act. However, the Constitution had adopted the *Native Customs (Recognition) Act* 1963 under Sch.2.6. This Act provides for the matters set out under Sch.2.1(3). In relation to matters of proof and pleading of custom, s.5 of the *Native Customs (Recognition) Act* [see now *Customs Recognition Act* Ch.19] provides the following:

(1) Subject to this section, questions of the existence and nature of native custom in relation to a matter, and its application in or relevance to any particular circumstances, shall be ascertained as though they were matters of fact.
(2) In considering a question referred to in the last preceding sub-section, a court is not bound to observe strict legal procedure or apply technical rules of evidence, but shall admit and consider such relevant evidence as is available (including hearsay evidence and expressions of opinion), and shall otherwise inform itself as it sees fit.
(3) For the purposes of the decision on a question referred to in Subsection (1) of this section, a court —
   (a) may refer to books, treatises, reports or other works of reference, or statements by Native Local Government Councils or committees thereof (whether published or not), and may accept any matter or thing stated therein as evidence on the question; and
   (b) may of its own motion call such evidence or require the opinions of such persons as it thinks fit,

but nothing in this subsection contained shall be deemed to limit in any way the discretion of the court in obtaining evidence or informing itself on the question.
(4) Notwithstanding the provisions of Subsection (1) of this section, where an appeal is made from a decision of a court, the court which hears the appeal may, if it thinks fit, consider de novo a question referred to in that subsection and which arises in the appeal.

S.C.R. No 4 of 1980; Re petition of M.T. Somare [1981] PNGLR 265 at p.289.

per Miles J.

The argument on behalf of the petitioner proceeded to a submission that there is a custom of the country that should be recognized, adopted, applied and enforced as part of the underlying law in accordance with Sch.2.1 to the effect that the petitioner has the legal standing to present to the National Court the petition filed herein. This submission was insofar as it related to law supported by argument and insofar as it related to fact supported by affidavit evidence. In some instance it was not clear whether the material in the affidavits was restricted to proving facts or whether it went on to argue matters of law. Schedule 2.1 would seem to treat custom in general as a matter of fact and custom as adopted applied and enforced as a matter of law. Some of the material in the affidavits was objected to as hearsay, outside the knowledge or expertise of the deponents and so on. Counsel for the petitioner himself swore an affidavit as to the custom of his own people which he withdrew upon objection and later replaced with a similar affidavit from another deponent. The Court received all the affidavit evidence subject to ruling on admissibility. I would take a very liberal view as to the admissibility of evidence relating to custom. I expect that most courts in the country would need all available assistance to inform themselves on relevant custom, particularly if it be as suggested in *Constitutional Reference No 1 of 1977 (Sch.2.3)* [1978] PNGLR 295 ('the enticement case'), that it is only nationwide custom that is to be adopted as part of the underlying law under Sch.2.1. Whilst there are good reasons why counsel appearing in a case should not also be a witness, the evidence of counsel is not inadmissible. If custom is not in dispute, the court may be assisted by statements from the Bar table but if there is a dispute such statements are of little value (see *Siwi Kurondo v Lindsay Dabiri* (1980 Unreported) N258). If a court is to adopt apply and enforce a particular custom as a rule of law under Sch.2.1, it should only do so after it has fully informed itself as to the precise nature and extent of that particular custom. If analogy with custom is to be used to formulate a rule of law in accordance with Sch.2.3(1)(c), then it need not be 'proved' at all. It is clear that custom for the purposes of Sch.2.3 is quite different from custom for the purposes of Sch.2.1 and is to be considered in the same light as relevant statutes, legislation and relevant decisions of courts in countries similar to Papua New Guinea and so on. In any event the *Native Customs (Recognition) Act* 1963 ousts the strict rules of evidence and enables a court to inform itself as it sees fit on any question as to custom.

S.C.R. No 4 of 1980; Re petition of M.T. Somare [1981] PNGLR 265 at p.304.

per Bredmeyer J.

Mr Lightfoot's third argument is that the magistrate failed to hear any evidence on customary law. This is a powerful argument. Section 5 of the *Native Customs (Recognition) Act* 1963 deals with proof of custom. Subsection (1) reads as follows:

(1) Subject to this section, questions of the existence and nature of native custom in relation to a matter, and its application in or relevance to any particular circumstances, shall be ascertained as though they were matters of fact.

This subsection means that native customs must be proved as a fact, that is by sworn evidence or affidavit evidence. The following subsections widen the court's powers somewhat — the court itself may call a witness, the evidence given can be unsworn, it can include hearsay and opinions, the court may refer to books, etc. Very often I suspect books will not be available. The court's basic duty under s.5(1) is to hear evidence of custom. This is necessary even though the magistrate may feel that he knows the customs very well. If he does not do so, he has erred at law. Unrepresented parties in the District Court are unlikely to lead evidence of custom so the best way for the magistrate to get evidence of it is to put questions to the complainant and defendant and their witnesses. The questions should be designed to ascertain the principles of customary law, for example, do you have a custom that if a wife leaves her husband for another man, the latter has to pay bride price to the husband? If so, does the amount depend on whether the wife leaves of her own will, or has been enticed there by the new man, or if her husband has ill-treated her? Does the amount depend on whether the wife is young or old; whether she has borne children or not; whether she is still capable of bearing children or not? Can the husband recover more than the bride price, for example for money spent on her food and clothes, or fares, for the shame caused to him, or for the less of her company and services? Having obtained evidence on the customary law applicable the magistrate should weigh up the evidence on custom stating which witness he believes or does not believe and resolving any conflicts of custom. The magistrate should state the customary law which he intends to apply. His reasons for decision should state his findings of facts, the law he considers applicable, and he should then apply the law to the facts to get the result. Sometimes magistrates in civil cases omit to state the law they are applying. They simply make findings of fact and then make an order for the complainant or defendant.

The magistrate did not hear evidence of native custom as required by s.5, that is an error of law which amounts to a substantial miscarriage of justice. I allow the appeal.
Henry Aisi v Malaita Hoala [1981] PNGLR 199 at pp.203,204.

GENERALLY

Referred to

by Kearney Dep.C.J. in *Camilus Billy v Jubilee* (1981 Unreported) N360(M) (following *Henry Aisi v Malaita Hoala* (above).

by Bredmeyer J. in *Aundak Kapil v The Independent State of Papua New Guinea* (1983 Unreported) N435 at pp.9,10 (*Customs Recognition Act* directs courts not to apply custom if to do so would result in an injustice).

PART 2. — RECEPTION OF A COMMON LAW, ETC.

Sch.2.2. — ADOPTION OF A COMMON LAW.

(1) Subject to this Part, the principles and rules that formed, immediately before Independence Day, the principles and rules of common law and equity in England are adopted, and shall be applied and enforced, as part of the underlying law, except if, and to the extent that —

(a) they are inconsistent with a Constitutional Law or a statute; or

(b) they are inapplicable or inappropriate to the circumstances of the country from time to time; or

(c) in their application to any particular matter they are inconsistent with custom as adopted by Part 1.

THAT FORMED IMMEDIATELY BEFORE INDEPENDENCE DAY

Comment

In a series of three powerfully argued judgments Kapi Dep.C.J. has drawn a distinction between two types of English post-Independence common law decisions. The first kind Kapi Dep.C.J. characterizes as decisions which further progress or develop the law. Such decisions, because Sch.2.2(1) adopts only those principles and rules that formed, immediately before Independence Day, the principles of rules of common law and equity in England, do not become part of the underlying law of Papua New Guinea.

The second kind of post-Independence decisions Kapi Dep.C.J. refers to are those which correct errors and declare what the common law has always been.

Kapi Dep.C.J. argues that if a competent court in England, after the date of Independence, declares that a principle of common law decided before that date was wrong law then that decision will have a retrospective effect. Corrections of this kind to the common law are adopted and become part of the underlying law of Papua New Guinea. The decisions in which Kapi Dep.C.J. has developed this analysis are *Waghi Savings and Loans Society Limited v Bank of South Pacific Limited* (1980 Unreported) SC185 at pp.17-19; *The State v Bisket Uranquae Pokia* [1980] PNGLR 97 at pp.99,100 (see extract below) and *S.C.R. No 4 of 1980; Re petition of M.T. Somare* [1981] PNGLR 265 at pp.290,291.

Notwithstanding Kapi Dep.C.J.'s persuasive advocacy this approach may be criticised on three grounds. First, it can be argued that the attempt to distinguish between those English post-Independence decisions which change the law by developing it as opposed to those which change the law by correcting former error is bound to result in arbitrary selections. Because most if not all decisions may with equal justification, be grouped in either class the choice of categorization becomes one of semantics not substance.

Second, the need to refer to post-Independence English case law appears inconsistent with the Constitution's object of severing the Papua New Guinean legal system from its colonial bedrock by making all further change to it a matter of indigenous decision.

Third, we are sceptical of Kapi Dep.C.J.'s underlying proposition that a court which finds a previously authorative decision to have been in error does not 'further progress or develop the law' but merely declares what has always been the law. That proposition presupposes a Blackstonian conception of the common law. Blackstonian theory was tersely but aptly criticised by Kearney J. in *The State v Allan Woila* [1978] PNGLR 99 at p.103 as being 'not [in] accord with the realities of the judicial process'.

Nonetheless, despite these theoretical objections, Kapi Dep.C.J.'s approach has been followed by Miles J. in *Vian Guatal v Papua New Guinea* [1981] PNGLR 230 at pp.243, 244 and the present balance of authority appears to be in its favour.

per Kearney J.

> It is unnecessary for me to speculate upon the position had *Director of Public Prosecutions v Ping Lin* [1975] 3 All ER 175 been decided after Independence; I consider however, that rules of the common law in England enunciated for the first time in decisions of English Courts handed down after Independence are not adopted as part of the underlying law by Constitution Sch.2.2(1). It seems clear enough that that provision adopts, subject to the important exceptions and limitations therein, as a residuary law, the great body of judge-made law as it stood, and was applied, in the courts in England on 16th September, 1975. That date was fixed for purposes of certainty. Judicial creativity thereafter is a matter for the courts of this country, and no other: Constitution Sch.2.4. In the light of the clear constitutional intention, no Blackstonian theory that 'judges do not make law, but only declare what has always been the law', can be relied upon to support the adoption under Constitution Sch.2.2(1) of rules of the common law in England first enunciated after Independence. In any event, in my opinion, the Blackstonian theory is now discredited, and does not accord with the realities of the judicial process.
> *The State v Allan Woila* [1978] PNGLR 99 at p.103.

per Kapi J.

> The common law of England has been described as fluid and progressive. Lord Denning, Master of the Rolls, in his recent book *The Discipline of Law* (1979) in the preface said the following:
> My theme is that the principles of law laid down by the Judges in the 19th century —

however suited to social conditions of that time — are not suited to the social necessities and social opinion of the 20th century. They should be moulded and shaped to meet the needs and opinion of today.

Over the years the common law has developed in this sense. A striking example of the progress of the common law in this sense is in the law of negligence. To give an example, before 1932 a plaintiff could not successfully sue a defendant for damages for negligent acts unless there was a contractual basis between the plaintiff and the defendant. However, the law was further developed in the famous case of *Donoghue v Stevenson* [1932] AC 562 to extend to those outside the contract between the plaintiff and the defendant in the neighbourhood theory [sic].

When the Constitution of the Independent State of Papua New Guinea adopted the common law as at immediately before Independence it froze the common law of England as at 15th September, 1975 and any further progress or development of the common law in the sense I have described above did not and does not become part of the underlying law of Papua New Guinea.

However, this does not mean that if a competent court in England after 15th September, 1975, as in *Wong Kam-ming* [1979] 1 All ER 939, declares that a certain principle of common law decided in 1941, as in the case of *Hammond's Case* [1941] 3 All ER 318, is wrong law, then the principle to be applied is in the latter case. The latter decision of a competent court in England after 15th September, 1975, will have a retrospective effect and all cases following the former principle would be regarded as wrongly decided. (*Wong Kam-ming*) [1979] 1 All ER 939 at p.943).

The principle decided in *Wong Kam-ming* (supra) is not a further development of the common law, as I have explained, but a declaration as to what the law should have been in 1941 in *Hammond's case* (supra).

It follows that the law that is to be applied under Sch.2.2 of the Constitution is the correct principle which is now declared in *Wong Kam-ming's* case (supra).
The State v Bisket Uranquae Pokia [1980] PNGLR 97 at pp.99, 100.

AS TO WHAT CONSTITUTES THE COMMON LAW OF ENGLAND

per Kearney J.

I do not think it is proper for this Court to decide that, where there is a decision of the House of Lords directly in point, the common law in England is as laid down in a conflicting decision of a court of another country. To the contrary: the decision of the House of Lords upon the point must be taken to be the authoritative expression thereon of the common law *in England*. The common law in Australia, or in Papua New Guinea, or elsewhere, is a matter for the courts of those countries.
The State v Allan Woila [1978] PNGLR 99 at p.111.

per Kapi J.

... As a matter of law the court should only consider the English cases declaring the common law as Sch.2.2 of the Constitution is only concerned with the common law of England. If there are cases from other common law countries such as Australia or Canada which declare common law as similar to common law declared by the English courts, then these cases may be used to supplement or strengthen the English cases. However, every precaution must be taken in referring to the decisions from these jurisdictions because the courts there might give their own interpretation or application of the common law principles. I consider that the Court should obtain the common law of England direct from English cases.
Iambakey Okuk v Fallscheer [1980] PNGLR 274 at p.280.

Referred to

by Pratt J. in *In the Matter of the State v Pep* (1983 Unreported) SC261 at p.42 (a decision of the Privy Council is not a part of the common law of England but forms part of the law of the country from which the appeal arises).

AS TO THE EFFECT OF PRE-INDEPENDENCE ENGLISH REPEAL OF THE COMMON LAW

Held

A rule or principle of common law which has been abolished by a United Kingdom Statute before the date of Independence is not received under Sch.2.2
Constitutional Reference No 1 of 1977 (Sch.2.3) [1978] PNGLR 295; see Prentice C.J. at p.297, Saldanha J. at p.300; see also *New Guinea Cocoa (Export) Co. Pty Ltd v Basis Vedbaek* [1980] PNGLR 205; see Bredmeyer J. at p.212.

AS TO THE 'JUDGES RULES'

Held

Having regard to Sch.2.2 of the Constitution the Judges Rules (Eng) are a part of the underlying law not as rules of law but as rules of practice for the guidance of police officers.
The State v Goli Golu [1979] PNGLR 11; see Saldanha J. at pp.12, 13.

AS TO THE MARITIME LAW

Held

The maritime law, the law in admiralty as it has developed in the English courts is no longer to be distinguished from the common law itself and accordingly is adopted as part of the underlying law pursuant to Sch.2.2.
Milan Capek v the Yacht 'Freda' (No 2) [1980] PNGLR 161; see Miles J. at p.169 but note also the comments of Bredmeyer J. in *New Guinea Cocoa (Export) Co. Pty Ltd v Basis Vedbaek* [1980] PNGLR 205 at p.211.

HELD INAPPLICABLE OR INAPPROPRIATE TO THE CIRCUMSTANCES OF THE COUNTRY

Held

The common law rule that in an action for defamation the defamatory words, if in a language other than that of the Court, must be written out in the vernacular language and followed by a literal translation, is inappropriate to the circumstances of the Papua New Guinea in cases in which the defamatory words are alleged to have been spoken in a vernacular which has not in ordinary usage been reduced to writing and is not reasonably capable of being accurately recorded by a Judge in the language of the Court. The contrary view would mean that such actions could never succeed.
Tei Abul v Anton Parau [1976] PNGLR 251; see Frost C.J. at p.254.

Held

If the principle of the judgment in *Trust Houses Ltd v Postlethwaite* [1944] 109 J.P. 12 operates to prevent compulsory discovery of a document actually and visibly in court then it should not be followed because it would be inappropriate to the circumstances of Papua New Guinea.
The State v Birch [1978] PNGLR 79; see Greville Smith J. at p.87.

Held

The traditional common law rule that an accused must be isolated in the dock is not appropriate to the circumstances of Papua New Guinea and is inconsistent with accused's rights under s.37.
The State v Allan Woila (No 2) [1978] PNGLR 113; see Kearney J. at p.117.

Held

The common law rule of practice which requires that a tribunal of the facts (jury) be warned that it is dangerous to act on uncorroborated evidence of an accomplice is neither appropriate or applicable to the circumstances of Papua New Guinea.
The State v Joseph Tapa [1978] PNGLR 134; see Pritchard J. at pp.141, 145-149; see also *The State v Titeva Fineko* [1978] PNGLR 262 (Prentice C.J. at p.263) but see contra *The State v Nataemo Waru* [1977] PNGLR 152 (Frost C.J. at pp.158, 159).

Held

Because most magistrates are not legally qualified and most policemen would not be expected to be acquainted with such niceties as the rule against duplicity, rigid adherence to the rule against duplicity is inappropriate and is likely to result in injustice being done.
Prai v Officer of the Government of Papua New Guinea [1979] PNGLR 1; see Greville Smith J. at p.9.

Held

Because cultural factors commonly render Papua New Guinean children reluctant to make an immediate complaint of rape, the common law principle (if it be such) that the lack of fresh complaint is evidence of consent, is totally unsuited to the situation of Papua New Guinea.
Birch v The State [1979] PNGLR 79; see Prentice C.J. at pp.81, 82, Raine Dep.C.J. at p.83, Kearney J. at p.86.

Held

The common law rule that in order to constitute provocation acts provoked must bear some reasonable relation to the initial provocative act has been excluded by the *Criminal Code Act*.
The State v Inawai Moroi [1981] PNGLR 132; see Kearney Dep.C.J. at p.8.

Held

The common law rules governing standing to bring an action in the Supreme Court under the Constitution are inappropriate and should not be followed in Papua New Guinea because of the different constitutional background against which the rules must operate.
S.C.R. No 4 of 1980; Re petition of M.T. Somare [1981] PNGLR 265; see Kidu C.J. at pp.270, 271, Kapi J. at pp.285-287, 290, Miles J. at p.303, but see also Greville Smith J. (dissenting) at pp.279, 280.

Held

The common law requirement that all parts of a damages award should be contained in a lump sum is inapplicable and inappropriate to the circumstances of the country.
Aundak Kapil v The Independent State of Papua New Guinea (1983 Unreported) N435 at pp.51-58.

PRINCIPLES AND RULES, APPLIED AND ENFORCED AS PART OF THE UNDERLYING LAW

Held

The common law principles which govern ratification of the acts of an agent by a principal apply in Papua New Guinea.
Johns v Thomason [1976] PNGLR 15; see Frost C.J. at p.19.

Held

The common law rules which govern domicile may be applied in Papua New Guinea.
In re the adoption of an Infant R [1976] PNGLR 81; see Prentice Dep.C.J. at p.83.

Held

The principles of the common law of England as to when and in which circumstances an award of damages for personal injuries may be set aside on appeal are 'entirely appropriate'.
The Government of Papua New Guinea v McCleary [1976] PNGLR 321 at pp.322, 323.

Held

The principle of the common law of England that 'clear and distinct legal authority' must be shown for the imposition of any fee charge or tax held applicable.
James Saleng Mileng v Alkan Tololo [1976] PNGLR 447; see Frost C.J. at pp.451,452, Prentice Dep.C.J. at p.459, Williams J. at p.426; see also *Mairi v Alkan Tololo and ors (No 2)* [1976] PNGLR 125; Frost C.J. at p.130, Prentice Dep.C.J. and Williams J. at p.139.

Held

The common law principle that possession of recently stolen property is good evidence of the possessor's guilt of house breaking of the premises from which the property has been stolen is 'entirely applicable and appropriate'.
State v Alpen Popo [1977] PNGLR 18 at p.21.

Held

'Proof beyond reasonable doubt' being the standard of proof required by the common law of England in criminal matters should remain the standard required to be met in Papua New Guinea for determining criminal proceedings.
John Beng v The State [1977] PNGLR 115; see Prentice Dep.C.J. and Williams J. at p.121.

Held

To be admissible in a criminal trial admissions by an accused must be proven beyond reasonable doubt to have been voluntary, which is the standard of proof required of such matters by the common law of England adopted under Sch.2.2.
The State v Allan Woila [1978] PNGLR 99; see Kearney J. at pp.102, 103, 110, 111.

Held

The common law rule of practice which requires a jury (tribunal of fact) to be given a warning of the danger of acting on the basis of uncorroborated evidence of an accomplice is 'clearly applicable to the circumstances of Papua New Guinea'.
The State v Nataemo Wanu [1977] PNGLR 152; see Frost C.J. at pp.158, 159; but see contra *The State v Joseph Tapa* [1978] PNGLR 134 (Pritchard J. at pp.141, 145-149) and *The State v Titeva Fineko* [1978] PNGLR 262 (Prentice C.J. at p.263).

Held

The rule of the common law of England that a date specified in an indictment is not a material matter unless it is an essential part of an alleged offence is applicable in Papua New Guinea; where the words 'on or about (a particular date)' are used in an indictment, proof that the offence was committed within some period having a reasonable approximation to the date mentioned in the indictment will suffice.
The State v Titeva Fineko [1978] PNGLR 262; see Prentice C.J. at pp.264, 265.

Held

The common law principles that a fall in the value of money may be taken into account so as to lead to an increase in the conventional sum of damages to be awarded for loss of expectation of life applied.
Rokan Buyave v Minisang Wankiar [1978] PNGLR 391; see Wilson J. at p.393.

Held

The common law rules governing admissibility of statements made in circumstances not in accordance with the Judge's rules applied.
The State v Goli Golu [1979] PNGLR 11; see Saldanha J. at p.13.

Held

The decision of the House of Lords in *British Transport Commission v Gourlay* [1956] AC 185 that in awarding damages in respect of loss of earnings the tax position should be taken into account is binding upon the National Court.
Charles Pupu v Pelis Tomilate and P.N.G. [1979] PNGLR 108; see Saldanha J. at p.114.

Held

The principles of the common law of England (c.f. those applying in Australia) are to be applied such that an award of damages for loss of earning capacity should be reduced by deducting a sum equivalent to the amount of tax which would have been payable in relation to these lost earnings.
Kerr v Motor Vehicles Insurance (P.N.G.) Trust [1979] PNGLR 251; see Andrew J. at p.272.

Held

The principles of the common law of England (c.f. those applying in Australia) are to be applied in determining the circumstances in which first hand hearsay is admissable in evidence.
Dowsett Engineering (New Guinea) Pty Ltd v Edwards [1979] PNGLR 426; see Kearney J. at p.435.

Held

The law applying in Papua New Guinea in respect of contempt of court is the English common law adopted under Sch.2.2.
Re Rooney (No 2) [1979] PNGLR 448; see Raine Dep.C.J. at p.466, Saldanha J. at p.472, Wilson J. at p.510.

Held

The principles of natural justice evolved by the English common law form part of the underlying law of Papua New Guinea and accordingly the General Manager of the National Airlines Commission appointed under s.22 of the *National Airlines Commission Act* 1973, has a right to be given reasons for his dismissal, and an opportunity to be heard in his own defence before being removed from office under s.23(2) of that Act.
Iambakey Okuk v Fallscheer [1979] PNGLR 274; see Kapi J. at pp.279, 285, Miles J. at pp.291, 293.

Held

The defence, recognised in Australia, that there is no breach of duty owed to a plaintiff who accepts the voluntary services of a driver affected by drink, is not part of the English common law. The English common law must be applied in Papua New Guinea.
Brown v Motor Vehicle Insurance (P.N.G.) Trust [1980] PNGLR 409; see Bredmeyer J. at pp.412, 413.

Held

The English common law action for damages flowing from negligent misrepresentation (as illustrated by the pre-Independence case *Hedley Byrne & Co Ltd v Heller & Partners Ltd* [1964] AC 465 is adopted as part of the underlying law pursuant to Sch.2.2.
Wahgi Saving and Loans Ltd v Bank of South Pacific Ltd (1980 Unreported) SC185; see Kearney Dep.C.J. at pp.4-6, Kapi J. at pp.17-22.

Held

The post-Independence 'declaration' of the common law by the Privy Council (see extract under earlier heading this Schedule) that an accused may not be examined as to the truth of a confession during a voir dire hearing upon its admissability, is to be applied under Sch.2.2.
The State v Bisket Uranquae Pokia [1980] PNGLR 97; see Kapi J. at pp.99, 100.

Held

Where a complaint of assault contains elements of a sexual nature the common law rules relating to the need for corroboration should apply. Such rules are applicable in the circumstances of Papua New Guinea.
Peter Townsend v George Oika [1981] PNGLR 12, see Greville Smith J. at p.18, Pratt J. at pp.22-24, Miles J. at pp.25, 26.

Held

In assessing damages for personal injuries in Papua New Guinea the rules of the common law of England that future inflation should not be taken into account in assessing the level at which future economic loss will be incurred should be followed. Inflation may however be properly taken into account in determining the interest discount rate.
Hassard v Bougainville Copper Ltd [1981] PNGLR 182; see Miles J. at pp.184-189.

Held

The common law rule regarding annexing of accessories (a motor) to chattels (a motor vessel) is that, prima facie, property is not to pass. This rule is applicable to Papua New Guinea.
Steamships Trading Company Ltd v Birner and ors (1981 Unreported) N363; see Kapi J. at pp.3, 4.

Held

Common law principles concerning the construction of the expression to 'extend' time, (such that time may be 'extended' after the period of time first allotted has expired) are to be applied.
Placer Holdings Pty Ltd v Independent State of Papua New Guinea [1982] PNGLR 16; see Greville Smith J. at pp.18,19, Kearney Dep. C.J. at p.17.

Held

The common law rules as to whether a court should hear an appeal from an appellant who has escaped from custody are applicable in the circumstances of Papua New Guinea.
Keko Aparo and ors v The State (1983 Unreported) SC249; see Bredmeyer J. at p.12, Gajewicz. J. at p.15.

per Bredmeyer J.

> The common law tort of negligence is not inconsistent with any Constitutional Law or statute .... A number of countries have opted for a no fault system of compensation for motor-vehicle injuries, others like Papua New Guinea have grafted a no-fault system onto the common law fault system, but the system of common law damages for injuries is so widely known and used in Papua New Guinea that I cannot say it is 'inapplicable or inappropriate to the circumstances of the country' at this time .... I follow the view that I expressed in *Brown v Motor Vehicle Insurance (P.N.G.) Trust* [1980] PNGLR 409 at pp.415 and 417 that I must under the Constitution apply the statutory defence of contributory negligence to the facts before the common law defence of *volenti non fit injuria* and that the latter defence is only likely to succeed where the plaintiff is wholly to blame [for his own injuries].
> *Aundak Kapil v The Independent State of Papua New Guinea* (1983 Unreported) N435 at pp.12-13, 28.

GENERALLY

Referred to

by Frost C.J. in *The State v Mogo Wonom* [1975] PNGLR 311 at p.315 (as to the relationship between the common law prerogative and express Constitutional provision);

by Prentice Dep.C.J. in *Paul Aika and ors v Caspar Uremany* [1976] PNGLR 46 at pp.53-55 (there are good reasons to reject common law rules relating to the number of times a person may apply for bail: but note however contrary holdings in the same case by Raine and Williams JJ.);

by Saldanha J. in *British and New Zealand Exempt Employees Association of Papua New Guinea v Papua New Guinea* [1976] PNGLR 67 at p.71 (common law principle that notwithstanding the fact that a statute may say that a decision of an inferior tribunal shall be final, there is power to bring up the decision by certiorari and quash it for error of law on the face of the record, referred to with approval);

by Raine J. in *Cory v Blyth (No 1)* [1976] PNGLR 274 at p.278;

by Frost C.J. in *Nai'u Limagwe and ors v The State* [1976] PNGLR 382 at p.391 (common law rules as to the exercise of discretionary power vested in the Court referred to with approval);

by Frost C.J. in *Mauga Logging Co Pty Ltd v South Pacific Oil Palm Development Pty Ltd (No 1)* [1977] PNGLR 80 at p.83;

by Kearney J. in *Garaiju Moruwu v Sabeme Uve and anor* [1978] PNGLR 161 at p.162 (queried whether judicial interpretation of long standing as to the construction of Part 4 of the *Law Reform (Miscellaneous Provisions) Act* 1962 should be followed);

by Prentice C.J. in *The Government of Papua New Guinea v Moini* [1978] PNGLR 184 at p.195 (principles of foreseeability with respect to third party 'pay back' killings following road accidents discussed); see also Pritchard J. at pp.195, 196;

by Prentice C.J. in *Sanguma Wauta v The State* [1978] PNGLR 326 at p.333;

by Pritchard J. in *Bromlay and Manton Pty Ltd v Eremus Andrew* [1978] PNGLR 498 at p.509;

by Pritchard J. (dissenting) in *Constitutional Reference No 1 of 1978 (s.19)* [1978] PNGLR 345 at p.377;

by Andrew J. in *Tapopwa Thomas v The State* [1979] PNGLR 140 at p.157 (common law referred to as illuminating the correct interpretation of ss.16 and 20 of the Criminal Code: person not to be twice punished for same offence);

by Pritchard J. in *Van der Kreek v Van der Kreek* [1979] PNGLR 185 at p.196 (expressing the tentative opinion that the *Foreign Judgement (Reciprocal Enforcement) Act* 1962 should be regarded as a codification);

by Saldanha J. in *Premdas v The Independent State of Papua New Guinea* [1979] PNGLR 329 at p.362 (discussion as to the adopting of the principles of natural justice pursuant to Constitution s.37(21)(a), s.59 and Sch.2.2); see also Wilson J. (dissenting) at pp.376, 382;

by Wilson J. in *P.L.A.R No 1 of 1980* [1980] PNGLR 326 at p.335 (referred to as relevant to formulating the general principles of statutory interpretation to be applied by the courts in Papua New Guinea);

by Bredmeyer A.J. in *Brown v Motor Vehicles Insurance (P.N.G.) Trust* [1980] PNGLR 409 at p.415 Fn;

by Kapi J. in *Acting Public Solicitor (sic) v Uname Aumane* [1980] PNGLR 510 at p.540 (common law is not written law for the purposes of Constitution s.37(2));

by Narakobi A.J. in *The State v Yale Gesie* (1980 Unreported) N254 at p.17;

by Miles J. in *Bogil Guma v The Independent State of Papua New Guinea and ors* (1980 Unreported) N262 at pp.6-10 (whether the defence of voluntary assumption of risk to an action in negligence and the doctrine of Crown or State immunity from liability for wrongful acts of police officers apply in Papua New Guinea; see also discussion of the applicable principles governing the question of vicarious liability);

by Greville Smith J. in *S.C.R. No 1 of 1980; Re s.22A(b) of Police Offences Act (Papua)* [1981] PNGLR 28 at pp.31, 32 (as to the interrelationship between s.37(4)(a) and Sch.2.2);

by Andrew J. in *Avia Aihi v The State* [1981] PNGLR 81 at p.99 (referred to in the context of ascertaining the meaning of the expression 'inherent jurisdiction' in s.155(2)(b) of the Constitution); see also Greville Smith J. (dissenting) at p.95, Kapi J. (dissenting) at p.109;

by Bredmeyer J. in *Henry Aisi v Malaita Hoala* [1981] PNGLR 199 at pp.201, 204 (the meaning of the expression 'personal action of law' in s.29 of the *District Courts Act* 1963 held to be wider than merely action at common law);

by Miles J. in *Schliebs v Singh* [1981] PNGLR 365 at pp.369-372 (common law authority referred to for assistance in illuminating the meaning of the expression 'knowingly in possession' as contained in s.7 of the *Dangerous Drugs Act* 1952);

by Kapi J. In *S.C.R. No 1A of 1981; Re Motor Traffic Act* [1982] PNGLR 122 at p.138;

by Greville Smith J. in *S.C.R. No 2 of 1981; Re s.19(1)(f) of the Criminal Code* [1982] PNGLR 150 at pp.166,167 (as to the correct approach of the judiciary to the development of the underlying law); see also Kapi J. at p.172;

by Bredmeyer J. in *Aundak Kapil v The Independent State of Papua New Guinea* (1983 Unreported) N435 at p.55 (the Supreme Court and National Court should not hesitate to declare parts of the English common law and equity inapplicable and inappropriate to the circumstances of Papua New Guinea).

(2) Subject to Subsection (1)(a), (b) and (c), the principles and rules adopted under Subsection (1) include principles and rules relating to the Royal Prerogative, except insofar as they provide for —
  (a) a power to declare martial law; or
  (b) a power to grant letters of denization or similar privileges; and
  (c) a power to do any other act, provision for the doing of which is made by a Constitutional Law or an Act of the Parliament.

AS TO THE CONTENT OF THE PREROGATIVE SO ADOPTED

per Frost C.J.

Leaving aside the legislative power, with which the Court is not concerned, whatever operation remains to be given to the express reservation of the principles and rules of the Royal Pregorative under Sch.2.2(2), there is no provision for any prerogative exercise of executive acts. Further the Royal Prerogative of the Monarch as the 'distributor' of justice has been displaced [referring to s.86(1), s.86(2), s.99(1), s.99(2), s.138 and s.139]. Accordingly the only conclusion open, in my opinion, is that the Head of State has no prerogative function to prosecute offences whether that is regarded as an executive function as, in my opinion, it is, or a judicial function.
The State v Mogo Wonom [1975] PNGLR 311 at p.316.

Held

Sch.2.2(2) and s.158 both confer power upon the National Court to exercise the special jurisdiction delegated in England by the Monarch as parens patriae.
Re The Adoption of Children Act 1968 (1980 Unreported N221; see Narokobi A.J. at p.3 but see also *Monomb Yamba v Geru* [1975] PNGLR 322 per Frost C.J. at p.323 (not relying upon Sch.2.2(2)).

GENERALLY

Referred to

by Greville Smith J (dissenting) in *Avia Aihi v The State* [1981] PNGLR 81 at p.95.

(3) The principles and rules of common law and equity are adopted as provided by Subsections (1) and (2) notwithstanding any revision of them by any statute of England that does not apply in the country by virtue of Section Sch.2.6 (*adoption of pre-Independence laws*).

GENERALLY

per Kapi J.

Before going into what the common law is, the basis of the application of the common law should be considered. Under Sch.2.2 of the Constitution the principles of common law and equity that applied in England immediately before Independence are adopted as part of the underlying law of Papua New Guinea. These principles apply notwithstanding revision of these by any Statute of England which does not apply in Papua New Guinea ... Schedule 2.2(3) of the Constitution in my view is an important provision because it removed the difficulties of construing what is the meaning of 'common law' as was posed in the High Court of Australia in *Booth v Booth* 53 CLR 1 .... It appears that this provision of the Constitution adopts 'common-law' as confined to 'unenacted' law as distinct from any revision of them by statute law.
Wahgi Saving and Loans Society Ltd v Bank of South Pacific Ltd (1980 Unreported) SC185 at pp.17,18.

Referred to

by Narokobi A.J. in *Ambi v Rabi and ors* (1980 Unreported) N279 at p.6;

by Kearney Dep.C.J. in *The State v Inawai Moroi* [1981] PNGLR 132 at p.138.

(4) In relation to any particular question before a court, the operation of Subsection (1)(b) shall be determined by reference, among other things, to the circumstances of the case, including the time and place of any relevant transaction, act or event.

AS TO CRITERIA FOR DETERMINING WHETHER A PRINCIPLE OF COMMON LAW IS OR IS NOT APPLICABLE.

per Kapi J.

... In considering the appropriateness or applicability of the common law principles to the circumstances of this country, one must not take it for granted that these common law principles should apply or (sic), on the other hand, care must be taken in rejecting these principles. This is well expressed by Lord Denning in the case of *Nyali Ltd v Attorney-General* [1956] 1 QB 1 at pp.16-17:

> The next proviso provides, however, that the common law is to apply 'subject to such qualifications as local circumstances render necessary'. This wise provision should, I think, be liberally construed. It is a recognition that the common law cannot be applied in a foreign land without considerable qualification. Just as with an English Oak so too with the English common law. You cannot transplant it to the African continent and expect it to retain the tough character it has in England. It will flourish indeed, but it needs careful tending. So with the common law. It has many principles of manifest justice and good sense which can be applied with advantage to peoples of every race and colour all the world over: but it has also many refinements, subleties and technicalities which are not suited to other folk.... In these far-off lands, the people must have a law which they understand and which they will respect. The common law cannot fulfil this role without considerable qualifications. *The task of making these qualifications is entrusted to the judges of these lands. It is a great task which calls for all their wisdom.* (Emphasis mine.)

As to what the circumstances are, in my view these will vary from case to case depending on whether the principle is dealing with a question of custom or whether dealing with a system of government or the law as provided by the Constitution or statutes of this country. *Iambakey Okuk v Fallsheer* [1980] PNGLR 274 at pp.285,286.

GENERALLY

Referred to

by Saldanha J. in *Prai v Officer of the Government of Papua New Guinea* [1979] PNGLR 1 at p.9 (the legal niceties of the rules against duplicity are inappropriate to the circumstances of the country at the present time).

Part 3 — DEVELOPMENT OF AN UNDERLYING LAW FOR PAPUA NEW GUINEA.

Sch.2.3. — DEVELOPMENT, ETC., OF THE UNDERLYING LAW.

(1) If in any particular matter before a court there appears to be no rule of law that is applicable and appropriate to the circumstances of the country, it is the duty of the National Judicial System, and in particular of the Supreme Court and the National Court, to formulate an appropriate rule as part of the underlying law having regard —

(a) in particular, to the National Goals and Directive Principles and the Basic Social Obligations; and

(b) to Division III.3 (*basic rights*); and

(c) to analogies to be drawn from relevant statutes and custom; and

(d) to the legislation of, and to relevant decisions of the courts of, any country that in the opinion of the court has legal system similar to that of Papua New Guinea; and

(e) to relevant decisions of courts exercising jurisdiction in or in respect of all or any part of the country at any time,

and to the circumstances of the country from time to time.

AS TO APPLICATION.

per Kapi J.

Thus I find that in this particular case there is no applicable rule of law. It is therefore a case of formulation of a new rule of law under Sch.2.3 of the Constitution. Schedule 2.3 of the Constitution directs that in formulating the appropriate rule the court shall have regard to:

(a) the National Goals and Directive Principles and the Basic Social Obligations;
(b) *basic rights*;
(c) analogies drawn from relevant statutes and custom;
(d) legislation and decisions of courts of any country which has a similar legal system;
(e) relevant decisions of courts in the country.

To have regard to these considerations does not mean the court should be strictly bound by them. What the court may eventually formulate may involve a combination of all these considerations. The point of this provision is that the court's formulation of the principle should be influenced more by these factors than anything else.

Under Sch.2.3(1)(c) the court shall have regard to *analogies to custom*. This is different from custom as adopted and applied under Sch.2.1. Under Sch.2.1 custom must be proven with some precision whereas the degree of precision may not be the same under Sch.2.3(1)(c). However, in practice custom must be decisively established under Sch.2.3(1)(c) if it is to play any part in the formulation of a new rule of law.

Whether or not custom has any influence in the formulation of principle depends on the evidence that is produced before the court. The court may, in appropriate cases, decline to formulate a law if it considers that not much assistance has been given on these considerations. Formulation of new law depends to a large extent on the evidence of these considerations. It is foreseeable that in appropriate cases the formulation of a new law may change from time to time on the subject depending on the evidence that is brought before the court. It is not satisfactory. For these reasons counsel appearing in these cases ought to give these matters the fullest research. This does not mean that the judges should not give the fullest research outside counsel's research. But it must be borne in mind that the judges of the Supreme Court are trial judges in the National Court and have very little time for full research. We do not have the benefit of law clerks as in the Supreme Court of the U.S.A. This undoubtedly puts a heavy burden on counsel who appear in these cases.

[Having so addressed himself generally, His Honour proceeded to examine, seriatum, each of the matters set out in sub-sections 1(a),(b),(c),(d) and (e) of Sch.2.3 before formulating a rule of the underlying law].

S.C.R. No 4 of 1980; Re petition of M.T. Somare [1981] PNGLR 265 at pp.292,293 (see also Kidu C.J. at pp.272,273, Greville Smith J. (dissenting) at p.281 and, in particular Miles J. at pp.303-312 advocating a slightly more flexible judicial methodology than that advanced by Kapi J (see also under Sch.2.1(1)).

AS TO JUDICIAL METHODOLOGY

Held

The duty to formulate a law pursuant to Sch.2.3 arises only when there is neither a rule of custom (applied under Sch.2.1) nor a rule of the common law of England (applied under Sch.2.2) covering the situation. If there remains a doubt that there may be an applicable rule of custom, the court should not proceed to formulate a new rule of law; it should decline to declare the law in the absence of any evidence as to matters of custom.

Constitutional Reference No 1 of 1977 (Sch.2.3) [1978] PNGLR 295: See Prentice C.J. at pp.297-299; Raine Dep.C.J. at p.299 and Saldanha J. at p.300.

Comment

The extremely cautious approach of the Court in *Constitutional Reference No 1 of 1977 (Sch.2.3)* [1978] PNGLR 295 has not always been followed. Thus for example in *Vian Guatal v Papua New Guinea* [1981] PNGLR 230 Miles J. stated, 'There has been no reference to custom on this issue and in the absence of any knowledge I can only find that there is no custom applicable' and proceeded upon that basis.

Although it must be conceded that the attempt to ascertain whether there are any applicable rules of custom ought always be made it is the authors' opinion that the rigid application of the methodology espoused in *Constitutional Reference No 1 of 1977* (*Sch.2.3*) will result in the court not undertaking its law-making duty leaving no law, bad law or, worse, uncertainty behind. In combatting that tendency the pragmatic approach exampled by Miles J. has much to commend it. A preferable approach, however, might require the court to adjourn its proceedings, and insist that counsel properly research the customary issue.

Referred to

by Kapi J. in *Acting Public Solicitor (sic) v Uname Aumane* [1980] PNGLR 510 at pp.540,543 (underlying law distinguished from the written law: development of the underlying law arises only when there is no rule of law applicable);

by Kapi J. (dissenting) in *Avia Aihi v The State* [1981] PNGLR 81 at p.112 (court may only formulate new law if there is no applicable rule of law);

by Bredmeyer J. in *Sausau v Police Commissioner* [1981] PNGLR 327 at pp.330,331, (court should not develop the underlying law when to do so would run counter to the intent of an Act of Parliament upon the subject);

by Greville Smith J. in *S.C.R. No 2 of 1981; Re s.19(1)(f) of the Criminal Code* [1982] PNGLR 150 at pp.146-166 (courts should be circumspect in developing the underlying law and it is not proper by judicial act to invade the province of the legislature);

by Kapi J. in *S.C.R. No 2 of 1981; Re s.19(1)(f) of the Criminal Code* [1982] PNGLR 150 at p.172 (discretionary power of the court under s.155(4) contrasted with the power of the court to develop the underlying law), see also Pratt J. at p.34;

by Kidu C.J. (Andrew J. concurring) in *Re James Allan Sannga: Peter Timereke v Duncan Ferrie and anor* (1983 Unreported) SC255 at p.17 (development of the underlying law only becomes relevant where there is no statutory law or accepted custom or common law), see also Kapi Dep.C.J. at pp.25,26,42.

EXAMPLES OF LAW DEVELOPED UNDER SCHEDULE 2.3

Held

The principles to be applied in Papua New Guinea when considering the evidence of accomplices declared and set forth in five paragraphs.
The State v Joseph Tapa [1978] PNGLR 134; see Pritchard J. at p.149.

Held

A Judge of the National Court who has imposed a sentence of imprisonment has power to recall the sentence and sentence afresh at any time before the circuit is formally closed.
The State v Kaupa Ungi [1980] PNGLR 199; see Narakobi A.J. at pp.203,204.

Held

The Leader of the Opposition has standing to invoke the powers of the Supreme Court under s.18(1) of the Constitution in order to determine whether the sending of troops overseas to Vanuatu for peacekeeping purposes is or is not constitutional because (per Kidu C.J. and Kapi J.) every citizen has the right to invoke the powers of the court to ensure the constitution is being adhered to and (per Miles J.) the Leader of the Opposition has a proper concern with the constitutional validity of the legislation and should, in the exercise of the court's discretion, be entitled to bring proceedings
S.C.R. No 4 of 1980; re petition of M.T. Somare [1981] PNGLR 265; see Kidu C.J. at p.273, Kapi J. at p.296, Miles J. at p.310-312; Kearney Dep.C.J. and Greville Smith J. dissenting.

GENERALLY

Referred to

by Prentice Dep.C.J. in *The State v Kewa Kai* [1976] PNGLR 481 at p.482;

by Prentice Dep.C.J. in *Reference No 1 of 1977* [1977] PNGLR 362 at p.374;

by Prentice Dep.C.J. in *The Government of Papua New Guinea v Moini* [1978] PNGLR 184 at p.195 ('I would be prepared to hold in the process of determining an underlying law ... that liability for negligence on the highway committed after Independence is capable of extending to foreseeable injury or death from payback ...'), see also Kearney and Pritchard JJ. at p.195;

by Andrew J. in *The State v Misimb Kais* [1978] PNGLR 241 at pp.244,252 (considered whether the function performed by Andrew J. was simply that of statutory interpretation rather than a function requiring consideration of Sch.2.3: see also the observations of Prentice C.J. in *Sanguma Wauta v The State* [1978] PNGLR 326 at p.329.);

by Prentice C.J. in *Premdas v The Independent State of Papua New Guinea* [1979] PNGLR 329 at p.342; see also Saldanha J. at p.362;

by Bredmeyer J. in *New Guinea Cocoa (Export) Company Pty Ltd v Basis Vedbaek* [1980] PNGLR 205 at pp.212,214 (declining to develop the underlying law when the common law of contract and quasi-contract is applicable to the circumstances of the country);

by Kapi J. in *Iambakey Okuk v Fallscheer* [1980] PNGLR 274 at pp.279,280 (Supreme Court yet to develop its own principles of natural justice);

by Miles J. in *Vian Guatal v Papua New Guinea* [1981] PNGLR 230 at pp.237,244,245;

by Pratt J. in *Re Passingam Taru* [1982] PNGLR 292 at pp.294,295 (arresting officer's duty includes a duty to appear to give evidence in court: if not a rule of the common law then required to be developed under Sch.2.3);

by Bredmeyer J. in *John Jaminan v The State* (1983 Unreported) SC262 at p.23 (a post-Independence common law decision concerning lies as corroboration held appropriate to the circumstances of Papua New Guinea and accordingly applied under Sch.2.3.).

(2) If in any court other than the Supreme Court a question arises that would involve the performance of the duty imposed by Subsection (1), then, unless the question is trivial, vexatious or irrelevant —

(a) in the case of the National Court — the Court may; and

(b) in the case of any other court (not being a village court) — the court shall,

refer the matter for decision to the Supreme Court, and take whatever other action (including the adjournment of proceedings) is appropriate.

TRIVIAL, VEXATIOUS OR IRRELEVANT

Comment

See note under s.18(2) discussing identical words.

Sch.2.4. — JUDICIAL DEVELOPMENT OF THE UNDERLYING LAW.

In all cases, it is the duty of the National Judicial System, and especially of the Supreme Court and the National Court, to ensure that, with due regard to the need for consistency, the underlying law develops as a coherent system in a manner that is appropriate to the circumstances of the country from time to time, except insofar as it would not be proper to do so by judicial act.

SPECIFIC APPLICATIONS

Held

Sch.2.4 provides justification for a judge to make general recommendations for the amendment of the statute law and/or the Constitution so that the law develops in accordance with principles of Sch.2.4.
Premdas v The Independent State of Papua New Guinea [1979] PNGLR 329; see Wilson J. (dissenting) at p.390.

Held

In construing an Act (the *Dangerous Drugs Act* 1952) it is desirable in the interests of consistency and coherence that where a term ('possession') is used which is not defined by the Act but is defined by another Act covering the same kind of subject matter (the Criminal Code) that the term be given the same meaning.
Schliebs v Singh [1981]PNGLR 364; see Miles J. at p.369.

GENERALLY

Referred to

by Prentice Dep.C.J. in *Reference No 1 of 1977* [1977] PNGLR 362 at p.374;

by Kearney J. in *The State v Allan Woila* [1978] PNGLR 99 at p.103 (after Independence judicial creativity is a matter for the courts of Papua New Guinea and no other);

by Prentice C.J. in *Constitutional Reference No 1 of 1977 (Sch.2.3)* [1978] PNGLR 295 at pp.297,298 (as warranting the conclusions that 'custom' in Sch.2.1 must mean 'custom obtaining throughout the country, and that in the absence of proper evidence and materials it is improper to embark upon the procedure of declaring the law under Sch.2.3);

by Prentice C.J. in *Sanguma Wauta v The State* [1978] PNGLR 326 at p.332 (as relevant to rejecting a construction of the provision of the Criminal Code relating to incest which would apply to sexual intercourse with children adopted under customary law);

by Pritchard J. in *Van Der Kreek v Van Der Kreek* [1979] PNGLR 185 (obiter remarks favouring the development of Papua New Guinea's own underlying law);

By Wilson J. in *P.L.A.R. No 1 of 1980* [1980] PNGLR 326 at p.335, see also Andrew J. at p.346 (Supreme Court should not abandon its own views to follow a decision of the High Court of Australia and thereby abandon consistency);

by Nakarobi A.J. in *The State v Wapulae, and ors* (1980 Unreported) N233 at p.20;

by Narakobi A.J. in *The State v Yale Gesie* (1980 Unreported) N254 (duty to interpret the Criminal Code in a way adapted to the changing circumstances of the country);

by Miles J. in *Acting Public Prosecutor v Konis Haha* [1981] PNGLR 205 at p.219 (post-Independence common law cases referred to in the interests of developing the law as a coherent system);

by Greville Smith J. (dissenting) in *S.C.R. No 4 of 1980; Re petition of M.T. Somare* [1981] PNGLR 265 at p.279: see also Kapi J. at p.286;

by Kapi J. in *S.C.R. No 1A of 1981: Re Motor Traffic Act* [1982] PNGLR 122 at p.138 (underlying law as embodying interalia the creation of new principles under Sch.2.3. and the development of these principles under Sch.2.4 discussed);

by Greville Smith J. in *S.C.R. No 2 of 1981: Re s.19(1)(f) of the Criminal Code* [1982] PNGLR 150 at pp.164,165 (the judiciary's duty to develop the underlying law is circumscribed by the words 'except insolar as it would not be proper to do so by judicial act'); see also Kapi J. at pp.169-172 (inherent power of the Supreme and National Courts pursuant to s.155(4) . . . 'to make remedial orders' distinguished from the application of principles of law and equity in relation to remedial orders of a similar nature);

by Pratt J. in *In the Matter of the State v Pep* (1983 Unreported) SC261 at p.42.

Sch.2.5. — REPORTS ON THE DEVELOPMENT OF THE UNDERLYING LAW

In their reports under Section 187(1) (*reports by Judges*), and in any report under Section 187(2) (*reports by Judges*) if in their opinion it is desirable to do so, the Judges shall comment on the state, suitability and development of the underlying law, with any recommendations as to improvement that they think it proper to make.

GENERALLY

Referred to

by Prentice Dep.C.J. in *Reference No 1 of 1977* [1977] PNGLR 362 at p.374;

by Greville Smith J. in *S.C.R. No 2 of 1981; Re s.19(1)(f) of the Criminal Code* [1982] PNGLR 150 at p.165 (as, inter alia the basis of His Honour's inference that judicial development of the underlying law should be confined and not invade the province of the legislature).

PART 4. — ADOPTION OF CERTAIN STATUTES.

Sch.2.6 — ADOPTION OF PRE-INDEPENDENCE LAWS.

(1) In Subsection (2), "pre-Independence law" means —
  (a) a law (including a law that had not yet come into operation) that was repealed by the *Laws Repeal Act* 1975 made by the pre-Independence House of Assembly for Papua New Guinea, and includes —
    (i) a law that was, and to the extent that it was, continued in force under or by virtue of any such law; and

(ii) a purported law that might have been (but had not been declared by a court to be) invalid by reason of a failure to comply with any other law in respect of the matter of its assent,

other than such a law that was repealed or superseded, or had expired or was spent, before the commencement of the *Laws Repeal Act* 1975; and

(b) the laws of Australia specified in Part I of Schedule 5 as in force in the country immediately before Independence Day; and

(c) the laws of England specified in Part 2 of Schedule 5 as in force in the country immediately before Independence Day; and

(d) subordinate legislative enactments under any such laws that were in force in the country immediately before the repeal, or immediately before Independence Day, as the case may be.

(2) Subject to any Constitutional Law, all pre-Independence laws are, by virtue of this section, adopted as Acts of the Parliament, or subordinate legislative enactments under such Acts, as the case may be, and apply to the extent to which they applied, or purported to apply, immediately before the repeal referred to in Subsection (1)(a), or immediately before Independence Day, as the case may be.

(3) For the avoidance of doubt it is hereby declared that where a pre-Independence law to which Subsection (2) applies has not been brought into operation, and does not itself express a date on which it is to come into operation, it may be brought into operation —

(a) in the case of an Act — on a date to be fixed by the Head of State by notice published in the National Gazette; and

(b) in the case of a subordinate legislative enactment — by publication in the National Gazette.

ADOPTED SUBJECT TO COMPLIANCE WITH THE CONSTITUTION

per Frost C.J.

Before turning to the relevant provisions of the Constitution, it is important to note the legal arrangements which were made to ensure that all laws in the country must stem from its autochthonous or 'homegrown' Constitution . . . The first step was the enactment by the pre-Independence House of Assembly of the *Laws Repeal Act* 1975 which came into operation immediately before the expiry of Independence Day, 15th September 1975. The purpose of that Act, which was achieved by one simple section and without reference to particular enactments, was the repeal in bulk, as it were, of all the legislation and subordinate legislation in Papua New Guinea, and any other country applying to Papua New Guinea immediately before the commencement of the Act. It was then by force of s.20(3) and Sch.2.6 of the Constitution, which came into effect on the 16th September, 1975, that all pre-Independence laws, which means for the purposes of this case all laws repealed by the *Laws Repeal Act* 1975, were adopted as Acts of the Parliament and were brought into application to the extent to which they applied immediately before

Independence Day. Just as the repeal was of the legislation in its entirety, so also was the adoption of that legislation under the Constitution ... Further as the provision construed in Sch.2.6 is expressly made subject to any Constitutional law, it is clear that the adopted laws are subject to the same constitutional limitations as an Act of Parliament ... [A law adopted under Sch.2.6 can be a valid law to the extent only that it can be brought within the legislative power of the National Parliament.]
Peter v South Pacific Brewery Ltd [1976] PNGLR 537 at pp.540,541; see also Prentice Dep.C.J. at pp.553,554.

Referred to

by Raine J. in *Cory v Blyth (No 1)* [1976] PNGLR 274 at pp.275-279 (obiter consideration of the relationship a law adopted as an Act of Parliament under Sch.2.6(2) and s.38 of the Constitution which prescribes that a law regulating or restricting a right or freedom conferred under Part III Division 3 Subdividion C of the Constitution must be made in a particular manner and form : see also notes under s.38);

by Kapi J. in *Minister for Lands v Frame* [1980] PNGLR 433 at pp.454,465 (Act adopted under Sch.2.6 must be construed subject to the Constitution).

AS TO THE ADOPTION OF FOREIGN STATUTES

per Kapi J.

At Independence Sch.2.6 of the Constitution ... adopted all pre-Independence laws as Acts of the parliament of the new Independent State of Papua New Guinea. Pre-Independence laws are defined under Sch.2 to include a law that was repealed by the *Laws Repeal Act* 1975. The *Papua and New Guinea Act* 1949 [an Act of Australia which applied to Papua New Guinea] and the *Supreme Court Act* 1949 [a subordinate legislative enactment by the Governor-General of Australia pursuant to the *Papua and New Guinea Act* 1949] were Acts repealed by the *Laws Repeal Act* 1975 and were therefore laws adopted under Sch.2.6 of the Constitution.
Milan Capek v The Yacht 'Freja' [1980] PNGLR 57 at p.61.

per Miles J.

The *Papua and New Guinea Act* 1949 (Aust.) (to give it its original title) repealed the 1945 Act and provided for the administrative union of the two Territories, but it went further. It established a Supreme Court s.58, and provided for the continuation of all laws in force in either or both Territories, s.32. The jurisdiction of the Courts of the Territories was given to the Supreme Court.

In my view the Supreme Court of Papua New Guinea (as it was originally called) acquired the same jurisdiction as a colonial court of admiralty but it could not be saïd that the *Colonial Courts of Admiralty Act* 1890 extended to either of the jointly administered Territories by virtue of its own force.

6. Independence: Laws Repeal Act 1975.

The stated purpose of this Act (a product of the pre-Independence House of Assembly) was to repeal all the legislation and subordinate legislation of Papua New Guinea and any other country applying to, adopted by or existing in Papua New Guinea immediately prior to Independence. It applied to an Act of Australia or England which was adopted, applied or continued in force as a law of one of the Territories but did not include an Act of Australia or England which extended of its own force to one of the Territories.

The *Laws Repeal Act* 1975 therefore applied to the *Colonial Courts of Admiralty Act* 1890 (Imp.), only indirectly in that the 1890 Act had been adopted, applied and continued in force in both Papua and New Guinea as at the time the *Laws Repeals Act*, 1975, came into operation, that is immediately before the expiry of 15th September, 1975, the day before Independence.

The *Colonial Courts of Admiralty Act* 1890 (Imp.), had not extended of its own force to Papua beyond 1906 and had never extended of its own force to New Guinea.

7. Independence: The Constitution.

By Sch.2.6(2) of the Constitution of the Independent State of Papua New Guinea all pre-Independence laws (that is to say laws repealed by the *Laws Repeal Act* 1975) are adopted as Acts of the Parliament of Papua New Guinea to the extent that they applied immediately before repeal by the *Laws Repeal Act* 1975.

For reasons I have indicated, this means that the *Colonial Courts of Admiralty Act* 1890 (Imp.), still governs the exercise of jurisdiction in admiralty in Papua New Guinea.

8. Papua New Guinea Independence Act 1975 (Aust.).

This Act of the Australian Parliament took effect on the expiration of the day preceding Independence Day, that is at the same time as the *Laws Repeal Act* 1975. It provided inter alia that, at that time, every Act of Australia, and every Imperial Act, extending to the whole or any part of Papua New Guinea as part of the law of Papua New Guinea ceases to so extend.

It may thus be seen that the effect of the *Laws Repeal Act* 1975, the *Papua New Guinea Independence Act* 1975 (Aust.) and the Constitution is to notionally repeal all laws of Papua New Guinea as at the moment of Independence and to adopt, at that same moment, all pre-existing laws except those Acts, Australian or Imperial, which had extended to Papua New Guinea not through adoption, application or continuation, but of their own force. If one takes the view (which I do not) that the *Colonial Courts of Admiralty Act* 1890 (Imp.) extended to Papua New Guinea immediately before Independence of its own force and not through adoption, application or continuance, then the attainment of Independence brought its operation in this country to an end. One would have to seek a basis for admiralty jurisdiction, if any, elsewhere.

My own conclusion therefore is that the National Court has a jurisdiction in admiralty matters similar to that of a colonial court of admiralty established under the 1890 Act. Because of changed circumstances and constitutional development I do not think that it is or ever was a colonial court of admiralty as such. (As to the application of antiquated legislation from other countries see Murphy J. in *Bistricic v Rokov & ors* [1976] 51 ALJR 163 at p.168.

Milan Capek v The Yacht 'Freja' (No 2) [1980] PNGLR 161 at pp.166–168.

per Bredmeyer J

The legislative steps by which the pre-Independence Supreme Court of Papua and New Guinea acquired admiralty jurisdiction are correctly related in the judgments of Kapi J. in *Milan Capek v The Yacht 'Freja'* (see above) and Miles J. in the case of *Milan Capek v The Yacht 'Freja' (No 2)* (see above). To reiterate briefly the *Colonial Courts of Admiralty Act* 1890 of United Kingdom conferred admiralty jurisdiction upon the Central Court of British New Guinea and that jurisdiction was continued in force in the territory of Papua by ss.6(1) and 8 of the *Papua Act* 1905. The *Colonial Courts of Admiralty Act* 1890 (Imp.) did not apply of its own force to the Mandated Territory of New Guinea because that territory was not a British possession but the Act was a law in force in Queensland and I agree with the learned editor of the *Laws of The Territory of New Guinea* 1927-1945 (Annotated), Vol.5 pp.67-68) that it was a law applicable to the circumstances of the territory and not repugnant to or inconsistent with any other law in force in the territory and hence it became an adopted law of New Guinea under s.14 of the *Laws Repeal & Adopting Ordinance* 1921. Also the *Judiciary Ordinance* 1921 of New Guinea created a Central Court for the territory, later renamed the Supreme Court, and by s.11 conferred on it the like 'jurisdiction, power and authority' as the Supreme Court of Queensland — which included its admiralty jurisdiction, inter alia, to try claims for necessaries supplied to ships.

The *Papua — New Guinea Provisional Administration Act* 1945 (Aust.) combined the two territories under an Administrator and by s.16 established the Supreme Court of the Territory of Papua New Guinea. It gave to that court the same jurisdiction as the previous Supreme Court of Papua had in relation to Papua and as the previous Supreme Court of New Guinea had in relation to New Guinea. That Act was replaced by the *Papua New Guinea Act* 1949 (Aust.) which also repealed the *Papua Act* 1905 and the *New Guinea Act* 1920. Section 32 of the *Papua and New Guinea Act* 1949 kept in force all the laws which previously applied in the respective territories of Papua and New Guinea which included the *Colonial Courts of Admiralty Act*. Section 58 of the *Papua and New Guinea Act* 1949 created a new Supreme court of the Territory of Papua and New Guinea and s.62 provided that its jurisdiction practice and procedure was to be established by an Ordinance. That Ordinance was the *Supreme Court Ordinance* 1949 which repealed the *Courts & Laws Adopting Ordinance* 1888 of Papua and the *Judiciary Ordinance* 1921 of New Guinea and which by s.6 gave to the new Supreme Court the same jurisdiction previously exercised by the Supreme Court of Papua New Guinea. Thus by the two provisions, s.32 of the *Papua and New Guinea Act* 1949 and s.6 of the *Supreme Court Ordinance* 1949, the *Colonial Courts of Admiralty Act* continued to apply and the Supreme Court of Papua and New Guinea continued to exercise the admiralty jurisdiction conferred by that British Act which had been exercised by the pre-war Supreme Courts of Papua and New Guinea.

That admiralty jurisdiction continued until Independence when the *Papua and New Guinea Act* 1949 was repealed by the *Papua New Guinea Independence Act* 1975 (Aust.) and the *Supreme Court Ordinance 1949* was repealed by the *Statute Law Revision (Independence) Act* 1975 (No.92 of 1975). Independent Papua New Guinea is not a British possession so the *Colonial Courts of Admiralty Act* does not apply to Papua New Guinea of its own force.

Has this admiralty jurisdiction survived Independence? As stated the *Colonial Courts of Admiralty Act* 1890 was adopted into the territories of Papua and New Guinea. I agree with Miles J. that the Act initially applied of its own force to British New Guinea but was them adopted in the *Papua Act* 1905, and it was adopted at the outset in New Guinea (see above). This adopted law was continued in force until Independence by virtue of s.32 of the *Papua and New Guinea Act* 1949. That Australian Act was repealed by another Australian Act, the *Papua New Guinea Independence Act* 1975 which means, ex facie, that the laws kept in force by s.32 of the 1949 Act were repealed by the 1975 Australian Act. However in an overlapping legislative provision, the *Laws Repeal Act* 1975 purports to repeal laws of the pre-war territories of Papua and New Guinea, including adopted English statutes, kept in force by the *Papua and New Guinea Act* 1949. It purports to repeal those laws, which would include the *Colonial Courts of Admiralty Act* 1890, and then Sch.2.6 of the Constitution adopts them as part of the laws of Independent Papua New Guinea. The *Laws Repeal Act* 1975 was a law passed by the House of Assembly which in turn was constituted and derived its powers from the *Papua and New Guinea Act* 1949 as amended. Faced with these overlapping statutory provisions and giving effect to the hierarchy of legislatures, the House of Assembly being dependent on the Australian Parliament for its powers, I conclude that the *Papua New Guinea Independence Act* 1975 repealed the operation of the *Colonial Courts of Admiralty Act* in Papua New Guinea and that the *Laws Repeal Act* 1975 did not do so; that its purported exercise of repealing power was not effective.

I am fortified in this view by a number of considerations. First, as explained above, in addition to the *Colonial Courts of Admiralty Act* 1890 being adopted into the territories of Papua and of New Guinea and then being kept in force in Papua New Guinea, s.6 of the *Supreme Court Ordinance* 1949 preserved the admiralty jurisdiction exercised by the pre-war Supreme Courts of Papua and of New Guinea. The *Supreme Court Ordinance* 1949 was repealed by the *Statute Law Revision (Independence) Act* 1975 which came into force immediately before the *Laws Repeal Act* 1975 which means that that admiralty jurisdiction was not revived under Sch.2.6 of the Constitution. Secondly, the sections in the Constitution conferring jurisdiction on the National Court of Justice do not preserve any jurisdiction exercised by the pre-Independence Supreme Court. Neither does the *National Court Act* 1975 save any pre-Independence jurisdiction although it also save the pre-Independence *Rules of Court*. Thirdly, the Constitution framers appear to have given considerable care to stipulate which Imperial statutes should apply after Independence and the *Colonial Laws of Admiralty Act* 1890 is not included among them. It is not one of the Imperial Statutes adopted in Sch.5 of the Constitution although seven of the eight Acts adopted in that Schedule relate to shipping. Neither is the 1890 Act — nor the relevant sections of the *Admiralty Courts Acts* of 1840 and 1861 — reenacted in the *Imperial Laws Replacement Act* 1975. For these reasons I have come to the opposite view to that expressed by Kapi and Miles JJ. in *Milan Capek v The Yacht 'Freja'* (see above). I consider that this Court no longer has the admiralty jurisdiction conferred on the pre-Independence Supreme Court by the *Colonial Courts of Admiralty Act* 1890.

I consider that s.6 of the *Admiralty Court Act* 1840 and s.5 of the *Admiralty Court Act* 1861 which are quoted above fall with the *Colonial Courts of Admiralty Act* 1890 and are no longer in force in Papua New Guinea. Those sections, so far as they concern this case, confer jurisdiction on the High Court of Admiralty to hear claims in rem for necessaries. I do not consider that they were adopted into Papua under the *Courts & Laws Adopting Ordinance* 1888 of British New Guinea or into New Guinea under the *Laws Repeal and Adopting Ordinance* 1921 of New Guinea, although the learned editor of the *Laws of The Territory of Papua* and the *Laws of The Territory of New Guinea* considered the 1840 Act (3 & 4 Vic. c. 65) was adopted, but that the 1861 Act (24 & 25 Vic. c. 10) was not (vol. 5 p.68.) I do not think that those Acts were, by themselves, applicable to the circumstances of those colonies. Those sections expressly conferred jurisdiction on the High Court of

Admiralty *in England*; they became relevant to Papua New Guinea only because the *Colonial Courts of Admiralty Act* 1890 conferred the English admiralty jurisdiction on colonial courts. The 1980 Act adopted in both Papua and New Guinea conferred English admiralty jurisdiction on the courts of those territories and the sections quoted of the 1840 and 1861 Acts defined part of that jurisdiction. I do not consider that the 1840 and 1861 Acts would have been applicable to either territory if there had been no 1890 Act. I consider that when the jurisdiction conferred by the adoption of the *Colonial Courts of Admiralty Act* 1890 and by s.6 of the *Supreme Court Ordinance* 1949 ceased to exist in Papua New Guinea the jurisdiction to hear claims in rem for necessaries ceased to exist with it.
New Guinea Cocoa (Export) Co Pty Ltd v Basis Vedbaek [1980] PNGLR 205 at pp.208-211.

Comment

The complex and unresolved debate (above) concerning the reception of pre-Independence foreign statutes into the law of Papua New Guinea appears to the authors to have been fundamentally misconceived.

Sch.2.6(2) adopts as Acts of the Parliament 'all-pre-Independence laws.' In turn the expression pre-Independence law is defined by Sch.2.6(1)(a) to mean, excepting matters not relevant to this note, 'a law ... that was repealed by the *Laws Repeal Act* 1975 made by the pre-Independence House of Assembly for Papua New Guinea ....'

Kapi, Miles and Bredmeyer JJ. despite their differences, are as one in implicitly accepting that the adjectival clause 'made by the pre-Independence House of Assembly for Papua New Guinea', qualifies the noun phrase 'the *Laws Repeal Act* 1975' in the above definition.

However, as a matter of ordinary grammar the adjectival clause could equally qualify the preceding noun, 'a law'. That this latter construction ought be preferred is suggested by two factors. First there would seem little point in regarding it as applying to the expression 'the *Laws Repeal Act* 1975', which expression would, without any qualification, convey an identical meaning. On such a reading the adjectival clause becomes mere surplusage.

The second reason to prefer the construction advocated by the authors, it is submitted, flows from the desirable consequences that such a reading would effect. It would restrict the re-adoption of pre-Independence statutes to those which had been passed by the indigenous pre-Independence House of Assembly. This would avoid the necessity for tortuous excursions though the statute law of England, the Commonwealth of Australia and the State of Queensland to determine whether a foreign statute is in force in Papua New Guinea. In so doing proper recognition would be given to: (a) the Constitution makers' goal of an autochthonous Constitution, (b) the circumstances of the country (where few adequate libraries for the sophisticated legal historiography required exist) and, (c) Sch.2.6(1)(b) and (c) and Sch.5, which as Bredmeyer J. noted in *New Guinea Cocoa (Export) Co. v Basis Vedbaek* at p.210 (see above) prescribe those foreign statutes which the Constitution framers thought fit to apply to Papua New Guinea after Independence. The express inclusion in the Constitution of a finite list of foreign statutes, it is submitted, clearly shows the legislative intent that the list be regarded as exhaustive.

Given these considerations, there is every justification, it is submitted, to reject an interpretation of Sch.2.6 which would leave the ascertainment of Papua New Guinea's laws dependent upon antiquitarian research of other foreign nations' legal systems.

GENERALLY

Referred to

by Frost C.J. in *The State v Mogo Wonom* [1975] PNGLR 311 at p.314;

by Prentice Dep.C.J. in *Public Curator of Papua New Guinea v Public Trustee of New Zealand* [1976] PNGLR 427 at p.431;

by Kearney J. in *Cory v Blyth (No 4)* [1976] 525 at p.527;

by Prentice Dep.C.J. in *Costello v The Controller of Civil Aviation (No 1)* [1977] PNGLR 229 at p.236 ('Agreement' between Australia and the pre-Independence Government of Papua New Guinea which did not have the force of law held not to have survived the attainment of Independence under Sch.2.6(2) as a pre-Independence 'law');

by Miles J. in *Milan Capek v The Yacht 'Freja' (No 2)* [1980] PNGLR 161 at p.168,169 (Section 166 of the Constitution must be read subject to Sch.2.6);

by Kapi J. in *S.C.R. No 4 of 1980; Re petition of M.T. Somare* [1981] PNGLR 265 at p.289;

by Kapi J. in *Wahgi Savings and Loan Society Ltd v Bank of South Pacific Ltd* (1980 Unreported) SC185 at p.18;

by Kapi J. in *S.C.R. No 1 of 1982; Re Bouraga* [1982] PNGLR 178 at p.191;

by Kearney Dep.C.J. in *S.C.R. No 2 of 1981; Re s.19(1)(f) of the Criminal Code* [1982] PNGLR 150 at p.158;

by Kapi Dep.C.J. in *Re James Allan Sannga; Peter Timereke v Duncan Ferrie and anor* (1983 Unreported) SC255 at pp.25,26,41 (there is no power given to the Court under the Schedule to question the appropriateness of an adopted statute to the circumstances of Papua New Guinea);

by McDermott J. in *Asi Burunge v John Kaupa* (1983 Unreported) SC258 at p.12 (*Native Regulations (Papua)* adopted at Independence by Sch.2.6(2)).

Sch.2.7. — ADAPTATION OF ADOPTED LAW.

(1) A law adopted by Section Sch.2.6 (*adoption of pre-Independence Laws*) takes effect subject to such changes as to names, titles, offices, persons and institutions, and to such other formal and non-substantive changes, as are necessary to adapt it to the circumstances of the country and to the Constitutional Laws.

(2) A Constitutional Regulation may prescribe changes to be made for the purposes of Subsection (1) and any such regulation is conclusive as to the changes so prescribed, but no omission to prescribe a change affects the generality of that subsection.

(3) A question as to a change to be made for the purposes of Subsection (1) is not a question relating to the interpretation or application of any provision of a Constitutional Law within the meaning of Section 18 (*original interpretative jurisdiction of the Supreme Court*), but this subsection does not affect the operation of Section 19 (*special references to the Supreme Court*).

AS TO INDICTMENTS

Held

Where the pre-Independence law adopted under Sch.2.6 prescribed a form of indictment entitled 'the Queen against AB' that law takes effect subject to the change of title from 'the Queen' to 'the State'.
The State v Mogo Wonom [1975] PNGLR 311, see Frost C.J. at p.317.

GENERALLY

Referred to

by Prentice Dep.C.J. in *Peter v South Pacific Brewery Ltd* [1976] PNGLR 537 at p.551 (questions as to the changes of titles etc. are not required to be referred by inferior courts for the attention of the Supreme Court under Sch.2.3(2));

by Kapi Dep.C.J. in *Re James Allan Sannga: Peter Timereke v Duncan Ferrie and anor* (1983 Unreported) SC255 at p.26 (Schedule 2.7 effects only formal non-substantive changes).

PART 5. — JUDICIAL PRECEDENT.

Sch.2.8 — EFFECT OF PART 5.

(1) Nothing in this part affects or is intended to affect, except to the extent specifically set out in this part —
(a) the legal doctrine of judicial precedent (also known as *stare decisis*); or
(b) the principles of judicial comity; or
(c) the rules of private international law (also known as *conflict of laws*); or
(d) the legal doctrine known as *res judicata*,
or the further development and adoption of those doctrines, principles and rules in accordance with Part 3 of this Schedule (*development of an underlying law for Papua New Guinea*).

(2) Except as provided by or under an Act of the Parliament, this Part does not apply to or in respect of village courts.

GENERALLY

Referred to

by Kearney J. in *The State v Allan Woila* [1978] PNGLR 99 at p.102;

by Narakobi A.J. in *Reva Mase v The Independent State of Papua New Guinea* (1980 Unreported) N260 at p.2 (as incorporating the doctrines of *res judicata* and *stare decisis* into the law of Papua New Guinea).

Sch.2.9. — SUBBORDINATION OF COURTS.

(1) All decisions of law by the Supreme Court are binding on all other courts, but not on itself.

(2) Subject to Section Sch.2.10 (*conflict of precedents*), all decisions of law by the National Court are binding on all other courts (other than the Supreme Court), but not on itself (except insofar as a decision of the National Court constituted by more Judges than one is of greater authority than a decision of the Court constituted by a lesser number).

(3) Subject to this Part, all decisions of law by a court other than the Supreme Court or the National Court are binding on all lower courts.

(4) In Subsection (3), 'lower court', in relation to a matter before a court, means a court to which proceedings by way of appeal or review (whether by leave or as of right) lie from the first-mentioned court in relation to the matter.

AS TO JUDICIAL METHODOLOGY

per Wilson J.

> I realize that the Supreme Court is not bound by earlier decisions of the Supreme Court . . . Nevertheless the legal doctrine of *stare decisis* and the principles of judicial comity are such that an earlier decision of the Supreme Court should only be over-ruled after great caution and in a clear case. I am of the opinion that, if the Supreme Court is to be invited to over-rule an earlier decision of the Supreme Court, or even an earlier decision of the pre-Independence Supreme Court, it is desirable that the Court be constituted by more than three judges and, if possible, the Chief Justice of the day should preside. I am also of the opinion that the Supreme Court should not consider over-ruling one of its earlier decisions . . . unless it has heard full argument . . . as to the desirability or otherwise of the Supreme Court at this stage in this country's development . . . changing the law by judicial as opposed to legislative decision.
> *The Public Prosecutor v John Aia of Mondo and anor* [1978] PNGLR 224 at p.232,233.

Referred to

by Raine Dep.C.J. in *Kerr v Motor Vehicles Insurance (P.N.G.) Trust* [1979] PNGLR 251 at p.255;

by Narakobi A.J. in *Reva Mase v The Independent State of Papua New Guinea* (1980 Unreported) N260 at p.2;

by Kidu C.J. in *The State v Paul Pokolau* (1983 Unreported) N404 at p.9 (duty of counsel to be mindful that lower courts are bound by decisions of higher courts).

Sch.2.10. — CONFLICT OF PRECEDENTS.

(1) Where it appears to a court other than the Supreme Court or the National Court that —
- (a) there are more decisions of law than one that are otherwise binding on it by virtue of the preceding provisions of this Part and that, in relation to the matter before it, the decisions are conflicting; or
- (b) a decision of law that is otherwise binding on it by virtue of the preceding provisions of this Part and that is otherwise applicable to the matter before it —
  - (i) is not, or is no longer, appropriate to the circumstances of the country or of the matter; or
  - (ii) is inconsistent with any custom that is part of the underlying law and is applicable in relation to the matter; or

(iii) is seriously inconsistent with the trend of the adaptation and development of the law in other respects,

then unless the question is trivial, vexatious or irrelevant the court may, and shall if so requested by a party to the matter, state a case to the court that made the decision or decisions or the equivalent court, or if there be no such court, to the National Court, and take whatever other action (including the adjournment of proceedings) is appropriate.

(2) Where a case is stated in accordance with Subsection (1), the court to which it is stated may require or permit the Minister responsible for the National Justice Administration to be represented by counsel to assist the court.

TRIVIAL VEXATIOUS OR IRRELEVANT

Comment

See note under s.18(2) discussing identical words.

Sch.2.11. PROSPECTIVE OVER-RULING.

(1) Subject to any decision of law that is binding upon it, in over-ruling a decision of law or in making a decision of law that is contrary to previous practice, doctrine or accepted custom, a court may, for a special reason, apply its decision of law only to situations occuring after the new decision.

(2) In the circumstances described by Subsection (1), a court may apply to a situation a decision of law that was over-ruled after the occurrence of the situation, or a practice, doctrine or custom that was current or accepted at the time of the occurence of any relevant transaction, act or event.

(3) In a case to which Subsection (1) or (2) applies, a court may make its decision subject to such conditions and restrictions as to it seem just.

Sch.2.12. — OUTSIDE DECISIONS.

(1) For the purposes of this section, except in a matter before the Supreme Court or the National Court —

(a) a decision of law by a Full Court of the pre-Independence Supreme Court, sitting in accordance with the pre-Independence law relating to sittings of the Supreme Court, or a decision of law on appeal from a decision of that court, has the same binding force as a decision of law of the Supreme Court; and

(b) a decision of law by a pre-Independence Supreme Court sitting otherwise than as a Full Court, or a decision of law on appeal from a decision of that court, has the same binding force as a decision of law of the National Court,

subject to any decision of law of the Supreme Court or the National Court, as the case may be, to the contrary, but otherwise no decision of law of a court or tribunal that was not established within the National Judicial System is binding on a court within it.

(2) Subsection (1) does not prevent recourse to the decisions of law or the opinions of courts or tribunals outside the National Judicial System (including courts or tribunals of jurisdictions other than Papua New Guinea) for their persuasive value.

BINDING: RES JUDICATA

per Narakobi A.J.

Under Sch.2.12(1)(a) decisions of the High Court of Australia [where that Court heard and determined a matter on appeal from Papua New Guinea before Independence] in so far as they apply to the parties in dispute and to the land in issue, have the same binding force as decisions of law of the Supreme Court. I would be bound by the [pre-Independence] High Court decision in a matter that has already been settled and in which the same parties have been the contestants or where possibly a party that could have joined issue stood by and did nothing. At least that is how I understand the interplay of the common law doctrines of judicial precedent, *stare decisis* and *res judicata* and estoppel.
Reva Mase v Independent State of Papua New Guinea (1980 Unreported) N260 at p.2 (see also at p.8).

GENERALLY

Referred to

by Frost C.J. in *The State v Tokai Koweri* (1976 Unreported) N63 (persuasive value of a decision of Griffith C.J. of the High Court of Australia applied in construing s.16 of the Criminal Code);

by Greville Smith J. in *The State v Marawa Kanaio* [1979] PNGLR 319 at p.322;

by Narakobi A.J. in *The State v Kaupa Ungi* [1980] PNGLR 199 at p.203.

PART 6. — THE LAW REFORM COMMISSION.

Sch.2.13. — ESTABLISHMENT OF THE COMMISSION.

(1) An Act of the Parliament shall make provision for and in respect of a Law Reform Commission.

(*See: Law Reform Commission Act* Ch.18).

(2) Only citizens may be members of the Commission.

Sch.2.14. — SPECIAL FUNCTIONS OF THE COMMISSION.

In addition to its other functions and responsibilities under any law, it is a special responsibility of the Law Reform Commission to investigate and report to the Parliament and to the National Executive on the development, and on the adaptation to the circumstances of the country, of the underlying law, and on the appropriateness of the rules and principles of the underlying law to the circumstances of the country from time to time.

C.P.C. Report Ch.5 Part 1 p.34

23. The proposed Law Reform Commission (referred to in Chapter 8, 'The Administration of Justice') or a special committee comprising Papua New Guinean public servants, and perhaps politicians also, with appropriate skilled staff and, if needed, outside consultants, should give careful consideration to all current legislation and government policies with a view to making recommendations, over a period of approximately two years, for the repeal and amendment of legislation which is contrary to the National Goals and Directive Principles, or to the proposed constitutional provisions concerning Human Rights and Obligations. This body should also recommend changes in policies of the government, including the institutions of government, in order to achieve conformity with the National Goals and Directive Principles. [Note: there is no reference in Chapter 8 to the proposed Law Reform Commission]

GENERALLY

Referred to

by Greville Smith J. in *S.C.R. No 2 of 1981; Re s.19(1)(f) of the Criminal Code* [1982] PNGLR 150 at p.165 (as inter alia, the basis of His Honour's inference that judicial development of the underlying law should be confined and not invade the province of the legislature).

Sec. Sch. 1.2(1). SCHEDULE 3.

DECLARATION OF OFFICE.

I, , do promise and declare that I will well and truly serve the Independent State of Papua New Guinea and its People in the office of

Sec. Sch.1.2(1) SCHEDULE 4

JUDICIAL DECLARATION.

I, , do promise and declare that I will well and truly serve the Independent State of Papua New Guinea and its People in the office of

that I will in all things uphold the Constitution and the laws of the Independent State of Papua New Guinea, and I will do right to all manner of people in accordance therewith, without fear or favour, affection or ill-will.

Sec. Sch.2.6.

SCHEDULE 5

ADOPTED LAWS OF OTHER COUNTRIES.

PART 1. — AUSTRALIA.

Continental Shelf (Living Natural Resources) Act 1968 — Section 9 and 14 only.
Explosives Act 1901-1973.
Judiciary Act 1903-1969 — Section 84 only.
Marine Insurance Act 1909-1966.
Navigation Act 1912-1973.
Patents Act 1903-1973 — Section 123 only.
Petroleum (Submerged Lands) Act 1967-1968 — Section 11 only.
Nationality and Citizenship Act 1911-1972 — Section 5(3) only.
Seamen's Compensation Act 1911-1972 — Section 4 only (in relation to a ship registered in the country under the *Merchant Shipping Act* 1894, as amended, of England).
Seamen's War Pensions and Allowances Act 1940-1974.
Submarine Cables and Pipelines Protection Act 1963-1973.

PART 2. — ENGLAND.

Merchant Shipping Act 1894.
Merchant Shipping Act 1897.
Merchant Shipping (Liability of Shipowners and Others) Act 1900.
Merchant Shipping Act 1906.
Merchant Shipping Act 1911.
Maritime Conventions Act 1911.
Merchant Shipping Act 1921.
Fees (Increase) Act 1923.

GENERALLY

Referred to

by Kapi J. in *Milan Capek v The Yacht 'Freja'* [1980] PNGLR 57 at p.61;

by Bredmeyer J. in *New Guinea Cocoa (Export) Co. Pty. Ltd. v Basis Vedbaek* [1980] PNGLR 205 at p.211 (see extract under Sch.2.6)

TABLE OF PAPUA NEW GUINEA CASES

TABLE OF FOREIGN CASES

TABLE OF STATUTES AND INTERNATIONAL CONVENTIONS

INDEX TO THE CONSTITUTION OF PAPUA NEW GUINEA AS AMENDED TO 1 JAN. 1984

www.ingramcontent.com/pod-product-compliance
Lightning Source LLC
LaVergne TN
LVHW062242200926
848484LV00006B/1598